Efficient Reading

Efficient Reading

SIXTH EDITION

James I. Brown *University of Minnesota*

D. C. Heath and Company   Lexington, Massachusetts   •   Toronto

In this print-filled world, academic success depends very largely on how well you can read. This book is intended to help you develop the reading efficiency so important in college and long afterwards.

To get down to particulars, suppose you decide to spend two hours of preparation for every hour spent in class. In carrying a normal load you will read an average of thirty hours a week. We'll say also that you read textbooks at about 200 words a minute with average comprehension.

Now what does increasing your reading efficiency mean? Well, an improvement in rate of only 100 words a minute without any loss in comprehension — a 50 percent gain — means you can do one hour's reading in forty minutes. That saves you 10 hours a week, 100 hours a quarter, and 300 hours a year. In four years of college that adds up to a grand total of 1200 hours saved, or the equivalent of 150 eight-hour days.

And that's only a beginning, for there's the much bigger problem of keeping up professionally for the rest of your life. In short, by taking the time somewhere along the way to develop greater reading efficiency, you literally *make* the time you need for additional reading as well as for a variety of other activities — social, professional, and otherwise. Yes, getting full value from the printed page with a minimum of time and effort is an ability well worth cultivating.

That brings us to another point you will want to remember. No matter how poorly or how well you now read, the chances are you are reading below your maximum potential. For example, that hypothetical 50 percent increase just mentioned should be relatively easy to attain. As a matter of fact, reports from reading centers and programs around the country usually mention much greater gains.

Excellent results can be achieved not only with classroom instruction but also in programs of individual study. The first fifty students who completed the University of Minnesota's home-study course using *Efficient Reading* improved their reading speed from 281 to 885 words per minute — an improvement of more than 200 percent — and their comprehension improved

as well. The Independent Study Division of the National University Extension Association awarded its prestigious certificate of merit to the University of Minnesota for this outstanding independent study course.

Furthermore, average and above-average readers seem to have as much room for improvement as others, if not more. A group of top executives, after ten class sessions, improved from an above-average initial rate of 318 to 834 words per minute, with 8 percent more comprehension — an increase of better than 160 percent in reading efficiency.

It is evidence of this kind that suggests that no matter how well you now read, you still have room for improvement.

But your progress in reading, if it is to be rapid and lasting, needs to be based on a solid foundation of communication, of which it is a part. Reading, writing, speaking, and listening are actually so closely interrelated that improvement in any one facilitates improvement in all the others, provided you capitalize on those interrelationships instead of on isolated skills. Since, according to research findings, 70 percent of your waking time is spent in reading, writing, speaking, or listening, the value of a broad approach seems obvious.

This book is organized into two parts to emphasize these interrelationships and to help you take full advantage of them as effective aids in learning to read.

The first section of Part One — "Background" — contains seventeen selections, chosen to bring you a better general understanding of the complex communication process. There are selections to sharpen your awareness of the part played by interest, attitude, habits, imagination, and observation in effective written and spoken communication. Other selections touch on the role of change in communications, the mushrooming growth of computers and word-processing, key principles of memory improvement, and ways of dealing more knowingly with common propaganda devices. Still other selections suggest ways of organizing your time and activities to best advantage.

The next five sections build on this foundation to help you use reading as a means for developing all communication skills. Section Two provides in-depth coverage of reading. Sections Three and Four give help with writing and speaking and point up relationships to further your reading growth. Section Five — on listening — treats skill in listening as a companion to skill in reading and should contribute much to your awareness of word meanings, to your building of general and specialized backgrounds, and to your acquaintance with methods of developing and organizing ideas. Section Six treats the one element underlying almost all communication — words. In a sense, one new word added to your vocabulary makes you a better reader, listener, speaker, and writer.

The last section, Section Seven, shifts the emphasis from *how* to communicate to *what* to communicate — a reminder that communication is a means toward an end and seldom an end in itself. As one educator put it: "In a very real sense the destiny of our society and of each of us individually will be determined by our ability to communicate with one another and with citizens of other nations about contemporary problems."

Your first step in using this book will be to get better acquainted with your strengths and weaknesses as a reader, writer, speaker, and listener. Do you write better than you read, for instance? One student, a poor reader, scored consistently low on objective tests where rapid, accurate reading was required. In one course where both objective and subjective tests were given, his grades on the objective type ranged from C down to F. On the subjective tests in the same course he never scored below a B. He told of spending twenty hours preparing for a botany quiz, which, because it was objective, brought him only a C. Yet, whenever he was asked to demonstrate his grasp of a subject in writing, he communicated well. Slow reading was, for him, a major handicap.

Your first move, then, will be to use this book to find out how fast you read and how much you comprehend. See at what difficulty levels you read with adequate understanding. Find out whether you read better than you listen, or listen better than you read. Check up on yourself, also, as a writer and speaker, noticing such things as your grasp of sentence and paragraph structure and your ability to organize material effectively. Find out if your vocabulary is adequate for your communication needs.

This book is designed to facilitate such explorations. For example, in Part Two, the ten questions testing each selection give you a check on comprehension. The first five measure how well you read for details. The last five measure how well you interpret, evaluate, draw inferences, or get central ideas — skills coming under the general heading of critical or reflective reading. These comprehension check questions are equally useful in exploring your listening ability. Get someone to read one of the selections aloud to you; then answer the questions to check your listening comprehension. The

five vocabulary questions provide an opportunity for checking the size and accuracy of your vocabulary as well as the effectiveness with which you use contextual clues in arriving at word meanings.

Whenever you disagree with the answers in the key (Appendix), go over the selection again carefully to find concrete evidence both for your answer and for the given answer. Discuss questionable items with someone else in an attempt to uncover all relevant data. Such analyses and discussions will do much to help you learn how to use emphasis, clarify organization, develop ideas, and avoid ambiguities in your own writing and speaking as well as how to improve reading comprehension.

Word counts and timing aids are for your convenience in exploring the relationship between word-per-minute rate and comprehension. (See Appendix, Conversion Table.) Read one selection at your normal rate, checking both rate and comprehension. Then read another selection for full comprehension to see if you can score a 90 or 100. Finally, read still another selection as fast as you can, again checking both rate and comprehension. The difference between your slowest and fastest rate is a kind of "index of flexibility," and indicates the range of rates at your command. Your comprehension on each of these trials will suggest the level of skill which accompanies those variations in rate.

Although all selections are arranged for self-timing, you should consider what specific purposes or what kinds of materials lend themselves most appropriately to rapid rates. When you are reading strictly for information, what rate is appropriate? Does slow reading tend to overaccent details and obscure the main ideas? And how rapidly should you read for enjoyment? Would seeing a full-length movie in slow motion tend to increase or lessen your enjoyment? Keep these questions in mind in your preliminary explorations.

The exercises in Part Two are based on each selection and provide you with further help in extending your effectiveness as reader, writer, speaker, and listener. (See the level of difficulty index on page 362.)

After you have a clear picture of yourself as a communicator from these initial explorations, you're ready for the next step — intelligently planned practice. Actually the first step insures the success of the second. Only when you know exactly what your problems are can you direct your attention properly for immediate results. For additional help turn to the Index of Exercises on page 187.

Suppose, for example, that your difficulty is comprehension. If the cause is lack of concentration, increasing your reading rate may be a helpful move. Other possible causes may be inadequate vocabulary or lack of experience with material at a certain difficulty level. Knowing that you tend to miss details or main ideas will help you direct attention more intelligently. As you work on the problem from several angles you will soon begin to see improvement.

Or suppose you find you are a "one-speed" reader. Again you will know where to direct your energies. Make a conscious effort to cultivate and use a much wider range of rates. Similarly in other areas, as you uncover specific needs, direct your practice efforts to best advantage.

Finally, as you work to attain the reading ability so necessary for college work, as well as for success after graduation, you have the satisfaction of knowing that you are getting skills basic to the highest educational endeavor. As Carlyle said: "If we but think of it, all that a university or final highest school can do for us is still but what the first school began doing — teach us to *read*."

The sixth edition of *Efficient Reading* marks the culmination of my thirty-five years of teaching college and adult reading classes to over 6,000 students. Following the first appearance of *Efficient Reading* in 1952, each subsequent edition has incorporated changes and improvements growing directly from classroom use of earlier editions. Feedback from both students and teachers has provided the needed insights and help.

This new edition, however, is the first and only one to bring together into a single volume those best-liked and most helpful selections from earlier editions. Twenty-one came from *Revised Form A* and thirty-two from *Revised Form B*. Thirty entirely new selections bring the total to eighty-three — eight more than in any previous edition. Thirteen short one- or two-page selections were also included as exercises to provide additional work on problem areas.

Like earlier editions, this one is designed for use in college and adult reading programs as well as in reading laboratories and clinics. It should also be useful in freshman English classes with an emphasis on reading. As Lamuth said in his *Golden Book on Writing,* the vocabulary, usage, and idiom "so essential to good writing can be acquired only by wide and intelligent reading. And in no other way whatsoever." The broad communication emphasis of the book provides a significant basis for study. After all, communication pervades every process of life, making the study of communication, in a sense, the study of society. This approach also provides the best possible foundation for maximum improvement in reading, through increased facility and growth in the companion skills of writing, speaking, and listening.

For this edition, item-analysis procedures, essential to the preparation of standardized tests, were used with nineteen of the comprehension tests. These tests are indicated by an asterisk in the Index According to Order of Difficulty on page 362. Items in the tests have an average validity of .47 — assurance of their high degree of discrimination. The use of such procedures in a text of this kind is unique.

As in the last edition, pacing sheets have been included. Using these sheets, students can pace at any of six speeds, thus eliminating the need for costly individual accelerators while employing a technique that students feel is the single most helpful device for improving reading efficiency. (For more detailed discussion of the pacing approach, read James I. Brown, "A Pacing Technique for Classroom Teaching of Reading," *College English,* December, 1956, pp. 164–5.)

With three available editions — *Revised Form A, Revised Form B,* and this *Sixth Edition* — all closely parallel in plan, treatment, and format, instructors have a wide choice of readings to draw from in meeting the specific needs and interests of their students. In *Revised Form A* there are still forty-nine readings not found in this edition; in *Revised Form B* there are forty-three, making a total of ninety-two. With thirty new selections in this edition, teachers have a total of one hundred and twenty-one different selections in the three texts. The three editions can be alternated from year to year for variety. Or, one edition can be used for in-class work and one of the others as the required text, an arrangement permitting more extensive coverage of any desired area and greater opportunity for accelerating or individualizing instruction.

As in earlier editions, selections rated from easy to difficult on the Flesch Scale[1] are included here to parallel the wide range of reading ability found among college students and adults in general. Incoming freshmen at the University of Minnesota, for example, range in reading ability from the sixth-grade to the college-senior level and beyond. In each of the seven main divisions, selections are arranged in order from easiest to most difficult. In addition, an index listing all selections according to difficulty, as indicated by Flesch "Reading Ease" scores, is provided on page 362. This wide range of difficulty facilitates the diagnosis of specific strengths and weaknesses and provides material appropriate for effective individualized instruction.

---

[1] See Rudolf Flesch, *The Art of Readable Writing* (New York: Harper & Row, 1949), and *The Art of Plain Talk* (New York: Harper & Row, 1946), for further details.

Users of earlier editions have asked for more detailed suggestions for structuring college or adult reading courses. Here are three possible course organizations that have been used at the University of Minnesota. Each plan provides a basic framework of developmental steps or stages using selections from this text.

1. The following nine-step sequence, found in *Guide to Effective Reading* (Heath) is one possibility. The *Guide* can be used as a source for classroom lectures and exercise suggestions with classes using only *Efficient Reading* as a text:

(1) Proper orientation and diagnosis of reading strengths and weaknesses; (2) Careful observation and analysis of performance; (3) Proper management of the learning process; (4) Skimming and scanning activities; (5) Establishing word-grouping habits; (6) Dealing with paragraph structure; (7) Managing organization; (8) Developing proper attitudes; (9) Dealing with examinations.

2. The following five-step organization is found in *Reading Power* (Heath):

(1) The Check-Up; (2) The Build-Up; (3) The Speed-Up; (4) The Shape-Up; (5) The Ease-Up.

Fourteen 1,000-word instructional readings amplify and develop these subpoints of the five divisions:

(1) Reading power — Key to personal growth; (2) How should you build up your vocabulary? (3) How do you best get the facts? (4) How can you speed up your reading? (5) Speeding by surveying; (6) Speeding by skimming; (7) Speeding by scanning; (8) Reading for meaning; (9) Reading words more effectively; (10) Reading paragraphs more effectively; (11) Reading entire selections more effectively; (12) Getting better grades; (13) Generating new and wider interests; (14) Reading for life.

3. For schools, learning centers or reading clinics with videotape playback facilities, a taped series of lectures[2] designed to be used with *Efficient Reading* is available. This series, which has been continually up-dated since 1960, introduces a twelve-step sequence for teaching reading. The lectures describe the various roads leading to improved reading efficiency:

(1) Know Thyself Road; (2) Visualizing Road; (3) Vocabulary Road; (4) Easy-Learning Road; (5) Pacing Road; (6) Formula Road; (7) Skimming-Scanning Road; (8) Main Idea Road; (9) Word Grouping Road; (10) Paragraph Reading Road; (11) Writer's Plan Road; (12) Dynamic Communication Road.

ACKNOWLEDGMENTS

Mention should be made of my obligation to those authors and publishers who have so generously granted permission for the use of their material and to my colleagues teaching reading at Minnesota. Eugene S. Wright deserves special mention for his leadership in adapting previous editions of this text to a wide range of individual differences in his classes in Efficient Reading. His doctoral research with an experimental group using an earlier edition as its basic text pointed up the importance of training in reading for academic success. And for much of the material on listening, special thanks must go to Dr. Ralph G. Nichols, whose book *Are You Listening?* provided so many useful insights for planning my own section on listening.

---

[2] Available through Telstar, 366 North Prior Avenue, St. Paul, Minnesota 55104.

CONTENTS

Part Two / Comprehension and Vocabulary Check Questions and Exercises

Part One

READING SELECTIONS

SELECTION 1

The Dynamics of Change

Don Fabun

Change! That's what this book focuses on. Use it to change your reading habits, skills, and interests. Use it to sharpen your awareness of the total communication picture — writing, speaking, and listening as well as reading. Use it to help you walk with increased confidence in this world of ever-accelerating change.

At exactly 5:13 a.m., the 18th of April, 1906, a cow was standing somewhere between the main barn and the milking shed on the old Shafter Ranch in California, minding her own business. Suddenly, the earth shook, the skies trembled, and when it was all over, there was nothing showing of the cow above ground but a bit of her tail sticking up.

For the student of change, the Shafter cow is a sort of symbol of our times. She stood quietly enough, thinking such gentle thoughts as cows are likely to have, while huge forces outside her ken built up all around her and — within a minute — discharged it all at once in a great movement that changed the configuration of the earth, and destroyed a city, and swallowed her up. And that's what we are going to talk about now: how, if we do not learn to understand and guide the great forces of change at work on our world today, we may find ourselves like the Shafter cow, swallowed up by vast upheavals in our way of life — quite early some morning.

One foot inextricably trapped in the clockwork mechanism of 19th Century science, and the other planted fearfully in the newly radiant soil of the 20th Century, Henry Adams, then 60 years old — and a student of change for forty of those — stood in the Gallery of Machines at the Great Paris Exposition of 1900 and saw — more clearly than most men of his time, or of now — one of the great fracture points in human history.

It was to be another sixty years and two World Wars later before the dimensions of the change he saw had become the common currency of popular journalism and awareness of change an accepted tool for survival.

For most of his life, Adams had been trying to make some sense out of history. It had not been an easy quest, for history appears to be what we want to make of it, and Adams found he could not make much of it.

In his *Education,* Adams said, "Satisfied that the sequence of men led to nothing and that the sequence of

society could lead no further, while the mere sequence of time was artificial and the sequence of thought was chaos, he turned at last to the sequence of force, and thus it happened, after ten years pursuit, he found himself lying in the Gallery of Machines . . . his historical neck broken by the irruption of forces totally new."

What Adams had seen was that change is observed motion, and motion is the product of applied force. Man had begun by acquiring fire — and that was a force — and then sometime later the use of wind and water, and then he put water and fire together and turned the steam engine loose on the world. The period of time between each new acquisition and application of power was successively shorter. It was only a little after steam that he began applying electrical force and even more shortly after that discovered and put to work nuclear force.

By 1900, the power of the electrical age was best symbolized in the dynamo, a force that Adams found parallel to the force of the Christian Cross in the affairs of men. And, in the discoveries of Roentgen and Curie, in the hidden rays of the suprasensual, the dimensions of a vast new world powered in its course by the dance of electrons, were — at the turn of the century — already visible to those few pairs of eyes curious enough to see them.

It was possible to plot the progress of these new forces in graphs, and when this was done, and the different graphs compared, it was seen that — in almost any application of force you wanted to measure — there was a constant acceleration; the changes became larger and they occurred more frequently as we moved forward in time.

Several years ago, *Scientific American* plotted Adams' "Law of Acceleration." Graphs were made up of such processes as the discovery of natural forces, and the time lag between each successive discovery; tables were made that plotted the isolation of natural elements, the accumulation of human experience, the speed that transportation has achieved from the pace of a man walking to space satellites, and the number of electronic circuits that could be put into a cubic foot of space. In every case, the rising curves on the graphs showed almost identical shapes, starting their rise slowly, then sharper and sharper until, in our times, nearly every trend line of force is embarked on a vertical course.

Some of the idea of the dimensions of change in our times, and the acceleration of it, can be found in the fact that, "Half of all the energy consumed by man in the past two thousand years has been consumed within the last one hundred." Kenneth Boulding, the economist and writer, finds that, "For many statistical series of quantities of metal or other materials extracted, the dividing line is about 1910. That is, man took about as much out of mines before 1910 as he did after 1910."

The picture of our world that emerges is as if all the rockets at Cape Kennedy were to go off at once, in some grand Fourth of July, and their skyward-soaring trails were the trend lines of our exploding technology.

Writing on "The Era of Radical Change," in *Fortune* magazine, Max Ways has said, "Within a decade or two it will be generally understood that the main challenge to U.S. society will turn not around the production of goods but around the difficulties and opportunities involved in a world of accelerating change and ever-widening choices. Change has always been a part of the human condition. What is different now is the pace of change, and the prospect that it will come faster and faster, affecting every part of life, including personal values, morality, and religions, which seem most remote from technology.

"So swift is the acceleration that trying to 'make sense' of change will come to be our basic industry. Aesthetic and ethical values will be evolving along with the choices to which they will be applied. The question about progress will be 'how good?' rather than 'how much?' "

He goes on to point out that, "The break between the period of rapid change and that of radical change is not sharp; 1950 is an arbitrary starting date. More aspects of life change faster until it is no longer appropriate to think of society as mainly fixed, or changing slowly, while the tide flows around it. So many patterns of life are being modified that it is no longer useful to organize discussion or debate mainly around the relation of the new to the old.

"The movement is so swift, so wide and the prospect of acceleration so great that an imaginative leap into the future cannot find a point of rest, a still picture of social order."

We are told that 25 per cent of all the people who ever lived are alive today; that 90 per cent of all the scientists who ever lived are living now; the amount of technical information available doubles every ten years; throughout the world, about 100,000 journals are published in more than 60 languages, and the number doubles every 15 years.

We are told these things, but we do not always act as if we believed them. "The fact is," says Alvin Toffler, " — and simple observation of one's own friends and associates will confirm it — that even the most educated people today operate on the assumption that society is relatively static. At best they attempt to plan by making simple straight-line projections of present trends. The result is unreadiness to meet the future when it arrives. In short, 'future shock.'

"Society has many built-in time spanners that help link the present generation with the past. Our sense of the past is developed by contact with the older generation, by our knowledge of history, by the accumulated heritage of art, music, literature and science passed down to us through the years. It is enhanced by immediate contact with the objects that surround us, each of which has a point of origin with the past, each of which provides us with a trace of identification with the past.

"No such time spanners enhance our sense of the future. We have no objects, no friends, no relatives, no works of art, no music or literature that originate in the future. We have, as it were, no heritage of the future."

And so, not having one, and needing it, we will have to develop one. This can be done, perhaps, by examining the forces of change around us and by trying to understand how they originated, where they are likely to be going, and how we can to some extent, by guiding them, cushion ourselves against "future shock."

We might begin by seeing ourselves in a somewhat different relationship to time than we are accustomed to. We can agree that there is not much we can do to affect the past, and that the present is so fleeting, as we experience it, that it is transformed into the past as we touch it. It is only the future that is amenable to our plans and actions. Knowing this, we can draw a broad general outline of the kind of future world we feel we would be most happy in. And because we have now arrived at a stage in our development, or shortly will arrive there, where our most pressing problems are not technological, but political and social — we can achieve the world that we want by working together to get it.

The forces of change *are* amenable to our guidance. If we seem to be hurried into the future by a runaway engine, it may be that the main reason it is running away is that we have not bothered yet to learn how it works, nor to steer it in the direction we want it to go.

Number of words 1680
See page 189 for Questions

Reading time in seconds _____
See page 358 for Conversion Table

I'll Remember It in a Minute
Corey Ford

Do you have trouble remembering things? Don't let that worry you. By the time you finish this article, you'll feel distinctly superior. After all, you can't be as forgetful as this fellow. Go ahead. Enjoy his difficulties.

Let's see, what was I going to say? It was right on the tip of my tongue. Oh, yes, about my memory.

Frankly, I've got a mind like a steel sieve. Things go in one ear, but that's as far as they get. Right now if you asked me, for instance, I couldn't tell you where I'm meeting my wife for lunch. I can't recall the license of my car, I have to look up my own phone number in the book, and I haven't the slightest idea what this string around my finger is for. People are always coming up to me and saying, "I bet you don't know who I am," and, what's more, they're always right. I never remember names.

Maybe I don't concentrate properly when I'm introduced. I'm so busy trying to look the other person smack in the eye — some book I read, I forget the title, said the first impression is very important — that I don't catch his name when he gives it. I thrust out my jaw — that's what the book said — seize his hand in a vice-like grip, yank it toward me and downward at the same time and pronounce my own name in a forceful tone: "Ford." As a result, the name "Ford" is fixed firmly in my mind, and I can remember it the rest of the evening, but when I meet the other person again I call him "Hi-ya boy," or "Hi," for short. Most of the people I know are named "Hi-ya boy."

On the other hand, I always forget a face. That is, I recognize the face, but I can't place the person it belongs to. When I join a cocktail party I'll snub the host completely, stare coldly at an important business client with whom I had dinner last night, and make a bee-line across the room to pump the hand of an old college classmate whom I've been trying to avoid for years and who takes advantage of my enthusiastic greeting to borrow ten dollars.

The safest solution, I've found, is to nod to everyone I meet, creating the impression that I'm running for public office. If I see anybody waving in a crowd, I smile and wave in return. Usually it turns out that he is trying to attract the attention of someone standing behind me, which means that I must arrest my gesture in midair and pretend that I was just reaching up to scratch my ear, or that I was waving at someone behind him. The trouble is that the person behind him is apt to wave back.

It's even worse when I spot a familiar-looking face on the street. I halt and stare intently into a store window, occasionally glancing over my shoulder to see if the owner of the face is still there. Unfortunately, he spots me at the same time and halts before another store window casting furtive looks in my direction. Sooner or later our glances meet, and we greet each other with well-feigned surprise, exclaiming, "Well, what do you know!" and clapping each other on the back to cover the fact that we're both a little guilty about having failed to keep in touch all these years.

We start walking down the street together, assuring each other that we haven't changed a bit and asking how everything is and what's new lately, while I thumb frantically through the pages of memory's album in search of some revealing clue. *Met him at Cape Cod last summer? Member of the club? Cousin Ettie's husband?* "How's the wife?" I try, just a feeler.

"Oh, Myrtle's fine thanks," he replies, dashing that hope.

I turn the corner, he turns it too. *Can't I ever get rid of him?* "Sure I'm not taking you out of your way?" I ask pointedly.

"Not a bit," he insists. "It's right in my direction."

By this time our conversation has dwindled to a few sporadic remarks like, "Hot enough for you?" or "How do you like the Giants?" and I wonder what I'll do if I meet somebody and have to introduce him. *Played golf together once? Sells insurance? Friend of Bill's?* "Ever hear from Bill?" I attempt.

"Bill who?" he counters, and we lapse into silence again.

I start down my own block, but he clings stubbornly to the last. I halt before my house in relief, and we shake hands. "Well, it's been great seeing you," I nod, starting up my path.

"We'll have to do it more often," he nods, and starts up the path of the house next door.

It's hard enough for me to remember a story I've heard, but it's even harder to remember where I heard it. Just as I'm halfway through a good one that somebody told me lately, I detect a certain glassy expression on my listener's face, which can be compared roughly to the sympathetic look you might give a doddering uncle who is well-meaning but not quite bright. The further I get with the story, the more patient his smile becomes. Along about the time I reach the point, the horrid realization dawns that I told the same story to him yesterday. Not only that, but he's the one who told it to me the day before.

I have the same trouble when I try to buy a shirt. Somehow the figure "36" sticks in my mind, but I'm not sure whether it's my neck size or the waistband of my trousers. Probably the number is printed on the bottom of the shirt I'm wearing, but I'd look pretty silly pulling out my shirttail in front of a storeful of people. I point vaguely to the pile on the counter and tell the clerk, "That one seems about right," which accounts for the way my sleeves hang down around my wrists — and is why my collar looks like that of a Rangeley guide who has driven into Bangor for the weekend.

I'm no good at all on birthdays or wedding anniversaries or dental appointments, but for some reason my wife never forgets a date. This isn't because women have better memories than men, I'm convinced, but because they forget different things. For instance, a woman can't recall where she put something, whereas a man knows right where he put it, but he can't think what it was he put there.

My wife has an uncanny faculty for remembering something I said six years ago, which she brings up triumphantly at the appropriate moment during an argument. She has never forgotten that I admitted once I had a weakness for redheads, and she hasn't let me forget it either. She's able to tell exactly when Elsie's baby is due, she'll report the entire menu they served at the bridge-club luncheon, and she can quote verbatim what that idiotic salesgirl said to her and what she told the salesgirl. On the other hand, when we start out of the house together she can never remember whether she left her cigarette burning.

It isn't that I don't retain. My mind is a veritable storehouse of assorted facts, like the names of all the living ex-Presidents, the declension of the Latin noun tuba (*tuba, tubae, tubae* or not *tubae*), the weight of the world's-record brook trout, or the first six verses of The Ancient Mariner. In short, I can remember anything, provided it is useless. I can count up to ten in Navajo, border the state of Tennessee and order a fried egg in Malay (*mata sapi,* in case you think I'm kidding); but when I try to give a taxi driver the address of my insurance company in the city, I draw a total blank. I'd go back to my hotel room and look it up, but I've forgotten the address of the hotel.

I suppose the answer is to train your memory. This book I was reading — I wish I could tell you its name — claims that the best way to remember a name is to associate it with the name of something else. It seems to me this means you'd have two things to remember instead of one, but probably the author knows what he's talking about. All right. Let's say, for instance, that I meet a Mr. Garden, and I want to establish his name in my mind. A garden needs fertilizer, and fertilizer suggests a barn, and a barn usually has cows in it, and cows produce butter, and butter reminds me of that grease spot on my necktie. So, the next time I meet Mr. Garden, I glance at my necktie — I assume I'm still wearing the same necktie — run through the list backward, extend my hand, smile pleasantly and say, "How do you do, Mr. Fertilizer." It's as easy as that.

It's just as easy to remember telephone numbers. Suppose I want to think of Ocean 9-2561. The 9 is a baseball team, of course, and 2 and 5 are the respective ages of my wife's sister's two children, and 6 plus 1 makes 7, which is my hat size. So I can think of my wife's sister's two children playing baseball with my hat in the ocean, or else I can look up the number in the directory and save myself all the trouble. The main thing to realize is that the mind is a muscle which can be developed with proper exercise, according to this book on memory. It's funny I can't think of the title. I know it as well as I know my own name —

My name? That's easy. It's right here at the top of this article, if I could remember where I put the magazine.

Number of words 1620
See page 191 for Questions

Reading time in Seconds _____
See page 358 for Conversion Table

How to Remember: Some Basic Principles

Robert L. Montgomery

Memory has both humorous and serious sides. Sample the serious. Why be content with a 10 percent level of remembering when you can tap three basic laws and triple your memory power? After all, improved memory means improved communication.

THE PREREQUISITES

Most of us, psychologists say, don't use more than 10 percent of our native ability to remember. That's comparable to running a car on one or two cylinders and just poking along.

Why don't we use more of our inherent memory power? There are several answers. First, because we haven't been trained to. Nowhere in our schooling were we taught how to use our powers of memory. And second, because we often just don't *care*. And that leads me to the three things that I feel are essential to a more powerful memory.

First, you must have a burning *desire* to improve your memory. *You must care about it.* Most people struggle along with poor memories, enduring endless frustrations and embarrassments in their daily lives, because they just don't want to be bothered remembering the constant barrage of names, numbers, facts, and information. What you have to do is remind yourself of the many benefits of a good memory: the increased confidence I promised you, the popularity, the peace of mind. Aren't those three alone enough to stir a desire in you to improve?

The second prerequisite is the ability to *concentrate*. You will be effective in remembering to the degree that you care enough to concentrate. A short period of intense concentration will often enable you to accomplish more than years of dreaming.

The third prerequisite was revealed to me by former Postmaster-General James Farley of New York City. Mr. Farley was cited by associates for having the most remarkable memory in this century. I asked him his secret.

"There's no real secret," he said. "You simply must *love people*. If you do, you won't have any trouble remembering their names, and a lot more about them than that."

And that's the third essential: You must *care about people*. It wasn't long after I talked to Mr. Farley that I came across an interesting line from Alexander Pope. "How vast a memory has love," he wrote. Certainly a

deeper interest in people, and in your work as well, should make your desire to remember and your concentration much easier.

THE BASIC LAWS

Visualize. Now you're ready to learn the basic techniques for developing your memory. The first essential is to *visualize*. Picture what you want to remember. Since 85 percent of all you learn and remember in life reaches you through your eyes, it is absolutely vital that you visualize the things you want to recall later. To do that, you must above all become *aware*. And awareness involves becoming both a keen observer and an active listener. You have to see clearly and hear accurately in order to picture vividly what you want to remember. Too many people go through life only partly awake, only partly aware. They don't forget names; they never hear them clearly in the first place. The art of *retention* is the art of *attention*.

Become curious, observant, and sensitive to everything around you. See the roof detail on that old building. Notice the difference between the tree greens of April and of August. Hear the difference between the sirens of an ambulance, a fire truck, a police car. Sharpen your senses of sight and hearing — they're the most important. Together, those two senses account for 95 percent of our memory power. Two ancient sayings highlight the importance of visualizing. "One time seeing is worth a thousand times hearing." And "A picture is worth ten thousand words."

Repeat. If school didn't bother to teach us formal memory work, it did teach us the need for *repeating*. We were taught to memorize by repeating a poem, a date, or the alphabet over and over again. Radio and television commercials rely heavily on repetition to remind listeners to buy, buy, buy.

Is there an American who doesn't recognize "Try it, you'll like it" or "I can't believe I ate the whole thing"? Burger King's famous "Have it your way" moved McDonald's, who got busy and created the line, "You, you're the one." When slogans like these are set to music, people don't just remember them — they even sing them. And there you have the secret of success: repetition.

Associate. Before we get into actual demonstrations of the kinds of memory and the application of techniques, there's one more key to memory, and it's the most important. The one indispensable fundamental is the requirement that you *associate* anything you want to recall later. Association is the natural as well as the easy way to assure instant recall. Your brain is more remarkable than even the most amazing computer in the world. And the principle on which it works is association. The brain is, in fact, an associating machine. To recall a name, date, or fact, what the brain needs is a cue, a clue.

Let's step back into history for a moment. Over 2,000 years ago Aristotle defined what he called the Primary Laws of Association. There is the Law of Resemblance or Similarity, where one impression tends to bring to mind another impression which resembles it in some way. There is the Law of Contrast or Opposites, which says that where there are two or more opposing impressions, the presence of one will tend to recall the others. And finally there is the Law of Contiguity or Togetherness. If two or more impressions occur at the same time, or follow close on one another in either time or space, thinking of one will recall the other.

There are secondary Laws of Association as well, and these are known as Recency, Frequency, and Vividness. *Recency* means we tend to recall associations made recently much better than those made months or years ago. *Frequency* implies that the more often you repeat an association, the easier it will be to recall. And *vividness* means that the more graphic or striking the association is, the quicker you'll be able to recall it.

In summary, the requirements for improving your memory are concentration, a desire to remember, and a love for people.

And the techniques for mastering the art of memory are visualizing, repeating, and associating.

One final note, this time on how to study: Memorizing anything is easier and faster when you practice for a half hour or so, and then go off and forget it for a while. Work again later for another half hour, then take another break. Tests have proved time and again that we learn better and faster when we alternate work and rest in a sort of wave pattern. The rest period actually reinforces the learning.

Now then, can you remember all that?

Number of words 1100
See page 193 for Questions

Reading time in Seconds _____
See page 358 for Conversion Table

The Open Window

Saki

Carl Gustav Jung, Swiss psychiatrist, once said, "The debt we owe to the play of imagination is incalculable." Yes — how dull communication would be without the spice of imagination, as the following story so well illustrates.

"My aunt will be down presently, Mr. Nuttel," said a very self-possessed young lady of fifteen; "in the meantime you must try and put up with me."

Framton Nuttel endeavoured to say the correct something which should duly flatter the niece of the moment without unduly discounting the aunt that was to come. Privately he doubted more than ever whether these formal visits on a succession of total strangers would do much towards helping the nerve cure which he was supposed to be undergoing.

"I know how it will be," his sister had said when he was preparing to migrate to this rural retreat; "you will bury yourself down there and not speak to a living soul,

and your nerves will be worse than ever from moping. I shall just give you letters of introduction to all the people I know there. Some of them, as far as I can remember, were quite nice."

Framton wondered whether Mrs. Sappleton, the lady to whom he was presenting one of the letters of introduction, came into the nice division.

"Do you know many of the people round here?" asked the niece, when she judged that they had sufficient silent communion.

"Hardly a soul," said Framton. "My sister was staying here, at the rectory, you know, some four years ago, and she gave me letters of introduction to some of the people here."

He made the last statement in a tone of distinct regret.

"Then you know practically nothing about my aunt?" pursued the self-possessed young lady.

"Only her name and address," admitted the caller. He was wondering whether Mrs. Sappleton was in the married or widowed state. An undefinable something about the room seemed to suggest masculine habitation.

"Her great tragedy happened just three years ago," said the child; "that would be since your sister's time."

"Her tragedy?" asked Framton; somehow in this restful country spot tragedies seemed out of place.

"You may wonder why we keep that window wide open on an October afternoon," said the niece, indicating a large French window that opened on to a lawn.

"It is quite warm for the time of the year," said Framton; "but has that window got anything to do with the tragedy?"

"Out through that window, three years ago to a day, her husband and her two young brothers went off for their day's shooting. They never came back. In crossing the moor to their favourite snipe-shooting ground they were all three engulfed in a treacherous piece of bog. It had been dreadful that summer, you know, and places that were safe in other years gave way suddenly without warning. Their bodies were never recovered. That was the dreadful part of it." Here the child's voice lost its self-possessed note and became falteringly human. "Poor aunt always thinks that they will come back some day, they and the little brown spaniel that was lost with them, and walk in at that window just as they used to do. That is why the window is kept open every evening till it is quite dusk. Poor dear aunt, she has often told me how they went out, her husband with his white waterproof coat over his arm, and Ronnie, her youngest brother, singing, 'Bertie, why do you bound?' as he always did to tease her, because she said it got on her nerves. Do you know, sometimes on still, quiet evenings like this, I almost get a creepy feeling that they will all walk in through that window—"

She broke off with a little shudder. It was a relief to Framton when the aunt bustled into the room with a whirl of apologies for being late in making her appearance.

"I hope Vera has been amusing you?" she said.

"She has been very interesting," said Framton.

"I hope you don't mind the open window," said Mrs. Sappleton briskly; "my husband and brothers will be home directly from shooting, and they always come in this way. They've been out for snipe in the marshes today, so they'll make a fine mess over my poor carpets. So like you men-folk, isn't it?"

She rattled on cheerfully about the shooting and the scarcity of birds, and the prospects for duck in the winter. To Framton it was all purely horrible. He made a desperate but only partially successful effort to turn the talk on to a less ghastly topic; he was conscious that his hostess was giving him only a fragment of her attention, and her eyes were constantly straying past him to the open window and the lawn beyond. It was certainly an unfortunate coincidence that he should have paid his visit on this tragic anniversary.

"The doctors agree in ordering me complete rest, an absence of mental excitement, and avoidance of anything in the nature of violent physical exercise," announced Framton, who laboured under the tolerably widespread delusion that total strangers and chance acquaintances are hungry for the least detail of one's ailments and infirmities, their cause and cure. "On the matter of diet they are not so much in agreement," he continued.

"No?" said Mrs. Sappleton, in a voice which only replaced a yawn at the last moment. Then she suddenly brightened into alert attention—but not to what Framton was saying.

"Here they are at last!" she cried. "Just in time for tea, and don't they look as if they were muddy up to the eyes!"

Framton shivered slightly and turned towards the niece with a look intended to convey sympathetic comprehension. The child was staring out through the open window with dazed horror in her eyes. In a chill shock of nameless fear Framton swung round in his seat and looked in the same direction.

In the deepening twilight three figures were walking across the lawn towards the window; they all carried guns under their arms, and one of them was additionally burdened with a white coat hung over his shoulders. A tired brown spaniel kept close at their heels. Noiselessly they neared the house, and then a hoarse young voice chanted out of the dusk: "I said, Bertie, why do you bound?"

Framton grabbed wildly at his stick and hat; the hall-door, the gravel-drive, and the front gate were dimly noted stages in his headlong retreat. A cyclist coming along the road had to run into the hedge to avoid imminent collision.

"Here we are, my dear," said the bearer of the white mackintosh, coming in through the window; "fairly muddy, but most of it's dry. Who was that who bolted out as we came up?"

"A most extraordinary man, a Mr. Nuttel," said Mrs. Sappleton; "could only talk about his illness, and dashed off without a word of good-bye or apology when you arrived. One would think he had seen a ghost."

"I expect it was the spaniel," said the niece calmly; "he told me he had a horror of dogs. He was once hunted into a cemetery somewhere on the banks of the Ganges by a pack of pariah dogs, and had to spend the night in a newly dug grave with the creatures snarling and grinning and foaming just above him. Enough to make any one lose their nerve."

Romance at short notice was her specialty.

Number of words 1210
See page 195 for Questions

Reading time in Seconds _____
See page 358 for Conversion Table

Love Is a Fallacy

Max Shulman

Perhaps a personal computer, not a raccoon coat, puts you in the swim today. College life may change over the years, but logical fallacies seem always the same, from Aristotle to the present. In the following selection, logical fallacies don't get the usual staid textbook treatment, as you'll soon find out.

Cool was I and logical. Keen, calculating, perspicacious, acute and astute — I was all of these. My brain was as powerful as a dynamo, as precise as a chemist's scales, as penetrating as a scalpel. And — think of it! — I was only eighteen.

It is not often that one so young has such a giant intellect. Take, for example, Petey Bellows, my roommate at the university. Same age, same background, but dumb as an ox. A nice enough fellow, you understand, but nothing upstairs. Emotional type. Unstable. Impressionable. Worst of all, a faddist. Fads, I submit, are the very negation of reason. To be swept up in every new craze that comes along, to surrender yourself to idiocy just because everybody else is doing it — this, to me, is the acme of mindlessness. Not, however, to Petey.

One afternoon I found Petey lying on his bed with an expression of such distress on his face that I immediately diagnosed appendicitis. "Don't move," I said. "Don't take a laxative. I'll get a doctor."

"Raccoon," he mumbled thickly.

"Raccoon?" I said, pausing in my flight.

"I want a raccoon coat," he wailed.

I perceived that his trouble was not physical, but mental. "Why do you want a raccoon coat?"

"I should have known it," he cried, pounding his temples. "I should have known they'd come back when the Charleston came back. Like a fool I spent all my money for textbooks, and now I can't get a raccoon coat."

"Can you mean," I said incredulously, "that people are actually wearing raccoon coats again?"

"All the Big Men on Campus are wearing them. Where've you been?"

"In the library," I said, naming a place not frequented by Big Men on Campus.

He leaped from the bed and paced the room. "I've got to have a raccoon coat," he said passionately. "I've got to!"

"Petey, why? Look at it rationally. Raccoon coats are unsanitary. They shed. They smell bad. They weigh too much. They're unsightly. They —— "

"You don't understand," he interrupted impatiently.

"It's the thing to do. Don't you want to be in the swim?"

"No," I said truthfully.

"Well, I do," he declared. "I'd give anything for a raccoon coat. Anything!"

My brain, that precision instrument, slipped into high gear. "Anything?" I asked, looking at him narrowly.

"Anything," he affirmed in ringing tones.

I stroked my chin thoughtfully. It so happened that I knew where to get my hands on a raccoon coat. My father had had one in his undergraduate days; it lay now in a trunk in the attic back home. It also happened that Petey had something I wanted. He didn't *have* it exactly, but at least he had first rights on it. I refer to his girl, Polly Espy.

I had long coveted Polly Espy. Let me emphasize that my desire for this young woman was not emotional in nature. She was, to be sure, a girl who excited the emotions, but I was not one to let my heart rule my head. I wanted Polly for a shrewdly calculated, entirely cerebral reason.

I was a freshman in law school. In a few years I would be out in practice. I was well aware of the importance of the right kind of wife in furthering a lawyer's career. The successful lawyers I had observed were, almost without exception, married to beautiful, gracious, intelligent women. With one omission, Polly fitted these specifications perfectly.

Beautiful she was. She was not yet of pin-up proportions, but I felt sure that time would supply the lack. She already had the makings.

Gracious she was. By gracious I mean full of graces. She had an erectness of carriage, an ease of bearing, a poise that clearly indicated the best of breeding. At table her manners were exquisite. I had seen her at the Kozy Kampus Korner eating the specialty of the house — a sandwich that contained scraps of pot roast, gravy, chopped nuts, and a dipper of sauerkraut — without even getting her fingers moist.

Intelligent she was not. In fact, she veered in the opposite direction. But I believed that under my guidance she would smarten up. At any rate, it was worth a try. It is, after all, easier to make a beautiful dumb girl smart than to make an ugly smart girl beautiful.

"Petey," I said, "are you in love with Polly Espy?"

"I think she's a keen kid," he replied, "but I don't know if you'd call it love. Why?"

"Do you," I asked, "have any kind of formal arrangement with her? I mean are you going steady or anything like that?"

"No. We see each other quite a bit, but we both have other dates. Why?"

"Is there," I asked, "any other man for whom she has a particular fondness?"

"Not that I know of. Why?"

I nodded with satisfaction. "In other words, if you were out of the picture, the field would be open. Is that right?"

"I guess so. What are you getting at?"

"Nothing, nothing," I said innocently, and took my suitcase out of the closet.

"Where you going?" asked Petey.

"Home for the week end." I threw a few things into the bag.

"Listen," he said, clutching my arm eagerly, "while you're home, you couldn't get some money from your old man, could you, and lend it to me so I can buy a raccoon coat?"

"I may do better than that," I said with a mysterious wink and closed my bag and left.

"Look," I said to Petey when I got back Monday morning. I threw open the suitcase and revealed the huge, hairy, gamy object that my father had worn in his Stutz Bearcat in 1925.

"Holy Toledo!" said Petey reverently. He plunged his hands into the raccoon coat and then his face. "Holy Toledo!" he repeated fifteen or twenty times.

"Would you like it?" I asked.

"Oh yes!" he cried, clutching the greasy pelt to him. Then a canny look came into his eyes. "What do you want for it?"

"Your girl," I said, mincing no words.

"Polly?" he said in a horrified whisper. "You want Polly?"

"That's right."

He flung the coat from him. "Never," he said stoutly.

I shrugged. "Okay. If you don't want to be in the swim, I guess it's your business."

I sat down in a chair and pretended to read a book, but out of the corner of my eye I kept watching Petey. He was a torn man. First he looked at the coat with the expression of a waif at a bakery window. Then he turned away and set his jaw resolutely. Then he looked back at the coat, with even more longing in his face. Then he turned away, but with not so much resolution this time. Back and forth his head swiveled, desire waxing, resolution waning. Finally he didn't turn away at all; he just stood and stared with mad lust at the coat.

"It isn't as though I was in love with Polly," he said thickly. "Or going steady or anything like that."

"That's right," I murmured.

"What's Polly to me, or me to Polly?"

"Not a thing," said I.

"It's just been a casual kick — just a few laughs, that's all."

"Try on the coat," said I.

He complied. The coat bunched high over his ears and dropped all the way down to his shoe tops. He looked like a mound of dead raccoons. "Fits fine," he said happily.

I rose from my chair. "Is it a deal?" I asked, extending my hand.

He swallowed. "It's a deal," he said and shook my hand.

I had my first date with Polly the following evening. This was in the nature of a survey; I wanted to find out just how much work I had to do to get her mind up to the standard I required. I took her first to dinner. "Gee, that was a delish dinner," she said as we left the restaurant. Then I took her to a movie. "Gee, that was a marvy movie," she said as we left the theater. And then I took her home. "Gee, I had a sensaysh time," she said as she bade me good night.

I went back to my room with a heavy heart. I had gravely underestimated the size of my task. This girl's lack of information was terrifying. Nor would it be enough merely to supply her with information. First she had to be taught to *think*. This loomed as a project of no small dimensions, and at first I was tempted to give her back to Petey. But then I got to thinking about her abundant physical charms and about the way she entered a room and the way she handled a knife and fork, and I decided to make an effort.

I went about it, as in all things, systematically. I gave her a course in logic. It happened that I, as a law student, was taking a course in logic myself, so I had all the facts at my finger tips. "Polly," I said to her when I picked her up on our next date, "tonight we are going over to the Knoll and talk."

"Oo, terrif," she replied. One thing I will say for this girl: you would go far to find another so agreeable.

We went to the Knoll, the campus trysting place, and we sat down under an old oak, and she looked at me expectantly. "What are we going to talk about?" she asked.

"Logic."

She thought this over for a minute and decided she liked it. "Magnif," she said.

"Logic," I said, clearing my throat, "is the science of thinking. Before we can think correctly, we must first learn to recognize the common fallacies of logic. These we will take up tonight."

"Wow-dow!" she cried, clapping her hands delightedly.

I winced, but went bravely on. "First let us examine the fallacy called Dicto Simpliciter."

"By all means," she urged, batting her lashes eagerly.

"Dicto Simpliciter means an argument based on an unqualified generalization. For example: Exercise is good. Therefore everybody should exercise."

"I agree," said Polly earnestly. "I mean exercise is wonderful. I mean it builds the body and everything."

"Polly," I said gently, "the argument is a fallacy. *Exercise is good* is an unqualified generalization. For instance, if you have heart disease, exercise is bad, not good. Many people are ordered by their doctors *not* to exercise. You must *qualify* the generalization. You must say exercise is *usually* good, or exercise is good *for most people*. Otherwise you have committed a Dicto Simpliciter. Do you see?"

"No," she confessed. "But this is marvy. Do more! Do more!"

"It will be better if you stop tugging at my sleeve," I told her, and when she desisted, I continued. "Next we take up a fallacy called Hasty Generalization. Listen carefully: You can't speak French. I can't speak French. Petey Bellows can't speak French. I must therefore conclude that nobody at the University of Minnesota can speak French."

"Really?" said Polly, amazed. *"Nobody?"*

I hid my exasperation. "Polly, it's a fallacy. The generalization is reached too hastily. There are too few instances to support such a conclusion."

"Know any more fallacies?" she asked breathlessly. "This is more fun than dancing even."

I fought off a wave of despair. I was getting nowhere with this girl, absolutely nowhere. Still, I am nothing if not persistent. I continued. "Next comes Post Hoc. Listen to this: Let's not take Bill on our picnic. Every time we take him out with us, it rains."

"I know somebody just like that," she exclaimed. "A girl back home — Eula Becker, her name is. It never fails. Every single time we take her on a picnic — "

"Polly," I said sharply, "it's a fallacy. Eula Becker doesn't *cause* the rain. She has no connection with the rain. You are guilty of Post Hoc if you blame Eula Becker."

"I'll never do it again," she promised contritely. "Are you mad at me?"

I sighed. "No, Polly, I'm not mad."

"Then tell me some more fallacies."

"All right. Let's try Contradictory Premises."

"Yes, let's," she chirped, blinking her eyes happily.

I frowned, but plunged ahead. "Here's an example of Contradictory Premises: If God can do anything, can He make a stone so heavy that He won't be able to lift it?"

"Of course," she replied promptly.

"But if He can do anything, He can lift the stone," I pointed out.

"Yeah," she said thoughtfully. "Well, then I guess He can't make the stone."

"But He can do anything," I reminded her.

She scratched her pretty, empty head. "I'm all confused," she admitted.

"Of course you are. Because when the premises of an argument contradict each other, there can be no

argument. If there is an irresistible force, there can be no immovable object. If there is an immovable object, there can be no irresistible force. Get it?"

"Tell me some more of this keen stuff," she said eagerly.

I consulted my watch. "I think we'd better call it a night. I'll take you home now, and you go over all the things you've learned. We'll have another session tomorrow night."

I deposited her at the girls' dormitory, where she assured me that she had had a perfectly terrif evening, and I went glumly home to my room. Petey lay snoring in his bed, the raccoon coat huddled like a great hairy beast at his feet. For a moment I considered waking him and telling him that he could have his girl back. It seemed clear that my project was doomed to failure. The girl simply had a logic-proof head.

But then I reconsidered. I had wasted one evening; I might as well waste another. Who knew? Maybe somewhere in the extinct crater of her mind a few embers still smoldered. Maybe somehow I could fan them into flame. Admittedly it was not a prospect fraught with hope, but I decided to give it one more try.

Seated under the oak the next evening I said, "Our first fallacy tonight is called Ad Misericordiam."

She quivered with delight.

"Listen closely," I said. "A man applies for a job. When the boss asks him what his qualifications are, he replies that he has a wife and six children at home, the wife is a helpless cripple, the children have nothing to eat, no clothes to wear, no shoes on their feet, there are no beds in the house, no coal in the cellar, and winter is coming."

A tear rolled down each of Polly's pink cheeks. "Oh, this is awful, awful," she sobbed.

"Yes, it's awful," I agreed, "but it's no argument. The man never answered the boss's question about his qualifications. Instead he appealed to the boss's sympathy. He committed the fallacy of Ad Misericordiam. Do you understand?"

"Have you got a handkerchief?" she blubbered.

I handed her a handkerchief and tried to keep from screaming while she wiped her eyes. "Next," I said in a carefully controlled tone, "we will discuss False Analogy. Here is an example: Students should be allowed to look at their textbooks during examinations. After all, surgeons have X-rays to guide them during an operation, lawyers have briefs to guide them during a trial, carpenters have blueprints to guide them when they are building a house. Why, then, shouldn't students be allowed to look at their textbooks during an examination?"

"There now," she said enthusiastically, "is the most marvy idea I've heard in years."

"Polly," I said testily, "the argument is all wrong. Doctors, lawyers, and carpenters aren't taking a test to see how much they have learned, but students are. The situations are altogether different, and you can't make an analogy between them."

"I still think it's a good idea," said Polly.

"Nuts," I muttered. Doggedly I pressed on. "Next we'll try Hypothesis Contrary to Fact."

"Sounds yummy," was Polly's reaction.

"Listen: If Madame Curie had not happened to leave a photographic plate in a drawer with a chunk of pitchblende, the world today would not know about radium."

"True, true," said Polly, nodding her head. "Did you see the movie? Oh, it just knocked me out. That Walter Pidgeon is so dreamy. I mean he fractures me."

"If you can forget Mr. Pidgeon for a moment," I said coldly, "I would like to point out that the statement is a fallacy. Maybe Madame Curie would have discovered radium at some later date. Maybe somebody else would have discovered it. Maybe any number of things would have happened. You can't start with a hypothesis that is not true and then draw any supportable conclusions from it."

"They ought to put Walter Pidgeon in more pictures," said Polly. "I hardly ever see him any more."

One more chance, I decided. But just one more. There is a limit to what flesh and blood can bear. "The next fallacy is called Poisoning the Well."

"How cute!" she gurgled.

"Two men are having a debate. The first one gets up and says, 'My opponent is a notorious liar. You can't believe a word that he is going to say.' . . . Now, Polly, think. Think hard. What's wrong?"

I watched her closely as she knit her creamy brow in concentration. Suddenly a glimmer of intelligence — the first I had seen — came into her eyes. "It's not fair," she said with indignation. "It's not a bit fair. What chance has the second man got if the first man calls him a liar before he even begins talking?"

"Right!" I cried exultantly. "One hundred per cent right. It's not fair. The first man has *poisoned the well* before anybody could drink from it. He has hamstrung his opponent before he could even start. . . . Polly, I'm proud of you."

"Pshaw," she murmured, blushing with pleasure.

"You see, my dear, these things aren't so hard. All you have to do is concentrate. Think — examine — evaluate. Come now, let's review everything we have learned."

"Fire away," she said with an airy wave of her hand.

Heartened by the knowledge that Polly was not altogether a cretin, I began a long, patient review of all I had told her. Over and over and over again I cited instances, pointed out flaws, kept hammering away without letup. It was like digging a tunnel. At first everything was work, sweat, and darkness. I had no idea when I would reach the light, or even *if* I would. But I persisted. I pounded and clawed and scraped, and finally I was rewarded. I saw a chink of light. And then

the chink got bigger and the sun came pouring in and all was bright.

Five grueling nights this took, but it was worth it. I had made a logician out of Polly; I had taught her to think. My job was done. She was worthy of me at last. She was a fit wife for me, a proper hostess for my many mansions, a suitable mother for my well-heeled children.

It must not be thought that I was without love for this girl. Quite the contrary. Just as Pygmalion loved the perfect woman he had fashioned, so I loved mine. I decided to acquaint her with my feelings at our very next meeting. The time had come to change our relationship from academic to romantic.

"Polly," I said when next we sat beneath our oak, "tonight we will not discuss fallacies."

"Aw, gee," she said, disappointed.

"My dear," I said, favoring her with a smile, "we have now spent five evenings together. We have gotten along splendidly. It is clear that we are well matched."

"Hasty Generalization," said Polly brightly.

"I beg your pardon," said I.

"Hasty Generalization," she repeated. "How can you say that we are well matched on the basis of only five dates?"

I chuckled with amusement. The dear child had learned her lessons well. "My dear," I said, patting her hand in a tolerant manner, "five dates is plenty. After all, you don't have to eat a whole cake to know that it's good."

"False Analogy," said Polly promptly. "I'm not a cake. I'm a girl."

I chuckled with somewhat less amusement. The dear child had learned her lessons perhaps too well. I decided to change tactics. Obviously the best approach was a simple, strong, direct declaration of love. I paused for a moment while my massive brain chose the proper words. Then I began:

"Polly, I love you. You are the whole world to me, and the moon and the stars and the constellations of outer space. Please, my darling, say that you will go steady with me, for if you will not, life will be meaningless. I will languish. I will refuse my meals. I will wander the face of the earth, a shambling hollow-eyed hulk."

There, I thought, folding my arms, that ought to do it.

"Ad Misericordiam," said Polly.

I ground my teeth. I was not Pygmalion; I was Frankenstein, and my monster had me by the throat. Frantically I fought back the tide of panic surging through me. At all costs I had to keep cool.

"Well, Polly," I said, forcing a smile, "you certainly have learned your fallacies."

"You're darn right," she said with a vigorous nod.

"And who taught them to you, Polly?"

"You did."

"That's right. So you do owe me something, don't you, my dear? If I hadn't come along you never would have learned about fallacies."

"Hypothesis Contrary to Fact," she said instantly.

I dashed perspiration from my brow. "Polly," I croaked, "you mustn't take all these things so literally. I mean this is just classroom stuff. You know that the things you learn in school don't have anything to do with life."

"Dicto Simpliciter," she said, wagging her finger at me playfully.

That did it. I leaped to my feet, bellowing like a bull. "Will you or will you not go steady with me?"

"I will not," she replied.

"Why not?" I demanded.

"Because this afternoon I promised Petey Bellows that I would go steady with him."

I reeled back, overcome with the infamy of it. After

he promised, after he made a deal, after he shook my hand! "The rat!" I shrieked, kicking up great chunks of turf. "You can't go with him, Polly. He's a liar. He's a cheat. He's a rat."

"Poisoning the Well," said Polly, "and stop shouting. I think shouting must be a fallacy too."

With an immense effort of will, I modulated my voice. "All right," I said. "You're a logician. Let's look at this thing logically. How could you choose Petey Bellows over me? Look at me — a brilliant student, a tremendous intellectual, a man with an assured future. Look at Petey — a knothead, a jitterbug, a guy who'll never know where his next meal is coming from. Can you give me one logical reason why you should go steady with Petey Bellows?"

"I certainly can," declared Polly. "He's got a raccoon coat."

Number of words 3850
See page 197 for Questions

Reading time in Seconds _____
See page 358 for Conversion Table

The Importance of Being Interested

H. Addington Bruce

Emerson once said: "Beware of what you want — for you will get it." Was this true with Franklin, Darwin, and Mozart? Perhaps it's want-to, not I.Q., that is most important. If so, how strong is your interest in improving your reading and communicating abilities?

Many years ago there lived in the city of Boston a small boy whose days were spent in a singularly wearisome way. At the age of ten, when most boys are dividing their time between school and play, he was busy all day boiling soap, cutting wicks for tallow candles, filling candle molds, and otherwise drudging as assistant to his father in the soap and candle business. It was a business in which the father took an honest pride, and in thus apprenticing his youngest son to it, he did so with the expectation of giving him full charge and ownership in later years.

As it happened, the son's mind was filled with thoughts of other things than soap and candles. He worked faithfully enough at the kettles and wicks and molds; but he worked with such scant enthusiasm and such little skill that his father soon perceived that he would never become an expert candle-maker. Bitterly disappointed, he nevertheless appreciated the folly of compelling his son to persist in an occupation manifestly uncongenial to him. To another and much older son he one day said:

"Will you take Ben into your printing shop? He will never be a successful chandler, but he may make a fair printer. At any rate, I wish you would give him a chance."

Into the printing shop, accordingly, young Ben went, somewhat against his will, for the handling of inky type seemed to him only a trifle less unpleasant than dealing with greasy molds. But he presently made the important discovery that through typesetting he was in a position both to gain knowledge for himself and to make knowledge available for other people by putting it into print. Forthwith he became interested in printing as he had never been in candle-making; also, he became fired with a desire to learn all he could about as many subjects as possible, and he developed, besides, an ambition to turn author and see his own thoughts take form on the printed page.

Behold him, then, sometimes sitting up the whole night long over Plutarch's *Lives, The Spectator,* Locke's *Essays,* and kindred works of information and literary power. Behold him in the fervor of his zeal turning vegetarian at the age of sixteen, because the greater cheapness of his meals would allow him more money

From the *Outlook*, July 18, 1914.

for books. Behold him scribbling and rescribbling in the effort to give clear expression to the ideas forming in his mind as a result of his wide reading and hard thinking. Finally, behold him timidly slipping under the door of his brother's newspaper office an unsigned essay written in a disguised hand — an essay so good that, on publication, its authorship was variously ascribed to leading writers of the day.

Thereafter he toiled more industriously than ever — printing, reading, thinking, writing. Ere he was thirty he was widely known, and long before his death he was acclaimed on two continents as one of the wisest of men. We of to-day, looking back from the vantage-point of more than a century later, feel that the praise of his contemporaries was not misplaced. For the whilom candle-maker who thus rose to eminence was none other than Benjamin Franklin, philosopher, scientist, diplomat, and apostle of America's freedom.

Take, similarly, the history of an English lad born some twenty years after Franklin died. More happily circumstanced, being the son of a successful physician, this boy was given all the advantages of good schooling. But he did not seem to draw much profit from his lessons. In fact, as he himself has told us, both his father and his teachers were inclined to regard him as "rather below the common standard in intellect." To make matters worse from the father's point of view, he showed a marked distaste for the tasks of the schoolroom, and an equally marked fondness for vagabondage.

Gun in hand, he would roam for hours through verdant lanes or across the open country. "You care for nothing but shooting, dogs, and rat-catching, and you will be a disgrace to yourself and all your family," his father once predicted, mournfully. As the boy grew older, his propensity for idling seemed only to increase. In spite of this, hoping against hope that he would settle down to serious things, his father entered him at the University of Glasgow, with the idea of fitting him for the practice of medicine. "It is no use," the boy frankly avowed after a few months at Glasgow. "I hate the work here, and I cannot possibly be a physician." So earnest were his protests that he was transferred to Cambridge University, on the understanding that he would study to be a clergyman.

At Cambridge, as good fortune would have it, he entered the natural history class of an eminent and enlightened scholar, Professor Henslow, who sent him into the woods and fields to make collections of plants and insects. Free again to roam under the clear blue skies, but this time with a lofty purpose set before his mind, a passion for achievement took possession of him. The boy whom other teachers had found dull and lazy proved himself, under Professor Henslow's inspiring guidance, a marvel of industry and mental vigor. There was no longer any thought of the "last resort"

plan of putting him into the ministry. He would, he assured his now delighted father, devote his whole life to the study of nature's laws.

Thus it came about that, when his college days were over, he eagerly accepted an opportunity to accompany a Government exploring expedition. During that long voyage in southern seas he accumulated a remarkable collection of specimens. What was far more important, he brought back with him to England, after a five years' absence filled with hardships, a mass of new ideas regarding fundamental principles in natural science — ideas which, being masterfully scrutinized and sifted, were afterwards to make him world-famous as Charles Darwin, originator of the doctrine of evolution.

Again, there was born in the German city of Salzburg, about the middle of the eighteenth century, a bright-eyed boy, the son of a Court musician. As was inevitable by reason of his father's vocation, this child, from the hour he first opened his eyes and ears to the world about him, daily heard melody from violin, clavier, and harpsichord. Before he was three years old it was noticed that he not only seemed to take great delight in listening to music, but also that he often attempted with his little fingers to strike harmonious intervals on the clavier. His father, amused but impressed, offered to give him lessons; joyfully the child accepted, and at once a start was made.

Thenceforth music dominated his waking thoughts. The toys of childhood were cast aside, and in their stead he played with the keyed and stringed instruments to which his father gave him ready access. From the first he astonished all around him by his wonderful skill. By the time he was four he could play several minuets on the harp and he was busily composing themes, and in his sixth year he was able to play the violin so well that he once assisted his father and a celebrated violinist in rehearsing trios which the latter had recently composed. Modest, unassuming, bending his every effort to progress in the art which had so fascinated him, the youngster passed in quick succession from one notable feat to another. On all sides the prediction was heard: "If this boy keeps on as he has begun, he will be one of the world-masters of music." Those who are familiar with Mozart's marvelous compositions for church, opera-house, and concert-room know well that the prediction was amply fulfilled.

Now, I have recalled these beginnings of the careers of Franklin, Darwin and Mozart because they strikingly illustrate a profound psychological truth the significance of which can scarcely be overestimated. It is a truth, to be sure, that has long been partially recognized. But its full meaning has not been — and could not be — appreciated until quite recently. Only within the past few years has scientific research effected sundry discoveries which make its complete recognition possible and of supreme importance — of such importance that practical application of the principles involved would make for an immediate and stupendous increase in human happiness, efficiency, and welfare.

Stated briefly, the truth in question is that success in life, meaning thereby the accomplishment of results of real value to the individual and to society, depends chiefly on sustained endeavor springing out of a deep and ardent interest in the tasks of one's chosen occupation. It is not enough merely to be a "hard worker." The world is full of people who slave faithfully at their respective duties, perhaps earn a handsome living, but know in their hearts that they have failed to achieve their possibilities. Yet the trouble with them simply is that they are not really interested in what they are doing. They are "misfits," as Franklin was in his father's candle-shop and Darwin at the University of Glasgow. Unlike Franklin and Darwin, they have not been so fortunate as to stumble eventually upon a vocation capable of inciting in them a passionate enthusiasm; unlike Mozart, they have not had a father wise enough to perceive their natural inclinations and brave enough to safeguard the development of these by an early education. Had they been thus circumstanced, who knows but that they might have attained results fairly comparable with the results attained by Franklin and Darwin and Mozart — all through the dynamic power of interest.

Indeed, evidence is accumulating that it is in this, rather than in any exceptional structure of the brain, that we have the true explanation of the wonderful achievements of so-called "men of genius." Looked at superficially, the mental processes of the man of genius undoubtedly seem to differ greatly from those of the ordinary man. In the case of the former, great ideal, marvelous "inspirations," often spring into consciousness seemingly of their own accord. Napoleon used to say that his battles frequently were won by tactics devised by him on the spur of the moment. "The decisive moment approached, the spark burst forth, and one was victorious." Goethe has testified that not a few of his themes, and sometimes whole poems, came to him from he knew not where. On Schiller's own testimony, when he was consciously at work, creating and constructing, his imagination did not serve him "with the same freedom as it had done when nobody was looking over its shoulder." Likewise we have Mozart's statement that his compositions "came involuntarily, like dreams."

All this, I say, seems very different from the workings of the mind of the ordinary man. Yet, after all, exactly the same sort of thing occurs to the latter. He, too, has his "happy thoughts," his occasional "flashings" of wise decisions, correct solutions of baffling problems, etc. Noticeably, however, his happy thoughts and flashings are always connected with matters to which he has devoted much conscious attention, matters which have been of great interest to him. It is as though, by thinking of them earnestly, he has set in motion some hidden mechanism that has enabled him, smoothly and easily, and all unknown to himself, to arrive at definite conclusions *beneath the threshold of consciousness.*

Precisely thus with the man of genius. A Napoleon's inspirations are not concerned with nature's laws; those of a Darwin have nothing to do with military conquest; those of a Mozart relate neither to problems of science nor problems of war. No, the inspirations of every man of genius are concerned solely with the subject in which, perhaps from earliest childhood, he has taken the greatest interest, and to which he has devoted the greatest thought. Napoleon, it is known, was so absorbed in military matters that, even at the opera, his mind would be incessantly occupied with some such problem as: "I have ten thousand men at Strasbourg, fifteen thousand at Magdeburg, twenty thousand at Würzburg. By what stages must they march so as to reach Ratisbon on three successive days?" The flowering of Darwin's great discovery was not the work of a moment, but was preceded by years of patient, arduous observation.

Mozart, beginning the study of music at the age of three, remained a zealous student all his days.

"Nobody," runs his own account, "takes as much pains in the study of composition as I. You could not easily name a famous master in music whom I have not industriously studied, often going through his works several times." Walking, or at the theater, or even while engaged in social amusements, he lived in a self-created atmosphere of music. "In Prague," Otto Jahn has recorded, "it once happened that Mozart, while he was playing billiards, was humming a motif, and from time to time would look into a book he had with him. Afterward he confessed he had been at work upon the first quintette of the 'Zauberflöte'!" And we have his wife's testimony: "In truth, his head was working all the time, his mind was ever moving, he composed almost unceasingly." As with Napoleon, Darwin, and Mozart, so with all men of genius of whose lives we have any detailed record.

It may, then, be stated as a well-established fact that intense interest plus persistent effort is the prime essential to the highest success in any sphere of human activity. . . .

Number of words 2250
See page 199 for Questions

Reading time in Seconds _____
See page 358 for Conversion Table

SELECTION 7
Computers and Word Processing
Money Magazine

The computer provides the newest mode of communication with such strange languages as BASIC, FORTRAN, PASCAL, and LOGO. Pen and typewriter are fast becoming outdated. Word processing introduces an amazingly different and improved way of writing, or communicating.

First off, computers don't *really* think. People just think they think. The most sophisticated computer is a tool, like a typewriter or a bench vice, only vastly more complicated. Actually, any problem that you can work out on a computer you could solve with bench vices if you had enough of them — a couple of hundred thousand, let's say — and someone stationed to open and close each one.

In reality, the heart of a computer is just so many thousands of microscopic electronic switches, known as gates, printed on a tiny silicon board known as a chip. An electrical charge is routed through these gates, opening some and closing others to create patterns that can be made to approximate the patterns of human logic. Simple enough? Hang on. It gets worse quickly.

These operations take place on the renowned microchip, which is also called a microprocessor or CPU (central processing unit) and is sometimes used synecdochically to refer to the whole motherboard, a platform on which a number of chips are fastened. From the CPU, electric current flows via circuits called buses to other nearby chips — first to ROM (read-only memory) chips. They are nonvolatile, meaning that they retain their information — gates opened in this or that pattern — even when the system isn't on. Then the current goes to the RAM (random-access memory) chips, essentially blank slates that you can program in any configuration manually with your computer's keyboard, or automatically by means of a tape cassette or disk drive. RAM chips are usually volatile, meaning that as soon as you shut off the system, they are wiped clean, so you will have space for new programs.

All these programs must be written in a language the machine understands, the two-digit system of binary mathematics. It's based on Boolean algebra, a system of logic devised in the nineteenth century for solving complex problems through a series of binary (yes or no) choices. On microchips, these choices, called bits, are represented by open or closed gates.

Since most people don't speak machine language or think in terms of Boolean algebra, languages had to be created, such as BASIC, FORTRAN and PASCAL, to allow nonmathematicians to use computers. Within

an eight-bit computer, the binary digits are organized in groups of eight. These units are called bytes. Each byte then has eight gates. By configuring the bytes into different patterns of opened and closed bits, each byte can be used to stand for a letter or a number. Thus you can address the machine by using words and phrases such as PRINT, GO TO 25 or HELP.

Inside the machine, each letter or numeral of the command has to be translated into the only terms the computer can really understand — the unfriendly binary digits of machine language — by means of a program already in place. It's called an interpreter or compiler. Each machine is designed to use only certain compilers and interpreters and thus can understand only certain languages. An interpreter translates each command, passes it on to the CPU and then forgets it. The interpreter is sometimes built right into the computer.

A compiler translates the instructions and saves them for later use. Compilers generally are optional. They come either as software programs on floppy disks or as firmware — small circuit boards that look like metallic water bugs and plug into slots in the machine's main circuit board. When you turn on your machine, the information from the interpreter or compiler is automatically loaded into memory and — with most computers — a menu of what is there comes up on the screen. The machine is said to have been booted, meaning it is ready to go to work.

Then what? Well, if you are fluent in computer languages, you can sit down and tap in instructions of your own on the keyboard. If you are not, or if you don't have time, you can feed these instructions into the CPU in the form of software. This you load into your machine from a tape cassette or from a disk drive, by far the faster and more convenient of the two storage devices.

But two things are needed before you can use a prerecorded program: a controller board to join the computer to a storage device such as a disk drive and a piece of software with the deceptively simple name of operating system. This is a special program that makes the CPU and its battalion of RAM chips ready to deal with additional software. Otherwise, they will stonewall it.

The operating system for a disk drive is called a DOS (disk-operating system), and you buy it when you purchase your disk. The DOS enables your disk drive not only to communicate with your central processor but also to catalogue the various programs — typically as many as 10 — that you may have on a single disk. The DOS also gives you a directory of them so that you can tell what's on the disk and get right to it.

To do this, though, you must first impregnate the disk with the operating system's instructions. In computer lingo, you initialize or "init" the disk. This is simpler than it sounds. You load the DOS into the computer's memory and then remove its disk from the drive. Next, you insert a blank disk into the drive and instruct the machine through the keyboard to initialize the blank disk. You do this only once. Ever afterward, when that disk is used, it will automatically be accepted by the operating system.

Each computer company usually has its own DOS, and this software (with a few exceptions such as the CP/M operating system) is not easily interchangeable. This is how each computer company hoped to corner the market. But with the assistance of a little piratical program known as an emulator, you can make an Apple behave like a NorthStar Advantage or enable an Olivetti to do a tolerably good imitation of an IBM PC.

Computer companies with a lot of software made for their particular DOS don't like emulators, but companies whose sales are suffering for lack of good software rather warm to the idea. No one, however, has come up with an emulator that can make a computer bend pipe like a good bench vice.

COMPUTER LANGUAGES

Some good news about the arcane languages that let you communicate with computers: you probably don't need to be fluent in any of them. If you're like most users — that is if you *don't* feel compelled to learn programming — all you'll need to know is a few simple commands. They will be explained in the instructions that accompany your machine and the software you buy. But if you intend to learn programming, get ready to encounter such computer argot as BEEP, BLOAD and GOSUB — all commands that tell your machine to do something.

Unless you want to become the S.I. Hayakawa of computerspeak, you'll most likely want — or need — to learn only one of the half a dozen or so programming languages in common use. Each has its own vocabulary, grammar and syntax — the ways in which commands are phrased and structured. Each has several variations, or dialects; which one you use is usually determined by the kind of computer you own. The four leading languages:

• BASIC. Because it is flexible, versatile and relies on such familiar English words as *print, read* and *data,* BASIC (the Beginner's All-purpose Symbolic Instruction Code) is the most popular computer language.

Fully 90% of the programs for personal computers are written in BASIC. One drawback: it's not as concise as some computer languages, requiring more programming steps to achieve the same end.

• PASCAL. Named for 17th-century French mathematician and philosopher Blaise Pascal, this language ranks second in popularity for personal computers. Because it's more rigid, structured and concise than BASIC, PASCAL handles complex programs faster. For this reason, it is often the language of choice for business programs.

• FORTRAN. Short for FORmula TRANslation, this language is for scientists, engineers and businessmen who use computers for complicated calculations. In FORTRAN, programming statements are expressed in algebraic forms and symbolic language. Like PASCAL, FORTRAN runs many programs faster than BASIC.

• LOGO. The new kid on the block, LOGO (from the Greek for "word") may become the language of the 1980s. It is easy to learn, having been designed at MIT to teach children how to program. In LOGO, a program is approached as a series of steps, which are then combined to create a whole.

DISKETTES

Diskettes have magnetism, the physical kind. Indeed, magnetism is why they work. A diskette is a magnetically treated circular sheet of flexible plastic that is encased in a stiff vinyl sleeve. A diskette — commonly called a floppy disk — files information as a series of magnetic traces. Its principal use: to store programs and feed them into your computer. A diskette is used on a disk drive, hardware that "reads" the diskette and can record data on it. Disk drives are either built into a computer or housed in a cigar-box-size cabinet.

The standard diskette for personal computers is 5¼ inches in diameter. It's a newer, sweated-down version of the original floppy disk, which is eight inches across and usually requires a bulkier drive. For most owners of personal computers, diskettes should offer sufficient storage. Each typically holds the equivalent of about 35 to 140 single-spaced pages of information, depending on the computer.

WORD PROCESSING

Word processing. Just the sound of it seems like a nasty thing to do to a word. And this perhaps explains why so many authors, letter writers and other people who have everything to gain from this basic computer application have shied away from it for so long. Certainly if there is any area in which the personal computer has indisputably improved upon the old ways of doing things, word processing is it.

And yet word processing is not magic. It is really just writing as we have always done. You sit at a keyboard, type, and see what you have written appear on a screen — not a page — in front of you. But with a word processor, there are a few mechanical tricks thrown in that make the task a little easier.

With a word processor you could:

• Word wrap. This computerese means that when you come to the end of a line, the next letter automatically begins at the start of the following line. The programs will then automatically pull the rest of the letters from the last word down to the second line so that the word isn't broken.

• Search and replace. By means of a simple command typed into the machine, you can find a particular word or phrase that occurs in your text. Suppose you want to correct a misspelled name throughout a five-page letter. Just type in the name as you misspelled it and again as spelled correctly, give the command and the cursor — a little lighted marker that tells where you are on the screen — will move through the text, stopping to correct the name at every spot where it appears.

• Justify. With the punch of a few keys, you can automatically cause the right-hand margin of your text to line up as neat and even as the left margin, just like a page in a book. To do this, the machine adjusts the spacing between each word. Some of the more sophisticated programs will make minuscule adjustments between each letter, so there aren't disconcertingly wide spaces between any of the words.

• Block move. This allows you to shift pieces of your text — from a word to several paragraphs — around like blocks. You also can add new blocks at whatever point you designate, and the entire text will automatically expand to accommodate them. Or, conversely, you can delete a block — and the text will shrink around the excised words, leaving no sign that they had ever been there in the first place.

• Typeover. When you want to substitute one word or phrase for another, you can type your change right over the existing text and the unwanted letters will vanish as the new ones fill their places.

There are many other wrinkles in word processors. One of the newest is an automatic dictionary that will check the spelling of each word you write against a word-processor program of 10,000 to 88,000 words, and make corrections. This feature usually is packaged as a separate program that you can add to your existing word-processing program.

Word processing is, hands down, the most common use for a personal computer.

PRINTERS

After you've done your word wrapping, typeovering and justifying with your word processor, you're going to need a printer if you want to fold up what you've written and send it to someone. Printers are expensive, temperamental and generally quite heavy. Yet printer technology is one of the most rapidly advancing wings of the computer industry.

There are basically three kinds of printers: daisy wheel, dot matrix and thermal. The first prints from a daisy-shaped wheel that bears a character on each spoke — or petal, if you will. The wheel spins until the right letter is in position, then a hammer strikes it, printing it onto the page. The dot matrix moves a little boxlike Gatling gun of blunt needles in front of the ribbon, shooting out only the needles that are needed to make the desired character. Thermal printers electronically burn impressions into specially treated paper.

Most letter-quality printers are daisy wheels. Typically they cost around $2,000. Dot-matrix printers are faster — some can print 250 characters a second —and generally cheaper than their daisy-wheel cousins. Thermal printers are the cheapest of all but you have to buy special paper for them and, in some cases, over time their print gradually fades from the page.

Most printers connect to the side or back of your computer through an RS-232 interface port, a socket for peripherals. Some computers can use electric typewriters as printers.

Number of words 2380
See page 201 for Questions

See page 201 for Questions

Reading time in Seconds _____
See page 358 for Conversion Table

The Fifty-First Dragon

Heywood Broun

"Believe that life is worth living, and your belief will help create the fact," said William James. Was belief the essential difference between the fiftieth and the fifty-first dragon in the story that follows? By comparison, how well do you tap the power of positive thinking — a facet of communication?

Of all the pupils at the knight school Gawaine le Cœur-Hardy was among the least promising. He was tall and sturdy, but his instructors soon discovered that he lacked spirit. He would hide in the woods when the jousting class was called, although his companions and members of the faculty sought to appeal to his better nature by shouting to him to come out and break his neck like a man. Even when they told him that the lances were padded, the horses no more than ponies and the field unusually soft for late autumn, Gawaine refused to grow enthusiastic. The Headmaster and the Assistant Professor of Pleasaunce were discussing the case one spring afternoon and the Assistant Professor could see no remedy but expulsion.

"No," said the Headmaster, as he looked out at the purple hills which ringed the school, "I think I'll train him to slay dragons."

"He might be killed," objected the Assistant Professor.

"So he might," replied the Headmaster brightly, but he added, more soberly, "we must consider the greater good. We are responsible for the formation of this lad's character."

"Are the dragons particularly bad this year?" interrupted the Assistant Professor. This was characteristic. He always seemed restive when the head of the school began to talk ethics and the ideals of the institution.

"I've never known them worse," replied the Headmaster. "Up in the hills to the south last week they killed a number of peasants, two cows and a prize pig. And if this dry spell holds there's no telling when they may start a forest fire simply by breathing around indiscriminately."

"Would any refund on the tuition fee be necessary in case of an accident to young Cœur-Hardy?"

"No," the principal answered, judicially, "that's all covered in the contract. But as a matter of fact he won't be killed. Before I send him up in the hills I'm going to give him a magic word."

"That's a good idea," said the Professor. "Sometimes they work wonders."

From that day on Gawaine specialized in dragons. His course included both theory and practice. In the morning there were long lectures on the history, anatomy, manners and customs of dragons. Gawaine did not distinguish himself in these studies. He had a marvelously versatile gift for forgetting things. In the afternoon he showed to better advantage, for then he would go down to the South Meadow and practice with a battle-ax. In this exercise he was truly impressive, for he had enormous strength as well as speed and grace. He even developed a deceptive display of ferocity. Old alumni say that it was a thrilling sight to see Gawaine charging across the field toward the dummy paper dragon which had been set up for his practice. As he ran he would brandish his ax and shout "A murrain on thee!" or some other vivid bit of campus slang. It never took him more than one stroke to behead the dummy dragon.

Gradually his task was made more difficult. Paper gave way to papier-mâché and finally to wood, but even the toughest of these dummy dragons had no terrors for Gawaine. One sweep of the ax always did the business. There were those who said that when the practice was protracted until dusk and the dragons threw long, fantastic shadows across the meadow Gawaine did not charge so impetuously nor shout so loudly. It is possible there was malice in this charge. At any rate, the Headmaster decided by the end of June that it was time for the test. Only the night before a dragon had come close to the school grounds and had eaten some of the lettuce from the garden. The faculty decided that Gawaine was ready. They gave him a diploma and a new battle-ax and the Headmaster summoned him to a private conference.

"Sit down," said the Headmaster. "Have a cigarette." Gawaine hesitated.

"Oh, I know it's against the rules," said the Headmaster. "But after all, you have received your preliminary degree. You are no longer a boy. You are a man. To-morrow you will go out into the world, the great world of achievement."

Gawaine took a cigarette. The Headmaster offered him a match, but he produced one of his own and began to puff away with a dexterity which quite amazed the principal.

"Here you have learned the theories of life," continued the Headmaster, resuming the thread of his discourse, "but after all, life is not a matter of theories. Life is a matter of facts. It calls on the young and the old alike to face these facts, even though they are hard and sometimes unpleasant. Your problem, for example, is to slay dragons."

"They say that those dragons down in the south wood are five hundred feet long," ventured Gawaine, timorously.

"Stuff and nonsense!" said the Headmaster. "The curate saw one last week from the top of Arthur's Hill. The dragon was sunning himself down in the valley. The curate didn't have an opportunity to look at him very long because he felt it was his duty to hurry back to make a report to me. He said the monster, or shall I say, the big lizard? — wasn't an inch over two hundred feet. But the size has nothing at all to do with it. You'll find the big ones even easier than the little ones. They're far slower on their feet and less aggressive, I'm told. Besides, before you go I'm going to equip you in such fashion that you need have no fear of all the dragons in the world."

"I'd like an enchanted cap," said Gawaine.

"What's that?" answered the Headmaster, testily.

"A cap to make me disappear," explained Gawaine.

The Headmaster laughed indulgently. "You mustn't believe all those old wives' stories," he said. "There isn't any such thing. A cap to make you disappear, indeed! What would you do with it? You haven't even appeared yet. Why, my boy, you could walk from here to London, and nobody would so much as look at you. You're nobody. You couldn't be more invisible than that."

Gawaine seemed dangerously close to a relapse into his old habit of whimpering. The Headmaster reassured him: "Don't worry; I'll give you something much better than an enchanted cap. I'm going to give you a magic word. All you have to do is to repeat this magic charm once and no dragon can possibly harm a hair of your head. You can cut off his head at your leisure."

He took a heavy book from the shelf behind his desk and began to run through it. "Sometimes," he said, "the charm is a whole phrase or even a sentence. I might, for instance, give you 'To make the' — No, that might not do. I think a single word would be best for dragons."

"A short word," suggested Gawaine.

"It can't be too short or it wouldn't be potent. There isn't so much hurry as all that. Here's a splendid magic word: 'Rumplesnitz.' Do you think you can learn that?"

Gawaine tried and in an hour or so he seemed to have the word well in hand. Again and again he interrupted the lesson to inquire, "And if I say 'Rumplesnitz' the dragon can't possibly hurt me?" And always the Headmaster replied, "If you only say 'Rumplesnitz,' you are perfectly safe."

Toward morning Gawaine seemed resigned to his career. At daybreak the Headmaster saw him to the edge of the forest and pointed him to the direction in which he should proceed. About a mile away to the southwest a cloud of steam hovered over an open meadow in the woods and the Headmaster assured Gawaine that under the steam he would find a dragon. Gawaine went forward slowly. He wondered whether it would be best to approach the dragon on the run as he did in his practice in the South Meadow or to walk slowly toward him, shouting "Rumplesnitz" all the way.

The problem was decided for him. No sooner had he come to the fringe of the meadow than the dragon spied him and began to charge. It was a large dragon and yet it seemed decidedly aggressive in spite of the Headmaster's statement to the contrary. As the dragon charged it released huge clouds of hissing steam through its nostrils. It was almost as if a gigantic teapot had gone mad. The dragon came forward so fast and Gawaine was so frightened that he had time to say "Rumplesnitz" only once. As he said it, he swung his battle-ax and off popped the head of the dragon. Gawaine had to admit that it was even easier to kill a real dragon than a wooden one if only you said "Rumplesnitz."

Gawaine brought the ears home and a small section of the tail. His school mates and the faculty made much of him, but the Headmaster wisely kept him from being spoiled by insisting that he go on with his work. Every clear day Gawaine rose at dawn and went out to kill dragons. The Headmaster kept him at home when it rained, because he said the woods were damp and unhealthy at such times and that he didn't want the boy to run needless risks. Few good days passed in which Gawaine failed to get a dragon. On one particularly fortunate day he killed three, a husband and wife and a visiting relative. Gradually he developed a technique. Pupils who sometimes watched him from the hill-tops a long way off said that he often allowed the dragon to come within a few feet before he said "Rumplesnitz." He came to say it with a mocking sneer. Occasionally he did stunts. Once when an excursion party from London was watching him he went into action with his right hand tied behind his back. The dragon's head came off just as easily.

As Gawaine's record of killings mounted higher the Headmaster found it impossible to keep him completely in hand. He fell into the habit of stealing out at night and engaging in long drinking bouts at the village tavern. It was after such a debauch that he rose a little before dawn one fine August morning and started out after his fiftieth dragon. His head was heavy and his mind sluggish. He was heavy in other respects as well, for he had adopted the somewhat vulgar practice of wearing his medals, ribbons and all, when he went out dragon hunting. The decorations began on his chest and ran all the way down to his abdomen. They must have weighed at least eight pounds.

Gawaine found a dragon in the same meadow where he had killed the first one. It was a fair-sized dragon, but evidently an old one. Its face was wrinkled and Gawaine thought he had never seen so hideous a countenance. Much to the lad's disgust, the monster refused to charge and Gawaine was obliged to walk toward him. He whistled as he went. The dragon regarded him hopelessly, but craftily. Of course it had heard of Gawaine. Even when the lad raised his battle-ax the dragon made no move. It knew that there was no salvation in the quickest thrust of the head, for it had been informed that this hunter was protected by an enchantment. It merely waited, hoping something would turn up. Gawaine raised the battle-ax and suddenly lowered it again. He had grown very pale and he trembled violently. The dragon suspected a trick. "What's the matter?" it asked, with false solicitude.

"I've forgotten the magic word," stammered Gawaine.

"What a pity," said the dragon. "So that was the secret. It doesn't seem quite sporting to me, all this magic stuff, you know. Not cricket, as we used to say when I was a little dragon; but after all, that's a matter of opinion."

Gawaine was so helpless with terror that the dragon's confidence rose immeasurably and it could not resist the temptation to show off a bit.

"Could I possibly be of any assistance?" it asked. "What's the first letter of the magic word?"

"It begins with an 'r,'" said Gawaine weakly.

"Let's see," mused the dragon, "that doesn't tell us much, does it? What sort of a word is this? Is it an epithet, do you think?"

Gawaine could do no more than nod.

"Why, of course," exclaimed the dragon, "reactionary Republican."

Gawaine shook his head.

"Well, then," said the dragon, "we'd better get down to business. Will you surrender?"

With the suggestion of a compromise Gawaine mustered up enough courage to speak.

"What will you do if I surrender?" he asked.

"Why, I'll eat you," said the dragon.

"And if I don't surrender?"

"I'll eat you just the same."

"Then it doesn't make any difference, does it?" moaned Gawaine.

"It does to me," said the dragon with a smile. "I'd rather you didn't surrender. You'd taste much better if you didn't."

The dragon waited for a long time for Gawaine to ask "Why?" but the boy was too frightened to speak. At last the dragon had to give the explanation without

his cue line. "You see," he said, "if you don't surrender you'll taste better because you'll die game."

This was an old and ancient trick of the dragon's. By means of some such quip he was accustomed to paralyze his victims with laughter and then to destroy them. Gawaine was sufficiently paralyzed as it was, but laughter had no part in his helplessness. With the last word of the joke the dragon drew back his head and struck. In that second there flashed into the mind of Gawaine the magic word "Rumplesnitz," but there was no time to say it. There was time only to strike and, without a word, Gawaine met the onrush of the dragon with a full swing. He put all his back and shoulders into it. The impact was terrific and the head of the dragon flew away almost a hundred yards and landed in a thicket.

Gawaine did not remain frightened very long after the death of the dragon. His mood was one of wonder. He was enormously puzzled. He cut off the ears of the monster almost in a trance. Again and again he thought to himself, "I didn't say 'Rumplesnitz'!" He was sure of that and yet there was no question that he had killed the dragon. In fact, he had never killed one so utterly. Never before had he driven a head for anything like the same distance. Twenty-five yards was perhaps his best previous record. All the way back to the knight school he kept rumbling about in his mind seeking an explanation for what had occurred. He went to the Headmaster immediately and after closing the door told him what had happened. "I didn't say 'Rumplesnitz,'" he explained with great earnestness.

The Headmaster laughed. "I'm glad you've found out," he said. "It makes you ever so much more of a hero. Don't you see that? Now you know that it was you who killed all these dragons and not that foolish little word 'Rumplesnitz.'"

Gawaine frowned. "Then it wasn't a magic word after all?" he asked.

"Of course not," said the Headmaster, "you ought to be too old for such foolishness. There isn't any such thing as a magic word."

"But you told me it was magic," protested Gawaine. "You said it was magic and now you say it isn't."

"It wasn't magic in a literal sense," answered the Headmaster, "but it was much more wonderful than that. The word gave you confidence. It took away your fears. If I hadn't told you that you might have been killed the very first time. It was your battle-ax did the trick."

Gawaine surprised the Headmaster by his attitude. He was obviously distressed by the explanation. He interrupted a long philosophic and ethical discourse by the Headmaster with, "If I hadn't of hit 'em all mighty hard and fast any one of 'em might have crushed me like a, like a — " He fumbled for a word.

"Egg shell," suggested the Headmaster.

"Like a egg shell," assented Gawaine, and he said it

many times. All through the evening meal people who sat near him heard him muttering, "Like a egg shell, like a egg shell."

The next day was clear, but Gawaine did not get up at dawn. Indeed, it was almost noon when the Headmaster found him cowering in bed, with the clothes pulled over his head. The principal called the Assistant Professor of Pleasaunce, and together they dragged the boy toward the forest.

"He'll be all right as soon as he gets a couple more dragons under his belt," explained the Headmaster.

The Assistant Professor of Pleasaunce agreed. "It would be a shame to stop such a fine run," he said. "Why, counting that one yesterday, he's killed fifty dragons."

They pushed the boy into a thicket above which hung a meager cloud of steam. It was obviously quite a small dragon. But Gawaine did not come back that night or the next. In fact, he never came back. Some weeks afterward brave spirits from the school explored the thicket, but they could find nothing to remind them of Gawaine except the metal parts of his medals. Even the ribbons had been devoured.

The Headmaster and the Assistant Professor of Pleasaunce agreed that it would be just as well not to tell the school how Gawaine had achieved his record and still less how he came to die. They held that it might have a bad effect on school spirit. Accordingly, Gawaine has lived in the memory of the school as its greatest hero. No visitor succeeds in leaving the building to-day without seeing a great shield which hangs on the wall of the dining hall. Fifty pairs of dragons' ears are mounted upon the shield and underneath in gilt letters is "Gawaine le Cœur-Hardy," followed by the simple inscription, "He killed fifty dragons." The record has never been equaled.

Number of words 3000
See page 203 for Questions

Reading time in Seconds _____
See page 358 for Conversion Table

The Future of Grammar

Paul Roberts

Being bad grammar, you shouldn't use no dangling participles. Furthermore, subject and verb has to always agree. Ain't it about time to look into this here grammar business to see what linguistic scientists are saying about grammar and communication. Do "ain't" and "isn't" communicate equally well?

The last few decades have witnessed an amiable but spirited battle between linguistic scientists and defenders of traditional ways of teaching English. Linguists have been in revolt against two assumptions that underlie the tradition: (1) that there are absolute criteria — logical, analogical, etymological, or whatever — by which correctness can be measured; and (2) that there are universal, nonlinguistic concepts through which the linguistic categories of any language can be identified and defined. Ultimately this revolt will succeed; there need be no doubt of that. Provided only that our society retains the orientation it has had for the past several centuries, nothing can prevent the establishment in the school system of the views of linguistic science. Wherever, in our civilization, science and non-science conflict, it is non-science that gives way, as astrology gave way to astronomy and alchemy to chemistry. In the same way, linguistic science and structural analysis will triumph over traditional language teaching, although it may take a similarly long time. It is true that astrology does not now play the role that it did in 1350, but astrologers are still around.

Our purpose here is not to discuss when or whether the transition will take place but rather to suggest what its effects on English teaching are likely to be.

Some effects there have been already, and not all of them are good. Linguists have long argued that correctness is altogether relative, having nothing to do with logic or the order of the universe, but depending on such variables as time, place, circumstance, age, sex. The language forms used, correctly, in addressing an umpire, may be incorrect in addressing a bishop. And vice versa. The sentence "We heard the sweetest little bird singing the dearest little song" is correct if you're a twelve-year-old girl but incorrect if you're a fifty-year-old bartender. In some circles, "Ain't you comin' back?" will get you blackballed; in others, "Shall you not return?" will get you tossed out on your ear.

Logic has nothing to do with it. When they ask, "Is it correct?" linguists don't mean, "Is it logical?" They mean, "Would it be well received — at this time, in this place, in this social situation — from a person of this age and sex?" It doesn't matter whether or not, in algebra, two negatives make a positive. What matters is whether, in the language area being considered, it is customary to say, "We don't want no trouble," and, if so, whether it would be generally understood that the speaker wants trouble or doesn't.

All this is old stuff. It is a principle now fully accepted by dictionaries, which don't tell us what to say but rather what we and our countrymen *do* say. It has also been accepted, to some degree, by most handbooks and by many teachers of English. But the implications for classroom procedure are still to be understood and faced.

One thing that the idea of relativity of correctness does *not* mean is that it doesn't matter how we talk or write. Recently some educators have been disposed to tell us: "It isn't important *how* you say a thing; what is important is what you say." This is a pious thought, and it may be true in the sight of God, but it isn't true as the world goes and never will be. Possibly this notion is the linguists' responsibility, but it isn't the linguists' notion.

Certainly it matters how you say a thing. Saying the right thing in the wrong way can get you fired, divorced, arrested, or expelled from the P.T.A. It's nice to be intelligible, but sometimes it is infinitely better to be unintelligible than incorrect. It makes a tremendous difference how you say a thing; it just doesn't always make the same difference. In fact, it probably never makes the same difference twice.

This is what the growing heaps of linguistic information, like the Linguistic Atlas and the dialect dictionaries, are showing ever more clearly. We may suppose that any bit of speech, any word or phrase or sentence, will, when uttered, be either correct or incorrect. But we cannot predict which without knowing all about the nonlinguistic environment in which the utterance occurs. The criteria of correctness are real enough, but they are staggeringly complex and constantly in motion, shifting subtly about us as we go from work to play, from night to morning, from anteroom to inner office, from Broadway to Cypress Street, from Peter to Paul. There is probably no American expression of which we can say, "This will always be correct." And none of which we can say, "This will always be wrong."

So far we have tried to meet this difficulty with the concept of "levels of usage," dividing usage into several strata, usually three — standard, colloquial, vulgate. Now this concept has its uses where the intent is purely descriptive, as for example in a dictionary or a descriptive grammar. But as a device for instructing students in how to behave linguistically, it is using nets to catch the wind. The "levels of usage" concept has not led us, as some would say, to teach descriptively rather than prescriptively. It has simply led us to be prescriptive in a much more complicated way — and yet in a way not nearly complicated enough for the linguistic reality which our students face. If we must be prescriptive, it is more reasonable to select some single, more or less graspable area of usage — say the usage of *The Atlantic Monthly* — and make the student learn that and only that and bat his ears down when he departs from it.

The alternative is to abandon the prescriptive idea altogether, to give up the notion of bringing the student to a fore-determined pattern of usage, and to seek other results entirely. We might aim not at conformity but at range, flexibility, adaptability. We might teach the student to observe his own language and the language of others and to describe them accurately. We might develop sensitivity for the nuances of speech and prose, an ear and an eye for the eternal subtle changes going on in them. We might train the student to use dictionaries as their makers intend them to be used — not as oracles but as collections of linguistic fact to be consulted in areas into which the user's experience does not reach and to be believed whenever they do not conflict with the user's own accurate observation.

Experiments in this direction are already underway in many schools throughout the country. But it may be generations before the thing is done in the school system generally. Our teaching materials will need to be thoroughly revised, the curriculum in teacher-training institutions drastically modified. Most important, beliefs and attitudes as deep-seated as the belief of the Middle Ages in astrology will have to give way. But there is no reason to believe that the change will not take place — in someone's lifetime — and that the change will not be generally for the better, resulting in a major improvement in the morale of English classes and in a general rise in the ability to speak and write fluently, intelligibly, gracefully, accurately, and even — in the best sense of the word — correctly.

Along with this must go a quiet revolution in our techniques for describing language. We are still tied to a superstition of "universal grammar," which rests in fact on the grammar of Latin. We can make it work in English only by the most rigorous exclusion of the realities of English, and what we study when we study "English grammar" is an artificial language, a concoction of made-up sentences with which no one could possibly communicate for any length of time on any subject of importance. Any student of English can prove this for himself simply by taking a page — any page — of actual English writing and trying to analyze it with the tools of what passes for English grammar.

But probably the most discouraging thing about traditional grammar is the set of tautologies in which it wanders: "a noun is a name," "a verb is an action," "an interrogative sentence is a sentence which asks a question." These statements are more or less true, but they don't tell us anything we don't already know, any more than would definitions like "a man is a man," "a rose is a rose." Let us grant that a noun is the name of something. What we want to discover is how we know, in any particular sentence, which words name things and are therefore nouns. We do not grasp this by any metaphysical intuition, but by our understanding of a complicated set of structural signals which mark off nouns from other word classes. These signals are indeed complex (and of course entirely different from language to language), but they are tangible, real and rather interesting. It is sometimes urged for grammar that it is valuable as an intellectual discipline, and it may be, provided it is real description of actual language. But when it is a half-baked hodge-podge of improbable abstractions, there is no intellectual discipline in it but only disillusion and despair.

Somebody will have to do something about this, and many people are already trying — seeking to look at the language and see what's there and find ways of describing it. Specialists disagree about whether to scrap everything and begin again or to try to save as much as possible from the tradition — terminology, for instance — and simply to change and add whatever is necessary. Whichever choice is made, the task will be long and difficult, but it will be done, and the grammar that emerges will make English studies more pleasant than they are now. People are disposed to believe that traditional grammar is dull and difficult, but useful. As generally taught, grammar is difficult and dull, but it isn't useful. The new grammar may not be useful either, and will be difficult, but won't be dull.

Number of words 1660
See page 205 for Questions

Reading time in Seconds _____
See page 358 for Conversion Table

SELECTION 10

The Educated Man

James Ansara

At what point in life can it be said that a person is truly educated? Lin Yutang once said, "The wise man reads both books and life itself." Does the following dramatic story say much the same thing? How differently can ideas be communicated!

My father was a man steeped in the aphorisms and parables of his race, with which he spiced even his everyday conversation. Best of all I liked the stories he often resorted to to illustrate truisms. I remember the first time he told the one about the education of Sheikh Yusif's son. I had finished college, and my problem was whether to continue my intellectual pursuits or to launch myself into the practical activities of the world. One evening I sought to discuss the matter with him, but instead of giving me his advice he offered to tell me a story that his father had once told him. It was after dinner and we were having black coffee flavored with the essence of roses. Between long, satisfying sips, this was the story he told: —

Once there was a sheikh, Yusif al-Hamadi, who was determined that some day his only son, Ali, should become a learned man.

When Ali completed his elementary studies under his tutors, the Sheikh called together his advisers and asked them where his son could acquire the best possible education. With one voice, they answered, "The University of El-Azhar, in Cairo."

So at El-Azhar, then the most renowned university in the whole world, the son of Sheikh Yusif studied with great energy and soon proved himself a true scholar. After eight years of study, the Ulama of the university pronounced Ali an educated man, and the son wrote that he was returning home.

As a scholar, Ali scorned the vanities of life and departed from Cairo riding a jackass and wearing the coarse raiment of an ascetic. Jogging along with his books behind him and his diploma fastened to his side, Ali lost himself in meditating upon the writings of the poets and philosophers.

When he was only a day's journey from his home, the young scholar entered a village mosque to rest for a while. It was Friday and the place was full of worshipers. A Khatib was preaching on the miraculous deeds of the Prophet.

Now Ali, as a result of his profound study of the teachings of the Prophet, had become an uncompromising puritan of the Faith. Therefore, when the Khatib told his credulous congregation that Mohammed caused springs to flow in the desert, moved mountains, and flew on his horse to heaven, Ali was outraged.

"Stop!" cried Ali. "Believe not this false man. All that he has told you are lies, not the true faith. Our

Reprinted by permission from *The Atlantic Monthly,* November 1937.

teacher, Mohammed, was not a supernatural being, but a man who saw the light, the truth —"

The Khatib interrupted to ask the young man upon what authority he contradicted him. Ali proudly informed him that he was a scholar, a graduate of the great University of El-Azhar. The preacher, with a sneer on his face, turned toward his congregation.

"This man, who calls himself a scholar, is a heretic, an atheist who dares come among you, the Faithful, and throw doubt upon the greatness of our Prophet Mohammed, blessed be his name. Cast him out of the mosque; he contaminates its sanctity."

The people seized Ali and dragged him to the street, beating and kicking him and tearing his clothes. Outside, his books and diploma were destroyed, and the unconscious Ali was tied to his jackass backward and stoned out of the village.

When word came of the approach of Ali, Sheikh Yusif and the neighboring sheikhs, whom the proud father had invited to join him to receive and honor his scholarly son, rode forth to meet the learned graduate of El-Azhar. But lo, the scholar was dangling from the back of a jackass, his learned head bouncing against its haunches. Bruised, half naked, he was muttering like an idiot.

Not for several days was Ali well enough to tell his father what had befallen him. When he finished, Sheikh Yusif sighed deeply and said, "Ali, you have come back to me only half educated. You must return to Cairo." The young man protested that there was nothing more the university could teach him, and Sheikh Yusif agreed. The rest of his education was to be outside of El-Azhar.

Back in Cairo, Ali was to discover a new world. According to his father's instructions, he spent the first six months in the shop of a merchant, bartering and wrangling in the busiest bazaar of Cairo. Following that, the chief of police took him in hand and introduced him to the life of the city in all its varied aspects. For a time he was a beggar outside one of the great mosques, a disciple of a magician, a waiter in a low café. Ali also came to know the life of a sailor, a wandering trader, and a laborer.

At the end of the fifth year, Ali informed his father that his education was completed and he was again returning home.

This time, the son of Sheikh Yusif left Cairo riding a spirited Arabian, dressed in silks and satins, and attended by a train of servants. His stops during the journey were brief, until he reached the village of the Khatib. It was again Friday and the same Khatib was declaiming the same miracles to the credulous peasants. Ali joined the congregation and listened to the words of the preacher with a rapture equal to that of his neighbors. His "Ah" and "Great is our Prophet" were even more fervent than those about him.

When the Khatib concluded his sermon, Ali humbly begged to be heard.

"In spite of my youth," said Ali, "I have studied much and traveled wide, seeking the truth and wisdom of our great Prophet, blessed be his name. But never have I heard or read a sermon equal in truth and piety to that of your reverend Khatib. Not only is he a learned man, but a holy one, for his knowledge of the life of the Prophet comes only from the deepest source of faith and piety, a knowledge denied to ordinary men. Fortunate are you in having such a saint. Fortunate am I too, for here ends my search for the holiest man of our age.

"O holy Khatib, fit companion of Caliphs, I beg of you a boon!"

The bewildered Khatib could only ask the nature of that boon.

"It is written in the Holy Koran that a relic from a saint brings endless blessings to the Faithful. A hair from they beard, O Saintly One!"

Still perplexed, the Khatib could not, before his whole congregation, deny such a pious request. The young man with bowed head slowly mounted the *mumbar* and, in sight of all the people, with two extended fingers pulled a hair from the outthrust, flowing beard. Ali kissed it with deep reverence, folded it meticulously in a white silk kerchief, and placed it inside his shirt next to his heart.

A murmur arose from the congregation — their Khatib was a holy man! Even before Ali left the *mumbar*, the stampede toward the preacher had begun. By the time the son of Sheikh Yusif had forced his way through the mad crowd to the street, not a hair was left on the Khatib's face or head, not a shred of clothing on his body, and he lay behind the *mumbar* writhing and gasping like a plucked rooster.

That evening, Ali arrived home and there was great rejoicing in his father's house. His wit and dignity, his profound store of knowledge, his tact and manners, charmed all the guests and swelled the heart of his father with pride.

When at last the guests departed and Ali was alone with his father, he recounted to him his second visit to the village of the Khatib. The old Sheikh nodded his head approvingly and said: —

"Now, my son, I can die in peace. You have tempered book learning with worldly wisdom and returned a truly educated man."

Getting Organized

Marlys Harris

According to research, seventy percent of your waking time is spent in doing one thing — communicating — through reading, writing, speaking, or listening. You may well need some help in organizing both communication time and noncommunication time. Read on. That help is at hand.

Deceptively, the principles of good organization — "First things first," "One thing at a time," "A place for everything and everything in its place," and "When in doubt, throw it out" — come right off Great-grandma Nettie's embroidered samplers. They're that obvious. So are the tactics: make lists, plan ahead, avoid distractions, clear away clutter. Getting organized is relatively easy. Staying that way is a lifetime project. You must hew to your goals with the ardor of a 12th-century monastic and avoid gossip sessions, unnecessary phone calls and long boozy lunches with the restraint of, well, a 12th-century monastic.

Despite all the professional and personal rewards it could provide, you've probably resisted getting yourself together. Yet to be organized, you don't have to arrange paper clips in symmetrical piles, eat your luncheon salad vegetables in alphabetical order or force your kids to make appointments to see you. You merely have to develop and use a system that helps you get things done. Says Margaret Cadman, a New York City management consultant who helps people and companies get organized: "There's no platonic ideal. Any system will work as long as it's a system."

But where to begin? Some people are wise to start with a cleanup because their mess has become so overwhelming. However, most consultants who help clients get organized believe that you should kick off your program by tackling the most difficult problem — time management. There always seems to be too much to do and not enough time to do it.

First, you should unjam your schedule by taking on less. Have the nerve to say no to those requests to head the Chip-and-Dip Committee for the company picnic or to write a memo on the Misuse of Company Stationery. Cutting down on the extras often helps you concentrate on what's important to you. Judy Lipton, 31, of Bellevue, Wash., focuses intently on her roles as wife, mother of four, full-time psychiatrist and civic activist. She rarely goes to parties, indulges in few social lunches, never watches TV and doesn't bother with theater or concerts. As she explains, "I eliminate unpleasant, unproductive or minimally useful activities."

Then there are the tasks that you can delegate to others. Tom Drucker, 36, a Los Angeles career consultant, and his wife, journalist Marcia Seligman, 45, took the extreme measure of hiring a 22-year-old man to be their "wife." He does the shopping, picks up the cleaning and performs the other household chores, which allows the couple to keep to a busy schedule of work and social activities. Of course, it comes as no surprise that you can pass the buck to subordinates and others whom you hire. However, you can also delegate work back to your boss. When she passes you in the hall, for example, you might remark, "Hi, Mrs. Bunbuster. I've been meaning to tell you that we've got a big problem with the spring curriculum plans and we'll need policy guidance." She will then have to look into the issue herself. That puts the mess on her desk. Naturally, if you are the boss, you must pass the hot potato back at once by replying, "Let me have your ideas by noon on Friday."

No matter how much or how little you want to accomplish, getting it all done usually requires following the standard practice of making a list. Writing it just before you leave work helps get you off to a fast start the next day. Stephanie Winston, author of *Getting Organized* (1978), suggests that you keep *two* lists. The first details all the foreseeable tasks you want to accomplish. Each day you pick 10 items from it to put on your daily list. "That's all anybody can reasonably do in a day," asserts Winston.

Lists work especially well in keeping complicated lives in hand. As senior partner of Rogers & Cowan, a big Hollywood public relations firm, Paul Bloch, 42, has his hands full catering to the needs of such film-star clients as James Caan, Dudley Moore and Elliot Gould. His workday, which starts at 7 a.m. so he can begin phoning clients in Paris, London and New York, consists of booking appearances, talking to newspaper columnists, arranging tours, negotiating deals and signing up new clients.

Twenty years ago Bloch got into the habit of writing a list before turning in for the night. Ritualistically, he uses yellow paper to set it apart from other paperwork and types his list in triplicate in red capital letters. Because he may list up to 50 tasks each weekday, including personal items such as buying a bottle of wine or asking a woman for a date, Bloch puts an asterisk next to high-priority items to make sure he gets them done that day. When he completes a job, he crosses it out with a black pen. Bloch carries one copy with him, leaves another with his secretary for safekeeping and brings the third along in his Mercedes as an aide-mémoire.

Unfortunately, lists don't work well for everyone. Says Larry Baker, co-owner of the Time Management Center, a St. Louis, Mo. training firm: "Lists can defeat you before you start." People tend to make out a long daily list without reference to the length of time any task will take. "You wind up transferring most of Monday's 'to-dos' to Tuesday."

His solution is a combination time-management and behavior-modification program. First you keep a time log, writing down everything you do for two weeks to get a sense of the amount of time tasks typically take you. Then you set long-range goals for whatever phases of your life you deem important — career, family, hobbies, finances and spiritual development — and list activities that might help you accomplish them. For each goal, you pick one step toward it that you could reasonably take in a year.

Suppose you are a chemist who aims to become vice president in charge of new-product development. You might decide to research and write a report on the feasibility of manufacturing a line of low-calorie food for dieters, say, coq au vin, lemonade and pizza. You divide the project into smaller activities and give yourself deadlines for each. Perhaps you set a two-month deadline for finishing an exhaustive survey of market-research reports on foods that dieters crave but should not eat. Each week you list what you will have to do to meet your deadline — perhaps read and analyze two reports. You then list that task and all of the other tasks that you have to complete that week along with estimates of the time needed for each. Then you whip out your calendar and schedule all your projects, including perhaps an hour a day for product development. Larry Baker pleads that you set aside long periods of uninterrupted time for a complex, brain-busting task such as blending the elements of the pizza sauce. These are best scheduled during "peak time" — the hours of the day when you have the most energy.

In a recent time-management lecture, Baker told his audience of 40 executives that he was sure no more than half of them would ever attempt to do long-range goal setting. Nonetheless, there are ways to plan ahead effectively without getting stuck on your reason for living.

A number of books can help you tailor an organizational system to your own needs. Among the best: *Getting Organized* (Warner Books) by Stephanie Winston, a paperback for the housewife (or househusband) covering everything from financial records to chaotic closets; *How to Get Control of Your Time and Your Life* (Signet) by Alan Lakein, a guide to setting your lifetime goals; *Manage Your Time, Manage Your Work, Manage Yourself* (Amacom) by Merrill and Donna Douglass, an organizing manual for corporate executives; *Getting Things Done* (Bantam Books) by Edwin Bliss, an easy-to-read treatment of the most essential organizational principles; and *Working Smart* (Warner Books) by Michael LeBoeuf, a time-management guide aimed specifically at the workaholic.

Number of words 1320
See page 209 for Questions

Reading time in Seconds _____
See page 358 for Conversion Table

SELECTION 12

The New Age of Reason

John M. Culkin

For a closer look at some problems inherent in our present familiar communication patterns, read the following criticisms and suggestions. Are you sold on the advantages? Do you see any difficulties? Would you like to see these changes?

Let's meet for lunch on September 30.

To produce that sentence I used four media: a typewriter, an alphabet, a number system, a calendar. The

First appeared in *Science Digest* © 1981 by The Hearst Corporation. Reprinted by permission of the author, John M. Culkin, Executive Director — Center for Understanding Media, New York City.

Arabic number system is unambiguous and efficient. Let's keep it. The other three media are a mess. Let's change them.

THE ALPHABET

And the worst shall be first. An alphabet — by definition, a system for mapping the sounds of a language — is an invention of a high order. Ideally, one letter stands for each sound and one sound for each letter. The genius of our phonetic system (as opposed to pictographic systems) is that the written symbols do not refer directly to the object described but to the pieces of sound that fall out of our faces.

The current English alphabet, however, is not as easy as ABC. Our 26 letters are at once too few and too many to handle the roughly 40 pieces of sound (phonemes) that constitute today's spoken English, the variety of speech used by Walter Cronkite and John Chancellor and scientifically analyzed by Bell Labs and most dictionaries. The alphabetic principle suggests that we have 40 letters in order to describe this spoken code accurately and completely. In fact, we have more than 200 spellings for the 40 basic sounds of spoken English. This is five times the number required; it produces an efficiency rating of 20 percent for our written code. A piano with that degree of effectiveness would have 440 keys.

Ask any child or foreigner about the vagaries of written English. They will chronicle the agonies of "one" and "eight" and "tough" and "through" and "though." English is a verbal melting pot, and we have never had an Academy, as do the French, to establish linguistic standards. As a result, we have 15 spellings for the long *o* sound (owe, beau, though, doe, etc.) and another 15 for the long *a* sound (may, maid, gauge, great, weight, etc.). Imagine the efficiency of our Arabic number system if any digit could randomly take on several other values: "7 (frequently) times 6 (occasionally) equals 42 (more or less)."

"Why," one asks, "can't we have a code that does for language what Arabic numerals do for mathematics?" We can. The question is whether we really want it. Alphabet reform has been around as long as there has been an alphabet. English-alphabet reform dates back to at least 1568; the movement has included Benjamin Franklin, Mark Twain and George Bernard Shaw.

The "most voluble player" in alphabet reform has been Shaw, who left part of his estate to establish a competition for the creation of a new phonetic alphabet. He wrote:

"This alphabet is reduced to absurdity by a foolish orthography [spelling system] based on the notion that the business of spelling is to represent the origin and history of a word instead of its sound and meaning. Thus an intelligent child who is bidden to spell *debt,* and very properly spells it *d-e-t,* is caned for not spelling it with a *b* because Julius Caesar spelled it with a *b.*"

Mark Twain also had a few words on the subject:

"The English alphabet is pure insanity. It can hardly spell any word in the language with any large degree of certainty. . . . The sillinesses of the English alphabet are quite beyond enumeration. Whereas the English orthography needs . . . simplifying, the English alphabet needs it two or three million times more."

Twain wanted a one-for-one alphabet in which each letter stood for one sound and vice versa.

To date, more than 300 new alphabets have been devised for the English language. You may have noticed that none of them has yet been adopted; the psychological and cultural resistance to such a change is obviously strong. In the past, formidable technological and economic barriers halted the move toward a new alphabet. Today, alphabet reform has a chance to work its logic *because of* technological and economic considerations. The presence of 25 million adult functional illiterates in our population and the increasing role of English as a world language provide additional impetus.

Have I got an alphabet for you! One hundred percent efficient, it is related to the existing alphabet and compatible with all computer technologies. It works as a reading system; it fits most other languages. Called UNIFON, the alphabet was devised by John Malone, a Chicago economist, 20 years ago.

ONE-FOR-ONE SYSTEM

UNIFON (single sound), a totally consistent 40-character alphabet, maps and matches the 40 sounds of standard spoken English. It is an isomorphic (one-for-one) system of 24 consonants and 16 vowels. One and only one letter stands for each sound. One and only one sound corresponds to each letter. Students need learn only one rule for its use: Spell everything as it sounds; sound everything as it is spelled. No silent letters and no double letters exist.

Here is how the UNIFON alphabet works:

UNIFON is a "capitalist" tool, based on the uppercase letters of the Roman alphabet. The new alphabet retains 23 existing letters. The three dropped letters are unnecessary: the abecedarian duties of *C* are taken on by either *K* or *S*, *Q* becomes *KW*, and *X* becomes *KS*.

Seventeen letters are added, all based on existing letters. The 6 new consonants include a symbol for the *-ng* sound and 5 that contain the *h* sound (*ch, sh, zh* and the two sounds for *th*). The 11 new vowels include the 5 long vowels, 5 diphthongs and the *e* before an *r* sound.

Much of the complexity of English is in the richness of its vowel system — 16 sounds. They can be remembered in their UNIFON order through the following mnemonic list of five names:

Cat Face Hall
Red Peters
Big Mike
Otto Cook Cowboy
Mud Mule Blue

If UNIFON or something similar became *the* alphabet, these improvements could follow:

Economics: UNIFON takes up 14 percent less space, with consequent savings in labor, storage, ink and paper.

Decline in Dyslexia: One author believes that more than 60 percent of the world's dyslexia occurs in English-speaking countries and blames the gap between our spoken language and our alphabet.

Voice-Activated Machines: UNIFON's one-for-one correspondence would simplify the programming of voice-activated computers and typewriters.

Foreign Languages: Already the official alphabet of several American Indian tribes, UNIFON also fits the major European languages with minor adjustments. The new alphabet can ease the acquisition of languages; it could be particularly useful in teaching English to those, such as Spanish speakers, who already have a consistent alphabet.

English as World Language: English has become the de facto world language, taught in the elementary schools of more than 100 countries. Although relatively easy to speak, English is one of the most difficult languages to learn from written materials. A sensible alphabet would greatly facilitate this process.

Spelling Bees: No more.

Our current alphabet and the reading thereof involve a "sort of" phonetic base, but schoolchildren must learn some words, like *one* and *eight,* as if they were Chinese symbols.

At present, UNIFON is being used as an initial reading system in the public schools of Indianapolis. First-graders spend six months with UNIFON, then transfer to traditional orthography. Because their first experience with print has been logical and consistent, the children score high in reading and writing skills.

Two books currently in preparation will make the system available to teachers and parents: *Reading for the TV Child* and *The UNIFON Double-Entry Dictionary,* which will allow readers to look up a word either according to its traditional spelling (e.g., physics) or according to its pronunciation (FIZIKS).

THE TYPEWRITER

Change the alphabet and you must change the typewriter. Few technologies are more in need of basic reform. We have improved and modernized every part of the typewriter — except for the 26 letter keys, throwbacks to the year 1867 when Christopher Latham Sholes of Milwaukee developed the first practical commercial machine. Attempts to produce such a device date back to 1714; Sholes has been referred to as "the fifty-second man to 'invent' the typewriter."

How did the conventional *QWERTY* keyboard arrangement, named for the first six of the top row of letters, come to be? Sholes originally arranged the letters in alphabetical order — a remnant of this system remains on the middle line of keys — on a keyboard with four rows of keys. He encountered serious problems with jamming when adjacent keys were struck in rapid succession. He and his brother-in-law rearranged the keyboard to disperse the most frequently recurring letters, then conned the public into accepting this as a scientific advance instead of a nontechnical answer to a technical problem. The common keyboard is programmed for inefficiency. To type almost any word in the English language, a maximum distance has to be covered by the fingers.

There are two roads out of Qwertyville: the keyboard can be entirely eliminated, or it can be reformed.

When the vocal cords can replace the fingers as typing instruments, as promised by voice-activated typewriters now in the works, the keyboard will ultimately be superfluous. We can make voice-activated typewriters the hard way by employing our existing alphabet and forcing computers to deal with the more than 2,000 exceptions that are part of our spelling system. Or we can get ourselves a proper alphabet (UNIFON comes to mind) with an unambiguous, one-for-one correlation between sound and letter and create simpler and cheaper voice-activated typewriters. Material typed or printed in such an alphabet would also easily lend itself to retranslation back into sound.

If, however, we are to be burdened for a few more years with what I affectionately call the stupid alphabet, we can still improve on the fingering futilities of our current keyboard (hereafter to be known as the stupid keyboard). Sholes didn't know much about frequency counts and finger movements when he produced his machine. By 1932, Dr. August Dvorak knew a great deal about both. As professor of measurements and statistics at the University of Washington, he studied letter frequencies and sequences and the digital movements of typists for several years before producing a new keyboard that reflected these facts. It is known as the Dvorak Simplified Keyboard (DSK) and, in a slightly modified form, as the American Simplified Keyboard (ASK). Smith-Corona manufactures a model using this keyboard.

16-TO-1 ADVANTAGE

As Casey Stengel, "the old perfessor," might observe: "The shortest distance between two points is the shortest distance between two points." Using this norm, we can report that for every 16 miles of "finger walking" on the QWERTY keyboard, the ASK typewriter requires only 1. All major international records for typing are currently held by operators using the ASK keyboard. The *Guinness Book of World Records* lists Barbara Blackburn of Everett, Washington, as a record holder for sustained rapid and accurate typing. She cruises at 170 words per minute, using a DSK typewriter. Her chief rival, Howard Hudson of Decatur, Georgia, also uses this machine.

THE CALENDAR

Compared with the alphabet and the typewriter, the calendar is in relatively good shape. It just needs a little fine tuning. The Julian and Gregorian reforms got the calendar calibrated with the length of the solar year. Externally the year has been tidied up, but internally things are a bit messy: the weeks don't divide evenly into the months or the year; the quarters are irregular; the months are uneven in length; the cycle takes 28 years to repeat itself.

When the League of Nations solicited proposals for calendar reform in 1923, it received 185 plans for a new calendar. The most popular submission and the one that has endured as a possible model for reform was that of Moses Bruines Cotsworth, an English statistician. It was called the International Fixed Calendar, or the Equal Month Calendar.

According to this scheme there would be 13 months of 28 days each. Each month would be exactly the same — beginning on Sunday the first and ending on Saturday the twenty-eighth. This adds up to 364 days. The extra day ("Peace Day" or "World Day") would occur on December twenty-ninth, but it would not be counted as a day of the week and thus not disrupt the cycle of 13 equal and identical months. In leap years, a similar "blank" day ("Leap Day") would be intercalated on June twenty-ninth. The thirteenth month would be inserted between June and July and would be named Sol, in honor of the sun. If this plan were put into effect on January 1 of a year that began with Sunday (1984 is the next such year), then the system would be in place and the Equal Month Calendar would serve for every month of the year — forever.

Under the Cotsworth system, the year can be divided evenly by weeks (but not by months) into half years and quarter years: the quarter points are April 7, Sol 14, September 21, December 28; each month begins on a Sunday and ends on a Saturday (February 1981 was such a month). Without even referring to a calendar, we would soon know the day of the week on which each day of the month would fall: the thirteenth is always a Friday; if today's the tenth, it must be Tuesday. The advantages are obvious.

Everyone would be inconvenienced a little, and some groups will be especially put upon — calendar manufacturers, astrologers and triskaidekaphobes (those who fear the number *13*).

THE "BLANK" DAYS PLAN

A more modest proposal offered to the League of Nations, the World Calendar, suggests that we maintain the current 12-month approach and arrange the months in each of the four quarters in a 31-30-30-day sequence. This plan would also use the "blank" days for the 365th and 366th days of our inconvenient year.

To many, the idea of reforming things as familiar as the alphabet, the typewriter and the calendar is comparable to tampering with the law of gravity or taking a referendum on the tides. We have a cultural and psychological investment in these institutions that discourages change. But as a planetary culture evolves and the interdependence of people becomes more crucial, the reasons for simplifying English, typing and the calendar will become even more compelling. We can't inflict on the next generation an inefficient alphabet, an illogical keyboard and an untidy calendar. We wouldn't fly an airplane with the 20 percent efficiency rate of our alphabet. Is human communication any less important?

Number of words 2400
See page 211 for Questions

Reading time in Seconds _____
See page 358 for Conversion Table

SELECTION 13

Habit! Make It Your Friend, Not Your Enemy

William James

In this world, what is strongest? Ovid, born back in 43 B.C., thought he knew. He put it this way — "Nothing is stronger than habit." How do you put habit formation directly behind all your efforts to improve reading and communication skills? Get help from this selection.

"Habit a second nature! Habit is ten times nature," the Duke of Wellington is said to have exclaimed; and the degree to which this is true no one probably can appreciate as well as one who is a veteran soldier himself. The daily drill and the years of discipline end by fashioning a man completely over again, as to most of the possibilities of his conduct.

"There is a story," says Professor Huxley, "which is credible enough, though it may not be true, of a practical joker who, seeing a discharged veteran carrying home his dinner, suddenly called out, 'Attention!' whereupon the man instantly brought his hands down, and lost his mutton and potatoes in the gutter. The drill had

From *Psychology: Briefer Course*, Henry Holt and Company, 1892.

been thorough, and its effects had become embodied in the man's nervous structure."

Riderless cavalry-horses, at many a battle, have been seen to come together and go through their customary evolutions at the sound of the bugle-call. Most domestic beasts seem machines almost pure and simple, undoubtingly, unhesitatingly doing from minute to minute the duties they have been taught, and giving no sign that the possibility of an alternative ever suggests itself to their mind. Men grown old in prison have asked to be readmitted after being once set free. In a railroad accident a menagerie-tiger, whose cage had broken open, is said to have emerged, but presently crept back again, as if too much bewildered by his new responsibilities, so that he was without difficulty secured.

Habit is thus the enormous fly-wheel of society, its most precious conservative agent. It alone is what keeps us all within the bounds of ordinance, and saves the children of fortune from the envious uprisings of the poor. It alone prevents the hardest and most repulsive walks of life from being deserted by those brought up to tread therein. It keeps the fisherman and the deck-hand at sea through the winter; it holds the miner in his darkness, and nails the countryman to his log-cabin and his lonely farm through all the months of snow; it protects us from invasion by the natives of the desert and the frozen zone. It dooms us all to fight out the battle of life upon the lines of our nurture or our early choice, and to make the best of a pursuit that disagrees, because there is no other for which we are fitted, and it is too late to begin again. It keeps different social strata from mixing. Already at the age of twenty-five you see the professional mannerism settling down on the young commercial traveller, on the young doctor, on the young minister, on the young counsellor-at-law. You see the little lines of cleavage running through the character, the tricks of thought, the prejudices, the ways of the "shop," in a word, from which the man can by-and-by no more escape than his coat-sleeve can suddenly fall into a new set of folds. On the whole, it is best he should not escape. It is well for the world that in most of us, by the age of thirty, the character has set like plaster, and will never soften again.

If the period between twenty and thirty is the critical one in the formation of intellectual and professional habits, the period below twenty is more important still for the fixing of *personal* habits, properly so called, such as vocalization and pronunciation, gesture, motion, and address. Hardly ever is a language learned after twenty spoken without a foreign accent; hardly ever can a youth transferred to the society of his betters unlearn the nasality and other vices of speech bred in him by the associations of his growing years. Hardly ever, indeed, no matter how much money there be in his pocket, can he even learn to *dress* like a gentleman-born. The merchants offer their wares as eagerly to him as to the veriest "swell," but he simply *cannot* buy the right things. An invisible law, as strong as gravitation, keeps him within his orbit, arrayed this year as he was the last; and how his better-clad acquaintances contrive to get the things they wear will be for him a mystery till his dying day.

The great thing, then, in all education, is to *make our nervous system our ally instead of our enemy.* It is to fund and capitalize our acquisitions, and live at ease upon the interest of the fund. *For this we must make automatic and habitual, as early as possible, as many useful actions as we can,* and guard against the growing into ways that are likely to be disadvantageous to us, as we should guard against the plague. The more of the details of our daily life we can hand over to the effortless custody of automatism, the more our higher powers of mind will be set free for their own proper work. There is no more miserable human being than one in whom nothing is habitual but indecision, and for whom the lighting of every cigar, the drinking of every cup, the time of rising and going to bed every day, and the beginning of every bit of work, are subjects of express volitional deliberation. Full half the time of such a man goes to the deciding, or regretting, of matters which ought to be so ingrained in him as practically not to exist for his consciousness at all. If there be such daily duties not yet ingrained in any one of my readers, let him begin this very hour to set the matter right.

In Professor Bain's chapter on "The Moral Habits" there are some admirable practical remarks laid down. Two great maxims emerge from his treatment. The first is that in the acquisition of a new habit, or the leaving off of an old one, we must take care to *launch ourselves with as strong and decided an initiative as possible.* Accumulate all the possible circumstances which shall re-enforce the right motives; put yourself assiduously in conditions that encourage the new way; make engagements incompatible with the old; take a public pledge, if the case allows; in short, envelop your resolution with every aid you know. This will give your new beginning such a momentum that the temptation to break down will not occur as soon as it otherwise might; and every day during which a breakdown is postponed adds to the chances of its not occurring at all.

The second maxim is: *Never suffer an exception to occur till the new habit is securely rooted in your life.* Each lapse is like the letting fall of a ball of string which one is carefully winding up; a single slip undoes more than a great many turns will wind again. *Continuity* of training is the great means of making the nervous system act infallibly right. As Professor Bain says:

"The peculiarity of the moral habits, contradistinguishing them from the intellectual acquisitions, is the presence of two hostile powers, one to be gradually raised into the ascendant over the other. It is necessary, above all things, in such a situation, never to lose a battle. Every gain on the wrong side undoes the effect of many conquests on the right. The essential precaution, therefore, is so to regulate the two opposing powers that the one may have a series of uninterrupted successes, until repetition has fortified it to such a degree as to enable it to cope with the opposition, under any circumstances. This is the theoretically best career of mental progress."

The need of securing success at the *outset* is imperative. Failure at first is apt to damp the energy of all future attempts, whereas past experiences of success nerve one to future vigor. Goethe says to a man who consulted him about an enterprise but mistrusted his own powers: "Ach! you need only blow on your hands!" And the remark illustrates the effect on Goethe's spirits of his own habitually successful career.

The question of "tapering off," in abandoning such habits as drink and opium-indulgence comes in here, and is a question about which experts differ within certain limits, and in regard to what may be best for an individual case. In the main, however, all expert opinion would agree that abrupt acquisition of the new habit is the best way, *if there be a real possibility of carrying it out.* We must be careful not to give the will so stiff a task as to insure its defeat at the very outset; but, *provided one can stand it,* a sharp period of suffering, and then a free time, is the best thing to aim at, whether in giving up a habit like that of opium, or in simply changing one's hours of rising or of work. It is surprising how soon a desire will die of inanition if it be *never* fed.

"One must first learn, unmoved, looking neither to the right nor left, to walk firmly on the strait and narrow path, before one can begin 'to make one's self over again.' He who every day makes a fresh resolve is like one who, arriving at the edge of the ditch he is to leap, forever stops and returns for a fresh run. Without *unbroken* advance there is no such thing as *accumulation* of the ethical forces possible, and to make this possible, and to exercise us and habituate us in it, is the sovereign blessing of regular work."

A third maxim may be added to the preceding pair: *Seize the very first possible opportunity to act on every resolution you make, and on every emotional prompting you may experience in the direction of the habits you aspire to gain.* It is not in the moment of their forming, but in the moment of their producing *motor effects,* that resolves and aspirations communicate the new "set" to the brain. As the author last quoted remarks: "The actual presence of the practical opportunity alone furnishes the fulcrum upon which the lever can rest, by means of which the moral will may multiply its strength, and raise itself aloft. He who has no solid ground to press against will never get beyond the stage of empty gesture-making. . . ."

As a final practical maxim, relative to these habits of the will, we may, then, offer something like this: *Keep the faculty of effort alive in you by a little gratuitous exercise every day.* That is, be systematically ascetic or heroic in little unnecessary points, do every day or two something for no other reason than that you would rather not do it, so that when the hour of dire need draws nigh, it may find you not unnerved and untrained to stand the test. Asceticism of this sort is like the insurance which a man pays on his house and goods. The tax does him no good at the time, and possibly may never bring him a return. But if the fire *does* come, his having paid it will be his salvation from ruin. So with the man who has daily inured himself to habits of concentrated attention, energetic volition, and self-denial in unnecessary things. He will stand like a tower when everything rocks around him, and when his softer fellow-mortals are winnowed like chaff in the blast.

The physiological study of mental conditions is thus the most powerful ally of hortatory ethics. The hell to be endured hereafter, of which theology tells, is no worse than the hell we make for ourselves in this world by habitually fashioning our characters in the wrong way. Could the young but realize how soon they will become mere walking bundles of habits, they would give more heed to their conduct while in the plastic state. We are spinning our own fates, good or evil, and never to be undone. Every smallest stroke of virtue or of vice leaves its never so little scar. The drunken Rip Van Winkle, in Jefferson's play, excuses himself for every fresh dereliction by saying, "I won't count this time!" Well! he may not count it, and a kind Heaven may not count it; but it is being counted none the less. Down among his nerve-cells and fibers the molecules are counting it, registering and storing it up to be used against him when the next temptation comes. Nothing we ever do is, in strict scientific literalness, wiped out. Of course this has its good side as well as its bad one. As we become permanent drunkards by so many separate drinks, so we become saints in the moral, and authorities and experts in the practical and scientific spheres, by so many separate acts and hours of work. Let no youth have any anxiety about the upshot of his education, whatever the line of it may be. If he keep faithfully busy each hour of the working day, he may safely leave the final result to itself. He can with perfect certainty count on waking up some fine morning, to find himself one of the competent ones of his generation, in whatever pursuit he may have singled out. Silently, between all the details of his business, the *power of judging* in all that class of matter will have built itself up within him as a possession that will never pass away. Young people should know this truth in advance. The ignorance of it has probably engendered more discouragement and faint-heartedness in youths embarking on arduous careers than all other causes put together.

Number of words 2245
See page 213 for Questions

Reading time in Seconds _____
See page 358 for Conversion Table

Your Words Make You What You Are
S. I. Hayakawa

To communicate effectively demands that you look more closely at the vocabulary and language habits of those around you as well as at your own. According to Wendell Johnson, your sanity and well-being depend on such an examination. Let S. I. Hayakawa explain.

Do you—well, let's not make it personal—do your friends talk too much? Are there some among them who are never happy unless they are hogging the conversation?

Do you know people who are so wound up inside that they seem to continue talking whether they want to or not, raising one difficult question after another, yet never listening to the answers offered so that they end up still asking the same questions? (That's "over-verbalization.")

Do you have friends who have only one or two topics of conversation and become bored the moment you start talking about anything else? (That's "content rigidity.")

Do you often have to listen to pointless stories that go on and on in endless circumstantial detail? (That's "dead level abstracting.")

Do you also know people whose talk consists entirely of predictable formulae—whether pompous academic clichés or slang phrases? (That's "formal rigidity.")

Do you have friends who are so afraid of making mistakes that they cannot open their mouths? (That's "underverbalization.")

And have you ever noticed that, in spite of the vast difference in output the oververbalized often don't get any more said than the underverbalized?

In short, what are the language habits of the people around you—and also, what are your own? For many of these people are in messes, always quarreling, or always overexcited, or always suffering from feelings of inadequacy, or always being victimized by their own prejudices. They are people in quandaries. Is there any connection between their quandaries and their language habits? Are they, as Wendell Johnson says,[1] merely the froth on the beer or an important ingredient of the beer itself?

It is Wendell Johnson's contention that one's language habits are a part of one's emotional and intellectual difficulties, as well as a part of one's sanity and well-being. Like other semanticists, he rejects the common notion that "peoples' words don't matter, it's what

they think and feel and do that counts." The common notion ignores the reverse possibility, namely, that people may think and feel and act as they do because of the words and the patterns of words in terms of which they have been taught to describe themselves, the world about them, and their problems.

You cannot get an intelligent answer to a stupidly formulated question. Most of what we call "thinking" is simply a matter of talking to oneself silently. What kind of questions, then, do you ask yourself—and is it any wonder that you get dopey answers—or no answers at all? And since action is the result of what we have "thought," is not language the central instrument of our adjustment—or maladjustment? And by language Professor Johnson means not only one's vocabulary and syntax, but one's unconscious assumptions about the relationship between words and things. If you believe that "thirteen" is an "unlucky number" or that "spit is a nasty word," what kind of a theory of language have you got? And does not that theory of language affect deeply your evaluation of reality, and, therefore, your behavior?

For people in quandaries, then, Professor Johnson suggests not merely the usual inquiries into physical health, the influences of childhood environment, present emotional conflicts, etc., but also into language habits—(1) the ways in which people verbally formulate their problems, (2) the ways in which they react to what other people say, and (3) the ways in which they react to their own formulations.

Of the three, all of them important, perhaps the most important is the last, since, as he says in one of his frequent penetrating observations, "Every speaker is usually his most interested and most affected listener." We are all like the Red Queen in "Alice." What we say three times is true. And, no matter how nonsensical the statement, it becomes even truer with each further repetition. Moreover, since the uttering of nonsense is rarely systematically discouraged, but is on the contrary actively promoted by a significant portion of our educators, our press, the radio, the advertising profession and the pulpit, it is hardly to be wondered at that we find ourselves, in our times, to be not only people in quandaries, but also labor unions in quandaries, employers in quandaries, political parties in quandaries, and nations in quandaries.

Field Enterprises, Inc. Article by S. I. Hayakawa, reprinted with permission.

[1] Wendell Johnson, *People in Quandaries: The Semantics of Personal Adjustment* (New York: Harper and Brothers, 1946).

For years, as director of the psychological and speech clinic at the State University of Iowa, Professor Johnson has been "company to misery, holding the damp, trembling hand of frustration." Coming to him with "speech difficulties" to be straightened out, his students (and their parents) reveal one neurotic quandary after another lying at the root of their troubles. The similarity of the patterns of frustration and despair shown by innumerable patients early led Professor Johnson to the conclusion that "conditions peculiar to our general culture" rather than individualized aberrations, are responsible for most of the difficulties. Starting as a psychological speech clinician, therefore, he soon found it necessary to become both a cultural anthropologist and a social critic.

In selecting our language habits as the most general and most pervasive of the cultural conditions that contribute to frustration and neurosis, Professor Johnson follows the trail marked out by Alfred Korzybski's *Science and Sanity* (1933), which is by far the most suggestive work in the study of the relations between language and life. (It is significant that Korzybski originally referred to his work as "general anthropology.") Language, as Korzybski and Johnson agree, is the principal instrument by means of which human cultures are created and transmitted.

Culture, indeed, might be defined as the patterns of reaction by means of which groups respond to socially transmitted sets of signs, symbols, and sign-situations; and even our responses to nonverbal signs (traffic lights, religious symbols, the alignment of players on a football field, etc.) are instilled in us mainly through accompanying verbal instructions. But throughout our culture, we have inherited patterns of reaction to signs and symbols (including especially verbal signs and symbols) that are essentially prescientific and primitive.

An example of this primitivism is the kind of person who, unconsciously believing that, because there is such a word as "success," there is such a thing, keeps trying to attain it—without ever having attempted to formulate what he means by "success." In spite of good positions or comfortable incomes, such persons manage to keep themselves miserable, because the goal they set up for themselves is so vaguely defined that *they can't ever tell whether they have reached it or not.* Hence a lifelong uneasiness, with hypertension or gastric ulcers to boot. (If the reader asks at this point, "But what is success?" he needs Johnson's book very badly.)

Maladjusted people, he points out, keep asking incredibly silly questions, "Why did this have to happen to me?" "Is it right to make a lot of money?" "How can I be popular?" "What is the unpardonable sin?" "What is the meaning of life?" "People in quandaries," he says, "are peculiar not only because they persist in asking themselves such vague and unanswerable questions, but also because they don't realize that their questions are unanswerable. In fact, they don't seem to realize that

their maladjustment is in any way related to their persistence in asking, and in trying to answer, such questions. They seem quite puzzled by the suggestion that their questions need rewording. They don't want to reword them. They want answers, absolute, now-and-forever, correct answers. And so they remain maladjusted, pursuing verbal will-o'-the-wisps with ever increasing tension and despair."

In other words, people in quandaries have no conception of language as an instrument or technique for the exploration of the realities concerning themselves and the external world. It is as if, just because they happened to find near them a pair of nail-clippers when they wanted to open a can of sardines, they were to keep on indefinitely trying to get at the sardines with the nail-clippers. In the discussion of personal problems, political and social issues, international war and peace, few of us do any better: we use any linguistic instrument that happens to be handy (left lying around by Dorothy Dix or Gabriel Heatter or your late lamented Aunt Harriet). The result is that, in our attempts at solving personal and social problems, we spend most of our time throwing verbal tools around without ever reaching the subverbal sardines—the world of not-words, where the facts, both of inner needs and of external reality, lie.

If the reader expects, on the basis of a cocktail party acquaintance with semantics, that what he has to do in order to be saved is to learn some extremely complex discipline having to do with "the correct meanings of words," he will be disappointed. The general semantics of Korzybski, upon which Professor Johnson relies heavily, is based on modern sociology, anthropology, psychoanalysis, biology and mathematical physics. Out of these and other modern disciplines, general semantics distills certain "rules for orientation." It seeks to train people to check their language with the facts, to have adequate flexibility in their approach to problems, to be constantly on the lookout for factors that may have been omitted from one's calculations, to understand and evaluate in the light of the great sociological and cultural fact of human interdependence, and to be wary of those unanswerable questions which scientists have been trained to leave alone, but which, when discussed, split people into warring factions.

It seeks, in short, to train people in the application of scientific method to all of life, instead of to just a part of it. "The fundamental thesis of this book," as the author says, "is simply that science, clearly understood, can be used from moment to moment in everyday life, and that it provides a sound basis for warmly human and efficient living."

In large part the method of science "consists in (a) asking clear, answerable questions in order to direct one's (b) observations . . . which are then (c) reported as accurately as possible . . . after which (d) any pertinent beliefs or assumptions that were held before the observations were made are revised in the light of observations made." As the reader can see (although scientists themselves often don't), such a method of inquiry can be applied to personal and social problems no less than to the action of hydrocarbons.

But the opposite habits of (a) asking unanswerable questions, (b) making no observations, but relying on the magic of snarlwords, (c) reporting as facts inferences based on fears and prejudices and (d) refusing to revise one's beliefs despite hell and high water, are systematically instilled into us by our cultural environment. The problem, therefore, is the restoration of the mother wit with which we were originally endowed.

Professor Johnson says that learning general semantics is like learning to float, both extremely easy and extremely difficult: "You don't do anything in order to float. What you have to learn is to do nothing that would keep you from floating." Similarly, general semantics is largely a matter of learning to do nothing that would prevent you from using your natural intelligence—a fantastically difficult task for anyone living within earshot of modern propaganda.

Reading Professor Johnson's account of how to achieve the relaxed, alert and healthy orientations of modern science and general semantics is, like all liberating experiences, exciting and exhilarating. He has a genuine knack for explanation and a happy way of summing up a whole series of sober observations in a vivid epigram. (On scientific agreement: "If a doctor, two interns and a nurse all agree that there are no grasshoppers on your suit jacket, you might as well quit trying to brush them off.")

The reader will have to do some serious thinking in the course of the book, but because every theoretical consideration is illumined by sharp and often amusing examples drawn from politics, folklore, business, parenthood, literature, race relations and everyday life, he will derive the sense of understanding that comes from knowing not only what the author thinks, but how it feels to think that way.

Finally, in addition to giving at the close many suggestions for further amateur and professional research in semantics so that the reader may check the truth of what he says, Professor Johnson applies general semantics to the specific problem of stuttering. Both the theoretical formulations in his book and the results he has obtained in his speech clinic at the University of Iowa show that, by following up the leads suggested by general semantics, he has apparently solved the problem. *People in Quandaries,* therefore, offers both the pudding of semantics and a major proof. I can't imagine what more a reader could ask.

Number of words 2108
See page 215 for Questions

Reading time in Seconds _____
See page 358 for Conversion Table

SELECTION 15

In Other Words

Peter Farb

If you want to say something, you have to use language and words. Or do you? Recently we have been made aware of silent or wordless language, part of which is sometimes called body language. Take a quick look now into this paradoxical area of wordless words.

Early in this century, a horse named Hans amazed the people of Berlin by his extraordinary ability to perform rapid calculations in mathematics. After a problem was written on a blackboard placed in front of him, he promptly counted out the answer by tapping the low numbers with his right forefoot and multiples of ten with his left. Trickery was ruled out because Hans's owner, unlike owners of other performing animals, did

From *Word Play: What Happens When People Talk,* by Peter Farb. Copyright © 1973 by Peter Farb. Reprinted by permission of Alfred A. Knopf, Inc.

not profit financially — and Hans even performed his feats whether or not the owner was present. The psychologist O. Pfungst witnessed one of these performances and became convinced that there had to be a more logical explanation than the uncanny intelligence of a horse.

Because Hans performed only in the presence of an audience that could see the blackboard and therefore knew the correct answer, Pfungst reasoned that the secret lay in observation of the audience rather than of the horse. He finally discovered that as soon as the problem was written on the blackboard, the audience bent forward very slightly in anticipation to watch

Hans's forefeet. As slight as that movement was, Hans perceived it and took it as his signal to begin tapping. As his taps approached the correct number, the audience became tense with excitement and made almost imperceptible movements of the head — which signaled Hans to stop counting. The audience, simply by expecting Hans to stop when the correct number was reached, had actually told the animal when to stop. Pfungst clearly demonstrated that Hans's intelligence was nothing but a mechanical response to his audience, which unwittingly communicated the answer by its body language.

The "Clever Hans Phenomenon," as it has come to be known, raises an interesting question. If a mere horse can detect unintentional and extraordinarily subtle body signals, might they not also be detected by human beings? Professional gamblers and con men have long been known for their skill in observing the body-language cues of their victims, but only recently has it been shown scientifically that all speakers constantly detect and interpret such cues also, even though they do not realize it.

An examination of television word games several years ago revealed that contestants inadvertently gave their partners body-language signals that led to correct answers. In one such game, contestants had to elicit certain words from their partners, but they were permitted to give only brief verbal clues as to what the words might be. It turned out that sometimes the contestants also gave body signals that were much more informative than the verbal clues. In one case, a contestant was supposed to answer *sad* in response to his partner's verbal clue of *happy* — that is, the correct answer was a word opposite to the verbal clue. The partner giving the *happy* clue unconsciously used his body to indicate to his fellow contestant that an opposite word was needed. He did that by shifting his body and head very slightly to one side as he said *happy,* then to the other side in expectation of an opposite word.

Contestants on a television program are usually unsophisticated about psychology and linguistics, but trained psychological experimenters also unintentionally flash body signals which are sometimes detected by the test subjects — and which may distort the results of experiments. Hidden cameras have revealed that the sex of the experimenter, for example, can influence the responses of subjects. Even though the films showed that both male and female experimenters carried out the experiments in the same way and asked the same questions, the experimenters were very much aware of their own sex in relation to the sex of the subjects. Male experimenters spent 16 percent more time carrying out experiments with female subjects than they did with male subjects; similarly, female experimenters took 13 percent longer to go through experiments with male subjects than they did with female subjects. The cameras also revealed that chivalry is not dead in the psychological experiment; male experimenters smiled

about six times as often with female subjects as they did with male subjects.

The important question, of course, is whether or not such nonverbal communication influences the results of experiments; the answer is that it often does. Psychologists who have watched films made without the knowledge of either the experimenters or the subjects could predict almost immediately which experimenters would obtain results from their subjects that were in the direction of the experimenters' own biases. Those experimenters who seemed more dominant, personal, and **relaxed during the first moments of conversation with their subjects** usually obtained the results that they secretly hoped the experiments would yield. And they somehow communicated their secret hopes in a completely visual way, regardless of what they said or their paralanguage when they spoke. That was made clear when these films were shown to two groups, one of which saw the films without hearing the sound track while the other heard only the sound track without seeing the films. The group that heard only the voices could not accurately predict the experimenters' biases — but those who saw the films without hearing the words immediately sensed whether or not the experimenters were communicating their biases.

A person who signals his expectations about a certain kind of behavior is not aware that he is doing so — and usually he is indignant when told that his experiment was biased — but the subjects themselves confirm his bias by their performances. Such bias in experiments has been shown to represent self-fulfilling prophecies. In other words, the experimenters' expectations about the results of the experiment actually result in those expectations coming true. That was demonstrated when each of twelve experimenters was given five rats bred from an identical strain of laboratory animals. Half of the experimenters were told that their rats could be expected to perform brilliantly because they had been bred especially for high intelligence and quickness in running through a maze. The others were told that their rats could be expected to perform very poorly because they had been bred for low intelligence. All the experimenters were then asked to teach their rats to run a maze.

Almost as soon as the rats were put into the maze it became clear that those for which the experimenters had high expectations would prove to be the better performers. And the rats which were expected to perform badly did in fact perform very badly, even though they were bred from the identical strain as the excellent performers. Some of these poor performers did not even budge from their starting positions in the maze. The misleading prophecy about the behavior of the two groups of rats was fulfilled — simply because the two groups of experimenters unconsciously communicated their expectations to the animals. Those experimenters who anticipated high performance were friendlier to their animals than those who expected low performance; they handled their animals more, and they did so more gently. Clearly, the predictions of the experimenters were communicated to the rats in subtle and unintended ways — and the rats behaved accordingly.

Since animals such as laboratory rats and Clever Hans can detect body-language cues, it is not surprising that human beings are just as perceptive in detecting visual signals about expectations for performance. It is a psychological truth that we are likely to speak to a person whom we expect to be unpleasant in such a way that we force him to act unpleasantly. But it has only recently become apparent that poor children — often black or Spanish-speaking — perform badly in school because that is what their teachers expect of them, and because the teachers manage to convey that expectation by both verbal and nonverbal channels. True to the teacher's prediction, the black and brown children probably will do poorly — not necessarily because children from minority groups are capable only of poor performance, but because poor performance has been expected of them. The first grade may be the place where teachers anticipate poor performances by children of certain racial, economic, and cultural backgrounds — and where the teachers actually teach these children how to fail.

Evidence of the way the "Clever Hans Phenomenon" works in many schools comes from a careful series of experiments by psychologist Robert Rosenthal and his co-workers at Harvard University. They received permission from a school south of San Francisco to give a series of tests to the children in the lower grades. The teachers were blatantly lied to. They were told that the test was a newly developed tool that could predict which children would be "spurters" and achieve high performance in the coming year. Actually, the experimenters administered a new kind of IQ test that the teachers were unlikely to have seen previously. After IQ scores were obtained, the experimenters selected the names of 20 percent of the children completely at random. Some of the selected children scored very high on the IQ test and others scored low, some were from middle-class families and others from lower-class. Then the teachers were lied to again. The experimenters said that the tests singled out this 20 percent as the children who could be expected to make unusual intellectual gains in the coming year. The teachers were also cautioned not to discuss the test results with the pupils or their parents. Since the names of these children had been selected completely at random, any difference between them and the 80 percent not designated as "spurters" was completely in the minds of the teachers.

All the children were given IQ tests again during that school year and once more the following year. The 20 percent who had been called to the attention of their teachers did indeed turn in the high performances expected of them — in some cases dramatic increases of 25 points in IQ. The teachers' comments about these children also were revealing. The teachers considered them more happy, curious, and interesting than the other 80 percent — and they predicted that they would be successes in life, a prophecy they had already started to fulfill. The experimenters plainly showed that children who are expected to gain intellectually do gain and that their behavior improves as well.

The results of the experiment are clear — but the explanation for the results is not. It might be imagined that the teachers simply devoted more time to the children singled out for high expectations, but the study showed that was not so. Instead, the influence of the teachers upon these children apparently was much more subtle. What the teachers said to them, how and when it was said, the facial expressions, gestures, posture, perhaps even touch that accompanied their speech — some or all of these things must have communicated that the teachers expected improved performance from them. And when these children responded correctly, the teachers were quicker to praise them and also more lavish in their praise. Whatever the exact mechanism was, the effect upon the children who had been singled out was dramatic. They changed their ideas about themselves, their behavior, their motivation, and their learning capacities.

The lesson of the California experiment is that pupil performance does not depend so much upon a school's audio-visual equipment or new textbooks or enriching trips to museums as it does upon teachers whose body language communicates high expectations for the pupils — even if the teacher thinks she "knows" that a black, a Puerto Rican, a Mexican-American, or any other disadvantaged child is fated to do poorly in school. Apparently, remedial instruction in our schools is misdirected. It is needed more by the middle-class teachers than by the disadvantaged children.

Number of words 1930
See page 217 for Questions

Reading time in Seconds _____
See page 358 for Conversion Table

The Feel

Paul Gallico

How does curiosity — the feel of things around you — relate to your ability to communicate? As you read on, you may wish to substitute names of sports heroes more current than the ones mentioned. No matter. The point of the article remains the same.

A child wandering through a department store with its mother, is admonished over and over again not to touch things. Mother is convinced that the child only does it to annoy or because it is a child, and usually hasn't the vaguest inkling of the fact that Junior is "touching" because he is a little blotter soaking up information and knowledge, and "feel" is an important adjunct to seeing. Adults are exactly the same, in a measure, as you may ascertain when some new gadget or article is produced for inspection. The average person says: "Here, let me see that," and holds out his hand. He doesn't mean "see," because he is already seeing it. What he means is that he wants to get it into his hands and feel it so as to become better acquainted.

I do not insist that a curiosity and capacity for feeling sports is necessary to be a successful writer, but it is fairly obvious that a man who has been tapped on the chin with five fingers wrapped up in a leather boxing glove and propelled by the arm of an expert knows more about that particular sensation than one who has not, always provided he has the gift of expressing himself. I once inquired of a heavyweight prizefighter by the name of King Levinsky, in a radio interview, what it felt like to be hit on the chin by Joe Louis, the King having just acquired that experience with rather disastrous results. Levinsky considered the matter for a moment and then reported: "It don't feel like nuttin'," but added that for a long while afterwards he felt as though he were "in a transom."

I was always a child who touched things and I have always had a tremendous curiosity with regard to sensation. If I knew what playing a game felt like, particularly against or in the company of experts, I was better equipped to write about the playing of it and the problems of the men and women who took part in it. And so, at one time or another, I have tried them all, football, baseball, boxing, riding, shooting, swimming, squash, handball, fencing, driving, flying, both land and sea planes, rowing, canoeing, skiing, riding a bicycle, ice-skating, roller-skating, tennis, golf, archery, basketball, running, both the hundred-yard dash and the mile, the high jump and shot put, badminton, angling, deep-sea, stream- and surf-casting, billiards and bowling, motorboating and wrestling, besides riding as a passenger with the fastest men on land and water and in the air, to see what it felt like. Most of them I dabbled in as a youngster going through school and college, and others, like piloting a plane, squash, fencing, and skiing, I took up after I was old enough to know better, purely to get the feeling of what they were like.

None of these things can I do well, but I never cared about becoming an expert, and besides, there wasn't time. But there is only one way to find out accurately human sensations in a ship two or three thousand feet up when the motor quits, and that is actually to experience that gone feeling at the pit of the stomach and the sharp tingling of the skin from head to foot, followed by a sudden amazing sharpness of vision, clear-sightedness, and coolness that you never knew you possessed as you find the question of life or death completely in your own hands. It is not the "you" that you know, but somebody else, a stranger, who noses the ship down, circles, fastens upon the one best spot to sit down, pushes or pulls buttons to try to get her started again, and finally drops her in, safe and sound. And it is only by such experience that you learn likewise of the sudden weakness that hits you right at the back of the knees after you have climbed out and started to walk around her and that comes close to knocking you flat as for the first time since the engine quit its soothing drone you think of destruction and sudden death.

Often my courage has failed me and I have funked completely, such as the time I went up to the top of the thirty-foot Olympic diving-tower at Jones Beach, Long Island, during the competitions, to see what it was like to dive from that height, and wound up crawling away from the edge on hands and knees, dizzy, scared, and a little sick, but with a wholesome respect for the boys and girls who hurled themselves through the air and down through the tough skin of the water from that awful height. At other times sheer ignorance of what I was getting into has led me into tight spots such as the time I came down the Olympic ski run from the top of the Kreuzeck, six thousand feet above Garmisch-Partenkirchen, after having been on skis but once before in snow and for the rest had no more than a dozen lessons on an indoor artificial slide in a New York department store. At one point my legs, untrained, got so tired that I couldn't stem (brake) any more, and I lost control and went full tilt and all out, down a three-foot twisting path cut out of the side of the mountain, with a two-thousand-foot abyss on the left and the mountain itself on the right. That was probably the most scared I have ever been, and I scare fast and often. I remember giving myself up for lost and wondering how long it would take them to retrieve my body and whether I should be still alive. In the meantime the speed of the descent was increasing. Somehow I was keeping my feet and negotiating turns, how I will never know, until suddenly the narrow patch opened out into a wide, steep stretch of slope with a rise at the other end, and *that* part of the journey was over.

By some miracle I got to the bottom of the run uninjured, having made most of the trip down the icy, perpendicular slopes on the flat of my back. It was the thrill and scare of a lifetime, and to date no one has been able to persuade me to try a jump. I know when to stop. After all, I am entitled to rely upon my imagination for something. But when it was all over and I found myself still whole, it was also distinctly worth while to have learned what is required of a ski runner in the breakneck *Abfahrt* or downhill race, or the difficult *slalom.* Five days later, when I climbed laboriously (still on skis) halfway up that Alp and watched the Olympic downhill racers hurtling down the perilous, ice-covered, and nearly perpendicular *Steilhang,* I knew that I was looking at a great group of athletes who, for one thing, did not know the meaning of the word "fear." The slope was studded with small pine trees and rocks, but half of the field gained precious seconds by hitting that slope all out, with complete contempt for disaster rushing up at them at a speed often better than sixty miles an hour. And when an unfortunate Czech skidded off the course at the bottom of the slope and into a pile of rope and got himself snarled up as helpless as a fly in a spider's web, it was a story that I could write from the heart. I had spent ten minutes getting myself untangled after a fall, *without* any rope to add to the difficulties. It seems that I couldn't find where my left leg ended and one more ski than I originally donned seemed to be involved somehow. Only a person who has been on those fiendish runners knows the sensation.

It all began back in 1922 when I was a cub sportswriter and consumed with more curiosity than was good for my health. I had seen my first professional prize-fights and wondered at the curious behavior of men under the stress of blows, the sudden checking and the beginning of a little fall forward after a hard punch, the glazing of the eyes and the loss of locomotor control, the strange actions of men on the canvas after a knockdown as they struggled to regain their senses and arise on legs that seemed to have turned into rubber. I had never been in any bad fist fights as a youngster, though I had taken a little physical punishment in foot-

ball, but it was not enough to complete the picture. Could one think under those conditions?

I had been assigned to my first training-camp coverage, Dempsey's at Saratoga Springs, where he was preparing for his famous fight with Luis Firpo. For days I watched him sag a spar boy with what seemed to be no more than a light cuff on the neck, or pat his face with what looked like no more than a caressing stroke of his arm, and the fellow would come all apart at the seams and collapse in a useless heap, grinning vacuously or twitching strangely. My burning curiosity got the better of prudence and a certain reluctance to expose myself to physical pain. I asked Dempsey to permit me to box a round with him. I had never boxed before, but I was in good physical shape, having just completed a four-year stretch as a galley slave in the Columbia eight-oared shell.

When it was over and I escaped through the ropes, shaking, bleeding a little from the mouth, with rosin dust on my pants and a vicious throbbing in my head, I knew all that there was to know about being hit in the prize-ring. It seems that I had gone to an expert for tuition. I knew the sensation of being stalked and pursued by a relentless, truculent professional destroyer whose trade and business it was to injure men. I saw the quick flash of the brown forearm that precedes the stunning shock as a bony, leather-bound fist lands on cheek or mouth. I learned more (partly from photographs of the lesson, viewed afterwards, one of which shows me ducked under a vicious left hook, an act of which I never had the slightest recollection) about instinctive ducking and blocking than I could have in ten years of looking at prizefights, and I learned, too, that as the soldier never hears the bullet that kills him, so does the fighter rarely, if ever, see the punch that tumbles blackness over him like a mantle, with a tearing rip as though the roof of his skull were exploding, and robs him of his senses.

There was just that—a ripping in my head and then sudden blackness, and the next thing I knew, I was sitting on the canvas covering of the ring floor with my legs collapsed under me, grinning idiotically. How often since have I seen that same silly, goofy look on the faces of dropped fighters—and understood it. I held onto the floor with both hands, because the ring and the audience outside were making a complete clockwise revolution, came to a stop, and then went back again counter-clockwise. When I struggled to my feet, Jack Kearns, Dempsey's manager, was counting over me, but I neither saw nor heard him and was only conscious that I was in a ridiculous position and that the thing to do was to get up and try to fight back. The floor swayed and rocked beneath me like a fishing dory in an off-shore swell, and it was a welcome respite when Dempsey rushed into a clinch, held me up, and whispered into my ear: "Wrestle around a bit, son, until your head clears." And then it was that I learned what those little love-taps to the back of the neck and the short digs to the ribs can mean to the groggy pugilist more than half knocked out. It is a murderous game, and the fighter who can escape after having been felled by a lethal blow has my admiration. And there, too, I learned that there can be no sweeter sound than the bell that calls a halt to hostilities.

From that afternoon on, also, dated my antipathy for the spectator at prizefights who yells: "Come on, you bum, get up and fight! Oh, you big quitter! Yah yellow, yah yellow!" Yellow, eh? It is all a man can do to get up after being stunned by a blow, much less fight back. But they do it. And how a man is able to muster any further interest in a combat after being floored with a blow to the pit of the stomach will always remain to me a miracle of what the human animal is capable of under stress.

Further experiments were less painful, but equally illuminating. A couple of sets of tennis with Vinnie Richards taught me more about what is required of a topflight tournament tennis-player than I could have got out of a dozen books or years of reporting tennis matches. It is one thing to sit in a press box and write caustically that Brown played uninspired tennis, or Black's court covering was faulty and that his frequent errors cost him the set. It is quite another to stand across the net at the back of a service court and try to get your racket on a service that is so fast that the ear can hardly detect the interval between the sound of the server's bat hitting the ball and the ball striking the court. Tournament tennis is a different game from week-end tennis. For one thing, in average tennis, after the first hard service has gone into the net or out, you breathe a sigh of relief, move up closer and wait for the cripple to come floating over. In big-time tennis second service is practically as hard as the first, with an additional twist on the ball.

It is impossible to judge or know anything about the speed of a forehand drive hit by a champion until you have had one fired at you, or, rather, away from you, and you have made an attempt to return it. It is then that you first realize that tennis is played more with the head than with the arms and the legs. The fastest player in the world cannot get to a drive to return it if he hasn't thought correctly, guessed its direction, and anticipated it by a fraction of a second.

There was golf with Bob Jones and Gene Sarazen and Tommy Armour, little Cruickshank and Johnny Farrell, and Diegel and other professionals; and experiments at trying to keep up in the water with Johnny Weissmuller, Helene Madison, and Eleanor Holm, attempts to catch football passes thrown by Benny Friedman. Nobody actually plays golf until he has acquired the technical perfection to be able to hit the ball accurately, high, low, hooked or faded and placed. And nobody knows what real golf is like until he has played around with a professional and seen him play, not the

ball, but the course, the roll of the land, the hazards, the wind, and the texture of the greens and the fairways. It looks like showmanship when a top-flight golfer plucks a handful of grass and lets it flutter in the air, or abandons his drive to march two hundred yards down to the green and look over the situation. It isn't. It's golf. The average player never knows or cares whether he is putting with or across the grain of a green. The professional *always* knows. The same average player standing on the tee is concentrated on getting the ball somewhere on the fairway, two hundred yards out. The professional when preparing to drive is actually to all intents and purposes playing his *second* shot. He means to place his drive so as to open up the green for his approach. But you don't find that out until you have played around with them when they are relaxed and not competing, and listen to them talk and plan attacks on holes.

Major-league baseball is one of the most difficult and precise of all games, but you would never know it unless you went down on the field and got close to it and tried it yourself. For instance, the distance between pitcher and catcher is a matter of twenty paces, but it doesn't seem like enough when you don a catcher's mitt and try to hold a pitcher with the speed of Dizzy Dean or Dazzy Vance. Not even the sponge that catchers wear in the palm of the hand when working with fast-ball pitchers, and the bulky mitt are sufficient to rob the ball of shock and sting that lames your hand unless you know how to ride with the throw and kill some of its speed. The pitcher, standing on his little elevated mound, looms up enormously over you at that short distance, and when he ties himself into a coiled spring preparatory to letting fly, it requires all your self-control not to break and run for safety. And as for the things they can do with a baseball, those major-league pitchers . . . ! One way of finding out is to wander down on the field an hour or so before game-time when there is no pressure on them, pull on the catcher's glove, and try to hold them.

I still remember my complete surprise the first time I tried catching for a real curve-ball pitcher. He was a slim, spidery left-hander of the New York Yankees, many years ago, by the name of Herb Pennock. He called that he was going to throw a fast breaking curve and warned me to expect the ball at least two feet outside the plate. Then he wound up and let it go, and that ball came whistling right down the groove for the center of the plate. A novice, I chose to believe what I saw and not what I heard, and prepared to catch it where it was headed for, a spot which of course it never reached, because just in front of the rubber, it swerved sharply to the right and passed nearly a yard from my glove. I never had a chance to catch it. That way, you learn about the mysterious drop, the ball that sails down the alley chest high but which you must be prepared to catch around your ankles because of the sudden dip it takes at the end of its passage as though someone were pulling it down with a string. Also you find out about the queer fade-away, the slow curve, the fast in- and out-shoots that seem to be timed almost as delicately as shrapnel, to burst, or rather break, just when they will do the most harm—namely, at the moment when the batter is swinging.

Facing a big-league pitcher with a bat on your shoulder and trying to hit his delivery is another vital experience in gaining an understanding of the game about which you are trying to write vividly. It is one thing to sit in the stands and scream at the batsman: "Oh, you bum!" for striking out in a pinch, and another to stand twenty yards from that big pitcher and try to make up your mind in a hundredth of a second whether to hit at the offering or not, where to swing and when, not to mention worrying about protecting yourself from the consequences of being struck by the ball that seems to be heading straight for your skull at an appalling rate of speed. Because, if you are a big-league player, you cannot very well afford to be gun-shy and duck away in panic from a ball that swerves in the last moment and breaks perfectly over the plate, while the umpire calls: "Strike!" and the fans jeer. Nor can you afford to take a crack on the temple from the ball. Men have died from that. It calls for undreamed-of niceties of nerve and judgment, but you don't find that out until you have stepped to the plate cold a few times during batting practice or in training quarters, with nothing at stake but the acquisition of experience, and see what a fine case of the jumping jitters you get. Later on, when you are writing your story, your imagination, backed by the experience, will be able to supply a picture of what the batter is going through as he stands at the plate in the closing innings of an important game, with two or three men on base, two out, and his team behind in the scoring, and fifty thousand people screaming at him.

The catching and holding of a forward pass for a winning touchdown on a cold, wet day always make a good yarn, but you might get an even better one out of it if you happen to know from experience about the elusive qualities of a hard, soggy, mud-slimed football rifled through the air, as well as something about the exquisite timing, speed, and courage it takes to catch it on a dead run, with two or three 190-pound men reaching for it at the same time or waiting to crash you as soon as your fingers touch it.

Any football coach during a light practice will let you go down the field and try to catch punts, the long, fifty-yard spirals, and the tricky, tumbling end-over-enders. Unless you have had some previous experience, you won't hang on to one out of ten, besides knocking your fingers out of joint. But if you have any imagination, thereafter you will know that it calls for more than negligible nerve to judge and hold that ball and even plan to run with it, when there are two husky ends bearing down at full speed, preparing for a head-on tackle.

In 1932 I covered my first set of National Air Races, in Cleveland, and immediately decided that I had to learn how to fly to find out what that felt like. Riding as a passenger isn't flying. Being up there all alone at the controls of a ship is. And at the same time began a series of investigations into the "feel" of the mechanized sports to see what they were all about and the qualities of mentality, nerve, and physique they called for from their participants. These included a ride with Gar Wood in his latest and fastest speedboat, *Miss America X*, in which for the first time he pulled the throttle wide open on the Detroit River straightaway; a trip with the Indianapolis Speedway driver Cliff Bergere, around the famous brick raceway; and a flip with Lieutenant Al Williams, one time U.S. Schneider Cup race pilot.

I was scared with Wood, who drove me at 127 miles an hour, jounced, shaken, vibrated, choked with fumes from the exhausts, behind which I sat hanging on desperately to the throttle bar, which after a while got too hot to hold. I was on a plank between Wood and his mechanic, Johnson, and thought that my last moment had come. I was still more scared when Cliff Bergere hit 126 on the Indianapolis straightaways in the tiny racing car in which I was hopelessly wedged, and after the first couple of rounds quite resigned to die and convinced that I should. But I think the most scared I have ever been while moving fast was during a ride I took in the cab of a locomotive on the straight, level stretch between Fort Wayne, Indiana, and Chicago, where for a time we hit 90 miles per hour, which of course is no speed at all. But nobody who rides in the comfortable Pullman coaches has any idea of the didoes cut up by a locomotive in a hurry, or the thrill of pelting through a small town, all out and wide open, including the crossing of some thirty or forty frogs and switches, all of which must be set right. But that wasn't sport. That was just plain excitement.

I have never regretted these researches. Now that they are over, there isn't enough money to make me do them again. But they paid me dividends, I figured. During the great Thompson Speed Trophy race for land planes at Cleveland in 1935, Captain Roscoe Turner was some eight or nine miles in the lead in his big golden, low-wing speed monoplane. Suddenly, coming into the straightaway in front of the grandstands, buzzing along at 280 miles an hour like an angry hornet, a streamer of thick, black smoke burst from the engine cowling and trailed back behind the ship. Turner pulled up immediately, using his forward speed to gain all the altitude possible, turned and got back to the edge of the field, still pouring out that evil black smoke. Then he cut his switch, dipped her nose down, landed with a bounce and a bump, and rolled up to the line in a perfect stop. The crowd gave him a great cheer as he climbed out of the oil-spattered machine, but it was a cheer of sympathy because he had lost the race after having been so far in the lead that had he continued he could not possibly have been overtaken.

There was that story, but there was a better one too. Only the pilots on the field, all of them white around the lips and wiping from their faces a sweat not due to the oppressive summer heat, knew that they were looking at a man who from that time on, to use their own expression, was living on borrowed time. It isn't often when a Thompson Trophy racer with a landing speed of around eighty to ninety miles an hour goes haywire in the air, that the pilot is able to climb out of the cockpit and walk away from his machine. From the time of that first burst of smoke until the wheels touched the ground and stayed there, he was a hundred-to-one shot to live. To the initiated, those dreadful moments were laden with suspense and horror. Inside that contraption was a human being who any moment might be burned to a horrible, twisted cinder, or smashed into the ground beyond all recognition, a human being who was cool, gallant, and fighting desperately. Every man and woman on the field who had ever been in trouble in the air was living those awful seconds with him in terror and suspense. I, too, was able to experience it. That is what makes getting the "feel" of things distinctly worth while.

Number of words 4470
See page 219 for Questions

Reading time in Seconds _____
See page 358 for Conversion Table

SELECTION 17

Of Happiness and of Despair We Have No Measure

Ernest van den Haag

What do the radio, television, movies, and newspapers do for us — or to us? Are they substitute gratifications — packaged dreams that encourage us to continue sleeping — or do they have the opposite effect, encouraging us to glimpse reality more clearly through an uncovering of essentials? See how convincing you find this selection.

All mass media in the end alienate people from personal experience and, though appearing to offset it, intensify their moral isolation from each other, from reality and from themselves. One may turn to the mass media when lonely or bored. But mass media, once they become a habit, impair the capacity for meaningful experience. Though more diffuse and not as gripping, the habit feeds on itself, establishing a vicious circle as addictions do.

The mass media do not physically replace individual activities and contacts — excursions, travel, parties, etc. But they impinge on all. The portable radio is taken everywhere — from seashore to mountaintop — and everywhere it isolates the bearer from his surroundings, from other people, and from himself. Most people escape being by themselves at any time by voluntarily tuning in on something or somebody. Anyway, it is nearly beyond the power of individuals to escape broadcasts. Music and public announcements are piped into restaurants, bars, shops, cafes, and lobbies, into public means of transportation, and even taxis. You can turn off your radio but not your neighbor's, nor can you silence his portable or the set at the restaurant. Fortunately, most persons do not seem to miss privacy, the cost of which is even more beyond the average income than the cost of individuality.

People are never quite in one place or group without at the same time, singly or collectively, gravitating somewhere else, abstracted, if not transported by the mass media. The incessant announcements, arpeggios, croonings, sobs, bellows, brayings and jingles draw to some faraway world at large and by weakening community with immediate surroundings make people lonely even when in a crowd and crowded even when alone.

We have already stressed that mass media must offer homogenized fare to meet an average of tastes. Further, whatever the quality of the offerings, the very fact that one after the other is absorbed continuously, indiscriminately and casually, trivializes all. Even the most profound of experiences, articulated too often on the same level, is reduced to a cliché. The impact of each of the offerings of mass media is thus weakened by the next one. But the impact of the stream of all mass-media offerings is cumulative and strong. It lessens people's capacity to experience life itself.

Sometimes it is argued that the audience confuses actuality with mass-media fiction and reacts to the characters and situations that appear in soap operas or comic strips as though they were real. For instance, wedding presents are sent to fictional couples. It seems more likely, however, that the audience prefers to invest

Excerpted from *The Fabric of Society* by Ernest van den Haag and Ralph Ross, Harcourt, Brace & World, Inc., 1957.

fiction with reality — as a person might prefer to dream — without actually confusing it with reality. After all, even the kids know that Hopalong Cassidy is an actor and the adults know that "I Love Lucy" is fiction. Both, however, may attempt to live the fiction because they prefer it to their own lives. The significant effect is not the (quite limited) investment of fiction with reality, but the de-realization of life lived in largely fictitious terms. Art can deepen the perception of reality. But popular culture veils it, diverts from it, and becomes an obstacle to experiencing it. It is not so much an escape from life but an invasion of life first, and ultimately evasion altogether.

Parents, well knowing that mass media can absorb energy, often lighten the strain that the attempts of their children to reach for activity and direct experience would impose; they allow some energy to be absorbed by the vicarious experience of the television screen. Before television, the cradle was rocked, or poppy juice given, to inhibit the initiative and motility of small children. Television, unlike these physical sedatives, tranquilizes by means of substitute gratifications. Manufactured activities and plots are offered to still the child's hunger for experiencing life. They effectively neutralize initiative and channel imagination. But the early introduction of de-individualized characters and situations and early homogenization of taste on a diet of meaningless activity hardly foster development. Perhaps poppy juice, offering no models in which to cast the imagination, was better.

The homogenizing effect of comic books or television, the fact that they neither express nor appeal to individuality, seems far more injurious to the child's mind and character than the violence they feature, though it is the latter that is often blamed for juvenile delinquency. The blame is misplaced. Violence is not new to life or fiction. It waxed large in ancient fables, fairy tales, and in tragedies from Sophocles to Shakespeare.

Mom always knew that "her boy could not have thought of it," that the other boys must have seduced him. The belief that viewing or reading about violence persuades children to engage in it is Mom's ancient conviction disguised as psychiatry. Children are quite spontaneously bloodthirsty and need both direct and fantasy outlets for violence. What is wrong with the violence of the mass media is not that it is violence, but that it is not art — that it is meaningless violence which thrills but does not gratify. The violence of the desire for life and meaning is displaced and appears as a desire for meaningless violence. But the violence which is ceaselessly supplied cannot ultimately gratify it because it does not meet the repressed desire. . . .

A little more than a hundred years ago, Henry David Thoreau wrote in *Walden*: "The mass of men lead lives of quiet desperation. . . . A stereotyped but unconscious despair is concealed even under what are called the games and amusements of mankind." Despair, we find, is no longer quiet. Popular culture tries to exorcise it with much clanging and banging. Perhaps it takes more noise to drone it out. Perhaps we are less willing to face it. But whether wrapped in popular culture, we are less happy than our quieter ancestors, or the natives of Bali, must remain an open question despite all romanticizing. (Nor do we have a feasible alternative to popular culture. Besides, a proposal for "the mass of men" would be unlikely to affect the substance of popular culture. And counsel to individuals must be individual.)

There have been periods happier and others more desperate than ours. But we don't know which. And even an assertion as reasonable as this is a conjecture like any comparison of today's bliss with yesterday's. The happiness felt in disparate groups, in disparate periods and places cannot be measured and compared. Our contention is simply that by distracting from the human predicament and blocking individuation and experience, popular culture impoverishes life without leading to contentment. But whether "the mass of men" felt better or worse without the mass-production techniques of which popular culture is an ineluctable part, we shall never know. Of happiness and of despair, we have no measure.

Number of words 1124
See page 221 for Questions

Reading time in Seconds _____
See page 358 for Conversion Table

SELECTION 18

How to Enjoy the Classics

Steve Allen

What's a classic? Clifton Fadiman put it nicely — "When you reread a classic you do not see more in the book than you did before; you see more in you than there was before." Does Steve Allen feel the same way about the classics?

Why is it? In school we learn one of the most amazing and difficult feats man has ever accomplished — *how to read* — and at the same time we learn to hate to read the things worth reading most!

It's happened to us all — with assignment reading! It happened to me. The teacher assigned *Moby Dick.* I didn't want to read it. So I fought it. I disliked it. I thought I won.

But I lost. My struggle to keep at arm's length from *Moby Dick* cost me all the good things that can come from learning to come to terms with those special few books we call the "classics."

I've come back to *Moby Dick* on my own since. I *like* it. And I've discovered a new level of pleasure from it with each reading.

What *is* a classic? A classic is a book that gives you that exhilarating feeling, if only for a moment, that you've finally uncovered part of the meaning of life.

A classic is a book that's stood the test of time, a book that men and women all over the world keep reaching for throughout the ages for its special enlightenment.

Not many books can survive such a test. Considering all the volumes that have been produced since man first put chisel to stone, classics account for an infinitesimal share of the total — less than .001 percent. That's just a few thousand books. Of those, under 100 make up the solid core.

Why should you tackle the classics? Why try to enjoy them?

I suggest three good reasons:

1. Classics open up your mind.
2. Classics help you grow.
3. Classics help you understand your life, your world, yourself.

That last one is the big one. A classic can give you insights into yourself that you will get nowhere else. Sure, you can get pleasure out of almost any book. But a classic, once you penetrate it, lifts you up *high!*

Aeschylus's *Oresteia* was written nearly 2,500 years ago — and it still knocks me out!

But I can hear you saying, "I've *tried* reading classics. They are hard to understand. I can't get into them."

Let me offer some suggestions that will help you open up this wondrous world. Pick up a classic you've always promised to try. Then take Dr. Allen's advice.

Know what you're reading. Is it a novel, drama, biography, history? To find out, check the table of contents, read the book cover, the preface, or look up the title or author in *The Reader's Encyclopedia.*

Don't read in bed. Classics can be tough going; I'll admit it. You need to be alert, with your senses sharp. When you read in bed you're courting sleep — and you'll blame it on the book when you start nodding off.

Don't let a lot of characters throw you. Dostoevsky tosses fifty major characters at you in *The Brothers Karamazov.* In the very first chapter of *War and Peace,* Tolstoy bombards you with twenty-two names — long, complicated ones like Anna Pavlovna Scherer, Anatole and Prince Bolkonski. Don't scurry for cover. Stick with it. The characters will gradually sort themselves out and you'll feel as comfortable with them as you do with your own dear friends who were strangers, too, when you met them.

Give the author a chance. Don't say "I don't get it!" too soon. Keep reading right to the end.

Sometimes, though, you may not be ready for the book you're trying to get into. I tackled Plato's *Republic* three times before it finally opened up to me. And man, was it worth it! So if you really can't make a go of the book in your lap, put it aside for another day, or year, and take on another one.

Read in big bites. Don't read in short nibbles. How can you expect to get your head into anything that way? The longer you stay with it, the more you get into the rhythm and mood — and the more pleasure you get from it.

When you read *Zorba the Greek* try putting bouzouki music on the record player; Proust, a little Debussy; Shakespeare, Elizabethan theater music.

Reprinted by permission of International Paper Company, from "The Power of the Printed Word" series.

Read what the author read. To better understand where the author is coming from, as we say, read the books he once read and that impressed him. Shakespeare, for example, dipped into North's translation of Plutarch's *Lives* for the plots of *Julius Caesar, Antony and Cleopatra* and *A Midsummer Night's Dream.* It's fun to know you're reading what *he* read.

Read about the author's time. You are the product of your time. Any author is the product of *his* time. Knowing the history of that time, the problems that he and others faced, their attitudes — will help you understand the author's point of view. *Important point:* You may not agree with the author. No problem. At least he's made you think!

Read about the author's life. The more you know about an author's own experiences, the more you'll understand why he wrote what he wrote. You'll begin to see the autobiographical odds and ends that are hidden in his work.

A writer can't help but reveal himself. Most of our surmises about Shakespeare's life come from clues found in his plays.

Read the book again. All classics bear rereading. If after you finish the book you're intrigued but still confused, reread it then and there. It'll open up some more to you.

If you did read a classic a few years back and loved it, read it again. The book will have so many new things to say to you, you'll hardly believe it's the same one.

A few classics to enjoy. You can find excellent lists of the basic classics compiled by helpful experts, like Clifton Fadiman's *Lifetime Reading Plan,* the *Harvard Classics* and Mortimer J. Adler's *Great Books.* Look into them.

But before you do, I'd like to suggest a few classics that can light up your life. Even though some might have been spoiled for you by the required reading stigma, try them. Try them. And *try* them.

Number of words 1290
See page 223 for Questions

1. Homer: *Iliad* and *Odyssey.* The Adam and Eve of Western literature. Read a good recent translation. My favorite is by Robert Fitzgerald.

2. Rabelais: *Gargantua and Pantagruel.* A Gargantuan romp. I recommend the Samuel Putnam translation.

3. Geoffrey Chaucer: *Canterbury Tales.* Thirty folks on a four-day pilgrimage swapping whoppers. Don't be surprised if the people you meet here are like people you know in *your* life.

4. Cervantes: *Don Quixote.* The first modern novel, about the lovable old Don with his "impossible dream." How could you go through life without reading it *once?*

5. Shakespeare: *Plays.* Shakespeare turned out 37 plays. Some are flops, some make him the greatest writer ever. All offer gold. His best: "Hamlet," "Macbeth" and "Romeo and Juliet." (See them on the stage, too.)

6. Charles Dickens: *Pickwick Papers.* No one can breathe life into characters the way Dickens can. Especially the inimitable Samuel Pickwick, Esq.

7. Mark Twain: *Huckleberry Finn.* Maybe you had to read this in school. Well, climb back on that raft with Huck and Jim. You'll find new meaning this time.

Of course, these few suggestions hardly scratch the surface.

Don't just dip your toe into the deep waters of the classics. Plunge in! Like generations of bright human beings before you, you'll find yourself invigorated to the marrow by thoughts and observations of the most gifted writers in history.

You still enjoy looking at classic paintings. You enjoy hearing musical classics. Good books will hold you, too.

Someone has said the classics are the diary of man. Open up the diary. Read about yourself — and *understand* yourself.

Reading time in Seconds _____
See page 358 for Conversion Table

How to Read a River

Mark Twain

The dictionary reminds us that we read many things besides words. You may read a person's character in his face. You may read someone's mind — particularly if it's like an open book. You may read the skies to determine the weather. And here is Mark Twain to help you read a river.

Now I had often seen pilots gazing at the water and pretending to read it as if it were a book; but it was a book that told me nothing. A time came at last, however, when Mr. Bixby seemed to think me far enough advanced to bear a lesson on water-reading. So he began:

"Do you see that long, slanting line on the face of the water? Now, that's a reef. Moreover, it's a bluff reef. There is a solid sand-bar under it that is nearly as straight up and down as the side of a house. There is plenty of water close up to it, but mighty little on top of it. If you were to hit it you would knock the boat's brains out. Do you see where the line fringes out at the upper end and begins to fade away?"

"Yes, sir."

"Well, that is a low place; that is the head of the reef. You can climb over there, and not hurt anything. Cross over, now, and follow along close under the reef — easy water there — not much current."

I followed the reef along till I approached the fringed end. Then Mr. Bixby said:

"Now get ready. Wait till I give the word. She won't want to mount the reef; a boat hates shoal water. Stand by — wait — *wait* — keep her well in hand. *Now* cramp her down! Snatch her! snatch her!"

He seized the other side of the wheel and helped to spin it around until it was hard down, and then we held it so. The boat resisted, and refused to answer for a while, and next she came surging to starboard, mounted the reef, and sent a long, angry ridge of water foaming away from her bows.

"Now watch her; watch her like a cat, or she'll get away from you. When she fights strong and the tiller slips a little, in a jerky, greasy sort of way, let up on her a trifle; it is the way she tells you at night that the water is too shoal; but keep edging her up, little by little, toward the point. You are well up on the bar now; there is a bar under every point, because the water that comes down around it forms an eddy and allows the sediment to sink. Do you see those fine lines on the face of the

water that branch out like the ribs of a fan? Well, those are little reefs; you want to just miss the ends of them, but run them pretty close. Now look out — look out! Don't you crowd that slick, greasy-looking place; there ain't nine feet there; she won't stand it. She begins to smell it; look sharp, I tell you! Oh, blazes, there you go! Stop the starboard wheel! Quick! Ship up to back! Set her back!"

The engine bells jingled and the engines answered promptly, shooting white columns of steam far aloft out of the 'scape-pipes, but it was too late. The boat had "smelt" the bar in good earnest; the foamy ridges that radiated from her bows suddenly disappeared, a great dead swell came rolling forward, and swept ahead of her, she careened far over to larboard, and went tearing away toward the shore as if she were about scared to death. We were a good mile from where we ought to have been when we finally got the upper hand of her again.

During the afternoon watch the next day, Mr. Bixby asked me if I knew how to run the next few miles. I said:

"Go inside the first snag above the point, outside the next one, start out from the lower end of Higgins's woodyard, make a square crossing, and — "

"That's all right. I'll be back before you close up on the next point."

But he wasn't. He was still below when I rounded it and entered upon a piece of the river which I had some misgivings about. I did not know that he was hiding behind a chimney to see how I would perform. I went gaily along, getting prouder and prouder, for he had never left the boat in my sole charge such a length of time before. I even got to "setting" her and letting the wheel go entirely, while I vaingloriously turned my back and inspected the stern marks and hummed a tune, a sort of easy indifference which I had prodigiously admired in Bixby and the other great pilots. Once I inspected rather long, and when I faced to the front again my heart flew into my mouth so suddenly that if I hadn't clapped my teeth together I should have lost it. One of those frightful bluff reefs was stretching its deadly length right across our bows! My head was gone

From *Life on the Mississippi*, 1883.

in a moment; I did not know which end I stood on; I gasped and could not get my breath; I spun the wheel down with such rapidity that it wove itself together like a spider's web; the boat answered and turned square away from the reef, but the reef followed her! I fled, but still it followed, still it kept — right across my bows! I never looked to see where I was going, I only fled. The awful crash was imminent. Why didn't that villain come? If I committed the crime of ringing a bell I might get thrown overboard. But better that than kill the boat. So in blind desperation, I started such a rattling "shivaree" down below as never had astounded an engineer in this world before, I fancy. Amidst the frenzy of the bells the engines began to back and fill in a curious way, and my reason forsook its throne — we were about to crash into the woods on the other side of the river. Just then Mr. Bixby stepped calmly into view on the hurricane-deck. My soul went out to him in gratitude. My distress vanished; I would have felt safe on the brink of Niagara with Mr. Bixby on the hurricane-deck. He blandly and sweetly took his toothpick out of his mouth between his fingers, as if it were a cigar — we were just in the act of climbing an overhanging big tree, and the passengers were scudding astern like rats — and lifted up these commands to me ever so gently:

"Stop the starboard! Stop the larboard! Set her back on both!"

The boat hesitated, halted, pressed her nose among the boughs a critical instant, then reluctantly began to back away.

"Stop the larboard! Come ahead on it! Stop the starboard! Come ahead on it! Point her for the bar!"

I sailed away as serenely as a summer's morning. Mr. Bixby came in and said, with mock simplicity:

"When you have a hail, my boy, you ought to tap the big bell three times before you land, so that the engineers can get ready."

I blushed under the sarcasm, and said I hadn't had any hail.

"Ah! Then it was for wood, I suppose. The officer of the watch will tell you when he wants to wood up."

I went on consuming, and said I wasn't after wood.

"Indeed? Why, what could you want over here in the bend, then? Did you ever know of a boat following a bend up-stream at this stage of the river?"

"No, sir — and I wasn't trying to follow it. I was getting away from a bluff reef."

"No, it wasn't a bluff reef; there isn't one within three miles of where you were."

Number of words 1734
See page 225 for Questions

"But I saw it. It was as bluff as that one yonder."

"Just about. Run over it!"

"Do you give it as an order?"

"Yes. Run over it!"

"If I don't, I wish I may die."

"All right; I am taking the responsibility."

I as just as anxious to kill the boat, now, as I had been to save it before. I impressed my orders upon my memory, to be used at the inquest, and made a straight break for the reef. As it disappeared under our bows I held my breath; but we slid over it like oil.

"Now, don't you see the difference? It wasn't anything but a *wind* reef. The wind does that."

"So I see. But it is exactly like a bluff reef. How am I ever going to tell them apart?"

"I can't tell you. It is an instinct. By and by you will just naturally *know* one from the other, but you never will be able to explain why or how you know them apart."

It turned out to be true. The face of the water, in time, became a wonderful book — a book that was a dead language to the uneducated passenger, but which told its mind to me without reserve, delivering its most cherished secrets as clearly as if it uttered them with a voice. And it was not a book to be read once and thrown aside, for it had a new story to tell every day. Throughout the long twelve hundred miles there was never a page that was void of interest, never one that you could leave unread without loss, never one that you would want to skip, thinking you could find higher enjoyment in some other thing. There never was so wonderful a book written by man; never one whose interest was so absorbing, so unflagging, so sparklingly renewed with every reperusal. The passenger who could not read it was charmed with a peculiar sort of faint dimple on its surface (on the rare occasions when he did not overlook it altogether); but to the pilot that was an *italicized* passage; indeed, it was more than that, it was a legend of the largest capitals, with a string of shouting exclamation-points at the end of it, for it meant that a wreck or a rock was buried there that could tear the life out of the strongest vessel that ever floated. It is the faintest and simplest expression the water ever makes, and the most hideous to a pilot's eye. In truth, the passenger who could not read this book saw nothing but all manner of pretty pictures in it, painted by the sun and shaded by the clouds, whereas to the trained eye these were not pictures at all, but the grimmest and most dead-earnest of reading-matter.

Reading time in Seconds _____
See page 358 for Conversion Table

The Bible's Timeless — and Timely — Insights

Smiley Blanton, M.D.

A well-known psychiatrist demonstrates the extraordinary wisdom of the Bible in dealing with problems that have haunted the human race from the beginning — and are more than ever with us today. Apparently reading can do more than inform. It can be bibliotherapy, bringing curative and restorative power.

The other day a new patient noticed a Bible lying on my desk. "Do you — a psychiatrist — read the Bible?" he asked.

"I not only read it," I told him, "I study it. It's the greatest textbook on human behavior ever put together. If people would just absorb its message, a lot of us psychiatrists could close our offices and go fishing."

"You're talking about the Ten Commandments and the Golden Rule?"

"Certainly — but more, too," I said. "There are dozens of other insights that have profound psychiatric value. Take your own case. For the past hour you've been telling me how you've done this, tried that, all to no avail. It's pretty obvious that you're worrying yourself into a state of acute anxiety, isn't it?"

"That," he said dryly, "is why I'm here."

I picked up the Bible. "Here's some advice that St. Paul gives to the Ephesians. Just four words: *Having done all, stand.* Now, what does that mean? Exactly what it says. You've done your best, what more can you do? Keep running in circles? Plow up the same ground? What you really need — far more than a solution to this particular problem — is peace of mind. And there's the formula: relax, stand quietly, stop trying to lick this thing with your conscious mind. Let the creative power in your unconscious mind take over. It may solve the whole thing for you, if you'll just get out of your own way!"

My patient looked thoughtful. "Maybe I should do a little Bible reading on my own," he said.

It does seem foolish not to make use of the distilled wisdom of 3000 years. Centuries before psychiatry, the Bible knew that "the kingdom of God is within you." We psychiatrists call it the unconscious mind — but only the words are new, not the concept. From beginning to end the Bible teaches that the human soul is a battleground where good struggles with evil. We talk about the forces of hostility and aggression contending with the love-impulses in human nature. It's the same thing.

What psychiatry has done is to bring scientific terminology to the truths that the Bible presents in poetry, allegory and parable. What, in essence, did Freud and the other pioneers discover? That the human mind functions on the conscious *and* the unconscious level. That the thing we call conscience does, too, and that many emotional pressures and dislocations are caused by its hidden action.

It is tremendously exciting to read the Bible with even this much knowledge of psychiatry. Here are a few of my favorite passages, words so full of insight that I think they might well be memorized and repeated periodically by anyone who values his mental health.

• **Underneath are the everlasting arms.** For hundreds of years, troubled people have found comfort in these words from the Book of Deuteronomy. This is not surprising. One of the few fears we are born with is the fear of falling, so the idea of a pair of loving arms, sustaining and eternal, is an answer to the yearning in all of us to feel safe, to find security. Furthermore, one of the deepest forms of communication is *touch*. And so this Biblical image brings a great sense of peace. If you suffer from tension and insomnia, try repeating these words to yourself at bedtime. You may find them more effective than any sleeping pill.

• **Love thy neighbor as thyself.** Many people think this noble concept comes from the New Testament. Actually you can also find it in Leviticus. The remarkable thing, to a psychiatrist, is its recognition that in an emotionally healthy person there must be self-love as well as love of others.

Lack of self-esteem is probably the most common emotional ailment I am called upon to treat. Often pressure from the unconscious mind is causing this sense of unworthiness. Suppose a woman comes to me, weighted down with guilt. I can't undo the things she has done. But perhaps I can help her understand why she did them, and how the mechanism of her conscience, functioning below the conscious level, is paralyzing her. And I can urge her to read and reread the story of the Prodigal Son. How can anyone feel permanently condemned or rejected in a world where this magnificent promise comes ringing down the centuries, the promise that love is stronger than any mistake, any error?

• **Take no thought for the morrow.** A modern rephrasing might well be, "Stop worrying about the future." Worry causes tension. Tension blocks the flow of creative energy from the unconscious mind. And when creative energy wanes, problems multiply.

Most of us know perfectly well that worry is a futile process. Yet many people constantly borrow trouble. "Sufficient unto the day," says the Bible, "is the evil thereof." There are plenty of problems in the here-and-now to tackle and solve. The only moment when you're really alive is the present one, so make the most of it. Have faith that the Power that brought you here will help you through any future crisis, whatever it may be. "They that wait upon the Lord," sang Isaiah, "shall renew their strength; they shall mount up with wings as eagles." Why? Because their faith makes them non-worriers.

• **As he thinketh in his heart, so is he.** This penetrating phrase from Proverbs implies that what you *think* you think is less important than what you really think. Every day in my office I see illustrations of this. Last week I was talking to a woman who had married during the Korean war. Her husband, a reserve officer, had volunteered for war duty and gone overseas, leaving her pregnant. He had been killed; she was left to bring up their son alone. Eventually she remarried, but now she was having difficulty with the 15-year-old boy.

It was apparent that she treated her son with unusual harshness and severity. "Why are you so strict with him?" I asked.

"Because I don't want him to grow up spoiled," she said instantly.

"Did it ever occur to you," I asked, "that when this boy's father went away voluntarily, leaving you, and got himself killed, something in you was enraged, something in you hated him? And isn't it just possible that some of this unadmitted hate has been displaced onto the child he left you with, although your conscious mind doesn't want to admit that either? Look into your heart and search for the truth there, below the rationalizations of your mind. Until you do, we're not going to get anywhere with this problem."

• **Where your treasure is, there will your heart be also.** Of course! *What* we shall love is the key problem of human existence, because we tend to become the reflection of what we love. Do you love money? Then your values will be materialistic. Do you love power? Then the aggressive instincts in you will slowly become dominant. Do you love God and your neighbor? Then you are not likely to need a psychiatrist!

We psychiatrists warn against sustained anger and hostility; we know that unresolved conflicts in the unconscious mind can make you physically ill. How does the Bible put it? *Let not the sun go down upon your wrath.* And: *A merry heart doeth good like a medicine.* Exactly so. These flashing sparks of truth from the pages of the Bible are endless!

If I were asked to choose one Bible passage above all others it would be this: *And ye shall know the truth, and the truth shall make you free.* In one tremendous sentence these words encompass the whole theory and method of psychotherapy. Nine times out of ten, when people come to me tormented by guilt, racked by anxiety, exhausted by unresolved hate, it is because they don't know the truth about themselves. It is the role of the psychiatrist to remove the camouflage, the self-deception, the rationalizations. It is his job to bring the unconscious conflicts into the conscious mind where reason can deal with them. As Freud said, "Reason is a small voice, but it is persistent." Once insight is gained, the cure can begin — because the truth *does* make you free.

We shall never have all the truth. Great questions of life and death, good and evil, remain unanswered — and must so remain, as the book of Job eloquently tells us. But this much seems plain to me: locked in the unconscious of each of us are the same elemental forces of love and hate that have haunted and inspired the human race from the beginning. With this hidden area of the human spirit psychiatry concerns itself — sometimes helpfully, sometimes not. But there is also an ancient book that deals with it, that understands it profoundly and intuitively, a book that for 3000 years has been a help in time of trouble to any person wise enough to use it.

Number of words 1490
See page 227 for Questions

Reading time in Seconds _____
See page 359 for Conversion Table

Feeding the Mind

Lewis Carroll

It has been said, "Tell me what you eat, and I will tell you what you are."
In the following selection Lewis Carroll seems to say that that is not so. It's not
so much what you eat but what you read that makes you what you are. Do you
find his case convincing?

Breakfast, dinner, tea; in extreme cases, breakfast, luncheon, dinner, tea, supper, and a glass of something hot at bedtime. What care we take about feeding the lucky body! Which of us does as much for his mind? And what causes the difference? Is the body so much the more important of the two?

By no means; but life depends on the body being fed, whereas we can continue to exist as animals (scarcely as men) though the mind be utterly starved and neglected. Therefore Nature provides that, in case of serious neglect of the body, such terrible consequences of discomfort and pain shall ensue as will soon bring us back to a sense of our duty; and some of the functions necessary to life she does for us altogether, leaving us no choice in the matter. It would fare but ill with many of us if we were left to superintend our own digestion and circulation. "Bless me!" one would cry, "I forgot to wind up my heart this morning! To think that it has been standing still for the last three hours!" "I can't walk with you this afternoon," a friend would say, "as I have no less than eleven dinners to digest. I had to let them stand over from last week, being so busy — and my doctor says he will not answer for the consequences if I wait any longer!"

Well it is, I say, for us, that the consequences of neglecting the body can be clearly seen and felt; and it might be well for some if the mind were equally visible and tangible — if we could take it, say, to the doctor and have its pulse felt.

"Why, what have you been doing with this mind lately? How have you fed it? It looks pale, and the pulse is very slow."

"Well, doctor, it has not had much regular food lately. I gave it a lot of sugar-plums yesterday."

"Sugar-plums! What kind?"

"Well, they were a parcel of conundrums, sir."

"Ah! I thought so. Now just mind this: if you go on playing tricks like that, you'll spoil all its teeth, and get laid up with mental indigestion. You must have nothing but the plainest reading for the next few days. Take care now! No novels on any account!"

Considering the amount of painful experience many of us have had in feeding and dosing the body, it would,

I think, be quite worth our while to try and translate some of the rules into corresponding ones for the mind.

First, then, we should set ourselves to provide for our mind its *proper kind* of food; we very soon learn what will, and what will not, agree with the body, and find little difficulty in refusing a piece of the tempting pudding or pie which is associated in our memory with that terrible attack of indigestion, and whose very name irresistibly recalls rhubarb and magnesia; but it takes a great many lessons to convince us how indigestible some of our favorite lines of reading are, and again and again we make a meal of the unwholesome novel, sure to be followed by its usual train of low spirits, unwillingness to work, weariness of existence — in fact by mental nightmare.

Then we should be careful to provide this wholesome food in *proper amount*. Mental gluttony, or overreading, is a dangerous propensity, tending to weakness of digestive power, and in some cases to loss of appetite; we know that bread is a good and wholesome food, but who would like to try the experiment of eating two or three loaves at a sitting?

I have heard of a physician telling his patient — whose complaint was merely gluttony and want of exercise — that "the earliest symptom of hypernutrition is a deposition of adipose tissue," and no doubt the fine long words greatly consoled the poor man under his increasing load of fat.

I wonder if there is such a thing in nature as a *fat* mind? I really think I have met with one or two minds which could not keep up with the slowest trot in conversation, could not jump over a logical fence to save their lives, always got stuck fast in a narrow argument, and, in short, were fit for nothing but to waddle helplessly through the world.

Then, again, though the food be wholesome and in proper amount, we know that we must not consume *too many kinds at once*. Take the thirsty haymaker a quart of beer, or a quart of cider, or even a quart of cold tea, and he will probably thank you (though not so heartily in the last case!). But what think you his feelings would be if you offered him a tray containing a little mug of beer, a little mug of cider, another of cold tea, one of hot tea, one of coffee, one of cocoa, and corresponding vessels of milk, water, brandy-and-water,

From *Feeding the Mind*, London: Chatto and Windus, 1907.

and buttermilk? The sum total might be a quart, but would it be the same thing to the haymaker?

Having settled the proper kind, amount, and variety of our mental food, it remains that we should be careful to allow *proper intervals* between meal and meal, and not swallow the food hastily without mastication, so that it may be thoroughly digested; both which rules for the body are also applicable at once to the mind.

First as to the intervals: these are as really necessary as they are for the body, with this difference only, that while the body requires three or four hours' rest before it is ready for another meal, the mind will in many cases do with three or four minutes. I believe that the interval required is much shorter than is generally supposed, and from personal experience I would recommend any one who has to devote several hours together to one subject of thought to try the effect of such a break, say once an hour — leaving off for five minutes only, each time, but taking care to throw the mind absolutely "out of gear" for those five minutes, and to turn it entirely to other subjects. It is astonishing what an amount of impetus and elasticity the mind recovers during those short periods of rest.

And then as to the mastication of the food: the mental process answering to this is simply *thinking over* what we read. This is a very much greater exertion of mind than the mere passive taking in the contents of our author — so much greater an exertion is it, that, as Coleridge says, the mind often "angrily refuses" to put itself to such trouble — so much greater, that we are far too apt to neglect it altogether, and go on pouring in fresh food on the top of the undigested masses already lying there, till the unfortunate mind is fairly swamped under the flood. But the greater the exertion, the more valuable, we may be sure, is the effect; one hour of steady thinking over a subject (a solitary walk is as good an opportunity for the process as any other) is worth two or three of reading only.

And just consider another effect of this thorough digestion of the books we read; I mean the arranging and "ticketing," so to speak, of the subjects in our minds, so that we can readily refer to them when we want them. Sam Slick tells us that he has learned several languages in his life, but somehow "couldn't keep the parcels sorted" in his mind; and many a mind that hurries through book after book, without waiting to digest or arrange anything, gets into that sort of condition, and the unfortunate owner finds himself far from fit really to support the character all his friends give him.

"A thoroughly well-read man. Just you try him in any subject, now. You can't puzzle him!"

You turn to the thoroughly well-read man: you ask him a question, say, in English history (he is understood to have just finished reading Macaulay); he smiles good-naturedly, tries to look as if he knew all about it, and

proceeds to dive into his mind for the answer. Up comes a handful of very promising facts, but on examination they turn out to belong to the wrong century, and are pitched in again; a second haul brings up a fact much more like the real thing, but unfortunately along with it comes a tangle of other things — a fact in political economy, a rule in arithmetic, the ages of his brother's children, and a stanza of Gray's *Elegy;* and among all these the fact he wants has got hopelessly twisted up and entangled. Meanwhile every one is waiting for his reply, and as the silence is getting more and more awkward, our well-read friend has to stammer out some half-answer at last, not nearly so clear or so satisfactory as an ordinary schoolboy would have given. And all this for want of making up his knowledge into proper bundles and ticketing them!

Do you know the unfortunate victim of ill-judged mental feeding when you see him? Can you doubt him? Look at him drearily wandering round a reading-room, tasting dish after dish — we beg his pardon, book after book — keeping to none. First a mouthful of novel — but no, faugh! he has had nothing but that to eat for the last week, and is quite tired of the taste; then a slice of science, but you know at once what the result of that will be — ah, of course, much too tough for *his* teeth. And so on through the old weary round, which he tried (and failed in) yesterday, and will probably try, and fail in, tomorrow.

Mr. Oliver Wendell Holmes, in his very amusing book *The Professor at the Breakfast-table,* gives the following rule for knowing whether a human being is young or old. "The crucial experiment is this. Offer a bulky bun to the suspected individual just ten minutes before dinner. If this is easily accepted and devoured, the fact of youth is established." He tells us that a human being, "if young, will eat anything at any hour of the day or night."

To ascertain the healthiness of the *mental* appetite of a human animal, place in its hands a short, well-written, but not exciting treatise on some popular subject — a mental *bun,* in fact. If it is read with eager interest and perfect attention, *and if the reader can answer questions on the subject afterwards,* the mind is in first-rate working order; if it be politely laid down again, or perhaps lounged over for a few minutes, and then, "I can't read this stupid book! Would you hand me the second volume of *The Mysterious Murder?*" you may be equally sure that there is something wrong in the mental digestion.

If this paper has given you any useful hints on the important subject of reading, and made you see that it is one's duty no less than one's interest to "read, mark, learn, and inwardly digest" the good books that fall in your way, its purpose will be fulfilled.

Number of words 1866
See page 229 for Questions

Reading time in Seconds _____
See page 359 for Conversion Table

Building a Home Library

The Royal Bank of Canada *Monthly Letter*

*Books are like friends, waiting patiently to inform or entertain you. You'll want
them conveniently close, of course — so start collecting. As Augustine Birrell said,
"Good as it is to inherit a library, it is better to collect one." For help, read on.*

Reading good books is not something to be indulged in as a luxury. It is a necessity for anyone who intends to give his life and work a touch of quality. The most real wealth is not what we put into our piggy banks but what we develop in our heads.

Books instruct us without anger, threats and harsh discipline. They do not sneer at our ignorance or grumble at our mistakes. They ask only that we spend some time in the company of greatness so that we may absorb some of its attributes.

You do not read a book for the book's sake, but for your own.

You may read because in your high-pressure life, studded with problems and emergencies, you need periods of relief and yet recognize that peace of mind does not mean numbness of mind.

You may read because you never had an opportunity to go to university, and books give you a chance to get something you missed.

You may read because your job is routine, and books give you a feeling of depth in life.

You may read because you see social, economic and philosophical problems which need solution, and you believe that the best thinking of all past ages may be useful in your age, too.

You may read because you are tired of the shallowness of contemporary life, bored by the current conversational commonplaces, and wearied of shop talk and gossip about people.

Whatever your dominant personal reason, you will find that reading gives knowledge, creative power, satisfaction and relaxation. It cultivates your mind by calling its faculties into exercise.

It is well to have some destination in mind. As Arnold Bennett remarks in *Literary Taste* (a Pelican Book), a man starting out for a walk says to himself that he will reach some given point, or that he will progress at a given speed for a given distance, or that he will remain on his feet for a given time. He makes these decisions according to his ambition, his physical capacity and his pleasure. So with reading.

Books are a source of pleasure the purest and the most lasting. They enhance your sensation of the interestingness of life. Reading them is not a violent pleasure like the gross enjoyment of an uncultivated mind, but a subtle delight.

Reading dispels prejudices which hem our minds within narrow spaces. One of the things that will surprise you as you read the Greek, Hebrew and Christian books; the Roman, French, Italian and British books; the books of philosophy, poetry and politics, and the books that just tell about people having fun, is that human nature is much the same today as it has been ever since writing began to tell us about it.

Some people act as if it were demeaning to wish to be well-read, but you can no more be a healthy person mentally without reading substantial books than you can be a vigorous person physically without eating solid food.

Perusal of good books will give you a mind of your own, bulwarked against the seduction of slogans. Through books you escape from the ephemeral challenge of a crossword puzzle to the actual challenge of working out the why and wherefore of a segment of life. By borrowing the aid of a superior understanding you double your own understanding, meeting what the writer says with your personal thoughts.

The proper function of books is associated with intellectual culture in which you steer clear of generalities and indefinite views. You enlarge your critical sense regarding events and personalities and trends, so that you are no longer at the mercy of theorists and demagogues.

It is perfectly possible for one who only gives to reading the leisure hours of a business life to acquire such a general knowledge of the laws of nature and the facts of history that every great advance made in science and government and business shall be intelligible and interesting.

CHOOSING BOOKS

In deciding what books to read and what books to have in your private library you need to take a wide sweep. There is a book to match your mood whatever it may be. There are books that are gentle and quieting, and books that are exciting and inspiring. All that mankind has done and thought, gained and lost: it is lying as in magic preservation in the pages of books. You should have a good selection of them within arm's reach.

As you read, your taste will become trained so as to increase your capacity for pleasure, enabling you to enter into a great variety of experiences. It will reject books that are fifth-rate, fraudulent and meretricious. You will not allow trash in books' clothing into your library.

You will, of course, have utility books on your shelves. There are some books which you must read if you are to progress in your job. The one who depends only upon his own experience is confined to narrow limits both of place and time. Non-readers are seldom remarkable for the exactness of their learning or the breadth of their thinking.

When you come to choose the general books for your library you may be torn between buying new books and buying old books. The good books of the hour, like the good books of all time, contain the useful or pleasant talk of some person whom you cannot otherwise converse with. They can be very useful often, telling you what you need to know; very pleasant often, as a personal friend's talk would be. They may be bright accounts of travel, good-humoured and witty discussions of events, lively or pathetic story-telling, or firm fact-reporting by men and women concerned in the events of passing history.

Perhaps the problem of old and new may be solved in this way: if you have not read a book before, it is to all intents and purposes new to you whether it was printed yesterday or three centuries ago. Apply the tests of appropriateness, taste and truth, and you can read ancient or modern with assurance.

READ GREAT BOOKS

Whatever you read, read "greats." A great book is one that, shining through time and space, lights our lives, illuminating depths within us we were not conscious of. It is one of the great thrills of life to uncover thoughts we did not know we were capable of having.

All the greatest books contain food for all ages, and have things of consequence to say to us here and now.

There is no positive hierarchy among books, but we cannot go wrong when we peruse masterpieces. These are not designed to rouse your admiration but to wake up your mind and spirit.

"A classic," Mark Twain said, "is something that everybody wants to have read and nobody wants to read." The word "classical" applied to books or music simply means what has worn best. The consent of the ages has marked them out for all time.

Why are the classics so often recommended? Arnold Bennett wrote in *Literary Taste*: "You are not in a position to choose among modern works. To sift the wheat from the chaff is a process that takes an exceedingly long time. Modern works have to pass before the bar of the taste of successive generations. Whereas, with classics, your taste has to pass before the bar of the classics."

Reading the classics is not to worship at the shrine of antiquity. We do not wish to look at life through the eyes of dead Greeks, but what those eyes saw of life is of help in interpreting what is going on today.

HOW TO READ

It is obvious that reading is not refined idleness. The person who hopes to make something worth while out of his reading cannot afford to disport himself in the flowery pastures of frivolous and trivial literature. It is legitimate to read a book for no other reason than to divert your mind from a troublesome idea, but it need not be a sleazy book.

It is impossible to give any method to our pursuit of the best till we get nerve enough to reject the weeds that threaten to overgrow our little patch of fruit-bearing reading.

You will find it unprofitable to approach a book with a blank mind and passive understanding, as one enters a cocktail party. Between these covers are thoughts worthy of your attention, ideas to solve your problems, inspiration that may enlighten your life. You have seen a child turning the pages of a Christmas catalogue, his eyes sparkling in anticipation of the new things to be seen. That is the sort of expectancy you should bring to your books.

Read boldly and in an unprejudiced way. Francis Bacon wrote: "Some books are to be tasted, others to be swallowed, and some few to be chewed and digested." Passive perusing may be all very well for escape stories, but it won't do at all for books which can improve one's mind, stir one's ambitions, pacify one's perturbations.

Some people are deterred from attempting what are regarded as stiff books for fear they should not understand them, but it is wise and stimulating to read close to the upper limits of your mental powers. Your mind is probably capable of more than you give it credit for, if only you press it somewhat, and accept the challenge of something a little difficult.

When you have your own books you can make reading easier, remembering more certain, and review quicker, if you read with pencil in hand. It is a poor objection to say "it would spoil the book," for you did not buy the book as a dealer to sell it again, but as a scholar. Intelligent marking gives a kind of abstract of the book, picking out the key sentences.

YOUR FAMILY LIBRARY

There are few hobbies more satisfying than the gradual collecting of good books.

Possession of books does not give knowledge, but it does make knowledge readily available. You may sit in a small home library and see the endless procession of human thought and passion and action as it passes. Even to build some shelves before you begin to stock books gives you exhilaration and excitement, because on those shelves you are going to place books that will become part of your intellectual life and that of your family.

When you have a number of selected books you do not need to decide beforehand what friends you will invite to spend the evening with you. When supper is over and you sit down for your hour of companionship with the great writers, you give your invitation according to your inclination at the time. And if you have made a mistake, and the friend is, after all, not the one you want to talk with, you can "shut him up" without hurting his feelings. These are friends who speak only when you want to listen, and keep silent when you want to think.

It may not suit the décor of your living-room to have shelves full of books there. But books are accommodating in this regard also: they can be stacked anywhere. E. M. Forster, author of *A Passage to India,* said that he had books not only in his library but in his bedroom, in his sitting-room, and in a bathroom cupboard.

A library is not to be regarded as a solemn chamber, but may be some small snug corner, perhaps in the cellar, almost entirely walled in by books. It is a place where you go to take counsel with all that have been wise and great and good and glorious among the men who have gone before you. It is pleasant to sit down in that corner just being aware that these authors, with their accumulated wisdom and charm, are waiting for you to open a conversation.

Number of words 2230
See page 231 for Questions

Building such a personal library is not an expensive undertaking. Millions of people have discovered books during the past thirty years through the book clubs and the paperback editions. Included are some of the very best books ever written.

No matter how tight your budget strings may be pulled, Shakespeare and Toynbee and Franklin and Whitehead and Socrates and Santayana and Churchill and Durant will visit you. They come dressed in faded leather from the secondhand book store, or in paper from the up-to-date book dealer. They represent, whether dressed in the brilliant finery of dust-covers or in ragged buckram, the world's accumulated hoard of mellow beauty and practical wisdom.

Children deserve such a library. Homes with no books, parents who read only the daily paper and an occasional magazine, have a negative influence upon the intellectual development of children.

Do not waste time in deciding what books to provide for your children: start giving them some of the best within their understanding. Books should be chosen, not for their freedom from evil, but for their possession of good. Dr. Johnson said: "Whilst you stand deliberating which book your son shall read first, another boy has read both."

Read and stock no mean books, but those which exalt and inspire. Literature exists so that where one man has lived finely thousands may afterwards learn to live finely. Reading a good book makes you feel warm and comfortable inside you. Your mind is cultivating appreciation of the excellent.

Reading time in Seconds _____
See page 359 for Conversion Table

SELECTION 23

Danger — Man Reading

Ralph Waldo Emerson

Emerson has earned a respected place among the foremost writers of American literature. Take his penetrating observations about reading. How true are they still? How well have they stood the test of time — well over a hundred years?

. . . The theory of books is noble. The scholar of the first age received into him the world around; brooded thereon; gave it the new arrangement of his own mind, and uttered it again. It came into him life; it went out from him truth. It came to him short-lived actions; it went out from him immortal thoughts. It came to him

business; it went from him poetry. It was dead fact; now, it is quick thought. It can stand, and it can go. It now endures, it now flies, it now inspires. Precisely in proportion to the depth of mind from which it issued, so high does it soar, so long does it sing.

Or, I might say, it depends on how far the process had gone, of transmuting life into truth. In proportion to the completeness of the distillation, so will the purity and imperishableness of the product be. But none is

From Ralph Waldo Emerson's *The American Scholar* (1837).

quite perfect. As no air-pump can by any means make a perfect vacuum, so neither can any artist entirely exclude the conventional, the local, the perishable from his book, or write a book of pure thought, that shall be as efficient, in all respects, to a remote posterity, as to contemporaries, or rather to the second age. Each age, it is found, must write its own books; or rather, each generation for the next succeeding. The books of an older period will not fit this.

Yet hence arises a grave mischief. The sacredness which attaches to the act of creation, the act of thought, is transferred to the record. The poet chanting was felt to be a divine man: henceforth the chant is divine also. The writer was a just and wise spirit: henceforward it is settled the book is perfect; as love of the hero corrupts into worship of his statue. Instantly the book becomes noxious: the guide is a tyrant. The sluggish and perverted mind of the multitude, slow to open to the incursions of Reason, having once so opened, having once received this book, stands upon it, and makes an outcry if it is disparaged. Colleges are built on it. Books are written on it by thinkers, not by Man Thinking; by men of talent, that is, who start wrong, who set out from accepted dogmas, not from their own sight of principles. Meek young men grow up in libraries, believing it their duty to accept the views which Cicero, which Locke, which Bacon, have given; forgetful that Cicero, Locke, and Bacon were only young men in libraries when they wrote these books.

Hence, instead of Man Thinking, we have the bookworm. Hence the book-learned class, who value books, as such; not as related to nature and the human constitution, but as making a sort of Third Estate with the world and the soul. Hence the restorers of readings, the emendators, the bibliomaniacs of all degrees.

Books are the best of things, well used; abused, among the worst. What is the right use? What is the one end which all means go to effect? They are for nothing but to inspire. I had better never see a book than to be warped by its attraction clean out of my own orbit, and made a satellite instead of a system. The one thing in the world, of value, is the active soul. This every man is entitled to; this every man contains within him, although in almost all men obstructed and as yet unborn. The soul active sees absolute truth and utters truth, or creates. In this action it is genius; not the privilege of here and there a favorite, but the sound estate of every man. In its essence it is progressive. The book, the college, the school of art, the institution of any kind, stop with some past utterance of genius. This is good, say they,— let us hold by this. They pin me down. They look backward and not forward. But genius looks forward: the eyes of man are set in his forehead, not in his hindhead: man hopes: genius creates. Whatever talents may be, if the man create not, the pure efflux of the Deity is not his;—cinders and smoke there may be, but not yet flame. There are creative manners, there are creative

actions, and creative words; manners, actions, words, that is, indicative of no custom of authority, but springing spontaneous from the mind's own sense of good and fair.

On the other part, instead of being its own seer, let it receive from another mind its truth, though it were in torrents of light, without periods of solitude, inquest, and self-recovery, and a fatal disservice is done. Genius is always sufficiently the enemy of genius by overinfluence. The literature of every nation bears me witness. The English dramatic poets have Shakspearized now for two hundred years.

Undoubtedly there is a right way of reading, so it be sternly subordinated. Man Thinking must not be subdued by his instruments. Books are for the scholar's idle times. When he can read God directly, the hour is too precious to be wasted in other men's transcripts of their readings. But when the intervals of darkness come, as come they must,—when the sun is hid and the stars withdraw their shining,—we repair to the lamps which were kindled by their ray, to guide our steps to the East again, where the dawn is. We hear, that we may speak. The Arabian proverb says, "A fig tree, looking on a fig tree, becometh fruitful."

It is remarkable, the character of the pleasure we derive from the best books. They impress us with the conviction that one nature wrote and the same reads. We read the verses of one of the great English poets, of Chaucer, of Marvell, of Dryden, with the most modern joy,—with a pleasure, I mean, which is in great part caused by the abstraction of all *time* from their verses. There is some awe mixed with the joy of our surprise, when this poet, who lived in some past world, two or three hundred years ago, says that which lies close to my own soul, that which I also had well-nigh thought and said. But for the evidence thence afforded to the philosophical doctrine of the identity of all minds, we should suppose some preëstablished harmony, some foresight of souls that were to be, and some preparation of stores for their future wants, like the fact observed in insects, who lay up food before death for the young grub they shall never see.

I would not be hurried by any love of system, by any exaggeration of instincts, to underrate the Book. We all know, that as the human body can be nourished on any food, though it were boiled grass and the broth of shoes, so the human mind can be fed by any knowledge. And great and heroic men have existed who had almost no other information than by the printed page. I only would say that it needs a strong head to bear that diet. One must be an inventor to read well. As the proverb says, "He that would bring home the wealth of the Indies, must carry out the wealth of the Indies." There is then creative reading as well as creative writing. When the mind is braced by labor and invention, the page of whatever book we read becomes luminous with manifold allusion. Every sentence is doubly significant, and the sense of our author is as broad as the world. We then see, what is always true, that as the seer's hour of vision is short and rare among heavy days and months, so is its record, perchance, the least part of his volume. The discerning will read, in his Plato or Shakespeare, only that least part,—only the authentic utterances of the oracle;—all the rest he rejects, were it never so many times Plato's and Shakspeare's.

Of course there is a portion of reading quite indispensable to a wise man. History and exact science he must learn by laborious reading. Colleges, in like manner, have their indispensable office,—to teach elements.

But they can only highly serve us when they aim not to drill, but to create; when they gather from far every ray of various genius to their hospitable halls, and by the concentrated fires, set the hearts of their youth on flame. Thought and knowledge are natures in which apparatus and pretension avail nothing. Gowns and pecuniary foundations, though of towns of gold, can never countervail the least sentence or syllable of wit. Forget this, and our American colleges will recede in their public importance, whilst they grow richer every year.

Number of words 1454
See page 233 for Questions

Reading time in Seconds _____
See page 359 for Conversion Table

SELECTION 24

What Is Reading?

Frank G. Jennings

Look at the history of the teaching of reading. Put yourself back in the nineteenth century, for example. How would you have been taught reading then? What changes have come since? Let Jennings give you an overview of those times.

What is reading? Where does it start? How can it be done well? With these questions you can make a fortune, wreck a school system or get elected to the board of education. Most people who try to think about reading at all conjure up these little black wriggles on a page and then mutter something about "meaning." If this is all it is, very few of us would ever learn anything. For reading is older than printing or writing or even language itself. Reading begins with wonder at the world about us. It starts with the recognition of repeated events like thunder, lightning and rain. It starts with the seasons and the growth of things. It starts with an ache that vanished with food or water. It occurs when time is discovered. Reading begins with the management of signs of things. It begins when the mother, holding the child's hand says that a day is "beautiful" or "cold" or that the wind is "soft." Reading is "signs and portents," the flight of birds, the changing moon, the "changeless" sun and the "fixed" stars that move through the night. Reading is the practical management of the world about us. It was this for the man at the cave's mouth. It is this for us at the desk, the bench or control panel.

The special kind of reading that you are doing now is the culmination of all the other kinds of reading. You are dealing with the signs of the things represented. You are dealing with ideas and concepts that have no material matter or substance and yet are "real." But you can not do this kind of reading if you have not become skilled in all the other kinds. Unless you know down from up, hot from cold, now from then, you could never learn to understand things that merely represent other things. You would have no language, as you now understand it, and you could not live in the open society of human beings. It is quite conceivable that a true non-reader can only survive in a mental hospital.

For most of the world's people the act of reading what is written down is still surrounded with an aura of mystery and the black arts. Throughout most of our history reading has been the prerogative of elite classes. Its earliest practitioners were priests and their special agents. The terrible power of the "remembering line" of writing held kings in bondage and made wisdom a commodity for sale at the temple. The owner of the book was the possessor of strong magic and so was respected, or feared, which amounted to the same thing. But the man who could wrest from a book its core of meaning and make it completely his own, was still stronger. The Egyptian god Horus, as a child, was able to possess the "wisdom" of a scroll merely by touching

From *This Is Reading* by Frank Jennings, published by Teachers College Press, 1965; republished by Plenum Publishing Corp., 1982. Reprinted by permission.

it. Everyone who hopes or wishes for some magical way of committing the printed word to understanding memory, without a struggle, is repeating the essence of this myth.

Until the beginning of the twentieth century, reading was thought of as a simple unitary act. Books were to be "mulled over," "studied" and struggled with. The teaching of reading was begun as a sort of matching game in which the child was trained to fit appropriate symbols together, beginning with the letters and building up to words and sentences. The child's formal introduction to the joys of reading began with the line, "A is for Adam. In Adam's fall, sinned we all." Here was a somber and sobering thought for the tyke. It was guaranteed to get rid of any notion that there ought or might be pleasure in reading.

The reading habits of any age are the direct products of the pressures of society and the world in which we live. You can easily see this in the ways in which we have used reading in this country. During colonial days and immediately thereafter in education, religion dominated the drama of life. The literature of the Bible and other kinds of religious writing provided almost all of the reading material available for most of the people. Some writers of the history of reading say that this kind of reading fulfilled a "felt need" (a favorite and not inaccurate phrase of many educators). They say that because of the hostile environment of the day-to-day struggle for some kind of security, man became sensitive to his spiritual resources. This is probably a superficial reading of our social history, but it is true that when all of the people, except for the usual cranks and subversives, keep their thoughts on God and their eyes on the acts of their neighbors, most people wouldn't be caught with anything other than an approved text. When the approvers happened to be New England divines who were quick with torch, rope and dunking stool, the intelligent and the wise would repair to the good book. And since pleasure whelped sin, they wisely suffered as they read.

This, of course was not true of all of the people, or even of some of the people all of the time. You have to read secular instructions if you are to survive in a world of waves and wilderness. You have to get the clear meaning out of what is written down if you are anxious to avoid financial or physical disaster. Road signs say their piece only once. The governor's edict in declarative prose had to be understood and acted upon. People in the colonies were busy trying to break even with life, so they had little time for reading that was not utilitarian.

The Industrial Revolution turned a lot of things upside-down, including our reading habits, and our notion of the proper place and function of religion. The New England theocracy was bound to shatter on the rock-bound coast of opportunity in the new world. If religion were to continue to suppress rather than to support the interests and capacities of man it would be ditched for a kinder contact with God, so religion, always willing, however reluctantly, to meet the "felt needs" of the people, turned a little toward the light and said that it was good. More and more, there was evidence that faith in the value of secular knowledge paid handsome dividends and more and more writers and speakers of influence announced that the printed word was in fact a safeguard against the corrosive influences of ignorance. Under the pressure of this kind of publicity many people read many books that their grandfathers would have burned, along with the reader, writer and publisher. The announcement of moral standards was no longer the central service sought from the book. Men wanted to know things and facts and if the book could instruct them, they would read.

Long before the middle of the nineteenth century, publishing in the United States had become a flourishing industry. Without the let or hindrance of copyright and with the aid of translators of widely varying talent, a flood of books carrying the world's knowledge was washed across the country. The hindsight of history always makes us out to be splendid solvers of jigsaw puzzles. With an expanding agrarian economy as a background and the bright light of an apparently limitless frontier to illumine the board, the pieces fell into their appointed places. In the last half of the nineteenth century, daily newspapers flourished. Public and private libraries were set up in the smallest cities. Jefferson's notion of appropriate educational opportunities was considerably expanded and public instruction in literacy was accepted as a social responsibility. Science was getting its hands dirty in mine and mill, filling the purses of the enterprising. The kind of power that was respected and sought was the kind that moved and made things and the knowledge of this power was eminently democratic. It required no school tie, no proper family connection, only an eagerness to know, a willingness to seek out the little truths that turned wheels and lighted the dark houses. With this explosive expansion of the desire for and the use of knowledge there came, too, a recognition of the obligation of anyone who would be anybody, to read widely and skillfully. So, although the teaching of the alphabet might still be a key to the library's treasure, it was a shining, inviting instrument, promised joys to children, pride for the parents and the world's riches for the whole community.

But change and development have always been most characteristic of the American community. And there have been enormous changes in our world during the last half-century. As Dr. La Brant said, "It would be absurd to think that the methods and purposes in the teaching and the learning of reading have not also changed with our world." Until this century, reading, talking and actual demonstration were the only ways in which information could be transmitted. Now we get our information and our entertainment from many sources. The world of words in which we are immersed is so radically different from that of our grandfathers'

and even our fathers' that some of them have been overwhelmed and have been forced to retreat from it. In many ways our children are living on a planet that differs from the one we knew.

Number of words 1560
See page 235 for Questions

Reading time in Seconds _____
See page 359 for Conversion Table

SELECTION 25

Reading for A's

Elisabeth McPherson and Gregory Cowan

Reading plays many different roles in our lives. Sometimes we read for pure pleasure, sometimes for inspiration, sometimes for specific problem-solving help — and, as explained in this selection — sometimes for better grades. Exactly how is that managed to best advantage?

Where and when and what you study are all important. But the neatest desk and the best desk light, the world's most regular schedule, the best leather-covered notebook and the most expensive textbooks you can buy will do you no good unless you know how to study. And how to study, if you don't already have some clue, is probably the hardest thing you will have to learn in college. Some students can master the entire system of imaginary numbers more easily than other students can discover how to study the first chapter in the algebra book. Methods of studying vary; what works well for some students doesn't work at all for others. The only thing you can do is experiment until you find a system that does work for you. But two things are sure: nobody else can do your studying for you, and unless you do find a system that works, you won't get through college.

Meantime, there are a few rules that work for everybody. The first is *don't get behind.* The problem of studying, hard enough to start with, becomes almost impossible when you are trying to do three weeks' work in one weekend. Even the fastest readers have trouble doing that. And if you are behind in written work that must be turned in, the teacher who accepts it that late will probably not give you full credit. Perhaps he may not accept it at all.

Getting behind in one class because you are spending so much time on another is really no excuse. Feeling pretty virtuous about the seven hours you spend on chemistry won't help one bit if the history teacher pops a quiz. And many freshmen do get into trouble by

spending too much time on one class at the expense of the others, either because they like one class much better or because they find it so much harder that they think they should devote all their time to it. Whatever the reason, going whole hog for one class and neglecting the rest of them is a mistake. If you face this temptation, begin with the shortest and easiest assignments. Get them out of the way and then go on to the more difficult, time-consuming work. Unless you do the easy work first, you are likely to spend so much time on the long, hard work that when midnight comes, you'll say to yourself, "Oh, that English assignment was so easy, I can do it any time," and go on to bed. The English assignment, easy as it was, won't get done.

If everything seems equally easy (or equally hard), leave whatever you like best until the end. There will be more incentive at half past eleven to read a political science article that sounded really interesting than to begin memorizing French irregular verbs, a necessary task that strikes you as pretty dull.

In spite of the noblest efforts, however, everybody does get a little behind in something some time. When this happens to you, catch up. Don't skip the parts you missed and try to go ahead with the rest of the class while there is still a big gap showing. What you missed may make it impossible, or at least difficult, to understand what the rest of the class is doing now. If you are behind, lengthen your study periods for a few days until you catch up. Skip the movie you meant to see or the nap you planned to take. Stay up a little later, if you have to. But catch up.

If you are behind not just in one class but in all of them, the problem is a little different. Maybe you have had a bad bout of mumps or an attack of the general

---

confusion common to students in their first quarter of school. Whatever your ailment was, if it has put you two weeks behind in everything, probably you cannot hope to catch up. Your best bet, in these circumstances, is to face the situation and drop a class. With one less course to worry about, you can spend both the class hours and the study time reserved for that class in catching up with your remaining classes. It's too bad to drop a course in the middle of a term, but it's a lot better to finish your first quarter with twelve hours of C than with seventeen hours of D or F.

The second rule that works for everybody is *don't be afraid to mark in textbooks*. A good student's books don't finish the term looking as fresh and clean as the day they were purchased: they look used, well used. Some sections are underlined. Notes are written down the margins. Answers to some of the questions are sketched in. In fact, the books look as though somebody had studied them.

If you are the well-brought-up product of a public school, this method of studying books may horrify you. Perhaps in kindergarten you learned that it was naughty to scribble in your books with your crayon. In grade school it was made clear that anyone who wrote in a book was headed for juvenile court. In high school you discovered that even the student who wrote on bathroom walls was more respectable than the evil character that marked in his books. And up to now there were good reasons for these restrictions. It does seem senseless and wasteful to let a child ruin a book with crayon scribbles or to let an idle student deface a book with aimless doodles or caricatures of his homeroom teacher's long nose. Besides, the school district didn't want you to produce all the answers for the student who would use the book next year.

In college your books belong to you. Even so, you are still dogged by the same advice, this time from the college bookstore: don't write in the book if you want to sell it. Of course, some students do sell their books. These students figure that books cost a lot of money, that the courses are dull anyway, and when these students finish the term, they think they never want to see those books again. These students count themselves fortunate if the manager of the bookstore offers anything at all for their books. These pseudo-students are more interested in saving a dollar or so next year than in learning much right now. On the other hand, the student who wants to make the most of his textbooks will not worry about selling them; he'll worry about keeping them and using them to the best advantage.

Let's assume that *you* plan to keep your book. First, put your name in it, in large, clear writing so that when you leave it in the coffee shop, some honest student can return it to you. Then start marking it up. We are not suggesting, of course, that you dig up your old crayons or draw cartoons of your teachers in the margins. But some kinds of marking are both useful and economically sound. To get your money's worth from your text, you must do more with it than just read it.

To begin with, when you first get a new textbook, look at the table of contents to see what material the book covers. Flip through the pages to see what study aids the author has provided: subheadings, summaries, charts, pictures, review questions at the end of each chapter. After you have found what the whole book covers, you will be better prepared to begin studying the chapter you have been asked to read.

Before you begin reading the chapter, give it the same sort of treatment. Skim through the first and last paragraphs; look with more care at the subheadings; if there are questions at the end of the chapter, read them first so you will know what points to watch for as you read. After you are thus forewarned, settle down to the actual business of reading. Read the chapter all the way through, as fast as you comfortably can. Don't mark anything this first time through except the words that are new to you. Circle them. When you have finished the chapter, find out what these unknown words mean, and write the definitions in the margin opposite the word.

Then look again at the questions, seeing whether you have found the answers to all of them. Guided by the things the questions emphasize and your knowledge of what the whole chapter covered, go rapidly through the chapter again, underlining the most important points. If the chapter falls into three major divisions, underline the three sentences that come closest to summing up the idea of each division. Number these points in the margin: 1, 2, 3. For each major point you have numbered, underline two or three supporting points. In other words, underline the sections you think you might want to find in a hurry if you were reviewing the chapter.

What happens in class the next day, or whenever this assignment is discussed, will give you some check on whether you found the important points. If the teacher spends a lot of time on a part of the text you didn't mark at all, probably you guessed wrong. Get yourself a red pencil and mark the teacher's points. You can make these changes during the study time you have set aside for comparing class notes with the textbook.

One word of warning: don't underline everything you read. If you mark too much, the important material won't stand out, and you will be just as confused as if you had not marked anything at all.

The third rule useful to everybody is *don't let tests terrify you*. If you have kept up in all your classes, if you have compared your class notes with your texts, if you have kept all your quizzes and gone over your errors, if you have underlined the important parts of each chapter intelligently, the chances are good that you can answer any questions the teacher will ask.

Being fairly sure that you can answer all the questions, however, is not the same thing as answering them. Nothing is more frustrating than freezing up during an important test, knowing all the answers but getting so excited at the sight of the test that half of what you actually know never gets written down.

Do you know the story of the lecturer who cured his stage fright by pretending that all the people listening to him were cabbages? A head of cabbage is no more capable of criticizing a lecture than cabbage soup would be. And who's afraid of a bowl of borsch? You might adapt this system to taking tests. Pretend that the test is only a game you are playing to use up an idle hour. Pretend that your test score is no more important than your score in canasta last night. But you tried to win at canasta; try for as high a test score as you can get without frightening yourself to death.

One way to insure a good score is to read the entire test before you answer any questions. Sometimes questions that come near the end will give clues to the answers on earlier questions. Even if you don't find any answers, you can avoid the error of putting everything you know into the first answer and then repeating yourself for the rest of the test.

Be careful, too, not to spend all your time on one question at the expense of the others. If you have sixty minutes to finish a test that contains ten questions, plan to spend five minutes on each question and save ten minutes at the end to read through what you have written, correcting silly mistakes and making sure you have not left out anything important. If some of the questions seem easier than others, answer the easiest first. There is no rule that says you must begin at the beginning and work straight through to the end. If you're going to leave something out, it might as well be the things you aren't sure of anyway.

Following these three suggestions, reading through the test, budgeting your time, doing the easy part first, will not guarantee A's on all your tests. To get A's on essay tests, you must be able to write well enough that your teacher is convinced you *do* understand. What following these suggestions *can* do, however, is help you make the most of what you know.

Number of words 2090
See page 237 for Questions

Reading time in Seconds _____
See page 359 for Conversion Table

SELECTION 26

Library in Your Lap — 2075 A.D.

James Cooke Brown

The science fiction of today often creates the reality of tomorrow. In this excerpt you question one who has just returned from the world of our future — the world of 2075 A.D. As she describes her favorite invention, the love of reading comes through loud and clear.

"Myra," James asked, "what was the invention of the next hundred years that pleased you most?"

She thought for a moment, and from the frown of concentration on her face, I gathered there were some close runners in that race. Finally she looked up and smiled. "The reader," she said firmly. "Yes; I think the reader was my favorite gadget. . . . It's the next development in the long history of the book. And it may well be the last, for it's the very essence of the book. So in that Platonic sense I guess it is heavenly. The reader itself is a light, flat, plastic box with a glass screen set into the top. They come in several sizes, but the most common is about the size of a magazine. Thicker but a little lighter. It's a television receiver coupled with a radio transmitter, essentially, but since they don't use cathode ray tubes any more, and since all their elec-

From *The Troika Incident,* Doubleday & Company, Inc., 1970.

tronic circuitry is grown, it's far, far lighter than you would expect for what it does. Just a few hundred grams, actually, with power cell and all.

"Along the lower edge of a typical reader is an alpha-numeric keyboard. If you know the title of the book you want, you key it into the set. If the title is unique, the first page of that book will appear before you on the screen in about three seconds. Thereafter, and until you release it, you have complete control of one copy of that book as well as the TV transmitter that happens to be looking at it. For example, by using certain simple controls you can turn its pages, leaf backward or forward . . . do anything you like with it. But if the title you have asked for is not unique, the list of all works which have that title will appear on the screen before you, together with the names of their authors, brief descriptions, dates, and so on; and you can then make your choice among them. And even if you don't know the title of the book you want, you can easily get it anyway by a slightly longer search that the reader will conduct for you, provided you know something about it — nearly any scrap of information will do — and provided it exists. Every book that does exist is available to any reader at any time of day or night.

"That, I suppose, is the most astonishing fact about the reader, James. Every book that has ever been written is . . . well, simply waiting to materialize in this little box sitting in your lap. It's an eerie feeling. At first, having a reader in your hands is a little like being drunk. Then it begins to be embarrassing . . . a surfeit of riches, I suppose. Then it's simply orgiastic. That stage lasts quite a long time. During our first month at Loma Verde, Mat and Jean-Jacques and Julie and I would rush back to our rooms at the slightest provocation, and there we would have orgies of reading. Reading aloud, browsing, looking things up, challenging one another, comparing authorities, looking things up again. Sometimes we did this when we were together, sometimes we did it alone. You can't imagine what a feeling of excitement, of sheer intellectual power, it gives you to know that you can learn anything, find anything out, look anything up, simply by fiddling with a little plastic box sitting in your lap. Later, months later, you calm down. But it takes some getting used to, this knowledge that all knowledge is available to you. You get the feeling there are no secrets you cannot share . . . if only you work hard enough to puzzle them out.

"Now the technical system that stands behind this little box is as straightforward as a wish. There is one central storage area — a library, I guess you'd call it — for the whole world. It happens to be in the middle of the Australian desert but it might be anywhere. The library is in direct radio contact, through satellite relay stations, with every reader transceiver in the world. When anyone requests a book his set is immediately linked to one of the millions of miniaturized, roving scanners that inhabit the immense building where the books are stored. There are as many of these scanners — bugs, the reader people call them — as the maximum number of clients the reader service can expect to be dealing with at any one time plus a margin. So no one ever has to wait for a scanner to be free. There are, I've heard, about one hundred million of these bugs on active duty at peak periods of the day. I've also been told that each of these little robots occupies the space of a 3-centimeter cube. The design of that tiny space is, of course, the technical heart of the system.

"The documents themselves are nothing but microprinted cards. They're so finely printed, in fact, that about nine hundred book pages can be recorded on a single card. Each card is three centimeters square. There are as many copies of each document as are ever likely to be called for at one time, plus another statistically computed safety margin. So again, no one ever has to wait for a book. Now these document cards are magnetically coded; and they're stored in coded racks that cover literally millions of square meters of floor space. When a reader calls for a certain document, the idle bug that happens to be closest to the address of that document is assigned to that particular reader. The first thing the bug does is go to the appropriately coded rack — never more than a few meters away — and remove a copy of the required document. Then it flashes the title page onto the distant reader's screen and awaits further orders. Thereafter, and until the user releases it, bug, document and reader are linked together in one integrated system which is completely under the user's control. Once released, the bug replaces the card and stands by ready for another call. . . ."

"I'll buy one, Myra," I said gladly. "In fact I'm not sure that I can get along without one. And you're right, such a system — in embryo at least — is technically possible right now."

Number of words 1040
See page 239 for Questions

Reading time in Seconds _____
See page 359 for Conversion Table

How Fast Should a Person Read?

George Cuomo

Some questions really can't be answered; some can and some must — or you're left forever in limbo. This author poses a must *question. After all, if you don't know how fast you should read, how can you set a specific goal? What do you think of his answer?*

It's probably futile to hope to talk sensibly any more about so-called speed reading. The extremists have overrun the field and, as usual, preposterous statements and foolish misconceptions make good copy. Amidst the din, quieter voices go unheard.

The extremists of the left—using such effective platforms as the Jack Parr show—tell us that we should be reading at ten thousand words a minute, fifteen thousand, twenty thousand . . .

Their right-wing counterparts thunder back with equal irrelevence. George Stevens's piece in the August 26, 1961, issue of this magazine, entitled "Faster, Faster!" is typical. Why not, he suggests, keep reading faster and faster until we can read all of Gibbon's *Decline and Fall* over a cup of instant coffee?

Why not, one could suggest in turn, carefully train ourselves to read slower and slower until it takes us a minute to read a single word? We could then blissfully spend something like 21,000 solid hours—or 2,625 eight-hour days—reading *Decline and Fall.*

To some, not knowing your reading rate is a source of pride. They don't want to know. One's reading rate is God-given, and to measure or question it or, heaven forbid, to try to improve it, is blasphemy. The assumption, of course, is that everybody's reading rate is just dandy as it is. Perhaps. But the facts scarcely encourage such blitheness of spirit.

At the other end of the scale, we have those whose pride springs from rates measured in rapidly multiplying tens of thousands. Bosh and foolishness, I say. Semantic humbug. Up in the rarified stratosphere of twenty or thirty thousand words a minute, a person is skimming, or surveying, or "getting the gist of the thing," but he isn't reading with anything resembling full or specific comprehension. With few exceptions, most people cannot read effectively at much better than two thousand words per minute.

Perhaps it would pay us to leave the extremes where they belong and look at the whole question realistically.

The average adult, for instance, reads about 250 words a minute. This is also the average I've found among college freshmen. But the variations in my classes run from 125 to 900. This means that some students were reading over *seven* times as fast as others.

There's probably an even greater spread among the general public.

All right, one is tempted to reply, some people are simply faster readers than others, as they may also be taller, fatter, or better looking.

But speed itself does not tell the whole story, and no one except the figure-worshippers of the left and the figure-haters of the right is concerned with speed alone. What counts is a person's overall reading ability, agreed. But in this, speed plays an important and usually misunderstood part. Every reputable study has shown that reasonably fast readers perform not only as well as their slower equivalents, but often better.

Probably the most common and groundless misconception about reading is the one that equates even moderate speed with sloppiness. Actually, the slow readers are the sloppy ones. They read aimlessly and passively and have more trouble concentrating than do faster readers. In addition, they do not understand as much, do not evaluate as well, and do not remember as effectively. The person who says he always reads slowly because he is being careful is just fooling himself. He is neither as careful nor as diligent as he likes to think. He is simply inefficient. He's driving along a smooth, clear highway in the same low gear he uses to get his car out of the mud.

The fast reader is fast because he is alert and skilful. He has been trained—or has trained himself—to use his ability and his intelligence effectively. Thousands of persons, including President Kennedy, have proved that such training is both possible and practical.

The methods used cannot be fully explained in a brief article, but they are based on sound principles and have been approved by many respected and conservative educators. More important, they have consistently worked. A person is taught, for instance, to read several words, or a phrase, or perhaps a whole line, at a single eye-stop, instead of making such a stop for every word. A person with a rate of less than 250 words per minute almost always reads word by word. This method is so slow and inefficient that it actually hinders comprehension. In learning to read by meaningful word groups, a person enables his brain to function much closer to its capacity and almost invariably improves his comprehension.

There are of course additional ways of improving both speed *and* comprehension, all of them based on nothing more outrageous than a basic understanding of the reading process. For no matter how hard some people try to ignore the fact, reading—for all its ethereal possibilities—is a learned process, in which certain techniques operate more successfully than others. No one is born knowing how to read; he must be taught. He can be taught well or poorly. What most often happens, however—and this seems to be what the "slower, slower" people are fighting for—is that he is not taught at all. Left to his own devices, he typically develops a surprising number of bad reading habits, among which is the habit of reading too slowly for maximum comprehension or enjoyment.

Ironically, the strongest opposition to the teaching of effective reading techniques comes from those who base their arguments on "literary" considerations. Yet these are the same people who complain that the schools aren't spending enough time teaching students how to write well. Give them more spelling, they demand, more punctuation, grammar, sentence structure, paragraph development. A knowledge of fundamental writing techniques thus seems most desirable, but any attempt to teach comparable reading techniques is considered immoral. Obviously, technique alone will not make a person a good writer *or* a good reader, but if training and knowledge help in one discipline, might they not also help in the other?

The real issue here is not whether a person should or shouldn't read twenty thousand words a minute, or even whether he can or can't. The real issue is much more mundane than that, and much more important. It is whether the average person—now reading 250 words a minute—would not be a better reader in every way if he learned to read effectively at 600, 800, or a thousand words a minute. The evidence is quite convincing that he would.

A person whose rate is 250 words a minute is not only kept from reading well, but is often kept from reading at all. Let's take another look at *Decline and Fall*. At 250 words a minute, a person will take eighty-three hours to read it. How often does he, faced with such a task, simply decide he hasn't got time for it? Rightly or wrongly, this is often his decision, for he has only two alternatives: to spend eighty-three hours on it, or no hours.

And this brings us to an important and generally neglected point. In actual fact, a person does not have a single reading rate. He has—or should have—many rates. He should be able to read as fast or as slow as he wants, or as the situation warrants.

But all people have what can be considered a "base" rate—the rate at which they normally read more or less average material. It is from this base rate that they should speed up or slow down in accordance with the demands of the material.

However, the reader with a low base rate—around 250—rarely does this. He reads Shakespeare and Spillane at essentially the same pace (which makes the "literary" arguments for slow reading that much more absurd). And even when he does try to shift gears, he isn't very successful. He can't get much faster because he's too unskilled, and he can't get much slower without coming to a dead halt.

The reader with a better base rate—say 800 words a minute—has a far broader range of potential variation. He can easily move up to a thousand words or better for casual reading, and can always slow down as much as he wants for studying, or for the reading of difficult or specialized material. The rapid reader is not a slave to speed; the slow reader *is* a slave to slowness.

Thus it's absurd to argue about "speed reading." The term is meaningless, because critics insist on interpreting it to mean that a person must read everything as fast as he possibly can, must race headlong through Yeats and Milton and Donne and dash madly through *Moby Dick*. Quite the contrary. For if a person learns his lesson well, he will not be limited, if he wants to read a good-sized novel, to a choice of either no hours or ten hours. He can spend on it any number of hours in between. He can spend on it as much time and effort as he feels it deserves. More than that no writer, not Gibbon, nor Shakespeare, nor Spillane, can fairly ask of any reader.

Now, for the life of me I can't see why encouraging sensible reading techniques, and pointing out that most people read too slowly for satisfactory comprehension or appreciation, should be considered evil or anti-intellectual. Perhaps the explanation lies in the startling emotional investment most people have in their reading habits. Almost everyone who has worked in the field has noticed this. You can with impunity criticize a person's ignorance of arithmetic or spelling or sex or politics, but mention his reading techniques and immediately he's insulted. Good, bad, or indifferent, they're his and he loves them.

The whole question can really be put quite simply. If someone can prove to me that a reasonable increase in a person's reading rate causes resultant disadvantages —such a loss of comprehension, or a lessening of that person's appreciation or enjoyment—I'll happily throw the whole business over and learn all the chants of the "slower, slower" crowd.

By the same token, I'd like to see these people agree that if a person *could* read faster—without any such losses, and usually with appreciable gains—then the increase in speed would be a desirable good, and worth working for.

This doesn't seem too much to ask. But the radicals will probably howl anyway.

Number of words 1734
See page 241 for Questions

Reading time in Seconds _____
See page 359 for Conversion Table

Handling the Knowledge Explosion

James I. Brown

Back in Biblical times, Solomon wrote, "Of making many books there is no end." Since then, thanks to burgeoning technology, publications have proliferated. Today scientific and technical literature rolls off the presses at a rate of a staggering 60 million pages a year. How can one best deal with such an avalanche of print? Apply the following suggestions.

As individuals, we can neither eliminate nor disregard the knowledge explosion. We can, however, do much to improve our ability to deal with it more effectively, for we are ourselves an integral part of such an explosion—the ones who must cope with it as it presently exists.

Since our greatest reading problem is finding time to read, we must be sure to use whatever free time we find to best possible advantage. That brings us to the key step of *making time*—quite a different thing from finding it. Even fifteen to thirty minutes a day is enough to bring dramatic change. With proper management, that thin sliver of time can let you make up to twenty-one additional hours a week.

Here is how it works. Suppose you now read at 250 wpm. If you read an hour a day, on the average, doubling your rate means you have, in a sense, made yourself seven extra hours a week. You can now do fourteen hours of reading in only seven hours' time. To put it another way, you will have stretched your customary seven hours of reading a week into fourteen hours. Over the long pull, that means an extra 365 hours a year. Furthermore, you should work toward tripling or quadrupling your rate, not merely doubling it. In short, invest fifteen minutes a day—make up to twenty-one extra hours a week.

The improvement of reading should, in fact, serve three functions, not one, acting as time-stretcher, problem-solver, and experience-extender. Carlyle catches this broad perspective so well when he says, "All that mankind has done, thought, gained, or been; it is lying as in magic preservation in the pages of books."

Now, how can this be done? By taking off the brakes! You would not think of driving your car with both foot and hand brake on. Yet, as a reader, you probably have several brakes slowing you down.

REGRESSING

One brake is regressing—looking back every now and then at something already read. It is like stepping backwards every few yards as you walk—hardly the way to move ahead in a hurry. Regression may be pure

habit, a lack of confidence, a vocabulary deficiency, or actual missing of a word or phrase. See what it does to a complex sentence like this, which seems even more tangled than tangled than usual as the eyes eyes frequently regress regress. Obviously this all-too-common habit plays havoc with reading speed, comprehension, and efficiency.

Eye movement photographs of some 12,000 readers show that college students regress an average of 15 times in reading only 100 words. To be sure, they perform better than the average ninth grader, who regresses 20 times. In short, regressions consume one-sixth or more of your precious reading time, making them a major retarding factor. Release this brake and enjoy an immediate spurt in reading speed, perhaps over 100 wpm. Class results show that awareness of the problem, which you now have, plus application of the suggestions to follow, should bring an 80% decrease in regressions.

VOCALIZING

A second brake is vocalizing or pronouncing words to yourself as you read. As beginning readers, we were all taught to pronounce words, syllables, and even letters. No wonder traces of this habit persist, interfering later on with general reading efficiency. To see how vocalizing slows reading speed, read these words s l o w l y, s o u n d i n g t h e s y l - l a - b l e s a n d l - e - t - t - e - r - s.

At the lip level, vocalizing pulls reading down to the speed of speech, probably below 200 wpm. To diagnose, put a finger over your lips as you read silently. Do you feel any movement? To get rid of that habit, keep a memory-jogging finger on your lips as you read.

Vocalizing at the voice-box level is far more common and much less obvious. If your top reading rate was close to 300 wpm, you have reason to suspect this kind of vocalizing. Check further by placing your thumb and forefinger lightly on each side of your voice-box. If, as you read silently, you feel faint movements, you know your problem, an important step toward its solution.

WORD-BY-WORD READING

The third major brake is word-by-word reading. To move 200 books, you would certainly not take 200 trips, one book a trip. Ten trips, twenty books a trip, would be more likely. As a reader, keep that same principle in mind.

Eye movement photographs reveal that in reading, the eyes move jerkily along a line of print, making a series of short stops to permit reading a portion of print. Research indicates that even college students are, without special training, word-by-word readers, taking in only 1.1 words per fixation or look. Obviously one way to double or triple your rate is by learning to take in two or three words at a glance instead of the usual one.

There they are—three major causes of reading inefficiency, three brakes that hold your reading to a snail's pace. Release them and enjoy immediate returns. Fortunately, one single key principle, properly applied, will do the job.

THE SOLUTION

Every successful reading improvement course relies heavily on the key principle of faster-than-comfortable reading, whether it be the least or most publicized, whether it costs 90 or 598 dollars. This principle automatically reduces regressions. You push ahead too fast to look back, Furthermore, you have less time to vocalize, so that bad habit begins to disappear. Finally, the added speed actually forces you to deal with word groups, not single words.

Put this principle to immediate use. Practice faster-than-comfortable speeds with the selections in this book, not worrying too much about comprehension. That will come later, as you gain added experience and skill at the faster speeds.

Keep an accurate wpm rate figure for each selection to enter in the back of the book.

Follow these suggestions faithfully. Make up to twenty-one extra hours a week for yourself. The need is imperative.

One word which sums up our age better than any other is the word *change*. But has change not always been present? True, but never before at such a breakneck pace. Today it is more than just change. It is unprecedented change, revealed largely through the explosion of print. In such a world, reading provides the best tool we have for keeping up and for avoiding future shock in a world continually being remade.

Number of words 1056
See page 243 for Questions

Reading time in Seconds _____
See page 359 for Conversion Table

SELECTION 29

Super-Speeds for the Knowledge Explosion
James I. Brown

Samuel Johnson once wrote, "The joy of life is variety." That can be paraphrased to read, "The joy of reading is variety": variety in things read and variety in specialized reading techniques, as described in the following article. See how much they add to your reading flexibility and versatility.

The knowledge explosion being what it is, doubling or tripling your reading rate is but a good beginning. You must now learn to make quantum-like jumps to cover twenty to thirty times more print without *increasing your rate*—to read faster, in short, *without reading faster*. To understand that paradox, you must tap the full potential of three special techniques: surveying, skimming, and scanning. They will put you, not where the action is, but where the essence is.

SURVEYING

Surveying is a special shortcut, designed to provide the best possible overview in the shortest possible reading time. With it, you make a gigantic leap in coverage, for you can survey twenty to thirty articles in the time normally taken to read one. This special technique is derived from certain common characteristics of written communication.

For example, with most articles or reports, the title usually provides the best concise indication of content. The first paragraph goes on to furnish the most complete orientation and foreshadowing of what is coming. From that point on, major subdivisions are likely to be marked with headings, other important parts emphasized by italics, heavy type, graphs, or tables. More often than not, the final paragraph summarizes or suggests pertinent implications or applications.

Translate those characteristics into action and you know exactly how to survey an article. You read the title, first and last paragraphs, and all headings, itali-

Adapted from "The LOOK 20-Day Course in Quick Reading," by James I. Brown, LOOK Magazine (February 10, 1970) © 1970 Cowles Broadcasting, Inc.

cized words, graphs, and tables in between. In a sense, a survey is like a reader-made abstract, a distilling of the essence of meaning into neat capsule form.

Surveying also works with books. Here you read the title, table of contents, preface, or foreword. Then you survey each chapter as you would a magazine article—title, first paragraph, headings, italicized words, graphs, tables, and last paragraph.

SKIMMING

The second super-speed technique to add to your repertoire is skimming, a careful reading of selected parts. It, too, is solidly grounded on certain basic characteristics of written expression.

Skimming is built around common characteristics of paragraph structure. For example, the bulk of our reading, an estimated 55 to 85%, is of *expository paragraphs,* where the main idea is usually expressed in a topic sentence. In 60 to 90% of such paragraphs, the *topic sentence* comes *first,* with the next more likely spot last. When the topic sentence leads off, the *last* sentence usually reiterates or *summarizes* the topic idea. In addition, certain *key words* through the paragraph *supply* further *detail* and support the idea being developed. In short, as in this paragraph, reading one fourth of the words still gives you the substance. *Skimming capitalizes on awareness of structure.*

You superimpose skimming on the survey technique, with its reading of title, first and last paragraphs, subheads, italicized words, graphs, and tables. All other paragraphs are skimmed. This means reading the first sentence in each one, shifting into high gear to pick key words, then reading the last sentence. The preceding paragraph illustrates the technique, italics indicating the words to be read in skimming. Notice how the essentials stood out.

Skimming is often three or four times faster than reading, depending upon style and average paragraph length. Furthermore, a skilled skimmer often gets more comprehension than an average reader. Develop more skimming skill by consciously skimming at least one article every day.

To stop here, however, is to miss the important role of skimming as a reading accelerator. As you work to improve, you may actually practice fast reading 15 minutes daily, but you probably read slowly several hours a day. How can you expect progress when you practice slow reading more than fast? It might look equally impossible for a 200-pound father to teeter-totter with his 20-pound son. But the solution is simple. He merely sits closer to the fulcrum and strikes a perfect balance, In the same way, skimming can be used to counteract and balance the slowing pull of normal reading.

For example, instead of reading an important 3,000-word article at 200 wpm, a fifteen-minute task, skim it at 1,500 wpm, then read it once at 250 wpm. This skimming-reading combination not only takes less time but usually means better comprehension and a distinct boost toward higher reading speeds.

SCANNING

Scanning, the third super-speed technique, also serves two functions. It lets you spot certain desired information as well as accelerate rate.

Scanning is a technique for finding a specific bit of information within a large body of printed matter—the proverbial needle in the haystack. This is the highest gear of all. Here you start with such specific questions as Who won? When? Where?

In my university reading classes, students scan initially, without special training or practice, at about 1,300 wpm. One intensive scanning session is enough to shoot the average up to about 14,000 wpm, without loss of accuracy, some few even passing the 25,000 mark.

Visualize the detail. Everyone has noticed how, in looking at a page of print, his own name jumps into sight. This psychological fact suggests one way to insure greater accuracy. If scanning for a date, for example, visualize exactly how it will look. Put a strong mind-set to work. For another example, compare the figures below. How many are identical?

The word "figures" was intended to establish the wrong mind-set, one to hinder you from seeing the word

in the illustration. Now let that new mind-set make the word (*tie*) pop out.

Use all available clues. If scanning for a proper name, focus on the capital letter. Synonyms, hyphens, italics, or quotation marks are other possible clues.

Use structural tips. If you are scanning for the word "rubles," a paragraph about Russia should be a useful tip. . . . If you want news about stock performance, let the phrase "Dow Jones average" pull you up short at the desired spot.

Use systematic scanning pattern. Zigzag down the column or middle of a page, the best way to cover a page of printed matter. Notice that if you look directly at the first and last words in the lines of print, you leave untapped the full perceptual span at your command. Looking as far in as the second or third word from each end should still let you see the words that come before and after. With a very narrow column, just run your eyes straight down the middle.

Number of words 1180
See page 245 for Questions

Scanning is particularly useful after reading an article when you want to fix pertinent details in mind. Increased skill will come by doing two or three scanning problems a day, in reading newspapers or magazines.

Augment your reading improvement plan by three super-speed techniques for extending coverage and accelerating progress. When fully developed and exploited, this hybrid combination of approaches should provide the potential for handling the knowledge explosion with enviable facility.

With exponential change the very essence of life today, a company can be prospering one day and facing ruin the next. This means that the individual who concentrates on the present is actually jeopardizing his future. Balancing today's demands with tomorrow's needs is a key problem reading can help solve with particular effectiveness.

Reading time in Seconds _____
See page 359 for Conversion Table

SELECTION 30

Why Do We Read?

Frank G. Jennings

Keep purpose uppermost in all your plans and activities and you'll soon taste the satisfaction of added achievement. Always ask, "Why?" That question puts purpose on a pedestal where you can't overlook it. Now — "Why read?"

We read to learn. We read to live another way. We read to quench some blind and shocking fire. We read to weigh the worth of what we have done or dare to do. We read to share our awful secrets with someone we know will not refuse us. We read our way into the presence of great wisdom, vast and safe suffering, or into the untidy corners of another kind of life we fear to lead. With the book we can sin at a safe distance. With Maugham's artist in *The Moon and Sixpence,* we can discommit ourselves of family responsibility and burn our substance and our talent in bright colors on a tropic isle. But this is no child's play. In this kind of reading there is profit and loss and to take the one and sustain the other our prior investments in psychological and intellectual securities must have been considerable and sound. Our maturity rating must be high enough to warrant the title *adult.*

Mature reading is more than and different from the mere application of the basic skills of "reading." It requires, of course, the cultivation of an ever growing vocabulary, in fact of several different though essentially related vocabularies. It requires some minimum level of physical well-being. It requires an ability to "shift gears," that is, to suit the way we read to what we read. Certainly a short story in a mass-circulation magazine neither requires nor deserves the attention we would give to one by Thomas Mann, Joseph Conrad, Sherwood Anderson or Katherine Mansfield. We would not study a sports column with the same intensity that we must bring to Albert Schweitzer's testament of faith. We don't read a cake recipe the way we read instructions on an income tax form. So, the adult must be able to read with discrimination as to the methods by which he reads. More especially he must be aware of the purposes for which he reads.

The same piece of writing may be read at many different levels, regardless of the author's obvious intent. If we choose to read for amusement, for recreation, for

From *This Is Reading* by Frank Jennings, published by Teachers College Press, 1965; republished by Plenum Publishing Corp., 1982. Reprinted by permission.

68

what is loosely now called escape, we should be able to do so, whether the writer be Plato or Mickey Spillane. This may shock some people's sensibilities, but it is hardly sensible to be so easily shocked. The book can be an instrument of widely different usage. It can be as fine and precise as a scalpel or as blunt and gross as a pole axe. Its service changes as we tell ourselves why we read.

Why ever we read, there are certain conditions that are present when we read as adults. We must be aware of all of them to some degree. For in the first place, an author is speaking to us. The child and the immature person is rarely aware that anyone is behind the book. We may avoid, if that is our purpose, any concern with the author's intent, even if he announces it loudly either in preface or in style. In the second place, even in the attitude of "escape," we work with our reading. We bring to bear upon the act of reading all that we are in terms of experience, all that we know, all that we are capable of feeling. Present at all times are clusters of attitudes, preconceptions, prejudices and preferences concerning the meanings of words and ideas. A white resident of Alabama cannot read Lillian Smith's *Strange Fruit* in quite the same way as a Philadelphia Quaker will read it. A labor leader won't read *The Legend of Henry Ford* by Keith Sward in quite the same way that a dedicated member of the Optimist Clubs might. A clergyman could not read Homer W. Smith's *Man and His Gods* with anything approaching the equanimity of a confirmed atheist.

A third condition that is present whenever we read as adults is really a corollary to the second. It is a kind of transaction between the writer and the reader. Although the author is done with his writing, he continues to work on the mind of each new or renewed reader. Marya Dmitievna in *War and Peace* never enters twice in the same way the room at the Rostov's dinner party — but her vitality, her boisterous aliveness, is always there for any reader. The way a reader feels when he reads and the conditions under which he reads, physical as well as psychological, all contribute to how he reads. This is more apparent in poetry with its concentrated compass but it is present in all forms of writing to some degree. Tolstoy has made Marya available, it is the reader who makes her live, and she will be alive differently for different readers and even for the same reader at different times. What we are and what we are living through at a particular time reworks what we read and makes it a unique experience fraught with new meanings that we never suspected. In the fall of 1941, Matthew Arnold's lines from "Dover Beach" referred to something he could never have known: ". . . on the French coast the light/ Gleams and is gone; the cliffs of England stand,/ Glimmering and vast, out in the tranquil bay." They will always have a particular quality for those who lived through World War II. For others who came before or after, these lines will have different and perhaps less-potent meanings.

A fourth condition which is present in the reading of all but the most abstract of technical writing is that mature reading provides and even requires a *living through* an experience, not merely getting knowledge *about* a real or imagined happening. We actually come *with* Isak in Knut Hamsun's *Growth of the Soil,* into the strange and desolate new country and, depending on our abilities as readers, we sense some of his feelings and taste some of his unspoken hopes. This is more and different from the adolescent identification of a boy or girl who has been picked up by some powerfully written story in the delight of helpless suffering or joy, and carried to some seeming world-shattering conclusion. The mature reader is past most seduction but is not blasé. In working with the author he may be learning something new in the experience but he is also, in a measure, controlling the shape of that experience. He has to accept the fact of the fiction but he need not either love or hate what he sees. In some ways he participates in the growth of the characters he is reading about. He takes the hints and suggestions of the author and amalgamates them with the substance of his own actual and vicarious experiences giving a flesh-and-blood roundness to the creatures of the writer's fancy.

These conditions then, the reader's awareness of the presence of the author, the reader working with the author, the pressure of current experience and the reader's ability and necessity to *live through* the constructed characters and events, all combine to direct and to color the aspects of every particular act of reading.

But maturity in reading goes far beyond this. In fact these conditions, by themselves, do not add up to the total act of reading. For, whatever we read, be it a mail-order catalogue or a treatise on the gods, we integrate it with the continuing flow of experiences and dealings that is our life. This explains in part why, through the writings of others, past and contemporary, we are able to live so richly in so short a time.

Number of words 1270
See page 247 for Questoons

Reading time in Seconds _____
See page 359 for Conversion Table

The Consolations of Illiteracy

Phyllis McGinley

Illiteracy! As with most words, illiteracy *has different meanings, different defini-tions. One meaning is "inability to read or write"; another meaning is "lack of education or culture." Which meaning did Phyllis McGinley have in mind in her article?*

There is something to be said for a bad education.

By any standards mine was deplorable; and I de-plored it for years, in private and in public. I flaunted it as if it were a medal, a kind of cultural Purple Heart which both excused my deficiencies and lent luster to my mild achievements. But as time goes on I murmur against it less. I find that even ignorance has its brighter side.

For if I grew up no better instructed about the world of books than was Columbus about global geography, I had in store for me, as he did, the splendors of discov-ery. There is such a thing as a literary landscape; to that, to nearly the whole length and breadth of classic English writing, I came as an astonished stranger. No one who first enters that country on a conducted tour can have any notion what it is like to travel it alone, on foot, and at his own pace.

I am not exaggerating. My education really was bad. As a child I lived on a ranch in Colorado with the near-est one-room schoolhouse four miles away and the roads nearly impassable in winter. Sometimes there was no teacher for the school, sometimes my brother and I were the only pupils. If there was a public library within practical distance I never learned of it. We were a reading family but my father's library ran chiefly to history and law and the collected works of Bulwer-Lyt-ton. I wolfed down what I could but found a good deal of it indigestible. In my teens neither the public high school of a very small Western town nor the decorous boarding school I later attended made much effort to mend the damage. It seems to me now that we were always having to make reports on "Ivanhoe" or repeat from memory passages from Burke's "Speech on Con-ciliation." I think in two separate English classes we spent most of the year parsing "Snowbound."

However, it was at college I seriously managed to learn nothing. My alma mater was one of those univer-sities founded and supplied by the state which in the West everybody attends as automatically as kindergar-ten. There are—or were then—no entrance examina-tions. Anybody could come and everybody did, for the proms and the football games; and they sat under a faculty which for relentless mediocrity must have out-stripped any in the land. So by putting my mind to it, I was able to emerge from four years there quite un-corrupted by knowledge. Let me amend that to literary knowledge. Somewhere along the line, out of a jumble of courses in Sociology, Household Chemistry, Hygiene, Beginner's German, I remember picking up bits and pieces of learning designed to enrich my life: the Theory of Refrigeration; the fact that Old German and Anglo-Saxon were two languages balefully akin and equally revolting; and the law about no off-spring's having eyes darker than the eyes of the darker of his two parents. I had also, in one semester, been made to bolt Shakespeare entire, including the sonnets; and the results of such forced feeding had left me with an acute allergy to the Bard I was years getting over. Otherwise, few Great Books had impinged on my life. Through a complicated system of juggling credits and wheedling heads of departments, I had been able to evade even the Standard General Survey of English Literature.

I had read things, of course, I was even considered quite a bookworm by my sorority sisters, who had given up going to the library after polishing off "The Wizard of Oz." But it was the contemporaries who occupied me. I had read Mencken but not Marlowe, Atherton but not Austen, Hoffenstein but not Herrick, Shaw but not Swift, Kipling but not Keats, Millay but not Marvell. Unbelievable as it may seem to an under-graduate, I had never even read A. E. Housman. Al-though I had scribbled verses in my notebooks during geology lectures, I had not so much as heard of Herbert or Donne or Gay or Prior or Hopkins. I had shunned Chaucer and avoided Dryden. Oliver Goldsmith I knew by hearsay as the author of a dull novel called "The Vicar of Wakefield." Milton had written solely in order to plague the young with "Il Penseroso." I hadn't read "Vanity Fair" or "Ethan Frome" or "Essay on Man" or "Anna Karenina" or "The Hound of Heaven" or "Dubliners." (Joyce was a contemporary but the furore over "Ulysses" was a mist that obscured his younger work.) Almost none of the alleged classics, under whose burden the student is supposed to bow, had I peered into either for pleasure or for credit.

As a consequence, although I came to them late, I came to them without prejudice. We met on a basis completely friendly; and I do not think the well-edu-cated can always claim as much.

I commiserate, indeed, with people for whom "Silas Marner" was once required reading. They tell me it left permanent scars on their childhood; and I am certain they could not approach George Eliot as open-mindedly as I did, only a year or two ago, when I tried "Adam Bede" as one might try for the first time an olive. "But it's magnificent!" I went around exclaiming to my friends. "I've been deceived! You told me Eliot was dull."

I pity the unlucky ones who wrote compositions on "Richardson as the Father of the English Novel." They could never come, relaxed and amused, upon "Pamela" as if it were a brand-new book. The literate may cherish as dearly as I do such disparate joys as "The Deserted Village" or "Pride and Prejudice" or "Old Curiosity Shop" or "The Bostonians." I do not think, however, they feel the same proprietary delight as I do toward them. Behind those pages, for me, hovers no specter of the classroom and the loose-leaf notebook. Each is my own discovery.

Often such discoveries have been embarrassing. Once I had begun to read for pleasure in a century not my own, I kept stumbling across treasures new to me only. I remember when I first pulled "Cranford" out of a boardinghouse bookcase shortly after I had left college. For weeks I kept buttonholing my friends to insist they taste with me that remarkable and charming tidbit written by some unheard-of wit who signed herself simply "Mrs. Gaskell." And I recall how I blushed to learn they had nearly all read it—and disliked it—as juniors. Although I no longer go about beating the drum for each masterpiece I unearth, neither am I apologetic about someone's having been there before me. After all, Cortez (or Balboa, if one insists on being literal) must have known, when he surveyed the Pacific from that peak in Darien, that generations of Indians had seen it earlier. But the view was new to him. His discovery was important because it came at the right time in his career.

So mine have come. There are books that one needs maturity to enjoy just as there are books an adult can come on too late to savor. I have never, for instance, been able to get through "Wuthering Heights." That I should have read before I was sixteen. I shall never even *try* "Treasure Island," which I missed at twelve.

On the other hand, no child can possibly appreciate "Huckleberry Finn." That is not to say he can find no pleasure in it. He can and does. But it takes a grownup to realize its wry and wonderful bouquet. Imagine opening it for the first time at forty! That was my reward for an underprivileged youth. For that Mark Twain shall have my heart and hand forever in spite of what he said about Jane Austen. "It's a pity they let her die a natural death," he wrote to William Dean Howells. Perhaps the young Samuel Clemens read her as part of a prescribed curriculum. Otherwise how could even that opinionated and undereducated genius have so misjudged an ironic

talent more towering than his own? Had I been younger than thirty when I first happened on Miss Austen I might have found her dry. Had I read her much later I might have been too dry, myself. Her season suited me.

For no matter how enchanting to the young are the realms of gold, maturity makes one a better traveler there. Do not misunderstand me. I wish all my heart that I had taken to the road earlier—I do not boast because I was provincial so long. But since I began the journey late, I make use of what advantages I have. So for one thing, I capitalize on my lack of impatience. I am not on fire to see everything at once. There is no goal I must reach by any sunset. And how fresh all the landscape is to me! I wander as far afield as I care to, one range of hills opens out into another which I shall explore in due time. I move forward or backward. I retrace my steps when I please. I fall in love with the formal grandeur of the eighteenth century and stop there for as many months as the mood holds. Boswell's "London Journal" leads me back into Johnson himself and into the whole great age. I read Pope and Gray and Goldsmith and backward still through Richardson and Fielding. I read the letters and diaries of Miss Burney because Dr. Johnson calls her his "dear little Fanny." (The view there is unimportant but amusing.) And that leads me forward once more to Jane Austen. I could not proceed at a pace so leisurely were I twenty once more and in haste to keep up with the fashionable cults. I go where I like. I read Gibbon one week and Sarah Orne Jewett the next, with catholic pleasure. Henry James entertains me not because he is in the mode but because he is enthralling, and I continue to prefer "The Bostonians" to "The Golden Bowl." I do not need to praise Kafka; and I can keep Montaigne and Clarence Day and Coleridge on the same bedside stand.

Because I am grown-up I am under no compulsion from either the critics or the professors to like *anything*. If I try "Tristam Shandy" and find it heavy going, I admit it and never open the second volume. If I do not agree with the world that "Moby Dick" is the Great American Novel, studded with the richest possible symbolism, I need not pretend to enjoy Melville. I think Trollope dull. That is nothing against Trollope; I need not dwell in the country he has invented.

And it is wonderful to be a member of no party! I pick my own way among the landmarks. No Baedeker distracts me from the scenery. I can be behind-times enough to like Tennyson and Browning. I can prefer Crawshaw to Donne and Willa Cather to Ronald Firbank. I can read (and disagree with) Virginia Woolf on Monday and on Tuesday begin an amiable quarrel with Newman; nor do I find it a dizzy flight. And so much still to see! Peak upon peak unfolds. But there are also delightful little fenced fields and flowery culverts where I can rest when I do not wish to climb. I have not yet read "War and Peace." But then I've never read anything by Rider Haggard, either, or Wilkie Collins, or anything of Mary Webb's except "Precious Bane." I haven't read Pepys's Diary or Katherine Manfield's. I have "The House of the Seven Gables" ahead of me, and I have also "Our Mutual Friend."

For all my discoveries, nearly the most breathless was Dickens, himself. How many of the educated can even suspect the delights of such a delayed encounter? I think we owned a "Collected Works" when I was a child. But I had tried "David Copperfield" too early and had believed all my life that he was not for me. One night last winter I was sleepless and somehow without a book. From our own shelves I took down "Little Dorrit," which people tell me now is one of the least beguiling of the lot. But Keats first looking on his Homer could have been no more dazzled than I first poring on my Boz. I felt as a treasure-hunter might feel had he tripped over the locked chest that belonged to Captain Kidd. "Oh, my America, my new-found land!" How many novels were there? Thirty-odd? And

every one of them still to be possessed! I got as drunk on Dickens for a while as I used to on the Cavalier poets when I first discovered *them*. I read in quick succession, "Great Expectations," "Martin Chuzzlewit," "Oliver Twist," "The Pickwick Papers," the very "David Copperfield" which had once put me off and then the preposterous, magnificent, exasperating, ridiculous, and utterly engrossing "Bleak House." I stopped there for fear I should have a surfeit; but it's consoling to know the rest of the novels are there waiting for me, none of them grown stale or too familiar for enjoyment.

There is still much to deplore about my education. I shall never read Latin verse in the original or have a taste for the Brontës, and those are crippling lacks. But all handicaps have compensations and I have learned to accept both cheerfully. To have first met Dickens, Austen, and Mark Twain when I was capable of giving them the full court curtsy is beatitude enough for any reader. Blessed are the illiterate, for they shall inherit the Word!

Number of words 2280
See page 249 for Questions

Reading time in Seconds _____
See page 359 for Conversion Table

SELECTION 32

Do You Need a Time Stretcher?

Eugene S. Wright

Have you ever said, "I don't have time"? According to the old Greek Theophrastus, "Time is the most valuable thing a man can spend." If that's so, a "time stretcher" should be most valuable. Read all about it. See what it can do and how it works.

Something new has been added to our stereotype of the American executive. Besides being a rugged individualist — a competitive-spirited woman or a two-fisted self-made man — the modern industrial tycoon now boasts (almost without exception) a beautifully developed set of stomach ulcers. Heckled, harassed, and hurried by overlings, underlings, and a mass of details, the current overlord of the corporate millions just plain doesn't have time to do all the things that have to be done in order to keep peace with the board of directors at the office and the high command at home.

The problem was dramatized the other day in a letter received by the writer. "If you know where I can buy a 'time stretcher,'" the communicant writes, "I will

give you a million dollars for it." And that's just what we must have, it seems, to restore our executive group to the fold of well-balanced, happy humanity. Nothing less than a "time stretcher" will enable overworked magnates to leave their bulging briefcases behind and return to the sanctuary of their homes without a mass of undigested reports standing in the way of a normal, relaxing home life.

Having for years proceeded on the assumption that time was an element which could not be tampered with, much less stretched, we felt that the plight of our business and industrial executives was quite hopeless indeed. But the offer of a million dollars often spurs men to extreme efforts and it is with such a reward in mind that the present observations are being made.

Granting, then, that some esoteric machine that is capable of stretching a minute into an hour or an hour into a day is quite beyond the realm of possibility even in this day of space travel, we are then faced with the necessity of finding a suitable substitute. And just such a substitute does exist. It is efficient reading.

Eugene S. Wright, "Do You Need a Time Stretcher?" *Journal of Communication.* Vol. 1, No. 2: pp. 25–29, November 1951. Reprinted by permission of the International Communication Association and the author.

"Now, just a minute," comes the clamor from the reading audience. "How can efficient reading be made to serve as a time stretcher?" The answer to that question is not difficult to explain, but some background is first required.

For years the general public has held to the notion that reading is a simple skill that, once mastered in about the third or fourth grade, will stick with you the rest of your life and will operate effectively in all types of reading situations. Not quite so, we now learn, as we realize that reading is a developmental process that begins early and continues along a path of ever-increasing complexity and refinement. Generally, however, the development stops when the pressures of the school are removed and the individual fails to meet and master material of increasing complexity. Of course, there are limits to this development placed upon each person by native ability, but seldom, if ever, does one encounter a reader who might be said to reach an optimum development in reading.

On the contrary, the author has encountered many college students and business people alike whose reading development was arrested at extremely low levels. Not uncommon are cases such as the graduate engineer who scored at the tenth grade level on a standardized reading test, or the M.D. who could not read college freshman material swiftly and meaningfully. Other notable instances where general ability and reading ability were far out of alignment have constantly been cropping up in the twenty-one years that the author has worked with reading programs at the college and extension level at the University of Minnesota.

Even though there is extreme danger in making generalizations with respect to reading, most of the students encountered fortunately exhibit only simple reading disabilities; that is, they possess the necessary tools but just need them sharpened. Some few cases don't have the tools at all and need individual clinical help.

Out of these many individual experiences evolved the program of Efficient Reading at the University of Minnesota under the guiding hand of Dr. James I. Brown. Almost an immediate success when first offered under the General Extension Division, the course soon attracted lawyers, doctors, students, university staff members, social workers, clerks, mail carriers, bankers, business and industrial executives, and members of many other vocational groups. The training, naturally, seeks to improve the reading efficiency of the students — that is, to increase their speed of comprehension, to improve their reading vocabularies, to stimulate versatility and flexibility in reading, and to instill confidence in their ability to read rapidly and still comprehend well. In order to accomplish these objectives, the course provides for a large amount of guided practice in a multiplicity of reading situations, provides visual training, touches lightly on the psychology of reading, and gives frequent and large-sized doses of motivation.

Among the devices employed are the tachistoscope, Controlled Reader, PDL perceptoscope, and the Master Word vocabulary building approach. Several complete sets of reading materials at various difficulty levels are also employed.

Observable results of the training seem to be manifold, ranging from testimonials from former students to the actual objective results computed in terms of rate and comprehension on material read. Naturally, most inquiries about the results of the training focus on the numerical evidences of gain, and in this department certain gratifying results can be reported. The average evening student, it may be concluded, after attending seventeen two-hour sessions over a period of one semester may expect to at least double his or her rate of reading in material of standard difficulty (measured by the Flesch formula) without affecting comprehension level.

It is easy to see now where the "time-stretching" feature of efficient reading comes in. Assume Ms. H. is an executive of a local industrial concern. In an effort to increase the effectiveness of her performance on the job she seeks to determine just how she is forced to occupy the time that she spends at her desk. She is startled to learn that approximately one-third of her 48-hour week is spent on various reading tasks — reading correspondence, reports, technical journals, general business publications, government directives, etc. Especially discouraging to Ms. H. is the fact that she feels the inefficiency of her reading skills and wishes she could read more rapidly, comprehend better, and retain more of what she reads. Motivated by an intense desire to do more with the time at her disposal, Ms. H. enrolls in the class in Efficient Reading. Shortly after the start of the first class she is further dismayed to find that she reads standard materials at the rate of only 200 words per minute and comprehends only 65 per cent of what she reads. At the start she is reluctant to part with reading habits of lifelong duration and therefore does rather poorly for the first couple of weeks of the course. Finally, in desperation, and with a "cost-nothing-to-try" attitude, she forcibly breaks with her old techniques and searches for new and better methods. For another short period she is completely "at sea" in reading, with not even her old inefficient habits as consolation. Finally she arrives at a new point of integration, and from there on improves rapidly.

At the end of the course of training she is reading comfortably at 300 words per minute and comprehending better than ever before. By forcing herself slightly she is able to achieve a rate of 400 words per minute with at least as good comprehension as at the start of the program.

Now let's total up these gains in terms of "time stretching." Because she is able to read twice as fast as before, the 16 hours per week which Ms. H. formerly spent in reading are now cut to 8 hours, leaving her a full working day per week to utilize in further reading or in more productive activities. This, it would seem, amounts to "time stretching" just as surely as if we had employed the hypothetical machine mentioned above to do the job.

Then there are those who like to see results of this type preceded by the dollar sign. Converting these time gains to monetary gains seems to impart a more dramatic quality to the results reported. Assume again that Ms. H. is a $40,000 a year executive. If she is able to provide services equivalent to an additional day per week because of her training in efficient reading, the company will be in line for a $6,672.00 annual saving on Ms. H's time.

Besides savings in time and money Ms. H. will realize other intangible gains. Apart from being able to read more work-type reading in a given time, Ms. H will find that her leisure readings skills have increased by an even greater percentage. Wider leisure reading will in turn impart greater understanding of social, political, and economic problems, allowing her to operate more knowingly in the areas of human relations and management. And in terms of personal development, few activities hold out such great potential as does wide reading.

Perhaps by now you have detected some personal references or interesting similarities to your present situation. Perhaps you have asked yourself, "Just what are the implications of these facts for me? How much of my working day could I save by doubling my reading rate? What would these savings amount to in terms of cash? What would my company be able to save by providing its complete executive force with training in efficient reading? What would doubled reading efficiency mean to me in terms of personal development?"

Throughout the country these questions have been asked and many industrial or professional groups have decided that this area holds forth great opportunities for corporate and personal benefits. Professional journals, trade journals, and house organs have reported results of these experimental programs. Without exception, these reports have been enthusiastically in favor of continued and improved courses of training in efficient reading.

From a seat at ringside it is easy to see that the future will bring a tremendous increase in training programs of this type. Business, professional, and industrial organizations have all expressed an interest in the training and have, on numerous occasions, requested that a demonstration of the activities of the course be presented at their meetings. As the result of one such demonstration a large St. Paul manufacturing company conducted a survey which turned up the astounding fact that a million dollar savings in management's time could be realized by training 200 of the company's top-level executives in efficient reading. Instances where such savings have already been effected are becoming more numerous in industrial management literature. Further expansion seems a certainty.

Considering the facts that no business or industrial area has a monopoly on reading and that our "time-stretching" device is not patentable, it might be well to investigate this matter of reading efficiency and attempt to determine just how much it could be made to serve the causes of personal and organizational development in a specific situation. And if a need is uncovered, the opportune time to start formulating a training program in this vital aspect of communication would seem to be now.

Most state universities at the present time have reading laboratories or reading clinics that serve the general public as well as the college population. In addition, various private "communication consultant" services offer training of the type described here. Such professional assistance in setting up a program appears to be a necessity if an adequate and sound program is to be developed. But whatever the source of the training, employ efficient reading as your "time stretcher" and help yourself to wider personal development and your company to greater job efficiency.

Number of words 1930
See page 251 for Questions

Reading time in Seconds _____
See page 359 for Conversion Table

You Can't Get Ahead Today Unless You Read

George Gallup

"When I get a little money, I buy books; and if any is left, I buy food and clothes"
— so said Erasmus. What an unusual priority! But — what an unusual man! Reading must have contributed its share, as it can still do today, according to George Gallup.

With knowledge in all fields expanding at a remarkable rate, and with competition growing keener for top positions in the business and professional world, the importance of reading must be carefully reassessed.

The cultural value of reading is well established. Likewise, the pleasures of reading have been widely extolled. These will not, therefore, be the chief concern of this article, but rather the very practical reasons why young and old should spend more time reading.

Fortunately, or unfortunately, competition starts at an early age in our highly competitive society. There was a time in America when the accepted formula for success was hard work. Today the formula calls for a college education.

Time was when a student who demonstrated a moderate interest in his work and who spent a reasonable amount of time in study could be fairly certain of getting a bachelor-of-arts degree. But those happy-go-lucky days are gone forever. College administrators do not feel justified in providing classroom and dormitory space to laggards. There are too many young men and women knocking at the door — students who are eager to make full use of this educational opportunity.

So the problem does not end with gaining admittance to a college or university. To keep one's grades at a high enough level to stay in college and to qualify for a degree requires a high order of scholastic ability.

What has this to do with reading?

A well-established fact is that students who possess verbal facility tend to score the highest on college-entrance examinations. And verbal facility is gained almost entirely through extensive reading.

Many of the best professional colleges, whether they be law, medicine or engineering, now require students to have had two or more years of liberal-arts courses as a prerequisite for admittance. Some, indeed, are including courses in the humanities in their professional curricula. Verbal skills are essential if the student wishes to pass these courses.

Why is so much emphasis placed on verbal facility? One reason is that *words are the tools of thought.* Abstract thinking is carried on by word concepts. The more extensive, the more precise one's vocabulary, the more exact one's thinking.

Undoubtedly this explains why there is such a high correlation between the results of a vocabulary and intelligence or "I.Q." test. Often a simple vocabulary test can be substituted for an intelligence test when circumstances make it impossible to administer a long test.

A simple vocabulary test can also reveal to a surprising extent one's educational attainment. This statement, of course, applies to the typical person, and not to that rare individual who without benefit of college education has managed to do a great deal of reading and who has, consequently, given himself the equivalent of a college education.

To see for yourself the high degree of relationship between educational attainment and vocabulary, try out the list of words given below.

These words have been carefully selected from general-magazine articles and from newspaper editorials. They are all useful words; not one can be properly described as a "trick" word.

Go over the list carefully and check the words that you think you know. Then look up the doubtful ones in the dictionary to be sure you are right before you credit yourself.

Here is the list:

elite	plebeian	enervate
obese	inane	laconic
ostracize	sagacious	nepotism
nostalgia	plebiscite	soporific
omnipotent	surfeit	recondite
avocation	banal	panegyric

If you are a high-school graduate you should know the correct meaning of two of these words. If you attended college, but left before graduation, you should be able to define five of these words. And if you are a college graduate, you should know eight of these words to equal the college average.

When this test was given to a national sample of high-school graduates it was found that one in every three could not define a single word correctly! And indicative of the lessened attention given to reading today, the most recent graduates tested had the lowest

From the *Ladies Home Journal,* August 1960. Reprinted by permission of the author.

scores of all. On the average they knew only one word in the list, and fully half of those tested were unable to define correctly a single word!

Many parents are concerned about the lack of interest in reading displayed by their children. But they have found no easy way to induce these youngsters to read more. Only thirty years ago reading was one of the chief sources of entertainment — but that was before radio and television became so widely available.

Part of the blame for today's situation must be placed on parents. In far too many homes there is a tendency for the parents to urge young Johnny or Mary to "Run off to your room and read a good book" while papa and mamma sit glued to the TV set looking at an exciting Western or mystery.

If mothers and fathers have little time to give to reading — whether it be newspapers, magazines or books — they can be absolutely certain that their example will have a powerful impact on their children.

There is mounting evidence of a decline in reading interest in America, especially on the part of high-school and college graduates. In fact, some studies have brought to light the cases of college graduates who have not read a single book in at least a year. And in one survey it was found that more than half of those who were graduated from high school had not read a book during the previous twelve months.

It is a matter of national shame that new houses are being built without any provision for books. This lack of concern for a home library would have shocked earlier generations who prided themselves on the number and quality of books available in their own homes.

Each generation, of course, has its own special likes and dislikes. Books which were exciting to parents and to their parents can be frightfully dull to young people today — a fact which should be kept in mind in trying to induce the upcoming generation to spend more time reading.

Too often the reading lists recommended by our public schools include books which are boring and unpalatable to present-day students. Requiring children to read these books is self-defeating. Often the result of forcing a child to read a book for which he is not properly prepared or psychologically attuned is to develop in him a distaste for all books.

Reading is a habit and parents should not be too much concerned as to whether critics or authorities have recommended a given book. The prime objective is to get young people to read, and obviously it is easier to get them to read what they like than to get them to read what they don't like. In the latter case it will be only a short time until they read nothing at all.

For this reason, I believe that teachers, parents and school librarians should co-operate in making up book lists, and these lists should be constantly revised. Books which students like, and books which they dislike, should be carefully identified. Equipped with this information,

librarians can be reasonably certain that the book which they put into the hands of a student is one which he will enjoy, and having read it, he will be back next week for another book.

I would make it a regular order of business in parent-teachers meetings to discuss the success which those parents present are having with this problem of reading in their own homes. This exchange of ideas could be most valuable in discovering interesting books and the most effective measures for getting students to read them. And of equal importance is the regular reading of magazines and newspapers.

Many years ago I taught a course in freshman English at the University of Iowa. My students, I discovered, had read rather few books before they entered the university to start their college careers, a situation which is common throughout the country. The English Department at that time required these freshmen to read many books which were beyond their comprehension and appreciation. The result of this forced feeding was inevitable: literary indigestion. Most of these students, I am certain, came to think of "good" books as "dull" books, a fact which may account for the generally low interest in book reading displayed today by many of our college graduates.

I am certainly not opposed to "good" books. In fact, I am so desirous that such books be read in America that I do not want the interest in all books — both good and bad — killed by policies pursued for the right ends but by the wrong methods. The only certain way to get young people to spend more time reading is to make certain that the reading they do is both interesting and rewarding. The constant reader slowly but surely cultivates a taste for the "good" books.

A few years ago I enlisted the aid of teachers in some thirty high schools in various parts of the country in a study dealing with this problem. I suggested that they ask their students to list the most interesting and rewarding books they had ever read, and the age at which they had read each of these books. The results of this study were most revealing. Some books found on the recommended lists were mentioned, but most were books not on these standard lists. On the other hand, the books the students had liked best were not "cheap" or "trashy" books. They reflected the tastes and interests of a new generation brought up in entirely different circumstances from their elders, who had made up the lists.

Why all this fuss about reading? The answer has already been given. If students increase the amount of their reading of books, magazines, newspapers, then more of them will pass the college-board examinations, more will win scholarships, more will earn degrees.

Stated another way, persons who read more write better, speak better, think better. And it goes without saying that they know more. As a result of a knowledge of the past they can think better about the present and future.

Parents who despair of the quality of education their children are receiving can take new hope. It is in their province to do something about it. They need not reform the local school system, or move to a community which has a better one. All they have to do is find a way to get their own children to read a great deal more. The deficiencies of almost any school can be remedied by a carefully planned reading program.

If reading is all-important today for children, it is equally important for their parents. Reading is the one certain way to improve oneself. In a world which grows more complex, it is almost inconceivable that any person who wishes to keep himself well informed on matters vital to himself and his children and who wishes to improve his lot can achieve these goals without spending at least *two hours each day in reading.*

Some years ago I seriously considered starting what I called the hour-for-hour club. Persons who joined this organization would agree to spend one hour in serious reading or study for each hour they spent being entertained. I still think the idea is a good one. And certainly if this country wishes to keep ahead of Russia in the future, then it will have to spend as much time as the Russians do in reading and study. We are not so much smarter than the Russians that we can spend less time than they do in these pursuits and still manage to keep ahead.

One of the great mistakes we in America so often make is to think of education almost entirely in terms of formal or school education. This view is not held in most European countries where school education is likely to end at an early age but self-education continues for many years. We need always to remember that learning is a process which begins at birth and ends only with death. There is no better way to spend some of our leisure hours — which grow in number constantly — than to devote a regular part of them to the reading of newspapers, magazines and books.

And this is not too much to ask. What we forget is that there is great excitement in learning, excitement which sometimes gets lost in our modern-day schools. We must find ways of bringing this excitement back to the learning process. We must recapture the spirit of Erasmus, who said, "When I get a little money, I buy books; and if any is left, I buy food and clothes."

Number of words 2110
See page 253 for Questions

Reading time in Seconds _____
See page 359 for Conversion Table

SELECTION 34

World's Best Directions Writer

Ken Macrorie

The poet Robert Frost wrote, "No tears in the writer, no tears in the reader." The world's best directions writer might rephrase this to say, "No care in the writing, no clarity in the reading." What is the secret to writing clear directions? You'll soon know.

As we turned to the elevator on the third floor of the Business Associates Building at 1115–20 Horace Street, we saw the scratched black letters on the frosted glass: "Edward Zybowski—Best Directions Writer in the World." We let the elevator go down without us.

Mr. Zybowski was willing to talk to us, he said, because at the moment he was stuck. "I've got 45 words for a label and I've got to get it down to 25."

As he spoke, he lifted the rod that held his paper against the typewriter roller and squinted at the words. He was ordinary-looking, about forty, the black hair at the back and sides of his head emphasizing the whiteness of the balding front part. Except for his face: it was kindly but looked mashed in.

"Not kicking about copy they gave me," he said. "Never do. More copy, more challenge to cut it till you wouldn't believe it was possible. That's what keeps customers comin' to me."

"We don't want to keep you from your work. . . ."

"That's O.K. I'm stuck. No use worryin' and worryin' over a label. Don't think consciously about it for a few hours when you're stuck. Then suddenly your unconscious comes through for you—wham! There it is. Needs only final touches. No ulcers for the writer that way."

"Inspiration?" we ventured.

"Inspiration! That's a literary myth. Purely a matter of the unconscious memories and tips your mind has stored up. Then they spill over.

"This job's more than just writing," he said. "Deciding position and size of type very important." He picked up a brightly colored jar lid. "Ad on top for radio program, see? Where's the direction? On side of lid where you put your fingers to open it. Why there? Most logical place in the world."

We read the instructions printed in blue along the fluted edge:

AFTER OPENING, KEEP IN REFRIGERATOR
DO NOT FREEZE

"You're opening the jar," he said, "and you see the word OPENING. Stops you, doesn't it? Same thing appears on other side of lid. Don't ordinarily believe in presenting any direction twice, but got to here. So important—food'll spoil if you don't follow these directions."

"We're just curious, Mr. Zybowski. What is difficult about writing a direction like that? Seems the only way one could say this idea."

Mr. Z. looked affronted for a second, then smiled. "Yeah, no one can see it at first. And that's really a compliment to me. Shows I did it the simplest and most natural way it could be done. Now take this jar-lid direction—copy came to me like this:

" 'When stored at normal refrigerator temperature this food will retain its taste, lightness, color, and value as a food product; but when exposed to air or kept at freezing temperature will suffer a chemical change which may render it unfit for human consumption. It is therefore recommended that it be kept at refrigerated temperature when not being used. However, it may be stored at room temperature safely if the lid has never been removed.'

"I get that essay on the subject, figure I got a space a half an inch high around the lid, and a damned important direction. So I write:

AFTER OPENING, KEEP IN REFRIGERATOR
DO NOT FREEZE

Our respect for Mr. Z. was growing. "You must be quite an expert on the English language," we said.

"I hate to put it this way," he said, "but I think I know more about English usage than 90 per cent of the college teachers in the country. And also how to use English—that's a different thing, you know. Under the how-to-use part, for example, there's this business of adjectives. The college experts who think they're up on the latest, say don't use adjectives. They got it from Hemingway, they claim. I read all the books and magazines on English, too. Almost never learn anything from them. When you got a space half an inch square facing you and an important idea to get across, you learn something about language. What was I going to say?"

From *College English* (February 1952). Reprinted with permission of the National Council of Teachers of English and Ken Macrorie.

"You were speaking of not using adjectives."

"Yeah. They say don't use 'em. In a way they're right. Adjectives are usually weak as hell." Without looking, he pointed to the wall behind him where hung a half-letter-size sheet of blue paper framed in black. "That one up there," he said, "has no adjectives. Shouldn't have any. It's true you should use 'em sparingly. But take this tea-bag carton." He pulled a box from a desk drawer. "After I told 'em how to make hot tea on the left panel here, then I say: 'For *perfect* iced tea, make hot tea and steep for 6 minutes.' The word *perfect* is a selling word there—plug. I don't like to write any plug angles into directions. Leave that slush to ad-writers, damn their lyin' souls. This business of mine you can be honest in. Givin' directions is really helpin' people, educatin' them."

We could see Mr. Z. was in the first glow of a long speech, but we wanted to find out how he wrote directions. So we interrupted. "We can see that it is an honorable occupation in a dirty business world. Would you mind telling us more about this tea-bag label? You said you used no adjectives except for *perfect,* but in the hot-tea instructions we see the words *warmed* teapot, *fresh, bubbling,* boiling water."

"Glad you mentioned it. Easy to misunderstand. You see, *warmed* teapot is what you've got to use, one of the important tricks of tea-making. So *warmed* isn't an idle little descriptive word thrown in. It's the kind of teapot you've got to use or else you don't get first-rate tea. And the same way with *fresh.* I hate a word like that usually because it sounds like those damned ad-writers' slush. You know how you always see the word on the package when you buy five-day-old stale cupcakes in a grocery store. But when used with water, the word *fresh* means something. When water stands around, it loses a lot—loses, to be exact . . ." He reached for a chemical dictionary.

"Oh, don't bother," we said. "We know you're right there."

"And *bubbling,*" he said, pushing the book back in the case behind him. "I'm sure you know there are many different stages of boiling, and 'bubbling' identifies the stage we want."

"Yes, so in that sense of basic meaning, you don't consider these words adjectives," we said.

"Right," he said, beaming with satisfaction as he leaned back in his chair. "One point those modern English teachers are straight on: use active verbs whenever possible. I use 'push,' 'lift,' 'scoop,' 'unscrew.' Never say anything like, 'The turn of the cap is accomplished by a twist.'" He smiled. "I would say, 'Twist cap to left.'"

"We'll have to go soon," we said. Mr. Z. looked crestfallen. "Could you show us the direction that you consider your masterpiece?"

"Well," he said, "there can be only one masterpiece done by any one artist. I couldn't pick which is best.

I try not to let any of 'em get out of this office till they're at least pared to the minimum. They may not always be brilliant, but they gotta be the minimum or they don't go out."

"How about that one in the frame? Any special significance in putting it on blue paper?"

He stood up and unhooked it from the wall. "Blue paper, use it for all final O.K.'d directions, so as not to make a mistake and let one of the earlier versions—call them scratches—get out when there's a better one been done." He held the frame out to us. "This one, I'll admit, is pretty good."

We read:

IF TOO HARD—WARM · IF TOO SOFT—COOL
PEANUT BUTTER SOMETIMES CONTRACTS
CAUSING AIR SPACE ON SIDE OF JAR
THIS MAY RESULT IN A WHITE APPEARANCE
WHICH IN NO WAY AFFECTS QUALITY OR TASTE.

"I like this one," he said, " 'cause no adjectives and no plug. First line there got the concentration of a line from Milton's *Samson,* my favorite poem."

We noticed the adjective *white* before *appearance,* but knew now that it wasn't an adjective to Mr. Z. and, for that matter, to us any more. "Why so little punctuation?" we asked. "One period at the end and then only two hyphens in the first line."

"Glad you asked," he said, wiping his forehead with a handkerchief. "Damnedest thing, punctuation! Spent years mastering American English punctuation when I started this business. Had to know it first but all along thought I wouldn't use it much," He picked up the framed direction from the desk. "Didn't either."

"Now first of all, you see these words," said Mr. Z.

BUTTER SOMETIMES CONTRACTS
CAUSING AIR SPACE

Ordinary punctuation usage says comma before 'causing,' but I take care of that by ending one line and starting another. Never need punctuation when eye has to stop and move over and down to a new line. In first line I use hyphen instead of dash because public doesn't know hyphen from a dash anyway. Hyphen saves space, and, when you don't use both in same copy, you don't need to differentiate between them. Remember, my context for a direction is not a chapter or a book or even a page, just the round top of a jar lid or one side of a package. Sometimes no other words except the direction. No chance for confusing with antecedents or references several pages before. And thank God! No footnotes! I won't allow any asterisks. Every explanation's gotta be complete in itself."

"How about that middle dot in the first line?" we said.

"Oh, that? I'm proud of that middle dot. Easier to see than period. A better stop really. We ought to use 'em in all writing, but you know the power of convention in usage. And this particular middle dot is in center of eight words, four on each side, with equal meaning and importance. A really logical and rational mark here, don't you think?"

We had to agree. "Anybody can see it's a very intelligent job of direction writing," we said. "There is only one thing that seems inconsistent with what you have said today."

"What's that?"

"After 'CAUSING AIR SPACE ON SIDE OF JAR,' you say 'THIS MAY RESULT.' It seems that the 'THIS' is a waste of words. Couldn't you say 'CAUSING AIR SPACE ON SIDE OF JAR AND RESULTING IN A WHITE . . .'?"

"Good point," said Mr. Z. "A really fine point of the trade. I'm glad, though, you didn't object to 'THIS' and say it is a vague reference. Anybody can see the reference is perfectly clear. But I'll tell you why I used the 'THIS.' Gettin' to be a pretty long sentence, that one. And if you say 'RESULTING,' you have to look back to be sure what the relationship is between 'RESULTING,' and 'CAUSING.' In a sense it would be no vaguer than 'THIS' in its reference, but in reality it would be harder to follow because that kind of parallelism is not in common everyday speech use. But the 'THIS' construction is. Remember my audience is everybody. A lot of those

everybodys really don't read, so you gotta talk, not write, to 'em."

"What would you say is the secret of this job, if there is one, Mr. Zybowski?"

"Funny thing," he said, "but I've thought that over a lot and come to an awfully egotistic conclusion. The secret is the same as for writing a great book or doing anything else that really gives something to people. That is to learn to put yourself in the other guy's place."

We knew nothing to say to such a statement. "It's been a pleasure," we said, getting up.

"Come in again. Sure enjoyed talkin' to you," he said.

As we got to the door, he looked up from the typewriter. "I forgot to tell you one other thing about this peanut-butter direction. Notice last phrase: 'IN NO WAY AFFECTS QUALITY OR TASTE.' That's the time I beat the ad-writers at their own game and still didn't misrepresent anything or slush the customer. The way I put it, it's a statement of fact, yet a subtle idea creeps into customer's mind that the quality and taste of this butter is exceptionally good. This time language did even more than it was expected to do."

"Goodbye," we said, shaking our head in wonder as we closed the frosted-glass door. We believed the words on it now.

Number of words 2100
See page 255 for Questions

Reading time in Seconds _____
See page 359 for Conversion Table

About Writing Letters
The Royal Bank of Canada *Monthly Letter*

What kind of writing are you most likely to do, now and for the rest of your life?
Not themes, exams and term papers! No, it's more likely to be letters — letters of
all kinds, business and personal. That's why this selection is particularly relevant.

We are so busy tending our time-saving devices that we can find little time for anything else. We are so snowed under by the news and views of other people that we find little chance to express our own ideas.

This is an invitation to escape for a while from subjection to things and people, and to pass around some ideas of your own. Writing letters is fun, it is useful, it is easy.

Every letter cannot be a masterpiece worthy of being put into a printed book, but every letter can be, at the

very least, a good journeyman job suited to its purpose. Its only purpose is to meet the needs of the reader.

People who write letters do not aspire to the fame reserved almost wholly in these days for writers of fiction. But writers of letters convey more thoughts to more people in a week than the fiction writers do in a year. They move more people to action. They give more people pleasure. They conduct the nation's business. For them there is no Governor General's medal or Canada Council grant. They do have, however, the sense of service and the tonic of self-expression.

A well written letter does not attract notice to itself. It has three points of focus: the writer, the message, and the reader. All you need is to have something to say, to know to whom you are going to say it, and then to write in such a way as to tell your story in a pleasing manner. This applies to both private and business letters.

Many people who think with regret of their lack of skill in talking well find relief through writing letters. Samuel Johnson said: "No man is more foolish than Goldsmith when he has not a pen in his hand, or more wise when he has." Napoleon was uncouth as a speaker, but became master of a quick, strong and lucid style which placed him among the great letter writers.

BUSINESS LETTERS

As to business letters: writing is part of your job, so why not make it a pleasant job?

Your work offers as much chance to be original, to persuade, and to apply logic, as any form of writing.

Business writing must be designed to perform a service. It must have something to say that matters. It has an instant impact; it involves both you and your reader. It has no room for airy frills.

William H. Butterfield, fruitful author of business textbooks, says in the latest edition of *Common Sense in Letter Writing* that there are seven steps to take: (1) get all the facts; (2) say what you mean; (3) don't take half a day saying it; (4) write courteously; (5) focus your message on the reader; (6) make your message sound friendly and human; (7) remember the "tact" in "contact."

Written with these points in mind, your letter may be received as a stroke of genius, which is pleasing. But you will know that it is the product of thought and work.

So, know what you are writing about. Don't depend upon starting out "Dear Sir" in the hope that the greeting will inspire you. Your reader's trust in what you say will be won only when you make it evident that you know your subject.

"Most correspondents," said Lord Chesterfield, "like most every learned man, suppose that one knows more than one does, and therefore don't tell one half what they could, so one never knows so much as one should."

Ideally, a business letter takes nothing for granted, but is written so as to be clear to any reader. It is written to accomplish a definite purpose, to explain something, or to get from its reader a definite kind of action.

No business letter should give the idea that it was written down to the twelve-year-old mental level. Give your reader the civility of treating him as if he were a cut above average.

The great merit in business writing is to be clear, and this includes using language that fits the purpose. Recall as a warning the wrath of a Queen when her prime minister addressed her "as if she were a public meeting."

If you think a letter you have dictated is stodgy or not clear, call in your secretary and read it aloud to her. Does it flow freely? Has it the right tone for your reader and your purpose? Does it cover the points you wish to make without excess words?

You must concentrate on getting your facts, but if your mind hits upon a good "angle" while you are scanning a sheaf of statistics, make a note of it quickly. It will likely illuminate what you have to write about the figures.

There is no reason why a touch of grace should not show itself in business letters. Some of the most potent letters are those that do not have to be written at all. They are "thank you" notes, words of praise for a job well done, good wishes on business and private anniversaries, and on fête days. Some firms, knowing the virtue in letters, have told their people to look for a timely excuse to write, even when there is no routine business object to be served.

LETTERS ARE WORDS

Someone quotes the Chinese as saying "A picture is worth a thousand words." But in a thousand words you could include the Lord's Prayer, the Sermon on the Mount, the Hippocratic Oath, a sonnet by Shakespeare, and Magna Charta — and no picture on earth can take the place of these.

In private correspondence we use good talking words, but whether business or private our letters must be made up of words which convey to the reader what is in our minds.

Saucy and audacious language unfit for the business office may be just the thing to lighten the day for a friend, while words weighty with the massive thoughts of business would add nothing to family fellowship.

When dealing with a serious subject, keep in mind that words are, after all, only nearly-correct ways of saying what we think, and try to use the best word, not its second cousin who is better known to you. A book of synonyms will help in this choice.

You do not need to have a big stock of tall opaque words, each having a great number of syllables. French shares with English the most elaborate compound: in-com-pre-hen-s-ib-il-it-y, with its root "hen" and its eight prefixes and suffixes — and it describes and illustrates what we must not have in our letters.

ABOUT BEING BRIEF

A belief common in our age is that anything can be improved by cutting, and that the shorter a letter is the better. This does not stand scrutiny. A condensed style such as some magazines use is far more difficult to follow intelligently than is the more relaxed style of newspapers.

Many short-cuts are self-defeating. They waste the reader's time. The only honest way to write shortly in letters is to choose words that are strong and sure-footed so as to carry the reader on his way toward comprehension.

Being brief does not mean being like a miser writing a telegram. To chop things down merely for the sake of shortness reminds us of the dreadful deeds of Procrustes. He was a bandit who tied his victims on a bed. If their length was greater than that of the bed, he cut short their limbs. It is, most of the time, more important to be courteous and clear, even if it takes more words, than to be brief.

When you are writing a business letter you can give it onward movement and pressure and make its purpose plain by leaving out all that has not a bearing upon your subject.

Keep in mind that most business letters are written to tell a reader something he wants to know, but not everything about the subject. A visitor to the Swiss pavilion at Expo asked an attendant the time, and was told how a watch is made.

When you finish a letter, stop. You are not a novelist, who must round things off in the last chapter, disposing of his characters neatly. Don't strive for a tuneful hearts and flowers closing. It will only put a hurdle between the real end of your message and your name.

Number of words 1390
See page 257 for Questions

Reading time in Seconds _____
See page 359 for Conversion Table

SELECTION 36

The Most Unforgettable Character I've Met

Henry Schindall

"Mint new coins — your own coins." For a would-be writer that advice is as good today as it was back when Wilmer T. Stone stepped into a high school English class. Sometimes it takes an unforgettable character to make such insights come through.

I remember vividly that first English class in the last term of high school. We boys (there were no girls in the school) were waiting expectantly for the new teacher to appear. Before long, through the door came a tall, unimpressive-looking man of about 40. He said shyly, "Good afternoon, gentlemen."

His voice had a surprising tone of respect, almost as if he were addressing the Supreme Court instead of a group of youngsters. He wrote his name on the blackboard — Wilmer T. Stone — then sat on the front of his desk, drew one long leg up and grasped his bony knee.

"Gentlemen," he began, "we are here this semester — your last — to continue your study of English. I know we shall enjoy learning with — and from — one another. We are going to learn something about journalism and how to get out your weekly school paper. Most important, we are going to try to feel the joy of good literature. Maybe some of us will really get interested in reading and writing. Those who do, I venture to say, will lead far richer, fuller lives than they would otherwise."

He went on like that, speaking without condescension, voicing a welcome message of friendliness and understanding. An unexpected feeling of excitement stirred in me.

During the term that followed, his enthusiasm spread through us like a contagion. He would read one of Keats's poems, for instance, and then say musingly, "I wonder whether we can say that better. Let's see." Then we'd all chip in, and voices would grow high-pitched in the melee of thoughts and phrases. Soon would come a glow of wonderment as we began to discover that there *was* no better way of saying it. By such devices he led us to an appreciation of the beauty and perfection of language and literature.

There was little formality about our sessions, but he never had to discipline us. Since he treated us with unfailing courtesy, we couldn't very well do anything except return it; approached as adults, we couldn't show ourselves childish. Besides, we were much too interested and too anxious to participate in the discussions to have time for foolishness.

We would point things out to one another, each contributing an idea, a viewpoint. We examined the subject as a child studies a new toy, turning it over in our hands, peering underneath, feeling its shape and finding out what made it go.

"Don't be afraid to disagree with me," he used to say. "It shows you are thinking for yourselves, and that's what you are here for." Warming to such confidence, we felt we had to justify it by giving more than our best. And we did.

Mr. Stone abhorred sloppy speech and lazy writing. I remember a book review in which I wrote, "At the

From *The Reader's Digest,* October 1949. Reprinted by permission of the author.

tender age of 17, he . . . ." Back came a sharp note: " 'Tender age' was a good phrase when first used, but now it's like a worn-out sock. Mint new coins — your own coins."

Mr. Stone gave us the greatest gift a teacher can bestow — an awakening of a passion for learning. He had a way of dangling before us part of a story, a literary character or idea, until we were curious and eager for more; then he would cut himself short and say, "But I suppose you have read so-and-so." When we shook our heads, he would write the title of a book on the blackboard, then turn to us. "There are some books like this one I almost wish I had never read. Many doors to pleasure are closed to me now, but they are all open for you!"

He was a great believer in wide reading outside class. "You know," he said once, "if I had to put all my advice into a single word, it would be: *browse*. In any library you will find awaiting you the best that has been thought and felt and said in all the ages. Taste it, sample it. Peek into many books, read a bit here and there, range widely. Then take home and read the books that speak to you, that are suited to your interests.

"How would you like to live in another century, or another country?" he went on. "Why not for a while live in France at the time of the French Revolution?" He paused and wrote on the blackboard: *Tale of Two Cities* — Dickens. "Or how would you like to take part in 14th-century battles?" He wrote: *The White Company* — Doyle. "Or live for a spell in the Roman Empire?" *Ben-Hur* — Wallace. He put the chalk down. "A man who reads lives many lives. A man who doesn't, walks this earth with a blindfold."

The end of the term came much too soon. The morning before graduation day the class suddenly and spontaneously decided to give Mr. Stone a literary send-off that afternoon — a good-bye party with poems and songs concocted for the occasion.

Bernie Stamm started a poem called "Farewell." We cudgeled our brains and each put in a line here and there. Then Herb Galen suggested a parody, and we went to work on Gilbert and Sullivan's "A Policeman's Lot Is Not a Happy One," changing it to "Poor Wilmer's Lot Is Not a Happy One." After we finished the verses

Larry Hinds sang it in his premature baritone, and we howled in glee.

That afternoon when Mr. Stone walked slowly into Room 318 we made him take a seat in the first row. Do you remember those old-fashioned school desks that you had to inch into from the side, with a small seat and a slightly sloping top? Mr. Stone, a tall, big-boned man, sat with his gawky legs spread out into the aisles and waited to see what would happen.

One of the boys, sitting in the teacher's chair, started off with a speech; the rest of us were grouped around him. Mr. Stone sat tight-lipped, until toward the end when he slowly turned to the right and then to the left, looking at each of us in turn as if he wanted to register the picture on his mind.

When we got to the last chorus of the parody, we saw tears rolling down Mr. Stone's high cheekbones. He didn't brush them off but just blinked hard once or twice. We sang louder so that nobody would seem to be noticing. As we came to the end, every throat had a lump in it that made singing difficult.

Mr. Stone got up and pulled out a handkerchief and blew his nose and wiped his face. "Boys," he began, and no one even noticed that he wasn't calling us "men" any more, "we're not very good, we Americans, at expressing sentiment. But I want to tell you you have given me something I shall never forget."

As we waited, hushed, he spoke again in the gentle musing voice of the natural-born teacher. "That is one of the secrets of life — giving; and maybe it is a fitting thought to leave you with. We are truly happy only when we give. The great writers we have been studying were great because they gave of themselves fully and honestly. We are big or small according to the size of our helping hand."

He stopped and shook hands with each of us. His parting words were: "Sometimes I think teaching is a heartbreaking way of making a living." Then as he glanced down the line and saw the boys looking at him reverently, he added with a wistful smile, "But I wouldn't give it up for all the world."

Part of Wilmer Stone, I know, stays in the hearts of all of us who once faced him across the desks of Room 318.

Number of words 1300
See page 259 for Questions

Reading time in Seconds _____
See page 359 for Conversion Table

"The" First Word

Marlys Millhiser

When you're writing a letter, theme, report, research paper, story — yes — even a novel, what's the first step? Writing the first word! Here's one person's suggestion for getting that word on paper — and telling you exactly what word to use.

I run for exercise and to keep down the pounds that add up so quickly in any sedentary occupation. I run different routes, most of them about four miles and most of them end at the top of the same steep hill. By the time I reach even the bottom of that hill my eyelashes are dragging.

When I begin my runs from my home, I try never to think of that hill and when I actually reach it, I try never to think of it either. I just lower my head and think of the next few feet and then the next and the next. (I lower my head so that I can't see the massive task ahead.) Pretty soon I'm at the top of the hill.

It has occurred to me from time to time that there is some similarity between writing and running. You feel so good when you stop. Sometimes if you dwell too long on what lies ahead you may not have the courage to start. But always, a four-mile run begins with the first step, and a novel begins with the first word.

For me, the thought of writing an entire novel approaches the madness of tackling the Boston Marathon with a broken leg. So I don't think of writing an entire novel; I think of writing a word. That word is usually "the." Not too exciting perhaps, but it certainly leaves the rest of the sentence open to an infinite number of possibilities.

The whole point, you see, is in getting started, and there are enough starts in this business to overwhelm beginner and pro alike. The decision to start writing novels at all can take some major reshuffling of your time and energies. But then you must decide where in the story to start the story, where to begin each new chapter. Then there's the problem of starting again each day or after your mind has blocked on the story and refuses to go on; after the break of a weekend, a phone call, a trip to the mail box.

Many of these starting problems stem, I suspect, from a basic lack of confidence that seems to plague those of us afflicted with the writing bug. But the mind and imagination will weary in any task of intense concentration, and reading about someone else's method can sometimes prove a useful tonic.

Where in a story do you begin a story? They are on-going organisms, remember, that exist before your page one and long after you type, "The End." Even if your story follows one character from birth to death, your beginning and your end may not be that straightforward. Family, community, even world events such as war have shaped the environment into which that child is born and must grow. And the character's actions, decisions and relationships with others will have effect on your story world long after his death.

You can start a story with the first scene or first character that occurred to you, the germ that enticed you to write this particular novel to begin with. You may rearrange things before you're through, and that original opening may no longer be in the book or it might turn up in the middle.

You could begin with a major action scene, especially if it's to be a suspense novel, and then fill in the events that led up to it later. Or you can start at what you first perceived the ending to be and spend the rest of the book showing the reader how this came to pass.

These same ideas can apply to starting each chapter. Also, if you are like me and like to keep readers up all night, there's the classic device of ending a chapter in the middle of a harrowingly suspenseful scene. It makes it much easier for you to start the next chapter and let us hope excruciatingly difficult for the reader to turn out the light, go to sleep and await the outcome of your cliffhanger until the next day.

But no matter where you begin your story or your chapter, you will have to begin with the first word.

I have a lucky friend who received a contract for a juvenile mystery, on the basis of an outline, from a publisher who had already bought several of her novels. She must have known a great deal about her story to have fully outlined it beforehand, but when she sat down to begin one morning she just stared at a silent typewriter until four o'clock in the afternoon. Waiting for that first word.

About half the published writers I know have their stories mapped out before they begin, and the other half, like me, just sort of muddle along until they figure out what's going on — allowing the story to grow from what has come before it. I have noticed between the two groups about an equal number of disasters and successes. But both groups admit to having trouble with starts.

Try the word "the." I defy you to go off and leave it sitting on a page all by itself. It is so incomplete, silly, and helpless it cries out for the next word. "The" what? And "the" combined with that next word will create a complication that demands another word, and so on until you have a sentence. You will need another sentence to explain, clarify, or extend the first sentence and then another, until you have a paragraph, eventually a page. But what you really have is a start. It might not be any good and you might want to go back and fix it up and rearrange it later, but that's a good deal easier than getting started to begin with.

Suppose you have only a vague idea of what your story will be about. But you are sitting there staring at that ridiculous "the" and it occurs to you that one of your characters is a woman. So — "The woman — " The woman what? What's she doing? Eating? Running? Dying? Taking a shower?

I expect you've about given up hope, but now is when this inanely simple little exercise in self-deception begins to make some sense. Because, whether you're aware of it or not, inside your head there is a movie screen on which you visualize your thoughts.

How often have you met someone you'd heard much about beforehand and been surprised to find she looked different from what you had expected? That's because your movie screen had been flashing you images of that person — albeit incorrect — made up of tidbits of other people's opinions, your own assumptions and past experiences in meeting similar types. That movie is always running, when you're asleep or awake. It's running in Technicolor; it's how you see your dreams. It's how you see a story, whether you're reading it or writing it. It's how you see a sentence. It's automatic, like breathing, and you use it without particularly noticing it.

Unless you're a writer.

Writers (and everyone from painters to interior decorators) learn quickly to locate and concentrate on that screen; to order the scenes of the film that would otherwise be random; to stop, start, reverse, focus, and edit the film. I used to project onto the wall in front of my desk, but now I purposely locate my screen on the inside of my forehead. It's more portable and immediate and somehow less open to the influence of stray images.

So, because you've been staring at two words on an otherwise blank piece of paper for some time now, your movie screen has been flashing you the image of a woman, with a lot of other junk, and if you'll just stop feeling unsure, inadequate, preposterous, and defeated, and concentrate — you'll notice her. She isn't clear enough to describe, or know or sympathize with, perhaps, but it's obvious she's just standing there. (Not a

terribly active way to begin but at least she's not lying dead.) And you have word number three. "The woman stood — "

Now if you can go off to sharpen pencils or raid the refrigerator with that half-formed sentence in your typewriter you're too incurious to be a writer. The woman stood where?

> The woman stood in the constant shadow of a cliff overhang in a gorge so deep and narrow the sun never reached the barren sand at her feet.

How do you know this? Because three weeks ago on your vacation you stood at the top of just such a gorge and felt almost sick looking down at the tiny black river below and wondered what it would be like being down there looking up. Remember now? That thought and accompanying visualization of this story germ have been imprinted on your mind film ever since, mixed up with all sorts of other images.

You have a whole sentence now, and you have another question to keep things going. You must know why that woman is standing at the bottom of a gorge.

> The voices of those who'd left her there faded and the sound of their paddles against the river. . . .

How do you know this? Well, you've stirred up some things in your head by now, and though there are no memory images to help you here, your imagination has become intrigued with the gaps and is offering suggestions for filling them in. Memory and imagination can combine to give you more on a mind film than you'd ever experience in a regular movie house. Besides sound and color and movement, they can offer smells, tastes and textures; the sensations of fear, loss, love, hunger — everything. It's all there. You just need a little confidence and a lot of sitting in that chair to find it. Memory and imagination can give you a sentence, a chapter, a novel. But don't worry about so steep a hill yet. Just think about completing that paragraph. You're already beginning to sort out what will prove useful, automatically beginning to edit and associate. You have a start. And it all began with the word, "the."

You'll notice this article did not.

That's because I had no trouble with this particular start. But it could just as well have been because I had gone back and rewritten it. I would probably not have allowed both the first two sentences to begin with "The" in the story about the woman in the gorge when I rewrote it, but for now I would hurry along with this start if I were you because it looks to be the beginning of a full dramatic scene. And what better way to begin a story?

What else is happening around that woman? Are there birds, insects, lizards? Is the river broad? Clear? Rushing? What shape would the sky have when seen from so deep a gorge? Why is she here? Who are the people who abandoned her? What are the colors, odors of this gorge? Is this story situated in the present or the past or the future? What is she feeling emotionally at this moment? What is she remembering? What is she planning to do? Who is she? Is she hungry? Does she hurt anywhere?

By the time you answer all these questions, you'll be into several pages and glad you didn't worry too long about that first word. You might run for hours, days or weeks on the momentum of this first scene but eventually you'll slow, become winded, wear down. That shouldn't stop you for long, though, because now you know where to catch your second wind or how to use your movie screen.

And your movie screen is just waiting for "the" first word.

Number of words 1950
See page 261 for Questions

Reading time in Seconds _____
See page 359 for Conversion Table

SELECTION 38

Ten Tips to Help You Write Better
Changing Times

Seventy percent of our waking time is spent in communication. Of our total communication time, 40 percent is spent in listening, 30 percent in speaking, 16 percent in reading, and 9 percent in writing. Get the message? Develop added skill in writing and you've got an exclusive skill. Here are ten tips to help you on your way.

1. Get to the point. Tell your reader right away what you plan to write about.

Ever notice how many writers tell you something else first, before getting to the business at hand? They recite anecdotes, allude to the classics, quote oft-quoted quotations, describe places, events or moods in loving detail — *anything* to avoid getting to the point.

One type of subject avoidance has been called NCD, noncommunicating discourse. NCD is talk that tells you nothing you don't know already. Examples: "We are gathered here tonight . . ." "I am writing you this letter . . ."

What audience needs to be told that it has assembled, or where or when? What letter reader needs to be informed that the writer of the letter he holds in his hand has written a letter? Or, for that matter, that the enclosed enclosure is enclosed?

A lot of opening wordage is mere warm-up material. Warming up is what a baseball pitcher does before he goes into the game. If you can't write without warming up, write your little warm-up — and throw it away. Don't ask your reader to catch before you're ready to pitch.

2. Get your facts together. Put everything on the same subject in the same place.

Some writers hate to tell all they know. They hoard facts, yielding them up one by one only as their text drives them to do so. This obliges the reader to piece the story together from scraps sprinkled sparsely along the way.

Some writers write piecemeal prose because they can't stick to the subject. At every opportunity they head out the exits hell-bent on unscheduled excursions. These side trips come to dead ends, of course. And then you read: "But, to get back to our story . . ."

There are fewer chances to digress when you put everything on the same subject in the same place. There are other advantages, too. A complete set of facts in one place helps your reader comprehend your meaning quickly and fully, which is a hallmark of good writing.

Just as important, putting facts together forces you, the writer, to consider whether all the necessary facts actually are present and in their proper order. If ends are left dangling, if items are omitted or arranged illogically, those faults will show in time for you to correct them.

3. Get your story in order. Remember, the object is exposition, not mystification. If you wish to tease and confuse, write a mystery. Then you can withhold facts, digress to mislead, relate events first and explain them later.

The purpose of exposition is to inform and clarify. Its aim is understanding. And there is no greater aid to understanding than logical sequence.

So put your thoughts in logical order even before you put them on paper. Then make an outline and tinker with it until you get it right. After that you can write. Then rewrite. Then write it all over again.

Laborious? Yes. Orderly thinking itself is hard work, and writing is nothing but the rigorous toil of analyzing and systematizing one's thoughts.

There is no way around it, either. Clear writing

never came from a mind that had not yet overcome its natural-born muddle.

4. Write simple. Use ordinary, everyday words. Don't write "configuration" when you mean "shape." If you mean "idea," don't say "conceptualization." And if you mean "too long," don't write "inordinately protracted."

Two-dollar words represent inflation. They puff up what you say, making you sound stiff and pompous. Worse yet, they often turn solid, accessible ideas into difficult abstractions.

Beware of words of three syllables or more that sound like Latin once removed. Usually there is a shorter word that says the same thing better.

5. Write short. Why? Because time is precious and readers don't want to have their time wasted by your long-windedness.

Pascal once wrote, "Please excuse such a long letter; I don't have time to write a short one." He was right. Brevity does take longer. And you have to sweat to achieve it.

There are three tricks to writing short. Point A, mentioned earlier, is to throw away everything you said before you got to your subject. Point C is to stop the instant you have said all you have to say. Point B is to be succinct en route from point A to point C.

And just in case you think that your normal writing style is sufficiently concise, here is a homework exercise to test yourself.

Write two pages on any subject. Then go back over it, crossing out words and phrases you can do without, eliminating redundancies, replacing long words with short ones. Keep at it until your two-page piece will fit on one page *yet include every fact and idea that was in your two-page first draft.*

Then shorten the one-page version by another third. This process hurts, but from the pain you will learn plenty about brevity.

6. Keep moving. We call the most enthralling stories page-turners. An enthusiastic reader's highest praise is, "I couldn't put it down!"

But what keeps readers reading?

Unfulfilled promise, partly. Suggest to your reader that you will reveal something interesting or useful and he will keep reading to find out what it is.

Partly it's involvement. Talk to your reader about his interests rather than yours and you have a chance to grip his attention.

Promise and involvement together still aren't enough, however. Your writing must also have momentum, a steady sense of movement, of getting somewhere. Once the pace stalls, you risk losing your reader.

Short sentences help keep things moving. When sentences are short, one idea succeeds another swiftly. There is less chance for interest to lag.

Straightforward sentences help, too. Suppose you write: "My subject is the catching of fish." That sounds stiff, inert, pedantic. Change that clumsy "the catching of fish" to the straightforward "catching fish."

"My subject is catching fish" is better, but you're still talking about yourself rather than your reader and not promising him much reward for his attention.

So make your implicit promise clear, put a more active twist on "my subject is" and speak directly to your reader and his concerns: "I'm going to tell you how you can catch more fish."

Now you're moving. And you have probably hooked a reader. Just keep up the momentum.

7. Be specific. Name names. Wherever possible, use exact numbers instead of indefinite terms.

Specifics evoke more vivid images than generalized words do. Say "a Mercedes" and you give a different picture than if you say "an automobile." "Tawny" is more precise than the indefinite "dark-hued." "Three" makes a sharper and stronger statement than "a number of," "a few," "several" or "some."

Use specifics even when there can be no doubt of your exact meaning. There is but one President of the U.S. and you won't be misunderstood if you write "the President." Nevertheless, the image becomes more vivid with the specific "President Carter."

Good specifics can stand repeating, too. Having mentioned Carter once, it's all right to call him by name if you mention him again. There is no reason to back away to any such circumlocutory evasion as "the nation's chief executive." Just call him President Carter.

One nonspecific worth avoiding is "not all that," as in "the pileated woodpecker is not all that plentiful." This fad usage has a vaguely negative connotation, yet it states nothing definite. The trouble with "not all that" is that it isn't all that specific.

8. Be positive. If you have something to say, find the courage to say it forthrightly.

Don't express things tentatively, in cautious, half-hearted ways. Avoid weakening modifiers like "rather," "somewhat," "kind of," "perhaps," "slightly." Even the nominally forceful "very" has a weakening effect when it props an assertion that ought to stand on its own.

So strike out all such attenuators. If you don't have the strength to make a declarative statement, be silent until you do.

9. Be frugal. If one word will do, don't use two.

For example, under guideline number 7 the phrase "circumlocutory evasion" appears. Since circumlocutions by definition are evasions, the phrase is redundant. Either "circumlocution" or "evasion" would have served as well as — or even better than — both.

Another example of superfluity: "an added plus." Think about that. A "plus" can only be something added, so "an added plus" adds up to an additional addition.

Redundancies aren't the worst type of spendthrift wordage, either. They at least mean 50% of what they say. Sometimes the ratio of content to volume is lower, as in the notorious "at this point in time," five words doing the work of "now."

10. Practice. No one ever learned to play the violin by attending seminars, taking courses, viewing training films, listening to cassettes or reading books and articles. It is the same with writing. To write better, you must practice, and practice a lot.

Workshops and courses may help if they force you to sit down and start writing. The instruction and criticism you get may be useful, too, depending on their quality, which is variable.

Books about writing can inspire, of course, and give you useful pointers. One book is invaluable, *The Elements of Style,* by William S. Strunk Jr. and E. B. White (Macmillan; paperback). If you're serious about writing better prose, study this small classic.

Still, the best instruction in the world and the sagest advice won't improve your writing one jot unless you work at your writing.

Practice, practice, practice.

Practice won't make you a great writer, but it may school you to become your own constant critic. And that is the first step toward making your writing better.

Number of words 1610
See page 263 for Questions

Reading time in Seconds _____
See page 359 for Conversion Table

Fell Swoop on a Fine Cliché Kettle

Bergen Evans

Samuel Goldwyn, famous motion-picture producer, heard that one of his writers was using clichés. He directed him to be more creative — to get some fresh new clichés. Difficult? That's the place for Goldwyn's comment, "In two words: impossible!"

Clichés flourish in our speech like crab grass in our lawns. Perhaps the sober times we live in have something to do with it. Without being entirely conscious of the fact, we lean toward the sententious, the emptily formal. Often it looks as if we did not want to use words at all, but only the husks of words to serve as recognition signals, passwords into the group, indications of not-too-committal amiability.

We are not wholly to blame. The torrent of printed and broadcast wordage that is dumped over us every day exceeds all possibility of fresh supply. The happiest day in the history of the language never produced one-thousandth of what the press and radio and television pour out every hour. And since most of this stuff is prepared in furious haste, it is bound to be repetitious, woven of the worn phrases that come to jaded minds writing under compulsion about things that don't really interest them. Ninety per cent of what the public reads and hears is expressed in fossilized fragments of once-living phrases.

There are times, of course, when triteness is not merely excusable, but a means to an end. One becomes forcibly aware of that fact during an election year such as this. Politicians, civil leaders and other such declaimers find clichés useful to avoid meaning and to win audiences. Before the third cliché has been delivered —usually around the end of the first sentence—the auditors relax, perceiving that they are listening to a sound man who is full of recognizable wisdom.

They know they are in the presence of a man who gets down to brass tacks, hits the nail on the head and doesn't beat about the bush; a man who means business, who is fully aware that although we have entered the atomic age we have not relinquished the faith of our fathers, and who believes that although we cannot rest upon our laurels we must not rush in where angels fear to tread. Such a speaker is a man after their own hearts. He has his feet on the ground. He knows the score.

The mark of a cliché is this intrinsic meaninglessness. Once it may have been clever or brilliantly precise or movingly passionate; chances are it was, or it wouldn't have been repeated so often. But after the ten-billionth repetition it no longer startles or shocks or amuses or excites. It simply doesn't register; it has become a conglomerate of syllables which the mouth pronounces while the mind rests.

Originally, most clichés had meaning beyond that of plain words. But all this has been battered out of them, and their use characterizes the user as a mere

From *The New York Times Magazine* (July 27, 1958). © 1958 by The New York Times Company. Reprinted by permission of the author and publisher.

parroter of musty turns of phrase—and as a dull person at the very moment he wants to be thought witty.

Thus, when John Bogart told a young reporter on *The New York Sun* sixty years ago, "When a dog bites a man, that is not news, because it happens so often. But if a man bites a dog that is news," he hit on a felicitous illustration that tickled the national fancy. Bogart was to be congratulated. And the first hundred million or so who repeated his words were to be envied for getting a good thing cheap. But when one hears them now, usually accompanied by the speaker's self-gratulatory chuckle, they can only be received with stoicism.

Many clichés are alliterative. Our minds seems to file our vocabularies in alphabetical order and if we scoop up a word carelessly it often brings with it another word beginning with the same consonant. It is not the thoughtful but the thoughtless who say *cool as a cucumber, slow but sure, rack and ruin, bag and baggage.*

And there are clichés that once were proverbs. But proverbs and clichés differ in the most fundamental way that forms of speech can differ: proverbs concentrate a people's wisdom, clichés concentrate their *lack* of thought.

Some have tried to defend clichés on the ground that, if usage establishes anything, they are surely established. If usage, they say, can change the meaning of words, alter grammar and gain acceptance for idioms that defy logic and grammar, surely it also makes clichés acceptable. But the difference is that usage has given the words and idioms their meaning; whereas overuse has drained clichés of theirs. So that those who insist that clichés must be accepted on this ground are arguing that there is no difference between meaning and non-meaning.

How worn many phrases that we hear daily actually are can scarcely be believed. It was said of ancient Athens that it was a wonderful place to visit but one wouldn't want to live there!

Jonathan Swift—our first cliché expert—published in 1738 a frightening book entitled "Complete Collection of Genteel Conversation * * * Now Used in the Best Companies of England," in which he gathered a huge heap of moldy platitudes, stale witticisms and meaningless tag ends of phrases to show what passed for sprightly talk among the members of the smart set of his time. And what makes the book frightening is that one could swear that most of it had been tape-recorded yesterday. Such tag ends as "talk of the devil," "It's all in the day's work" and "a sight for sore eyes." Such profundities as "Marriages are made in heaven," "You can't have your cake and eat it" and "Oh, the wonderful works of nature, that a black hen should lay a white

egg" (William Jennings Bryan wowed the Chautauqua circuits with that one for forty years). Such gastronomic witticisms as "I love it [some food], but it doesn't love me" and "He was a bold man that first ate an oyster."

Swift assured the reader that "there is not one single witty phrase in the whole collection which hath not received the stamp and approbation of at least one hundred years."

But then, as now, there was one use of clichés so satisfying that it almost justified their existence: as the basis of a great deal of wit. The familiarity of a cliché can be relied on to lead the listener's or hearer's mind into a definite groove where the wit can lie in wait for him. The opening words suggest an inevitable conclusion and in the expectation of this inevitability is the wit's chance.

So Oscar Wilde's "Punctuality is the thief of time," Samuel Butler's "It's better to have loved and lost than never to have lost at all," and Addison Mizener's "None but the brave desert the fair."

Exquisite wits will sometimes use a cliché unaltered, but in a context where its common meaning becomes ludicrous. And sometimes, most delicious of all, where its literal and original meaning is thrust upon us with unexpected freshness and force. Thus Clifton Fadiman, speaking of the cool reception accorded the first number of "Pickwick," says that it was successful "only in a Pickwickian sense."

But these, of course, are anti-clichés, golden transmutations of some of the world's dullest lead. Intent is all. If a phrase has meaning for speaker and hearer, then no matter how often it may have been uttered, it is not a cliché. No one who heard Edward VIII's abdication broadcast can forget the pathos of the opening "At long last." All triteness was purged and the hackneyed phrase was vibrant with meaning.

When the writer or speaker has his metaphor vividly in mind, he isn't using a cliché. Haystacks do not come naturally to our urban minds, and it has been centuries since jack was a generic term for men. But if one actually thinks of a needle in a haystack as an effective trope for something difficult to find, or of a jack-of-all-trades as a concise and vivid way of describing a man of many abilities but few talents, then he should speak these words.

If the phrase is sincerely meant, spoken deliberately with a full awareness of its exact meaning and its shop-worn state, or gaily borrowed in ridicule, it is not a cliché, no matter how often it has been spoken. It is a cliché only when it comes without meaning, though often with a most pompous pretense of meaning, from an unmeaning mind.

Number of words 1375
See page 265 for Questions

Reading time in Seconds _____
See page 359 for Conversion Table

Write a Résumé That Gets the Job

Changing Times

Perhaps the most important writing you'll ever do is writing the "paper you" — the résumé to get yourself a much-wanted job. That writing assignment may actually be repeated several times in a lifetime — whenever you want to change occupations. How is it best done? You need to know.

A personal advertisement . . . a condensed self-analysis . . . a ledger of your accomplishments . . . the paper you. That's what a job résumé has been called. As such it's a key part of landing a job. Its purpose is to get you job interviews. To do that, it must attract the attention of prospective employers and interest them in what you have to offer as a potential employee.

"It used to be that people were hired for some jobs by word of mouth," said an employment counselor recently. "Now employers want a résumé on everybody from the janitor to the chairman of the board."

Your résumé is one of the first things you should get in order when you decide to look for a new job. You'll want to include a copy with every job-hunting letter you mail and with every answer to a want ad. You should have copies available for job interviewers and employment agency counselors. It's also a smart idea to give copies to friends, associates and people you've asked to be your references to bring them up-to-date on your job goals and qualifications so they can help in your hunt.

ORGANIZING YOUR STORY

A résumé is not a full-fledged autobiography but a shorthand sketch aimed at getting your foot in the door. If it works, you'll have time later, in a personal interview, to go into detail about your background. The shape your résumé takes will depend to some extent on your own experience and qualifications and the sort of job you are looking for. But there are some basic elements that every résumé should contain. Present them in a simple, uncluttered, eye-pleasing outline form, usually in this priority.

Identification. Right up at the top put your name, address and telephone number (office as well as home phone if you can take job calls at work).

Your objective or job goal. Handle this carefully. If you're too specific, you could rule yourself out for related jobs you'd actually want to consider. If you are vague about what you want to do, an employer might not bother to try to figure out where he could use you. One job counselor suggests that instead of a specific

job title, such as "contract procurement officer," you include a one- or two-line summary of your abilities: "Comprehensive background in all phases of contract negotiation and administration."

Work experience. This is the heart of your résumé. Give it the most space and emphasis, and don't waste time getting to it. Describe briefly the development of your career to date. Work in this information about each job you've held: name and location of the firm (for a small or unknown company identify the type of business; for a giant corporation indicate the department you worked in); dates of your employment; your title and responsibilities if not apparent; and, above all, your specific accomplishments, presented so that they are immediately apparent, not buried in a long paragraph. Examples are money-saving innovations or promotions within one firm. Give the most space to your latest or highest-level position.

There are several ways of presenting this information. You can do it job by job in chronological order, starting with your present or last job and working backward. This format works best for most people and particularly well when you have held a series of progressively better jobs. On the other hand, you can outline your work experience by the kinds of positions you've held, giving first priority to your most important job function, lesser attention to other job functions regardless of actual employment chronology. This is a good idea with occupations where you perform several functions or where there are frequent changes of assignment in each job. Another possibility is to combine features of both formats.

Education and training. List your high school or college, degree and major. Also note postgraduate and special training courses or seminars you have completed. Cite special job-related skills, such as knowledge of foreign languages or specialized certification.

If you are a new graduate with little work experience, you might cover your educational background before your work experience. And flesh out the education section with more details to show how your studies and extracurricular activities relate to the work you seek. Note the areas of emphasis in your major.

Personal data. This is where you might include information on your age, marital status and health, especially if you think it has a bearing on your application, though in most cases it really isn't necessary. Do include such things as business, professional, social and civic affiliations; honors and awards; military service; hobbies or outside interests.

References. At the end of your résumé, include the statement, "References will be provided upon request."

Don't omit any of the sections noted above, no matter how meager you think your material is. The absence of any section will only raise questions and could eliminate you from consideration before you have a chance to explain. There's no reason to dwell on information you consider negative. Put it down in a way that minimizes its importance without misrepresenting the facts. A company sales manager might be embarrassed about being a fifth-grade dropout. But if he omitted any reference to his schooling, an employer would wonder why and might reject him on principle. Included, the fact of curtailed schooling would seem inconsequential in view of his career record, and it just might say something to the employer about his enterprise and initiative.

PUTTING IT IN WRITING

Should you resort to a professional résumé-writer? Given the proper material, a professional can craft for you an attractive résumé with an excellent chance of catching the eye of an employer.

But that's only half the job of a résumé. It also tells an employer something of a person's ability to marshal and present facts. An employer who recognizes that your résumé was professionally prepared may decide not to take the time to test you in some other way. Writing your own covering letter could take the edge off a prepared résumé. One personnel manager says that if both a résumé and its covering letter are obviously factory-made, he wonders about the job applicant's ability to communicate. If you need advice from a pro, get it, but turn out the basic products yourself.

You don't have to pay for résumé-writing help. Look over ones that friends have used to get good jobs. Also check model résumés in books such as these, available in libraries and bookstores: *Job Résumés, How to Write Them, How to Present Them,* by J.I. Biegeleisen (Grosset & Dunlap), and *How to Get a Better Job Quicker,* by Richard A. Payne (Taplinger).

A word of caution about model résumés: Don't copy the format rigidly; use them as guides to write your own. The personnel director of a large company said he frequently receives — and rejects out of hand — résumés from different job applicants who've obviously used the same model.

Begin by collecting and jotting down on scratch paper all the data you'll need. Organize the material under the headings of the outline described earlier.

Then you're ready to begin writing. Here are some tips to guide you:

• *Be positive.* Demonstrate a confidence in your abilities and your experience. Don't dwell on your adversities. One job applicant explained in her résumé that she wanted to leave her present job because she had to get up at 5 A.M. and take three different buses each way to and from work and she was exhausted when she got home at the end of the day. A prospective employer isn't interested in hearing about your problems; he wants to know if you can solve *his* problems. Also, never attempt to build yourself up by knocking a former employer or fellow employee. The only thing negative information can do for you is scotch your chance for the job.

• *Be brief.* One-page résumés are best; two-pagers are okay; longer ones are a poor idea unless there are extraordinary reasons for such length. An employer can't spend all morning studying your résumé. Make it easy for him to get at the key points of your background quickly and easily.

• *Stick to the facts.* Avoid flowery adjectives and personal opinions. What counts is what you have done ("Sales volume rose 34% during my control of the department"), not what you think about it ("I feel I contributed greatly to the over-all success of the company"). Don't lie. If you can't back something up, don't include it. Even little white lies have a way of tripping you up. Things you fudged on will seem much worse than they are when you have to explain why you tried to hide them.

• *Make yourself clear.* Use correct, straightforward English — active verbs, short and simple words. You needn't use complete sentences, but your phrases should read smoothly. Avoid using stilted language, abbreviations and obscure terms of your trade.

• *Keep things in focus.* Emphasize background and credentials that best establish your qualifications for the work you seek. Tailor your résumé as closely as you can to specific job fields or employers, even if it means writing several versions. For example, if you are interested in landing a job as a research assistant, a copywriter or an English teacher, don't use the same résumé for all three jobs. Write separate ones to emphasize your background related to each job goal.

• *Write, rewrite and polish.* Obviously, you'll go through a number of rough drafts before your résumé begins to fall into shape. When you think you've come up with a final draft, give it yet another once-over. See whether you can edit it a bit more, cut out every unnecessary word or phrase, and give it that extra punch.

• *Make it neat.* Be sure your résumé is expertly typed on standard-sized, good-quality paper. Use underlines and words in capital letters to set things off. Leave lots of white space in margins and between sections of type. Don't try to attract attention with wild gimmicks or somebody's idea of an unusual format. And make clean, legible copies — by offset printing or Xerox, for instance, not mimeograph or carbon copies.

The appearance of your résumé says perhaps as much about you as its content. One employment manager says about 15% of the ones he receives are re-

jected purely on the basis of their appearance — full of typos, smeared and smudged, coffee stained. Will your résumé identify you as a slob, or as a neat, organized individual with originality and the ability to get essential information across quickly and forcefully?

Number of words 1780
See page 267 for Questions

Reading time in Seconds _____
See page 359 for Conversion Table

SELECTION 41

On Learning How to Write

Benjamin Franklin

The allusions may be obscure, the style antiquated — after all, Franklin wrote this over 200 years ago — but it's still clear and vigorous writing. And what Franklin says about learning to write has been proved by experience, for he did work — and write — his way to fame. Why not try his method yourself?

From a child I was fond of reading, and all the little money that came into my hands was ever laid out in books. Pleased with the Pilgrim's Progress, my first collection was of John Bunyan's works in separate little volumes. I afterward sold them to enable me to buy R. Burton's Historical Collections; they were small chapmen's books, and cheap, forty or fifty in all. My father's little library consisted chiefly of books in polemic divinity, most of which I read, and have since often regretted that, at a time when I had such a thirst for knowledge, more proper books had not fallen in my way, since it was now resolved I should not be a clergyman. Plutarch's *Lives* there was in which I read abundantly, and I still think that time spent to great advantage. There was also a book of De Foe's, called an *Essay on Projects,* and another of Dr. Mather's, called *Essays to do Good,* which perhaps gave me a turn of thinking that had an influence on some of the principal future events of my life. . . .

And after some time an ingenious tradesman, Mr. Matthew Adams, who had a pretty collection of books, and who frequented our printing-house, took notice of me, invited me to his library, and very kindly lent me such books as I chose to read. I now took a fancy to poetry, and made some little pieces; my brother, thinking it might turn to account, encouraged me, and put me on composing occasional ballads. One was called *The Lighthouse Tragedy,* and contained an account of

the drowning of Captain Worthilake, with his two daughters; the other was a sailor's song, on the taking of Teach (or Blackbeard), the pirate. They were wretched stuff, in the Grub Street ballad style; and when they were printed he sent me about the town to sell them. The first sold wonderfully, the event being recent, having made a great noise. This flattered my vanity; but my father discouraged me by ridiculing my performances, and telling me verse-makers were generally beggars. So I escaped being a poet, most probably a very bad one; but as prose writing has been of great use to me in the course of my life, and was a principal means of my advancement, I shall tell you how, in such a situation, I acquired what little ability I have in that way.

There was another bookish lad in the town, John Collins by name, with whom I was intimately acquainted. We sometimes disputed, and very fond we were of argument, and very desirous of confuting one another, which disputatious turn, by the way, is apt to become a very bad habit, making people often extremely disagreeable in company by the contradiction that is necessary to bring it into practice; and thence, besides souring and spoiling the conversation, is productive of disgusts and perhaps enmities where you may have occasion for friendship. I had caught it by reading my father's books of dispute about religion. Persons of good sense, I have since observed, seldom fall into it, except lawyers, university men, and men of all sorts that have been bred at Edinburgh. . . .

About this time I met with an odd volume of the *Spectator.* It was the third. I had never before seen any of them. I bought it, read it over and over, and was

From Benjamin Franklin, *Autobiography and Other Writings,* edited with an introduction and notes by Russel B. Nye, Riverside Editions; copyright 1958 by Houghton Mifflin Company. Reprinted by permission.

much delighted with it. I thought the writing excellent, and wished, if possible, to imitate it. With this view I took some of the papers, and making short hints of the sentiment in each sentence, laid them by a few days, and then, without looking at the book, tried to complete the papers again, by expressing each hinted sentiment at length, and as fully as it had been expressed before, in any suitable words that should come to hand. Then I compared my *Spectator* with the original, discovered some of my faults, and corrected them. But I found I wanted a stock of words, or a readiness in recollecting and using them, which I thought I should have acquired before that time if I had gone on making verses; since the continual occasion for words of the same import, but of different length, to suit the measure, or of different sound for the rhyme, would have laid me under a constant necessity of searching for variety, and also have tended to fix that variety in my mind, and make me master of it. Therefore I took some of the tales and turned them into verse; and, after a time, when I had pretty well forgotten the prose, turned them back again. I also sometimes jumbled my collections of hints into confusion, and after some weeks endeavored to reduce them into the best order, before I began to form the full sentences and complete the paper. This was to teach me method in the arrangement of thoughts. By comparing my work afterwards with the original, I discovered many faults and amended them; but I sometimes had the pleasure of fancying that, in certain particulars of small import, I had been lucky enough to improve the method or the language, and this encouraged me to think I might possibly in time come to be a tolerable English writer, of which I was extremely ambitious. My time for these exercises and for reading was at night, after work, or before it began in the morning, or on Sundays, when I contrived to be in the printing-house alone. . . .

Number of words 920
See page 269 for Questions

Reading time in Seconds _____
See page 359 for Conversion Table

SELECTION 42

The Practical Writer

The Royal Bank of Canada *Monthly Letter*

Written words! They form the mainstay of communication in organizations and business. But they also fail to do their job. Why? Lean on the following pragmatic guide to find out.

From time to time most educated people are called upon to act as writers. They might not think of themselves as such as they dash off a personal note or dictate a memo, but that is what they are. They are practising a difficult and demanding craft, and facing its inborn challenge. This is to find the right words and to put them in the right order so that the thoughts they represent can be understood.

Some writers deliberately muddy the meaning of their words, if indeed they meant anything to begin with. When most people write, however, it is to get a message across. This is especially so in business and institutions, where written words carry much of the load of communications. The written traffic of any well-ordered organization is thick and varied — letters, memos, reports, policy statements, manuals, sales literature, and what-have-you. The purpose of it all is to use words in a way that serves the organization's aims.

Unfortunately, written communications often fail to accomplish this purpose. Some organizational writing gives rise to confusion, inefficiency, and ill-will. This is almost always because the intended message did not get through to the receiving end. Why? Because the message was inadequately prepared.

An irresistible comparison arises between writing and another craft which most people have to practise sometimes, namely cooking. In both fields there is a wide range of competence, from the great chefs and authors to the occasional practitioners who must do the job whether they like it or not. In both, care in preparation is of the essence. Shakespeare wrote that it is an ill cook who does not lick his own fingers; it is an ill writer who does not work at it hard enough to be reasonably satisfied with the results.

Unlike bachelor cooks, however, casual writers are rarely the sole consumers of their own offerings. Reclusive philosophers and schoolgirls keeping diaries are about the only writers whose work is not intended for other eyes. If a piece of writing turns out to be an indigestible half-baked mess, those on the receiving end are usually the ones to suffer. This might be all right in literature, because the reader of a bad book can always toss it aside. But in organizations, where written communications command attention, it is up to the recipient of a sloppy writing job to figure out what it means.

The reader is thus put in the position of doing the thinking the writer failed to do. To make others do your work for you is, of course, an uncivil act. In a recent magazine advertisement on the printed word, one of a commendable series published by International Paper Company, novelist Kurt Vonnegut touched on the social aspect of writing: "Why should you examine your writing style with the idea of improving it? Do so as a mark of respect for your readers. If you scribble your thoughts any which way, your readers will surely feel that you care nothing for them."

In the working world, bad writing is not only bad manners, it is bad business. The victim of an incomprehensible letter will at best be annoyed and at worst decide that people who can't say what they mean aren't worth doing business with. Write a sloppy letter, and it might rebound on you when the recipient calls for clarification. Where one carefully worded letter would have sufficed, you might have to write two or more.

Muddled messages can cause havoc within an organization. Instructions that are misunderstood can set people off in the wrong directions or put them to work in vain. Written policies that are open to misinterpretation can throw sand in the gears of an entire operation. Ill-considered language in communications with employees can torpedo morale.

A CAREFUL WRITER MUST
BE A CAREFUL THINKER

In the early 1950s the British Treasury grew so concerned with the inefficiency resulting from poor writing that it called in a noted man of letters, Sir Ernest Gowers, to work on the problem. Out of this Gowers wrote an invaluable book, *The Complete Plain Words,* for the benefit of British civil servants and anyone else who must put English to practical use. (Her Majesty's Stationery Office, London, 1954.)

Gowers took as his touchstone a quotation from Robert Louis Stevenson: "The difficulty is not to write, but to write what you mean, not to affect your reader, but to affect him precisely as you wish." To affect your reader precisely as you wish obviously calls for precision in the handling of language. And to achieve precision in anything takes time.

Gowers suggested that the time spent pursuing precision more than cancels out the time wasted by imprecision. People in administrative jobs might well protest that they were not hired as writers, and that their schedules are crammed enough without having to fuss over the niceties of grammar and the like. The answer to this is that it is an important part of their work to put words on paper. It should be done just as thoroughly and conscientiously as anything else for which they get paid.

No one should be led to believe writing is easy. As great a genius as Dr. Samuel Johnson described composition as "an effort of slow diligence and steady perseverance to which the mind is dragged by necessity or resolution." Writing is hard work because *thinking* is hard work; the two are inseparable. But there is some compensation for the effort invested in trying to write well.

The intellectual discipline required to make thoughts come through intelligibly on paper pays off in clarifying your thoughts in general. When you start writing about a subject, you will often find that your knowledge of it and your thinking about it leave something to be desired. The question that should be foremost in the writer's mind, "What am I really trying to say?" will raise the related questions, "What do I really know about this? What do I really think about it?" A careful writer has to be a careful thinker — and in the long run careful thinking saves time and trouble for the writer, the reader, and everybody else concerned.

The problem is that many people believe that they *have* thought out ideas and expressed them competently on paper when they actually haven't. This is because they use nebulous multi-purpose words that may mean one thing to them and something quite different to someone else. Gowers gave the example of the verb "involve," which is used variously to mean "entail," "include," "contain," "imply," "implicate," "influence," etc., etc. "It has . . . developed a vagueness that makes it the delight of those who dislike the effort of searching for the right word," he wrote. "It is consequently much used, generally where some more specific word would be better and sometimes where it is merely superfluous."

THE RIGHT WORD WILL ALMOST
TELL YOU WHERE IT SHOULD GO

There are plenty of other lazy man's words lurking about, threatening to set the writer up beside Humpty Dumpty, who boasted: "When I use a word, it means just what I want it to mean." It is therefore wise to avoid words that can be taken in more than one way in a given context. This ties in with the first commandment of practical writing, which is: "Be Specific." "Specify, be accurate, give exact details — and forget about fine writing and original style," Rudolph Flesch says in his book, *How to Be Brief.*

Style tends to take care of itself if you select the right words and put them in the most logical order; so, to a large extent, do grammar and syntax. Find the right word, and it will almost tell you where in a sentence it should go.

VOCABULARY IS USUALLY THE LEAST OF A WRITER'S PROBLEMS

Since words come first, an ample vocabulary is an asset in conveying meaning. Oddly enough, though, people who have difficulty getting their written messages across rarely lack the vocabulary required. They know the apt words, but they don't use them. They go in for sonorous but more or less meaningless language instead.

People who are perfectly able to express themselves in plain spoken language somehow get the idea that the short, simple words they use in everyday conversation are unworthy to be committed to paper. Thus where they would say, "We have closed the deal," they will write, "We have finalized the transaction." In writing, they "utilize available non-rail ground mode transportation resources" instead of loading trucks. They get caught in "prevailing precipitant climatic conditions" instead of in the rain. They "utilize a manual earth removal implement" instead of digging with a shovel. When so many words with so many meanings are being slung about, nobody can be quite sure of just what is being said.

The guiding principle for the practical writer should be that common words should always be used unless more exact words are needed for definition. The reason for this is so plain that it is all but invisible. It is that if you use words that everybody knows, everybody can understand what you want to say.

A common touch with language has always distinguished great leaders. Winston Churchill comes immediately to mind; he "mobilized the English language and sent it into battle."

Churchill was an admirer of H. W. Fowler's *A Dictionary of English Usage,* to which he would direct his generals when he caught them mangling the language. Fowler set five criteria for good writing — that it be direct, simple, brief, vigorous and lucid. Any writer who tries to live up to these is on the right track.

By keeping in mind two basic techniques you can go some way towards meeting Fowler's requirements. These are:

Prefer the active voice to the passive. It will make your writing more direct and vigorous. It's a matter of putting the verb in your sentence up front so that it pulls along the rest of the words. In the active voice you would say, "The carpenter built the house"; in the passive, "The house was built by the carpenter." Though it is not always possible to do so in the context of a sentence, use the active whenever you can.

Prefer the concrete to the abstract. A concrete word stands for something tangible or particular; an abstract word is "separated from matter, practice, or particular example." Churchill used concrete terms: "We have not journeyed all this way, across the centuries, across the oceans, across the mountains, across the prairies, because we are made of sugar candy." If he had couched that in the abstract, he might have said: "We have not proved ourselves capable of traversing time spans and geographical phenomena due to a deficiency in fortitude." Again, there are times when abstractions are called for by the context because there are no better concrete words, but try not to use them unless you must.

The combination of the active and the concrete will help to make your prose direct, simple, vigorous, and lucid. There is no special technique for making it brief; that is up to you.

The first step to conciseness is to scorn the notion that length is a measure of thoroughness. It isn't. Emulate Blaise Pascal, who wrote to a friend: "I have made this letter a little longer than usual because I lack the time to make it shorter."

Use your pen or pencil as a cutting tool. No piece of writing, no matter what its purpose or length, should leave your desk until you have examined it intensely with a view to taking the fat out of it. Strike out anything that does not add directly to your reader's understanding of the subject. While doing this, try to put yourself in his or her shoes.

Be hard on yourself; writing is not called a discipline for nothing. It is tough, wearing, brainracking work. But when you finally get it right, you have done a service to others. And, like Shakespeare's cook, you can lick your metaphorical fingers and feel that it was all worthwhile.

Number of words 2015
See page 271 for Questions

Reading time in Seconds _____
See page 360 for Conversion Table

But, Please George, Write It in English!

Muriel Beadle

Ideas can be expressed in many different ways. You can write literary English, newspaper English, scientific English, or gobbledygook. A whole new field — technical communication — is opening up now to those seeking a challenging career. This selection suggests the central problem.

Once upon a time a long time ago, I managed to satisfy my full science requirement at Pomona College by taking a lecture course in chemistry. (That's right; no lab.) I got an A on my term paper, which had to do with the use of sulfur dioxide in preserving fruit. Thirty years later, I rediscovered the paper — in a beat-up carton which also contained a desiccated corsage — and I gave it to my husband to read. He nearly died laughing.

Much had happened during those thirty years. Such faint interest as I may have had in science had vanished under the pressures of the depression, the war, marriage, motherhood, widowhood, and the necessity of making regular payments on the mortgage. I'd racked up some experience in the advertising business and, by the 1950s, was a newspaper reporter.

The literary approach to these two specialties is, by the standards of scientific writing, somewhat imprecise. In retail advertising, before the Federal Trade Commission concerned itself with the proper labeling of furs, I had thought up as many aliases for rabbit as any other imaginative copywriter; and I had mastered the art of generalization.

As for the newspaper: It was a tabloid. My editor's credo was: "Keep it gutsy!" He pruned away all tendencies on my part to use polysyllables or the passive tense, taught me to build sentences from small, strong words and keep paragraphs short.

Then, in 1953, I married a scientist.

Talk about living in an ivory tower! George W. Beadle didn't know who Marilyn Monroe was. He'd never seen a horse race. And although he talked about zygotes with diploid sets of autosomes as if he were speaking English, he'd blink and look puzzled when I said I'd had trouble telescoping eight graphs into one in time for the bulldog lockup.

We'll, we've both learned a lot.

George is a geneticist. Within this field of science, there has recently been an explosion of knowledge comparable in significance to Mendel's discoveries about inheritance in the nineteenth century. What has been learned is of great import to the whole of society.

But all you have to do to scare my generation out of its wits is to say "deoxyribonucleic acid." It's immaterial that our *children* understand what DNA is; insofar as we oldsters are concerned, familiarity with modern molecular biology is in the same class as a complicated income tax return. We leave it to the experts and hope for the best.

Unfortunately, the experts can't (or at least *shouldn't*) make decisions for all of us on the control of radioactive fallout or the right of people with inherited diseases to reproduce as freely as people without such diseases. Whether one race has an inherited superiority to another race is no longer a purely academic question, either.

In our kind of society, the formation of intelligent opinion about such matters isn't going to occur until ordinary citizens understand the new genetics much better than they do now. Which is why my husband so often used to make speeches on the subject to any group of nonscientists who were curious enough and concerned enough to try to understand it.

He developed great skill in the art of keeping people awake long enough to learn something of what's been happening in biology since they dissected a frog back in '48. For example, our Siamese cats often shared the platform with him. (Their pigmentation illustrates an important point about genetic control of body chemistry.) Audiences also found themselves participating in George's demonstrations. And he made much use of analogies drawn from everyday life.

It was one of these analogies, in fact, that got me into my recent difficulties.

As George told it, there was once a housewife who made such good angel food cake that many people asked for her recipe. On one occasion when she wrote it out, however, she listed thirteen egg whites instead of the twelve egg whites she should have specified. The cook who followed that copy of the recipe got a cake so light and delicate that *her* recipe for angel food cake became the one that all the members of the Ladies' Guild requested. The twelve-egg cake thus became extinct and the thirteen-egg cake survived.

The original cook's mistake when copying the recipe, George pointed out, was a mutation; and the subsequent replacement of the twelve-egg cake by the thirteen-egg cake was a perfect example of evolution by natural selection. It may have been that some of the ladies in his audiences felt that it was also a perfect example of the foolishness of sharing your recipes with anyone; but, for whatever reason, they listened.

On the evening that George first used the angel food cake analogy, I was full of praise. Riding home afterwards, I said, "That cake idea was great. So is your comparison of DNA code to Morse code. And to describe transfer RNA as a postman delivering packages. . . . Say! I'll bet there would be a market for your lectures in written form. Books that are supposedly written for 'the intelligent layman' all seem to degenerate into scientific double-talk by the third chapter. Why don't you write a really simple one?"

Telling someone in academic life that he ought to write a book is like telling a pretty girl that she ought to be in the movies. They can't resist the idea. But in this case, I oversold it. George decided that *I* ought to do the writing. His theory was that if I understood the hydrogen bonding of nucleotides well enough to describe it, *anybody* would understand it. He'd determine the content and provide the outline, of course; I'd have to do little more than substitute language for the sections where, on the speaker's platform, he waves his arms around. . . .

That was three years ago.

The publisher's jacket blurb will undoubtedly describe the book as a collaborative venture, but that's because we've kept the sordid details secret. I don't know how it is with the Overstreets or the Lockridges, but with us it hasn't been collaboration — it's been controversy and compromise every step of the way.

1. We disagreed about structure.

I wanted short paragraphs, a picture on every page, and at least one joke per chapter. George believes that you should start with a topic sentence and refrain from paragraphing until you've fully developed the thought, which is likely to be three pages later.

2. We disagreed about style.

My first draft was full of eureka-type prose. (Upon returning to the laboratory, Smith glanced at the rack of test tubes. They were cloudy. Could this be the breakthrough he had hoped for?") George had a fit. And you should have seen him wince when I wrote that something or other had been proved. According to my mentor, it's preferable to say that the analysis undertaken by several investigators was not without success.

3. We disagreed about vocabulary.

It wasn't difficult to decide on the basic scientific vocabulary that we would expect our readers to master. After all, if your subject was genes, chromosomes, and nucleic acids, you might as well name them. And we agreed on the elimination of truly exotic terminology. It cannot be disputed that there is a net gain in clarity when one refers to a T_2 phage as a virus.

But we quarreled about use of the jargon that characterizes not only genetics but every other profession, art, or craft — from the psychologists' *sibling* (for "brother or sister") to the astronauts' *mach number* (for "the ratio of the speed of a body to the speed of sound in the surrounding atmosphere"). To groups that use such terms, they are quick and precise. To groups that don't, they're incomprehensible.

Naturally, George opted for the jargon of genetics. And his reason was sound: To translate specialized terms into layman's language usually requires whole phrases that, by comparison to the original, are long-winded and cumbersome. It *is* simpler to say that a person is heterozygous for curly hair (seven words) than to explain that he has received a gene for curly hair from one parent and a gene for straight hair from the other parent (twenty-one words).

Nevertheless, I preferred the longer way home. If I said it once, I said it a thousand times: "But, George, it's more *readable* in everyday English." Sometimes, I convinced him.

4. On content, we disagreed about depth and scope.

Oddly, it was I — not George — who pressed for the inclusion of material that was too complicated for Joe Doakes.

Scientific research, I had discovered, is a highly creative process. At its best, it proceeds via great leaps of imagination into the unknown; and the elegance and sophistication of the thinking behind such leaps excited me. I therefore attempted to write excessively detailed accounts of research methods, and engaged in long forays into chemistry, mathematics, or physics.

For example, when I reached the point of writing about discoveries that had been made possible by invention of the electron microscope, I realized that to understand this instrument one should know something about the physical nature of light. So I undertook some independent research on the subject. The result was three pages in which I summarized all of twentieth-century physics.

When George read it, he said, "Honey, where did you get that stuff?"

"From the *Encyclopedia Britannica* and the *Life Science Library*," I replied. "Furthermore, I think it's a remarkably lucid exposition of difficult material."

"Oh, it is," he agreed. "But it also happens to be wrong."

Our book is now in final draft. The manuscript will be ready to send to the publisher as soon as I do a little surgery on an addition of George's that begins, "These data would seem to confirm. . . ."

I should be happy, after all these months, to be getting rid of the heap of pages on my desk. But I'm not. Once they've gone, what on earth are we going to talk about after dinner?

Number of words 1662
See page 273 for Questions

Reading time in Seconds _____
See page 360 for Conversion Table

SELECTION 44

Simple Secrets of Public Speaking

Dale Carnegie

We spend a good share of our communication time in speaking — about 30 percent.
Of course that figure includes both public and private speaking or talking. For most
of us, however, public speaking is by far the more difficult. Here are some secrets
to make it much less so.

I am going to let you in on a secret that will make it easy for you to speak in public immediately. Did I find it in some book? No. Was it taught to me in college? No. I had to discover it gradually, and slowly, through years of trial and error.

Stated in simple words, it is this: *Don't spend ten minutes or ten hours preparing a talk. Spend ten years.*

Don't attempt to speak about anything until you have earned the right to talk about it through long study or experience. Talk about something that you know, and you know that you know. Talk about something that has aroused your interest. Talk about something that you have a deep desire to communicate to your listeners.

To illustrate, let's take the case of Gay Kellogg, a housewife of Roselle, New Jersey. Gay had never made a speech in public before she joined my class in New York. She was terrified: she feared that public speaking might be a hidden art way beyond her abilities. Yet at the fourth session of the course she made an impromptu talk that held the classroom audience in the palm of her hand.

I asked her to speak on "The Biggest Regret of My Life." Six minutes later, the listeners could hardly keep the tears back. Her talk went like this:

"The biggest regret of my life is that I never knew a mother's love. My mother died when I was only six years old. I was brought up by a succession of aunts and relatives who were so absorbed in their own children that they had no time for me. I never stayed with any of them very long. They never took any real interest in me, or gave me any affection.

"I knew I wasn't wanted by any of them. Even as a little child I could feel it. I often cried myself to sleep because of loneliness. The deepest desire of my heart was to have someone ask to see my report card from school. But no one ever did; no one cared. All I craved as a little child was love — and no one ever gave it to me."

Had Mrs. Kellogg spent ten years preparing that

talk? No. She had spent twenty years. She had been preparing herself to make that talk when she cried herself to sleep as a little child. She had tapped a gusher of memories and feelings deep down inside her. No wonder she held her audience spellbound.

Poor talks are usually the ones that are written and memorized and sweated over and made artificial. A poor speaker, like a poor swimmer, gets taut and tense and twists himself up into knots — and defeats his own purpose. But, even a man with no unusual speaking ability can make a superb talk if he will speak about something that has deeply stirred him.

Do beginning speakers know that? Do they look inside themselves for topics? No; they are more likely to look inside a magazine. Some years ago, I met in the subway a woman who was discouraged because she was making little progress in a public-speaking course. I asked her what she had talked about the previous week. I discovered that she had talked about whether Mussolini should be permitted to invade Ethiopia.

She had gotten her information from a weekly news magazine. She had read the article twice. I asked her if she had some special interest in the subject, and she said "No." I then asked her why she had talked about it.

"Well," she replied, "I had to talk about something, so I chose that subject."

I said to her: "Madame, I would listen with interest if you spoke about how to rear children or how to make a dollar go the farthest in shopping; but neither I nor anyone else would have the slightest desire to hear you try to interpret Mussolini's invasion of Ethiopia. You don't know enough about it to merit our respect."

Many students of speaking are like that woman. They want to get their subjects out of a book or a magazine rather than out of their own knowledge and convictions.

You are prepared right now to make at least a dozen good talks — talks that no one else on earth could make except you, because no one else has ever had precisely the same experiences. What are these subjects? I don't know. But you do. So carry a sheet of paper with you for a few weeks and write down, as you think of them, all the subjects that you are now prepared to talk about through experience — subjects such as "The Biggest

---

From "A Quick and Easy Way to Learn to Speak in Public," by Dale Carnegie, and from *Coronet*, February 1949. Reprinted by permission of *Esquire*, Inc. © 1949.

Regret of My Life," "My Biggest Ambition," and "Why I Liked (or Disliked) School." You will be surprised how quickly this list will grow.

Talking about your own experiences is obviously the quickest way to develop courage and self-confidence. But later you will want to talk about other subjects. What subjects? And where can you find them? Everywhere.

I once asked a class of executives that I was training for the New York Telephone Company to jot down every idea for a speech that occurred to them during the week. It was November. One man saw Thanksgiving Day featured in red on his calendar and spoke about the many things he had to be thankful for. Another man saw some pigeons on the street. That gave him an idea. He spent a couple of evenings in the public library and gave a talk about pigeons that I shall never forget.

But the prize winner was a man who had seen a bedbug crawling up a man's collar in the subway. He went to the library, uncovered some startling facts about bedbugs, and gave us a talk that I still remember after fifteen years.

Why don't you carry a "scribbling book"? Then, if you are irritated by a discourteous clerk, jot down the word "Discourtesy." Then try to recall two or three other striking examples of discourtesy. Pick the best one and tell us what we ought to do about it. Presto! You have a two-minute talk on Discourtesy.

Don't attempt to speak on some world-shaking problem like "The Atomic Bomb." Take something simple — almost anything will do, provided the idea gets you, instead of you getting the idea. Once you begin to look for topics for talks, you will find them everywhere — in the home, the office, the street.

Here are seven rules that will help immensely in preparing your speeches:

1. *Don't Write Out Your Talks.* Why? Because if you do, you will use written language instead of easy, conversational language; and when you stand up to talk, you will probably find yourself trying to remember what you wrote down. That will keep you from speaking with naturalness and sparkle.

2. *Never Memorize a Talk, Word for Word.* If you do, you are almost sure to forget it; and the audience will probably be glad, for nobody wants to listen to a canned speech. Even if you don't forget it, you will have a faraway look in your eyes and a faraway ring in your voice. If you are afraid you will forget what you want to say, then make brief notes and hold them in your hands and glance at them occasionally.

3. *Fill Your Talk with Illustrations and Examples.* By far the easiest way to make a talk interesting is to fill it with examples. Years ago, a congressman made a stormy speech accusing the government of wasting money by printing useless pamphlets. He illustrated what he meant by a pamphlet on "The Love Life of the Bullfrog." I would have forgotten that speech years ago if it hadn't been for that one specific illustration.

4. *Know Forty Times as Much About Your Subject as You Can Use.* The late Ida Tarbell, one of America's most distinguished biographers, told me that years ago while in London, she received a cable from McClure's Magazine asking her to write a two-page article on the Atlantic cable. Miss Tarbell interviewed the London manager of the Atlantic cable and got all the information she actually needed for a 500-word article. But she didn't stop there.

She went to the British Museum library and read articles and books about the cable, and the biography of Cyrus West Field, the man who laid it. She studied cross sections of cables on display in the British Museum; then visited a factory on the outskirts of London and saw cables being manufactured.

"When I finally wrote those two pages," Miss Tarbell said, "I had enough material to write a small book. But that vast amount of material which I had and did not use enabled me to write what I did write with confidence and clarity and interest. It gave me reserve power."

Ida Tarbell had learned through years of experience that she had to earn the right to write even 500 words. The same principle goes for speaking. Make yourself something of an authority on your subject. Develop that priceless asset known as reserve power.

5. *Rehearse Your Speech by Conversing with Your Friends.* Will Rogers prepared his famous Sunday-night radio talks by trying them out as conversation on the people he met during the week. If, for example, he were going to speak on the gold standard, he would wisecrack about it during the week. He would then discover which of his jokes went over with his listeners, which remarks elicited interest. That is an infinitely better way to rehearse a speech than trying it out with gestures in front of the bathroom mirror.

6. *Instead of Worrying about Your Delivery, Get Busy with the Causes That Produce It.* A lot of harmful nonsense has been written about delivery of a speech. The truth is that when you face an audience, you should forget all about voice, breathing, gestures, posture, emphasis. Forget everything except what you are saying.

Don't imagine that expressing your ideas and emotions before an audience is something that requires years of technical training, such as you have to devote to mastering music or painting. Anybody can make a splendid talk at home when he is angry. If somebody hauled off and knocked you down this instant, you would get up and make a superb talk. Your gestures, your posture, your facial expression would be perfect because they would be the expression of emotion.

To illustrate, a rear admiral of the Navy once took my course. He had commanded a squadron during World War I. He wasn't afraid to fight a naval battle, but he was so afraid to face an audience that he made weekly trips from his home in New Haven, Connecticut, to New York City to attend the course. Half a dozen sessions went by, and he was still terrified. So one of our instructors, Prof. Elmer Nyberg, had an idea that he felt would make the admiral forget himself and make a good talk.

There was a wild-eyed communist in this class. Professor Nyberg took him to one side and said: "Now, don't let anybody know that I told you to do this, but tonight I want you to advocate that we grab guns, march on Washington, shoot the President, seize the government and establish communism in the U. S. I want you to get the admiral angry, so he will forget himself and make a good talk."

The Bolshevik said: "Sure, I'll be glad to." He had not gone far in his speech, however, when the rear admiral leaped to his feet and shouted: "Stop! Stop! That's sedition!" Then the old sea dog gave this communist a fiery lecture on how much he owed to this country and its freedom.

Nyberg turned to the officer and said: "Congratulations, Admiral! What a magnificent speech!" The rear admiral snapped back: "I'm not making a speech; but I am telling that little whippersnapper a thing or two."

This rear admiral discovered just what you will discover when you get stirred up about a cause bigger than yourself. You will discover that all fears of speaking will vanish and that you don't have to give a thought to delivery, since the causes that produce good delivery are working for you irresistibly.

7. *Don't Try Imitating Others: Be Yourself.* Act on the sage advice that the late George Gershwin gave to a struggling young composer. When they first met, Gershwin was famous while the young man was working for $35 a week in Tin Pan Alley. Gershwin, impressed by his ability, offered the fellow a job as his musical secretary at almost three times the salary he was then getting.

"However, don't take the job," Gershwin advised. "If you do, you may develop into a second-rate Gershwin. But if you insist on being yourself, some day you'll become first-rate on your own."

The young man heeded the warning, turned down the job and slowly transformed himself into one of the significant American composers of this generation.

"Be yourself! Don't imitate others!" That is sound advice both in music and in public speaking. You are something new in this world. Never before, since the dawn of time, has anybody been exactly like you; and never again, throughout all the ages to come, will there ever again be anybody exactly like you. So why not make the most of your individuality?

Your speech should be a part of you, the very living tissue of you. It should grow out of your experiences, your convictions, your personality, your way of life. In the last analysis, you can speak only what you are. So, for better or for worse, you must cultivate your own little garden. For better or for worse, you must play your own little instrument in the great orchestra of life.

Number of words 2320
See page 275 for Questions

Reading time in Seconds _____
See page 360 for Conversion Table

Mark Twain's Speechmaking Strategy
Lydel Sims

You probably think of Mark Twain as author of Tom Sawyer, Huckleberry Finn, *or* Connecticut Yankee in King Arthur's Court. *In his own day, however, he was equally well known for his ability as a speaker. You'll know why when you read about his strategy.*

The schoolboy in the old story explained the technique nicely. "Strategy," he wrote, "means that when you run out of bullets you keep on firing." It hasn't caught on in military circles, but speechmakers have been practicing that kind of strategy for generations.

Reprinted from *TWA Ambassador* Magazine with permission of the author and publisher. Copyright 1976 by Trans World Airlines, Inc.

Consider the problem:

You're going to a sales conference, a convention, a testimonial dinner, a meeting of department heads. You're scheduled to speak, or you know you'll be called on. So you organize your thoughts, scribble notes on a piece of paper . . . and worry.

You worry, because like all good speakers, you want people to believe the words just flow out — all the humor, the motivation, the drive, the matchless grasp of detail, the fresh and sparkling anecdotes.

But speakers who hold audiences in the palm of their hand don't speak from notes. Are you going to pause and consult those plaguey notes, thus admitting mere mortality? Or are you going to wing it and risk forgetting your best story, omitting your most important point? And if you run out of ammunition, are you going to try to keep on firing?

Mark Twain faced that very same dilemma and solved it, becoming one of the most successful speakers in America's history.

In his early days on the lecture circuit, Mark Twain worked out a solution to the speechmaker's dilemma by trial and error, but he didn't explain it until years later in a little-known essay that was published after his death. The system was so good, he testified, that a quarter-century after he had given a lecture he could remember the whole thing by a single act of recall.

You have Twain's posthumous guarantee that it'll work for you.

When he first began his speaking career, Twain recalled, he used a full page of notes to keep from getting mixed up. He would write down the beginnings of key sentences, to take him from one point to another and to protect him from skipping. For a typical evening's lecture, he would write and memorize 11 key beginnings.

The plain failed. Twain would remember the sentences, all right, but forget their order. He would have to stop, consult his notes, and thereby spoil the spontaneous effect of the whole speech.

Twain then decided to memorize not only his key sentences, but also the first letter of each sentence. This initial-letter method didn't work either. Not even when, as he solemnly alleged, he cut the numbers of letters to 10 and inked them on his fingernails.

"I kept track of the fingers for a while," he wrote in his essay, "then I lost it, and after that I was never quite sure which finger I had used last."

He considered licking off the inked letters as he went along. People noticed he seemed more interested in his fingernails than his subject; one or two listeners would come up afterwards and ask what was wrong with his hands.

Then Mark Twain's great idea came — that it's hard to visualize letters, words and sentences, but *pictures* are easy to recall. They take hold. They can make things stick . . .

Especially if you draw them yourself.

Twain was no artist, mind you, but that didn't stop him. "In two minutes I made six pictures with a pen," he reported, "and they did the work of the 11 catch-sentences, and did it perfectly."

Having once drawn the pictures, he found he could throw them away. He discovered [and you can test it for yourself] that, having once made a crude series of drawings, he could recall their image at will.

He left us samples of three of those first six pictures, and they are pathetic things, indeed, by artistic standards. But they got the job done.

The first was a haystack with a wiggly line under it to represent a rattlesnake — that was to tell him to begin talking about ranch life in the West. Alongside it, he drew a few slanting lines with what could just possibly be an umbrella and the Roman numeral II — that referred to a tale about a great wind that would strike Carson City at 2 o'clock every afternoon. Next, he drew a couple of jagged lines — lightning, of course — telling him it was time to move on to the subject of weather in San Francisco, where the point was that there *wasn't* any lightning. Nor thunder either, he noted.

From that day, Twain was able to speak without notes, and the system never failed him. Each portion of his speech would be represented by a picture. He would draw them, all strung out in a row, then look at them and destroy them. When the time came to speak, there was the row of images sharply in his mind.

Twain observed you can even make last-minute notes based on the remarks of an earlier speaker. Just insert another figure in your set of images.

The magic of the Twain technique should be immediately obvious to the speaker who organizes remarks around anecdotes. Are you introducing your first point with a story about a nervous doctor in Dubuque? Draw the doctor. Are you following that with the principle that's best illustrated with the tale of the fellow who treed a wildcat? Draw a tree alongside the doctor. And so on.

The remarkable thing is that Twain's method can work just as well for concepts as it does for anecdotes. Sales must be increased? Draw a vertical arrow with a dollar sign. Something about productivity? A lopsided circle representing a wheel is sufficient. Research and development? Even you can draw what will be recognized — by you — as a mad scientist. And if you need figures, put them in the pictures, too, coming out of people's mouths, piled in pyramids, outlined in exclamation marks, lurking under bridges.

The wilder the image, the easier it'll be to remember. And once you have your scrawls in sequence and take a good look, you're fixed. Instant memory.

Mark Twain didn't mention it, but there's one more thing you might do. When you reach the end of your drawings, hence the end of your speech, you could add one more — a drawing of an octagonal sign: STOP!

That would be smart strategy, for then you really *are* out of bullets. No need to keep on firing.

Read Aloud — It's Fun

Charles Laughton

Robert Louis Stevenson once told of an illiterate Welsh blacksmith who happened to hear someone reading Robinson Crusoe *aloud. He became so fascinated that he immediately set about learning to read, eventually finishing the book himself. Have you ever become interested in a book because you heard some of it read aloud? Laughton has a suggestion. Why not give it a try?*

Not long ago I read passages from Will Shakespeare's *Twelfth Night* to a group of college English teachers. Afterward a young instructor confronted me. "That wasn't quite fair," he said. "You edited those passages to make them livelier."

"But I didn't skip a word," I protested and opened my book to show him the unmarked passages I had read from. When he seemed convinced, I asked him, "Whatever made you think that?"

"Well," he replied simply, "this is the first time I ever really liked the play."

I won't take credit for explaining Shakespeare to a scholar. I feel certain, however, that his new appreciation of the play was inspired mostly by the enjoyment of hearing it read aloud. Reading aloud is an old and well-loved pastime now somewhat neglected. These days we may drone through a few bedtime stories for our youngsters, but by and large we regard books as something to be taken silently, swiftly and alone. For recreation and entertainment, the temptation—more often than not—is to look outside our homes, outside ourselves. This is not a good omen. For the attitude that we are necessarily incapable of entertaining ourselves is, if I may say so, poppycock.

I plead for more reading aloud. It is a friendly, quiet and thoroughly refreshing thing to do. It makes us participants rather than spectators. Instead of sitting by to let the professionals amuse or enlighten us, *we* can get into the act, make contact with new ideas, exercise our imagination.

More than that, it is a shared experience which draws people closer together. Husbands and wives, families or groups of friends can enjoy the comfortable satisfaction that comes from laughing together, learning together— from doing the same thing at the same time, together. There is nothing better than old-fashioned family reading to form a warm bond between parents and teenagers.

Is this important? I think so. I have felt it was ever since I began reading to people during the war.

Not fit for juggling or singing but anxious to do something, I decided to read to whoever would listen. My first audiences were in Army hospitals. Before long,

I met men who pronounced the Bible a dull book, then sat spellbound as we read the old stories together. I saw wounded men, embittered by pain, discover that their troubles were not unique and find solace in the sufferings of Shakespeare's tragic heroes.

More recently, on my reading tours of the United States, I have seen the good feeling of companionship grow in crowds of from several hundred to several thousand because we were bent on something together.

How, then, do you begin reading aloud? Many people find taking the plunge the hardest part. Some feel they will be expected to declaim like Fourth of July orators or bellow like Captain Bligh. Others are shy. Dozens of service men have told me they wanted to read poems to their wives or sweethearts, but didn't know how to start.

To such as these, I say, brace up! I am delighted to tell you that there are no hard and fast rules. Wanting to begin is the only requirement. After that, choose a book you're comfortable with. Anything is worth reading if you enjoy it.

Read nothing because you think you should. A book read from sense of duty is almost certain to be a crushing bore. The pleasure in reading aloud comes principally from sharing something you like with someone you like.

Near the top of my own list of favorites are the Bible, Shakespeare, Charles Dickens, the Fables of Aesop, and the witty works of James Thurber. I also like Mark Twain, the short stories of O. Henry, the verse of Rudyard Kipling.

Not all Shakespeare suits me, I must confess. I would warn beginners away from his sonnets, even as I imagine young violinists are urged not to break their hearts on a Beethoven Sonata. In *Look Homeward, Angel,* Thomas Wolfe, another of my favorites, describes neatly the plight of a man who tackled the sonnets. "Their woven density (he writes) was too much for his experience." I agree heartily.

Henry James and his rarefied vocabulary get a wide berth from me, and I find the great John Milton—alas! —rather wearing. Mr. Dostoevski and I do poorly together, regardless of what his countless admirers say, and I confess I have on occasion hurled the Brontës across the room.

But these are only my own preferences. The nice thing is that you are bound by none of them. If Milton defeats me, for you his words may turn handsprings. Time and again, when I have finished reading to groups in private homes, someone will fetch a book and say, "Do you know this?" and then read, far more beautifully than I could, a passage that has special meaning for him.

In choosing something to read aloud, don't feel that you have to limit yourself to one book. If a volume loses its savor, drop it. Be selective. Experiment with several books at once, taking a short story from one, a chapter from another, a poem from a third. One couple I know never approaches the end of one book without dipping into the opening chapters of another—a sort of "Coming Attraction," or promise of things to come.

Having started out, go at your own pace. You know best how many evenings a week are free for reading and what part of each evening you want to spend. One quick way to lose enthusiasm for reading aloud is to let it become a nightly chore, like washing the dinner dishes. There is no harm done if you skip a few evenings.

But once you start, stay with it. Don't let interruptions cool you off before your author has a chance to get his story under way.

I think you'll find at first that an hour is the reading period you can handle most comfortably. Later, perhaps, you can lengthen it, but stop before your voice becomes hoarse and froggy, and the heroine of your book begins to sound like a galloping case of asthma.

Remember that reading aloud takes some degree of concentration. When your attention begins to wander, you've had enough. This is not to say that everyone must sit stiffly alert with hands folded. Ladies may knit. Gentlemen may overhaul their fishing tackle.

As for the technique of reading aloud, above all be natural. Many people try to disguise their home-grown accents and cultivate an affected, stagy voice. Don't do it. Your normal speaking voice will be your best read-ing voice. And if you're interested in what you're reading, you'll read well. Shakespeare didn't write "Julius Caesar" in Latin. There's no reason for you to try to sound like an Elizabethan Englishman when you read it.

More than anything, you will need practice. Only with practice will you gain fluency and learn to keep from stumbling over words or from running out of breath or pausing in the wrong spots.

These, however, are refinements. They may add pleasure to your reading, but you are not striving for an elocution medal and can enjoy yourself thoroughly without them.

One of the best ways to practice I know is to gather a group together and read plays. Collect as many copies of the plays as you can and let each person take several parts. Watching your cues and answering the other players, measure for measure, is a grand way to lose self-consciousness and build a small fire of excitement in your delivery.

Old hands at this frequently find whole passages sticking in their memories. In my own case, I'm told that I once "read" a considerable section from Mr. Dickens while holding my book upside down.

Finally, do not end your evening with the closing of your book. When you stop reading, begin talking. Reading aloud is fun in itself, but it is better yet when it prompts lively conversation after you've put the book aside. That is when it truly becomes a shared experience, as well as a rewarding one.

Two young people once told me that they had been reading *War and Peace* for a year and a half. "It's not that we're slow readers," they explained. "It's just that every few pages seem to suggest something fresh to us, and then we're off, talking, thinking, planning. We're not sure that we'll ever finish the book, but we've learned a great deal about ourselves and our life together."

This, to me, is how to enjoy reading aloud.

Number of words 1430
See page 279 for Questions

Reading time in Seconds _____
See page 360 for Conversion Table

The 11 Toughest Job Interview
Questions . . . and How to Answer Them
Bruce E. Moses

Getting a responsible job usually involves writing the kind of letter of application that opens the way to still another hurdle — the personal interview. Two you's are thus revealed — you the writer and you the talker or the social creature. Can you handle the interview effectively? Here's an article to help you.

As the food commercial jingle on TV suggests . . . "Anticipation . . ."

The job hunter must anticipate and be prepared for the so-called "curve" questions which no doubt will be thrown out during the interview. Everyone is vulnerable to "loaded" or "curve" questions. This is especially true if there is a "red flag" on your resume to call attention to a particularly delicate subject. But not everyone is vulnerable to the same questions in the same way because we all bring different strengths and weaknesses to an interview.

Following is my selection of the 11 toughest questions which are asked during the interview . . . and how to answer them. It is based on composite feedback received from candidates I have recruited as well as corporate clients I have served during 15 years as an executive recruiter.

1. Several jobs in a short period of time. The best defense is an offense. As long as the "Dates Employed" are glaring at the interviewer from the resume, you should explain why you had so many jobs *before* the question is even raised.

For instance, suppose you were fired for incompetence after just one year on a particular job. Depending on how long ago it was, you might indicate that, "Although the job did not work out, I gained quite a bit from it because . . ." and then proceed to tell why. You might also list some of your accomplishments, even though you were there only a short time. You might have taken some additional courses to help improve your background — so that you will be better prepared the next time around. Use empathy and make sure you are coming across in a sincere and positive manner. For all you know, the same thing may have happened to the interviewer at one time. Avoid transparent excuses — candor is refreshing!

2. Weak formal education. Turn the liability into an asset. Explain what responsibilities you had when you were young, and how you have studied on your own. If it is true, you might explain that no matter where you were employed, you were usually the only non-college graduate at your job level. If there is a possibility of night school, tell that to the interviewer, too.

3. What are your long-range goals? This question seems to baffle a lot of people. Whatever you say, avoid indicating that "What I really want is a business of my own" . . . even if you do! You certainly will not encourage an employer by indicating you will give the company the privilege of training you for a couple of years, but then plan on going out on your own to compete with them. You may even change your mind once you begin to work for the company. Frequently, I will hear from an employee who has spent twenty or more years with his company who says, "When I first joined my employer more than twenty years ago, I had absolutely no intention of staying more than just a couple of years — just for the experience."

Answer the "long-range goal" question as you really believe . . . outside of "leaving the company." If you feel that someday you could become president of the company, then tell the interviewer so. Also, offer reasons that support your ambitious plans. Maybe you plan on obtaining your MBA, or some other positive accomplishment to help you meet your goals.

4. What is your greatest weakness? Nobody is perfect. When answering this question, you had better use empathy. The wrong answer could instantly disqualify you for the job.

I will never forget the candidate I once recruited for the position of corporate comptroller who told the president of the company that, "My greatest weakness is detail. I hate detail work!" Needless to say, that particular candidate was not hired. The irony of it all was that he had been a successful comptroller for almost fifteen years. Be honest, but try to think of a "greatest single weakness" which will not immediately eliminate you from any further consideration for the job.

5. Physical handicap or health problem. Not everyone is blessed with perfect health or appearance. If you have an obvious physical handicap or health problem, it is usually best to discuss it openly with the interviewer, provided it will not automatically disqualify you. Be honest with both the interviewer and yourself.

I once recommended a candidate who was confined to a wheelchair because of a childhood accident. He explained very positively that his handicap was really not

This article has been reprinted through the courtesy of Halsey Publishing Co., publishers of Delta *Sky* magazine and by permission of the author.

a hindrance but a mere inconvenience. His attitude was marvelous. This man very candidly admitted that because of his handicap he always tried a little harder to overcome it . . . and most certainly did.

6. Recently divorced. This is a common subject which, when discussed with applicants, frequently causes discomfort — especially if there are children involved. Some companies will not hire a recent divorcee until after the so-called "adjustment period" (whatever that is) is completed. Some people never completely adjust to divorce, while others were never completely adjusted to marriage — and therefore become much better immediately after the divorce.

The trepidation employers sometimes have about the recently divorced is that any new job requires total concentration and commitment. If a new employee has to tackle, simultaneously, the adjustment to a new job plus putting life back together after a recent divorce, then the pressures may be too great.

When the subject comes up in an interview, it is best to be candid about it. If the divorce is fairly recent, try to explain to the interviewer that because your marital problems are now over, you are prepared to give 110% to the job. Be positive!

7. Recently retired military officers. The typical "curve" question which may be thrown at a recently retired military officer: "Do you think you may have difficulty adapting to civilian life?" Your response could be: "The responsibility and exposure that I received in the military are directly applicable for the following reasons . . ." then proceed to explain those reasons. Try to draw analogies between what you accomplished in the military and what you perceive the job requiring.

If the interviewer brings up the fact that you are earning a handsome retirement salary and therefore should not require too much money . . . you might indicate politely, but firmly, "My pension pay should have no bearing on the salary the employer has set for the job opening. I will contribute as much to the company as someone who is not on a pension, and therefore should be compensated appropriately."

You want to convince the interviewer that your military experience is an asset in fulfilling the requirements of the job. Use civilian terminology which you know will be positive. You want the interviewer to think of you as a "business executive" rather than a "retired officer looking for a way to spend his free time."

8. Why should the company hire you? This is one of the most frequently asked questions, yet most job hunters fail to take advantage of it. Prepare for this question prior to your interview and be ready to answer it with enthusiasm and in a manner of controlled confidence. Summarize your experience and accomplishments in a concise positive statement as to why you are the best qualified candidate for the job. Do not bore the interviewer with a long dissertation, but be sure to convey the benefits the company will receive by hiring you.

9. Why are you leaving your present position? The job may be dull, the boss a boor, and the pay low . . . however, you want to avoid the negative cliches and use more positive reasons. You might be seeking greater advancement opportunities where you could take on added responsibilities and earn more money. Your prospects for career development could be limited because of a lack of promotional opportunities. You do not want to appear as a job-hopper who is just running away from another problem. Use reasons which the interviewer can relate to and identify with.

10. Age — Too young or too old? If you are young, you want to come across as mature and level-headed. You want to illustrate that you have already handled business situations and possess the experience and good judgment to do an excellent job. Cite some examples of your success.

If you are "middle aged" or older (and I am not sure I know what "middle aged" is), you want to appear full of vim and vitality. Talk about your most recent accomplishments and the future goals you have set for yourself. Substantiate to the interviewer that your most recent years have been most productive. Highlight your most recent achievements.

11. Unemployed executive. If you are unemployed and there is no way you can cover yourself with your prior employer — like remaining on the payroll — then just indicate that you are unemployed . . . but have several offers pending.

It just does not pay to try and cover yourself with the "I am presently doing consulting" routine, unless you really are. Any astute interviewer will see right through your facade, and you will only further weaken your position.

One approach you may consider is that you found it difficult taking time off from work to explore other opportunities. You felt that as long as your prior employer was paying you, you owed him a fair day's work. So rather than lie or make excuses for taking time off, you elected to pursue your job campaign on a full-time basis.

The above subjects and questions are the 11 toughest, but there are many more which could be just as important, depending on your circumstances. Do not be caught by surprise. Make a list of every conceivable question an interviewer might ask. You will be amazed at what you come up with. Remember, these same questions could be thrown at you!

Successful interviews do not happen by chance. Everyone has the desire to do well in an interview, but the job hunter who will ultimately receive the offer is the one who has the greatest desire to prepare for the interview.

Number of words 1670
See page 281 for Questions

Reading time in Seconds _____
See page 360 for Conversion Table

New Hope for Audiences
National Parent-Teacher

Discussion is, in a sense, a variety of public speaking. A discussion can, of course,
be lively, stimulating, and purposeful. But all too often it is just the opposite.
In short, discussion often needs new hope to give it new life.

The late Eduard C. Lindeman, who ended his teaching days at the New York School of Social Work and spent much of his life in conference activities, was one of the first men of our time to recognize that new ground rules are needed for small group discussions. He pointed out how much we still continue to use the "fight symbol" in all our meetings, which advertises and encourages disagreement. An audience is invited by the chairman to "go after" the speaker. Debates are prized for their pugilistic effects. Discussions are considered lively only if the line of battle is drawn.

CIRCULAR RESPONSE

Professor Lindeman saw that it was not enough merely to get people together around a table. The result might be disastrous unless there were some clearly defined purpose and some method of discussion that would help achieve this purpose. The group, in a word, must learn to think together, not merely provide a setting in which two or three members do all the talking and lambaste each other while the other members of the group sit passive and bored. So he proposed this arrangement:

The members of the group — not more than twenty and preferably fifteen — are seated in a circle. The chairman or leader proposes the question to be taken up. The discussion begins with the man or woman at his right. That person has the first opportunity to express his views. Then the person at *his* right has a chance to talk, and so on until the discussion has gone around the circle. No member of the group can speak a second time until his turn comes again.

If, for example, you are sitting fourth from the leader's right, you may express your views on the subject and also, if you must, on the opinions advanced by the leader and the three who have spoken before you. But if the person on your right says something that arouses your ire or excites your response, you have no chance to comment until the next time around.

So much for the mechanics of the circular response procedure. And the mechanics alone accomplish wonders toward remedying the bad manners and monopolistic practices that mar many a small group discussion.

Extreme views belligerently presented are modified by the restraints imposed. The timid person speaks more freely when he knows that it is his natural right as a member of the group. In some places where there is a Quaker influence a member may even delay speaking and invoke a moment of silence on the part of the whole group. This is likely to improve the quality of what follows, for good discussion often needs a measure of silence.

FROM MANY VIEWS, A NEW VIEW

One special advantage of the circular response method is its suitability for mixed age groups. Students as young as fourteen have taken part in groups made up mostly of adults. When their turn comes, they speak freely and as members, not as individuals segregated because of their age.

It is not merely because of the ground rules that the young and the timid both speak more freely under this method. Another reason is to be found in the fact that circular response, by its very nature, encourages every person in the group to make his particular contribution to the problem at hand. The skillful chairman will make the most of this feature. He will visualize a common pot of experience as existing in the very center of the group and will help members to put their contributions into this pot instead of throwing remarks at each other. The whole effort is to arrive at a consensus — and understanding. Naturally such an object will not always be attained, but the direction is toward creative thinking by the group, a mingling and distillation of many views, so that something new is actually brought into being.

If circular response is used in the discussion of political or economic problems — as part of a larger adult education program — the chairman and the group will of course need a certain amount of careful preparation. Circular response is not a substitute for reading and thinking or a convenient way of pooling ignorance. But it offers many blessings and benefits, regardless of the subject, for it reminds those who take part that the aim of discussion is reflection and not fireworks.

Two pages out of the literature of group dynamics may be taken and applied to circular response. One is to appoint a person whose function is to summarize the findings of the group at the end of the discussion. The other is to have another person, sitting with but not of the group, to act as observer. He is not concerned with

---

Reprinted by permission from *National Parent-Teacher.*

the content of the discussion. His duty is to spend a few moments at the end of the discussion period commenting on the procedure itself and the behavior of the members, pointing out how the whole business can be carried on better next time.

ROLE PLAYING

Where the issue is one that concerns a delicate or difficult problem of human relations, the method known as role playing can be of great value. In role playing members of a group act out a real-life situation. They have no script, no set dialogue, and they make up their parts as they go along.

The situation to be acted out may be based on some clash or conflict — perhaps in the home, on the job, or in the community. But role playing need not center on conflict. It may be a practice session to put people at ease in assignments like interviewing an official, calling on a voter to remind him to register, or conferring with a school board member. However, role playing is put to its best use when it dramatizes a situation that most people in the group face and feel somewhat strongly about.

Suppose a parent education study-discussion group is exploring the age of adolescence. Most of the members are parents of teen-agers, and most of them feel quite strongly about the matter of getting home on time after a date. They can imagine a situation in a household where a fifteen-year-old girl resents the rule that she must be in by ten o'clock. So three group members volunteer to act it out, playing the roles of mother, father, and daughter.

After the parts have been decided upon, an inexperienced group might take a little time to discuss the kind of person each player is to portray. The young girl might be rebellious and quick-tempered, the mother given to worry and nagging, and the father a strict disciplinarian. This discussion of roles, or warming-up period, may not be necessary in groups familiar with the technique.

At this point the players may need some reassurance. It is not always easy for adults to throw themselves into a part, even though all of us have some sense of drama. They may be self-conscious before a group. Or they may be reluctant to act out in public their own thoughts and feelings — or thoughts and feelings that might rightly or wrongly be construed as theirs.

To overcome these obstacles it is suggested that the leader say something like this: "Keep in mind that this is make-believe. You're playing a part. You're not going to show what *you* consider right. You're going to talk and act as you think the person you are playing would talk and act."

Once the players understand the problem and their own roles, the drama may start. It need not last long. Often two or three minutes are enough to bring out the point and show how human relations operate in such a situation.

A still further possibility is to replace some or all of the cast, thus giving other members of the group a chance at role playing.

The situation, the roles, and the solution may have to be discussed and played several times before the actors and the group feel that they have worked out a satisfactory handling of the problem. In this way each drama can mean new learning and new insight for both players and observers.

The advantages of role playing are many. It offers groups a dramatic way of calling attention to problems that involve strong emotions. It provides a way of learning the skills needed to carry out the goals of the group. It gives each player a chance to take on the personality of another human being — to enter into his feelings and for the moment to think and act from his point of view. Through it the whole group has an opportunity to see several solutions to a problem, some of them better than others. Finally, it offers practice in handling problems under two big advantages. When mistakes are made in this setting, the players are spared the penalties exacted in real life. Better still, an audience is at hand — observing, weighing, seeking along with the players better ways of coping with problems that await answers from actors and watchers alike.

REVIEWING THE ROLES

After the role playing comes discussion. The leader invites comments from the group with such questions as these: "Do you agree with the way the roles were played?" "Would you have played any of them differently?" "What would you have said or done? Why?" Or he may be more specific and ask: "What made the girl rebellious?" "Why was her mother particularly worried?" "What was at the root of the father's attitude?" "What could the girl have done to ease matters?" "How else could the father have handled the problem?" "What suggestion could the mother have made?"

When members have arrived at a new understanding of the roles and of possible solutions the whole drama may be tried again, incorporating the changes agreed upon by the group. The same members may play the same roles, thus gaining experience in trying out various ways of handling feelings. Or the same players may continue but this time take different parts. The player who had been the mother may now take the role of the girl. The one who played the girl may now be the father; and the father, the mother. This recasting of characters helps create understanding of another's feelings and point of view.

Number of words 1704
See page 283 for Questions

Reading time in Seconds _____
See page 360 for Conversion Table

Ask, Don't Tell

Nardi Reeder Campion

Have you ever wondered why some people are such good company and others are not? Perhaps you'll find one answer as you read this article. Afterwards, start observing friends and acquaintances. See how many know how to unlock doors with questions.

You start a question and it's like starting a stone. You sit quietly on the top of a hill; and away the stone goes, starting others.—Robert Louis Stevenson

How wonderful it is when a conversational stone we throw out brings an avalanche of response from those around us; when our interest and concern open a wide path to another's personality. How wonderful—and how rare! So often we feel shut out from the true thoughts of our friends and loved ones. They may be overflowing with ideas, but it is difficult for us to establish real contact. Yet each of us can learn the magical power of asking the right question at the right time, and gain the joy of unlocking the floodgates of true communication.

This exciting idea was first presented to me by the principal of our school. "When I talk to our 10-year-old son, Russell," I complained, "he pretends to be listening, but he's not. Later I find out that he didn't hear one word I said."

Miss Markham smiled and suggested, "Don't tell him, ask him—and then *you* really listen to what *he* says."

"Ask him what?" I countered.

"Well, what do you think he'd like to talk about?"

As I paused to mull over my answer, it suddenly dawned on me that Miss Markham was using the very technique she was telling *me* to use. Because she had answered my question with a question, I was thinking about the problem as I never would have if she had spelled out exactly what questions I should ask. Her apt question engaged my attention completely.

"It could be all the difference between sitting on a beach and swimming in the waves, if you can convince your son you'll heed any answer he gives you, no matter how unacceptable it seems. Genuine interest and acceptance . . . these are the keys to real communication."

Don't tell, ask. I doubted if such a simple suggestion could be of any real value, although I can understand that it is dangerous to "tell" too much. Most of us

at some time have blundered into the booby-trap of repeating ideas until our children dial out.

Could it be possible, I asked myself, that Miss Markham's idea could really help me to bridge the gulf that separated me from others? I decided to test it by trying a few "asking" experiments in the laboratory of my own living room, to see whether the idea offered a fresh attack on "the disease of not listening."

I didn't have to wait long for an opportunity. Our 15-year-old daughter Cissa and I clash with clock-like regularity over the time she should come home at night. I usually say, "I want you to be in by 10.30."

"But, Mother," she moans, *"everybody* stays out until 11."

"How many times have I told you—everybody's business is nobody's business?" I answer. And then we are off on a collision course.

This Saturday when Cissa started out for the basketball game I tried Miss Markham's advice. I simply asked, "What time do you think you'll get back?"

"Oh," she said, "I'll make it by 10:30 all right."

I almost fell over. I felt as though I had been pushing against a door that was already open. Communications hadn't exactly flowed forth, but by asking one small question I had by-passed our usual head-on crash, and it left the door open between us.

I made up my mind right then to take as my motto those cheerful words from the Sermon On The Mount. "Knock, and it shall be opened unto you." My optimism increased when I read in a magazine that Norman Vincent Peale, who is more qualified than most of us to be a "teller," is a genius at the art of asking. When his children were growing up, Dr. Peale used to bring home letters people had written to him about their problems, and ask his children how they would answer them. He would say, "Here's a lady who's upset because her son lies to her. What advice can we send her?"

As Dr. Peale's children spelled out their answer they did some serious thinking about truth. Knowing their father valued their opinion made them clarify their own convictions. They knew he would give thoughtful consideration to their answers, however zany they might sound. If his son said, "I think it helps to be a good liar," Dr. Peale wouldn't register disapproval. He would say, "Can you explain what you mean?" And then the dialogue would begin.

Encouraged, I started asking questions right and left. At first I ran into a number of blank walls. Some questions, I discovered, come equipped with built-in discouraging answers. When our high school senior came home from the spring dance I asked eagerly, "How was the party, Toby?" The words were no sooner out of my mouth than I knew what the answer would be.

"Okay."

"Do you want to tell me about it?"

He shrugged his broad shoulders. "Not really."

End of conversation, if that's what you can call it.

I wasn't much more successful with Russell when I quizzed him about his new baseball club. He answered me patiently at first and then said, "Gosh, Mom, what is this? Twenty Questions?"

I'm glad to say my husband opened up much more freely than the boys had. When he came home from work I discarded the usual "What did you do today?" for a more definite question: "What was the most interesting thing that happened all day?"

"The cost control meeting."

"Cost control? Can you explain that to me?"

He eyed me skeptically. "You mean it?"

"Of course."

"Well, the whole area of cost control is sensitive . . ." and away he went. *Can you explain that?* turned out to be a leading question all right. Ten minutes later my husband said, "You're not listening."

"But I *want* to hear more about your work," I insisted.

"Don't try to bluff it," he laughed. "You're not all that crazy about cost control."

Clearly I had a lot to learn about the art of asking questions. Some of mine apparently closed more doors than they opened. Toby seemed to feel my questions didn't really concern him; Russell thought I was overly inquisitive; and my husband accused me of insincerity, however well-intentioned.

While brooding moodily over my ineptness, a picture suddenly flashed before my mind's eye. I was a young girl again, all dressed up for my first formal dance. My mother, who grew up in the southern-belle tradition, was counseling me, "Try to get your beau to do the talking, my dear. It's better for a girl to ask the right questions than to know all the answers."

"What *are* the right questions?"

"The ones that flatter your young man, of course. 'What's your opinion of this?' or 'Would you explain that?' Men like to feel important, and most of them can't resist a girl who asks leading questions and pays rapt attention to their answers."

My mother reassured me that the feminine "asking" role is marvelously effective. "It goes all the way back to Biblical times," she said, "and probably accounts for the Queen of Sheba's dazzling conquest of King Solomon. You remember in the Second Book of Chronicles it says the Queen of Sheba 'communed with him of all that was in her heart. And Solomon told her all her questions.' "

What was it, I asked myself, that the Queen of Sheba knew about the art of asking questions that I didn't know?

I am lucky to have as a friend and neighbor one of America's wisest men, a great preacher now in his eighties—Dr. Harry Emerson Fosdick. Like the rest of his friends, when I have a problem, I call on him. Dr. Fosdick had written: "My father's typical method in getting something done he wanted done was to ask us what we really thought about it ourselves, and even when I asked him for counsel I was fairly certain to have the question thrown back at me—what did I think myself? So from the beginning we were trained for independence." When I consulted him about the secret of asking good questions, he thought a minute and then said, "I suppose the secret, if there is one, is to realize that questioning and listening are inseparable. The asking of good questions represents listening on its highest plane, and of course true listening can never be faked or turned on. It must come from within. In order to sound sincere, a person has to *be* and *act* sincere, and I believe it's the quality of attention that makes all the difference."

I resolved to concentrate on the "quality of attention" with my husband, too. That evening, instead of too many eager-beaver questions, I waited for him to start our conversation when and where he wanted it to start. After years of plunging right in, this took a little doing, but I managed to keep quiet. At first there was a long silence, and then my husband said, "I'm quite concerned about a new committee I'm working on at the plant . . ."

As he talked I had no difficulty appearing interested, for I *was* interested—simply because what he was talking about was so important to him. After he finished he smiled at me and said, "You know, it's encouraging to have you listen to me like that." What a rewarding moment that was when I felt the magic of communication that grows out of a real concern for another!

What could actually be more encouraging than to make someone feel that you want to hear more fully what he thinks? A person who can do this naturally must have an invaluable gift. John F. Kennedy, for instance, was famous for the incisive questions he asked, and the intent way he listened to replies. Robert Saudek, who conferred with President Kennedy at the White House while he was producing *Profiles in Courage* for television, later told friends, "President Kennedy made you think he had nothing else to do except ask you questions and listen, with extraordinary concentration, to your answer. You knew that for the time being he had blotted out both the past and the future. More than anyone else I have ever met, President Kennedy seemed to understand the importance of *now*."

The phrase, "the importance of now" struck me like lightning. Suddenly I realized I had just been playing games with my family. If I were serious about trying to communicate with them, I would have to watch keenly for every fleeting chance to do so. Instead of trying to create those moments artificially, I would have to grasp every possible opportunity to bridge the gap by asking the right question at the right time.

I noticed how spontaneously my young neighbor responded to "the importance of now," even when the one asking questions was a small child. One day when we were having tea, her muddy 3-year-old son burst into the room, babbling about some question he wanted to ask. His mother excused herself, knelt down to get on an eye-level with the little boy, and listened carefully. Then she answered him as gravely as if he had been an adult. He nodded and trotted happily out of the room. When I commented on her patience with a rambling childish question she said, "I'm sure that question did sound silly, but right now it is the most important thing in the world to Peter." During their brief dialogue, the mother had conferred dignity on the child simply because she felt his needs to be as important as her own.

Thinking over my all-out attack on *Ask, don't tell,* I decided I had, by trial-and-error, learned a number of things. I sat down and made a list of what I now knew about the art of asking questions.

℞ FOR GOOD QUESTIONS

1. Grasp every possible chance to ask a searching question—*then keep quiet.* (When you're talking, *you're* not learning anything.)
2. One thoughtful question is worth a dozen inquisitive ones. The prod-and-pry approach makes people clam up fast.
3. Questions that come close to the other person's true interest get the best answers—provided the listener is interested, too.

4. Be prepared to wait. Sometimes a long silence can be more rewarding than plunging in with another question.
5. *In every case,* the quality of an answer depends on the quality of attention given by the questioner.
6. Questions must spring from honest inquiry, not from attempts at flattery or efforts to manipulate the other person's thinking.
7. Questions that deal with a person's *feelings* are more provocative than those dealing with *facts.*
8. A good questioner must really want to hear the answers, even if they are unpleasant.

I read and re-read my list. It seemed all right, as far as it went, but something essential was lacking. To my surprise, it was my high school boy who supplied the missing ingredient. Toby came downstairs one night after he had finished studying and announced, "I think Hamlet's an idiot."

"Why?"

"Because he's putty in his mother's hands."

I asked him to explain what he meant and he launched into a diatribe that was the beginning of a long, often heated, dialogue. We started out with Hamlet and Queen Gertrude, and ended with a lively discussion of the mother-and-son relationship. It was one of those rare and wonderful interludes when communication flows like wine.

The next morning at breakfast I said, "I enjoyed our conversation, Toby."

"Me, too," he mumbled, addressing the cereal bowl.

"Why was it so good?" I said. "When I asked you about the spring dance, you gave me the old deep freeze. What was different last night?"

Toby grinned at me. "Well," he said, "I guess it was because you weren't just leading me on. For once I knew you really cared."

There, I submit, in a simple sentence, is the essence of true communication: "You really cared." To ask good questions we have to care, and care very much, about what the other person feels and says. True dialogue begins when we really want to share another's thoughts, for only a listening, loving heart has power to penetrate the coat of armour that encases us.

Number of words 2394
See page 285 for Questions

Reading time in Seconds _____
See page 360 for Conversion Table

Conversation Is More Than Talk

Gelett Burgess

Conversation! Is it really a lost art? What general principles, if followed, can transform conversation into that rarity, good conversation? After all, conversing is something you do far more often than public speaking. That's why it's well worth reading and thinking about.

Good talkers are common, but good conversation is rare. Yet, like good manners, conversation is an essential requisite for anyone who wishes to be friends with those people who are usually most worth while. The man or woman who understands that good conversation is a social exchange of ideas is welcome everywhere.

There is a fundamental principle underlying good conversation. It is the basis of all good manners. This principle is the avoidance of friction in social contacts — a friction caused by irritation, boredom, envy, egotism, ridicule, and such emotions.

In San Francisco I once was a member of a small group which met weekly for the purpose, we proudly claimed, of reviving the lost art of conversation. Here are some of the rules we finally adopted that guided our talks and made our conversation a delightful game.

1. *Avoid all purely subjective talk.* Don't dilate on your intimately personal affairs — your health, your troubles, domestic affairs; and never, never discuss your wife or husband.

Streams of personal gossip and egotism destroy, in any group, all objective discussion — of art, science, history, timely topics, sports, or whatever. Such monologues not only bore the listener, but, as the talker is repeating only what he or she already knows, he learns nothing from others.

2. *Don't monopolize the conversation.* One of my friends long ago was a laughing, attractive person, who told stories well, with a mixture of highbrow terms and slang that was most amusing. But his stories were too long and too many. You roared with laughter, but after a while you grew restless and yearned for a more quiet, comfortable talk with plenty of give-and-take. You couldn't help remembering what old John Dryden said about those "who think too little, and who talk too much."

3. *Don't contradict.* Flat contradiction is another conversation-stopper. You may say, "I don't quite agree with that," but conversation, to be pleasant and profitable, should never descend to the level of emotional argument.

To get the most benefit from a conversation one should instead seek to find points of agreement. In that way, the subject develops in interest with each one's contribution to the discussion, and you both advance in knowledge. I had a postal-card correspondence with a friend, once, on the subject of God. We found we had so many ideas in common that, if I were not converted to his thought, my own thinking was considerably broadened.

4. *Don't interrupt.* Of course, when you toss a few grace notes into the talk such as, "How wonderful!" or "You mean she didn't know?" it doesn't throw the train of conversation off the track. But to interpolate views of your own is not only discourteous, but leaves what the speaker has to say unfinished when he perhaps hasn't yet made his point. Conversation is like an ordered dinner where each is served in turn. It should have rhythm and tempo to be gracious and truly social.

One perfect conversational dinner party is still alive in my memory. It was given in Boston by Mrs. James T. Fields, widow of the publisher who had entertained every visiting writer from Dickens to Kipling. There were present Mr. and Mrs. Thomas Bailey Aldrich; the brilliant Mrs. Bell, daughter of Rufus Choate; Bliss Perry, then editor of The Atlantic Monthly; and myself.

Six is the ideal number for an intimate dinner; if you have more the conversation is apt to break up into separate side dialogues. At Mrs. Fields' each of us talked and each of us listened. No one interrupted; no one contradicted; no one monologued. The affair had the charm and pleasing restfulness of music.

5. *Don't abruptly change the subject.* Some people virtually interrupt, after patiently and painfully waiting for a talker to cease, by jumping into the conversation with a new subject.

In our Conversation Club it was an unwritten rule that after one person had stopped talking there should be half a minute or so of silence in which to reflect, digest, and appreciate what had been said. It is the proper tribute to anyone who has offered an idea for consideration.

There is no surer way to make people like you than to pay them the compliment of interest and sympathy. Prolong their subject, ask more about it, and they expand like flowers in the sun. Yet what usually happens

---

Reprinted by permission of the author from *Your Life,* December 1947.

is that, should you venture to describe some misfortune or accident that has happened to you, they immediately narrate a similar mischance that they have suffered.

6. *Show an active interest in what is said*. You need not only your ears to listen well, but your eyes, hands, feet, and even posture. I have often tested the merits of a story or an article I have written by reading it aloud to one or two friends. What they said about it never helped me much since one often liked what another didn't.

But if their eyes went up to the ceiling, or to a picture on the wall, if their fingers moved or their feet tapped the floor or swung from a knee, I had indisputable evidence that the manuscript wasn't holding their interest and I marked the dull spots for revision.

And so in good conversation your social duty is to manifest an alert interest in what is said. It brings out the best in the speaker and it insures his confidence in your sympathy.

7. *After a diversion, return to the subject*. There is no surer test of being able to converse well than this. Often while a subject is not yet fully considered it is completely lost in some conversational detour. To reintroduce this forgotten topic is not only polite and gracious, but it is the best evidence of real interest.

If it is your own story, it is futile for you yourself to bring it back to persons who have by-passed it. Let it go, and see that you don't commit their error.

8. *Don't make dogmatic statements of opinion*. The Japanese tea ceremony, when gone through according to the old rules, was perhaps the most refined and idealistic social form ever practiced. Everything about the special tea house, every stone on the path to it, every gesture in partaking of the tea was strictly prescribed. It was a cult of simplicity and self-effacement.

One of the rules of behavior concerned conversation during the ritual. It was considered vulgar and inartistic for host or guest to make any definite, decisive statement. One might speak of anything — the symbolism of the one *kakemono* on the wall, perhaps, or the beauty of a flower arrangement — but never with an expression of finality. The remark was left up in the air, so to speak, for the next guest to enlarge upon or add to, so that no one was guilty of forcing any personal opinion upon the others.

It is a good game, but difficult; try it some time with your friends. The principle applies well to almost any conversation where opinions are concerned. You may state facts as facts; but your application of them should be tentative, with such qualifications as "In my opinion," or "It seems to me," or "Isn't it possible that . . .?"

If you associate with people of wisdom and understanding, you'll find they probably use such qualifying phrases, "with the meekness of wisdom," as St. James says, while the ignoramus is always for cut-and-dried pronouncements.

9. *Speak distinctly*. Even a bore can attain a certain consideration if he enunciates his words well, while another person with a great deal more intellect will not be listened to simply because he mumbles or whispers.

While I was a member of the executive committee of the Authors' League I was fascinated by the fact that one or two men were always listened to, while the others often had to force their way into the conversation. Those who spoke slowly dominated the meeting. High, hurried voices simply couldn't compete with Ellis Parker Butler's deliberate words, and his voice helped him maintain his leadership for years.

If you observe a group talking, you'll find that the one with a low, controlled voice always gets the most respect. The eager, temperamental contenders dash up against him like waves against a rock, and the rock always withstands them.

10. *Avoid destructive talk*. Did you ever attempt to live for a single day without saying anything destructive in tone? At a house party, long ago, I was one of half a dozen guests who agreed to try it. If one of us went to the window and said, "It looks like rain," there would be a whoop of glee, and a fine of one dollar. If you said you didn't like bananas, another dollar; and so on.

At the end of the day we agreed that nothing but optimism and Pollyanna was a good deal of a bore, and we liked a little pepper in our conversational soup; but we did realize for the first time how many quite unnecessary derogatory remarks we were all likely to make.

Evil, of course, must be condemned and opposed. But the unnecessary criticism, the desire to raise a laugh through ridicule, the general tendency to look on the unpleasant side of life, puts lines and a cynical expression in your face, and makes people shun you no matter how clever you are.

Now this little decalogue may seem simple, even axiomatic. But you will be amazed to find how often these primary rules are violated even by those who are supposed to be cultivated people, and how often their infringement causes unpleasantness.

So much for the negative side. What about the constructive view? How to create and maintain an agreeable conversation?

The secret is simple. To talk well one must think well. If you merely relate an incident that has happened — the facts in the case — it is nothing but anecdote. To make good conversation you must think underneath, above, and all around the subject.

This kind of thinking is well illustrated in the conversation of baseball enthusiasts. Are they content with telling the score, the number of base hits, errors, and home runs? Not at all. They discuss a team's potentialities, its comparison with another, the characteristics of the different players and their values, the theory and technique of the game. The same principle applies to all kinds of conversation.

Anyone who finds it hard to talk should learn to think about what he sees and hears and reads, and get something out of it. Ask why, and what it means. Discover what you can learn from it.

As you ponder, try to associate the subject with your own experience and observations and with ideas previously acquired.

Furthermore, if you mingle only with your own set or trade, your conversation inevitably degenerates into shop talk, or sport talk, or dress talk.

Get out of your rut and enlarge your interests by making acquaintances engaged in other pursuits. Develop a genuine curiosity about what is outside your ken, not a cheap inquisitiveness with regard to personalities. Join clubs. Join the church actively. Develop a hobby. Read up on subjects that have interested you. Study Spanish or nature or numerology — anything that has been outside your field of view.

If you fertilize and enrich your thinking in such ways you need not worry about being able to converse well. Every new experience will make your talk more interesting and more valuable.

Number of words 1930
See page 287 for Questions

Reading time in Seconds _____
See page 360 for Conversion Table

SELECTION 51

Man the Talker

Peter Farb

Language — what a mysterious part of our make-up. We can't even fathom its slow, ever-changing nature. Yet, as Washington Irving points out, some writers are proof against such change. Why? "Because they have rooted themselves in the unchanging principles of human nature." Human nature, linguistic creativity, grammar — for more about language, read on.

Some twenty-five hundred years ago, Psamtik, an Egyptian pharaoh, desired to discover man's primordial tongue. He entrusted two infants to an isolated shepherd and ordered that they should never hear a word spoken in any language. When the children were returned to the pharaoh several years later, he thought he heard them utter *bekos,* which means "bread" in Phrygian, a language of Asia Minor. And so he honored Phrygian as man's "natural" language. Linguists today know that the story of the pharaoh's experiment must be apocryphal. No child is capable of speech until he has heard other human beings speak, and even two infants reared together cannot develop a language from scratch. Nor does any single "natural" language exist. A child growing up anywhere on earth will speak the tongue he hears in his speech community, regardless of the race, nationality, or language of his parents.

Every native speaker is amazingly creative in the various strategies of speech interaction, in word play and verbal dueling, in exploiting a language's total re-

sources to create poetry and literature. Even a monosyllabic yes — spoken in a particular speech situation, with a certain tone of voice, and accompanied by an appropriate gesture — might constitute an original use of English. This sort of linguistic creativity is the birthright of every human being on earth, no matter what language he speaks, the kind of community he lives in, or his degree of intelligence. As Edward Sapir pointed out, when it comes to language "Plato walks with the Macedonian swineherd, Confucius with the headhunting savage of Assam."

And at a strictly grammatical level also, native speakers are unbelievably creative in language. Not every human being can play the violin, do calculus, jump high hurdles, or sail a canoe, no matter how excellent his teachers or how arduous his training — but every person constantly creates utterances never before spoken on earth. Incredible as it may seem at first thought, the sentence you just read possibly appeared in exactly this form for the first time in the history of the English language — and the same thing might be said about the sentence you are reading now. In fact, if conventional remarks — such as greetings, farewells, stock phrases like *thank you,* proverbs, clichés, and so forth — are disregarded, in theory all of a person's speech consists of sentences never before uttered.

A moment's reflection reveals why that may be so. Every language groups its vocabulary into a number of different classes such as nouns, verbs, adjectives, and so on. If English possessed a mere 1,000 nouns (such as *trees, children, horses*) and only 1,000 verbs (*grow, die, change*), the number of possible two-word sentences therefore would be 1,000 × 1,000, or one million. Of course, most of these sentences will be meaningless to a speaker today — yet at one time people thought *atoms split* was a meaningless utterance. The nouns, however, might also serve as the objects of these same verbs in three-word sentences. So with the same meager repertory of 1,000 nouns and 1,000 verbs capable of taking an object, the number of possible three-word sentences increases to 1,000 × 1,000 × 1,000, or one billion. These calculations, of course, are just for minimal sentences and an impoverished vocabulary. Most languages offer their speakers many times a thousand nouns and a thousand verbs, and in addition they possess other classes of words that function as adverbs, adjectives, articles, prepositions, and so on. Think, too, in terms of four-word, ten-word, even fifty-word sentences — and the number of possible grammatical combinations becomes astronomical. One linguist calculated that it would take 10,000,000,000,000 years (two thousand times the estimated age of the earth) to utter all the possible English sentences that use exactly twenty words. Therefore, it is improbable that any twenty-word sentence a person speaks was ever spoken previously — and the same thing would hold true, of course, for sentences of greater length, and for most shorter ones as well.

For a demonstration of just why the number of sentences that can be constructed in a language is, at least in theory, infinite, show twenty-five speakers of English a cartoon and ask them to describe in a single sentence what they see. Each of the twenty-five speakers will come up with a different sentence, perhaps examples similar to these:

> I see a little boy entering a magic and practical-joke shop to buy something and not noticing that the owner, a practical joker himself, has laid a booby trap for him.

> The cartoon shows an innocent little kid, who I guess is entering a magic shop because he wants to buy something, about to be captured in a trap by the owner of the shop, who has a diabolical expression on his face.

It has been calculated that the vocabulary and the grammatical structures used in only twenty-five such sentences about this cartoon might provide the raw material for nearly twenty *billion* grammatical sentences — a number so great that about forty human life spans would be needed to speak them, even at high speed. Obviously, no one could ever speak, read, or hear in his

lifetime more than the tiniest fraction of the possible sentences in his language. That is why almost every sentence in this book — as well as in all the books ever written or to be written — is possibly expressed in its exact form for the first time.

This view of creativity in the grammatical aspects of language is a very recent one. It is part of the revolution in ideas about the structure of language that has taken place since 1957, when Noam Chomsky, of the Massachusetts Institute of Technology, published his *Syntactic Structures*. Since then Chomsky and others have put forth a theory of language that bears little resemblance to the grammar most people learned in "grammar" school. Not all linguists accept Chomsky's theories. But his position, whether it is ultimately shown to be right or wrong, represents an influential school in theoretical linguistics today, one that other schools often measure themselves against.

Chomsky believes that all human beings possess at birth an innate capacity to acquire language. Such a capacity is biologically determined — that is, it belongs to what is usually termed "human nature" — and it is passed from parents to children as part of the offspring's biological inheritance. The innate capacity endows speakers with the general shape of human language, but it is not detailed enough to dictate the precise tongue each child will speak — which accounts for why different languages are spoken in the world. Chomsky states that no one learns a language by learning all of its possible sentences, since obviously that would require countless lifetimes. For example, it is unlikely that any of the speakers who saw the cartoon of the child entering the magic store ever encountered such a bizarre situation before — yet none of the speakers had any difficulty in constructing sentences about it. Nor would a linguist who wrote down these twenty-five sentences ever have heard them previously — yet he had no difficulty understanding them. So, instead of learning billions of sentences, a person unconsciously acquires a grammar that can generate an infinite number of new sentences in his language.

Such a grammar is innately within the competence of any native speaker of a language. However, no speaker — not even Shakespeare, Dante, Plato, or the David of the Psalms — lives up to his theoretical competence. His actual performance in speaking a language is considerably different, and it consists of numerous errors, hesitations, repetitions, and so forth. Despite these very uneven performances that a child hears all around him, in only a few years — and before he even receives instruction in reading and writing in "grammar" school — he puts together for himself the theoretical rules for the language spoken in his community. Since most sentences that a child hears are not only unique but also filled with errors, how can he ever learn the grammar of his language? Chomsky's answer is that children are born with the capacity to learn only grammars that accord with the innate human blueprint. Children disregard performance errors because such errors result in sentences that could not be described by such a grammar. Strong evidence exists that native speakers of a language know intuitively whether a sentence is grammatical or not. They usually cannot specify exactly what is wrong, and very possibly they make the same mistakes in their own speech, but they know — unconsciously, not as a set of rules they learned in school — when a sentence is incorrect.

Number of words 1420
See page 289 for Questions

Reading time in Seconds _____.
See page 360 for Conversion Table

SELECTION 52

America's Penniless Millionaire
Farnsworth Crowder

What can you do to become a millionaire? Do as Conwell did. Develop one *speech so inspiring that it will make you a fortune of five million. Then, after you've made your million, how do you make yourself a penniless millionaire? You'll soon find that out, too.*

Statistically, the most extraordinary speech of all time was a collection of two dozen true stories woven into an inspirational lecture called *Acres of Diamonds*. It had a "run" of fifty years; it was repeated no less than 6000 times to an audience of millions throughout the world. It crowded little provincial churches and packed the largest auditoriums in the biggest cities. It hypnotized gatherings of the widest diversity, from handfuls of prairie homesteaders in crossroads school houses to metropolitan assemblies of the elect. It drew fees ranging from a chicken dinner to $9000. Its net earnings, conservatively husbanded, easily could have built for its author a fortune of five million. That it did nothing of the sort was due to the fact that, as rapidly as the money rolled in, the author gave it away. During certain long periods, though he was making tens of thousands, he would rarely have more than a hundred ready dollars of his own at one time. Russell Herman Conwell was "America's penniless millionaire."

His fabulous lecture was a defense, by means of anecdotes, of the theme that the world is a vast acreage strewn with diamonds. The wise man snatches up the dull stone that others have been kicking around. He chips a corner to find an eye of blue-white fire looking at him and then laboriously polishes it down to the form of a splendid jewel.

Opportunity, said Conwell, is no chance visitor who knocks but once and flees. It stands, very possibly, in our own boots, wearing our own socks. It is in our own back yard. It sits on the door step beside the milk bottle, waiting to be brought in. It is here, now; not over the horizon, tomorrow. It wanders about in unlikely and forlorn and even trampish guises, while heedless people kick it aside in their frantic rush to find a spectacular golden goddess called Luck.

With respect to this particular deity, Russell Conwell was an atheist. "The most hopeless proposition in the world," he would say, "is the fellow who thinks that success is a door through which he will sometime stumble if he roams around long enough." Good Luck he would define as a product of purpose, will, training and industry; Bad Luck as a face-saving excuse rather than an explanation. Golden Apples were to him a harvest from hard work, not chance sports on neglected trees.

To support his thesis, he scarcely could have found a more pat illustration than his own life. He mined and minted his own Good Luck. It was said of him that he could see the promise and design of a mountain in a molehill and then bring the mountain into being. He uncovered opportunities on the most unexpected and discouraging sites. He could snatch up thin suggestions and develop them into monuments.

From earliest youth, he seemed to realize, with some compelling intuitive wisdom, that he must make the best of whatever raw material was under his own hat and within immediate reach of his hands. He might have to live in poverty on a Massachusetts rock pile that his father called a farm. He might have to get up at four in the morning and work like a man. There might be no well-staffed neighborhood school with a rich curriculum. But he could learn to read. He carried a book wherever he went, down the furrows, to the pasture, out to the barn. It was a habit he never broke and never ceased to advocate: "Remember, you can carry a university in your coat pocket."

He so far developed the power to read, and with it his memory, that he could fix a page in mind and later recall it, word for word, as if he held the book in his hand. The capacity of his memory became an astonishment to his friends: though he believed he had only an average memory given an extraordinary discipline.

He never allowed it to break training. He never practiced the gentle vices of loafing and wool-gathering. During his services with the Union Army, he employed idle hours to commit the whole of Blackstone. Years later, while commuting by train to and from his law offices in Boston, he learned to read five languages.

No time, no occasion, no suggestion was ever left unexploited. As a boy, he made the farm livestock his first audience. The power, as orator and preacher, which was to make him the platform peer of William J. Bryan, was first exercised in the chicken house.

By the time he entered Yale College, his habits of application and self-command enabled him to carry the academic and law courses simultaneously, while supporting himself with employment in a New Haven hotel. When the Civil War broke, it was as if he had anticipated the opportunity to become "the recruiting orator of the Berkshires." He raised and captained the Mountain Boys of Massachusetts and was later returned from the South to assemble a company of artillery.

There is an event of his military service which demonstrates his facility for laying hold of symbols, suggestions and incidents and fixing them tenaciously into the dynamic pattern of his life. A diminutive orderly, John Ring, attached to the company, became profoundly devoted to big fine-looking Captain Conwell — and to the Captain's sword, which represented, to John, both his beloved officer and all the glory of war. One day, near New Bern, a surprise Confederate advance routed the company from its position. Retreating across a river, the men fired a wooden bridge to cut off their pursuers. They had also cut off escape for their orderly: Johnnie Ring had dashed back to bring the Captain's sword. He appeared with it at last and gained the blazing bridge. But with clothes in flames he fell into the river. Dragged out and returned to consciousness, his first thought was for his Captain and the sword. He smiled to find it safe beside him, took it in his arms and died.

"When I stood over his body," Conwell recollected, "and realized that he had died for love of me, I made a vow that I would live, thereafter, not only my own life, but also the life of John Ring, that it might not be lost."

And from then on, for sixty years, Russell Conwell

literally worked a double day — eight hours for himself and eight for Johnnie. And always over the head of his bed hung the sword to keep bright his extravagant vow. That he kept it, one can well believe after a glance at a mere catalogue of his activities.

Following a European interlude to recover his health, broken by war injuries, he settled down to an intensive, versatile career in Boston. He opened two law offices in Boston. He lectured. He launched the Boston Young Men's Congress. He wrote editorials for the *Traveler*, corresponded for outside newspapers and went abroad frequently to interview celebrities. He managed a political campaign. He made money in real estate. He founded the *Journal* in suburban Somerville and maintained a free legal clinic for the poor.

Conwell had lost his first wife and had married again, a woman who freshened his interest in religious work. One day, an elderly lady visited his office for legal counsel on selling a distressed church property in Lexington. To give his advice, he journeyed out to a meeting of the discouraged and pastorless congregation. There was such melancholy in the little group, some of whom had worshiped there all their lives, that Conwell was moved to blurt, "Why sell it? Why not start over again!"

They objected that the structure was too dilapidated and money too dear. But young Conwell's eye for the hidden chance was wide awake and challenged. "You can make repairs," he shouted. "I'll help you!"

On the appointed day he borrowed tools and came out. No one else showed up, but he pitched in on the rickety front steps. A livery-stable proprietor of the town paused to ask what he was going to do. "Build a new church," Conwell answered. They fell to chatting and before he left, the man had pledged $100 toward a new building.

It was all the prospect that Russell Conwell needed to set imagination and energy to working. He made the hundred-dollar kernel grow. While the new church was going up, he preached to the congregation in rented rooms. Within eighteen months he had been ordained as their minister and had built around them a flourishing institution.

From Lexington he was invited to another hapless, debt-ridden little church in Philadelphia. He accepted and, characteristically, saw great possibilities in the discouraging new scene. The salary offered him was only $800, but the trustees stipulated that every time he could double the congregation, they would match the feat with a doubled salary. Six weeks after taking charge, Conwell had done it. Within six years he was drawing $10,000. Thereafter, he mercifully excused the trustees from their agreement. Had he held them to it, his salary would have climbed to over $25,000.

The popularity of his services was soon straining the capacity of the auditorium. One Sunday, from the many being turned away, he rescued a particularly unhappy little girl and saw her to a place inside. She was so grateful for the kindness and so distressed at the smallness of the room that she resolved to save her money for a building that would be big enough. Before she had advanced far on her grand project, she died. Her father turned over her fund, just fifty-seven cents in pennies.

Conwell reported the gift to his trustees. They were touched, but he was inspired. If $100 could be the nucleus of a building fund in Lexington, fifty-seven cents could do similar duty in Philadelphia! Accordingly, he went to the owner of a certain fine lot on Broad Street. The price was $10,000. Conwell made the outrageous offer of a down payment of fifty-seven cents. It was accepted. In due time the balance was paid off and upon that property, in 1891, was dedicated the largest church auditorium of its day.

The design of Russell Conwell's achievements might be called horticultural — the discovery of a seed; an uncanny insight into its fertility; a prodigious amount of work to make it grow.

From the modest ambitions of a young man came a university. Conwell was solicited for advice by a student who wanted to better his education, but was handicapped by having little money and a mother to support. As to all such, Conwell's first admonition was: "Read. Make a traveling library of your pocket." And then he added: "Come to me one evening a week and I'll begin teaching you to be a minister myself."

The first week, the student appeared with six friends in tow. The second week, forty were in the class. More volunteer teachers had to be invited. A house was rented. By the end of the first year, 250 were studying in this informal night college. A second house was hired. Buildings rose beside the great Temple church into the physical form of Temple University. "Our aim from the first," said President Conwell, "was to give education to those unable to get it through the usual channels." He lived to see more than 100,000 such pupils take work in his school.

Similar and equally unpretentious was Conwell's founding of Philadelphia's big Samaritan Hospital. Two rented rooms, one nurse, one patient. That was all. But it was enough for a beginning. In its expansion, the Samaritan acquired Goodheart Hospital and Garretson in the industrial quarter of the city and all became affiliated with Temple University.

But the heading up of a huge institutional church, a University and three hospitals was not enough for the dual capacities of Russell Conwell-Johnnie Ring. Out of the daily stint of sixteen hours was found the time to go on the platform for more than 8000 lectures — usually *Acres of Diamonds;* to maintain contacts with scores of the leading men of his time and with hundreds of the boys and girls he was helping through school; and to write thirty-seven volumes — biographies, travel books and legal treatises. In authorship, his vast reading and disciplined memory served him like a reference library. It was told that, on the train between lecture dates, without notes or books, he dictated a best-selling biography of Charles H. Spurgeon, the eminent evangelist, in twelve days.

His famous lecture was one more work developed from a rudiment. Any number of people might have heard — did hear — the story which an Arab guide along the Euphrates River was fond of telling. They might have thought it interesting, even worthy a place in their repertoire of traveler's tales. But to Russell Conwell's ears, it was dramatically suggestive; its lesson squared with his own philosophy of success; it could be made the germinal anecdote of a strong lecture.

The Arab's story was that of the wealthy and contented farmer, Ali Hafed, who was made to feel wretchedly poor and miserable by a visitor who infected him with a passion for diamonds. So covetous did Ali become that he sold the farm, abandoned his family and set out to prospect the world. And while he found no precious stones and at last threw his spent and starving body into the sea, the man who had purchased his farm discovered along its familiar stream beds the diamond mines of Golconda. "Ali would have been better off to remain at home and dig in his own cellar."

Throughout his lecture, Conwell hammered with his massive force at that simple moral. The impact of the message on many lives was crucial. As the years went by, testimonials poured in on him from governors, mayors, teachers, merchants, engineers and professionals, thanking him for the impetus his lecture had given their lives.

And from the thousands of college young people benefited by his largess came testimonials even more gratifying. Conwell was only thirty-three, and far from rich, when he determined to devote the proceeds of his lecturing to students fighting the kind of material odds and social discriminations he had experienced at Yale. His program of donations was continued for over forty years. He always kept a list of candidates for aid, most of them recommended by college presidents. His one rigid and unvarying requirement before extending help was that a student must be trying to help himself. He wanted his gifts to be, not chance windfalls, but premiums for diligent effort already made.

When, in 1925, Russell Conwell entered his eighty-second and last year, with all his enormous work behind him, books written, institutions founded and prospering, honors, degrees, prizes and medals to his name, there was one old-man satisfaction that he could not have. He could not mull over huge bank accounts and vast accumulated investments. He had distributed his fortune as he made it. He remarked, shortly before his death, that his riches lay in the men and women he had started on the road to accomplishment and happiness; and that was all, in the way of assets, he needed now.

Number of words 2530
See page 291 for Questions

Reading time in Seconds _____
See page 360 for Conversion Table

Your Voice Gives You Away

John E. Gibson

When you read a Sherlock Holmes story, you're supposed to be amazed at how the great detective notices things others never see. Take that intimate part of yourself, your voice. Does it take a Sherlock Holmes to unravel its secrets? No — apparently it reveals more about you than you think, much more than what you say.

Did you know that your voice can reveal how old you are, whether you're short or tall, fat or thin; whether you are an introvert or an extrovert? It's true! In fact, research conducted at leading universities and research centers has shown that in a surprisingly large percentage of cases, a person's voice even can reveal the general type of work he is engaged in. And tests at Harvard's psychological laboratories show that another person, just by listening to your voice, can judge your personality traits—and be right 90 per cent of the time!

It has been scientifically established by studies conducted both in the U.S. and Britain that a person's voice can give an incredibly accurate picture of many of his mental and physical characteristics. To test these findings, the Psychological Institute of the University of Vienna conducted a fascinating experiment.

The voices of nine persons who differed widely in age, personality, and occupation, were broadcast from a radio station. Questionnaires were distributed in advance to the radio audience, announcing the experiment, and requesting the audience to listen carefully to each of the nine voices, and then judge the age, physical appearance, personality, and vocation of the speakers. This information was to be written on the questionnaire form, and mailed back to the university.

The speakers whose voices were broadcast were: a stenographer (age 27), a college professor (age 48), a tavern keeper (age 53), a minister (age 58), a grade-school teacher (age 39), a mathematician (a woman, age 46), a taxi driver (age 30), a boy (age 12), and a girl (age 14).

At the time set for the broadcast, each of these persons stood before a microphone and read aloud from a script for two minutes. Then followed a period of organ music, during which members of the listening audience were requested to write down their judgments on the form provided for the purpose.

Twenty-seven hundred listeners sent in completely filled-out questionnaires. Analysis of these revealed a strikingly large percentage of correct judgments. The average estimate of the age of the speakers was almost "on the nose" in a number of cases. For example, the average guess for the 27-year-old stenographer was 26; average guess for the 39-year-old school teacher was

38; and most listeners were only two years off in estimating the boy's age.

In judging the age of the persons who were over 45 however, the estimates tended to be less accurate. The investigators' conclusions: age can be judged by a person's voice with a high degree of accuracy until he or she reaches middle age. After that the voice tends to sound younger than the person actually is.

So far as judging temperament and physique were concerned, the psychologists found that the average guess was remarkably accurate—except in the case of the taxi driver and the two children. In all of the other cases the listeners were able to classify the speakers' builds correctly and make accurate judgments as to their personality characteristics.

An astonishingly high percentage of the radio listeners was able to correctly classify the speakers' occupation—just, mind you, by listening to their voices. Almost half judged the professor to be a member of the academic profession.

From 27 per cent to 35 per cent of the listeners put the mathematician, tavern keeper, minister, and the school teacher in the right occupational bracket. And as for the taxi driver—out of the 2,700 persons who filled out the questionnaires, over *2,000* judged his occupation correctly!

The only one they didn't do so well on was the stenographer. Ninety-three per cent guessed her to be just about everything but what she was. Most, however, did come within a year of guessing her age—and made substantially accurate judgments as to her body build and temperament.

A number of the radio listeners who participated in the experiment were totally blind. And it is extremely interesting to note that they were invariably more accurate in their judgments than the others. This fact is easily explained. When a person loses his sight, his other senses, including hearing, seem to become more sensitive and acute because he places greater reliance upon them.

Impressed by the findings of the Vienna study, Harvard University scientists conducted a similar test in the United States. They installed complete broadcasting equipment in the psychological laboratory and broadcast the voices of 18 speakers—each carefully selected for the experiment. Listeners were asked to make judgments regarding each speaker's age, temperament, vocation, etc. A total of 587 responded.

The results more than corroborated the conclusions of the University of Vienna investigators. In the majority of cases, the average guess for a speaker's age came within a year of hitting the exact mark—when the speakers were under 40.

But, as in the Vienna experiment, speakers past middle age tended to sound younger than they were. The listeners also showed a marked ability to classify occupations correctly. They also were able to successfully match sketches of the speakers—which were distributed—with their voices. And a majority were able to judge which of the voices belonged to introverts and which to extroverts.

Most striking evidence of the extent to which a person's voice reveals both appearance and personality was furnished by a further test in which the judges were asked to decide whether each speaker was "moody," "nervous," "precise," "dapper," and so on. *Ninety-one per cent of the judgments were wholly correct!*

Another interesting point brought out by the Harvard study was that when tests were repeated, using a curtain rather than the radio to conceal the speaker, the listeners were about seven per cent more accurate in their judgments. This finding, the investigators believe, indicates that a slight degree of distortion was produced when the voices were transmitted over the radio.

Another test to determine what your voice reveals about you was conducted at DePauw University. Voices were broadcast over a public address system, and students were asked to identify the body build of the speakers. It was found that the easiest type to identify by voice alone was the person who is tall and slender; the short, stocky type ranked a close second.

Only type that couldn't be identified with a high degree of accuracy was the well-proportioned, or "athletic" build. That the tone of a short, stocky (pyknic type) individual tends to differ appreciably from the leptosome (tall, thin), and from the athletic type, was borne out by the DePauw tests. (Editor's Note: However, the nuances of timbre, modulation and tonal qualities are too subtle for accurate verbal description in this article.)

The study also showed that certain professions can be judged better than others from the individual's voice. It was found, for example, that it's easier to identify a preacher or a lawyer than it is a musician or a detective.

To what extent a man's voice gives away his thoughts has not yet been scientifically established. But university tests have shown that in most cases you can tell whether a person is lying or not—just from the way his voice sounds!

Student subjects at DePauw were asked to label the statements of hidden speakers as "the truth" or "a lie." The speakers then made statements about themselves, such as "I'm wearing a green tie," or "My name is Fred," or "I had ham and eggs for breakfast," etc. In the majority of instances the listeners were able to correctly label each statement as being true or false.

The women subjects turned in a higher percentage of correct judgments than the men did. And another phase of the test showed that when a woman tells an untruth, her voice doesn't give her away to the extent that a man's does!

Psychologists have demonstrated that a person's voice frequently reveals things about him which ordinarily could be ascertained only by psychoanalysis. Studies at Kent State University, Kent, Ohio, for example, have shown that an unpleasant voice indicates the likelihood of neurotic tendencies.

Analysis of hundreds of men and women showed that pleasant-voiced individuals tend to be better adjusted. The studies indicated that voices of persons with neurotic tendencies tend to fall into three different categories: (1) breathy, (2) nasal whine, (3) harsh and metallic. The whiny-voiced individuals are found to be the most emotionally unstable.

At Brooklyn College, students whose voices were classified as harsh and unpleasant were given clinical examinations. In about three-fourths of the cases investigators found no direct physical cause. But when personality tests were administered, almost half of the subjects were found to be definitely maladjusted. The study further showed that when better personality adjustment was brought about, the unpleasant quality in the subject's voice tended to disappear.

There are many types of unpleasant voices, and all of them have been found to indicate, to a greater or lesser extent, the likelihood of neurosis. Take, for example, the person who speaks in a dull monotone. Stanford University investigations show that these individuals are, more often than not, lacking in mental and emotional stability.

In a recent Smith College study, a group of fifth-grade children who spoke in a continuous and unvaried monotone, was selected for careful personality analysis. *It was found that 100 per cent of the group was definitely maladjusted!* This does not mean, of course, that every person who speaks in a monotone possesses neurotic tendencies. But it does suggest that a strong likelihood does exist in a high percentage of the cases.

Dr. Paul J. Moses of Stanford University Medical School, has made a study of thousands of voice recordings and related them to the personal characteristics of the speakers. His conclusions are in general agreement with those of other studies cited in this article.

Indeed, he finds that the human voice offers so many vital clues to an individual's make-up and temperament, as to be of value to both layman and specialist in assessing the personality of their fellowmen!

Number of words 1660
See page 293 for Questions

Reading time in Seconds _____
See page 360 for Conversion Table

SELECTION 54

We Quit Talking — and Now the Cupboard Is Bare

Ewart A. Autry

Ambrose Bierce, in his book The Devil's Dictionary, *defines the word* bore. *A bore is "a person who talks when you wish him to listen." That suggests that listening is the communication key to social acceptance. Here's a married couple to show you both the advantages and disadvantages of listening.*

"We're talking too much," my wife announced one morning at breakfast. "But these are the first words we've said since we sat down," I protested. "I mean when we're out in public or have company," she explained. "We carry too much of the conversation. It must bore others."

I thought it over. "Well," I finally agreed, "it's true we rarely run out of words."

"And we're always eager to get them in," she continued. "We talk so much that people learn everything about us while we're learning nothing about them. So let's do something about it."

"Tape our lips?" I suggested.

She ignored that, with reason. "Let's agree to limit our part of the conversation when others are around," she said. "We'll set up some signals. When you think I'm talking too much just touch your forehead and I'll slow down. When I think you're talking too much, I'll use the same signal."

I was skeptical but willing to try. So we did. On our very next visitor.

It wasn't a successful experiment. He was a phlegmatic neighbor who never used any more words than were absolutely necessary. That, coupled with our resolve to let guests carry most of the conversation, produced long, awkward silences. Intermittently the three of us stared into our open fire and there was little sound except the crackling of my hickory logs. When our visitor had gone, my wife looked chagrined. "I kept hoping you'd talk," she said, "but I didn't know how to get you started. The only signal we agreed on was the one to cut down on the talking."

There was another repercussion from that fiasco. Our visitor reported to the neighbors that we weren't well and they kept calling to inquire about our health. "That's some reputation to have," I grumbled. "When we don't rattle on all the time, people think we're sick."

Most visitors, though, unknowingly cooperated with our new scheme. They kept the conversation rolling with no more than an occasional word from us. It was amazing how much some people talked. I commented on it one day after a visit from Dan and Ina Blake. "Dan was really wound up," I said. "I thought he'd never finish that story about the big bass he caught Christmas day."

"This is the first chance he's had to finish it," advised my wife. "Always before you've interrupted to tell some wild fish story of your own."

"And I noticed Ina got in the full account of her latest operation," I retorted. "Other times you've put your stitches in before she could even begin on hers."

"It takes will power to keep your mouth shut," said my wife thoughtfully. "Especially when you have something more interesting to tell than what's being told."

The signals actually worked well and we didn't have to use them too often. But sometimes we'd let our tongues get ahead of our brains. Like when I was telling Don Duke about a bass I'd hooked. The fish was weighing about nine pounds and I had him on the way to the boat when I saw my wife touch her forehead. I immediately cut the bass down to three pounds and let him get away.

Then there's the time my wife was telling some friends about a recent vacation trip to the ocean. She was waxing poetic as she described a sunset over the water. I noticed our visitors beginning to wiggle restlessly, so I caught her eye and touched my forehead. You never saw a sun drop so quickly into the sea.

There were times when others noticed our signals. Once we were visiting friends and I was talking too much. My wife touched her forehead. When I didn't react immediately she kept touching it. In a few minutes our hostess left the room and returned with a glass of water and an aspirin. "You poor thing," she said to my wife. "You have a headache. Take this."

A few days later I had a bad crick in my neck. I went to a doctor who is a family friend. At his invitation my wife came into the consultation room. She began to tell him my various symptoms. I thought she was telling too much so I touched my forehead. The

Reprinted from *Minutes,* Magazine of Nationwide Insurance, Fall 1970.

doctor noticed it immediately. "Ah, ha," he said. "Just as I thought. You have sinus trouble."

He tilted my chin and sprayed my nose with the hottest stuff I ever felt. My eyes watered for an hour. But I must have touched the right spot. My neck was better before we got home.

Our talk curb has been in effect for a year now. We've talked less and heard more. Not all of it has been worthwhile but at least it's been as good as some of the stuff we were putting out.

And we've learned one thing for certain — talk less and you'll have more company. More people came to our house this past year than in any of the thirty we've been married. One of our regular visitors said why. "I like to visit here," he beamed. "You're interesting people to talk to."

"To." Not "with."

We have a problem though. Much of our company has been at mealtime. Sometimes our pantry has been stripped to the danger point. Right now we're trying to decide whether to buy more groceries each week or forget our conversation moratorium.

When I mention the second possibility, my wife gets an eager gleam in her eyes. And come to think of it, there are a few things I'd like to say too. So, if you're planning to come to our house, you'd better hurry. Before we start talking again.

Number of words 950
See page 295 for Questions

Reading time in Seconds _____
See page 360 for Conversion Table

SELECTION 55

The Listener

John Berry

You may not understand French, Italian, Spanish, or Russian; still you can enjoy music from any of those countries. There are no language barriers. Music is indeed a universal language. But do you actually respond to music as if that were so — as if music spoke to you? Does the listener in this story?

Once there was a puny little Czech concert violinist named Rudolf, who lived in Sweden.* Some of his friends thought he was not the best of musicians because he was restless; others thought he was restless because he was not the best of musicians. At any rate, he hit upon a way of making a living, with no competitors. Whether by choice or necessity, he used to sail about Scandinavia in his small boat, all alone, giving concerts in little seaport towns. If he found accompanists, well and good; if not, he played works for unaccompanied violin; and it happened once or twice that he wanted a piano so badly that he imagined one, and then he played whole sonatas for violin and piano, with no piano in sight.

One year Rudolf sailed all the way out to Iceland and began working his way around that rocky coast from one town to another. It was a hard, stubborn land; but people in those difficult places do not forget the law of hospitality to the stranger — for their God may decree that they too shall become strangers on the face of the earth. The audiences were small, and even if Rudolf had been really first-rate, they would not have been very demonstrative. From ancient times their energy had gone, first of all, into earnest toil. Sometimes they were collected by the local schoolteacher, who reminded them of their duty to the names of Beethoven and Bach and Mozart and one or two others whose music perhaps was not much heard in those parts. Too often people sat stolidly watching the noisy little fiddler, and went home feeling gravely edified. But they paid.

As Rudolf was sailing from one town to the next along a sparsely settled shore, the northeast turned black and menacing. A storm was bearing down upon Iceland. Rudolf was rounding a bleak, dangerous cape, and his map told him that the nearest harbor was half a day's journey away. He was starting to worry when he saw, less than a mile offshore, a lighthouse on a tiny rock island. At the base of the lighthouse was a deep, narrow cove, protected by cliffs. With some difficulty, in the rising seas, he put in there and moored to an iron ring that hung from the cliff. A flight of stairs, hewn out of the rock, led up to the lighthouse. On top of the cliff, outlined against the scudding clouds, stood a man.

"You are welcome!" the voice boomed over the sound of the waves that were already beginning to break over the island.

Darkness fell quickly. The lighthouse keeper led his

From *New World Writing*, #16. Copyright © 1960, by J. B. Lippincott Company. Published by J. B. Lippincott Company.
* Karl Almegaard told me this story. If it were not true, he would not have told it to me.

guest up the spiral stairs to the living room on the third floor, then busied himself in preparation for the storm. Above all, he had to attend to the great lamp in the tower, that dominated the whole region. It was a continuous light, intensified by reflectors, and eclipsed by shutters at regular intervals. The duration of light was equal to that of darkness.

The lighthouse keeper was a huge old man with a grizzled beard that came down over his chest. Slow, deliberate, bearlike, he moved without wasted motion about the limited world of which he was the master. He spoke little, as if words had not much importance compared to the other forces that comprised his life. Yet he was equable, as those elements were not.

After the supper of black bread and boiled potatoes, herring, cheese and hot tea, which they took in the kitchen above the living room, the two men sat and contemplated each other's presence. Above them was the maintenance room, and above that the great lamp spoke majestic, silent messages of light to the ships at sea. The storm hammered like a battering ram on the walls of the lighthouse. Rudolf offered tobacco, feeling suddenly immature as he did so. The old man smiled a little as he declined it by a slight movement of the head; it was as if he knew well the uses of tobacco and the need for offering it, and affirmed it all, yet — here he, too, was halfway apologetic — was self-contained and without need of anything that was not already within his power or to which he did not relinquish his power. And he sat there, gentle and reflective, his great workman hands resting on outspread thighs.

It seemed to Rudolf that the lighthouse keeper was entirely aware of all the sounds of the storm and of its violent impact upon the lighthouse, but he knew them so well that he did not have to think about them; they were like the involuntary movements of his own heart and blood. In the same way, beneath the simple courtesy that made him speak and listen to his guest in specific ways, he was already *calmly* and mysteriously a part of him, as surely as the mainland was connected with the little island, and all the islands with one another, so commodiously, under the ocean.

Gradually Rudolf drew forth the sparse data of the old man's life: He had been born in this very lighthouse eighty-three years before, when his father was the lighthouse keeper. His mother — the only woman he had ever known — had taught him to read the Bible, and he read it daily. He had no other books.

As a musician, Rudolf had not had time to read much either — but then, he had lived in cities. He reached down and took his beloved violin out of its case.

"What do you make with that, sir?" the old man asked.

For a second Rudolf thought his host might be joking; but the serenity of the other's expression reassured him. There was not even curiosity about the instrument, but rather a whole interest in him, the person, that included his "work." In most circumstances Rudolf would have found it hard to believe that there could exist someone who did not know what a violin was; yet now he had no inclination to laugh. He felt small and inadequate.

"I make —music with it," he stammered in a low voice.

"Music," the old man said ponderously. "I have heard of it. But I have never seen music."

"One does not see music. One hears it."

"Ah, yes," the lighthouse keeper consented, as it were with humility. This too was in the Nature of Things wherein all works were wonders, and all things were known eternally and were poignant in their transiency. His wide gray eyes rested upon the little fiddler and conferred upon him all the importance of which any individual is capable.

Then something in the storm and the lighthouse and the old man exalted Rudolf, filled him with compassion and love and a spaciousness infinitely beyond himself. He wanted to strike a work of fire and stars into being for the old man. And, with the storm as his accompanist, he stood and began to play — the Kreutzer Sonata of Beethoven.

The moments passed, moments that were days in the creation of that world of fire and stars: abysses and heights of passionate struggle, the Idea of Order, and the resolution of these in the greatness of the human spirit. Never before had Rudolf played with such mastery — or with such an accompanist. Waves and wind beat the tower with giant hands. Steadily above them the beacon blazed in its sure cycles of darkness and light. The last note ceased and Rudolf dropped his head on his chest, breathing hard. The ocean seethed over the island with a roar as of many voices.

The old man had sat unmoving through the work, his broad, gnarled hands resting on his thighs, his head bowed, listening massively. For some time he continued to sit in silence. Then he looked up, lifted those hands calmly, judiciously, and nodded his head.

"Yes," he said. "That is true."

On Listening and Not Listening
Lyman K. Steil

In 1979, interest in listening led the author of this article to organize the International Listening Association. Its purpose? To promote the study and development of effective listening. How important is listening? Let Dr. Steil answer that question. He's uniquely qualified to do just that.

An insurance agent called his company for background on a potential client and received instructions not to insure him — he was a bad risk. But the agent misunderstood. He thought his company had given him the go-ahead, and drew up a contract for multimillion dollar coverage. A few months later the client filed a substantial claim. The insurance company was forced to pay and the agent lost his job.

A phone conversation overheard in the Seattle airport: "Guess what!" said the man in the booth next to mine. "I'm not supposed to be here until tomorrow. I could have sworn they told me to come today." "What will you do?" the voice at the other end must have asked. "What can I do?" said the man. "I'll stay overnight and absorb the cost."

On an airplane recently, I talked with the president of a small company. I asked whether his firm had experienced any problems because of employees' inability or failure to listen. The man's eyebrows went up. He told me how the company had recently lost a million dollar sale. "Two of my employees were involved," he said. "One didn't hear the important message at all, and the other one misinterpreted it. The upshot was that we lost out on a bid that we should have won hands down."

The incidents differ, but there is a common denominator: In each case someone failed to listen. A mistake was made. Money was lost. With more than 100 million workers in this country, a simple $10 mistake by each of them as a result of poor listening adds up to a cost of a billion dollars. And most people make more than one listening mistake every day.

My point is this: The failure or the inability to listen has costs associated with it — in time, relationships and productivity. And what is the price of an idea not heard? These are avoidable costs, which, to the extent avoided, have a direct impact on the profit and loss statement.

Don't be misled: Listening problems aren't limited to the workaday world. Actually, bad listening habits encroach deeply into the territory of our personal lives too. It's just that business is more noticeably vulnerable to the quantitative results of a bad habit. Dollars are lost, and that affects the bottom line. With all of the computerization in businesses today, large and small, the automation, and the organizational and management counseling that is available, it's both heartening and discouraging to know that a simple human error, an "I forgot," or "I thought you said you were going to mail the proposal," are still at the heart of our enterprise.

Indeed, the effects of bad listening are to be seen all around us: The sinking of the *Titanic,* Pearl Harbor, the Jonestown, Guyana incident, the MGM Grand fire and some of the recent airplane disasters, though dramatic, are classic examples of a breakdown in communication. A message was sent, listening failed, and lives were lost.

And poor listening affects our emotional lives. Parenting and marriage provide examples most of us understand. Listening audits show that respondents usually rate themselves as poorer listeners with spouses than with friends or business associates. But even sadder is that while newlyweds rate each other very highly as listeners — close to the level of best friend, which ranks highest — that ranking falls steadily downhill as the marriage goes on. In a household where the couple has been married for 50 years, chances are that while there may be a lot of talking going on, very little listening will be going on to reciprocate. The result? Clearly, a great many of the one million divorces each year are related to the inability or unwillingness to listen.

With all the talk about poor communication being at the root of so many ills, there is surprisingly little thought given to what that means. Communication is most often considered something we do unto others, when actually about half of that activity has to do with the willingness to receive from others: People spend about 80 per cent of their waking hours communicating, and about 45 per cent of that time is spent listening. And most people, even by their own admission, are at best average listeners.

After hearing a ten-minute oral presentation, the average listener has heard, understood, properly evaluated and retained only half of what was said, according to some studies. Within another 48 hours that drops off another 50 per cent, meaning that an audience only effectively comprehends and retains one-quarter of what is said.

By Dr. Lyman K. Steil, President, Communication Development, Inc., 25 Robb Farm Road, St. Paul, Minnesota 55110. Reprinted by permission.

Back to business. Add the chain of command of a large corporation to the statistics on how humans misconstrue messages: Ideas can be distorted by as much as 80 per cent as they're stretched, condensed, twisted and hurried along the sometimes tortuous organizational path. The cost of that distortion is more than dollars. Productivity is affected and profits suffer. Letters have to be retyped, appointments rescheduled, shipments rerouted. And as many married couples feel increasingly distant and alienated from one another, employees can feel distant from the objectives of a department or the goals of a corporation, and ultimately feel alienated from its day-to-day operations.

For each of us, one of our greatest needs is to be listened to.

The solution? Unfortunately, that activity which we do most in life — listening — is taught least. This is unfortunate because listening is so much more complex than say, reading. What we read is locked on the printed page. If you're distracted, you can put it aside and return to it later. If you don't understand, you can read it over again. But in listening, the message is written on the wind. If you don't get it the first time, there's no going back.

Fortunately, listening *can* be taught. People aren't born good listeners. Listening is learned. If you exercise the listening muscles, your listening skills will improve. A number of primary and secondary schools — still the exceptions — are teaching listening, along with the old standards reading, writing, and arithmetic. After all, students spend 60–70 per cent of classroom time *listening* to what the teacher is saying. Hundreds of companies are recognizing the same need.

One study of the 20 most critical managerial competencies lists "Listen Actively" at the very top. In comparison, number two on the list is "Give Clear, Effective Instructions." Number five, "Manage Time and Set Priorities"; number twelve, "Write Effectively"; and number twenty, still listed as a critical activity, "Participate in Seminars and Read."

The higher one advances in management, the more critical listening skill becomes. It's the heart of success. But like everyone else, managers often don't hear the messages of others. They may be busy, preoccupied, distracted, or they misunderstand and don't respond.

Poppycock to the individual who says, "When I need to listen well, or when I want to listen well, I can will myself to listen." More than three decades of research proves that we can only listen at any moment at the level of skill we've developed. For most of us, that's simply not good enough. We cannot simply "will" ourselves to listen well.

Listening is more complex than wills and won'ts and dos and don'ts. *There is no quick fix.* Hearing is only the beginning. There's also interpretation, which leads to understanding or misunderstanding. There's evaluation, which is when you decide how to use the information, and then there's the reaction itself. Taken together, that's listening.

Whether it be a company-wide effort, sales training, or a separate group project, much can be done to improve one of the most mutually endearing — and necessary — of our human attributes, the ability to listen. And the benefits of better listening far outweigh the costs.

Semper bene ausculpabis!

Number of words 1290
See page 299 for Questions

Reading time in Seconds _____
See page 360 for Conversion Table

SELECTION 57

Are You a Good Listener?

Robert L. Montgomery

Zeno, the old Greek philosopher, once argued the importance of listening with rather startling logic. He said, "We have two ears and one mouth that we may listen the more and speak the less." Despite that questionable logic, Zeno was right — we actually do listen more and speak, read, or write less — which brings us to the question "How well do you listen?"

Do you listen to others as you like to be listened to? It takes skill and determination to speak, but it takes even more skill and determination to listen to others. It also takes energy.

We listen more than we do any other human activity except breathe. Listening is essential to our personal, professional, social and family success. If working people were taught to listen effectively, the efficiency of American business could be doubled.

Listening is the most neglected and the least understood of the communications arts. It has become the weakest link in today's communications system. Poor listening is a result of bad habits that develop because we haven't been trained to listen. Fortunately, it is a skill that can be learned.

Here are six basic guidelines for better listening. You can improve your listening the day you start practicing them.

First, look at the other person. Look at the person who is talking to you. Also, always look at the person you're talking to. Looking directly at the person who is speaking shows dynamic interest. I don't mean staring at the other person, just looking into his or her eyes, but looking toward the person as he or she talks to you. You can look at the hairline, the neckline, watch the mouth as the person speaks, even notice the color of the eyes of the speaker.

But don't look at the floor or ceiling or out the window. And don't turn your eyes to view every distraction around you. People tell me they don't trust the person who doesn't look at them. They also sense suspicion, trickery or distrust from such people. And distrust will block communication. It's a huge block also to motivation. There's little or no motivation when there is no respect. Concentrate on the other person as you listen. Looking at the person will enable you to judge the intent of the message as well as the content. So give your undivided attention as you listen to others. If you project genuine, active attention, you will convey sincere interest. When the eyes are elsewhere, the mind is elsewhere.

Rule 2 is ask questions. This is the best way for anyone to become a better listener fast. It's a necessity for parents, teachers, managers and salespeople. To keep from doing all the speaking yourself and to get the other person talking, develop the tools of the reporter, the art of asking questions. Master the different types of questions you'll learn now. Start using them today. Practice is the best instructor.

Some types of questions help you discover facts. You might want to know where someone works or lives, what they do, where they're from. Questions that get specific, concise facts for answers are called closed-end questions. You rarely get more than a word or two in reply. "What is your name?" is one example. "How old are you?" is another.

The opposite type is called open-ended questioning. You can find out most of the facts about a person by asking just one or two open-ended questions. For example, I might ask you, "How did you get into the line of work you're in now?" That question will usually get a person talking for at least five minutes and more likely for 15. Of course, you could simply say to someone, "Tell me about yourself." That's open-ended and will accomplish the same purpose.

I've often wondered how many sales are lost each week because the salesperson doesn't listen to the prospect or customer. There has been a revolution in selling. The change has taken us from the product-pusher of the past to the counselor-type salesperson who asks questions first. Contrary to the belief of many people, you actually save time and make the sale faster by asking the prospect some questions to discover his or her needs, problems or objectives.

To illustrate the power of questions, I think of the experience of a famous sales trainer and speaker, the late Fred Herman. Herman was introduced on the Mike Douglas television show one day as "the greatest salesman in the world." What happened next was purely spontaneous; Herman vowed he had no idea what Mike Douglas would ask him.

Douglas began by saying, "Fred, since you're hailed as the No. 1 salesman in the world, sell me something!" Without any hesitation, Fred Herman responded instantly and instinctively with a question: "Mike, what would you want me to sell you?"

Mike Douglas, who is paid a couple of million dollars a year for asking questions, was now on the defensive. Surprised, Douglas paused, looked around and finally answered, "Well, sell me this ashtray."

Fred Herman again spoke instantly, "Why would you want to buy that?" And again, Mike Douglas, surprised and scratching his head, finally answered, "Well, it's new and shapely. Also, it's colorful. And besides, we are in a new studio and don't want it to burn down. And, of course, we want to accommodate guests who smoke."

At this point, Mike Douglas sat back in his chair, but not for long. Instantly Fred Herman responded, "How much would you pay for the ashtray, Mike?"

Douglas stammered and said, "Well, I haven't bought an ashtray lately, but this one is attractive and large, so I guess I'd pay $18 or $20." And Fred Herman, after asking just three questions, closed the sale by saying, "Well, Mike I'll let you have the ashtray for $18."

That's selling by questioning and listening. I call it selling with a professional ear. The whole sale took less than one minute. Fred Herman said he simply reacted as he always does in selling, by asking questions.

Make it your personal goal to ask a lot of questions. But have a purpose for each question. There are two basic categories: to get specific information or to learn opinions and feelings. It's easier to gain rapport and get a person to open up by relating your questions to the other person's background or experience. Use open-ended questions to draw out. Remember, closed-end questions will make it difficult to get another person to speak and share ideas or information. Nobody likes to feel he's being investigated.

Finally, remember the advice of the famous statesman of some years ago, Bernard Baruch, who said: "You can win more friends in two months by showing interest in others than you can in two years by trying to interest others in you." Looking at people as you converse with them and asking questions will help show genuine interest.

Rule 3 is don't interrupt. It's just as rude to step on people's ideas as to step on their toes.

It's a human tendency to want to jump right into a conversation when we get an idea or are reminded of something by someone's words. And that's why there's a problem. We need to continually practice letting other people finish their sentences or ideas. Speak only in turn is the answer.

Most of us avoid interrupters. We even go out of our way to avoid them. In fact, a desire to prevent interruptions motivated Thomas Jefferson to invent the dumbwaiter, a mechanical lift to take food and drink by pulley from the kitchen to an upstairs dining room. Jefferson disliked being interrupted in conversation by servants; with the dumbwaiter, no servants were necessary and he couldn't be interrupted.

Nobody likes to be cut off while speaking. So work at letting others finish what they have to say. Bite your tongue and count to 10 if you have to, but practice Rule 3.

Rule 4 is don't change the subject. This is a little different from Rule 3. Interrupting is bad enough, but going right on and changing the subject at the same time is positively rude. Some people do this so much they are dodged by others who don't want to be their next victim.

Consider a group of people who are talking and one of the members says, "I was watching television the other night and Sen. Hayakawa of California spoke about . . ." Now at this point another member of the group, hearing the word *California,* interrupts immediately and changes the subject. "Oh, California, have you been out there to Disneyland? It's terrific! We took the kids there last summer and had a ball. You know, they have an island there, Tom Sawyer Island. And they have tree houses, caves, all kinds of things to do. Why, you could spend a couple of days there. You get to the island on a raft or one of those old Mississippi steamboats. Boy, it was just like being Robinson Crusoe on that island. Now what were you saying?"

Well, the speaker who was going to say something about Sen. Hayakawa of California has no doubt buried that idea forever. In fact, the person who was cut off will not offer any more ideas and will probably find a reason to get out of the presence of the interrupter who also changed the subject.

Interrupting and changing the subject are sure ways to alienate people quickly. So try to curb both tendencies. You can be certain of this: If you cut people off while they're speaking and also change the subject, you'll be cutting them out of your life as friends or associates as well. A little restraint will pay big dividends.

Rule 5 is to check your emotions. Some people are prone to anger and get excited about certain words. It doesn't pay to get overstimulated and overreact to the words and ideas of others.

Words such as gasoline, taxes, 7 percent, abortion and communism can stir one's emotions instantly. Curb your emotions. Control your urge to interrupt and stifle the other person's idea. It's a free country. People are entitled to their opinions and the right to complete their thoughts. Hear others out.

Let them explain their points of view. Cutting them off won't accomplish anything. Try to understand them first. Then give your own ideas in a controlled manner. Little is gained through arguing and fighting. On the contrary, loss of time and injured relationships usually result.

Evaluate when the idea is complete, not before, or only when you fully understand the other person's meaning.

I know a fellow who went storming into his boss' office. He was shouting and complaining that someone not as long with the company had received a promotion he thought he should have gotten. The boss told him that because of his quick temper he couldn't be trusted to manage others.

Besides, getting overly excited causes us to mentally debate or fight any idea that differs from our personal conviction, experience or bias. So we don't hear what the speaker is saying at these times. Remember, the biggest problem in listening is failing to concentrate on the other person's communication. Getting overly emotional about something is one of the causes of the problem. Check your emotions. Hear the other person out first.

Rule 6 stands for an essential principle of better listening and therefore better understanding: responsiveness. Be a responsive listener. Be responsive in your demeanor, posture and facial expression. Let your whole being show you are interested in other people and their ideas.

As you listen, look at the other person and show some signs of hearing and understanding. Nod your head occasionally — gently, not vigorously. Nod slightly with a yea for agreement or a no when it's something sad or unhappy. Show through your posture, whether seated or standing, that you are concentrating on listening totally.

We show our interest in others also when we say occasionally "Um-mm" or "Uh-huh." These simple signs encourage speakers. They show that we're interested in them and that we're listening to what they're saying. However, others won't talk long unless we are responsive in our listening and offer some nonverbal and even some slight verbal signs of understanding.

To understand this important principle of being responsive, it helps to ask, "How do we turn people off?" The answers come quickly, by not looking at them, not asking questions, not showing any positive response; by looking out the window, shuffling papers, interrupting or giving other negative types of feedback.

But we want to turn people on, not off. Whether

we're teachers, managers, doctors, parents or salespeople, we want to encourage others to communicate with us so that we can gain understanding.

And there's one more important part to being responsive in listening to others: The one time it is all right, even desirable, to interrupt is to clarify what is said.

For example, as soon as you hear someone's name when you are introduced, inquire right at that moment how to spell the name if it is a difficult one. Or if you aren't sure of a statistic, date, place or other fact someone mentions, it shows responsive, concentrated listening to interrupt to clarify.

You can cushion your interruption with "Pardon me." But sometimes that isn't necessary. You might simply inquire, "How many?" or "When did it happen?" or "What's the name?" The interruption to clarify will actually help you focus on the other person's message more actively.

With a little knowledge and practice you can double your listening ability.

Listening is a gift you can give, no matter who you are. And you can give it to anyone. It doesn't cost a cent, but it is priceless to a person who needs a listener.

Number of words 2210
See page 301 for Questions

Reading time in Seconds _____
See page 360 for Conversion Table

SELECTION 58

Listening Is a 10-Part Skill

Ralph G. Nichols

When you sit down by Dr. Nichols at his desk, what do you see? A sign of name-plate size that reads, "I'm listening"! For the first time you may realize the significance of listening in interpersonal relations. It's important to be listened to — and to listen.

White collar workers, on the average, devote at least 40 percent of their work day to listening. Apparently 40 percent of their salary is paid to them for listening. Yet tests of listening comprehension have shown that, without training, these employes listen at only 25 percent efficiency.

This low level of performance becomes increasingly intolerable as evidence accumulates that it can be significantly raised. The component skills of listening are known. They boil down to this:

Learning through listening is primarily an inside job — inside action on the part of the listener. What he needs to do is to replace some common present attitudes with others.

Recognizing the dollar values in effective listening, many companies have added courses in this skill to their regular training programs. Some of the pioneers in this effort have been American Telephone & Telegraph Co., General Motors Corporation, Ford Motor Company, The Dow Chemical Company, Western Electric Co., Inc., Methods Engineering Council of Pittsburgh, Minnesota Mining & Manufacturing Co., Thompson Products, Inc., of Cleveland, and Rogers Corp. of Connecticut.

Warren Ganong of the Methods Engineering Council has compared trainees given a preliminary discussion of efficient listening with those not provided such discussion. On tests at the end of the courses the former achieved marks 12 to 15 percent higher than did the latter.

A. A. Tribbey, general personnel supervisor of the Wisconsin Telephone Company, in commenting on the results of a short conference course in which effective listening was stressed, declared: "It never fails to amaze us when we see the skill that is acquired in only three days."

The conviction seems to be growing that upper-level managers also need listening skill. As Dr. Earl Planty, executive counselor for the pharmaceutical firm of Johnson & Johnson, puts it: "By far the most effective method by which executives can tap ideas of subordinates is sympathetic listening in the many day-to-day informal contacts within and outside the work place. There is no system that will do the job in an easier manner. . . . Nothing can equal an executive's willingness to hear."

A study of the 100 best listeners and the 100 worst listeners in the freshman class on the University of Minnesota campus has disclosed ten guides to improved listening. Business people interested in improving their own performance can use them to analyze their personal strengths and weaknesses. The ten guides to good listening are:

1. FIND AREA OF INTEREST

All studies point to the advantage in being interested in the topic under discussion. Bad listeners usually declare the subject dry after the first few sentences. Once this decision is made, it serves to rationalize any and all inattention.

Good listeners follow different tactics. True, their first thought may be that the subject sounds dry. But a second one immediately follows, based on the realization that to get up and leave might prove a bit awkward.

The final reflection is that, being trapped anyhow, perhaps it might be well to learn if anything is being said that can be put to use.

The key to the whole matter of interest in a topic is the word *use*. Whenever we wish to listen efficiently, we ought to say to ourselves: "What's he saying that I can use? What worth-while ideas has he? Is he reporting any workable procedures? Anything that I can cash in, or with which I can make myself happier?" Such questions lead us to screen what we are hearing in a continual effort to sort out the elements of personal value. G. K. Chesterton spoke wisely indeed when he said, "There is no such thing as an uninteresting subject; there are only uninterested people."

2. JUDGE CONTENT, NOT DELIVERY

Many listeners alibi inattention to a speaker by thinking to themselves: "Who could listen to such a character? What an awful voice! Will he ever stop reading from his notes?"

The good listener reacts differently. He may well look at the speaker and think, "This man is inept. Seems like almost anyone ought to be able to talk better than that." But from this initial similarity he moves on to a different conclusion, thinking "But wait a minute. . . . I'm not interested in his personality or delivery. I want to find out what he knows. Does this man know some things that I need to know?"

Essentially we "listen with our own experience." Is the conveyer to be held responsible because we are poorly equipped to decode his message? We cannot understand everything we hear, but one sure way to raise the level of our understanding is to assume the responsibility which is inherently ours.

3. HOLD YOUR FIRE

Overstimulation is almost as bad as understimulation, and the two together constitute the twin evils of inefficient listening. The overstimulated listener gets too excited, or excited too soon, by the speaker. Some of us

are greatly addicted to this weakness. For us, a speaker can seldom talk for more than a few minutes without touching upon a pet bias or conviction. Occasionally we are roused in support of the speaker's point; usually it is the reverse. In either case overstimulation reflects the desire of the listener to enter, somehow, immediately into the argument.

The aroused person usually becomes preoccupied by trying to do three things simultaneously: calculate what hurt is being done to his own pet ideas; plot an embarrassing question to ask the speaker; enjoy mentally all the discomfiture visualized for the speaker once the devastating reply to him is launched. With these things going on subsequent passages go unheard.

We must learn not to get too excited about a speaker's point until we are certain we thoroughly understand it. The secret is contained in the principle that we must always withhold evaluation until our comprehension is complete.

4. LISTEN FOR IDEAS

Good listeners focus on central ideas; they tend to recognize the characteristic language in which central ideas are usually stated, and they are able to discriminate between fact and principle, idea and example, evidence and argument. Poor listeners are inclined to listen for the facts in every presentation.

To understand the fault, let us assume that a man is giving us instructions made up of facts A to Z. The man begins to talk. We hear fact A and think: "We've got to remember it!" So we begin a memory exercise by repeating "Fact A, fact A, fact A. . . ."

Meanwhile, the fellow is telling us fact B. Now we have two facts to memorize. We're so busy doing it that we miss fact C completely. And so it goes up to fact Z. We catch a few facts, garble several others and completely miss the rest.

It is a significant fact that only about 25 percent of persons listening to a formal talk are able to grasp the speaker's central idea. To develop this skill requires an ability to recognize conventional organizational patterns, transitional language, and the speaker's use of recapitulation. Fortunately, all of these items can be readily mastered with a bit of effort.

5. BE FLEXIBLE

Our research has shown that our 100 worst listeners thought that note-taking and outlining were synonyms. They believed there was but one way to take notes — by making an outline.

Actually, no damage would be done if all talks followed some definite plan of organization. Unfortunately, less than half of even formal speeches are carefully organized. There are few things more frustrating than to try to outline an unoutlineable speech.

Note-taking may help or may become a distraction.

Some persons try to take down everything in shorthand; the vast majority of us are far too voluminous even in longhand. While studies are not too clear on the point, there is some evidence to indicate that the volume of notes taken and their value to the taker are inversely related. In any case, the real issue is one of interpretation. Few of us have memories good enough to remember even the salient points we hear. If we can obtain brief, meaningful records of them for later review, we definitely improve our ability to learn and to remember.

The 100 best listeners had apparently learned early in life that if they wanted to be efficient note-takers they had to have more than one system of taking notes. They equipped themselves with four or five systems, and learned to adjust their system to the organizational pattern, or the absence of one, in each talk they heard. If we want to be good listeners, we must be flexible and adaptable note-takers.

6. WORK AT LISTENING

One of the most striking characteristics of poor listeners is their disinclination to spend any energy in a listening situation. College students, by their own testimony, frequently enter classes all worn out physically; assume postures which only seem to give attention to the speaker; and then proceed to catch up on needed rest or to reflect upon purely personal matters. This faking of attention is one of the worst habits afflicting us as a people.

Listening is hard work. It is characterized by faster heart action, quicker circulation of the blood, a small rise in bodily temperature. The overrelaxed listener is merely appearing to tune in, and then feeling conscience-free to pursue any of a thousand mental tangents.

For selfish reasons alone one of the best investments we can make is to give each speaker our conscious attention. We ought to establish eye contact and maintain it; to indicate by posture and facial expression that the occasion and the speaker's efforts are a matter of real concern to us. When we do these things we help the speaker to express himself more clearly, and we in turn profit by better understanding of the improved communication we have helped him to achieve. None of this necessarily implies acceptance of his point of view or favorable action upon his appeals. It is, rather, an expression of interest.

7. RESIST DISTRACTIONS

The good listeners tend to adjust quickly to any kind of abnormal situation; poor listeners tend to tolerate bad conditions and, in some instances, even to create distractions themselves.

We live in a noisy age. We are distracted not only by what we hear, but by what we see. Poor listeners tend to be readily influenced by all manner of distractions, even in an intimate face-to-face situation.

A good listener instinctively fights distraction. Sometimes the fight is easily won — by closing a door, shutting off the radio, moving closer to the person talking, or asking him to speak louder. If the distractions cannot be met that easily, then it becomes a matter of concentration.

8. EXERCISE YOUR MIND

Poor listeners are inexperienced in hearing difficult, expository material. Good listeners apparently develop an appetite for hearing a variety of presentations difficult enough to challenge their mental capacities.

Perhaps the one word that best describes the bad listener is "inexperienced." Although he spends 40 percent of his communication day listening to something, he is inexperienced in hearing anything tough, technical, or expository. He has for years painstakingly sought light, recreational material. The problem he creates is deeply significant, because such a person is a poor producer in factory, office, or classroom.

Inexperience is not easily or quickly overcome. However, knowledge of our own weakness may lead us to repair it. We need never become too old to meet new challenges.

9. KEEP YOUR MIND OPEN

Parallel to the blind spots which afflict human beings are certain psychological deaf spots which impair our ability to perceive and understand. These deaf spots are the dwelling place of our most cherished notions, convictions, and complexes. Often, when a speaker invades one of these areas with a word or phrase, we turn our mind to retraveling familiar mental pathways crisscrossing our invaded area of sensitivity.

It is hard to believe in moments of cold detachment that just a word or phrase can cause such emotional eruption. Yet with poor listeners it is frequently the case; and even with very good listeners it is occasionally the case. When such emotional deafness transpires, communicative efficiency drops rapidly to zero.

Among the words known thus to serve as red flags to some listeners are: mother-in-law, landlord, redneck, sharecropper, sissy, pervert, automation, clerk, income tax, communist, Red, dumb farmer, pink, "Greetings," antivivisectionist, evolution, square, punk, welsher.

Effective listeners try to identify and to rationalize the words or phrases most upsetting emotionally. Often the emotional impact of such words can be decreased through a free and open discussion of them with friends or associates.

10. CAPITALIZE ON THOUGHT SPEED

Most persons talk at a speed of about 125 words a minute. There is good evidence that if thought were measured in words per minute, most of us could think easily at about four times that rate. It is difficult — almost painful — to try to slow down our thinking speed. Thus we normally have about 400 words of thinking time to spare during every minute a person talks to us.

What do we do with our excess thinking time while someone is speaking? If we are poor listeners, we soon become impatient with the slow progress the speaker seems to be making. So our thoughts turn to something else for a moment, then dart back to the speaker. These brief side excursions of thought continue until our mind tarries too long on some enticing but irrelevant subject. Then, when our thoughts return to the person talking, we find he's far ahead of us. Now it's harder to follow him and increasingly easy to take off on side excursions. Finally we give up; the person is still talking, but our mind is in another world.

The good listener uses his thought speed to advantage; he constantly applies his spare thinking time to what is being said. It is not difficult once one has a definite pattern of thought to follow. To develop such a pattern we should:

Try to anticipate what a person is going to talk about.

Number of words 2490
See page 303 for Questions

On the basis of what he's already said, ask yourself: "What's he trying to get at? What point is he going to make?"

Mentally summarize what the person has been saying. What point has he made already, if any?

Weigh the speaker's evidence by mentally questioning it. As he presents facts, illustrative stories and statistics, continually ask yourself: "Are they accurate? Do they come from an unprejudiced source? Am I getting the full picture, or is he telling me only what will prove his point?"

Listen between the lines. The speaker doesn't always put everything that's important into words. The changing tones and volume of his voice may have a meaning. So may his facial expressions, the gestures he makes with his hands, the movement of his body.

Not capitalizing on thought speed is our greatest single handicap. The differential between thought speed and speech speed breeds false feelings of security and mental tangents. Yet, through listening training, this same differential can be readily converted into our greatest asset.

Reading time in Seconds _____
See page 360 for Conversion Table

SELECTION 59

"After This Manner, Therefore, Listen"

B. W. Overstreet

Here's General George Marshall's formula for success in dealing with people: (1) listen to the other person's story; (2) listen to the other person's complete story; (3) listen to the other person's complete story first. Do you think Overstreet would agree with such a formula? And where does reading fit into the picture?

Stop—Look—Listen. That is good advice at a railroad crossing; and equally good advice in a lot of other places: places where there are things to see that we do not see; things to hear that we do not hear; things which, if they could hold our attention and become part of our understanding, would make us more safe to be allowed at large in a worried and suffering world. It is good advice. Particularly the word "listen." For most of us do not listen.

This need not mean that we do more than our share of the talking. It may mean that. But quite as likely it means that we are mentally awake only when we are doing the talking—that we slide into a coma when it

comes our turn to keep still. Our comatose state may be disguised—if we are expert in the use of the fixed bright expression; the eager smile; the little nod that says, "Of course," and the shake of the head that says, "Oh, dear, what a shame!" I have even known people who could appear to be thinking—weighing carefully every word that was being said—with the effect achieved by their muscles instead of their minds. This accomplishment involves a certain furrowing of the brow, and a rhythm of smoothing and deepening the furrows; a certain drooping of the jowls as though under the weight of a problem. It does not, however, involve thinking. Nor real listening. Just enough clue-listening to be sure that the muscular responses hit the right rhythm.

Wordsworth, in brief, was more of an optimist than a psychologist when he wrote:

The eye—it cannot choose but see;
We cannot bid the ear be still. . . .

Eyes that are not seeing and ears that are not hearing are the rule rather than the exception—if we take seeing and hearing to be mental and emotional, as well as purely physical, experiences.

There is a kind of common notion that talking is a more active form of behavior than listening: that more of the self is engaged. Probably this error stems from the fact that our lips move when we talk, but our ears do not wiggle when we listen. So far as the active involvement of the brain is concerned, however, the two processes—talking and listening—should be equal parts of one experience: the experience of breaking down our own separateness, our own psychological isolation, and linking ourselves in mutual understanding with other people.

Sometimes even our talking seems curiously related to mental activity. Words keep on coming out of the mouth for no better reason, apparently, than because nothing has happened to stop them. But even more frequent is a condition of imitation listening: of silence that is not the silence of mental receptivity.

Real listening is a very active business. Rightly understood, our power to listen is the power to escape the limitations of our own experience and learn more about life than we can ever have a direct, personal chance to learn.

We are all partial, narrow, biased, walled around by our own memories and habits. We cannot help being so. For very few of the whole multitude of things that can happen to human beings ever happen to any one of us. And since it is what happens to ourselves that we feel most vividly, we easily think of our partial experience as typical experience. Listening—listening with the mind and heart, as well as with the ears—is the best means we have of supplementing our narrow experience with the wider experience of the race.

But to listen in this fashion we have to lend ourselves fully to the speaker. Hearing his words, we have also to feel the person who speaks them: the person for whom they represent experience and value. This person-who-is-not-ourselves may be talking about the house where he grew up; or about the high cost of living; or about refugees from Europe; or about Congress, or the younger generation, or a trip across country, or a new hat. But always and inevitably he is describing himself. By talking about a subject, he is telling what he thinks is worth talking about. By choosing to say one thing rather than another about a person he knows or a magazine article he has read, he is telling what he values. The art of listening, then, is the art of imaginatively moving ourselves over into the speaker's mind, the art of locating his few spoken words in the context of all his memories and hopes, beliefs, and doubts. If we form the habit of thus actively listening when others talk, we will be continually broadening and deepening our knowledge of what it feels like to be human, what it feels like even in situations utterly different from our own.

Perhaps it is stretching a point to say that the art of reading is actually the art of listening—just another form of it: a form that allows us to cock a receptive ear toward a speaker a world away from us in space or centuries away from us in time. Yet that is how I myself like to think of reading.

After all, it is still a new thing for the human race to be able to read. For more generations than we can number, listening was the only means man possessed of enlarging his own experience by the borrowed experience of others. Philosophy, religion, drama, history, story, poetry: these no less than the small incidents of his friends' lives came to man, if at all, because they were spoken by someone and he listened to them. He listened to them and built up feelings around them and used them as a measure of his own behaviors, as company for himself when he was alone, as a stimulus to his own powers when they needed stimulus, as wisdom to pass on in his turn to other folk. The individual who, in the long preliterate stages of history, had no keen ability as a listener must have remained a prisoner within his own small cell of experience.

But we learned after a while, after many centuries. We learned, as it were, to take liquid speech and freeze it on the printed page: fix it there for keeps, fix it there so that people could look with their eyes at what was formerly accessible only to their ears. But this meant that the reader had to know how to listen—with mind and heart—to whoever was speaking to him in the soundless code of print. Here, again, he had to learn how to imagine his way into the other person's mind; he had to learn the art of looking out at life from the angle of the other person's experience. He had to listen with his eyes.

When we do thus learn to listen to the printed page, we move into a far wider company of talkers than we can ever expect to know by just listening with our ears to audible voices. We can open a novel and listen to people worrying their way through problems that we never thought about before, but that suddenly become real to us: the problems, perhaps, that are faced by sharecroppers, or members of some minority group, or men and women who earn their living at jobs we have never tackled. We can open a book of philosophy and listen to Socrates talking on an Athenian street corner. We can open a book of poetry and hear voices that astonish us with beauty, or stab us with a new sense of the world's old sorrow. We can, in brief, invite into our own living room any speaking company to which we choose to lend the ears of our understanding.

And these people who speak to us from books speak with an astonishing lack of inhibition. They tell us, in the first half-hour that we spend with them, more about their own inner thoughts and their past lives than even our intimate friends ever bring themselves to tell. By listening, then, to those who speak from the pages of novels, histories, and dramas, we acquire a store of insight about human experience and feeling that it would take many lifetimes to acquire from words that reach the ear from the speaking lips of our own acquaintances.

It is a rich and subtle art, this art of listening. He who learns it well may also learn well, as a by-product, the art of speaking with wisdom.

Number of words 1434
See page 305 for Questions

Reading time in Seconds _____
See page 360 for Conversion Table

SELECTION 60

Listen to This, Dear

James Thurber

Sometimes reading and listening come into sharp conflict. Attentive reading hinders listening; attentive listening hinders reading. See how Thurber suggests dealing with this problem. Unfortunately Thurber, well-known humorist, is also a well-known misogynist. We tolerate one side to enjoy the other.

It is a commonplace that the small annoyances of the marriage relationship slowly build up its insupportabilities, as particles of sediment build up great deltas. And yet I have never seen, even among the profundities of our keenest researchers into divorce, a competent consideration of the problem that is created by the female's habit of interrupting the male when he is reading. It is, indeed, more than a habit; I believe it is a law of woman's behaviorism as deeply rooted as her instinct to attract the male. And it causes almost as much trouble.

In the early ages of mankind, woman's security, and hence her contentment, were assured by the activity of the male and jeopardized by his inactivity. The male rampant — killing animals for food and for clothing, digging out caves, and putting up huts, driving off enemies — early came to be associated in the mind of the elemental female with warmth, well-being, safety, and the kindred creature comforts. Lying down, or even sitting down, the male was a symbol of possible imminent disaster: famine, exposure, capture and servitude, even death. Any masculine posture of relaxation or repose, therefore, became a menace which must be removed.

The reasonable dismay of the primeval female at the sight of her mate doing nothing was so powerful that it remains ineradicable in the mind and the heart of the female of today, although logical motivation for her original dread has largely disappeared with the shaping up of our civilization. The softer centuries, it is true,

have reduced her primal terror to a kind of hazy uneasiness, just as they have tempered the violence of her protest, but the instinct to prod the inert male into action nevertheless persists. Where once woman shook man, or struck him with a rock, or at least screamed imprecations at him, when he sat down to draw pictures on the walls of the cave, she now contents herself with talking to him when he is reading. The male's ability to lose himself in the printed page brings back to the female, from vanished wildernesses, the old, dim fear of masculine inertia.

"I must tell you what happened to the base of the Spencers' child's brain," a wife will begin when her husband has just reached the most exciting point in the sports extra's account of a baseball game or a prizefight, and she will proceed to go into details which, although interesting, or even horrific, lack the peculiar excitement of competitive competition to which the husband has adjusted his consciousness. Or she will say, "I want you to listen to this, dear," and she will read him a story from her section of the evening paper about a New Jersey dentist who tried to burn up his wife and collect her insurance. Telling the plots of plays, and speculating as to why a certain couple were drawn together, or drifted apart — as the case may have been — are other methods a wife frequently uses to interrupt her husband's reading.

Of the various ways of combating this behavior of the female, open resentment, manifested by snarling or swearing or throwing one's book or newspaper on the floor in a rage, is the worst, since nine times out of ten it will lead to quarrels, tears, slamming of doors, and even packing of suitcases, and the disruption of family life. The husband may gain, by this method, the privacy of his club, but he will no longer be in the proper frame of mind for quiet reading. He will find himself wondering where his wife is, whether she has gone home to her mother, whether she has taken veronal (I am dealing, of course, with those high-strung, sensitive couples who make up such a large percentage of present-day families). He will then fall to recalling miserably the years of their happiness, and end up by purchasing a dozen roses for his wife, and five or six rye highballs for himself, after which he must still face the ordeal of patching things up, a business made somewhat easier perhaps by the fact of the roses, but correspondingly harder by the fact of the highballs. This whole method of protest, in a word, takes a great deal out of a man and is not to be recommended.

The best way of dealing with a wife who tells long stories of the day's happenings, or reads accounts of murders aloud when her husband has settled down to his book or journal, is to pretend to listen but not really to listen at all. To the uninitiated this may seem simple, but the husband who has perfected the method knows that it calls for a unique bifurcation of the faculty of attention, and a remarkable development of the power of concentration. In order to go right on with his own reading while his wife is talking, the husband must deaden his mind to the meaning of her words and at the same time remain conscious of the implications of her inflections. Thus he will be able, at the proper places in her recitation, to murmur an interested "Yes?" or an incredulous "No!," although not following her narrative at all and still getting the sense of what he is reading. "Um," "Hm," and "Um hm" should also be freely used, but never "Hm?" for it denotes a lapse of attention. Exclamations of astonishment or high interest, such as "You don't say!" are extremely dangerous and should be interjected only by the oblivious husband who is so sensitive to the tempo and pitch of his wife's voice that he can be positive when she has reached some (to her) important climax in whatever she is relating.

This form of deception is, of course, fairly easy to practice when the female is reading aloud, for her eyes must naturally be upon the printed page before her. It is not so easy when she is relating an occurrence, or a chain of occurrences, for her eyes are then likely to be upon the male. In this case he should contrive, as soon as she begins, to drop his magazine or newspaper on his knee, as if he had abandoned it — all the time, however, keeping the type within range. I know of one husband who drops his newspaper on the floor before him and then bends over it with his hand to his brow, shielding his eyes, his elbow on his knee, as if he were intent upon his wife's words. He continues to read right along, however.

A defense against forward passes, as they say in football, must also be carefully built up by the inattentive husband. By forward passes, I mean sudden and unexpected questions which the wife is likely to fling at any minute, such as, for example, "Would you think Hilda Greeb capable of a thing like that?" In building up a defense against this trick play, the husband must keep a little corner of his consciousness alert, like the safety man on a defensive football team, for all sentences beginning with "would," "should," "are," "have," "can," and the like. In this way he can spot a question coming in time to have some sort of response ready. In the case of the question we have already cited, "Would you think Hilda Greeb capable of a thing like that?" it is probable that either a "Yes" or "No" would see the husband safely by the crisis. If he says "Yes," the wife will probably say, "Well, of course I would, knowing her as well as I do." However, each particular husband, knowing the twists and turns of his particular wife's mind, must work out his own system of defense against forward passes. The greatest care should be taken by every husband, however, to answer only those questions which are directed to him. He must, I mean, be on guard against "inner-quote queries." For example, if a wife should say, in the course of whatever she is telling, "So I asked her, 'what time is it?' " the husband is lost if he is caught off guard and replies, "About a quarter after eight, I think." This is bound to lead to accusations, imprecations, quarrels, tears, slamming of doors, etc.

I know a few husbands who simply evade the whole problem by giving up reading. They just don't read anything any more. It seems to me that this is cowardly.

Number of words 1400
See page 307 for Questions

Reading time in Seconds _____
See page 360 for Conversion Table

I Keep Hearing Voices

Cornelia Otis Skinner

Have you ever caught yourself making subtle or not-so-subtle changes in your voice to fit different occasions? Have you ever tried to label any of those changes? For example, do you have a false-heartiness voice or a solemn-regret voice? See if you find some of the author's voices typical of some of your own.

It comes as a shock suddenly to discover in oneself some eccentricity of behavior which one may have had for years without ever before being aware of it. Take voices, for instance. I find, to my fascination, that many persons, myself in particular, have a curious collection of varying voices.

I don't mean accents picked up during exposure to regional pronunciation. (I return from a trip through the South with an accent of Georgia peach-fuzz, while 24 hours in London finds me as British as a Trafalgar lion given the power of speech.) I refer to the tone and manner of delivery we use on specific occasions.

For example, the ways in which people address the elderly. It seems to be a universal conclusion that to be advanced in years means *ipso facto* to be advanced in deafness. Whoever is presented to, say, a venerable old gentleman starts conversing in a deferential bellow. The opposite approach is the hospital voice of muted concern coupled with a note of awe indicating that to grow old automatically means to grow holy.

I have a woman cousin who is a chipper 89 and when I've introduced people to her I have watched them shake her hand as if it might be a fragile bluebell and speak to her with the solemn reverence of addressing a saint not long for this world. Actually the old girl is about as fragile as a sturdy oak, has probably just downed a double whisky-sour and is rarin' to get to the Canasta table.

Certain variations in voices seem to be peculiar to male behavior—as the looking-forward-to-breakfast halloo, particularly on Pullman trains at an early hour when you're trying to sleep. As they march Indian file through your car, the leader calls out in the cry of a lumberjack poling in turbulent rapids, "OH BOY! AM I LOOKING FORWARD TO THAT CUP OF COFFEE!" Each member of the doughty crew clarions a yes siree what isn't he going to do to those ham 'n eggs, and another wants jubilantly to know what the betting is on old W. G. here having himself a big stack of pancakes.

Women are not without their own peculiar noises of enthusiasm. Take, for example, the chance meeting of former schoolmates after the hiatus of years. All of a sudden the staggering fact dawns that the one is . . . not surely *Mary Smith!!!* and the other . . . it isn't possible, *Sally Jones!!!* The emotion of recognition is expressed in the mounting melodics of gleeful and slightly hysterical sirens—and I don't refer to the sort who sat on rocks and lured mariners with dulcet sounds.

Then there is the delivery the female uses when talking to her own child in the presence of company. Plunging into a dewy-eyed motherhood act, she lilts out sweet suggestions such as "Isn't it time we went to beddy-bye?" while what she'd like to say, and what the child expects her to shrill out, is "You little pain-in-the-neck, get the hell up to bed!" Even when the child grows older the mother employs a parlance suggestive of a Victorian elocution mistress giving the proper reading of "Birds in their little nests agree." As my own son once rudely summed it up, "For Pete's sake, Mom, when you're talking about me do you have to *sing?*"

Then there is the conspiratorial voice, often used when there is no need for secrecy, as in the case of that husband-and-wife code exchange toward the end of a social gathering: the husband rises and, in the manner of a second-story man passing the signal to his partner, mutters, "I think we'd better be . . ." and she, rising cautiously, echoes the sinister password "Yes, we'd better be . . ." What should be so hush-hush about making the simple announcement that it's late and they ought to go home?

Of the barnyard imitations and birdcalls women employ when addressing household pets, it is almost too embarrassing to speak. A shameless weakness for dogs releases from me a flow of baby talk and babbling asininities. My dogs don't seem to mind my gurgling endearments, but my family does. My parakeet voice is also pretty dreadful, being a stream of baby jargon in a falsetto soprano, giving the effect of a leaking steam valve. In fact, all domestic animals appear to reduce me to a state of infantilism, and I have even heard myself addressing a police horse as though it were swaddled in diapers and cooing in a bassinet.

I am aware that I have a voice of cheer full of ersatz sunshine that makes its nauseating appearance when I am suddenly confronted by the children of my friends —young creatures on whom I've not set eyes for years. This voice with hypocritical eagerness utters banalities like "How's the new math teacher?" or "Your dad says you're coming along just fine with your surfboard!"

Only a week ago I shared a train seat with an attractive young woman who turned out to be the daughter of former neighbors. I didn't recognize her until she introduced herself saying that she was Penelope E. I immediately came out with a loud "Why Penny *Pen!*" and pumping her hand with splendid vigor exclaimed, "Last time I saw you, you were covered with poison ivy!" What she was covered with then was discomfort. Obviously she hadn't been called by the distressing nickname in years. However, she smiled indulgently and replied politely to my elephantine inquiries as to how was the family, did she enjoy school and mercy it wasn't possible that she had graduated from *college!* Shortly Penny Pen, under pretext of smoking a cigarette, sought refuge in another car.

Another locution I have recently discovered is my doctor voice. Not the confiding mutter used in situations of illness or consultation, but the one I catch myself using when I meet one of the medical profession socially. Possibly out of a desire to give the impression that I have no need for his professional services, I talk with great animation in tones vibrant with radiant health. If he happens to be a psychiatrist also, I have the disquieting feeling that the chair I am sitting on is about to let down into a couch and that my every gesture is indicative of deep-rooted neuroses. The result is a careful enunciation to show how frightfully normal I am.

However, there is nothing to equal my talking-with-a-foreigner delivery. And I don't refer to someone who speaks only a foreign tongue, with whom one decides the only means of communication is through a bellow of English. I mean the cultured linguist who speaks my language with far greater elegance than I. If through the perfection of his Oxford verbiage there comes the slightest hint of foreign accent, I slow down to LP speed, mouthing each syllable with meticulous deliberation and using the basic words of a *First Primer*. It is the form of painstaking peroration William Penn must have used when explaining his treaty to the Indians.

Then there is my chatting-with-clergymen parlance. The sudden sight of a clerical collar makes me go right into my voice of piety: a combination of the hostess of a Cape Cod tea shoppe and Beth in *Little Women,* hushed and not a little hallowed, as though we were about to step into the next room and view the remains. It is somewhat reassuring to note that others carry on conversations with parsons in the same funereal manner. It must be one of the more doleful exactions of the dedicated life.

Finally there is my losing-interest voice, which is less a voice than a fade-out. This creeps slowly upon me during some interminable tête-à-tête with say, a golf enthusiast or someone just back from Europe and determined to present an unillustrated travelogue. What issues from my mouth is quite mechanical; in fact, I usually have no idea what I am saying. This is disturbing for it creates that eerie sensation of standing outside yourself and listening to a complete stranger.

This listening to myself is making me uncomfortably self-conscious. Perhaps I had better stop enumerating all my varying forms of speech.

Perhaps, as a matter of fact, in certain situations it might be best for me to stop speaking altogether.

Number of words 1380
See page 309 for Questions

Reading time in Seconds _____
See page 360 for Conversion Table

SELECTION 62

Thanks for a Terrible Try

R. J. Hicks

Your words reveal much of your life history — your background, your family, your education, and your interests. With that in mind, watch how the Quiz Master mercilously torments his word-impoverished contestants.

It sounded at first like the usual quiz show—studio audience bellowing, oozy commercials, gasp-making patter about the size of the kitty—but there was something about the Quiz Master's tone which stayed my hand on the knob.

"So you're Mrs. Boheme Quiltman, and you come from McClusky, North Dakota? Hmm." The way he uttered these words (a touch of Basil Rathbone in an unsympathetic role) caused the audience to applaud a shade uncertainly.

"McClusky must be over a thousand miles from Hollywood," he continued. "Tell me, Mrs. Quiltman, what possessed you to come all the way?"

"Wanted a little vacation. Been saving up for years. Came by bus," said Mrs. Quiltman.

"Ah, yes. It is, after all, a free country. But once here, Mrs. Quiltman, what strange whim induced you to appear on a quiz program?"

"Want ta win a little money, I guess. Tee-hee. Could use it back home in McClusky!"

"Could you? Well, let's see what sort of figure you cut. Incidentally, the makers of Chewy Chewettes will pay you $11,000 if you contrive to answer this one question correctly." (A wail of muffled cupidity from Mrs. Quiltman.) "All right. How many decades are there in twenty years?"

"Dec—Jer mind repeating that, Mister?"

"You heard it all right, but I will. How many decades in twenty years? . . . You don't know, do you, you pinhead? As a matter of form I must wait for the sound of the gong."

The Quiz Master waited in sadistic silence, with none of the little goadings and sympathetic gigglings customary with his more normal confreres. From the audience there came sounds of puzzled restiveness. The gong sounded.

"I sometimes wonder about people like you, Mrs. Quiltman," continued the Quiz Master in blue-diamond tones. "You must hear such words as 'decade' occasionally, and read them in a newspaper, even in McClusky. Why don't you ever ask what they mean?"

Reprinted by permission from *The Atlantic Monthly*, January 1947.

"Well I ——"

"Or look in that handsomely engraved leather-covered dictionary which I'm sure you display prominently in the Quiltman place on Elm Street. Yet you go on, year after year, taking 'decade' for granted, and scores —hundreds—of other words as well. You probably haven't the slightest idea how long a generation is?"

"I — well, I ——"

"As I thought. What grade did you end up in, in school?"

"Why, the same one everyone ends up in."

"Have you any real interests in life?"

"Interests?"

"Ah, well, let's not go into that." (Renewed signs of restiveness from the audience.) "Do you ever read any books, Mrs. Quiltman?"

Mrs. Quiltman by this time sounded distinctly defiant. "I should just say so!"

"And, what, if one may ask, was the title of the last one that you read?"

"Why—er—why, it was a very good best-seller. Very good."

"Ever write any letters?"

"Don't have any call to, Mister Smartypants!" (A cheer from the audience.)

"I see, Mrs. Quiltman. Well, I wish you luck, I suppose; but I honestly think you'd do well to stay away from any too public demonstration of your mental attainments. I'm pretty sure that you would have been incapable of answering any question put to you tonight. It isn't a matter of being flustered, or of not being able to think on your feet (capacious though I observe them to be). You are just an ignoramus. Good night."

"Now," continued the Quiz Master, to a background of rather plaintive growling, "Chewy Chewettes simply double the kitty each time a question is muffed. So we have $22,000 awaiting Mister—what is your name, sir?"

"Mortimer Flange. Just call me Mort. And my home town's right here in Hollywood. I'm a bus boy at the Hotel Hibiscus."

"I see. And are you a film fan?"

"Am I! You kiddn, Mister?"

"Good. I take it that you are familiar with the names of Bette Davis and Charlie Chaplin?"

"You kiddn?" asked Mort again.

"Very well. Bette Davis often appears in tragedy; $22,000 if you can tell me what kind of films Chaplin appears in."

"What kind of films?"

"Yes. In other words, the opposite of tragedy. Charlie Chaplin makes—what kind of films?"

"Funny uns?"

"Yes, but they are known as—what?"

Long pause. Crash of gong. "The answer is, of course, comedy," said the Quiz Master. "Comedy is the opposite of tragedy."

"It is?"

"Yes. Surely you knew that?"

"Seems like I heard the word before some place, but you don't hear it much around the Hotel Hibiscus." (Applause.) "Dunno what it means, anyway."

"How old are you?"

"Nineteen—going on twenty."

"Do you read much?"

"Sure—fan magazines; and the funnies."

"But what kind of imbecile are you that you don't know that Chaplin is a comedian?"

"Hunh? What was that you just called me?"

"Only an imbecile."

"Oh, for a minute there I thought you was maybe gettn fresh."

"Do you break many dishes while you work?"

"Fair number."

"I don't doubt it. I can just picture your puzzled frown each time you start to pile them on the tray, never learning the knack, amazed each time again at the renewed complexity of existence. What do you want out of life? What would you like to be? Surely not just a bus boy? . . . Well, I won't detain you, Mortimer. You are a moron, but at least a happy one, apparently. Good night."

"Your name, please?"

"Miss Imogene Cusack. I am just twenty-three." The voice was mincingly self-possessed. Its owner evidently had well-defined ideas about Poise—keep the tone level at all times . . . watch yourself . . . the girls from the office are out there listening.

"Your profession?"

"Stenographer. I work in an office—in a business house, that is—in Pasadena."

"Good. Now, Miss Cusack, the sum of $44,000 awaits you if you answer this correctly. You are standing on the eastern shore of England, looking out eastward across the English Channel and the North Sea. Name any one country towards which you are looking."

"Well—er—I think I know —"

"Good. But time is slipping past, so let me put it this way: name any country besides England and Scotland which has its coastline on the North Sea or the English Channel. . . . Think of D Day."

"Think of what?"

"Never mind—think of a map of Europe."

"Maps. Oh, I don't look at maps much."

"Well, guess!"

Miss Cusack's veneer was cracking fast. She cried excitedly: "Ireland!" (Wild pandemonium from the audience, which apparently thought her right.)

"Wrong, you little silly, utterly wrong," said the Quiz Master wearily. "Why don't you look at a map now and again? You do realize, I hope, that the United States is now a great world power?"

"Why certainly," retorted Miss Cusack, with hauteur. "My boy friend hopes to get on the next Olympic Games track squad." (Applause.)

"And why don't you cut out that phony bored look? Nobody expects every woman to be a beauty, but you could attain some degree of charm and attractiveness if you would relax—be natural. That's to say, you might have done so—it's probably much too late now. To me you look almost repellent, minus all the feminine graces. No kindliness, no sympathy, no warmth. Just a desiccated imitativeness. How sorry I am for your boy friend."

Miss Cusack said, "Am I being insulted?"

"Yes," returned the Quiz Master with gusto. Miss Cusack burst into tears and withdrew. "All right, next. Come on, ladies and gentlemen, not much more time."

The audience was in uproar. Some voices could be heard maintaining that it was all just a gag, as when Hope insults his guest stars.

"Ah, we have here?"

"Jonathan Spawnson."

"And this, doubtless, is Mrs. Spawnson. Here goes for $88,000. Last spring we had visiting us in the United States a Good Neighbor from the south. He is the head of the Neighboring state directly to the south of us, a country with which we had a war just one hundred years ago. What is his name?"

Mrs. Spawnson: "General Eisenhower!"

Quiz Master, evenly: "You, Mr. Spawnson?"

Spawnson gave a sudden shout: I got it—you mean he was from Mexico, don't you?"

"Yes, that's the country. Who is its president?"

Spawnson, fortissimo: "President Alamo!"

Quiz Master: "Good God. Well, our time is practically up, but I must ask you both one more question: Have you any children?"

The Spawnsons replied in chorus, "Five fine sons and two fine daughters."

"And I suppose your seven children are sitting out there in the audience or listening at home? What must they think of such parents! If either of you had a sense of the fitness of things you would have taken a good deal of trouble to ensure that you did not expose your ludicrous inadequacies in public like this. Why undermine whatever lingering faith they may still have ——"

The telephone rang insistently: I answered it in hot impatience, aware of what sounded like blows and imprecations flowing from the radio. When at last I was free to dash back, the program had ended. Silence reigned. Since then I have worn my fingers to the bone twiddling at the dials, but, alas, never to this day have I been able to find again that beautiful, beautiful Quiz Master.

Number of words 1540
See page 311 for Questions

Reading time in Seconds _____
See page 360 for Conversion Table

SELECTION 63

The Romance of Words

Wilfred Funk and Norman Lewis

Words are not dead things. They are born, they mature — they even die. Take the word ducemptologist. *It was just now born and is not in a single dictionary. It means "salesman." After all, a salesman practices the science* (ology) *of leading* (ducere) *us to buy* (emere). *There is romance in words.*

From now on we want you to look at words intently, to be inordinately curious about them and to examine them syllable by syllable, letter by letter. They are your tools of understanding and self-expression. Collect them. Keep them in condition. Learn how to handle them. Develop a fastidious, but not a fussy, choice. Work always towards good taste in their use. Train your ear for their harmonies.

We urge you not to take words for granted just because they have been part of your daily speech since childhood. You must examine them. Turn them over and over, and see the seal and superscription on each one, as though you were handling a coin. *We would like you actually to fall in love with words.*

Words, as you know, are not dead things. They are fairly wriggling with life. They are the exciting and mysterious tokens of our thoughts, and like human beings, they are born, come to maturity, grow old and die, and sometimes they are even re-born in a new age. A word, from its birth to its death, is a process, not a static thing.

Words, like living trees, have roots, branches and leaves.

Shall we stay with this analogy for a few moments, and see how perfect it is?

The story of the root of a word is the story of its origin. The study of origins is called *etymology,* which in turn has *its* roots in the Greek word *etymon* meaning "true" and the Greek ending — *logia* meaning "knowledge." So *etymology* means the true knowledge of words.

Every word in our language is a frozen metaphor, a frozen picture. It is this poetry behind words that gives language its overwhelming power. And the more intimately we know the romance that lies within each word, the better understanding we will have of its meaning.

For instance, on certain occasions you will probably say that you have "calculated" the cost of something or other. What does this term "calculate" really mean? Here is the story. Years ago, ancient Romans had an instrument called a *hodometer,* or "road measurer," which corresponds to our modern taximeter. If you had hired a two-wheeled Roman vehicle to ride, say, to the Forum, you might have found in the back a tin can with a revolving cover that held a quantity of pebbles. This can was so contrived that each time the wheel turned the metal cover also revolved and a pebble dropped through a hole into the receptacle below. At the end of your trip you counted the pebbles and *calculated* your bill. You see the Latin word for pebble was *calculus,* and that's where our word "calculate" comes from.

There are, of course, many words with much simpler histories that this. When you speak of a "surplus," for instance, you are merely saying that you have a *sur* (French for "over") *plus* (French for "more") or a *sur-plus.* That is, you have an "over-more" than you need.

Should you be in a snooty mood for the nonce, and happen to look at someone rather haughtily, your friends might call you *supercilious,* a word which comes from the Latin *supercilium,* meaning that "eyebrow" you just raised. That person you are so fond of, who has become your companion, — [*cum* (Latin for "with") and *panis* (Latin for "bread")] — is simply one who eats bread with you. That's all. Again, "trumps" in bridge is from the French "triomphe" or triumph, an old-time game of cards. In modern cards one suit is allowed to triumph over, or to "trump" the other suits. And still again, in the army, the *lieutenant* is literally one who takes the place of the captain when the latter is not around. From the French *lieu* (we use it in "in lieu of") and *tenir,* "to hold." The captain, in turn, derives from the Latin word *caput* (head); colonel comes from *columna* (the "column" that he leads).

If, by any chance, you would like to twit your friend, the Wall Street broker, just tell him that his professional title came from the Middle English word *brocour,* a *broacher,* or one who opens, or broaches, a cask to draw off the wine or liquor. We still employ the same word in the original sense when we say "he broached (or opened up) the subject." Finally the broacher, or broker, became a salesman of wine. Then of other things, such as stocks and bonds.

These are the roots of words. We next come to the branches. The branches of our language tree are those many groups of words that have grown out from one original root.

Let's take an example. The Latin term *spectare* which means "to see" contains the root *spec,* and from this one root have sprouted more than 240 English words. We find the root hidden in such words as *spec*tacles, those things you "see" through; in re*spect,* the tribute you give to a person you care to "see" again; in*spect,* "to see" into; disre*spect* (*dis* — unwilling; *re* — again; *spec* — to see) therefore, when you treat someone with disrespect, you make it plain that you do not care to see him again; intro*spec*tion, looking or seeing within; *spec*tator, one who "sees" or watches.

Turning to the Greek language, which has so largely enriched our own, we discover the root appearing in English as *graph.* This means "to write" and has been a prolific source of words for us. We have tele*graph,* which literally means "far writing"; phono*graph,* "sound-writing"; photo*graph,* "light-writing"; steno*grapher,* one who does "condensed writing"; a *graphic* description, one that is just as clear and effective as though it had been written down; mimeo*graph,* "to write a copy or imitation."

We have in our language a host of roots such as these. There is the Latin *spirare,* meaning "to blow or breathe," from which we get such English words as in*spire* (breathe into); ex*pire* (breathe out); per*spire*

(breathe through); re*spir*ation (breathing again or often). And there is also our word "liable" that comes from the Latin *ligare,* "to bind." This fascinating root *lig* has branched out into ob*lige* and ob*lig*ate (to bind to do something); *lig*ature (bandage or binding); *lig*ament (something that ties two things together); and, with the root no longer so obvious, "league" (those nations or other organizations that are bound together); and even the word "ally" which is from *ad* and *ligare,* to bind to one another.

These, then, are the branches. We turn now to the leaves. If the roots are the origins of words and the branches are the word families that stem out of them, the leaves of this language tree would be the words themselves and their meanings.

Each given word, in its beginning, had, no doubt, only one meaning. But words are so full of life that they are continually sprouting the green shoots of new meanings.

Shall we choose just one word as an instance of the amazing vitality of language? The simple three letter word *run,* up to this moment of writing, has more than 90 dictionary definitions. There is the *run* in your stocking and the *run* on the bank and a *run* in baseball. The clock may *run* down but you *run* up a bill. Colors *run.* You may *run* a race or *run* a business or you may have the *run* of the mill, or, quite different, the *run* of the house when you get the *run* of things. And this little dynamic word, we can assure you, is not yet through with its varied career.

Is it any wonder that our unabridged dictionaries contain as many as 600,000 living and usable words, words sparkling with life, prolific in their breeding, luxuriant in their growth, continually shifting and changing in their meanings?

Words even have definite personalities and characters. They can be sweet, sour, discordant, musical. They can be sweet or acrid; soft or sharp; hostile or friendly.

From this time on, as we enter our word studies, try to become self-conscious about words. Look at them, if possible, with the fresh eyes of one who is seeing them for the first time. If we have persuaded you to do this, you will then be on the way to the success that can be won with a more powerful vocabulary.

Number of words 1380
See page 313 for Questions

Reading time in Seconds _____
See page 361 for Conversion Table

Test Your Vocabulary

William Morris

It pays to increase your vocabulary. Where have you heard that before? But before you start, why not find out how much you need to improve? Would you call your vocabulary average, above-average, or below-average? Check up on yourself. Work through this article and test.

If you think you have a pretty good vocabulary, you feel pleased with yourself. You may keep this pride hidden, of course, but it is there all the same. If, however, you are a little uncertain of your word prowess—as most of us are—you may be one of the reasons why vocabulary-building books sell so well, even though they aren't much help.

The basic reason for this interest in words is the big American urge for self-improvement. We all admire the person who has a ready command of words. We instinctively feel that to know more words ourselves would increase our self-confidence and prestige. We also hear that people who rise to the top usually are those who express their ideas easily and accurately, and we see a correlation between the size of vocabulary and the size of pay check.

Naturally we want all these good things. If words will give them to us, let's learn more.

How many words do you know, and how many ought you to know?

Accompanying this article is a quiz which will answer the first part of that question. The test was devised exclusively for *Changing Times* by William Morris, editor-in-chief of Grosset & Dunlap, New York book publishing firm, and author of a syndicated column on words.

If you score high, you can give yourself a pat on the back. If you don't, don't worry too much. Vocabularies can be improved, as you will see.

Nobody knows exactly how many words there are in the English language, but the figure 750,000 is widely accepted. A foreigner probably could get along here on about 350, and Basic English—an English for international use—depends on only 850.

But all of us use many times that number. A child of eight, for example, knows about 3,600 words and a child of fourteen, about 9,000. Men and women with little formal education probably recognize between 9,000 and 10,000 words.

Shakespeare used some 24,000 different words in his plays and undoubtedly knew many more than that. The total recognition vocabulary for the adult high school graduate has been placed as high as 25,000 words. The literate college graduate who reads a few books a year knows 35,000 or more.

How do you go about increasing your fund of words? The word-building books have it all figured out. They offer word-a-day plans, 30-day plans, or even lists of 5,000 or so supposedly high-powered words which, if learned, will give you a vocabulary second to none.

The trouble with these plans is that they don't work. You buy a book and study it faithfully—15 or 30 minutes a day, whatever is called for. But the words don't stick. The system is too artificial.

Crossword puzzles are equally useless. They are concerned too much with freak words. Magazine and newspaper word columns are more helpful, and so is the plan of writing down unfamiliar words when you come across them and looking them up in a good dictionary.

But the sure way to increase your vocabulary—and, say the experts, the only real, workable way—is to read.

Vocabulary building is a process of mental absorption. You soak up words automatically if you see or hear them frequently enough. Their meaning becomes clear through context, and your mind retains them.

The next question is what to read. Here is where most articles on vocabulary building stop short. But despite the fact that reading is largely a matter of personal preference, there is some good advice to be had.

If you happen to have read *A Tree Grows in Brooklyn,* you may recall that Katie's mother advised Katie to read Shakespeare and the King James Version of the Bible if she wanted to raise herself by her bootstraps.

That's still good advice. You couldn't get better. Only you've heard this before.

Here is some other reading you can do. Start on the classics. Yes, it will take a little more effort than reading the sports or women's pages. But it is not as formidable as you may think, and if you are really serious about building up your vocabulary, this is the best way to do it.

Take Washington Irving, the first great American stylist. You probably read *The Sketch Book* in high school. But get it out and read it again. Not just *Rip Van Winkle* and *The Legend of Sleepy Hollow*. Read the essays too.

In the novel, the possibilities are, of course, endless. Read *Treasure Island* again, or anything by Stevenson. Or perhaps Thomas Hardy's *Return of the Native*, Henry James's *Turn of the Screw*, Conrad's *Lord Jim*, Thackeray's *Vanity Fair*, Trollope's *Barchester Towers*, Emily Brontë's *Wuthering Heights*, George Eliot's *Adam Bede*.

Then go into other fields—history, biography, political science. Try Parkman's *The Oregon Trail;* Stra-chey's *Queen Victoria; The Federalist;* or H. G. Wells's *Outline of History.*

All these books are readily available. Your library has them. Your bookstore has them. Many can be had in paper-bound editions.

Does it all sound too highfalutin? It isn't really. If you had thought of spending 3 minutes a day studying words, try using the 30 minutes to read books like these instead. Their authors had a fine command of the English language, and some of it is bound to rub off on you.

(Now turn to page 315 and check your comprehension before going ahead with the test which follows.)

Number of words 890
See page 315 for Questions

Reading time in Seconds _____
See page 361 for Conversion Table

SELF-SCORING VOCABULARY TEST*

This is really tough, no fooling. You probably have never seen a lot of these words. The test has to be made hard in order to accommodate the few individuals who are whizzes with words. So don't get discouraged—even people with sizable vocabularies may miss half the words.

Another thing: Speed does not count, so take your time. But no peeking into the dictionary, or at the scoring key which follows the quiz.

Directions for Sections I and II: Before each word in column A write the letter of the word from column B that most nearly matches it in meaning. You will find it helpful to strike out words in column B as you use their letters in column A.

SECTION I

	A		B
1.	_____amenable	a.	amnesty
2.	_____bizarre	b.	confident
3.	_____captious	c.	faultfinding
4.	_____commensurate	d.	grotesque
5.	_____compassionate	e.	incipient
6.	_____contumacious	f.	inflexible
7.	_____guileless	g.	inherent
8.	_____immanent	h.	irresolute
9.	_____inane	i.	lively
10.	_____incessant	j.	insipid
11.	_____inchoate	k.	perverse
12.	_____jejune	l.	prank
13.	_____lachrymose	m.	proportionate
14.	_____monkeyshine	n.	risky
15.	_____obdurate	o.	showy
16.	_____ostentatious	p.	sincere
17.	_____palpable	q.	sympathetic
18.	_____pardon	r.	tangible
19.	_____precarious	s.	tearful
20.	_____renegade	t.	toady
21.	_____salubrious	u.	tractable

22.	_____sanguine	v.	turncoat
23.	_____sprightly	w.	uninterrupted
24.	_____sycophant	x.	vacuous
25.	_____vacillating	y.	wholesome

SECTION II

1.	_____abrogate	a.	annihilate
2.	_____aggravate	b.	annul
3.	_____ameliorate	c.	antiquated
4.	_____augur	d.	boldness
5.	_____contravene	e.	cunning
6.	_____crotchety	f.	dexterous
7.	_____dawdling	g.	elicit
8.	_____deft	h.	enervated
9.	_____diminutive	i.	enthusiastic
10.	_____ebullient	j.	exact
11.	_____educe	k.	favorable
12.	_____effrontery	l.	foretell
13.	_____extirpate	m.	intensify
14.	_____haphazard	n.	laggard
15.	_____irascible	o.	minute
16.	_____laconic	p.	mitigate
17.	_____naive	q.	mulish
18.	_____obdurate	r.	odd
19.	_____precise	s.	random
20.	_____propitious	t.	splenetic
21.	_____senile	u.	verse
22.	_____shipshape	v.	tidy
23.	_____slovenly	w.	unkempt
24.	_____spiritless	x.	unsophisticated
25.	_____wily	y.	violate

SECTION III

Check the lettered word or phrase nearest in meaning to the numbered words below.

1. **banal**   (a) vivid, (b) imaginative, (c) fraternal, (d) commonplace

2. **chicanery**   (a) poultry, (b) admiration, (c) petty trickery, (d) stubborn pride

3. **diffident**   (a) unusual, (b) unconfident, (c) various, (d) routine

4. **quixotic**   (a) swift, (b) insane, (c) practical, (d) romantically idealistic

---
*Prepared especially for *Changing Times* Magazine by William Morris, noted editor and lexicographer.

5. **potable**   (a) drinkable, (b) transportable, (c) elementary, (d) poisonous

6. **mundane**   (a) pecuniary, (b) worldly, (c) municipal, (d) weekly

7. **necropolis**   (a) a large city, (b) cemetery, (c) lovers' lane, (d) site of a guillotine

8. **didactic**   (a) poetic, (b) entertaining, (c) instructive, (d) pertaining to diets

9. **truculent**   (a) portable, (b) amiable, (c) stiffly formal, (d) fiercely resentful

10. **opulent**   (a) wealthy, (b) industrious, (c) overweight, (d) impoverished

11. **effulgent**   (a) filling to overflowing, (b) feeding until corpulent, (c) pouring out a stream of radiant light, (d) retiring in nature

12. **euphony**   (a) repetitious sound, (b) musical variation, (c) characteristic of organization, (d) sweet sound

13. **prescience**   (a) preliminary investigation, (b) a phase of science, (c) crystal clear, (d) foresight or knowledge of the future

14. **postulate**   (a) protest, (b) reply to a statement, (c) a musical phrase, (d) proposition taken for granted

15. **ephemeral**   (a) effeminate, (b) lasting, (c) interesting, (d) short-lived

16. **persiflage**   (a) light raillery, (b) disguise, (c) anger, (d) thermal

17. **desultory**   (a) dreary, (b) designing, (c) aimless, (d) lonely

18. **profligate**   (a) set fire to, (b) recklessly extravagant, (c) humdrum, (d) hateful

19. **blatant**   (a) dark, (b) bland, (c) flattering, (d) noisy

20. **foment**   (a) extinguish, (b) smooth out, (c) nurse to life, (d) make bubblelike

21. **soporific**   (a) dreamy, (b) sleep-inducing, (c) of exceptional swiftness, (d) viscous

22. **collate**   (a) to eat a meal, (b) gather and compare, (c) clot, (d) add

23. **uxorious**   (a) slavishly devoted to one's wife, (b) urgent, (c) usurping, (d) laborious

24. **pariah**   (a) father, (b) an outcast, (c) an ancient, (d) a foreigner

25. **vestige**   (a) power of office given to officials, (b) a trace of something no longer existent, (c) early sign of sprouting seeds, (d) evidence of destruction

26. **accolade**   (a) an award or decoration, (b) a verdict handed down by courts, (c) decision rendered by international court, (d) a special dispensation

27. **redolent**   (a) harsh in scent, (b) pleasingly fragrant, (c) overflowing, (d) repetitious in nature

28. **anomalous**   (a) similar to another, (b) routine and regular, (c) diminutive (d) out of the ordinary

29. **hebdomadal**   (a) occurring at intervals of seven days, (b) varying at long intervals, (c) any idolatrous worship, (d) a seasonal variation

30. **insensate**   (a) undeveloped, (b) small in size (c) with high sensory reaction, (d) without sensation

31. **calumny**   (a) catastrophic action, (b) false accusation, (c) just accusation before a court, (d) a settling of guilt

32. **porcine**   (a) characteristically hoggish in appearance, (b) round-bodied and smooth, (c) high-handed, (d) lacking energy

33. **tautology**   (a) to pull something taut or tight (b) a kind of philosophy, (c) terseness in diction, (d) needless repetition of meaning in other words

34. **lucubration**   (a) system of oiling machinery, (b) state of being slippery, (c) laborious study, (d) process of cultivating land

35. **enucleate**   (a) to tie things together, (b) to raze a structure, (c) to peel out of a shell, (d) to break something

36. **verisimilar**   (a) closely resembling, (b) related mathematically, (c) contrary to reality, (d) appearing to be true

37. **depurate**   (a) to appoint a deputy, (b) to free of impurities, (c) to delegate authority, (d) to incorporate a group

38. **lustrate**   (a) to make pure by offerings, (b) to point out something, (c) to show by illustration, (d) to pay homage

39. **cozenage**   (a) study of family relations, (b) a type of humorous play, (c) organized play, (d) art or practice of fraud

40. **polyandry**   (a) a kind of mischievous ghost, (b) having more than one husband, (c) having more than one wife, (d) having many names

41. **ominous**   (a) thunderous or noisy, (b) inauspicious, (c) vacillating in action, (d) definitely true

42. **hegemony**   (a) leadership in government, (b) marriage between reigning families, (c) line of succession, (d) organization of political adherents

43. **flatulent**   (a) explosive, (b) without order or plan, (c) pretentious, (d) flat

44. **pother**   (a) to confuse, (b) to be contrary, (c) to plan, (d) to organize

45. **fecund**   (a) sourish, (b) hateful, (c) miserly, (d) prolific

46. **apostatize**   (a) to proclaim a saint, (b) to request, (c) to renounce one's faith, (d) to petition

47. **cortege**   (a) a procession, (b) a jury for a high court, (c) flowers worn on a dress, (d) a funeral

48. **eleemosynary**   (a) electing by popular vote, (b) receiving alms or favors, (c) sanguine in disposition, (d) apathetic in attitude

49. **pertinacious**   (a) loosely held, (b) with a tendency to give up, (c) proceeding on a straight line, (d) unyielding

50. **tumid**   (a) swollen, (b) dampish, (c) gigantic, (d) characterized by tumult

Now turn to the key on page 316 and check your answers.

How to Improve Your Vocabulary

Edgar Dale

It's not enough just to recognize the importance of word power. The next step is much more important. Exactly how do you improve your vocabulary? In this selection you'll find seven specific suggestions. Put them to immediate use and start enjoying the added confidence that follows.

The best readers usually have the best vocabularies. No really good reader has a poor one. A good reader is word-conscious, word-sensitive; he knows that words are an excellent way to share ideas and feelings. So one way to improve our reading is to improve our vocabulary, and vice versa.

What is an improved vocabulary? Certainly it is larger and broader. But also it has greater depth and precision. What can we do to develop a richer vocabulary?

Let's look first at the difference in size between an inadequate, poverty-stricken vocabulary and the rich vocabulary of an able, mature reader. About how many words are known by the average eighth-grader, the high-school graduate, the college graduate? How many does the ablest reader know?

There are about 600,000 words in a big, unabridged dictionary such as *Funk and Wagnalls New College Standard* or *Webster's New International. Webster's New Collegiate Dictionary* has more than 125,000 entries, and the 896-page *Thorndike-Barnhart Comprehensive Desk Dictionary* includes over 80,000.

The big, unabridged dictionaries, however, contain many forms of the same word, as well as many rare and obsolete words, and names of thousands of places, persons, rivers, and towns. So I find it more useful to think in terms of the 80,000-word Thorndike-Barnhart dictionary.

The average eighth-grader knows at least 10,000 of these words, the average high-school graduate about 15,000, and the average college graduate not fewer than 20,000. But even college graduates have trouble with such words as *adumbrate, attenuate, avuncular, deprecate, egregious, germane, ingenuous, jejune, plethora, temerity, unconscionable, unctuous.* An able reader increases his vocabulary well beyond the college graduate's 20,000 words.

The best way to improve your vocabulary is through firsthand experiences. If you have had experience in cooking, you know such words as *dredge, sear, draw, marinate, parboil, sauté, braise, frizzle, coddle.* A sports fan will know baseball terms, such as *fungo, Texas leaguer, infield fly.* You don't usually learn such vocabularies by reading books or magazines. But cooks and sports fans do read in these fields and thereby increase the range and depth of their vocabularies.

So a first rule in improving your vocabulary is to improve the range and depth of your experiences. Visits to museums, art exhibits, the legislature, or Congress bring increased vocabulary. So do working with the Community Chest, a nature hike, political activity, or a visit to the seashore. Think of the terms that sailing may bring into your active vocabulary: *scupper, topsail, dinghy, starboard, luff.*

A second suggestion is to work at your vocabulary a little every day. You can do this in several ways. Underline in pencil the hard words you run across in magazines, books, or newspapers. You need not even look them up. Just fix your attention on them, guess their meaning, and go right ahead with your reading. The next time you see one of these words, test your previous guess about its meaning. Maybe your guess fits now, and maybe it doesn't. Check it with your desk dictionary. You might also note its origin and get an additional memory hook on which to hang this word. If you check the pronunciation and say the word aloud, you get another boost in remembering it. You can also check on words you may mispronounce, such as *acclimate, archipelago, niche, orgy, schism, succinct.*

Third, you can sharply improve your vocabulary by reading more. You will see the hard words more often and in a variety of contexts. Of the many ways to increase your vocabulary by indirect experience, reading is the best.

Fourth, start using some of your "new" words in ordinary conversation.

Fifth, read aloud. Years ago, when I started to read "Penrod and Sam" to a seventh-grade class, I discovered that my speaking vocabulary was way behind my reading vocabulary. I did not know how to pronounce such words as *conversant, dolorous, primordial, flaccid, solaced.*

Sixth, you can increase your word power by becoming conscious of key roots and important suffixes and prefixes. A root such as *folium,* meaning *leaf,* gives us *foil, cinquefoil, foliaceous, foliage, foliate, folio, portfolio, trefoil.*

Do you know the prefixes *crypto-, hyper-, hypo-,*

neo-? They appear in words like *cryptocommunist, cryptograph, hyperbole, hypertension, hypertrophy, hypochondriac, neoclassic, neologism, neophyte.*

A single root such as the Greek *nym*, meaning name, yields *antonym, homonym, acronym, pseudonym, synonym, anonymous. Nom*, from the Latin *nomen*, also meaning name, gives us *nominate, nominative, nomination, denomination, nomenclature, nominee.*

A seventh way to improve your vocabulary is to develop an interest in the origins of words. Thus you learn that a *nightmare* is not a night horse but an evil spirit formerly supposed to cause bad dreams. A *nasturtium* is a nose twister. *Recalcitrant* means kicking back. *Excoriate* means to take the hide off. The *devil* in "between the devil and the deep blue sea" is a part of a boat.

Finally, it will help if you become conscious of the four stages by which vocabulary grows.

In the first stage, you see a word and are certain you have never seen it before. You never saw *shug* and *bittles*, hence don't know them. They are not words at all; I just made them up.

But you probably have seen words like *lethargic, lissome, serendipity.* If so, you may be in the second stage and may say, "I've seen these before, but I haven't any notion what they mean."

In the third stage, you are able to place the word in a broad classification. You may say, "I know that *lethargic* is an unfavorable word, that *lissome* and *serendipity* are attractive, favorable words, but I don't know exactly what they mean."

You are in the final stage when you know the word accurately.

Many of us have a large number of words in stage three, the twilight zone between words being known and yet not known. Are some of the following words in your twilight zone: *lares and penates, abscond, garrulous, dolorous, ingenuous, friable, tedium, savant, sedulous, sine qua non?*

Also, you may move a word toward a more scientific definition. You may have used *respiration* as a synonym for breathing; later you may learn it is the name for the body's process of absorbing oxygen and giving off carbon dioxide and water. A child may think of a *whale* as a fish, but the adult thinks of it as a mammal that nurses its young. A *spider* is not an insect. A *star* is not a planet. Botanically, a *tomato* is a fruit.

And there is precision of vocabulary — Wordsworth's "choice word and measured phrase." A tree isn't just a tree; it is a *cryptomeria*, a *locust*, a *white pine*, a *yellow poplar.* The ground may be *moist, sodden, arid,* or *parched.* Is a person *sulky, petulant,* or perhaps *bilious*? Why not learn the difference between a *jackanapes* and

a *jackal,* a *winch* and a *wench, pretentious* and *portentous*? The educated person is one who sees life with increasingly finer discriminations. And certainly this applies to his discrimination about the words he uses in speech and recognizes in reading.

Sometimes we may say, "Why should I study words before I need to use them? If I meet them in my reading, I'll look them up." But, curiously, a brief acquaintance with a word may cause us to see it later. Haven't you ever looked up an unusual or rare word and then suddenly found it in later reading?

Once, to illustrate an article, I chose four words from a list — *alb, valerian, periwinkle,* and *fichu.* I didn't know what they meant, but within three months I had "accidentally" seen and learned all of them. *Alb* appeared on a label in an exhibit of religious garments; *fichu* on a label describing the neckerchief worn by a young woman in a painting. I saw *valerian* in a display at the old country drugstore in the Farmers' Museum in Cooperstown, New York. And the color *periwinkle* blue turned up in the film *Artists and Models.*

I can draw two conclusions. First, just looking carefully at an unknown word and noting its spelling, as I suggested earlier, may cause us to be ready to see it later. And second, exhibits, galleries, and museums are good places to improve our vocabularies. Just looking sharply at an unknown word can thus be the cause of further experience as well as a result. A chance acquaintance with words sometimes brings them into our vocabulary. We become restless when we don't know what a *pied piper* is, the difference between a *monogram* and a *monograph*, between a *connoisseur* and a *dilettante*, between *ingenious* and *ingenuous.*

The best way of all to improve your vocabulary is to get fun out of words. I enjoy collecting interesting misuses and mispronunciations, such as: "He stepped on the exhilarator." "We are studying jubilant delinquency." "I don't deserve all this oolagoozing." "I don't like to sing solo; I like to sing abreast." "Minch pie." "My boy can't come to school. He has indolent fever."

If we accept the late John Erskine's theory that we have a moral obligation to be intelligent, we should improve our vocabularies. Then, we can read magazines and books that wake us up mentally. We can "argue" with the authors. We can discuss what we have read, improve our dinner-table conversation, be more interesting people.

Your vocabulary gives you away. It may suggest that you are a person with a rich and varied experience, for it tells where you have been, what you have read, talked about, reflected upon. And it tells how far you have traveled along the road to intellectual maturity and discriminating living.

Number of words 1600
See page 317 for Questions

Reading time in Seconds _____
See page 361 for Conversion Table

In Defense of Gender

Cyra McFadden

In the English language we're blessed with three genders — masculine, feminine, and neuter. And that's where we have the problem of desexing English. He/She/It must not feel slighted, of course. Take a closer look at the desexing problem.

So pervasive is the neutering of the English language on the progressive West Coast, we no longer have people here, only persons: male persons and female persons, chairpersons and doorpersons, waitpersons, mailpersons — who may be either male or female mailpersons — and refuse-collection persons. In the classified ads, working mothers seek childcare persons, though one wonders how many men (archaic for "male person") take care of child persons as a full-time occupation. One such ad, fusing nonsexist language and the most popular word in the California growth movement, solicits a "nurtureperson."

Dear gents and ladies, as I might have addressed you in less troubled times, this female person knows firsthand the reasons for scourging sexist bias from the language. God knows what damage was done me, at 15, when I worked in my first job — as what is now known as a newspaper copyperson — and came running to the voices of men barking, "Boy!"

No aspirant to the job of refuse-collection person myself, I nonetheless take off my hat (a little feathered number, with a veil) to those of my own sex who may want both the job and a genderless title with it. I argue only that there must be a better way, and I wish person or persons unknown would come up with one.

Defend it on any grounds you choose; the neutering of spoken and written English, with its attendant self-consciousness, remains ludicrous. In print, those "person" suffixes and "he/she's" jump out from the page, as distracting as a cloud of gnats, demanding that the reader note the writer's virtue. "Look what a nonsexist writer person I am, avoiding the use of masculine forms for the generic."

Spoken, they leave conversation fit only for the Coneheads on "Saturday Night Live." "They have a daily special," a woman at the next table told her male companion in Perry's, a San Francisco restaurant. "Ask your waitperson." In a Steig cartoon, the words would have marched from her mouth in the form of a computer printout.

In Berkeley, Calif., the church to which a friend belongs is busy stripping its liturgy of sexist references. "They've gone berserk," she writes, citing a reading

from the pulpit of a verse from I Corinthians. Neutered, the once glorious passage becomes "Though I speak with the tongues of persons and of angels . . ." So much for sounding brass and tinkling cymbals.

The parson person of the same church is now referring to God as "He/She" and changing all references accordingly — no easy undertaking if he intends to be consistent. In the following, the first pronoun would remain because at this primitive stage of human evolution, male persons do not give birth to babies: "And she brought forth her firstborn son/daughter, and wrapped him/her in swaddling clothes, and laid him/her in a manger; because there was no room for them in the inn. . . ."

As the after-dinner speaker at a recent professional conference, I heard a text replete with "he/she's" and "his/her's" read aloud for the first time. The hapless program female chairperson stuck with the job chose to render these orally as "he-slash-she" and "his-slash-her," turning the following day's schedule for conference participants into what sounded like a replay of the Manson killings.

Redress may be due those of us who, though female, have answered to masculine referents all these years, but slashing is not the answer; violence never is. Perhaps we could right matters by using feminine forms as the generic for a few centuries, or simply agree on a per-woman lump-sum payment.

Still, we would be left with the problem of referring, without bias, to transpersons. These are not bus drivers or Amtrak conductors but persons in transit from one gender to the other — or so I interpret a fund-drive appeal asking me to defend their civil rights, along with those of female and male homosexuals.

Without wishing to step on anyone's civil rights, I hope transpersons are not the next politically significant pressure group. If they are, count on it, they will soon want their own pronouns.

In the tradition of the West, meanwhile, feminists out here wrestle the language to the ground, plant a foot on its neck and remove its masculine appendages. Take the local art critic Beverly Terwoman.

She is married to a man surnamed Terman. She writes under "Terwoman," presumably in the spirit of *vive la différence.* As a letter to the editor of the paper for which she writes noted, however, "Terwoman" is not ideologically pure. It still contains "man," a syllable reeking of all that is piggy and hairy-chested.

Why not Beverly Terperson? Or better, since "Terperson" contains "son," "Terdaughter"? Or a final refinement, Beverly Ter?

Beverly Terwoman did not dignify this sexist assault with a reply. The writer of the letter was a male person, after all, probably the kind who leaves his smelly sweat socks scattered around the bedroom floor.

No one wins these battles anyway. In another letter to the same local weekly, J. Seibert, female, lets fire at the printing of an interview with Phyllis Schlafly. Not only was the piece "an offense to everything that Marin County stands for," but "it is even more amusing that your interview was conducted by a male."

"This indicates your obvious assumption that men understand women's issues better than women since men are obviously more intelligent (as no doubt Phyllis would agree)."

A sigh suffuses the editor's note that follows: "The author of the article, Sydney Weisman, is a female."

So the war of the pronouns and suffixes rages, taking no prisoners except writers. Neuter your prose with all those clanking "he/she's," and no one will read you except Alan Alda. Use masculine forms as the generic, and you have joined the ranks of the oppressor. None of this does much to encourage friendly relations between persons, transpersons or — if there are any left — people.

I also have little patience with the hyphenated names more and more California female persons adopt when they marry, in the interests of retaining their own personhood. These accomplish their intention of declaring the husband separate but equal. They are hell on those of us who have trouble remembering one name, much less two. They defeat answering machines, which can't handle "Please call Gwendolyn Grunt-Messerschmidt." And in this culture, they retain overtones of false gentility.

Two surnames, to me, still bring to mind the female writers of bad romances and Julia Ward Howe.

It's a mug's game, friends, this neutering of a language already fat, bland and lethargic, and it's time we decide not to play it. This female person is currently writing a book about rodeo. I'll be dragged behind a saddle bronc before I will neuter the text with "cowpersons."

Number of words 1125
See page 319 for Questions

Reading time in Seconds _____
See page 361 for Conversion Table

SELECTION 67

Two Words to Avoid, Two to Remember

Arthur Gordon

Back near the turn of the century, Emile Coué, a French psychotherapist, devised a system of autosuggestion which he brought to America. To start the day his way, you said three times, "Every day in every way I'm getting better and better." It's the verse from the Bible all over again: "As he thinketh in his heart, so is he." Here's still another example to apply.

Nothing in life is more exciting and rewarding than the sudden flash of insight that leaves you a changed person—not only changed, but changed for the better. Such moments are rare, certainly, but they come to all of us. Sometimes from a book, a sermon, a line of poetry. Sometimes from a friend. . . .

That wintry afternoon in Manhattan, waiting in the little French restaurant, I was feeling frustrated and depressed. Because of several miscalculations on my part, a project of considerable importance in my life had fallen through. Even the prospect of seeing a dear friend (the Old Man, as I privately and affectionately thought of him) failed to cheer me as it usually did. I sat there frowning at the checkered tablecloth, chewing the bitter cud of hindsight.

He came across the street, finally, muffled in his ancient overcoat, shapeless felt hat pulled down over his bald head, looking more like an energetic gnome than an eminent psychiatrist. His offices were nearby; I knew he had just left his last patient of the day. He was close to 80, but he still carried a full case load, still acted as director of a large foundation, still loved to escape to the golf course whenever he could.

By the time he came over and sat beside me, the waiter had brought his invariable bottle of ale. I had not seen him for several months, but he seemed as indestructible as ever. "Well, young man," he said without preliminary, "what's troubling you?"

I had long since ceased to be surprised at his perceptiveness. So I proceeded to tell him, at some length, just what was bothering me. With a kind of melancholy pride, I tried to be very honest. I blamed no one else for my disappointment, only myself. I analyzed the whole thing, all the bad judgments, the false moves. I went on for perhaps 15 minutes, while the Old Man sipped his ale in silence.

When I finished, he put down his glass. "Come on," he said. "Let's go back to my office."

"Your office? Did you forget something?"

"No," he said mildly. "I want your reaction to something. That's all."

A chill rain was beginning to fall outside, but his office was warm and comfortable and familiar: book-lined walls, long leather couch, signed photograph of Sigmund Freud, tape recorder by the window. His secretary had gone home. We were alone.

The Old Man took a tape from a flat cardboard box and fitted it onto the machine. "On this tape," he said, "are three short recordings made by three persons who came to me for help. They are not identified, of course. I want you to listen to the recordings and see if you can pick out the two-word phrase that is the common denominator in all three cases." He smiled. "Don't look so puzzled. I have my reasons."

What the owners of the voices on the tape had in common, it seemed to me, was unhappiness. The man who spoke first evidently had suffered some kind of business loss or failure; he berated himself for not having worked harder, for not having looked ahead. The woman who spoke next had never married because of a sense of obligation to her widowed mother; she recalled bitterly all the marital chances she had let go by. The third voice belonged to a mother whose teen-age son was in trouble with the police; she blamed herself endlessly.

The Old Man switched off the machine and leaned back in his chair. "Six times in those recordings a phrase is used that's full of subtle poison. Did you spot it? No? Well, perhaps that's because you used it three times yourself down in the restaurant a little while ago." He picked up the box that had held the tape and tossed it over to me. "There they are, right on the label. The two saddest words in any language."

I looked down. Printed neatly in red ink were the words: *If only.*

"You'd be amazed," said the Old Man, "if you knew how many thousands of times I've sat in this chair and listened to woeful sentences beginning with those two words. 'If only,' they say to me, 'I had done it differently—or not done it at all. If only I hadn't lost my temper, said that cruel thing, made that dishonest move, told that foolish lie. If only I had been wiser, or more

unselfish, or more self-controlled.' They go on and on until I stop them. Sometimes I make them listen to the recordings you just heard. 'If only,' I say to them, 'you'd stop saying *if only,* we might begin to get somewhere!' "

The Old Man stretched out his legs. "The trouble with 'if only,' " he said, "is that it doesn't change anything. It keeps the person facing the wrong way—backward instead of forward. It wastes time. In the end, if you let it become a habit, it can become a real roadblock, an excuse for not trying anymore.

"Now take your own case: your plans didn't work out. Why? Because you made certain mistakes. Well, that's all right: everyone makes mistakes. Mistakes are what we learn from. But when you were telling me about them, lamenting this, regretting that, you weren't really learning from them."

"How do you know?" I said, a bit defensively.

"Because," said the Old Man, "you never got out of the past tense. Not once did you mention the future. And in a way—be honest, now!—you were enjoying it. There's a perverse streak in all of us that makes us like to hash over old mistakes. After all, when you relate the story of some disaster or disappointment that has happened to you, you're still the chief character, still in the center of the stage."

I shook my head ruefully. "Well, what's the remedy?"

"Shift the focus," said the Old Man promptly. "Change the key words and substitute a phrase that supplies lift instead of creating drag."

"Do you have such a phrase to recommend?"

"Certainly. Strike out the words 'if only'; substitute the phrase 'next time.' "

"Next time?"

"That's right. I've seen it work minor miracles right here in this room. As long as a patient keeps saying 'if only' to me, he's in trouble. But when he looks me in the eye and says 'next time,' I know he's on his way to overcoming his problem. It means he has decided to apply the lessons he has learned from his experience, however grim or painful it may have been. It means he's going to push aside the roadblock of regret, move forward, take action, resume living. Try it yourself. You'll see."

My old friend stopped speaking. Outside, I could hear the rain whispering against the windowpane. I tried sliding one phrase out of my mind and replacing it with the other. It was fanciful, of course, but I could hear the new words lock into place with an audible click.

"One last thing," the Old Man said. "Apply this little trick to things that can still be remedied." From the bookcase behind him he pulled out something that looked like a diary. "Here's a journal kept a generation ago by a woman who was a schoolteacher in my hometown. Her husband was a kind of amiable ne'er-do-well, charming but totally inadequate as a provider. This woman had to raise the children, pay the bills, keep the family together. Her diary is fully of angry references to Jonathan's weaknesses, Jonathan's shortcomings, Jonathan's inadequacies.

"Then Jonathan died, and all the entries ceased except for one—years later. Here it is: 'Today I was made superintendent of schools, and I suppose I should be very proud. But if I knew that Jonathan was out there somewhere beyond the stars, and if I knew how to manage it, I would go to him tonight.' "

The Old Man closed the book gently. "You see? What she's saying is 'if only'; if only I had accepted him, faults and all; if only I had loved him while I could." He put the book back on the shelf. "That's when those sad words are the saddest of all: when it's too late to retrieve anything."

He stood up a bit stiffly. "Well, class dismissed. It has been good to see you, young man. Always is. Now, if you will help me find a taxi, I probably should be getting on home."

We came out of the building into the rainy night. I spotted a cruising cab and ran toward it, but another pedestrian was quicker.

"My, my," said the Old Man slyly. "If only we had come down ten seconds sooner, we'd have caught that cab, wouldn't we?"

I laughed and picked up the cue. "Next time I'll run faster."

"That's it," cried the Old Man, pulling his absurd hat down around his ears. "That's it exactly!"

Another taxi slowed. I opened the door for him. He smiled and waved as it moved away. I never saw him again. A month later, he died of a sudden heart attack, in full stride, so to speak.

More than a year has passed since that rainy afternoon in Manhattan. But to this day, whenever I find myself thinking "if only," I change it to "next time." Then I wait for that almost-perceptible mental click. And when I hear it, I think of the Old Man.

A small fragment of immortality, to be sure. But it's the kind he would have wanted.

Number of words 1596
See page 321 for Questions

Reading time in Seconds _____
See page 361 for Conversion Table

SELECTION 68

My Alma Mater

Malcolm X

Have you ever observed, personally, a man who commanded total respect with his words? Malcolm X once did. That started him on a word-building program without parallel. The heart of his program was the dictionary. Here's what he did with it.

The first man I met in prison who made any positive impression on me whatever was a fellow inmate, "Bimbi." I met him in 1947, at Charlestown. He was a light, kind of red-complexioned Negro, as I was; about my height, and he had freckles. Bimbi, an old-time burglar, had been in many prisons. In the license plate shop where our gang worked, he operated the machine that stamped out the numbers. I was along the conveyor belt where the numbers were painted.

Bimbi was the first Negro convict I'd known who didn't respond to "What'cha know, Daddy?" Often, after we had done our day's license plate quota, we would sit around, perhaps fifteen of us, and listen to Bimbi. Normally, white prisoners wouldn't think of listening to Negro prisoners' opinions on anything, but guards, even, would wander over close to hear Bimbi on any subject.

He would have a cluster of people riveted, often on odd subjects you never would think of. He would prove to us, dipping into the science of human behavior, that the only difference between us and outside people was that we had been caught. He liked to talk about historical events and figures. When he talked about the history

From *The Autobiography of Malcolm X*, by Malcolm X and Alex Haley. Copyright © 1964 by Alex Haley and Malcolm X. Copyright © 1965 by Alex Haley and Betty Shabazz. Reprinted by permission of Random House, Inc.

148

of Concord, where I was to be transferred later, you would have thought he was hired by the Chamber of Commerce, and I wasn't the first inmate who had never heard of Thoreau until Bimbi expounded upon him. Bimbi was known as the library's best customer. What fascinated me with him most of all was that he was the first man I had ever seen command total respect . . . with his words.

Bimbi seldom said much to me; he was gruff to individuals, but I sensed he liked me. What made me seek his friendship was when I heard him discuss religion. I considered myself beyond atheism — I was Satan. But Bimbi put the atheist philosophy in a framework, so to speak. That ended my vicious cursing attacks. My approach sounded so weak alongside his, and he never used a foul word.

Out of the blue one day, Bimbi told me flatly, as was his way, that I had some brains, if I'd use them. I had wanted his friendship, not that kind of advice. I might have cursed another convict, but nobody cursed Bimbi. He told me I should take advantage of the prison correspondence courses and the library.

When I had finished the eighth grade back in Mason, Michigan, that was the last time I'd thought of studying anything that didn't have some hustle purpose. And the streets had erased everything I'd ever learned in school; I didn't know a verb from a house. . . .

Many who today hear me somewhere in person, or on television, or those who read something I've said, will think I went to school far beyond the eighth grade. This impression is due entirely to my prison studies.

It had really begun back in the Charlestown Prison, when Bimbi first made me feel envy of his stock of knowledge. Bimbi had always taken charge of any conversation he was in, and I had tried to emulate him. But every book I picked up had few sentences which didn't contain anywhere from one to nearly all of the words that might as well have been in Chinese. When I just skipped those words, of course, I really ended up with little idea of what the book said. So I had come to the Norfolk Prison Colony still going through only book-reading motions. Pretty soon, I would have quit even these motions, unless I had received the motivation that I did.

I saw that the best thing I could do was get hold of a dictionary — to study, to learn some words. I was lucky enough to reason also that I should try to improve my penmanship. It was sad. I couldn't even write in a straight line. It was both ideas together that moved me to request a dictionary along with some tablets and pencils from the Norfolk Prison Colony school.

I spent two days just riffling uncertainly through the dictionary's pages. I'd never realized so many words existed! I didn't know which words I needed to learn. Finally, to start some kind of action, I began copying.

In my slow, painstaking, ragged handwriting, I copied into my tablet everything printed on that first page, down to the punctuation marks.

I believe it took me a day. Then, aloud, I read back, to myself, everything I'd written on the tablet. Over and over, aloud, to myself, I read my own handwriting.

I woke up the next morning, thinking about those words — immensely proud to realize that not only had I written so much at one time, but I'd written words that I never knew were in the world. Moreover, with a little effort, I also could remember what many of these words meant. I reviewed the words whose meanings I didn't remember. Funny thing, from the dictionary first page right now, that "aardvark" springs to my mind. The dictionary had a picture of it, a long-tailed, long-eared, burrowing African mammal, which lives off termites caught by sticking out its tongue as an anteater does for ants.

I was so fascinated that I went on — I copied the dictionary's next page. And the same experience came when I studied that. With every succeeding page, I also learned of people and places and events from history. Actually the dictionary is like a miniature encyclopedia. Finally the dictionary's A section had filled a whole tablet — and I went on into the B's. That was the way I started copying what eventually became the entire dictionary. It went a lot faster after so much practice helped me to pick up handwriting speed. Between what I wrote in my tablet, and writing letters, during the rest of my time in prison I would guess I wrote a million words.

I suppose it was inevitable that as my word-base broadened, I could for the first time pick up a book and read and now begin to understand what the book was saying. Anyone who has read a great deal can imagine the new world that opened. Let me tell you something; from then until I left that prison, in every free moment I had, if I was not reading in the library, I was reading on my bunk. You couldn't have gotten me out of books with a wedge. Between Mr. Muhammad's teachings, my correspondence, my visitors — usually Ella and Reginald — and my reading of books, months passed without my even thinking about being imprisoned. In fact, up to then, I never had been so truly free in my life. . . .

As you can imagine, especially in a prison where there was heavy emphasis on rehabilitation, an inmate was smiled upon if he demonstrated an unusually intense interest in books. There was a sizable number of well-read inmates, especially the popular debaters. Some were said by many to be practically walking encyclopedias. They were almost celebrities. No university would ask any student to devour literature as I did when this new world opened to me, of being able to read and *understand.*

I read more in my room than in the library itself. An inmate who was known to read a lot could check out more than the permitted maximum number of books. I preferred reading in the total isolation of my own room.

When I had progressed to really serious reading, every night at about ten P.M. I would be outraged with the "lights out." It always seemed to catch me right in the middle of something engrossing.

Fortunately, right outside my door was a corridor light that cast a glow into my room. The glow was enough to read by, once my eyes adjusted to it. So when "lights out" came, I would sit on the floor where I could continue reading in that glow.

At one-hour intervals the night guards paced past every room. Each time I heard the approaching footsteps, I jumped into bed and feigned sleep. And as soon as the guard passed, I got back out of bed onto the floor area of that light-glow, where I would read for another fifty-eight minutes — until the guard approached again. That went on until three or four every morning. Three or four hours of sleep a night was enough for me. Often in the years in the streets I had slept less than that.

I have often reflected upon the new vistas that reading opened to me. I knew right there in prison that reading had changed forever the course of my life. As I see it today, the ability to read awoke inside me some long dormant craving to be mentally alive. I certainly wasn't

seeking any degree, the way a college confers a status symbol upon its students. My homemade education gave me, with every additional book that I read, a little bit more sensitivity to the deafness, dumbness, and blindness that was afflicting the black race in America. Not long ago, an English writer telephoned me from London, asking questions. One was, "What's your alma mater?" I told him, "Books." You will never catch me with a free fifteen minutes in which I'm not studying something I feel might be able to help the black man. . . .

Every time I catch a plane, I have with me a book that I want to read — and that's a lot of books these days. If I weren't out here every day battling the white man, I could spend the rest of my life reading, just satisfying my curiosity — because you can hardly mention anything I'm not curious about. I don't think anybody ever got more out of going to prison than I did. In fact, prison enabled me to study far more intensively than I would have if my life had gone differently and I had attended some college. I imagine that one of the biggest troubles with colleges is there are too many distractions, too much panty-raiding, fraternities, and boola-boola and all of that. Where else but in prison could I have attacked my ignorance by being able to study intensely sometimes as much as fifteen hours a day?

Number of words 1720
See page 323 for Questions

Reading time in Seconds _____
See page 361 for Conversion Table

See page 323 for Questions
See page 361 for Conversion Table

SELECTION 69

A Master-Word Approach to Vocabulary

James I. Brown

A master word is like a master key. An ordinary key unlocks only one or two doors. A master key for a building may unlock over a hundred doors. Master words provide that same kind of comprehensive help in unlocking not one word meaning but hundreds.

How would you like a way of getting acquainted with words, a thousand at a time?

A few minutes with each of the following fourteen words will help you master well over 14,000 words. These words, the most important in the language to speed you along a superhighway toward vocabulary and success, do even more. They furnish invaluable background for further word study and give you a technique, a master key, which has endless possibilities.

You see, most of our English words are not English at all, but borrowings from other languages. Eighty percent of these borrowed words come to us from Latin

and Greek and make up approximately sixty percent of our language.

Since this is so, the most important of these classical elements offer amazingly useful short cuts to a bigger vocabulary. The words in the list at the end of this article contain twelve of the most important Latin roots, two of the most important Greek roots, and twenty of the most frequently used prefixes. Over 14,000 relatively common words, words of collegiate dictionary size, contain one or more of these elements (or an estimated 100,000 words of unabridged dictionary size).

Now, how to put these words to work, converting them into keys to the meanings of thousands of related words?

First, look up each of the fourteen words in the dic-

Reprinted by permission from the May 1949 issue of *Word Study* © 1949 by Merriam-Webster, Inc., Publishers of the Merriam-Webster ® Dictionaries.

tionary, noticing the relationship between derivation and definition. For example, take the word "intermittent." Let's chop it in two and chase it back to its birthplace. The two halves you come up with are a Latin prefix "inter-," which means "among" or "between," and a root word "mittere," which to a Roman meant "to send." "To send between!"

That does it. That drags the ghosts out of the Latin closet and arranges their bones so you can tell what goes on. An *intermittent* sound is one that is "sent between" periods of silence. Maybe those Romans had something, when you dust away the cobwebs caused by a dislike of high-school Latin. Now compare that derivational meaning, "to send between," with the dictionary definition, "coming or going at intervals."

This step develops an understanding of the many relationships existing between derivation and definition, relationships from almost exact agreement — as with *prefix,* by derivation and definition meaning "to fix before," — to varied extensions and restrictions of the derivational meaning.

Next, look up each prefix. When you look up "pre-," for example, you'll find five somewhat different specific meanings, all denoting priority — priority in time, space, or rank. The dictionary entry will fix those meanings in mind and will often indicate assimilative changes.

The third step is to list at least ten words containing the prefix, checking each with the dictionary to avoid mistakes. You'll find some prefixes as changeable as chameleons. *Offer* is really *ob-fer,* but *offer* is easier to say. And there's the word *cooperation,* "to operate or

work together." But doesn't *com-* mean "together?" Yes, but *comoperation* is awkward to say, so we say *cooperation.* This prepares you for the changes that occur when *com-* is combined with *-stant, -relation, -laboration,* and *-cil* to make *constant, correlation, collaboration,* and *council.* There's your background for recognizing similar chameleon-like changes of *ob-, ad-, ex-,* and others.

Finally, list at least ten words containing the root, checking each carefully with the dictionary. A few examples are listed for each root which should suggest others. Try to discover less common forms by some intelligent guessing.

Take the root *plicare,* "to fold" — the one that's part of *complication.* First of all, you'll think of *application, implication,* and *duplication. Duplication* may suggest *duplex* as well as *perplex* and *complex. Complex* may open the way to *comply,* which may in turn remind you of *apply, imply, pliant, supply, deploy,* and *employ.* Each discovery you make of a variant form adds that much to your background and understanding of the large family of words for which that root is key. Your dictionary will keep your guesses in line with the facts.

So much for method. Now, just how useful is your newly acquired knowledge of roots and prefixes?

Suppose you see the strange word *explication.* You know *ex-* means "out" and you know *plicare* means "to fold" — "to fold out." With the help of the sentence — "his explication was confused and difficult to follow" you see that explication refers to an unfolding

THE FOURTEEN WORDS

KEYS TO THE MEANINGS OF OVER 14,000 WORDS

WORDS	PREFIX	COMMON MEANING	ROOT	COMMON MEANING
1. *Precept*	pre-	(before)	capere	(take, seize)
2. *Detain*	de-	(away, from)	tenere	(hold, have)
3. *Intermittent*	inter-	(between)	mittere	(send)
4. *Offer*	ob-	(against)	ferre	(bear, carry)
5. *Insist*	in-	(into)	stare	(stand)
6. *Monograph*	mono-	(alone, one)	graphein	(write)
7. *Epilogue*	epi-	(upon)	legein	(say, study of)
8. *Aspect*	ad-	(to, towards)	specere	(see)
9. *Uncomplicated*	un-	(not)	plicare	(fold)
	com-	(together with)		
10. *Nonextended*	non-	(not)	tendere	(stretch)
	ex-	(out of)		
11. *Reproduction*	re-	(back, again)	ducere	(lead)
	pro-	(forward)		
12. *Indisposed*	in-	(not)	ponere	(put, place)
	dis-	(apart from)		
13. *Oversufficient*	over-	(above)	facere	(make, do)
	sub-	(under)		
14. *Mistranscribe*	mis-	(wrong)	scribere	(write)
	trans-	(across, beyond)		

or folding out of meaning — or an explanation, in other words. Sometimes knowing only part of the word is enough. A student reading of a man's *predilection* for novels need only notice the *pre-* to assume that the man places novels "before" other books, that he has a "preference" or "partiality" for novels. Take another example. Is a *precocious* child one who has matured before or later than the average child? Again the prefix is your key to the meaning.

This procedure puts certain psychological laws of learning to work for you overtime. It forces you to discover meaningful relationships between derivation and definition. It stimulates you to use your knowledge to analyze strange words and understand familiar words better. It leads you to discover important principles of language development. In short, it forces you to take the initiative necessary to speed toward vocabulary and success.

And spelling is easier. If you continually misspell *prescription*, spelling it with a *per-*, you have only to remember the meanings of the prefixes. Since a prescrip-

tion is written *before* being filled, you'll have to spell it with a *pre-*. You'll also know how to spell such demons as *misspell* or *misstep*, for you know they're combinations of *mis-* with *spell* and *step*. And what about someone who migrates into this country? Is he an *immigrant* or *emigrant*? Since he's coming *into* the country, he is an *in-migrant* or by assimilation an *immigrant*.

In this way you begin to understand the intricacies of our language. At first you'll have trouble spotting the root *facere* in such a word as *benefactor*. But soon you'll be a regular Sherlock Holmes, able to ferret out that root in such varied disguises as *artifice, affair, feature, affection, facsimile, counterfeit, fashion, facilitate*. You'll soon have no trouble finding the prefix *ex-* in *effect*, or *in-* in *illiterate*, or *dis-* in *differ*.

And best of all, you'll have a master key to unlock the meanings of thousands of other words, a technique to use with other classical elements. Yours is the magic touchstone, curiosity about derivations, which will bring words to life and lead you eventually to an awareness and understanding of words reached by relatively few.

Number of words 1090
See page 325 for Questions

Reading time in Seconds _____
See page 361 for Conversion Table

SELECTION 70

Vocabulary First-Aid

Paul Witty

For a student, a new word a day keeps the low grades away. For someone in business, a new word a day speeds success on its way. And for all of us, a new word a day adds zest right away. Words are indeed important. Vocabulary first-aid deserves major attention.

Before you attempt to build your vocabulary, consider for a moment what words really are. Words are similar to money, as the following comparison shows.

You may have heard someone say that money is "a medium of exchange." Money itself—the paper and metal out of which bills and coins are made—has only a small actual value. The real value of money is in what it stands for. And that *what* includes among other things groceries, clothing, shelter, automobiles, movies, and medical care.

Words, like money, have little value in and of themselves. They are important because they stand for real things—objects, actions, sounds, thoughts, and feelings. They are also important because they are a medium for the exchange of ideas.

If you want to get a clearer notion of what words mean to you every day, try getting along without them. When you sit down to dinner this evening. "tell" your family something you did today. Instead of using words, try to use sign language only. You will find it difficult if not impossible to exchange many ideas. Then, tell your story in words. You will quickly decide that, as a medium of communication, words are truly wonderful.

WORDS PROMOTE BETTER LIVING

If you are short on words, you may also be short on ideas. This will handicap you in school or college, on the job, at home, or elsewhere. But if you know many words, you are likely to have a wealth of ideas. You are better able to understand what you read or hear. You are also better able to express yourself when you talk or write.

Studies of successful people clearly show that they usually have large vocabularies. They know the exact

From *How to Become a Better Reader* by Paul Witty. © 1953, Science Research Associates, Inc. Reprinted by permission of the publisher.

meanings of words. And they use the right word in the right place at the right time.

Because words are an aid to good living, you will want to build your vocabulary. As you do so, you will improve your reading.

WORDS CAN BE WALLS OR GATEWAYS TO UNDERSTANDING

Assume that you have a very small vocabulary. Also assume that you do not know how to get the meanings of new words. When you come across an unfamiliar word, that word may block, like a wall, your understanding of the material. Your eyes pause too long on the word as you try to get its meaning. You go back and read the word again trying to obtain its meaning from the context —the words in the sentence where the word appears. As a result, you read much more slowly than you should— and you find that the hard word is a wall to your comprehension.

Suppose, however, that you know many words and that you are skilled in finding the meanings of new words. Then, your eyes move quickly and you read rapidly. You comprehend instantly what you are reading. To you, words are gateways which lead to better understanding.

If you have a good vocabulary, moreover, you are more likely to read for ideas. As your eyes move along a line of print, you do not think of words as words. When you see a word group, you think an idea—the idea for which the word group stands.

YOU CAN MASTER NEW WORDS

No matter how good your vocabulary may be, you can always improve it. To strengthen your word power, you should set up your own program. This lesson will suggest ways to do it.

After you finish this lesson, you will want to continue your word-building program. If you do, you will maintain your interest in vocabulary growth. You will expand your vocabulary. And this will challenge your thinking, broaden your ideas, and increase the information and enjoyment that you get from reading.

Your bigger and better vocabulary will also help you increase the speed and accuracy of your reading. New and hard words will no longer master you, for you will have become their master.

WHAT ARE THE MAIN TYPES OF VOCABULARY?

If you take a close look at the words you use, you will find that you really have two main types of vocabulary. The first type is your general vocabulary; the second type is made up of your technical vocabularies.

Your general vocabulary includes the words you commonly use in conversation and correspondence, and the words you read in newspapers, books, and magazines. Your technical vocabularies include the words you find in specialized subjects or fields such as English history, chemistry, engineering, medicine, farming, auto repair, and cooking.

You can build your general vocabulary indirectly through extensive reading—that is, through reading widely in different fields. You can also increase your general vocabulary directly through studying words.

Through your reading and your other experiences, you can develop your technical vocabularies. You, of course, do not want to master the technical vocabularies of all the different professions or trades, for example. In fact, you could not learn all these vocabularies even though you spent a lifetime trying to do so. Yet, you will need to acquire a technical vocabulary in each subject or field in which you are especially interested.

HOW CAN YOU BEST LEARN THE MEANINGS OF NEW WORDS?

As mentioned before, you use words in four main ways:

1. You read what other people have written.
2. You listen to other people.
3. You talk to other people.
4. You write to other people.

In each of these ways, you can increase your word power. With this greater word power, you can improve your reading, your conversation, and your writing.

Because you are using this book to become a better reader, this lesson tells you how you can build your vocabulary through reading and for reading. To increase your word knowledge, here are some suggestions:

1. *Look and listen for new words.* Keep your eyes and ears open for words that you do not know. You will see them in reading. You will hear them in talking with other people, in watching movies, and in listening to radio or television programs.
2. *Write down your new words.* Get yourself a pocket notebook and label it, "My Vocabulary Notebook." Carry this notebook with you. In it, write down every new word that you see or hear. Do this immediately. If you wait, you may forget the new word.
3. *Find the meanings of new words.* In the dictionary, look up the meanings of the new words that you have written in your vocabulary notebook. At the right of each word, write the dictionary definition or meaning that applies to the word as it was used in what you read or heard.
4. *Make the new words your own.* Use each new word in talking with your family or friends. Pronounce the word accurately. Also, use this word in what you are writing. Spell the word correctly. In speaking or writing, be sure that you use the word as it should be used.

5. *Enter several new words in your vocabulary note-book each day.* Keep building your word power. At the end of the week, quickly review the new words you entered during the seven-day period just ended. This review will help you remember the meanings of these words.

BUILD YOUR VOCABULARY WHILE YOU READ

When you meet a new word in your reading, guess its meaning. Using your pencil, mark a check near the word so that you can find it later. Then keep on reading until you finish the entire story or part of the story. In this way, you do not allow a new word to slow down your reading speed or to interrupt your understanding of the flow of the story.

Number of words 1380
See page 327 for Questions

After you finish the story or part of it, go back and find the new words that you did not know. Write each word in your vocabulary notebook. Then take these steps.

1. Try to guess the meaning of the word. Write down your guess.
2. Try to get the word's meaning by reading again the sentence in which the word appears. Copy the sentence.
3. Look up the word in the dictionary. Find the definition or meaning that applies to the sentence in which the word appears. Then write down this meaning.
4. Write your own sentence that includes this word.

Reading time in Seconds _____
See page 361 for Conversion Table

SELECTION 71

The Freshman and His Dictionary

Mitford M. Mathews

As every English teacher knows, too many students believe that a dictionary contains little more than the spelling and meaning of words. Here Mathews suggests that it has riches and resources far beyond mere definitions. Let him share some insights.

When I was a small boy a carpenter once said in my presence that few workmen, even among master mechanics, knew more than a fraction of the uses of an ordinary steel square. The remark amazed me, as at that early age I thought a carpenter's square was a very simple tool. It certainly appeared so to me — nothing more than two flat pieces of metal forming a right angle, and useful in marking a plank that one wished to saw in two in something like a workmanlike manner. True, the instrument has numerous markings and numbers on it, but I had never seen anyone making the slightest use of these, so I had concluded they might be ignored.

When I became older and found that large books have been written on the uses of the steel square, I changed my mind about the simplicity of the tool and the limited range of its usefulness. For many years as I have observed the use made of dictionaries by even good students, I have been reminded of that remark by the carpenter about steel squares.

Dictionaries are tools, and they are much more complicated, and capable of many more uses than students

suspect. All of us know students need encouragement and guidance in the use of dictionaries, and perhaps there are few teachers of freshman composition but that devote a part of their program to an effort to help students form the habit of consulting dictionaries. Composition books for freshmen point out the need for instruction of this kind.

Despite what is being done, however, the fact is easily observable that few students are able to use their dictionaries with anything like efficiency. Certainly there must be very few of those who come up through the grades these days who are not familiar with the details of looking up words in dictionaries, but it is one thing to find a word in a dictionary and quite another to understand fully the information there given about it. It seems to me that college freshmen are fully prepared for and could profit by a well-planned introduction to the larger English dictionaries, and an acquaintance with what they contain. Such a program might well include material of the following kinds.

1. Students should know something about the large, unabridged dictionaries to which they have ready access in college. They might well be given brief sketches of the *Oxford English Dictionary,* the *English Dialect Dictionary,* by Joseph Wright, the old *Century Dictionary* (12 volumes), and the modern unabridged

From *College Composition and Communication* (December 1955). Reprinted by permission of the author and the National Council of the Teachers of English.

Webster. These may be called the "Big Four" in the dictionary field, and while it is certainly not anticipated that the freshman will ever provide himself with all of them, it is a cultural experience for him to become acquainted with the circumstances under which each of them was produced, and with the special excellencies each exhibits.

An acquaintance with these larger works will not only make the student aware of what kind of information about words is available in them, but it will leave him much better prepared to make efficient use of the desk-size dictionary with which he has some familiarity.

Many years ago a graduate student inconvenienced himself greatly to come a long distance to see me to ask if I could help him secure some information about the term "poll tax." He was preparing a doctor's thesis, he told me, and needed to know how long this term had been in the language, what its basic meaning was, and what other meanings it may have had in the course of its use in English. He was most surprised when I opened the *OED* to the appropriate place and showed him that all he needed to know about this term had been available within a few feet of his desk in the school where he was studying. It is not at all likely that any but the exceptional student will ever need all the information about words that the larger dictionaries afford, but it is well worth the while of every student to become acquainted with the fact that such information is available for those who at any time need to make use of it.

It is to be hoped that in such general instruction as may be given about the different dictionaries, some emphasis will be placed on the fact that modern dictionaries do their utmost to *record* usage, not to *prescribe* it. The tendency to regard the lexicographer as a linguistic legislator is so deep-seated that it will probably never be entirely overcome. The habit of thought that is back of such expressions as "the dictionary now permits us to pronounce it thus," has been with us for a long time, and will continue. But every student should have the wholesome experience of being taught that dictionaries attempt to give commonly accepted usage, and that correctness in the use of language varies sometimes according to time and place.

2. Along with some information about the origin and scope of the large dictionaries mentioned, there should be given some elementary information about the history of the English language and the place it occupies with reference to the others of the Indo-European group. I am certainly not foolish enough to suggest that all teachers of freshman composition become instructors in Germanic philology. What I have in mind is nothing more detailed than could be easily covered in one, or at most two, class sessions, the over-all relationships of the languages being presented briefly, with a few well chosen examples to indicate the relationship of a few of them.

The desirability of this elementary acquaintance with the linguistic position occupied by English is brought out quite clearly by Professor Pei in his *Story of Language*:

> Many years ago I was requested to tutor in French a young girl who had to take College Entrance Examinations. Knowing that she had had four years of Latin as well as three years of French, I spared no occasion in the course of the tutoring to remind her that certain French words which she had difficulty in remembering came from Latin words she knew. For a time she took it patiently, though with a somewhat bewildered air. But one day she finally blurted out: "Do you mean to tell me that there is a *connection* between Latin and French?" In the course of four years of one language and three of the other, it had never occurred to any of her Latin teachers to inform her that Latin had descendants, or to her French teacher to tell her that French has a progenitor!

3. The attention usually devoted to instruction in the use of the dictionary apparently stresses spellings, meanings, and pronunciations somewhat in the order here given. Certainly these are conspicuous features of any dictionary, and it is altogether desirable for students to be encouraged to turn to these works when they are confronted with a problem of the kind indicated.

The impression, however, inevitably conveyed by instruction restricted altogether to employing the dictionary as a problem-solver, is that such a book is of no particular use unless there is a problem requiring immediate attention. Students are sorely tempted to so manipulate things as to avoid encountering problems that drive them to a dictionary. It is to be feared that, for many of them, the dictionary is a form of medicine to be resorted to only in time of unavoidable need. They associate it perhaps with castor oil or some other undesirable, dynamic type of cathartic. It is a most helpful thing for the student to learn that dictionaries are filled with interesting information from which one can derive much pleasure and instruction, even though he may not be confronted with an urgent problem of any kind.

Students should be encouraged to develop a wholesome curiosity about words that present no particular problem in spelling, pronunciation, or meaning. As a rule, the words we know well do not rise to the surface of our consciousness. It is only rarely that some common, everyday term forces itself upon our attention so urgently that for the first time we turn to the dictionary to see what lies back of it.

This use of the dictionary when there is no immediate, pressing need to do so, this giving attention to words we have known for a long time but have never grown curious about, is most rewarding. This kind of use of the dictionary we may think of as the labor of free men; the forced use is more properly likened to that of slaves.

On every hand there are words of fascinating backgrounds about which the dictionary has much to teach us. Certainly the name *Jesus,* that of the founder of Christianity, is well known to all those with whom you and I come in contact. Perhaps few of us have ever felt impelled to look the word up in a dictionary, or even realized that dictionaries contain it. An examination of the dictionary, however, reveals that the name his parents gave the Savior was Joshua, and it was by this thoroughly Jewish name that He was known by those He lived among.

The first accounts of His life were written in Greek, and in these writings *Joshua* was transliterated into *Jesus,* a name that is certainly not Jewish in its present dress and at the same time appears odd as a Greek name.

Not even a grade-school pupil is likely to be baffled by *ostrich,* but one who is allergic to words may well become curious about it. Allow it to become the focus of your attention for a moment and see how odd the word appears. Make a guess as to where you think it might have come from, and then check up on yourself by turning to the dictionary. You might be surprised, as I was, to find the word is made up of two, one from Latin and one from Greek, which have so blended as to obscure altogether the fact that the expression signifies "bird-bird" or "bird-sparrow." It is a good term to bear in mind and use upon those of our brethren who insist that only "pure English" should be used, and profess to be pained by such obvious hybrids as *cablegram* and *electrocute.*

There may be few teachers who have discovered how rewarding it is to look curiously at the scientific terms used in dictionaries in the definitions of plants and animals. These expressions are usually hurried over by most of us as being the exclusive property of scientists and of very little interest for others.

It is surprisingly interesting to linger over such terms. It is a gratifying experience to discover one that yields its significance somewhat readily. Our common mocking bird, for instance, is *Mimus polyglottos.* The ingenuity needed for deciphering this expression is possessed by all of us. *Mimic* and *polyglot* are all we need to see that our expression means "the many-tongued mimic," a fitting description of the bird in question.

In the spring when the snow has melted, and the earth is warming up from its long cold sleep, the cheer-ful piping notes of a very small frog begin to be heard in the woods and marshes. People call this little creature a *spring peeper* because of the season when his little peeping notes are first heard, but scientists dub him *Hyla crucifer.* As we puzzle over this name we are likely to give up on *Hyla* for there is no other word in the English language with which we can, perhaps, associate it properly. It has descendants among us, but we are not likely to be acquainted with them.

Crucifer though is easier. Even if we do not know that a *crucifer* is one who carries a cross, especially in a church procession, we can reason out the two elements in the word and see that it must have the meaning of one who carries a cross. Our ability to reason out this much of the scentific expression may increase our curiosity about the first element *Hyla.* Here is a helpful hint. As we all know, these scientific genus names are often from Greek. So we are reasoning sensibly when we suppose *Hyla* is Greek.

The fact is elementary that when we are confronted with a Greek word which begins with an *h,* i.e. with a rough breathing, it behooves us as cautious scouts to cast about in our minds for a possible Latin cognate beginning with an *s.* Substituting an *s* in *hyla* we come up with *syla.* Let us study *syla* a bit. It is almost a word. If we might be so bold as to insert a -v- and make it *sylva* we have a word that is in our dictionary, and one we met in a slightly different form, *silva,* when we studied first-year Latin.

The little detail of why this -v- is necessary need not bother us in the slightest at this point, because we are just having fun with no idea of becoming linguisticians. And this is it. *Hyla* and *sylva* go together and they both mean wood or forest. Now we can interpret this *Hyla crucifer* "the (little) fellow who lives in the woods and carries a cross," and when we find that this spring peeper has a dark marking on his back shaped like a cross, we are indeed gratified that now light is shining where previously all was darkness.

A teacher who is fortunate enough to have an assiduously cultivated curiosity about words will over and over again bring to a class gleanings of unexpected sorts from dictionaries. Such sharing of treasures will do more than anything else to bring home to students the fact that dictionaries are not dull, enlarged spelling books. They are filled with such a number of things that we can never exhaust their treasures but we can all be as happy as kings as we come time after time upon interesting nuggets of the kind just mentioned.

Number of words 2340
See page 329 for Questions

Reading time in Seconds _____
See page 361 for Conversion Table

SELECTION 72

The Myth of Supermom

Betty Friedan

Have women really won choices — or simply traded a feminine *mystique for a* feminist *mystique? Ms. Friedan's conclusions will startle women who care deeply and men who care deeply about them.*

These past few years, I have been nagged by an uneasy feeling of urgency. Listening to my own daughter and sons, and others of their generation whom I've met while lecturing at universities and attending professional conferences around the world, I sense something *off,* out of focus, going wrong, in the terms by which these young people are trying to live the equality we in the women's movement fought for.

In the voices of these daughters and sons, I've begun to sense undertones of pain and puzzlement, a queasiness, an uneasiness, almost a bitterness that they hardly dare admit. Despite all the opportunities we won for them, and for which we envy them, they seem afraid to ask certain questions. And they continue to be troubled by those old needs which shaped our lives and trapped us, those needs against which we rebelled.

• In California, in the office of a television producer who prides himself on being an "equal opportunity employer," I am confronted by his new "executive assistant." She wants to talk to me alone before her boss arrives. Lovely, in her late 20's and "dressed for success," she is not just a glorified secretary with a fancy title in a dead-end job. The woman she replaced has just been promoted to the position of "creative vice president."

"I know I'm lucky to have this job," she says, defensive and accusing, "but you people who fought for these things had your families. You already had your men and children. What are we supposed to do?"

• A young woman in her third year at Harvard Medical School tells me, "I'm going to be a surgeon. I'll never be a trapped housewife like my mother. But I would like to get married and have children, I think. They say we can have it all. But how? I work 36 hours in the hospital, 12 off. How am I going to have a relationship, much less kids, with hours like that? I'm not sure I can be a superwoman. I'm frightened that I may be kidding myself. Maybe I can't have it all. Either I

won't be able to have the kind of marriage I dream of or the kind of medical career I want."

• In New York, a woman in her 30's who has just been promoted says, "I'm up against the clock, you might say. If I don't have a child now, it will be too late. But it's an agonizing choice. I've been supporting my husband while he gets his Ph.D. We don't know what kind of job he'll be able to get. There's no pay when you take off to have a baby in my company. They don't guarantee you'll get your job back. If I don't have a baby, will I miss out on life somehow? Will I really be fulfilled as a woman?"

I sense victories we thought were won yielding illusory gains; I see new dimensions to problems we thought were solved. After 15 years of the women's movement, the gap between women's earnings and men's is greater than ever, with women earning on the average only 59 cents to every dollar men earn; the average male high-school dropout today earning $1,600 more a year than female college graduates.

An unprecedented majority of women have entered the work force in these years, but the overwhelming majority of women are still crowded into the poorly paid service and clerical jobs traditionally reserved for females. (With the divorce rate exceeding 40 percent, it turns out that 71 percent of divorced women are now working compared to only 78 percent of divorced men; the women must be taking jobs the men won't touch.)

Even in the "new girls" network of the women who've broken through to the executive suite and enjoyed the tokens of professional and political equality, I sense the exhilaration of "superwoman" giving way to a tiredness, a certain brittle disappointment, a disillusionment with "assertiveness training" and the rewards of power. Matina Horner, the high-powered president of Radcliffe, calls it a "crisis of confidence."

What worries me today is that many of the "choices" women have supposedly won are not turning out to be viable options. How can a woman freely "choose" to have a child when her paycheck is needed for the rent or mortgage, when her job isn't geared to taking care of a child, when there is no national policy for parental leave and no assurance that her job will be waiting for her if she takes time off to have a child?

What also worries me is that despite the fact that more than 40 percent of the mothers of children under 6 are now working because of economic necessity due to inflation, compared with only 10 percent in 1960 (and, according to a Ford Foundation study, it is estimated that by 1990 only one out of four mothers will be at home full time), no major national effort is being made for child-care services by Government, business, labor, Democratic or Republican parties — or by the women's movement itself.

In the 15 or 20 years after World War II we were bombarded with the image of woman as being completely fulfilled in her role as wife and mother. It was an image I called the "feminine mystique," and it denied the very existence in women of the need to be recognized as persons, individuals in their own right.

In the 1960's we broke through that image. So for nearly 20 years now, the words written about, by and for women have been about women's need to be themselves, find themselves and fulfill themselves — to free themselves from submission as servants of the family and take control of their own bodies, their own lives; to find their own identities apart from men, marriage and child-rearing; to demand equal opportunity and power of their own in corporate office, Senate chamber, spaceship, ballfield, battlefield, at whatever price.

As feminist Ellen Goodman writes, "We were to be the first generation of superwomen. We were the women who would — in fact, should — have dazzling careers and brilliant, satisfied husbands and remarkable, well-adjusted children" (*Washington Post,* June 7, 1980).

But the new image, which has come out of the women's movement, cannot evade the continuing tests of real life. That uneasiness I have been sensing these past few years comes from personal truth denied and questions unasked because they do not fit the new accepted image — the *feminist* mystique. It may take only a few years for the feminist image to harden into a similarly confining, defensive mystique. Does our feminist image already leave out important new, or old, dimensions of female possibility and necessity?

I want to help women break through the mystique I helped to create. They have to ask new questions, speak the unspeakable again, admit new, uncomfortable realities and secret pains and surprising joys of their personal truth that are hard to put into words because they do not fit either the new or old images of women.

The simple, heartfelt questions I've been hearing from young women all over the country this past year seem to me to indicate a blind spot in feminism that is both personal and political in its implications and consequences. The younger women have the most questions:

"How can I have it all? Do I *really* have to choose?"

"How can I have the career I want and the kind of marriage I want and be a good mother?"

"How can I get my husband to share more responsibility at home? Why do I always have to be the one with the children, making the decisions at home?"

"I can't count on marriage for my security — look what happened to my mother — but can I get all my security from my career?"

"Can I make it in a man's world, doing it the man's way? What other way is there? But what is it doing to me? Do I want to be like men?"

"Will the jobs open to me now still be there if I stop working in order to have children?"

"Does it really work, that business of 'quality, not quantity' of time with the children? How much is enough?"

"How can I fill my loneliness, except with a man?"

"Do men really want 'equal' women?"

"If I put off having a baby till I'm 38 and can call my own shots on the job, will I ever have kids?"

"How can I juggle it all?"

"How can I put it all together?"

"Can I risk losing myself in marriage?"

"Do I have to be a superwoman?"

I think we can only find the answers by sharing our new uncertainties, the seemingly insoluble problems and unremitting pressures, our fears and shameful weaknesses. Do we deny certain painful feelings, certain yearnings, certain simple needs for fear we will drown in them, be trapped again in the weakness, the helplessness, the terrible dependence that was woman's lot before? If we suddenly suggest that old experiences supposedly irrelevant or distracting to new women are, in fact, more important than we wanted to admit — experiences like motherhood, which the old feminine mystique and the new enemies of equality claim are the only important experiences for women — do we thereby deny the importance of the gains won in the women's movement: Would we want to go back?

That is the fear, of course. That is why we do not want to face new questions, new tests. But if we go on parroting or denouncing or defending the cliches of women's liberation in the same old terms until they harden into a new mystique, denying the realities of our personal experience and the new problems, *then* we are in real danger of going back. *Then,* we invite a real backlash of disillusioned, bitter women — and outraged, beleaguered men.

The balance of power is undeniably shifting now between the sexes, everywhere in the world, as women move into jobs. But the tradeoffs have not been worked out in the family. In fact, for the real tradeoffs to take place, the sharp demarcation between family and home as "woman's world," and work (and politics and war) as "man's world" will have to be redrawn. Equality in jobs, without domestic equality, leaves women doubly burdened. And equality in the family isn't real for women if it is isolated from economic measures of worth and survival in the world.

Part of the problem comes from the lack of either real economic measures or political attention to the previously private woman's work, in home and family, an irreducible minimum of which is necessary for the survival of humans and their society.

The new imbalance is becoming visible, at least. Equal job opportunities for women "will turn out to be a recipe for overwork" unless "the sharing of unpaid household labor between men and women becomes a reality," said a research report issued by the World Watch Institute in 1980. Although half of the world's adult women are in the labor force out of choice or necessity, "they have retained an unwilling monopoly on unpaid labor at home. The result is a pronounced imbalance between male and female workloads, with unhappy consequences for women, men and children."

In a certain sense, the roles of women and men in the labor force have virtually come full circle. Historically, both men and women worked to "support the household in subsistence production," states the World Watch report. Then came the split "between women's unpaid work in the household and men's breadwinning." In the current transition, the report continues, "women increasingly share the breadwinning role with men but retain most of the responsibility for the house." In "the as-yet-unrealized ideal," the family will again become symmetrical, when "both the financial support and the physical maintenance of the family are equally shared between men and women."

Between 1950 and 1975, the number of women considered "economically active" rose from 344 million to 576 million, both because of women's rising demand for equality and inflationary pressures requiring them to seek jobs outside the house. Since this trend was not matched by an increased involvement of men in housework, women are now carrying a double burden.

When supposed solutions such as part-time work, flextime and child-care centers are sought as "women's benefits," instead of easing the strain between work and family, they actually do the reverse, merely "reinforcing the idea that home and family belong to women's sphere rather than being a joint responsibility."

We weren't wrong, in the women's movement, to focus the first stage on equal opportunity for jobs and education. Women have to experience at least the beginnings of equality in the world before they can trade off that supreme, excessively burdensome power in the family.

The transition to the next stage of the women's movement won't be easy. The same shadow of the idealized family of the past — that compulsion to be a Perfect Mother left over from excessive female dependence — keeps many women *and* the experts from coming to grips with the new problems. But for the sake of women and men and families, we must begin to break through the feminist mystique — and the myth of supermom.

Number of words 2210
See page 331 for Questions

Reading time in Seconds _____
See page 361 for Conversion Table

SELECTION 73

From *The Road to Wigan Pier*

George Orwell

Machines — we'd be lost without them, wouldn't we? Or, as Orwell suggests, are we actually lost with *them? Are you convinced by his reasoning? How do we manage the technological monster we have created?*

The function of the machine is to save work. In a fully mechanised world all the dull drudgery will be done by machinery, leaving us free for more interesting pursuits. So expressed, this sounds splendid. It makes one sick to see half a dozen men sweating their guts out to dig

From *The Road to Wigan Pier* by George Orwell. Reprinted by permission of Harcourt Brace Jovanovich, Inc. and the estate of the late Sonia Brownell Orwell and Martin Secker & Warburg Ltd.

a trench for a water-pipe, when some easily devised machine would scoop the earth out in a couple of minutes. Why not let the machine do the work and the men go and do something else. But presently the question arises, what else are they to do? Supposedly they are set free from "work" in order that they may do something which is not "work." But what is work and what is not work? Is it work to dig, to carpenter, to plant trees, to fell trees, to ride, to fish, to hunt, to feed chickens, to play the piano, to take photographs, to build a house, to cook, to sew, to trim hats, to mend motor bicycles? All of these things are work to somebody, and all of them are play to somebody. There are in fact very few activities which cannot be classed either as work or play according as you choose to regard them. The labourer set free from digging may want to spend his leisure, or part of it, in playing the piano, while the professional pianist may be only too glad to get out and dig at the potato patch. Hence the antithesis between work, as something intolerably tedious, and not-work, as something desirable, is false. The truth is that when a human being is not eating, drinking, sleeping, making love, talking, playing games or merely lounging about — and these things will not fill up a lifetime — he needs work and usually looks for it, though he may not call it work. Above the level of a third- or fourth-grade moron, life has got to be lived largely in terms of effort. For man is not, as the vulgarer hedonists seem to suppose, a kind of walking stomach; he has also got a hand, an eye and a brain. Cease to use your hands, and you have lopped off a huge chunk of your consciousness. And now consider again those half-dozen men who were digging the trench for the water-pipe. A machine has set them free from digging, and they are going to amuse themselves with something else — carpentering, for instance. But whatever they want to do, they will find that another machine has set them free from *that*. For in a fully mechanised world there would be no more need to carpenter, to cook, to mend motor bicycles, etc., than there would be to dig. There is scarcely anything, from catching a whale to carving a cherry stone, that could not conceivably be done by machinery. The machine would even encroach upon the activities we now class as "art"; it is doing so already, via the camera and the radio. Mechanise the world as fully as it might be mechanised, and whichever way you turn there will be some machine cutting you off from the chance of working — that is, of living.

At a first glance this might not seem to matter. Why should you not get on with your "creative work" and disregard the machines that would do it for you? But it is not so simple as it sounds. Here am I, working eight hours a day in an insurance office; in my spare time I want to do something "creative," so I choose to do a bit of carpentering — to make myself a table, for instance. Notice that from the very start there is a touch of artificiality about the whole business, for the factories can turn me out a far better table than I can make for myself. But even when I get to work on my table, it is not possible for me to feel towards it as the cabinet-maker of a hundred years ago felt towards his table, still less as Robinson Crusoe felt towards his. For before I start, most of the work has already been done for me by machinery. The tools I use demand the minimum of skill. I can get, for instance, planes which will cut out any moulding; the cabinet-maker of a hundred years ago would have had to do the work with chisel and gouge, which demanded real skill of eye and hand. The boards I buy are ready planed and the legs are ready turned by the lathe. I can even go to the wood-shop and buy all the parts of the table ready-made and only needing to be fitted together; my work being reduced to driving in a few pegs and using a piece of sandpaper. And if this is so at present, in the mechanised future it will be enormously more so. With the tools and materials available *then,* there will be no possibility of mistake, hence no room for skill. Making a table will be easier and duller than peeling a potato. In such circumstances it is nonsense to talk of "creative work." In any case the arts of the hand (which have got to be transmitted by apprenticeship) would long since have disappeared. Some of them have disappeared already, under the competition of the machine. Look round any country churchyard and see whether you can find a decently-cut tombstone later than 1820. The art, or rather the craft, of stonework has died out so completely that it would take centuries to revive it.

But it may be said, why not retain the machine *and* retain "creative work"? Why not cultivate anachronisms as a spare-time hobby? Many people have played with this idea; it seems to solve with such beautiful ease the problems set by the machine. The citizen of Utopia, we are told, coming home from his daily two hours of turning a handle in the tomato-canning factory, will deliberately revert to a more primitive way of life and solace his creative instincts with a bit of fretwork, pottery-glazing or handloom-weaving. And why is this picture an absurdity — as it is, of course? Because of a principle that is not always recognised, though always acted upon: that so long as the machine *is there,* one is under an obligation to use it. No one draws water from the well when he can turn on the tap. One sees a good illustration of this in the matter of travel. Everyone who has travelled by primitive methods in an undeveloped country, knows that the difference between that kind of travel and modern travel in trains, cars, etc., is the difference between life and death. The nomad who walks or rides, with his baggage stowed on a camel or an ox-cart, may suffer every kind of discomfort, but at least he is living while he is travelling; whereas for the passenger in an express train or a luxury liner his journey is an interregnum, a kind of temporary death. And yet so long as the railways exist, one has got to travel by train — or by car or aeroplane. Here am I, forty miles from London. When I want to go up to London why do I not pack my luggage on to a mule and set out on foot, making a two days' march of it? Because, with the Green Line buses whizzing past me every ten minutes, such a journey would be intolerably irksome. In order that one may enjoy primitive methods of travel, it is necessary that no other method should be available. No human being ever wants to do anything in a more cumbrous way than is necessary. Hence the absurdity of that picture of Utopians saving their souls with fretwork. In a world where everything could be done by machinery, everything would be done by machinery. Deliberately to revert to primitive methods, to use archaic tools, to put silly little difficulties in your own way, would be a piece of dilettantism, of pretty-pretty arty and craftiness. It would be like solemnly sitting down to eat your dinner with stone implements. Revert to handwork in a machine age, and you are back in Ye Olde Tea Shoppe or the Tudor villa with the sham beams tacked to the wall.

Number of words 1380
See page 333 for Questions

Reading time in Seconds _____
See page 361 for Conversion Table

SELECTION 74

How to Live 24 Hours a Day

Arthur Gordon

To live fully is, of course, a major problem. A Gallup Poll asked, "Do you find life exciting, pretty routine, or dull?" Of the 1,521 questioned, 51 percent found life "dull" or "routine." Going to college makes the most difference; only 24 percent of the college-bred replied "dull" or "routine." What else helps twenty-four hours a day?

Like several million other people, my wife is a faithful reader of a lady columnist who gives advice on all subjects. Pretty good advice, too, most of the time. But the other night I noticed the faithful reader frowning over the newspaper. "Here," she said, "take a look at this."

In the column, a married woman in her mid-30s was voicing a wistful complaint. She got on well with her husband, they had three well-adjusted children, there were no great health or financial problems. But something was wrong. There was busyness in her life, but no fulfillment. There was a coping with day-to-day problems, but no sense of adventure or joy. She had every reason to be contented, but she felt only half alive. What should she do? What *could* she do? She signed herself, *The Unenviable Mrs. Jones.*

In reply, the columnist urged the woman to be satisfied with what she had. Other people, she pointed out, had far more serious difficulties. "Count your blessings," she advised . . . and moved on to the next problem.

"The trouble with that reply," my wife said, "is that it doesn't answer the question. And the question needs to be answered, because it's just about the most important one there is. I know exactly how that woman feels. She wants to overcome her sense of futility. She wants somebody to tell her how to escape from ordinariness and start living — really be alive — 24 hours a day."

"Can anyone," I said skeptically, "really be alive every single hour?"

"Oh," said my wife impatiently, "you know what I mean. In terms of time we all live 24 hours a day, but that's just horizontal living. In terms of emotions, people live vertically. At least, they should. That's what this Mrs. Jones is groping for: Depth in living and feeling. Intensity — that's the word, I guess. If you ask me, the main enemy in most marriages today isn't cruelty or infidelity or poverty or alcoholism. It's monotony. And frustration. I feel very sorry for Mrs. Jones."

"So do I," I said.

"Well," my wife said, "why don't you *do* something about it? In your work you meet all sorts of people who are supposed to be experts in the field of human behavior. Surely they'd have something to offer that would be helpful. Why don't you pick a psychiatrist and a minister and ask them what they'd say if Mrs. Jones came to them with her problem?"

"I might talk to Herb Smith about it," I said, "the next time we go fishing. He's about as good a psychiatrist as I know. And the next time I go to New York I could ask Norman Peale what he would say."

"Do that," my wife replied. "This is a tough question. People need some answers."

"It's a very widespread thing," Dr. Herbert D. Smith said, "this nagging uneasiness, this feeling that life is hiding from you, that you've lost the capacity to enjoy or appreciate the ordinary pleasures of existence. I think women are more susceptible to it than men — partly because men tend to be absorbed in their work, partly because, being more emotional, women can become emotionally starved more easily.

"Now, what would I say to Mrs. Jones? I think I'd start by trying to reassure her a little. I'd tell her that her feelings are understandable, that many people have similar ones, that it takes courage to admit that you're dissatisfied with your life.

"Next, I'd try to inject some realism into her thinking. I'd say, 'Mrs. Jones, let's talk for a moment about something called acceptance. It's important, because unless you start with a degree of acceptance, you're going to go right on being discontented no matter what I say to you. We all have certain limitations in our lives. We all yearn for more excitement and pleasure than we have. There are times when I wish I were an explorer or an astronaut, but I'm just a doctor, you're just a housewife, and I can't radically change my circumstances any more than you can. What I *can* change — if I work at it — is my attitude toward these circumstances, and, to some degree, my performance within those circumstances.'

"Finally, I'd give Mrs. Jones three specific suggestions to follow. She's really in a prison, partly of her own making. These three suggestions are designed to help her break out. Here they are:

"1. *Pay more attention to people.* Attention is a dialogue, and a dialogue is an escape from self. You can't be totally self-imprisoned when you pay deep attention to what another person feels, or says, or is.

"It doesn't matter who the other person is. Let's say your neighbor Martha drops in from next door for a cup of coffee. You're fond of Martha, but you take her completely for granted, and at times you feel she's a bit of a trial because she's always complaining about something.

"But take a new look at Martha. Why is she the way she is? What is she trying to say to you that she doesn't know how to say in words? What needs does she have that you might possibly supply? Ask yourself, 'Who is this person?' On the surface she may seem like the same old Martha, complaining this time because her feet hurt or her husband snores. But actually, you have, right there in your kitchen, sitting at your table, a creature so fantastically complex that all the psychiatrists in the world couldn't fully explain her to you — or to herself.

"And don't limit yourself to Martha. Learn to observe and study all kinds of people. It's endlessly fascinating — and it will take your mind off yourself.

"2. *Give your emotions more elbowroom.* You can't expect them to have much vitality if you're constantly overcontrolling them. Too many of us are hesitant about expressing affection — we're afraid it may be misinterpreted or even rejected. Too many of us are ashamed of flashes of anger even when there's a valid cause. Too many of us have forgotten how to roar with laughter. These stifled emotions fence us in, cut us off from life and people. If Mrs. Jones would let herself go occasionally, instead of mutely enduring her frustrations, she might be a lot better off.

"3. *Start a one-woman rebellion against routine.* This is the greatest single cause of emotional numbness: The unvarying repetition of basically uninteresting tasks. Life tries to clamp a pattern down on all of us, and it's not easy to fight back. But it's imperative to try, even in small things. I remember I once ordered a man to drive to work by a different route every day, no matter how much extra time it consumed. He thought this was foolish, but it wasn't. He was encrusted with old, stale habits. We had to start somewhere.

"So I would say to Mrs. Jones, 'When routine begins to stifle you, look for new ways of doing things. Even with chores that have to be done, try to dramatize them somehow. Set new performance goals. Try to cut your shopping time or your vacuuming time in half; compete with yourself.

" 'Force yourself to do something unexpected now and then. Walk in the summer rain without an umbrella or a raincoat. Get up before dawn and watch a sunrise. Strike up a conversation with a stranger. Write a letter without using the words *I* or *me, my* or *mine.* In a restaurant, order a meal consisting exclusively of things you have never tasted before.

" 'In other words, Mrs. Jones, fight deadening routine as if it were your mortal enemy. Because it is.'

"If Mrs. Jones or anyone like her will take those suggestions seriously," Dr. Smith concluded, "I think she'll find that her problems grow less."

"What this Mrs. Jones is suffering from," Norman Vincent Peale said thoughtfully, "is a form of soul-sickness that is a peculiarly modern disease. Part of it, I think, is the result of a kind of emotional isolation. One or two generations ago, children grew up in large families with uncles and aunts scattered up and down the block and grandparents readily available. There wasn't so much shifting around; people knew and counted on their neighbors. But now we tend to live in tight family units — two antagonistic generations crowded together with all the interpersonal strains concentrated relentlessly day after day. Just parents and kids, no buffer personalities at all. No wonder people feel stifled and depressed.

"As for Mrs. Jones, I would make a few suggestions designed to get her into better alignment with the universe that surrounds her. I'd try to keep them practical, not pious. And I'd try to make them short.

"I'd say to her, 'Mrs. Jones, one of the things you need most is a heightened sense of awareness. This is not a gift that anyone can hand you; you must develop it yourself. You must make a conscious and deliberate effort to become more sensitized to the beauty and mystery and magic of things. Take life to pieces and what do you have? Miraculous fragments of reality. Not one of them is really commonplace. It's our reactions to them that grow dull if we let them.

" 'Learn to look beyond the obvious. If, let's say, you see a furry caterpillar walking on your windowsill, you must sometimes — not always, but *sometimes* — regard it not just as an unwelcome intruder that deserves to be squashed, but as a manifestation of the life force that in its own way is just as remarkable as you are.'

"I knew a woman once who had a serious illness followed by a long convalescence. Day after day she lay in bed, weak and listless. Her doctors were very concerned; the vital spark seemed almost to have flickered out. Then, suddenly, she began to improve dramatically.

"Later, when asked about her recovery, she pointed to a magnifying glass, small but powerful. 'This has a lot to do with it,' she said. 'When a friend brought it to me, I had almost lost interest in living. But when I began to look through it, commonplace things became astonishing. You have no idea what you can see in a simple flower, or a leaf, or a piece of cloth. I believe that something in me decided that this world was too beautiful to leave — and so I began to get well.'

"I would say to Mrs. Jones that this kind of discovery is available to all of us. Not everyone can be a Thoreau, perhaps, and live by a remote lake with no companionship but his own thoughts. But it should be possible for each of us to find his own small wilderness in a garden or a seashore or even a cramped backyard — any place where things grow and the seasons change and small creatures exist in their own tiny worlds. Even a city dweller can go up on the roof at night, or out into the street and stare at the stars and think about the incomprehensible distances and magnitudes involved. I remember once being told by an astronomer about one star so huge that if a creature existed on it in the same proportion to his star as we are to our Earth, he could swallow our sun without burning his throat. 'Ponder that, Mrs. Jones, and feel your mind reel — as it should!'

"What else can you do to develop a sense of wonder? All sorts of mental tricks! Imagined scarcity, for example. Suppose the common alley cat you see crossing the road were the *only* cat in existence. What a fabulous creature it would be considered — beautiful, sinuous, superb and priceless. Or suppose this were the last time you could ever see a sunset, or hear great music, or tuck your child into bed. Just a supposition, sure — but it creates a sense of wonder and gratitude.

"I would also advise Mrs. Jones to align herself with goodness now and then. I know that's what a preacher is expected to say, but there's more to it than that. 'This is an ethical universe,' I'd say. 'You are part of it, Mrs. Jones. Therefore it's important to put yourself in tune with those powerful unseen forces.'

"How do you do this? It's simple. Visit a sick friend. Take on some worthwhile civic responsibility. Help someone less fortunate. Give somebody an unexpected gift. Put yourself out when you'd much rather not. Do these things as often as you can.

"What does this have to do with intensity of living? Just this: The person who is bored or unfulfilled is almost always the person who is uninvolved. And often he's uninvolved because his self-esteem and, consequently, his self-confidence are low. Performing a kindness; helping another person makes you like yourself better. And the more you like yourself, the more outgoing and unbored you are going to be.

"Finally," the minister said, "I'd talk to Mrs. Jones about love, because this is the key that will open the doors that she feels are closed to her. I'd probably talk to her mainly about married love, which someone has called 'the persistent effort of two persons to create for each other conditions under which each can become the person God meant him to be.' If a woman — or a man, for that matter — can even come close to this ideal, *everything* is going to be colored by it. Every one of the 24 hours in a day is going to be richer and brighter.

"I rather suspect that if Mrs. Jones ever had this kind of relationship, it has become dimmed by the dust of daily living. That's what's at the heart of her discontent. And so I would recommend that she and her husband find a quiet place and quiet time and ask themselves three basic questions. Perhaps they could think them over alone at first.

" '1. In the life that you are leading today, what gives you most satisfaction, what seems most worthwhile? Is it sex, religion, children, work, some form of recreation? Do you agree, between yourselves, as to what it is? Do you share it — or does it separate you? Don't try in one sitting to solve the problems the question may raise. Just look at them honestly.

" '2. Thirty years from now, when you look back at your life as it is today, how will you feel about the way you are investing your time? Will you think some of your activities were unnecessary and meaningless? Will you wish you had used the priceless days of hours differently? Sit quietly — and discuss — and think.

" '3. If you could change just one thing in your husband-wife relationship, if each of you had one magic wish that could be instantly granted, what would that wish be? Listen carefully to what your partner says, because in it may lie a clue to your own happiness — or to what is keeping you from it.'

"And that," Dr. Peale concluded, "is approximately what I'd say to the unhappy Mrs. Jones."

"Well," I said later, when I had put their thoughts on paper and showed them to my wife, "what do you think?"

"They're good answers," she said. "But it's still an enormous question."

"Of course it is," I said. "People have been wrestling with it since the beginning of time."

"Maybe," she said, "maybe there are no complete blueprints. Maybe each of us has to grope and struggle and find the answers for ourselves as we go along."

"Perhaps," I said.

"I think your minister friend came closest when he said that the central love-relationship is the main thing. If that's right, everything else will follow. If it's wrong, everything else will be in shadow."

"So we sit here in the sunshine counting our blessings, eh?"

She laughed. "As a matter of fact," she said, "sometimes I do."

Number of words 2654
See page 335 for Questions

Reading time in Seconds _____
See page 361 for Conversion Table

If London Cleans Its Air and Water, Why Can't Our Large Cities?

Donald Gould

Pollution! It's a growing contemporary problem of worldwide scope. What does it take to give our antipollution efforts proper momentum? This story about London could help. It provides a possible pattern plus some needed encouragement.

A few days ago I was walking down Fleet Street in the city of London on a Saturday afternoon so hot that my feet flinched each time I put one down on the burning sidewalk. Fleet Street is almost empty on a Saturday, so I was bound to notice two American matrons hobbling wearily toward me in the heat, and I was bound to overhear one complain to the other about the fellow from whom they had asked directions. He had told them to plod on if they wanted to see St. Paul's Cathedral, but he must have been fooling, for there was still no sign of anything like a cathedral.

Just then they rounded a half bend, and there suddenly, huge and glowing, was Wren's great stone anthem, alive and alight in the summer sunshine, filling and shaping and commanding the entire scene.

These two good, tired, disgruntled ladies simply stopped in their tracks and said, "Oh, my!"

A few years ago this wouldn't have happened. St. Paul's was not a glowing monument, but a soot-black hulk, hardly to be distinguished from its equally grimy surroundings. Like everything else in London, Wren's cathedral was thickly coated with greasy filth which millions of chimneys daily poured into the sky — a filth which for generations fell softly in a malignant mist on all the lovely shapes of columns, spires, porticoes and gables of the town, so that the richness of the place was smothered into a dirty mass.

London suffered the full impact of the garbage of the new industrial age. Her air was poisoned and her river stank. Two happy accidents have been responsible for stimulating today's vigorous corrective measures. First is the fact that the Houses of Parliament stand alongside the Thames.

A river can tolerate some organic waste without turning sour. It contains bacteria which break down dead plant and animal matter into inoffensive substances. But to do this job, bacteria need oxygen.

A certain amount of oxygen from the air becomes dissolved in river water. If a lot of rubbish must be dealt with, the bacteria will get more oxygen by breaking down nitrates and so releasing nitrogen, a bland gas

which makes up something like 80 percent of the air we breathe. However, if the quantity of organic rubbish is so large that neither dissolved oxygen, nor oxygen from nitrates, can deal with it, the bacteria will start breaking down sulfates.

When you take oxygen away from a sulfate, you are left with the foul-smelling gas, hydrogen sulfide — the stuff that rotten eggs smell of. It is also a highly aggressive chemical which likes combining with other materials, and can therefore do a lot of damage.

About a century ago the load of organic waste in the Thames became so large that hydrogen sulfide began to rise from the river. Riverside citizens became accustomed to the permanent whiff of stale eggs, but sometimes the stench grew so great that parliamentary sittings were adjourned. This, of course, focused official attention wonderfully upon the problem.

The second lucky accident for London happened more recently and concerned the Englishman's curious regard for animals. The English country gentleman will get on his horse, and go out and harass foxes, but he would, on the whole, feel easier after beating his wife than his dog. We show, indeed, an enormous kindness to animals, except those which may be ritually destroyed. But our national conscience in this matter got a tremendous jolt in the winter of 1952.

London had long been accustomed to its own ugly brand of winter fog, which inspired the term "smog," for it resulted from a dreadful mixture of smoke and water droplets. During the foul British winters, water would condense in tiny globules around specks of soot, and the water would also contain dissolved sulfur dioxide (a major component of chimney gases). So London smogs consisted of countless billions of tiny specks of tarry dust encapsulated in small globules of dilute sulfuric acid — exactly the type of chemical weapon which the generals would be happy to pay some imaginative scientist a handsome sum to invent.

Smog killed people quite effectively. Every time London was subjected to attack by one of these miasmas the death rate showed a sharp peak spiking above the normal for the time of year. Most victims were old and nobody bothered a great deal.

Smogs also caused chaos on roads and railways, but Londoners are used to that, so it caused small reaction.

In truth, many of us rather enjoyed our smogs. They were something extra to grumble about, and they broke up the grim routine of the winter working day.

Then came the terrible smog of December 1952. An unfortunate duck, flying blind, crashed through the glass roof of Victoria Station and fell at the feet of passengers bravely waiting for trains which were quite unable to move. A performance of *La Traviata* ended when the singers could no longer see the conductor. In cinemas only front-seat customers could follow what was happening on the screen. Yet Londoners enjoyed the same feeling of togetherness that they had achieved during the blitz. Then the really shocking news began to spread around town.

The Smithfield Show was in progress — an annual festival of butchers, where live animals, raised for the table, are awarded prizes before they go to slaughter. When the smog struck, many died before they could be judged or butchered. About 4,000 Londoners also died as a result of that particular smog. But I believe it was the death of a few steers which made people decide that enough was enough. We are accustomed to the idea of people dying, but when you bring a great mass of beef into the center of your city, and it lies down and dies, then you begin to sense that something might be seriously wrong.

Anyway, the smog of 1952 convinced Londoners that something had to be done about their poisonous air, and only four years later the first effective Clean Air Act was passed.

It was hardly ahead of its time. At the beginning of this century just under 400 tons of soot settled on each square mile of London every year. Between the wars, this continuing inky blizzard eased off slightly, dropping to around 300 tons. This was simply the result of the growing use of fuels like anthracite, coke, oil, gas and electricity.

The cost of living with all this filth was incalculable. Even a recent estimate has put the annual national bill for air pollution damage at around $850 million. Chief material victims are buildings and engineering works. Steel and bricks are attacked by acids formed from sulfur gases escaping from chimneys in homes and factories using fossil fuels — coal or oil. Far graver is the damage done to people.

The commonest result of breathing smoke is chronic bronchitis. This amounts to a slow destruction of the lungs. In Britain the disease kills an estimated 30,000 people every year, and makes many more into virtual cripples who struggle, coughing and breathless, through each night and day. The huge total of 35 million working days is lost annually by sufferers. All this makes clean air a sound economic proposition.

The British Clean Air Act of 1956 was so relatively modest a measure that some American experts claimed it couldn't possibly impinge upon so prickly a problem.

Principally, it gave to local authorities the power to designate smokeless zones. Here citizens are not allowed to burn smoky fuels in their grates. Local authorities meet 70 percent of the cost of changing over household equipment to burn smokeless fuel.

This simple measure has worked miraculously well, particularly in London, where boroughs applied their powers with enthusiasm. Some 80 percent of London's smoke came from domestic chimneys, so that smoke suppression in an entire area could be achieved simply by telling a few merchants to sell only smokeless fuel. Any reluctant householder would soon change his heating system and accept his 70 percent subsidy once he could no longer buy the coal to burn in his old smoky grate.

Since the Clean Air Act, London has become a wonderfully brighter city. Graceful structures like Admiralty House, the National Gallery, and the Guildhall were built of a mellow stone which has been hidden under layers of soot for generations. Only within the past decade has it become worthwhile to scrape off the grime and show these places as their architects meant them to be seen.

Now that much of the cleaning has been done, Londoners delight in new beauty, but to begin with there was some uneasiness. We had become so accustomed to the blackness of our great buildings that many people felt that this was their proper state. When the dean and chapter of St. Paul's decided that the new purity of the London air justified the huge expense of cleaning the cathedral stone, they asked the public to subscribe the necessary money. For many weeks afterwards letters appeared in the *Times* protesting the sacrilege. How dare anyone wreak such a change on the dear familiar blackness of St. Paul's! There were even claims that Sir Christopher Wren, knowing what happened to buildings in the London air, had meant his cathedral to be black, and had designed it with that color in mind.

But the protests have disappeared in the face of the rejuvenated stone. London is a more exciting place to move around in now than it has been for many years.

More birds are moving into town. London has always been a wonderful aviary — on the line of a number of migration routes, but recently birds which have not been seen here for a long time have been nesting in the city. We now have swifts, house martins and even swallows — insect-eating birds. Ornithologists at the London Natural History Society believe that our cleaner air has encouraged the return of insects that don't care for soot.

Measurements made by the meteorological office show that since the passing of the Act of 1956, the amount of winter sunshine enjoyed by Londoners has increased by 50 percent. The frequency of what are officially described as "dense" fogs has fallen by about 80 percent, and of "thick" fogs by 75 percent. The killer smogs have gone completely.

The same kind of success has marked efforts to clean up the Thames. The Thames doesn't stink any more. We have yet to see salmon making their way through the London docks toward spawning grounds in the Berkshire hills. But there is now no part of the river which is absolutely starved of oxygen. Freshwater fish are venturing farther down toward the sea, and sea fish are moving farther in. There are anglers on the river bank at Hammersmith after silver and scarlet roach which are busying the water there. Elvers — young eels — which used to be a favorite dish of Londoners, are coming upstream again.

Wordsworth, gazing from Westminster Bridge more than 150 years ago, saw his city "like a garment, wear the beauty of the morning. . . ." Then industrial man spewed his garbage upon it, and all that beauty began to suffocate. But at last the sickness is being cured. London is living again, thanks importantly to the quiet cooperation of local borough governments. Perhaps there is a lesson here for all the world's sick cities.

Number of words 1898
See page 337 for Questions

Reading time in Seconds _____
See page 361 for Conversion Table

SELECTION 76

Too Many Divorces, Too Soon

Margaret Mead and Rhoda Metraux

"Let me not to the marriage of true minds
Admit impediments. Love is not love
Which alters when it alteration finds. . . ."

From Shakespeare on, marriage has been a favorite subject. What about divorce —
the other side of the coin? Why the shift of attention?

In our generation divorce has become part of the American way of life.

We have not stopped believing in marriage. We are still among the most married people in the world, and increasingly Americans are willing to try a second, a third and even a fourth marriage. But over the past 30 years the proportion of women whose first marriage has broken down in divorce has continued to increase and in the last ten years alone the total annual number of divorces has risen steeply.

What has changed is not our belief that a good marriage is the most important adult relationship, but our expectation about the durability of marriage. We no longer deeply believe that two people who once have made the choice to marry necessarily should try to weather the storms that shake any vital, intimate relationship. Instead, and more and more, our answer to a difficult marriage is: Try it again — with someone else. And marriages are dissolved even though in reality, for too many people — particularly young mothers with children to care for and nowadays young fathers with children to rear — divorce means going it alone.

It is true that many young people in their 20s are deciding to remain single or are experimenting with alternatives to marriage. As yet we cannot know whether they will succeed in setting new styles in relationships between men and women or what the consequences will be for the kind of fragile marriage we now have.

One thing we do know is that these experiments with new styles have not yet reached down to a still younger age group — to the adolescents who fall in love and want to establish an exclusive pair relationship. For them marriage remains the answer they prefer — indeed, the only answer that promises freedom from parental control and the right always to be together. Equally important, it is the only solution — aside from breaking off the relationship — that most parents will tolerate. Whatever their reservations may be, where their adolescent sons and daughters are concerned, parents usually accept marriage with the idea that it may help — or force — the young pair to "settle down." And if it doesn't work out, they can always get divorced.

Certainly this is not the point of view of two young people deeply in love for the first time. They enter marriage, however hurriedly, with the happy conviction that it will work, that they are different from those who fail. Some of them *are* different and *do* succeed magnificently in growing into adulthood and parenthood serene and confident.

But many do not — too many, especially when there are children who later are shuffled about from one parent to the other. Especially when a second marriage with a second baby or a third does not work either — and unsuccessful second marriages tend to have a shorter life span than the first. Especially when the young mother does not find a new partner and, totally inexperienced and saddened, must both work and try, alone, to do what it has always taken two parents to do well, and then often with the help of other adults — to bring up children to be full human beings.

Knowing that the proportion of early marriages has dropped, many people simply shrug off the problems of early marriage and divorce. But the fact is that in absolute numbers teen-age marriages are increasing. The children of the "baby boom" are growing up and very many of them are marrying early. By ignoring their problems we are creating new difficulties, I think, for their generation and the next as well.

For their marriages are the most fragile of all. Compared to the marriages of young people in their 20s, statistics show, the marriages of teen-agers are of shorter duration and end in the catastrophe of divorce more than twice as frequently. And even when such marriages survive for many years, they carry a high risk. After ten years and 20 years, the likelihood that they will end in divorce remains twice as high as the marriages of young people who were only a few years older when they married.

Whatever we may think about divorce in general, I believe it is crucially important that we think very hard about the fate of the thousands of young people whose marriages falter and fail before they reach their mid-20s. It is not enough to say: They were too immature to make so important a decision, too inexperienced to handle their problems. This may well be true — in our society. But need it be?

Statistics tell part of the story of the hazards in early marriage:

Marriage and early pregnancy are the main reasons today why girls drop out of school, perhaps never to return. In most communities there is no place in the high-school system for a young married woman, let alone for a young mother. Often, too, young husbands fail to go on with their education. The freedom gained by leaving home and school becomes the obligation to work — to be self-supporting and, for a young father, to support a family. Lack of education in turn means that a very large proportion of the very young married live at the poverty level without any reserves to fall back on or any hope of getting out of poverty and debt by getting jobs that require greater skills and practice in using those skills.

There are, of course, young families that are supported by parents. Sometimes this works out happily, particularly when parents are furthering the education of their married children so that they can better make their own way. But mere financial support can mean a prolongation of parental control and childhood dependence and lead to resentment that invades all the family relationships.

In young marriages there is also the problem of health for mothers and their babies. Childbirth can be very safe today. But for many mothers under 20 there are still heavy risks in carrying and bearing a child. And the chances for that baby to be well born are far less than for those whose mothers are only a few years older. Today 25 percent of the low-birth-weight babies are born to mothers in their teens. We know this, and yet it is very difficult for teen-aged adults to get the counseling they need or the medical care and support young mothers especially should have.

But such statistics can tell only part of the story of why so many young marriages end up as young divorces.

More significant is the dull and frightening sense of isolation that so often takes the place of feelings of freedom and the delight in being alone with a loved partner. Married and living alone, the young husband and wife no longer move among older adults, whose concerns they no longer share, and they have no place among their unmarried peers. All the social supports of their lives fall away in their total dependence on each other.

In most societies in which there is teen-age marriage, the young couple are given a great deal of time to find themselves in their new life. The young wife goes back and forth between her parents' home and her own, and when the first baby comes she is in the center of a group of mothering women while she gains her own experience of motherhood. The young husband too can count on help and companionship.

But with our insistence that marriage, as an adult relationship, means living in and fending for one's own home, the high price of early marriage too often is unprotected isolation and extreme loneliness. Unprepared for parenthood, two young people who have become very close may see the new baby as an interloper. Or if they are already restless, the baby may become just one more obstacle to pleasure and freedom. The mother is permanently stuck at home. The father is almost equally confined — or goes out alone. There is no money now for pleasure and almost nowhere the young couple can go for amusement with the baby.

Then our current belief that a speedy divorce is the way out of the dilemma begins to take effect. From the time a young wife gets pregnant, fear of divorce hangs over her. Will he stay with her? Will he help take care of the baby? Will he still love her? Or will he, like so many other young fathers, throw up his responsibilities because the load is too heavy, the future too bleak? And her anxieties feed his. Looking around, she becomes much more aware of the fatherless families she knows about; looking around, he sees the defecting fathers who are going their own way. And each accuses the other of things they both fear and long for — freedom from responsibility, a chance to get away, longing for better opportunities in life, a way out of their unhappy situation.

But is the divorce that so often follows the only solution? For a marriage that has irretrievably failed, it may be. But need it have failed?

The greatest enemy of young marriages, I believe, is the fact that from the beginning we anticipate their failure. Almost no one — neither the friends of the young couple nor their parents, teachers and employers — expects a very young marriage to grow in stability and happy mutuality. When it does fail, most people say: "I told you so!" And the failure is the more poignant because of this ultimate rejection.

Where primitive peoples waited for young married couples to attain some maturity before they settled down, we all too often use marriage as the means of getting young people to settle down — the girl safely in her home, the boy firmly tied to his job. Since they are married, we expect them to behave as adults. But at the same time, because they are so young and inexperienced, we expect them to fail.

It is this ambivalence in our social attitudes toward young marriage that sets it apart from other marriages and compounds the problems of early-marriage failure and early divorce. It is also this ambivalence that prevents us from considering in all seriousness what can be done to protect these marriages while a young husband and wife are growing each other up, are learning to become parents before they are fully adult and are searching for a significant place for themselves in a world they have only begun to explore.

We shall not solve the problems of early marriage and early divorce until the climate of opinion about marriage and divorce in general changes. This may involve a much stronger feeling that it is valuable to remain single in the years in which a man and a woman are finding themselves as individuals. It may include a fresh appreciation of friendship as a basic adult relationship. Almost certainly, as we continue to value marriage we shall realize that a good marriage — and a good divorce too — does take a lot of devotion and hard work.

All that will help. But for young marriages it will not be enough.

Looking at young people who are trying to make a go of it, the thing that is most obvious is that they exist in a kind of limbo. They are treated neither as full adults nor as children. They are accorded neither the full rights that go with adult responsibilities nor the protections that go with childhood dependence. So they are left without the major sources of support provided in our kind of society.

Communities, educators, counselors and families all can contribute to providing a legitimate place in life for those who enter marriage early. They need to live where they can keep in touch with their peers, married and single, and where they have some continuing communication with older adults. Group living — as married students live close together during their college years — can keep them in touch with each other and give some unmarried young people a way to try out living away from home. Facilities for continuing their education and access to the kinds of education that will help them find their way as young adults are essential, both for their future and to keep them moving with their peers. The right to family counseling and medical care — without adult intervention — can ease many of their difficulties.

But above all they need opportunities to belong — to have the support of small groups of their own choice. They need to know that other people, young and not so young, have trouble getting adjusted to each other; they need to learn how to talk things out. Consciousness-raising for young couples is a much safer and more constructive enterprise than consciousness-raising for one sex, where women — or men — talk about their spouses who aren't present until often they are turned into monsters. They need to know what their spouses are troubled about as a first step in reaching out to help each other. And they need ideas — things to think about and things to do together outside the narrow walls of their marriage.

Young couples need a chance to continue to become persons. Some will grow together; some will grow apart. But whatever the outcome for the marriage, they will have had a *good* experience of being and living with a growing human person.

Number of words 2225
See page 339 for Questions

Reading time in Seconds _____
See page 361 for Conversion Table

The Fifth Freedom

Seymour St. John

"If a nation values anything more than freedom, it will lose its freedom; and the irony of it is that if it is comfort or money that it values more, it will lose that too" — so said Somerset Maugham. Is the fifth freedom one that addresses itself to that very problem?

More than three centuries ago a handful of pioneers crossed the ocean to Jamestown and Plymouth in search of freedoms they were unable to find in their own countries, the freedoms we still cherish today; freedom from want, freedom from fear, freedom of speech, freedom of religion. Today the descendants of the early settlers, and those who have joined them since, are fighting to protect these freedoms at home and throughout the world.

And yet there is a fifth freedom — basic to those four — that we are in danger of losing: *the freedom to be one's best.* St. Exupéry describes a ragged, sensitive-faced Arab child, haunting the streets of a North African town, as a lost Mozart: he would never be trained or developed. Was he free? "No one grasped you by the shoulder while there was still time; and nought will awaken in you the sleeping poet or musician or astronomer that possibly inhabited you from the beginning." The freedom to be one's best is the chance for the development of each person to his highest power.

How is it that we in America have begun to lose this freedom, and how can we regain it for our nation's youth? I believe it has started slipping away from us because of three great misunderstandings.

First, the misunderstanding of the meaning of democracy. The principal of a great Philadelphia high school is driven to cry for help in combating the notion that it is undemocratic to run a special program of studies for outstanding boys and girls. Again, when a good independent school in Memphis recently closed some thoughtful citizens urged that it be taken over by the public-school system and used for boys and girls of high ability; that it have entrance requirements and give an advanced program of studies to superior students who were interested and able to take it. The proposal was rejected because it was undemocratic! Out of this misunderstanding comes the middle-muddle. Courses are geared to the middle of the class. The good student is unchallenged, bored. The loafer receives his passing grade. And the lack of an outstanding course for the outstanding student, the lack of a standard which a boy or girl must meet, passes for democracy.

The second misunderstanding concerns what makes for happiness. The aims of our present-day culture are

avowedly ease and material well-being: shorter hours; a shorter week; more return for less accomplishment; more softsoap excuses and fewer honest, realistic demands. In our schools this is reflected by the vanishing hickory stick and the emerging psychiatrist. The hickory stick had its faults, and the psychiatrist has his strengths. But the trend is clear: *Tout comprendre c'est tout pardonner.* Do we really believe that our softening standards bring happiness? Is it our sound and considered judgment that the tougher subjects of the classics and mathematics should be thrown aside, as suggested by some educators, for doll-playing? Small wonder that Charles Malik, Lebanese delegate at the U.N., writes: "There is in the West" — in the United States — "a general weakening of moral fiber. [Our] leadership does not seem to be adequate to the unprecedented challenges of the age."

The last misunderstanding is in the area of values. Here are some of the most influential tenets of teacher education over the past fifty years: there is no eternal truth; there is no absolute moral law; there is no God. Yet all of history has taught us that the denial of these ultimates, the placement of man or state at the core of the universe, results in a paralyzing mass selfishness; and the first signs of it are already frighteningly evident.

Arnold Toynbee has said that all progress, all development come from challenge and a consequent response. Without challenge there is no response, no development, no freedom. So first we owe to our children the most demanding, challenging curriculum that is within their capabilities. Michelangelo did not learn to paint by spending his time doodling. Mozart was not an accomplished pianist at the age of eight as the result of spending his days in front of a television set. Like Eve Curie, like Helen Keller, they responded to the challenge of their lives by a disciplined training: and they gained a new freedom.

The second opportunity we can give our boys and girls is the right to failure. "Freedom is not only a privilege, it is a test," writes De Nöuy. What kind of a test is it, what kind of freedom where no one can fail? The day is past when the United States can afford to give high-school diplomas to all who sit through four years of instruction, regardless of whether any visible results can be discerned. We live in a narrowed world where we must be alert, awake to realism: and realism

Reprinted by permission of the author.

demands a standard which either must be met or result in failure. These are hard words, but they are brutally true. If we deprive our children of the right to fail we deprive them of their knowledge of the world as it is.

Finally, we can expose our children to the best values we have found. By relating our lives to the evidences of the ages, by judging our philosophy in the light of values that history has proven truest, perhaps we shall be able to produce that "ringing message, full of content and truth, satisfying the mind, appealing to the heart, firing the will, a message on which one can stake his whole life." This is the message that could mean joy and strength and leadership — freedom as opposed to serfdom.

Number of words 934
See page 341 for Questions

Reading time in Seconds _____
See page 361 for Conversion Table

SELECTION 78

Seven Keys to the Puzzle of Coping with Life
Roy Menninger, M.D.

Coping with life happens to be a universal problem. A psychiatrist is perhaps especially well qualified to share with us insights that will provide significant help. Menninger gets us back to the basics. As the Greeks put it, "Know thyself." Menninger adds, "in seven ways."

In this incredibly complex world each of us needs to examine ourselves — our motivations, our goals. As a search for a clearer idea of what we stand for, toward what we are headed, and what we think is truly important, this kind of continuing self-scrutiny can help to stabilize us in a world of explosive change. A close look at ourselves contributes to that sought-after capacity for autonomy, and gives us greater ability to make wise and useful choices, to exert some control over our own destiny.

It is never easy for any of us to look closely at ourselves — the ancient aphorism of "physician, heal thyself" notwithstanding. Most of us do so only when forced by crisis, anxiety, or a blunt confrontation with reality. Some of us have spouses or friends who help us look at the sore spots within, the personal rough spots which cause us and others pain. But for most of us, it is far easier to look outside, to look at others, whether to admire or to find fault, whether to seek guidance or to castigate.

As important as this self-knowledge is, the daily pressures to act, to do, to decide make it difficult to stop and think, to consider, to examine one's life goals, one's directions, one's priorities — the basic choices one faces in managing his own world. Indeed, it is more than probable that few of us would pause to undertake such a vital inventory unless someone else said, as I am saying now, "Stop! Think about these issues for a while;

defer those other 'important' things that pre-empt your daily routine!"

How are we to go about this? I ask you to focus on several rhetorical questions — rhetorical because the answers are to be offered to yourself, not to the public scene. The questions are intended to be a framework around which you may organize ideas about yourself and your relationships with your environment. Though they are questions which focus on the inner world, though they are here raised by a psychiatrist, and though they might be considered a kind of "mental health check-up," they will unquestionably strike you as rather nonmedical and perhaps even more philosophic than scientific. But pre-eminently they are intended to provoke honest thought — never an easy task in relation to one's self.

I

The first of these questions is perhaps the most global for it invites a review of your basic life direction: What are your goals in life? Put otherwise, toward what objectives are you aiming and how realistic are they? How well do they incorporate what is *really* important to you, and how well do they accurately express your values? Are they for real, or only for show?

The network of queries arising from the central question provokes several observations. In an era when planning and setting objectives are bywords for every organization, it is ironic to see how few people have adopted the same strategy for themselves. Perhaps only in late middle-age does the lack of a clear sense of direction and the absence of specific goals become an appalling

From *The Menninger Perspective,* Vol. 3, No. 4 (June/July 1972).

reality. Many people reach that point in life with a bitter sense of loss and regret, wondering where time and opportunity have gone. The lack of intrinsic value in the materialistically oriented goals some people adopt is obvious when they helplessly wonder what to do next with their lives, now that they have the million dollars they planned to make. The acquisition of a bigger house, a bigger car, and a bigger boat, plus all the status that money will buy has taken on the appearance of a logical goal for many — but would that truly represent your central values?

One cannot think about one's own life goals without asking still other difficult questions: To what purposes do you dedicate your efforts and your lives? What are your personal priorities, and how well does your life's work reflect those priorities? Most of us find such difficult questions easy to avoid, presuming that time will answer them — as indeed it will, though not necessarily to our ultimate satisfaction. A close, comfortable, and accepting relationship with another person — a spouse, a colleague, a friend, or even a psychotherapist — can be of great help in considering such questions. The dilemma is, will you find such an opportunity?

II

Closely related to the question about goals is one which bears on your use of time and energy: Does your use of your vital resources truly reflect your priorities? Without much thought most of you would certainly answer "yes," failing to appreciate that for 90 percent of us the answer is almost assuredly "no." Executives with broad responsibilities are presumed to use their time for the things that are important — such things as planning, policy preparation, and the "big" decisions. With a consistency that is hard to believe, studies have repeatedly shown that this is rarely true, and that much more often the busy executive is spending 90 percent of his time on matters that could better be done by others, are simply a part of the daily routine, and have limited relation to the vital responsibilities which he carries.

Most of us will recognize in a moment of more somber thought that the "important things" in our lives are frequently deferred with some comforting but self-deceiving assumption that there will always be time tomorrow.

From yet another perspective, there is a high probability that your use of time and energy reflects serious imbalances within the life space of each of you. In spite of public protestations about the importance of the family, about the needs of the community, about the troubles in our world, most of us devote the smallest proportion of our time to these areas. Indeed, it could be fairly said of many of you that you are married to your jobs, not your husbands or wives, that you are invested in your colleagues, not your children, that you are committed to your business, not your society. The point is not that these imbalances are wrong, but that it

is quite probable that they are decidedly inconsistent with your own statements about what is important and what constitute your personal priorities.

It is this inconsistency which produces a subtle but corrosive tension as your conscience cries out for one commitment while your activities express another. At times this reflects a distorted conception of responsibility, at times an impulsive response to the demands of others, but most often it is the outcome of unthinking behavior, the consequence of a general failure to consider your goals, your priorities, and your plans for reaching them.

Nowhere is the imbalance in the use of time and energy more obvious than in regard to ourselves. Executives are dedicated people, and for many this dedication implies and finally comes to mean considerable self-sacrifice. Time for one's self is discouraged, pleasure is deemed to be selfish, and one's own needs come last.

Again drawing upon information from a study of executives, I can report that less than 40 percent of some 4,000 executives studied had an avocational pursuit. They appeared to have had few sources of personal gratification and gave themselves few opportunities for fulfilling personal pursuits. Why do they not think better of themselves than that, and are they so different from you?

III

The third question is to ask if your sense of responsibility is also out of balance. In its extreme forms, it is easy to find examples of those who will assume no more responsibility for anything than absolutely necessary; certainly the fragmentation of our contemporary culture encourages us to restrict our efforts to smaller and smaller sectors of the human community. Executives demonstrate that same pattern, pointing out that the quality of information is so great that fragmented specialization is inevitable and even advisable. And perhaps it is, but are we guilty of hiding an unduly narrow concept of our responsibility to others behind that rationalization?

Considerably more common in the field of industry is a pattern that reflects the other extreme: an excessive sense of responsibility that keeps us moving like a driven animal. Again, the needs of our organization and the endless call for our services make it hard to define a sense of responsibility which simultaneously expresses our commitment to our organization, to ourselves, and to our family and world as well. Failing to do so exposes us to the ravages of guilt feelings and failure, and of all the feelings known to the human psyche, guilt is probably the most painful.

It is easy to confuse a concept of responsibility with a command for action, connecting a notion of obligation with a need to do something about it. When one begins to discover how big the problem is about which he is worrying, his growing sense of helplessness leads him to turn away, disconnect, and assume that someone else will worry instead.

A more difficult but more effective concept of responsibility is an acknowledgement of the importance of continuing to think about problems and dilemmas, neither turning away in frustration nor hurling one's self forward into them under the pressure of guilt. Continuing to think about the problems of delinquency in one's community, the need for better school programs for the limited as well as the gifted, and the hundreds of other things for which responsible concern is needed is a way of staying engaged, remaining open to alternatives and opportunities, and being ready to respond when the occasion permits.

In more personal terms, the concept of balanced responsibility implies a willingness to accept the responsibility for one's own attitudes, feelings, failures and prejudices, forsaking the easier and unfortunately more frequent tendency to project or displace these feelings and attitudes onto persons or forces external to one's self. It is worth asking: Do each of you demonstrate a readiness to acknowledge your anger, your bias, or your limitations — at least to yourself, and to others when this is germane to the situation?

IV

My fourth query is to ask about your courage — not the sort more commonly associated with the battlefield, challenging or embarrassing situations or the like — important though that is. I refer to the courage we need to face the internal foe, for we are in most cases our own worst enemies. In the inimitable words of Pogo, "We have met the enemy — and they is us." This kind of courage is exemplified in an ability to look at yourself honestly and fairly — an expression of the responsibility I noted earlier. It is not easy to entertain the questions I am posing without fluctuating wildly between extremes of excessive personal criticism and total denial that these thoughts have any bearing on you at all.

It is this courage which enables us to face, to articulate, and finally to accept our disappointments and losses — one of the most difficult tasks the human psyche faces.

Perhaps this is not so apparent until one stops to realize that life itself is a succession of losses — beginning with the loss of the warmth and comfort of the uterus which nurtured us for the first nine months of our existence; progressing through childhood and its many losses: dependent infant status, our favorite childhood toys, our privileged status; the loss of the family as adolescence separates us from childhood; the loss of irresponsible pleasures of youth with the advent of maturity; the loss of jobs, or positions, or self-esteem, money, opportunity; the loss of one's friends with advancing age; these and a million others, and finally the

ultimate loss of life itself. It is something to ponder how extensive the experience of each of us is with loss, big and small, and to note that these are experiences with profound effects upon our mental health. Even as losses vary in their impact upon us, our psychic structure varies in its capacity to handle them, and not all of us do it with equal success.

It has been said that the quality which distinguishes a great man from another otherwise like him is his capacity to manage disappointment and loss. One thinks of the experiences of Winston Churchill and the crushing disappointments of his early career, or those of Franklin Roosevelt with a disabling onslaught of polio, and begins to realize the wisdom in that observation.

Accepting loss is to accept the reality of it, to allow one's self to feel the pain and anguish of it. One can then come to terms with its meaning. Doing so is vital if the spirit is to continue to grow, and in some cases even to survive. It is relevant to note that the successful rehabilitation of a person newly blind depends upon his first having accepted the painful reality of his loss of vision, in a process of mourning akin to grieving the loss of a loved one.

It brings me to ask: What can you say about your courage to face and to accept the anguish of loss?

V

The fifth query is to ask you to examine the consistency and the quality of your personal relationships. Most of us accept the truism that people are important to people, yet we fail to perceive how often human relationships are superficial, meager, and unrewarding. Is this true of your own? Which of your relationships can you say has a quality of involvement with the other, expressing a depth of emotional investment which is real and mutually experienced? It is again too easy to explain that the pressures of our lives and the demands upon us, the superficial materialism of the age and all the rest are what account for a deep sense of poverty in our relationships with others. To call again upon that element of courage to which I earlier referred, can we examine the quality of the relationships of those who are closest to us to question how honest, how open, how real they are?

It is clear that the capacity to establish close, significant emotional ties with others is characteristic of emotional maturity. It is clear, moreover, that the work, the effort, and sometimes the pain of doing so is quite enough to discourage many, especially when the trends in our society are moving in the same direction. And yet we are still disdainful of the empty superficiality of the cocktail party, even when lessened by the illusion of intimacy which alcohol can provide.

The phenomenon of parallel play in the nursery school — two children in close physical contact with each other but playing entirely alone — is expectable at the age of 2 or 3. When it can be said to characterize a pattern of living at the age of 20 to 40, it hints at relationships eroded by infantile expectations and a lack of mutual commitment. Relationships which show a depth of emotional involvement require a willingness to engage, to share, to listen, to give. What can you say about these qualities in your human relationships?

VI

Not unrelated to a question about your human relationships is a query about sources of your emotional support: From whom do you receive it and to whom do you give it? I have referred to the lack of fulfilling avocation in the lives of many executives — the absence of a rewarding investment in art, in music, in physical activity, in stamp collecting, or a hundred others. Does this also describe you?

It is also clear that many people who are imbued with an especially strong sense of responsibility have great difficulty in seeking or accepting support from others. For some, this is reminiscent of a profoundly unpleasant sense of helplessness from an earlier phase of life. For some it is an unacceptable admission of weakness, of inadequacy; for some it is a contradiction of one's sense of strength and commitment to help others. Ironically, those whose careers lead to increasing responsibility to others must therefore provide increasing support for others at the very moment when they are progressively more isolated, less able to fend for help for themselves, and less able to receive it when it is available. Greater responsibility generates greater personal need — and greater obstacles to receiving it.

Number of words 3010
See page 343 for Questions

VII

Lastly, any survey of your mental health must ask about the role of love in your lives. For most of us the very use of this word threatens a deluge of sentimentality. It is a word which too readily conjures images of Technicolor Hollywood and cow-eyed adolescents. But it is a respectable feeling. I use it to refer to a capacity to care. Perhaps we are not fully aware that it implies a willingness to invest ourselves in others, to be involved with them, to listen to them — in short, to care about them. It should therefore be a hallmark of all our relationships with others. This is the true sense of helping, for it is the only antidote to hate we know, and it is also the foundation stone for that indispensable pillar of good human relationships — trust. Both are always in short supply.

Without intending to promote egocentricity, I would have to ask how truly and how well you love yourself — not in irrational or narcissistic and overblown terms, but as an object of pride and self-esteem, a thing of value, a person of worth. As one can love himself in this mature and realistic way, so he is able to extend the help of love to others in ways which are not demeaning, not controlling, not condescending or patronizing, but respectful and genuinely caring.

Your relationships to others do indeed mirror your relationship to yourself. How well you deal with others may depend upon your success in managing yourself in relation to the provocative and difficult questions I have posed for you today. No one has suggested these questions are easy; in some sense they may be unanswerable. But they do need to be thought about by each of you, talked about with those you love and are close to, and examined repeatedly in the months and years ahead.

Reading time in Seconds _____
See page 361 for Conversion Table

SELECTION 79

The Road to Safe Driving

The Royal Bank of Canada *Monthly Letter*

Must a civilized society, Canadian or American, tolerate thousands of needless traffic "accidents" every year? Somehow we do — and think little of it unless we ourselves become victims. Should we view the carnage on the road as a social problem — someone else's fault — or recognize our individual failings as drivers?

In a debate on violence in society in the British House of Lords a few years ago, a member pointed out to the assembled peers that they each ran a dozen times more risk of death or injury from auto accidents than from

all other forms of aggression. "The reminder was timely," commented *The Guardian,* "since to talk about violence without mentioning cars is rather like discussing 'Macbeth' without mentioning blood."

It may feel strange to the average driver to have his car thus looked upon as an instrument of aggression, but the fact is that the motor vehicle has killed and maimed more people in its brief history than any bomb or fire-arm ever invented. The yearly toll of blood and tears exacted by unsafe driving is incomparably greater than by murder or any other crime.

So the relentless carnage on the roads may properly be regarded as a critical social problem. It is hardly overstating the case to call it, as a safety official once did, "another manifestation of man's inhumanity to man." For much of the blood on the pavement flows essentially from the refusal of drivers to respect the legal and moral rights of others. Those who would dispute this statement on the grounds that "accidents are bound to happen" should consider the following facts:

- Most so-called traffic "accidents" are avoidable. Most happen in fair weather and under good road conditions. Some accident experts speculate that most occur as a result of people disregarding either the law or well-known safety rules.
- In Canada, where traffic accidents take the lives of 6,000 people annually, the use of alcohol is involved in up to half of these fatal incidents.
- Accident researchers say that most people who drive dangerously defective cars and trucks are aware of the defects and are gambling — often with the lives of strangers and family or friends as passengers — on not having trouble. Mechanical defects are responsible for an estimated 20,000 serious accidents in Canada every year.

It has been observed that in the western world today, there is no longer such a thing as a "motorist." So prevalent has the use of cars and trucks become that traffic is simply the public at large on wheels.

It follows that a person operating a motor vehicle has the same social obligation to keep the peace on the streets and highways as a person in any other public area. The only difference is that one's capacity to inflict injury on others is magnified enormously when one is behind the steering wheel of a potential juggernaut weighing a ton and a half and capable of hurtling through space at more than 150 kilometres an hour.

Yet the enemies of society on wheels are ordinarily rather harmless people. They are the respectable working man who takes a chance on driving home after he has had a few drinks; the housewife preoccupied with a family problem as she tailgates the car in front of her; the young fellow who says, "let's see how fast this thing will go on the straight stretch"; the salesman with thousands of driving hours behind him who feels it is beneath his dignity to signal; the vacationer who sets out on an overnight run to his destination when he hasn't had enough sleep.

Just ordinary people acting carelessly, you might say. But it is a principle both of law and common morality that carelessness is no excuse when one's actions are liable to bring death or damage to others. Sins of omission and commission are equally reprehensible if they cause human grief.

The only real and lasting solution, say the experts, is to get it into peoples' heads that driving is a skilled task requiring constant care and concentration. A driver in today's traffic is called upon to perform a complex range of functions simultaneously — not only operating the vehicle itself, but surveying the entire fast-moving traffic picture and anticipating potential problems. A driver must assess the actions of others, make decisions while in motion, and exercise acute timing. Those who fail to do all these things present a menace to those with whom they share the road.

An exhaustive study designed to get to the roots of the traffic accident problem in the United States established that "inadequate driving skills" figure much more prominently in accidents than had been previously imagined. Poor driving not only gives rise to innumerable accidents, but adds to their severity. It was found that many drivers, when faced with a crisis, did not know the correct way to steer or stop their cars.

Ironically, another study conducted in the U.S. at about the same time showed that nine-tenths of the people covered by a broad survey rated themselves as "above average" in driving skills and safety awareness. Even those with a record of convictions for traffic violations felt that public exhortations to safer driving were not applicable to them.

This was a vivid illustration of what policemen call "the other guy syndrome," whereby "the other guy" is always a bad driver and always to blame for an accident. This mythical figure stands as a formidable opponent of any general improvement in driving habits. The difficulties inherent in promoting safer driving can be clearly seen when one considers that practically everyone concerned feels immune from responsibility for the appalling accident rate.

Is it too much to ask that some day all drivers will drive responsibly? Probably. But we can hope nonetheless for a pronounced improvement on the grisly situation that prevails at present.

The question of how to make our public thoroughfares as safe as humanly possible is one that encompasses the fields of law, education, and public attitudes. Not until society makes a broad and determined commitment to improve mass driving habits will the needless injury and loss of life cease.

Number of words 970
See page 345 for Questions

Reading time in seconds _____
See page 361 for Conversion Table

174

A Few Words on Choosing Your Dictionary

Barbara Currier Bell

Poor Shakespeare. Back in his day there was no such thing as a dictionary. Today? Not one, but many. If, as it's said, a dictionary is a student's best friend, certainly choosing the right one — the best one for you — becomes a matter of special concern.

When you set off on a college education, of course a general dictionary should go along. But which one? Here are some pointers to help you choose.

First, a hardcover dictionary will serve you much better than a paperback. Although it is more expensive, it is also more durable, more convenient and more readable. Think of it as a businessman does the cost of equipment.

Next, studies suggest that a "collegiate" dictionary, with 130,000 to 170,000 entries, will be a better buy than most abridged dictionaries ("desk," "concise," "compact," "pocket"), which range down below 55,000 entries. It is probably also better for your purposes than the other extreme, an unabridged dictionary, with over 250,000 entries.

The five most commonly recommended collegiate dictionaries are:

• American Heritage Dictionary, New College Edition.

• Funk & Wagnalls Standard College Dictionary.

• The Random House College Dictionary.

• Webster's New Collegiate Dictionary, 8th Edition.

• Webster's New World Dictionary, 2d College Edition.

Besides having about the same number of words, and costing, weighing and measuring about the same, these dictionaries are all authoritative. All stay as current as possible. They make about equal efforts with vocabulary coverage, and they contain roughly the same amount of encyclopedic material. Most important, they all do more than define words: they provide pronunciations, syllabications, synonyms and antonyms, grammatical forms and functions, usage labels and etymologies.

Despite these similarities, some comparisons among the five are instructive. Below are five criteria for evaluating a collegiate dictionary.

1. Readability. This is one aspect of a dictionary not usually given top billing, but it is critical. You should not be embarrassed about paying attention to such "unscholarly" matters as typographic design, format and illustration.

2. Clarity of Definition. Clarity matters more than other aspects of definition for the college student because so often the word to be looked up is abstract or general.

3. Etymology. The histories of words record essential dimensions of meaning. Etymologies encourage you to appreciate the organic quality of words, the way each one takes on a life of its own, and the extent to which that life is linked with others.

4. Usage Level. Usually, concern centers on "good" language and "bad." Those who prefer a prescriptive approach either want to see only "good" words in the dictionary or, if all sorts are included, to have usage level stressed. Those on the descriptive side want to include as many words as possible and to play down usage level.

5. Front-Matter. This can make or break you in your use of the dictionary as a learning tool. It is the instruction manual, telling you how the dictionary is put together. It also includes articles on the English language, the structure of languages in general and ours in particular, and on language usage.

With these five criteria in mind, you can look at the main collegiate dictionaries more closely:

American Heritage is the newest. It has the most spacious format of the five, a type design that aids visual discrimination, and many more illustrations than its competitors. Its definitions are not always as clear as those of its competitors, but it balances that deficiency with the largest number of illustrative quotations and staff-written examples. It stresses etymology the most. It also contains extensive and unique usage-level information. Finally, it has more prefatory essays than its rivals.

Funk & Wagnalls has the greatest number of illustrations after the American Heritage, and the largest type size of any of the dictionaries reviewed here, so that its graphics are a plus. It draws on an unabridged dictionary, the Funk & Wagnalls Standard, with particularly well-respected scholars in charge; however, in striving for simplicity, its definitions become too brief. Etymologies are not extensively pursued. On usage level, it provides more than at least one competitor; obscenities are limited.

Random House falls in the middle for readability. Lexically, it is based on an excellent unabridged dictionary, though a smaller one than either Webster's Third International or the Funk & Wagnalls Standard. Its prefatory material is thorough, but does not try to move into new territory.

Webster's New Collegiate — "the" Webster's — has the greatest name recognition of the five and is the dictionary most often found on reference librarians' desks. However, it is cramped and scrimps on illustrations, with about one-fourth the number in the American Heritage. Drawing on Webster's Third, it offers somewhat longer definitions than its competitors, but the length does not guarantee clarity; the frequent use of illustrative quotations is more help. It does not carry its etymologies particularly far. Priding itself on being descriptive, in particular contrast to American Heritage, it dismays the same group that criticizes Webster's Third. Collegiate users, however, regret its relative lack of usage-level labels. Its prefatory material is definitely a plus.

Webster's New World — the "other" Webster's — is a rival in more than name. It has a more comfortable type face than the New Collegiate, but besides its relative deficit in illustrations it does not employ as many typographical aids as American Heritage for discrimination, nor does it offer as much space. Webster's New World has no connection with the Merriam-Webster Company that publishes the New Collegiate, and is not derived from an unabridged dictionary, but its definitions have been acclaimed by reference authorities and publications as the best in any of the dictionaries reviewed here. One strength is its coverage of Americanisms. It is also strong on etymology in general. It does not include obscenities.

Number of words 905
See page 347 for Questions

Reading time in Seconds _____
See page 361 for Conversion Table

SELECTION 81

Democracy Will Fail

Thomas Babington Macaulay

Letters make fascinating reading — even old ones. Do you see any signs that Macaulay's dire prophecy is finally coming to pass, some one hundred twenty years after he predicted it? What about the key deterring factor — our boundless stretch of fertile, unoccupied land?

HOLLY LODGE,
KENSINGTON, LONDON, *May* 23, 1857.

DEAR SIR, — The four volumes of the *Colonial History of New York* reached me safely. I assure you that I shall value them highly. They contain much to interest an English as well as an American reader. Pray accept my thanks, and convey them to the Regents of the University.

You are surprised to learn that I have not a high opinion of Mr. Jefferson, and I am surprised at your surprise. I am certain that I never wrote a line, and that I never, in Parliament, in conversation, or even on the hustings — a place where it is the fashion to court the populace — uttered a word indicating an opinion that the supreme authority in a state ought to be intrusted to the majority of citizens told by the head; in other words, to the poorest and most ignorant part of society. I have long been convinced that institutions purely democratic must, sooner or later, destroy liberty or civilization, or both.

In Europe, where the population is dense, the effect of such institutions would be almost instantaneous.

What happened lately in France is an example. In 1848 a pure democracy was established there. During a short time there was reason to expect a general spoliation, a national bankruptcy, a new partition of the soil, a maximum of prices, a ruinous load of taxation laid on the rich for the purpose of supporting the poor in idleness. Such a system would, in twenty years, have made France as poor and barbarous as the France of the Carlovingians. Happily the danger was averted; and now there is a despotism, a silent tribune, an enslaved press. Liberty is gone, but civilization has been saved. I have not the smallest doubt that, if we had a purely democratic government here, the effect would be the same. Either the poor would plunder the rich, and civilization would perish, or order and prosperity would be saved by a strong military government, and liberty would perish.

You may think that your country enjoys an exemption from these evils. I will frankly own to you that I am of a very different opinion. Your fate I believe to be certain, though it is deferred by a physical cause. As long as you have a boundless extent of fertile and unoccupied land, your laboring population will be far more at ease than the laboring population of the Old World, and, while that is the case, the Jefferson policies may continue to exist without causing any fatal calamity. But the time will come when New England will be as thickly peopled as old England. Wages will be as low, and will fluctuate as much with you as with us. You will have your Manchesters and Birminghams, and in those Manchesters and Birminghams hundreds of thousands of artisans will assuredly be sometimes out of work. Then your institutions will be fairly brought to the test.

Distress everywhere makes the laborer mutinous and discontented, and inclines him to listen with eagerness to agitators who tell him that it is a monstrous iniquity that one man should have a million while another cannot get a full meal. In bad years there is plenty of grumbling here, and sometimes a little rioting. But it matters little. For here the sufferers are not the rulers. The supreme power is in the hands of a class, numerous indeed, but select; of an educated class; of a class which is, and knows itself to be, deeply interested in the security of property and the maintenance of order. Accordingly, the malcontents are firmly yet gently restrained. The bad time is got over without robbing the wealthy to relieve the indigent. The springs of national prosperity soon begin to flow again: work is plentiful, wages rise, and all is tranquillity and cheerfulness. I have seen England pass three or four times through such critical seasons as I have described.

Through such seasons the United States will have to pass in the course of the next century, if not of this. How will you pass through them? I heartily wish you a good deliverance. But my reason and my wishes are at war, and I cannot help foreboding the worst. It is quite plain that your government will never be able to restrain a distressed and discontented majority. For with you the majority is the government, and has the rich, who are always a minority, absolutely at its mercy.

The day will come when in the State of New York a multitude of people, none of whom has had more than half a breakfast, or expects to have more than half a dinner, will choose a Legislature. Is it possible to doubt what sort of a Legislature will be chosen? On one side is a statesman preaching patience, respect for vested rights, strict observance of public faith. On the other is a demagogue ranting about the tyranny of capitalists and usurers, and asking why any body should be permitted to drink Champagne and to ride in a carriage while thousands of honest folks are in want of necessaries. Which of the two candidates is likely to be preferred by a working-man who hears his children cry for more bread? I seriously apprehend that you will, in some such season of adversity as I have described, do things which will prevent prosperity from returning; that you will act like people who should in a year of scarcity devour all the seed-corn, and thus make the next a year not of scarcity, but of absolute famine.

There will be, I fear, spoliation. The spoliation will increase the distress. The distress will produce fresh spoliation. There is nothing to stop you. Your Constitution is all sail and no anchor. As I said before, when a society has entered on this downward progress, either civilization or liberty must perish. Either some Caesar or Napoleon will seize the reins of government with a strong hand, or your republic will be as fearfully plundered and laid waste by barbarians in the twentieth century as the Roman Empire was in the fifth, with this difference, that the Huns and Vandals who ravaged the Roman Empire came from without, and that your Huns and Vandals will have been engendered within your own country by your own institutions.

Thinking thus, of course, I cannot reckon Jefferson among the benefactors of mankind. I readily admit that his intentions were good and his abilities considerable. Odious stories have been circulated about his private life; but I do not know on what evidence those stories rest, and I think it probable that they are false or monstrously exaggerated. I have no doubt that I shall derive both pleasure and information from your account of him.

I have the honor to be, dear Sir, your faithful servant,

T. B. MACAULAY.

H. S. RANDALL, Esq., etc., etc., etc.

Number of words 1140
See page 349 for Questions

Reading time in Seconds _____
See page 361 for Conversion Table

The Four Frontiers of Global Security

Thomas W. Wilson, Jr.

It's a difficult step from our little individual microcosm to a world macrocosm.
However, Thomas W. Wilson, Jr., formerly advisor to the U.S. Mission to NATO,
is particularly well qualified to bring us just such a needed global perspective.

The problem of national security today is fundamentally a conceptual problem. The question is whether we can expand our concept of the national interest to include the integrity of the global systems that sustain human society and life itself. Can we not perceive that there can be no security for any nation if the planet itself is at risk? And that world security has become the precondition for national defense? Surely the point of departure for a modern defense policy is an understanding that national security is conceivable in these latter years of the twentieth century only within the framework of a wider world security.

There are four strategic frontiers of world security that must be defended if we are to retain even a potential capacity to cope with many of the most dangerous world problems of the 1980s and 1990s. Each of these frontiers is threatened increasingly. None is adequately protected as of today. Indeed, national governments do not even seem to be aware of some of the gravest perils to world security on the contemporary scene. These are the four frontiers:

First, the strategic systems of the natural biosphere. These are the basic biological systems that, over the millennia, created conditions favorable to life on earth — and that ever since have nourished the only life we know to exist in the cosmos: the croplands, the pasturelands, the forests and the fisheries. These are the master strategic systems of a living planet; without them, nothing survives.

And there is no doubt that these strategic systems are vulnerable and subject to impairment; no doubt that their integrity is threatened increasingly by the rising impact of human activities; no doubt that, as things stand today, these planetary systems already are deteriorating on a global scale; and there is no doubt that the world at large is neglecting the security of this global frontier.

Governments simply have not yet perceived the connection between their national security and the viability of global strategic systems. Yet the point is supremely simple and straightforward; no nation — no people — can ever be secure within their political borders if the

planet as a whole is physically insecure. Nothing very difficult or complex about that.

Second, there is the strategic frontier of critical services in the artificial, man-made environment or, as it is sometimes called, the technosphere. These are the vital technological systems and supporting services and institutions that make it possible for the tribes of mankind to communicate with each other, to travel far and quickly, to navigate safely, to engage in commerce, to keep accounts, to deal with endless minor conflicts, to exchange knowledge, data and technology, to take part in thousands of meetings for as many purposes around the globe, year in and year out — in brief, to cope with the multifarious and complex daily affairs of an interdependent contemporary world with an increasingly differentiated division of labor.

These socially created systems, like the natural systems of the biosphere, are globally integrated and provide a vital metabolism for the international society of nations. And, like biological systems, they are vulnerable to overload, deterioration and breakdown. They also are subject to physical attack and to political sabotage. It is simply impossible to envision world security without an elaborate system of reliable global utilities and services — all requiring international agreement, international cooperation and international organization.

Again, the point is simple: The modern world would grind to a crashing stop without a functioning network of reliable global services. And, again, governments seem unaware of these crucial services as an essential frontier of a workable world security system. This seems especially curious in the case of the major powers — for they are much more dependent than others upon the reliability of critical global services, and hence are much more vulnerable in the event of malfunction, paralysis or collapse of the systems.

The third frontier involves the security of the global commons, where it is essential to have agreed-upon rules of conduct if chaos and conflict are to be contained. These commons are the great shared resources of the oceans, the atmosphere, outer space and the polar continent of Antarctica.

As things stand now, we have a treaty reserving Antarctica for cooperative scientific research, but it will expire before long and there have been some threats of a return to conflicting national claims and free-for-all

Reprinted with permission from *Sierra* magazine (Jan/Feb 1983) pp. 124–125.

exploitation of marine and other resources; we have a treaty reserving outer space for peaceful uses, but this has not prevented a creeping militarization of that global domain; we have a treaty designating the surface of the moon as the common heritage of mankind, but it may not be ratified by key countries; and we may or may not have a treaty for the rational management of the global ocean systems after more than seven years of complex and tedious negotiations.

In brief, the security outlook for the global commons is anything but encouraging. Yet these dangers are given little or no weight in debates about national security or in the allocation of resources to national defense.

The fourth and final frontier for world security is a basic capacity for political action on priority issues at the world level. This, of course, is the very heart of a workable system of world security — for without the ability to make decisions about matters beyond national jurisdiction, it manifestly would be impossible to do anything at all about the security of the strategic planetary systems or the critical global services or the endangered global commons — which together sustain the biosphere and the technosphere alike, the living systems and the man-made systems that constitute the human environment.

It is perfectly obvious that there can be no world security without the political capacity to cope with an agenda of inherently transnational problems that will not take care of themselves and will not oblige us by going away — no matter how hard we may try to ignore them. To be secure we have to be able to exist in peace, and to exist in peace we have to be able to cope with our most urgent and threatening problems. Without that, disintegrative forces take charge of events and drag the world toward that unmarked but fateful threshold between a state of peace and a state of war.

Today there is evidence on all sides that our political capacity for coping with contemporary problems is seriously strained — to put it very mildly. Almost every national government in the world is in trouble today — regardless of its ideological beliefs, social structure, economic system, stage of development or length of experience. On the international level we are facing something close to a pervasive political paralysis — along the East-West axis and the North-South axis as well.

This paralysis in political systems is deadly dangerous. It is all too likely to lead to political polarization. And when issues become polarized, the next stage is almost certain to be the outbreak of violence. How much evidence do we need of the progression from paralysis to polarization to mindless violence — what with Ireland, Lebanon, Iran, Cambodia, Ethiopia and El Salvador staring us in the face?

World security is threatened, then, on all four frontiers: the biospheric strategic systems that sustain all life; the critical services that sustain international society; the global commons beyond national jurisdiction; and the political systems that underlie any capacity for action on the other frontiers of world security.

If one still has to ask what all this has to do with the national security of the United States, it is because the subject of national security has been isolated, fenced off in a special compartment of thought, belief and action. And this artificial and arbitrary separation of perceptions of security from perceptions of political, social and strategic realities in the world today has deceptive and dangerous results:

First, we fail to see that demographic, economic and environmental world trends have combined in recent years to create a qualitatively distinct class of unavoidable world-level problems that are virtually unknown to traditional diplomacy, that are beyond the reach of national governments, that cannot be fitted into perceived traditions of international relations, that cannot be wished away, that are coming increasingly to dominate world affairs, that have powerful implications for national security and that are indifferent to military force.

Second, more specifically, we fail to identify the security significance of direct threats to the strategic natural systems of planet Earth or to the vital man-made systems that sustain the interdependent society of nations.

Third, we fail to see that political paralysis is a threat to security — because paralysis leads to polarization, which leads to violence, which is all too likely to have international dimensions difficult to foresee and even more difficult to control.

Finally, by keeping our perceptions of security isolated from the political, social and strategic conditions of the real world, we limit our concepts of the national interest and of national security to a perilously narrow military base.

This is doubly perilous. On the one hand, nonmilitary threats to national security are on the rise. On the other hand, even a casual inspection of the recent record brings to light some hard questions about relevance of military force to real-world problems and conditions in the 1980s and beyond.

• In the last two wars we have fought, our most powerful military weapons have remained in their arsenals because the United States could not find an acceptable way to use them.

• In Iran, the weapon used to destroy a regime holding all the cards of conventional military and police power was a general strike.

• For the past several years, the economically and technologically most powerful nations in the world have been staring down the barrel of something known as an "oil weapon" wielded by a group of nations of almost insignificant military capability.

• Remote desert sheikdoms, without benefit of a single aircraft carrier among them, have the power today to make major nations sit up and take notice.

• After six years of strenuous effort the United States was unable to produce a military victory in Indochina; the Chinese attempt to "teach a lesson" to Vietnam was costly and inconclusive; and the modern military might of the Soviet Union has yet to pacify the primitive countryside of Afghanistan.

Meanwhile, the search for effective military options for action in world trouble spots turns out to be less and less productive — as the practice of power politics, based on reliance upon military force, looks more and more like a loser's game. Armaments pile up at record rates, but national security policy verges on doctrinal bankruptcy.

The United States and the Soviet Union share a special responsibility for expanding obsolete concepts of national defense to embrace the strategic frontiers of world security. Both nations have the military capacity to destroy each other's society under worst-case assumptions; yet both feel militarily insecure vis-a-vis the other. For this reason alone, they should be the first to perceive that there is something fundamentally wrong with their inherited concepts of national defense.

Beyond that, Soviet and American scientists are well aware that man-made changes in the global climate system could have devastating impacts on the viability of national societies — that depletion of the ozone layer, destruction of tropical forests, deterioration of coastal zones and estuaries, extinction of animal and plant species, loss of genetic resources — all this on top of degradation of cropland, pastureland, fisheries and forests on a worldwide scale, necessarily places the modern security issue squarely in a global context. In sum, East and West now share the knowledge that mankind can put an end to the human experiment not only through nuclear war but through destruction of the natural systems that sustain all life on the planet.

Still and all, it might seem naive, in the present political climate, to hope that the superpowers could break out of the conceptual traps that drive the "mad momentum" of the strategic arms race. Except for one thing: A strictly military concept of national defense has become a central threat to world security — and thus, inescapably, to the national security of both nations.

Number of words 2050
See page 351 for Questions

Reading time in Seconds _____
See page 361 for Conversion Table

SELECTION 83

Which Career Is the Right One for You?

David P. Campbell

More than anything else, your choice of career is going to determine how you live — and probably even where you live. The following article, excerpted from Dr. Campbell's book, If You Don't Know Where You're Going, You'll Probably End Up Somewhere Else, *should help you see yourself from a different angle.*

(Before reading the article, you should turn to page 354 and take the self-scoring Career Compatibility Test. You can then be your own career counselor.)

When you are trying to plan your career, try out a variety of jobs, work in many different settings, volunteer for different tasks.

There are six basic categories of occupations. The six types of jobs, as developed by Professor John L. Holland, a psychology professor from Johns Hopkins University, are described here in some detail. Recognize that when I talk about the characteristics of people in the jobs, no one person has all of these characteristics. I am talking about trends, but they are strong trends.

TYPE A — REALISTIC JOBS

These are mainly skilled trades or technical jobs, usually involving work with tools or machines, frequently called "blue-collar" positions.

People who are attracted to realistic jobs are usually rugged, robust, practical, physically strong and frequently competitive in outlook. They usually have good

From *If You Don't Know Where You're Going, You'll Probably End Up Somewhere Else* by David P. Campbell, Ph.D. © 1964 Argus Communications, a Division of DLM, Inc., Allen, TX 75002.

physical coordination, but sometimes they have trouble expressing themselves in words or in talking with others. They prefer to deal with things rather than with ideas or with people. They enjoy creating things with their hands. They have good motor coordination, but they are frequently uncomfortable in social settings, and lack verbal and interpersonal skills. They usually see themselves as mechanically and athletically inclined and are stable, natural and persistent. They prefer concrete to abstract problems. Realistic people tend to see the world in simple, tangible and traditional terms. Possessions are important to them, and they usually put their recreational money into cars, boats, campers, snowmobiles, motorcycles, airplanes or other machinery.

Realistic people describe themselves in interviews as "conforming, frank, genuine, normal, persistent, practical, stable, thrifty, materialistic, shy and uninvolved."

One unique reward of most realistic jobs is that the worker can quickly see the results of her labors.

In general, in realistic jobs, life is not complicated by intricate problems between people or organizations, nor by troublesome choices between conflicting philosophies.

TYPE B — CONVENTIONAL JOBS

These are usually office jobs where people work with organizations, files and regular schedules.

Conventional occupations include bookkeeper, statistician, bank teller, inventory controller, payroll clerk, secretary, financial analyst, office manager, computer operator, bank cashier and accountant. Conventional jobs usually require a fair amount of writing, but it is usually the writing of business letters and regular reports.

People who enjoy conventional jobs describe themselves as "conforming, conscientious, efficient, inhibited, obedient, orderly, persistent, practical and calm."

They like for life to be orderly and to go according to plan. They like to know what is expected of them, and they enjoy carrying out their assignments.

Conventional people prefer the highly ordered activities, both verbal and numerical, that characterize office work. They dislike ambiguity and prefer to know precisely what is expected of them. They describe themselves as "conventional, stable, well-controlled and dependable." They have little interest in problems requiring physical skills or intense relationships with others and they are most effective at well-defined tasks. They value material possessions and status, although they usually prefer conforming and subordinate roles.

The rewards of working in conventional jobs center around seeing offices and organizations run smoothly, and in understanding how the individual's contribution helps in making that happen.

People in conventional positions are frequently the glue that holds the entire operation together. Because of the nature of their work, they are not always publicly recognized as much as perhaps they should be, but they themselves have some appreciation of the contribution they are making to the organization, and this is one of the pleasant aspects of conventional occupations.

TYPE C — INVESTIGATIVE JOBS

These are scientific and laboratory jobs, jobs where people investigate how the world is put together.

The tasks involved in investigative jobs are scientific or laboratory in nature, and usually involve trying to solve some puzzles, whether the puzzle is a large, mysterious problem such as how the universe came into being, or a more normal, daily problem such as figuring out the composition of a sample of blood taken from a patient in a medical clinic.

Investigative workers are usually found in research laboratories or clinical settings, but they also work in a wide range of other places — highway departments where they study issues such as traffic control and composition of highway materials; in advertising agencies where they work on market surveys; in food-producing companies where they work on nutritional aspects of food; in military settings where they work on new weapons or new military strategies; in financial departments where they work on questions of economic strategy, money flow and inventory problems — in general, in any place where problems are being attacked in a systematic, scientific way.

Investigative tasks frequently involve the use of computers, microscopes, telescopes, high-speed centrifuges or any of an incredible array of other laboratory and scientific equipment. The investigative job differs from the realistic job in that the realistic job is usually more concerned with machines that produce products, while the investigative job is concerned with machines that produce data or information.

People in investigative jobs are task-oriented, which means they get all wrapped up in the problem they are working on. They sometimes perceive themselves as lacking in leadership or persuasive abilities, but they are confident of their scholarly and intellectual abilities.

They prefer to think through problems rather than act them out. They enjoy ambiguous challenges and do not like highly structured situations with lots of rules. They frequently have unconventional values and attitudes and tend to be original and creative, especially in scientific areas.

They describe themselves as "analytical, curious, independent and reserved." They especially dislike repetitive activities and sales activities. They are very curious.

The unique reward of many investigative jobs is the worker's opportunity to satisfy an innate curiosity, analyzing situations, trying to understand what is going on in whatever field they are working.

TYPE D — ARTISTIC JOBS

These are creative jobs where people work with words or music or art.

The tasks involved in artistic occupations usually involve working with words, music or other art forms. Decorating rooms, designing homes or doing portrait photography are other examples of artistic activities.

Artistic jobs are found in settings such as art museums, art galleries, music departments, interior decorating offices, music stores, theater groups, photographic studios, radio and television studios and any place where artistic skills are used and/or taught.

People who enjoy working in artistic jobs describe themselves as "complicated, disorderly, emotional, idealistic, imaginative, impractical, impulsive, independent, introspective, intuitive, nonconforming and original." They like to work in free environments that allow them to express themselves in a wide variety of media — writing, music, drawing, photography, fabrics — in general, any art form.

They value beauty and aesthetic qualities, and don't care much for social entanglements. They like to make things, especially new and different things, and are willing to take risks to try something new, even if the chances of failure are high.

The artistic person has a distaste for appearing conventional or undistinguished. Such people like to use their creativity to help them stand out from the crowd.

Artistic people have little interest in problems that are highly structured or that require a lot of physical strength, preferring those problems that can be dealt with with self-expression and artistic media. They resemble investigative people in preferring to work alone, but have a greater need for individualistic expression, are usually less assertive about their own capabilities, and are more sensitive and emotional.

The continual stimulation for the new and the different, for quality in creativity, is a primary reward of artistic jobs.

TYPE E — SOCIAL JOBS

These are jobs where people work with people — healing them, teaching them, helping them.

The tasks involved in social jobs are those concerned with working with other people, teaching them, or training them, or curing them, or leading them, or organizing them or enlightening them. Social tasks include explaining things to others, entertaining other people, planning the teaching of other people, helping other people solve their difficulties, organizing and conducting charities, and straightening out differences between people.

People who enjoy working in social jobs describe themselves as "cooperative, friendly, generous, helpful, idealistic, responsible, social, tactful and understanding." They like to work in groups, especially small groups that are working on problems common to individuals in the group.

They dislike working with machines or in highly organized situations such as military units. They like to discuss philosophic questions — the purpose of life, what constitutes right or wrong.

They like attention and seek situations that allow them to be at or near the center of the group. They prefer to solve problems by discussions with others, or by arranging or rearranging relationships between others. Social people also describe themselves as "cheerful, popular, achieving and good leaders."

The rewards of working in social jobs center around the warm glow that comes from helping other people solve their problems or improve themselves. People in social jobs usually have co-workers who are like themselves, and these groups are usually warm and supportive of each other. They make each other feel wanted, have great respect for each other's abilities, and have many opportunities for close interpersonal relationships.

TYPE F — JOBS OF LEADERSHIP

These are jobs where people persuade other people to do something — sales jobs, political jobs, merchandising jobs.

Also included are many business executive jobs, making speeches, running for an elected office, heading up a fund-raising campaign and many other jobs of leadership, as well as taking a course in leadership development.

Other examples of jobs of leadership include public relations directors, stock and bond brokers, buyers, hostesses, retailers, fashion merchandisers and industrial consultants.

People who enjoy working in jobs of leadership describe themselves as "adventuresome, ambitious, argumentative, domineering, energetic, flirtatious, impulsive, optimistic, self-confident, sociable and talkative."

Such people enjoy competitive activities and like to work in groups where they can have some influence over what the group is doing. They are self-confident and usually see themselves as good leaders.

Generally, such enterprising people dislike science and systematic thinking.

People in leadership jobs usually have a great facility with words, which they put to effective use in selling, dominating and leading. They are impatient with detail work or work involving long periods of heavy thinking. They have strong drives to organizational goals or economic aims. They see themselves as aggressive, popular, self-confident, cheerful and sociable. They generally have a high energy level and lots of enthusiasm.

The unique reward from jobs of leadership is the sense of achievement that comes from making things happen, whether it is conducting a sales campaign, or winning an election, or persuading a board of directors to accept new policies.

Number of words 1750
See page 353 for Questions

Reading time in Seconds _____
See page 361 for Conversion Table

Part Two

COMPREHENSION AND VOCABULARY
CHECK QUESTIONS AND EXERCISES

Perhaps the best measure of reading comprehension is your ability to reexpress with a minimum of loss or distortion what you have just read. That is, however, a very time-consuming process and does not lend itself to easy objective evaluation. The ten objective COMPREHENSION CHECK QUESTIONS are intended to provide a quick, convenient approximation or supplement to any such re-expression.

Your score on the first five questions will suggest how well you note details and is spoken of as *Receptive Comprehension*. Your score on the last five questions will suggest how well you get the central idea, draw inferences, reach conclusions, note relationships, and recognize pattern and organization. These last five questions come under the heading of *Reflective Comprehension*. The sixth question is always on the central idea. Indicate your answer by entering the number of the correct choice in the space following the question. When you have finished, check your answers with the key on page 357.

The VOCABULARY CHECK QUESTIONS are meant to encourage increased attention to context. In a general way they parallel the twofold division of the COMPREHENSION CHECK QUESTIONS. The distinction here is between knowing a word without further study, and having to depend upon a reflective analysis of context in order to arrive at an accurate understanding of its meaning. Low comprehension, in both reading and listening, is often attributable to inadequate vocabulary (Column I score) or to inability to make effective use of contextual clues in arriving at word meanings (Column II score).

Without looking back at the selection, you are to enter a set of answers in Column I, headed *without context*. This provides a measure of your word knowledge without the help of context. Next, turn back to the selection containing the words, find the word, and study it in its full context to see if you can arrive at a better understanding of its meaning. Use Column II, headed *with context,* for entering your second set of answers. When you have completed both sets, check your results by using the key on page 357 or by referring to your dictionary.

If you are as skilled as you should be in using contextual clues to word meanings, your scores in the second column should be almost perfect. If they are low, you have particular reason for developing added skill with context to facilitate your mastery of new words and improve comprehension. In the first few selections you read, if your answers in Column I are all correct, you may wish to omit working through the items a second time with the help of context. In that case, take 20 off for each mistake to get your WORD COMPREHENSION SCORE.

A careful record of your performance as you work through the various tests should do much to hasten your progress. Enter all your test results on the PROGRESS RECORD at the end of the book, pages 363 following.

The eighty-three EXERCISES on the reverse side of the Check Questions provide for added practice, reinforcement, and extension of reading and study-related skills. Eleven of the twelve exercises for the selections in Section VII are, for example, focused on writing skills. The format is based on Franklin's method, described in Selection 41, but modified here to make it more objective for easier checking. For specific matters of style, usage, diction, grammar, and the like, refer to a standard handbook of English, such as *The Heath Handbook of Composition,* 10th edition, by Elsbree and Bracher.

INDEX OF EXERCISES

NAME——————————————— DATE——————— READING RATE——————— W.P.M.

COMPREHENSION CHECK QUESTIONS

1. The earthquake occurred (1) in the afternoon; (2) in the evening; (3) at night; (4) in the morning.   1. ————

2. Adams attended an exposition in (1) London; (2) Rome; (3) Paris; (4) Brussels.   2. ————

3. The author mentions (1) Edison; (2) Newton; (3) Galileo; (4) Roentgen.   3. ————

4. What date was said to mark the change from rapid to radical change? (1) 1880; (2) 1900; (3) 1920; (4) 1950.   4. ————

5. The amount of technical information doubles every how many years? (1) ten; (2) twenty; (3) thirty; (4) forty.   5. ————

Receptive Comprehension ————

6. The main idea is to (1) reveal the importance of change; (2) help us understand and guide the forces of change; (3) point up the acceleration of change; (4) explain the function of time-spanners.   6. ————

7. The Shafter cow incident was intended primarily to show what about change? (1) its suddenness; (2) its importance; (3) its severity; (4) its unexpectedness.   7. ————

8. The article is organized basically (1) from past to present; (2) from the ordinary to the unusual; (3) from basic to less basic; (4) from cause to effect.   8. ————

9. Adams was most concerned about (1) change; (2) time; (3) thought; (4) force.   9. ————

10. The author's outlook is best described as (1) optimistic; (2) pessimistic; (3) uncertain; (4) casual.   10. ————

(10 off for each mistake)   *Reflective Comprehension* ————

TOTAL READING COMPREHENSION SCORE ————

VOCABULARY CHECK QUESTIONS

		without context I	with context II
1. *ken*	(1) area; (2) thought; (3) knowledge; (4) intent; (5) love.	1. ————	————
2. *quest*	(1) end; (2) pursuit; (3) doubt; (4) twist; (5) question.	2. ————	————
3. *irruption*	(1) fall; (2) trick; (3) blow; (4) breakdown; (5) bursting into.	3. ————	————
4. *arbitrary*	(1) military; (2) dated; (3) disputed; (4) fixed; (5) curved.	4. ————	————
5. *amenable*	(1) responsive; (2) immoral; (3) entertaining; (4) combined; (5) repairable.	5. ————	————

(10 off for each mistake)   *Word Comprehension* without *contextual help* (I) ————

Word Comprehension with *contextual help* (II) ————

TOTAL WORD COMPREHENSION SCORE ————

EXERCISES

Noting organizational clues: With reading as with driving, looking ahead is imperative. With a dense fog obscuring your view, you must of necessity creep along or risk running off the road. The same is true with reading. You must cultivate the habit of noting any and all clues that suggest the direction the writer is taking.

Read the first words of the opening paragraph of *The Dynamics of Change* — "At exactly 5:13 a.m. . . . ." Ask yourself what those words suggest about the remainder of the paragraph. Mention of a specific time suggests a chronological ordering of events. Notice the first word of the second sentence — "Suddenly, ..."

Taste the satisfaction of having looked ahead with accuracy to the second sentence — even before reading it. That kind of foreshadowing means better comprehension and more rapid reading, for you are less likely to get off the track because of the clear way ahead.

Try the second paragraph in the same way. Read the first few words — "For the student of change . . . ." Again ask yourself what those words suggest about direction. In the first place, the word *change* stands out, reminding you that that word summarizes the first paragraph nicely. It also suggests that change will be further developed in the second paragraph, perhaps in a way analogous to that of the first.

As you read on, you note the cow is called a "symbol of our times." Again, ask yourself what is foreshadowed by that statement. You will expect some explanation to follow. When you come to the words "like the Shafter cow," you see confirmation of your expectations. Furthermore, you're told exactly what to expect in the remainder of the article — what's going to be talked about now.

To take further steps in establishing habits of using words to point the road ahead, move on to the end of the article.

At exactly 5:13 a.m., the 18th of April, 1906, a cow was standing somewhere between the main barn and the milking shed on the old Shafter Ranch in California, minding her own business. Suddenly, the earth shook, the skies trembled, and when it was all over, there was nothing showing of the cow above ground but a bit of her tail sticking up.

For the student of change, the Shafter cow is a sort of symbol of our times. She stood quietly enough, thinking such gentle thoughts as cows are likely to have, while huge forces outside her ken built up all around her and — within a minute — discharged it all at once in a great movement that changed the configuration of the earth, and destroyed a city, and swallowed her up. And that's what we are going to talk about now; how, if we do not learn to understand and guide the great forces of change at work on our world today, we may find ourselves like the Shafter cow, swallowed up by vast upheavals in our way of life — quite early some morning.

Take the sentence "Society has many built-in time spanners that help link the present generation with the past." What would you expect to follow in the remaining part of the paragraph? Write down your expectations in the space below, then check back to the article to see how accurately you were foreshadowing what was said.

Do the same with the next paragraph. Here is the opening sentence: "No such time spanners enhance our sense of the future." What do you think follows that sentence on down the road?

Establish this way of reading as your normal habit. Let it keep you on track.

NAME_____ DATE_____ READING RATE_____ W.P.M.

COMPREHENSION CHECK QUESTIONS

1. The author says his mind is like (1) an empty pail; (2) a butterfly net; (3) alphabet soup; (4) a steel sieve.   1. _____

2. When he is introduced to someone, he (1) looks him in the eye; (2) smiles; (3) throws his chest out; (4) repeats the name of the person forcefully.   2. _____

3. When he is buying a shirt, what figure sticks in his mind? (1) 36; (2) 25; (3) 18; (4) 9.   3. _____

4. He refers to (1) the Jabberwocky; (2) Kubla Khan; (3) the Ancient Mariner; (4) Mandalay.   4. _____

5. The telephone exchange mentioned was (1) Parkway; (2) Midway; (3) Ocean; (4) Federal.   5. _____

Receptive Comprehension _____

6. This is primarily to (1) help us remember better; (2) illustrate the problems posed by a poor memory; (3) reveal the author's personal troubles in remembering; (4) poke fun at memory books.   6. _____

7. The chief purpose is to (1) amuse; (2) clarify; (3) moralize; (4) convince.   7. _____

8. The bit about Mr. Garden was intended to (1) illustrate the value of associations; (2) demonstrate the author's foggy memory; (3) ridicule the association technique; (4) explain how association works. 8. _____

9. In style, this is best described as (1) humorous; (2) conversational; (3) witty; (4) farcical.   9. _____

10. The idea is presented largely through (1) narrative bits; (2) details; (3) comparisons; (4) analysis of difficulties.   10. _____

(10 off for each mistake)   *Reflective Comprehension* _____

TOTAL READING COMPREHENSION SCORE _____

VOCABULARY CHECK QUESTIONS

		without context I	with context II
1. *furtive*	(1) useless; (2) mad; (3) sharp; (4) rapid; (5) stealthy.	1. _____	_____
2. *well-feigned*	(1) well-timed; (2) friendly; (3) well-pretended; (4) tired; (5) well-fed.	2. _____	_____
3. *sporadic*	(1) occasional; (2) spontaneous; (3) playful; (4) sparkling; (5) germlike.	3. _____	_____
4. *verbatim*	(1) spoken; (2) word for word; (3) idiotic; (4) talkative; (5) part of speech.	4. _____	_____
5. *veritable*	(1) valuable; (2) vernacular; (3) skilled; (4) true; (5) springlike.	5. _____	_____

(10 off for each mistake)   *Word Comprehension* without *contextual help* (I) _____

Word Comprehension with *contextual help* (II) _____

TOTAL WORD COMPREHENSION SCORE _____

EXERCISES

1. Spotting the central idea: The good reader is one who is able to see past all the details and development to grasp the central or topic idea of a paragraph. Try this with some of the paragraphs in this selection, expressing the topic idea below in a word or phrase. Just turn back to the selection, find the paragraph in question, read it over rapidly, then summarize the topic idea briefly.

Example: the paragraph beginning, "Frankly, I've got . . . ," is chiefly about

```
his sievelike mind
```
_____

A. The paragraph beginning, "Maybe I don't . . . ," is chiefly about

_____

B. The paragraph beginning, "It's hard enough . . . ," is chiefly about

_____

C. The paragraph beginning, "I have the . . . ," is chiefly about

_____

D. The paragraph beginning, "I'm no good . . . ," is chiefly about

_____

E. The paragraph beginning, "It isn't that . . . ," is chiefly about

_____

2. Reading to remember: Good reading should include good remembering. Use associations to connect things you want to remember with things you already know. For example, is it *indispensable* or *indispensible?* Use associations. Just remember that an *able* man is indeed indispens*able*. Let that association remember the right spelling for you. And is it *attendance* or *atendence?* If you're not sure, remember that a good time to start dancing is at ten — *at-ten-dance.* List below five words that you tend to misspell, then make up some association or mnemonic for each, to help you remember the correct form.

List below five words that you tend to misspell, then make up some association or mnemonic for each, to help you remember the correct form.

Word	**Association or Mnemonic**
1.	
2.	
3.	
4.	
5.	

3. Levels in the cognitive domain: The cognitive domain is the domain of intellect, of intellectual development. Ideally, comprehension check questions should touch on all levels of cognition in order to provide maximum stimulus for the reader's intellectual development. Only recently have levels of cognition been rather clearly delineated. Seven levels deserve particular attention.

(1) Memory (remembering what was expressly said)
(2) Translation (putting what was said into other words or form)
(3) Interpretation (noting unstated relationships)
(4) Application (applying a principle recognized)
(5) Analysis (breaking a subject down into its parts for examination)
(6) Synthesis (fusing parts into a whole)
(7) Evaluation (formulating a standard and using it to judge the worth of something)

Now how are you going to remember those seven levels? Just remember this sentence:

```
My  Thinking  Is  All  About  Saving  Effort.
 |      |      |   |     |       |       |
Memory  |      |  Analysis      |
 |   Translation |      |    Synthesis
      Interpretation         Evaluation
           |
      Application
```

192

NAME————————————————— DATE——————— READING RATE—————— W.P.M.

COMPREHENSION CHECK QUESTIONS

1. Most of us don't use more than what percent of our ability to remember? (1) ten; (2) twenty; (3) thirty; (4) forty. 1. ———

2. One essential for better memory is (1) training; (2) desire; (3) practice; (4) discipline. 2. ———

3. How many basic laws were discussed? (1) only one; (2) two; (3) three; (4) four. 3. ———

4. Specific mention was made of (1) Plato; (2) Virgil; (3) Crito; (4) Aristotle. 4. ———

5. The author discusses how to (1) memorize poetry; (2) study; (3) take notes; (4) listen better. 5. ———

Receptive Comprehension ———

6. This article is mainly about (1) prerequisites for remembering; (2) how to improve memory; (3) the Laws of Association; (4) the need to love people. 6. ———

7. Mention of commercials was made to point up the value of (1) repetition; (2) humor; (3) the personal; (4) cleverness of expression. 7. ———

8. To improve memory, it's most important to (1) associate; (2) visualize; (3) repeat; (4) understand. 8. ———

9. This article is chiefly to (1) entertain; (2) describe; (3) explain; (4) inspire. 9. ———

10. The line from Alexander Pope was to emphasize the importance of (1) visualizing; (2) caring; (3) concentrating; (4) associating. 10. ———

(10 off for each mistake)   *Reflective Comprehension* ———

TOTAL READING COMPREHENSION SCORE ———

VOCABULARY CHECK QUESTIONS

		without context I	*with context* II
1. *native*	(1) inborn; (2) national; (3) general; (4) rude; (5) foreign.	1. ———	———
2. *inherent*	(1) pure; (2) essential; (3) harmless; (4) sticky; (5) indirect.	2. ———	———
3. *cited*	(1) mentioned; (2) built; (3) strengthened; (4) played; (5) read.	3. ———	———
4. *retention*	(1) thought; (2) memory; (3) plan; (4) holder; (5) reach.	4. ———	———
5. *contiguity*	(1) contagion; (2) emergency; (3) nearness; (4) series; (5) sameness.	5. ———	———

(10 off for each mistake)   *Word Comprehension* without *contextual help* (I) ———

Word Comprehension with *contextual help* (II) ———

TOTAL WORD COMPREHENSION SCORE ———

EXERCISES

Reading paragraphs: A close inspection of a well-planned paragraph will suggest how important it is to read for ideas, not words. Often from a fourth to a half of the words in a paragraph are unessential modifiers and connectives or words needed to fit the ideas into conventional English sentence patterns.

Reading the skeleton versions below should suggest how mind and eye should work together to focus on the essentials and suggest the place of stylistic connectives and modifiers. After reading the versions over several times, try filling in some of the gaps, then check back with the original paragraph.

Version A (Skeleton topic idea and forward step—7% of total paragraph)

Lack of self-confidence . . . . one of . . . great problems . . . .

Version B (Skeleton topic idea, supporting development, and forward step—43% of total paragraph)

Lack of self-confidence . . . . one of . . . great problems . . . . survey . . . . six hundred students . . . . asked to state . . . . . most difficult . . . . problem. Seventy-five percent listed lack . . confidence. . . . . same . . . . true . . . . . population generally. Everywhere . . . . people . . . . afraid, . . . shrink . . . . life, . . . suffer . . . . . deep . . . . inadequacy . . . insecurity, . . doubt . . . . . own powers. . . . . mistrust . . . . . ability . . meet responsibilities or . . grasp opportunities. . . . . beset by . . . . fear . . . . something . . not . . . . right. . . . . . . not believe . . . . be what they want . . . . , . . . so . . . . make . . . . content with . . . . less than . . . . capable. Thousands . . . . go . . . . through life . . . ., defeated . . . afraid. . . . in most cases such . . . . is unnecessary.

in most cases such . . . . is unnecessary.

Drawing inferences from main or topic ideas: After a cursory reading of an article, you are apt to feel that your answers to the questions are just guesses. To demonstrate the difference between guesses based on pure chance and inferences, a class of thirty was asked to choose a number between 0 and 100. Since there was little reason to select either a high or low number, the class average was roughly midpoint—an average of 46.

The class was then asked to infer from their own experience, what percent of a sample of 600 college students listed lack of self-confidence as one of their major problems. Here the class average was 56 percent, still roughly toward the midpoint mark.

To point up the role of the topic sentence in affecting the accuracy of an inference, the topic sentence of the paragraph was read aloud to the class. The students were then asked to give the percent figure. Here the class average was 72 — only three points away from the actual figure given later in the paragraph, which was 75 percent.

In short, there is an observable difference between (1) pure chance, (2) personal experience and background, and (3) intelligent use of a specific topic sentence. Inferences drawn from general ideas should not be confused with pure chance reactions. If a rapid reading of a selection does give you the main ideas, intelligent use of that information should lead to quite accurate information about details which you actually did not read.

Paragraphing dialogue: By referring back to the selection and examining the way dialogue is paragraphed, try to formulate a rule covering the situation. Check your formulation with a handbook statement. Most people remember the things they think through and discover for themselves much better than those things someone else puts into a book to be memorized. You might as well capitalize on that by trying to formulate a rule *before* checking the matter in your handbook.

NAME_____ DATE_____ READING RATE_____W.P.M.

COMPREHENSION CHECK QUESTIONS

1. Framton called on the Sappletons (1) to please his mother; (2) to help cure his nervousness; (3) to renew a former acquaintance; (4) to bring greetings from his sister.   1. _____

2. Framton had a letter of introduction to (1) no one; (2) one person; (3) two persons; (4) an unspecified number of persons.   2. _____

3. Framton's sister had once stayed in this rural retreat at (1) a relative's; (2) a friend's; (3) the inn; (4) the rectory.   3. _____

4. Mrs. Sappleton said that Framton only talked about (1) his work; (2) his sister; (3) the weather; (4) his illness.   4. _____

5. The niece said Mrs. Sappleton had lost her husband (1) only last year; (2) two years ago; (3) three years ago; (4) an unspecified number of years ago.   5. _____

Receptive Comprehension _____

6. The theme of this story is (1) the troubles of a nervous individual; (2) the gullibility of most adults; (3) the mischievous romancing of a child; (4) the value of a vivid imagination.   6. _____

7. This story is told from the point of view of (1) Framton; (2) the niece; (3) a third person; (4) Mrs. Sappleton.   7. _____

8. The plausibility of the niece's tragic story depends most strongly on (1) Mrs. Sappleton's actions; (2) the open window; (3) the details mentioned; (4) the niece's own emotional reactions.   8. _____

9. Mrs. Sappleton's attitude toward Framton is best described by the word (1) friendly; (2) apprehensive; (3) bored; (4) amused.   9. _____

10. The story is best described as (1) humorous; (2) fantastic; (3) stirring; (4) dramatic.   10. _____

(10 off for each mistake)   *Reflective Comprehension* _____

TOTAL READING COMPREHENSION SCORE _____

VOCABULARY CHECK QUESTIONS

		without context I	*with context* II
1. *endeavoured* (1) ate; (2) entered; (3) attempted; (4) planned; (5) departed.	1.	_____	_____
2. *unduly* (1) pleasantly; (2) formally; (3) stupidly; (4) cleverly; (5) excessively.	2.	_____	_____
3. *delusion* (1) false belief; (2) conclusion; (3) new idea; (4) covering; (5) departure.	3.	_____	_____
4. *imminent* (1) prominent; (2) impending; (3) time-honored; (4) immortal; (5) helpful.	4.	_____	_____
5. *pariah* (1) outcast; (2) equal; (3) trained; (4) package; (5) part.	5.	_____	_____

(10 off for each mistake)   *Word Comprehension* without *contextual help* (I) _____

Word Comprehension with *contextual help* (II) _____

TOTAL WORD COMPREHENSION SCORE _____

EXERCISES

Reading narration: In writing or telling a story you have the problem of communicating certain necessary facts — the *Who? Where? What? Why?* and *When?* of the story. That necessary introductory explanation or exposition is where your skill as a story teller receives its first test — and where your appreciation as a story reader begins.

Try your hand at translating the following beginning of the story from exposition into narration, getting action into the picture from the very start and bringing the characters to immediate life. When you finish, compare with the original to note essential differences between exposition and narration. Can you make any generalizations about the essential nature of narration? Notice the implications for a reader.

Who?   The two principal characters in this story are a man by the name of Framton Nuttel and a young lady of fifteen, with a Mrs. Sappleton, aunt of the young lady, playing a minor role.

Where?   The story takes place in a room of Mrs. Sappleton's home in a quiet rural retreat.

What?   Mr. Nuttel is making a call on Mrs. Sappleton, whom he has never met before. The young lady is entertaining him until the aunt comes downstairs.

Why?   Mr. Nuttel left his home to come to a quiet spot to settle his nerves. His sister has suggested that he call on a few people so as not to develop more nerves because of loneliness.

Description and narration: Character may be delineated by direct or indirect means. The direct method is through simple description or labeling, as, for example, "He was a shy young man." In the indirect method his shyness would be revealed by his words and actions. As a reader, you should take advantage of that knowledge.

After each of the names below, list those words and phrases which are used to characterize the individual either directly or indirectly. How many descriptive details are given? How much of the characterizing is done indirectly?

     Mr. Nuttel:

     The young lady of fifteen:

     Mrs. Sappleton:

NAME————————————————— DATE——————— READING RATE——————— W.P.M.

COMPREHENSION CHECK QUESTIONS

1. Looking at Petey, his roommate diagnosed (1) mumps; (2) acute indigestion; (3) appendicitis; (4) low back pain.   1. ————

2. The raccoon coat belonged to the story teller's (1) uncle; (2) cousin; (3) brother; (4) father.   2. ————

3. Mention was made of a (1) Stutz Bearcat; (2) Olds; (3) Willys Overland; (4) Cord.   3. ————

4. There was a reference to the University of (1) Minnesota; (2) Chicago; (3) Michigan; (4) Indiana.   4. ————

5. Polly wanted more movies with (1) John Barrymore; (2) Van Johnson; (3) Walter Pidgeon; (4) Robert Taylor.   5. ————

Receptive Comprehension ————

6. This article was written mainly to (1) show that love is a fallacy; (2) have fun with logical fallacies; (3) show how unstable Petey is; (4) show how fickle women are.   6. ————

7. The central character was predominantly (1) brainy; (2) studious; (3) farsighted; (4) sympathetic.   7. ————

8. Polly's language — "terrif, wow-dow, marvy" —emphasized her (1) interest; (2) dumbness; (3) enthusiasm; (4) faddishness.   8. ————

9. "Reading is good" is an example of (1) Post Hoc; (2) Dicto Simpliciter; (3) Contradictory Premises; (4) Ad Misericordium.   9. ————

10. You would infer that Polly's eventual grasp of logic was due primarily to her (1) teacher's persistence; (2) strong interest; (3) intelligence; (4) teacher's ability in presenting the material.   10. ————

(10 off for each mistake)   *Reflective Comprehension* ————

TOTAL READING COMPREHENSION SCORE ————

VOCABULARY CHECK QUESTIONS

		without context I	*with context* II
1. *perspicacious*	(1) shrewd; (2) warm; (3) stubborn; (4) obvious; (5) clear.	1. ————	————
2. *veered*	(1) repeated; (2) vowed; (3) hid; (4) deviated; (5) neared.	2. ————	————
3. *waif*	(1) wail; (2) box; (3) homeless child; (4) drink; (5) long walk.	3. ————	————
4. *desisted*	(1) left; (2) ceased; (3) opposed; (4) stated; (5) deserved.	4. ————	————
5. *fraught*	(1) tricked; (2) filled; (3) frank; (4) free; (5) proud.	5. ————	————

(10 off for each mistake)   Word Comprehension without *contextual help* (I) ————

Word Comprehension with *contextual help* (II) ————

TOTAL WORD COMPREHENSION SCORE ————

EXERCISES

1. *Using your time effectively:* For one entire week, Monday through Sunday, keep an accurate, detailed record of how you spend your time. If it is to be accurate, you will have to keep your record during the day, not at the end of the day by memory. Otherwise you will miss recording or noting how long you talked with a friend after class or how long it took you to eat or to get from home to school. Then, and only then, are you in a position to know how effectively you are using your time and what changes can be made to real advantage.

At the end of the week, a total of 168 hours, summarize your findings, using such headings as the following:

Sleep	Meals	Class and laboratory	Study	Outside work	Personal care	Travel	Leisure	Social	Waste time	Total
____	____	_____	____	_____	_____	____	____	____	_____	168

If you have never kept an accurate, detailed record of this kind, you have much to learn about yourself. The next step of course, is to plan with care exactly how to make more effective use of time to insure having sufficient time for all major activities.

Now try working out a personal study schedule so as to develop the work and study habits which will serve you to best advantage. Remember, the student who looks and plans ahead is the one who gets ahead.

2. *Using parallelism as an aid in reading:* Parallelism is putting similar or contrasting ideas in identical or similar word patterns in order to sharpen and clarify their likenesses. Look at a few famous examples to get a clearer picture. Patrick Henry knew enough to capitalize on parallelism in his stirring words, "Give me liberty or give me death." Abraham Lincoln's memorable phrase "of the people, by the people, for the people" is another famous example.

List two other examples below:

A. _____

B. _____

Notice how you can rely on parallelism to supply words you have not actually read. Read the following sentences from the selection, filling in the blanks by relying on expectations stemming from parallel structure.

A. My brain was as powerful as a dynamo, _____ precise _____ _____ chemist's scales, _____ penetrating _____ _____ scalpel.

B. It is, after all, easier to make a beautiful dumb girl smart than _____ _____ _____ ugly _____ _____ _____.

C. "What's Polly to me or _____ _____ _____?"

D. "If there is an irresistible force, there can be no immovable object. If _____ _____ _____ immovable _____, _____ _____ _____ _____ _____ _____. Get it?"

Now check back to the article to see if you can actually read words without seeing them. Develop the awareness of parallelism that will give you that kind of guidance, leading to more rapid reading without loss of meaning.

NAME_____ DATE_____ READING RATE_____ W.P.M.

COMPREHENSION CHECK QUESTIONS

1. Franklin sometimes sat up all night reading (1) *Pilgrim's Progress;* (2) Plutarch's *Lives;* (3) *Paradise Lost;* (4) *Gulliver's Travels.*   1. _____

2. Darwin's father sent him to the University of Glasgow to study (1) medicine; (2) music; (3) for the ministry; (4) for government service.   2. _____

3. Mozart attempted to strike harmonious intervals on the clavier at the age of (1) three; (2) four; (3) five; (4) six.   3. _____

4. One of the following was *not* mentioned: (1) Napoleon; (2) Henslow; (3) Goethe; (4) Shakespeare.   4. _____

5. "Men of genius," when compared with ordinary men, are (1) quite different; (2) more imaginative; (3) essentially the same; (4) more temperamental.   5. _____

Receptive Comprehension _____

6. The purpose of this selection is to suggest the (1) importance of hard, sustained effort; (2) role of deep and ardent curiosity; (3) significance of flashes of inspiration; (4) special insights of men of genius.   6. _____

7. The author implies that Franklin learned to write chiefly because he (1) was urged to write; (2) read so widely; (3) practiced so hard; (4) wanted to so much.   7. _____

8. By implication good speaking probably results from (1) intelligent practice; (2) strong desire; (3) hard work; (4) wide reading.   8. _____

9. In selecting reading for an anthology, the author would probably favor most strongly getting the reactions of (1) the teachers using the book; (2) the students using the book; (3) well-known writers and critics; (4) literary figures and reviewers.   9. _____

10. The author implies that in selecting reading material the most important consideration would be (1) difficulty; (2) literary merit; (3) timeliness; (4) personal appeal.   10. _____

(10 off for each mistake)   *Reflective Comprehension* _____

TOTAL READING COMPREHENSION SCORE _____

VOCABULARY CHECK QUESTIONS

		without context I	*with context* II
1. *scant*	(1) limited; (2) rapid; (3) frightening; (4) colorful; (5) designed.	1. _____	_____
2. *fervor*	(1) search; (2) intensity; (3) charm; (4) fete; (5) sickness.	2. _____	_____
3. *verdant*	(1) colorful; (2) populated; (3) golden; (4) verbal; (5) green.	3. _____	_____
4. *propensity*	(1) liking; (2) scheme; (3) propellent; (4) hatred; (5) expression.	4. _____	_____
5. *sundry*	(1) bright; (2) various; (3) costly; (4) warm; (5) sullen.	5. _____	_____

(10 off for each mistake)   *Word Comprehension* without *contextual help* (I) _____

Word Comprehension with *contextual help* (II) _____

TOTAL WORD COMPREHENSION SCORE _____

EXERCISES

Dealing with synthesis and analysis: The good reader is one who is familiar with a variety of ways of organizing material. In the same way, a good driver is one who is familiar with a wide variety of highway signs and markers and can travel with a minimum of error. Synthesis and analysis are patterns of organization that should be well known.

Suppose we look more closely at each. Synthesis is essentially a fitting together of parts or ideas to form a whole — a generalization or thesis. For example, when you add the prefix *in-* to the prefix *de-* to the root *pend* to the suffix *-ence,* you get the word *independence,* formed from a synthesis of language elements. Analysis is just the opposite. You start with a whole and break it down into its parts so as to understand it better. With *independence,* that would mean breaking the word down into the two prefixes, root, and suffix forming the word.

Now think back to the article on interest. Notice how the author turns to three careers, synthesizing from each the parts that can be put together to form a single generalization or thesis. Look back to see exactly what words he uses as road markers to call attention to a new thought division. Write the first six words of each paragraph that marks the beginning of his treatment of another individual. Use the following spaces.

(1) _____

(2) _____

(3) _____

To pull together the threefold pattern, the elements to be synthesized, the author uses what might be called a summary statement serving as a transition leading on to his generalization. The paragraph that serves this important function begins with what fourteen words? Enter them below.

_____

_____

What generalization comes from the synthesis of these three careers — the truth to be distilled as a matter of major concern? Enter the statement of that truth below.

_____

_____

_____

The remaining paragraphs lead on to a somewhat modified final truth, growing out of the additional development. State that final truth below, underlining the portion added to the initial generalization synthesized from the three careers.

_____

_____

_____

Examining your reading interests: Analyze your own reading interests below, listing two conclusions — one focused on a major strength, one on a major weakness.

A. _____

_____

B. _____

_____

NAME——————————————— DATE————— READING RATE————— W.P.M.

COMPREHENSION CHECK QUESTIONS

1. Computers are likened to (1) doors; (2) bench vices; (3) gates; (4) light switches.   1. ——————

2. When a computer is "booted," it (1) starts printing; (2) starts searching the memory; (3) is turned off; (4) is ready to go.   2. ——————

3. About what percent of programs for personal computers use the BASIC language? (1) 45%; (2) 60%; (3) 75%; (4) 90%.   3. ——————

4. Disk drives are said to be about what size? (1) Kleenex-box size; (2) book-box size; (3) record-changer-cabinet size; (4) cigar-box size.   4. ——————

5. How many kinds of printers were discussed? (1) four; (2) three; (3) two; (4) one.   5. ——————

Receptive Comprehension ——————

6. This article is mainly (1) a guide to purchasing; (2) a discussion of how to operate the equipment; (3) an overview; (4) an explanation of word processing.   6. ——————

7. The style of this article is best described as (1) witty; (2) forceful; (3) factual; (4) lively.   7. ——————

8. Emphasis is on the (1) who; (2) why; (3) how; (4) what.   8. ——————

9. If intending to purchase, you would infer you should hold off purchase of which longest? (1) disk drive; (2) printer; (3) word processor; (4) computer.   9. ——————

10. Points are developed largely by use of (1) definitions; (2) quoted experts; (3) descriptive details; (4) illustrative examples.   10. ——————

(10 off for each mistake)   *Reflective Comprehension* ——————

TOTAL READING COMPREHENSION SCORE ——————

VOCABULARY CHECK QUESTIONS

		without context I	*with context* II
1. *binary*	(1) solid; (2) blank; (3) flexible; (4) brittle; (5) twofold.	1. ——————	——————
2. *arcane*	(1) old; (2) foreign; (3) warm; (4) little-known; (5) curved.	2. ——————	——————
3. *argot*	(1) argument; (2) phrase; (3) area; (4) accent; (5) dialect.	3. ——————	——————
4. *excised*	(1) treated; (2) removed; (3) exploded; (4) trained; (5) carried.	4. ——————	——————
5. *peripherals*	(1) patients; (2) intervals; (3) externals; (4) segments; (5) studies.	5. ——————	——————

(10 off for each mistake)   *Word Comprehension* without *contextual help* (I) ——————

Word Comprehension with *contextual help* (II) ——————

TOTAL WORD COMPREHENSION SCORE ——————

EXERCISES

Noting transitional and connective devices: The efficient reader is alert to any words or phrases which let him follow with increased ease the path set by the writer. When a skillful reader reads, "To go back now to our general maxims . . . ," he knows he should look on the preceding development as somewhat of a digression from the main outline and the following paragraph as a return to another division. Other words suggest cause or result, comparison, repetition, and the like as a step in the development of the subject.

A. Classify the following words and phrases, using the following divisions:

| 1. Addition | 3. Repetition | 5. Contrast |
| 2. Example | 4. Comparison | 6. Definition |

a. "just as" _____   f. "a certain Rudolph Somebody, who" _____

b. "That is," _____   g. "when people use the word 'habit' " _____

c. "in short" _____   h. "This leads to a fourth" _____

d. "But, if" _____   i. "in the sense that" _____

e. "good or" _____   j. "is like" _____

(Note answers below)

B. Now try a differently structured exercise, again dealing with the transitional and connective words and phrases. In the left-hand column below, you'll find five phrases taken from the article about computers. In the right-hand column, you'll find descriptive phrases that can be matched with each of the phrases in the left-hand column. On the spaces beween the two columns, enter the number identifying the proper matching of the phrases —a suggestion as to what will probably follow.

a. "In reality"   _____   1. next step in a sequence

b. "Then what?"   _____   2. discussion of next procedure

c. "But two things"   _____   3. expect more details

d. "With a word processor you could" _____   4. description of things

e. "After you're done"   _____   5. listing of possibilities

When you've checked your answers with the key below, turn back to the article and find the phrases, noting exactly what follows. This exercise sharpens your awareness of such phrases and their function in keeping you, the reader, on track.

C. Suppose the subheadings in this article were all eliminated. When and how soon would you know that a new division was being discussed? For example, if the subheading "Computer Languages" were eliminated, what specific clue to the change of subject could you find? In the blanks below, write all the words up to those that mark the change of subject.

1. Computer Languages: _____

2. Diskettes: _____

3. Word Processing: _____

4. Printers: _____

Can you make any generalizations on the basis of this exercise that will help you as you read articles where subheadings are not used?

_____

_____

_____

_____

Answers to B: a, 3; b, 2; c, 4; d, 5; e, 1.

Answers to A: a, 4; b, 3; c, 3; d, 5; e, 5; f, 2; g, 6; h, 1; i, 6; j, 4.

202

NAME——————————————— DATE———————— READING RATE———————— W.P.M.

COMPREHENSION CHECK QUESTIONS

1. To kill the dragons Gawaine used a (1) sword; (2) lance; (3) battle-ax; (4) spear.   1. ————

2. When Gawaine is first told he is to kill dragons, he asks for (1) an enchanted cap; (2) a magic word; (3) more training; (4) some other job.   2. ————

3. After killing a dragon, Gawaine would always bring back (1) the claws; (2) a lock of hair; (3) a tooth; (4) the ears.   3. ————

4. Gawaine said he thought some of the dragons were (1) 50 feet long; (2) 100 feet long; (3) 200 feet long; (4) 500 feet long.   4. ————

5. The dragon that finally killed Gawaine was (1) a small one; (2) a fair-sized one; (3) a large one; (4) of unknown size.   5. ————

Receptive Comprehension ————

6. This story illustrates the importance of (1) training; (2) courage; (3) attitude; (4) magic.   6. ————

7. Gawaine's record of fifty killings was primarily attributable to (1) his skill; (2) his assurance; (3) his training; (4) none of those factors.   7. ————

8. You would infer that the Headmaster regarded Gawaine (1) highly; (2) with some aversion; (3) as likable but a mediocre student; (4) as a capable but lazy student.   8. ————

9. The humor of this article is best described as (1) mildly satiric; (2) rather obvious; (3) farcical; (4) stilted.   9. ————

10. You would infer from this that to read well one should be (1) well educated; (2) interested in books; (3) confident; (4) experienced.   10. ————

(10 off for each mistake)   *Reflective Comprehension* ————

TOTAL READING COMPREHENSION SCORE ————

VOCABULARY CHECK QUESTIONS

		without context I	with context II
1. *restive*	(1) subdued; (2) limited; (3) nervous; (4) respected; (5) happy.	1. ————	————
2. *versatile*	(1) upright; (2) dizzy; (3) visible; (4) competent; (5) vested.	2. ————	————
3. *impetuously*	(1) rudely; (2) furiously; (3) impassively; (4) imperfectly; (5) fairly.	3. ————	————
4. *indulgently*	(1) slowly; (2) ravishingly; (3) with lenience; (4) with a smile; (5) honestly.	4. ————	————
5. *debauch*	(1) outlet; (2) rubbish; (3) collapse; (4) dissipation; (5) evening.	5. ————	————

(10 off for each mistake)   *Word Comprehension* without *contextual help* (I) ————

Word Comprehension with *contextual help*   (II) ————

TOTAL WORD COMPREHENSION SCORE ————

EXERCISES

Interpreting what you read: The difference between what is stated and what is unstated focuses on the difference between receptive questions — those among the first five — and reflective questions — those among the last five. To see that difference more clearly, take a typical question on "The Fifty-first Dragon." Find in that article the actual statement answering the following question:

"The dragon that finally killed Gawaine was (1) a small one; (2) a fair-sized one; (3) a large one; (4) of unknown size."

Enter the exact stated words from the article that answer the question:

_____

In answering such questions the reader must read and remember a stated fact.

Now take a typical question from among the last five, which demand interpretation. Here it is often a matter of drawing inferences or conclusions based on certain relevant evidence. To understand the problem, examine the article closely for evidence bearing on each of the four choices. Enter the exact words under the appropriate choice to see what evidence supports each possibility.

Here is the question. Space is given under each choice for entering relevant evidence.

"You would infer that the Headmaster regarded Gawaine (1) highly; (2) with some aversion; (3) as likable but a mediocre student; (4) as a capable but lazy student."

(1) highly _____

_____

(2) with some aversion _____

_____

(3) as likable but a mediocre student _____

_____

(4) as a capable but lazy student _____

_____

Try still another question from the last five. This time, imagine that you are arguing with someone, not only about which is the right answer but about why you think the other answers are wrong. List under each of the four choices the specific evidence you would use in making your point. Here is the question.

"Gawaine's record of fifty killings was primarily attributable to (1) his skill; (2) his assurance; (3) his training; (4) none of those factors."

(1) his skill _____

_____

(2) his assurance _____

_____

(3) his training _____

_____

(4) none of those factors _____

_____

NAME_____ DATE_____ READING RATE_____ W.P.M.

COMPREHENSION CHECK QUESTIONS

1. The article mentions (1) astrology; (2) geometry; (3) metaphysics; (4) graphology.   1. _____

2. Appropriateness is a principle of language now (1) fully accepted by dictionaries; (2) not yet accepted by dictionaries; (3) just beginning to be accepted by them; (4) accepted in theory but not in practice.   2. _____

3. Usage is said to be divided into how many levels? (1) not given; (2) two; (3) three; (4) four.   3. _____

4. The author mentions (1) *The Reader's Digest;* (2) *Harper's;* (3) *The Atlantic Monthly;* (4) *Vogue.*   4. _____

5. The new emerging grammar is predicted to be more (1) dull; (2) difficult; (3) useful; (4) interesting.   5. _____

Receptive Comprehension _____

6. This is mainly about (1) whether the linguists will succeed; (2) the concept of difficulty levels; (3) the effects of the change on teaching English; (4) the relative nature of correctness.   6. _____

7. According to linguists, "Ain't you coming?" is (1) logically unacceptable English; (2) correct English; (3) incorrect English; (4) sometimes correct, sometimes not.   7. _____

8. The best statement about criteria of correctness is that they are (1) quite complex; (2) absolute; (3) nonexistent; (4) dependent upon dictionary authority.   8. _____

9. The concept of levels of usage is particularly useful in (1) avoiding prescriptive grammar; (2) teaching writing; (3) teaching descriptive grammar; (4) preparing a dictionary.   9. _____

10. We are asked to analyze a page of English so as to appreciate the (1) complexity of language; (2) failure of traditional grammar; (3) value of grammar as a discipline; (4) importance of well-established grammatical distinctions.   10. _____

(10 off for each mistake)   *Reflective Comprehension* _____

TOTAL READING COMPREHENSION SCORE _____

VOCABULARY CHECK QUESTIONS

		without context I	*with context* II
1. *criteria*	(1) complaints; (2) standards; (3) wrinkles; (4) credits; (5) keys.	1. _____	_____
2. *strata*	(1) clouds; (2) streaks; (3) levels; (4) wanderers; (5) strains.	2. _____	_____
3. *nuances*	(1) shades; (2) strings; (3) annoyances; (4) numbers; (5) proofs.	3. _____	_____
4. *fluently*	(1) irregularly; (2) correctly; (3) highly; (4) smoothly; (5) cleverly.	4. _____	_____
5. *tangible*	(1) confused; (2) hopeful; (3) breakable; (4) false; (5) definite.	5. _____	_____

(10 off for each mistake)   *Word Comprehension* without *contextual help* (I) _____

Word Comprehension with *contextual help* (II) _____

TOTAL WORD COMPREHENSION SCORE _____

EXERCISES

Using the topic sentence survey: The average person would not think of making an extended auto trip without first consulting some road maps. On the other hand, few individuals think of surveying a book or chapter before reading it. Yet traveling through print in a direct, meaningful way is usually much more difficult than traveling through countryside. If maps are useful to drivers, surveys are even more useful to readers.

Since that is so, just how do you go about surveying a chapter, article, or book? The best survey should bring you a maximum of information in a minimum of time. Furthermore, it should bring you the most important information. With these things in mind, suppose we try to survey this informative article, using the topic sentence survey type.

Here are the two essential steps:

1. Read the title, getting yourself properly oriented to its implications.
2. Read the first sentence of each paragraph in the article. Since, in expository writing, that is usually the topic sentence, you should be getting most of the ideas of key importance.

Now suppose we see what a survey of this article would bring us, either as a preliminary to reading or as a review of reading:

THE FUTURE OF GRAMMAR

The last few decades have witnessed an amiable but spirited battle between linguistic scientists and defenders of traditional ways of teaching English. . . . .

Our purpose here is not to discuss when or whether the transition will take place but rather to suggest what its effects on English teaching are likely to be.

Some effects there have been already, and not all of them are good. . . . .

Logic has nothing to do with it. . . . .

All this is old stuff. . . . .

One thing that the idea of relativity of correctness does *not* mean is that it doesn't matter how we talk or write. . . . .

Certainly it matters how you say a thing. . . . .

This is what the growing heaps of linguistic information, like the Linguistic Atlas and the dialect dictionaries, are showing ever more clearly. . . . .

So far we have tried to meet this difficulty with the concept of "levels of usage," dividing usage into several strata, usually three — standard, colloquial, vulgate. . . . .

The alternative is to abandon the prescriptive idea altogether, to give up the notion of bringing the student to a fore-determined pattern of usage, and to seek other results entirely. . . . .

Experiments in this direction are already underway in many schools throughout the country. . . . .

Along with this must go a quiet revolution in our techniques for describing language. . . . .

But probably the most discouraging thing about traditional grammar is the set of tautologies in which it wanders: "a noun is a name," "a verb is an action," "an interrogative sentence is a sentence which asks a question." . . . .

Somebody will have to do something about this, and many people are already trying — seeking to look at the language and see what's there and find ways of describing it. . . . .

As you can see, this look at a tenth part of the original article does bring you into contact with most of the major points developed and discussed, giving you an ideal background for rereading the article with much more intelligence.

It also suggests a potential weakness. If the first sentence is *not* the topic sentence, your survey is to that degree somewhat short of bringing you all the important ideas. Note how often the topic sentence comes first.

Check further by turning to the article to see which sentence is the topic sentence. Enter the number below; then re-examine all paragraphs to see if there is some typical clue in the first sentence that suggests the topic sentence is still to come. Enter a zero if no topic sentence is found.

Paragraph   Number of topic sentence

Paragraph #1: Topic sentence is #_____   Paragraph #8: Topic sentence is #_____

Paragraph #2: Topic sentence is #_____   Paragraph #9: Topic sentence is #_____

Paragraph #3: Topic sentence is #_____   Paragraph #10: Topic sentence is #_____

Paragraph #4: Topic sentence is #_____   Paragraph #11: Topic sentence is #_____

Paragraph #5: Topic sentence is #_____   Paragraph #12: Topic sentence is #_____

Paragraph #6: Topic sentence is #_____   Paragraph #13: Topic sentence is #_____

Paragraph #7: Topic sentence is #_____   Paragraph #14: Topic sentence is #_____

Compare the topic sentence survey type with the short survey type on page 222.

Name_____ Date_____ Reading Rate_____ w.p.m.

COMPREHENSION CHECK QUESTIONS

1. When Ali started home after his University experience, he came on (1) a jackass; (2) foot; (3) a spirited Arabian; (4) a camel.   1. _____

2. How many years did Ali study at the University of El-Azhar? (1) two; (2) four; (3) six; (4) eight.   2. _____

3. At his first stop in the village, Ali found the Khatib preaching about the (1) prophetic powers of Mohammed; (2) miraculous deeds of Mohammed; (3) nature of God as revealed by Mohammed; (4) punishment of sinners and unbelievers as described by Mohammed.   3. _____

4. What indignity was *not* suffered by Ali at the hands of the villagers? (1) stoning; (2) imprisonment; (3) beating; (4) destruction of his diploma.   4. _____

5. When Ali came to the village of the Khatib a second time, (1) he was dressed in silks and satins; (2) he was dressed in the coarse raiment of a scholar; (3) he was dressed in the garb of a foreigner; (4) no mention was made of his dress.   5. _____

Receptive Comprehension _____

6. The purpose of this selection is to show the need for (1) worldly wisdom; (2) book learning; (3) tact and cleverness; (4) a well-rounded development.   6. _____

7. The selection was intended primarily to (1) entertain; (2) persuade; (3) describe; (4) explain.   7. _____

8. When Ali and the Khatib first met, (1) Ali was apparently in the right in their argument; (2) the Khatib was apparently in the right; (3) both were mistaken; (4) both were equally well informed about Mohammed.   8. _____

9. You would infer from Ali's first experience with the Khatib that in an argument the deciding factor is most likely to be (1) the truth; (2) tact; (3) authority; (4) personality.   9. _____

10. You would judge from this that the best way of convincing someone is to (1) cite direct evidence; (2) contradict the opposite viewpoint; (3) appeal to authority; (4) present your case indirectly without seeming to disagree.   10. _____

(10 off for each mistake)   *Reflective Comprehension* _____

TOTAL READING COMPREHENSION SCORE _____

VOCABULARY CHECK QUESTIONS

		without context I	with context II
1. *aphorisms*	(1) insects; (2) drugs; (3) peaks; (4) visitors; (5) sayings.	1. ____	____
2. *raiment*	(1) beams; (2) surface; (3) curve; (4) parapet; (5) garments.	2. ____	____
3. *credulous*	(1) easily convinced; (2) critical; (3) shy; (4) apt; (5) worthy of praise.	3. ____	____
4. *boon*	(1) log; (2) sound; (3) structure; (4) favor; (5) fate.	4. ____	____
5. *meticulously*	(1) hurriedly; (2) decisively; (3) very carefully; (4) actually; (5) quite gayly.		

(10 off for each mistake)   *Word Comprehension* without *contextual help* (I) _____

Word Comprehension with *contextual help* (II) _____

TOTAL WORD COMPREHENSION SCORE _____

EXERCISES

Reading for imagery: One of the important differences between reading exposition and narration is in savoring the mental pictures typical of narration. These demand a special response by the reader to the sense impressions provided — a vicarious enjoyment of things seen, heard, tasted, felt, or smelled.

As a means of sharpening your awareness of such sense impressions, make a list of from three to ten specific sensory images in each of the following five categories. For example, "black coffee" is primarily a sight impression, but if you are reading imaginatively it should also be listed under *taste* or *smell.*

Sights	Tastes	Smells	Feels	Sounds

Look back over each of the quoted word or phrases listed; then concentrate your full attention on each, imagining as vividly as possible what is described. How well did you imagine the taste of "black coffee"? Did you think of it as deliciously hot, pleasantly warm as it ran down your throat? Did you imagine its aroma? Did you visualize the steam slowly rising from the cup? In short, did you imaginatively bring together the whole range of sensory impressions found in "black coffee"?

Developing an idea: Actually, as a reader, when you get the main idea, you strip away the author's development of a thesis or point to get the kernel. To understand the process better, look at it from the writer's point of view. Starting with a main idea, the writer then goes on to develop it fully.

See how this works with a single sentence. Contrast the sentence "Ali then took a hair from the Khatib's beard" with the original passage describing that act. How does an author develop parts of a narrative and bring them to life?

Getting the main idea: This is a story told to illustrate a general principle. Write the thesis or central idea developed, using the author's phrasing. To be truly educated, one should

---

NAME————————————————————————— DATE————————— READING RATE————————— W.P.M.

COMPREHENSION CHECK QUESTIONS

1. You were told to act like a 12th-century (1) scribe; (2) monastic; (3) artisan; (4) apprentice.   1. ————

2. One couple hired (1) an efficiency expert; (2) a relative; (3) a secretary; (4) a "wife."   2. ————

3. How many listed items are considered reasonable? (1) twenty; (2) fifteen; (3) ten; (4) five.   3. ————

4. One man used what color of paper for his lists? (1) yellow; (2) pink; (3) buff; (4) orange.   4. ————

5. One expert named was (1) Mary Grieve; (2) Larry Baker; (3) Lucille Nichols; (4) William Cadman.   5. ————

Receptive Comprehension ————

6. This article is mainly about (1) sources of help for getting organized; (2) managing time better; (3) how to get organized; (4) eliminating unproductive activities.   6. ————

7. Mention of Great-grandma was to show that the basic principles of good organization (1) are laughable; (2) are old; (3) need revision; (4) are outdated.   7. ————

8. The Judy Lipton illustration was to get you to (1) make lists; (2) learn to delegate; (3) eliminate unproductive activities; (4) call in an expert.   8. ————

9. Which word best describes this article? (1) practical; (2) stimulating; (3) theoretical; (4) entertaining.   9. ————

10. Points are developed largely by (1) citing figures; (2) logical reasoning; (3) concrete illustrations; (4) personal opinion.   10. ————

(10 off for each mistake)   *Reflective Comprehension* ————

TOTAL READING COMPREHENSION SCORE ————

VOCABULARY CHECK QUESTIONS

		without context I	*with context* II
1. *tactics*	(1) traces; (2) problems; (3) methods; (4) hopes; (5) trends.	1. ————	————
2. *hew*	(1) help; (2) stick; (3) save; (4) depart; (5) smell.	2. ————	————
3. *delegate*	(1) delay; (2) please; (3) detract; (4) convince; (5) entrust.	3. ————	————
4. *deem*	(1) dread; (2) think; (3) desire; (4) appear; (5) order.	4. ————	————
5. *feasibility*	(1) amiability; (2) regulation; (3) feature; (4) action; (5) practicability.	5. ————	————

(10 off for each mistake)   *Word Comprehension* without *contextual help* (I) ————

Word Comprehension with *contextual help* (II) ————

TOTAL WORD COMPREHENSION SCORE ————

EXERCISES

Reading paragraphs: Increased awareness of paragraph structure is an important step toward intelligent adjustment of rate to material. Just as a driver who sees a clear, straight stretch of highway ahead can accelerate without fear of consequences, so the reader who makes effective use of a topic sentence can shift into high for the remainder of the paragraph. A topic sentence is, in a sense, a highway marker to facilitate our attempts to follow the writer's thoughts.

Analyze the following five paragraphs to determine (a) whether the topic idea is expressed or implied, (b) if expressed, what it suggests by way of development. If the topic idea is implied, skip (b) and (c).

EXAMPLE: Paragraph beginning "First, you . . . ."   (Skim through the selection until you find the paragraph, then go ahead with the analysis.)

    (a) Expressed __✔__ or implied _____
    (b) The topic sentence is the 1st in the paragraph
    (c) It suggests that the rest of the paragraph will deal more specifically with how to unjam your schedule.

Paragraph beginning "Then there are the tasks . . . ."

    (a) Expressed _____ or implied _____

    (b) The topic sentence is the _____ in the paragraph

    (c) It suggests that the rest of the paragraph _____

Paragraph beginning "Lists work especially well . . . ."

    (a) Expressed _____ or implied _____

    (b) The topic sentence is the _____ in the paragraph

    (c) It suggests that the rest of the paragraph _____

Paragraph beginning "Twenty years ago, ..."

    (a) Expressed _____ or implied _____

    (b) The topic sentence is the _____ in the paragraph

    (c) It suggests that the rest of the paragraph _____

Paragraph beginning "Suppose you are a chemist . . . ."

    (a) Expressed _____ or implied _____

    (b) The topic sentence is the _____ in the paragraph

    (c) It suggests that the rest of the paragraph _____

Paragraph beginning "A number of books . . . ."

    (a) Expressed _____ or implied _____

    (b) The topic sentence is the _____ in the paragraph

    (c) It suggests that the rest of the paragraph _____

Compare your results with those of other students; discuss any differences in an attempt to resolve them.

NAME———————————————————— DATE——————————— READING RATE——————— W.P.M.

COMPREHENSION CHECK QUESTIONS

1. Spoken English has roughly how many phonemes or sounds? (1) 40; (2) 36; (3) 28; (4) 26.   1. ————

2. Who left part of his estate to create a new alphabet? (1) Mark Twain; (2) Shaw; (3) Franklin; (4) Churchill.   2. ————

3. What was *not* mentioned as an advantage of UNIFON? (1) a decline in dyslexia; (2) a saving in space; (3) ease of translation to other languages; (4) voice-activated machines.   3. ————

4. Dr. Dvorak worked to improve the (1) typewriter; (2) calendar; (3) alphabet; (4) none of the preceding.   4. ————

5. Who solicited proposals for calendar reform? (1) League of Nations; (2) United Nations; (3) U.S. Government; (4) British House of Parliament.   5. ————

Receptive Comprehension ————

6. The main emphasis is on (1) problems; (2) methods; (3) reasons for change; (4) solutions.   6. ————

7. The opening bit about "lunch September 30" was to (1) suggest possible solutions; (2) uncover areas for discussion; (3) suggest need for change; (4) get attention.   7. ————

8. What reason for reform of the alphabet received most emphasis? (1) inefficiency; (2) learning difficulties; (3) spelling problems; (4) the space-consuming aspect.   8. ————

9. Apparently the major problem with the typewriter is (1) letter placement; (2) key jamming; (3) speed of action; (4) ribbon feed and action.   9. ————

10. The three parts are organized in order from (1) the most difficult to the easiest; (2) the simple to the complex; (3) the less important to the more important; (4) the past to the present.   10. ————

(10 off for each mistake)   *Reflective Comprehension* ————

TOTAL READING COMPREHENSION SCORE ————

VOCABULARY CHECK QUESTIONS

		without context I	with context II
1. *vagaries*	(1) changes; (2) losses; (3) oddities; (4) ends; (5) gaps.	1. ————	————
2. *voluble*	(1) voluntary; (2) talkative; (3) greedy; (4) massive; (5) worthy.	2. ————	————
3. *impetus*	(1) improve; (2) beg; (3) blame; (4) force; (5) touch.	3. ————	————
4. *de facto*	(1) definite; (2) dependent; (3) existing; (4) factual; (5) impartial.	4. ————	————
5. *conned*	(1) put to rest; (2) compared; (3) concluded; (4) conquered; (5) tricked.	5. ————	————

(10 off for each mistake)   *Word Comprehension* without *contextual help* (I) ————

Word Comprehension with *contextual help*   (II) ————

TOTAL WORD COMPREHENSION SCORE ————

EXERCISES

Reading punctuation: What do you read? Words! Yes, but you also read the punctuation marks that help you make sense out of the words. For example, try reading the following words in a meaningful way:

Bill where Jim had had had had had had had had had had the approval of the language experts.

Without the help of punctuation that sentence is probably meaningless. Try reading the same sentence, this time *with* punctuation:

Bill, where Jim had had "had had," had had "had"; "had had" had had the the approval of the language experts.

Punctuation does indeed make for easier, more meaningful reading.

Try the following matching exercise to sharpen your awareness of some of the most common meanings of punctuation marks. Enter the most appropriate word or words from the right in the space after each mark of punctuation on the left.

Matching Exercise

1. ? _____		a. namely
2. ! _____		b. stop
3. " " _____		c. startling, isn't it
4. , _____		d. and
5. : _____		e. said
6. . _____		f. stop-and-go
7. ; _____		g. who, what, when, where, how
8. — _____		h. an aside
9. ( ) _____		i. interruption

Insert the following marks of punctuation in the following passage to improve its readability: ( ), :, -, —, ;, ,.

To produce that sentence I used four media a typewriter an alphabet a calendar The Arabic number system . . . .

An alphabet by definition a system for mapping the sounds of a language is an invention of a high order Ideally one letter stands for each sound . . . .

The genius of our phonetic system as opposed to pictographic systems is that the written symbols do not refer directly to the objects described . . . .

After you have added the punctuation, check with the article to see if there is agreement. Notice also how much more easily you read the punctuated version.

NAME————————————————————— DATE———————— READING RATE———————— W.P.M.

COMPREHENSION CHECK QUESTIONS

1. According to the Duke of Wellington, habit is what? (1) stronger than nature; (2) ten times nature; (3) nature personified; (4) our hidden nature.

    1. ————

2. The critical age period for forming intellectual habits was said to be (1) between twenty and thirty; (2) below twenty; (3) the first ten years; (4) the first six years.

    2. ————

3. The writer quotes (1) Goethe; (2) Shakespeare; (3) the Bible; (4) Alexander Pope.

    3. ————

4. The author says there is no more contemptible type of character than the (1) agitator; (2) drifter; (3) dreamer; (4) exploiter.

    4. ————

5. The article refers specifically to (1) Robinson Crusoe; (2) Rip Van Winkle; (3) Shylock; (4) Samson.   5. ————

Receptive Comprehension ————

6. The primary purpose of this selection is to (1) suggest the key role of habit in education; (2) prove that habit is our best friend; (3) explain the difficulties of habit formation; (4) contrast habit with thought.   6. ————

7. The story about the discharged veteran and the practical joker was to show (1) the thoroughness of military training; (2) how absent-minded the veteran was; (3) our natural tendency to obey; (4) the strength of habit.

    7. ————

8. Apparently the best way to break the smoking habit would be to (1) stop abruptly; (2) taper off gradually; (3) first cut down to only two cigarettes a day; (4) stay away from other smokers.   8. ————

9. You would conclude that a tendency to act comes primarily from (1) motivation; (2) reasoning; (3) willing; (4) doing.

    9. ————

10. You would infer that the author would particularly favor (1) meeting things as they come; (2) avoiding too rigid a schedule; (3) relaxing during the weekends; (4) following a weekly schedule.   10. ————

(10 off for each mistake)   *Reflective Comprehension* ————

TOTAL READING COMPREHENSION SCORE ————

VOCABULARY CHECK QUESTIONS

		without context I	*with context* II
1. *ordinance*	(1) statement; (2) reputation; (3) movement; (4) established custom; (5) new publication. 1.	————	————
2. *inanition*	(1) ridicule; (2) anger; (3) worry; (4) growth; (5) exhaustion. 2.	————	————
3. *squalid*	(1) nasty; (2) flat; (3) worn; (4) sober; (5) exhausted 3.	————	————
4. *concomitants*	(1) references; (2) rules; (3) accompaniments; (4) contradictions; (5) plots. 4.	————	————
5. *gratuitous*	(1) useful; (2) meaningful; (3) casual; (4) unnecessary; (5) grateful. 5.	————	————

(10 off for each mistake)

Word Comprehension without *contextual help* (I) ————

Word Comprehension with *contextual help*   (II) ————

TOTAL WORD COMPREHENSION SCORE ————

Reading paragraphs: Each paragraph should have a single central idea. If it is expressed in a sentence, the sentence is called a topic sentence and may come at the beginning, middle, or end of the paragraph. But at times the main idea is not expressed — only implied.

Analyze the specified paragraphs from the article on habit. If the paragraph contains a topic sentence, write it in the space provided below. If the main idea is implied, try to compose an appropriate topic sentence for the paragraph, writing it in the space provided below.

For example, reread the first paragraph in the article. Check the appropriate choice.

Is the topic idea expressed   _____

                or implied?   _____

If the topic idea is expressed, enter the exact words that express it:

If the topic idea is implied, express it in a sentence that you devise and write here:

It seems to be expressed in the phrase — "habit is ten times nature." The words, "degree to which this is true" lead on to the example of the soldier who, by years of discipline and the ingraining of habit, is fashioned "completely over again."

Now take the next paragraph and analyze it in similar fashion.

Paragraph 2:

Is the topic idea expressed   _____

                or implied?   _____

If the topic idea is expressed, enter the exact words that express it:

If the topic idea is implied, express it in a sentence that you devise and write here:

Paragraph 3:

Is the topic idea expressed   _____

                or implied?   _____

Notice how much of the paragraph deals with "domestic beasts." How much deals with "men"? How much with wild animals?

If the topic idea is expressed, enter the exact words that express it:

If the topic idea is implied, express it in a sentence that you devise and write here:

Paragraph 4:

Is the topic idea expressed   _____

                or implied?   _____

What is the function of the single word *it*, which is used to begin the six sentences immediately following the first sentence? Does this help you in your analysis?

If the topic idea is expressed, enter the exact words that express it:

If the topic idea is implied, express it in a sentence that you devise and write here:

NAME_____ DATE_____ READING RATE_____W.P.M.

COMPREHENSION CHECK QUESTIONS

1. People who have only one or two topics of conversation illustrate (1) dead level abstraction; (2) content rigidity; (3) formal rigidity; (4) underverbalization.

    1. _____

2. Wendell Johnson is called a (1) grammarian; (2) psychiatrist; (3) sociologist; (4) semanticist.

    2. _____

3. *Science and Sanity* was written by (1) Johnson; (2) Heatter; (3) Hayakawa; (4) Korzybski.

    3. _____

4. The author talked about learning to (1) swim; (2) dive; (3) tread water; (4) float.

    4. _____

5. Johnson is concerned with the specific problem of (1) amnesia; (2) pronunciation; (3) stuttering; (4) inflections.

    5. _____

    Receptive Comprehension _____

6. The chief purpose of the article is to (1) stress the importance of vocabulary; (2) discuss Johnson's research; (3) review Johnson's book; (4) provide a general introduction to semantics.

    6. _____

7. The general thesis that is developed is that a person's language habits (1) are determined by heredity; (2) are less important than his feelings and actions; (3) influence his life; (4) grow out of his life experience.

    7. _____

8. The opening descriptions of kinds of people was largely intended to point up (1) verbal peculiarities; (2) language habits; (3) common problems; (4) classification categories.

    8. _____

9. Discussion of the word *success* was to show the importance of (1) a life goal; (2) a comfortable income; (3) formulating word meanings; (4) achieving a given goal.

    9. _____

10. The reference to a can of sardines and the nail-clippers was to show (1) the reality of the world of not-words; (2) the importance of the right words; (3) the need for verbal tools; (4) the importance of outside help.

    10. _____

(10 off for each mistake)   *Reflective Comprehension* _____

TOTAL READING COMPREHENSION SCORE _____

VOCABULARY CHECK QUESTIONS

		without context I	*with context* II
1. *clichés*	(1) clippings; (2) statements; (3) clues; (4) books; (5) platitudes.	1. _____	_____
2. *affected*	(1) loving; (2) natural; (3) ambiguous; (4) influenced; (5) helpful.	2. _____	_____
3. *aberrations*	(1) savages; (2) sores; (3) deviations; (4) skills; (5) oaths.	3. _____	_____
4. *pervasive*	(1) cranky; (2) agitated; (3) penetrating; (4) relevant; (5) oppressive.	4. _____	_____
5. *epigram*	(1) parasite; (2) plague; (3) gourmet; (4) folk song; (5) witty saying.	5. _____	_____

(10 off for each mistake)   *Word Comprehension* without *contextual help* (I) _____

Word Comprehension with *contextual help* (II) _____

TOTAL WORD COMPREHENSION SCORE _____

EXERCISES

Parallelism to mark organization: At times a writer will use parallelism to fuse several paragraphs into a larger unit. In this selection, for example, how many paragraphs make up what would be called the introduction?

How does each paragraph begin?

What two-word phrase accents the pulling together of the previous paragraphs and serves as a transition into the main part of the article?

Noting words that link: Read the paragraph on the left below. Then study the linking words indicated on the right.

In short, what are the language habits of the people around you—and also, what are your own? For many of *these people* are in messes, always quarreling, or always being victimized by their own prejudices. *They* are people in quandaries. Is there any connection between *their quandaries* and their language habits? Are *they,* as Wendell Johnson says, merely the froth on the beer or an important ingredient of the beer itself?

(of the people around you)
↖ *these people*

They

their quandaries

(language habits)◄——they

Notice how frequently pronouns with antecedents in the previous sentence provide the essential link between sentences. To reinforce the connection, repetition is also used, as with *people* and *quandaries.*

Using words that link: The following sentences make up one paragraph but are jumbled so that they lack proper order. First, underline all words that link sentences with sentences. Next, through attention to those linking words, reorder the sentences to make a readable, coherent paragraph. Check back to the original passage (paragraph 4, p. 35) when you have finished to see if there is agreement.

In spite of good positions or comfortable incomes, such persons manage to keep themselves miserable, because the goal they set up for themselves is so vaguely defined that *they can't ever tell whether they have reached it or not.* An example of this primitivism is the kind of person who, unconsciously believing that, because there is such a word as "success," there is such a thing, keeps trying to attain it —without ever having attempted to formulate what he means by "success." (If the reader asks at this point, "But what is success?" he needs Johnson's book very badly.) Hence a lifelong uneasiness, with hypertension or gastric ulcers to boot.

NAME—————————————————————— DATE————————— READING RATE————————— W.P.M.

COMPREHENSION CHECK QUESTIONS

1. Pfungst was spoken of as a (1) linguistic scientist; (2) psychologist; (3) horse trainer; (4) writer.   1. ————

2. The selection specifically refers to television (1) talent contests; (2) interviews; (3) panel discussions; (4) word games.   2. ————

3. Filmed sequences showed that trained experimenters (1) treated both sexes alike; (2) varied question wording depending on sex of subject; (3) sat closer to subjects of the opposite sex; (4) took longer with subjects of the opposite sex.   3. ————

4. One experiment involved training rats (1) to trip a lever for food; (2) to learn a simple sequence of two actions; (3) to push a button to avoid a shock; (4) to run a maze.   4. ————

5. Specific mention was made of (1) the University of California; (2) Princeton; (3) Harvard University; (4) San Diego State College.   5. ————

Receptive Comprehension ————

6. This is mainly about (1) bias in interviewing; (2) animal intelligence; (3) nonverbal communication; (4) development of I.Q.   6. ————

7. In the title "In Other Words," the word *words* is used in what sense? (1) literal; (2) unimaginative; (3) figurative; (4) limited.   7. ————

8. The Clever Hans illustration was used to show (1) how observant horses are; (2) how important body language is; (3) how uniformly people act; (4) how easily the horse's behavior should be explained.   8. ————

9. This selection discusses behavior that is primarily (1) obvious; (2) unsophisticated; (3) unconscious; (4) mechanical.   9. ————

10. From this selection you would infer that it is most important that (1) others think that you can succeed; (2) you think you can succeed; (3) tests show that you can succeed; (4) your initial efforts show that you can succeed.   10. ————

(10 off for each mistake)   *Reflective Comprehension* ————

TOTAL READING COMPREHENSION SCORE ————

VOCABULARY CHECK QUESTIONS

		without context I	with context II
1. *uncanny*	(1) free; (2) common; (3) serious; (4) wise; (5) limited.	1. ————	————
2. *imperceptible*	(1) undesirable; (2) unnoticeable; (3) imperfect; (4) unexpected; (5) self-conscious.	2. ————	————
3. *inadvertently*	(1) unintentionally; (2) helpfully; (3) daringly; (4) admittedly; (5) foolishly.	3. ————	————
4. *elicit*	(1) glide over; (2) draw out; (3) raise; (4) trap; (5) steal.	4. ————	————
5. *blatantly*	(1) glaringly; (2) frequently; (3) noisily; (4) soundly; (5) criminally.	5. ————	————

(10 off for each mistake)   *Word Comprehension* without *contextual help* (I) ————

Word Comprehension with *contextual help* (II) ————

TOTAL WORD COMPREHENSION SCORE ————

EXERCISES

1. Developing skill in interpretation: Interpretation is one of the important cognitive levels, focusing on how effectively you deal with *unstated relationships*. As an alert reader you will want to develop maximum skill in anticipating what will either be stated or implied.

Take this sentence from another article on nonverbal communication: "Anyone who owns a cat, a dog, or a baby is well aware that certain meanings can be clearly expressed without the use of words." After such a generalization, what would you anticipate next? Can you make a supposition?

The next sentence actually begins: "The cat sits up politely for a morsel of turkey, the _____?" What specific word do you anticipate next? Hopefully, as you looked back at the series, "a cat, a dog, or a baby," you were led to anticipate the word *dog*. If you did, congratulate yourself. You anticipated well. The next word is *dog*.

Suppose we go a step further. Which of the following choices would best fit your anticipation? The dog (1) sleeps on the floor; (2) sniffs the air; (3) scratches on the door. If you selected the third choice, you are again anticipating well, for that was the phrase used.

For further practice, see if you can supply the missing words exactly in the following passage. Every fifth word of the original is omitted. By anticipating and reasoning, fill in all the blanks. Then check back to the original to see how accurate you were. A score of 15 out of 17 exactly right would be good.

Early in this century, _____ horse named Hans amazed _____ people of Berlin by _____ extraordinary ability to perform _____ calculations in mathematics. After _____ problem was written on _____ blackboard placed in front _____ him, he promptly counted _____ the answer by tapping _____ low numbers with his _____ forefoot and multiples of _____ with his left. Trickery _____ ruled out because Hans' _____, unlike owners of other _____ animals, did not profit _____ — and Hans even performed _____ feats whether or not _____ owner was present.

2. Think over the day. What examples of nonverbal communication do you remember? List some examples below:

3. How would you communicate nonverbally the following ideas?

A. I'm tired

B. I'm sleepy

C. I'm thirsty

D. I'm a friend

NAME_____ DATE_____ READING RATE_____W.P.M.

COMPREHENSION CHECK QUESTIONS

1. This selection begins by showing a child wandering through (1) a clothing store; (2) a supermarket; (3) a hardware store; (4) a department store.

    1. _____

2. The author boxed with (1) Firpo; (2) Louis; (3) Dempsey; (4) Levinsky.

    2. _____

3. The author discusses in some detail (1) basketball; (2) bowling; (3) tennis; (4) wrestling.

    3. _____

4. The author speaks particularly about (1) fielding a long hit; (2) playing first base; (3) pitching to a crack hitter; (4) catching a curve-ball.

    4. _____

5. On the race track the author went (1) 90 miles per hour; (2) 107 mph; (3) 126 mph; (4) 180 mph.

    5. _____

Receptive Comprehension _____

6. The central idea of this selection is to establish (1) the difficulty of understanding the skills required of sportsmen; (2) the importance of first-hand experience and observation; (3) the difference between spectators and participants; (4) the way to develop skill in reporting.

    6. _____

7. Levinsky's statements ("It don't feel like nuttin' " and "in a transom") were intended to suggest that (1) experience is most important; (2) the gift of expression is most important; (3) the same experience affects people differently; (4) experience and expression are equally important.

    7. _____

8. This selection is organized chiefly around (1) specific sports; (2) types of sports; (3) personal experiences in chronological order; (4) the two headings—participants and spectators.

    8. _____

9. With respect to the gap between reading about something and actually doing it, you would infer that good reporting (1) eliminates it; (2) has no effect on it; (3) increases it; (4) decreases it.

    9. _____

10. The author apparently thinks of the average spectator with feelings of (1) irritation; (2) respect; (3) indifference; (4) amusement.

    10. _____

(10 off for each mistake)   *Reflective Comprehension* _____

TOTAL READING COMPREHENSION SCORE _____

VOCABULARY CHECK QUESTIONS

		without context I	with context II
1. *admonished*	(1) urged; (2) admired; (3) limited; (4) reproved; (5) selected.	1. _____	_____
2. *ascertain*	(1) arise; (2) join; (3) learn; (4) create; (5) look up.	2. _____	_____
3. *donned*	(1) put on; (2) started; (3) took off; (4) sat down; (5) sounded.	3. _____	_____
4. *vacuously*	(1) engagingly; (2) stupidly; (3) freely; (4) lightly; (5) hopelessly.	4. _____	_____
5. *truculent*	(1) mechanical; (2) truthful; (3) trusting; (4) strong; (5) fierce.	5. _____	_____

(10 off for each mistake)   Word Comprehension without *contextual help* (I) _____

Word Comprehension with *contextual help*   (II) _____

TOTAL WORD COMPREHENSION SCORE _____

EXERCISES

Checking paragraph coherence: One important characteristic of a well-written paragraph is its coherence—the closeness with which the sentences are related. One test of coherence is to jumble the sentences around so that they are completely out of order, then see if you can put them together again by relying on the many devices a writer uses to relate sentence to sentence and show gradual progression of thought.

To develop added insight into paragraph structure, coherence, and writing, try rearranging the following sentences into the most coherent order. In each of the paragraphs there is one sentence which does not belong. First, decide which sentence is out of place and eliminate it; then rearrange the remaining sentences in the most coherent order. Finally, check your arrangement with the original paragraph.

A. 1. I was always a child who touched things and I have always had a tremendous curiosity with regard to sensation.

   2. The average person says: "Here, let me see that," and holds out his hand.

   3. Mother is convinced that the child only does it to annoy or because it is a child, and usually hasn't the vaguest inkling of the fact that Junior is "touching" because he is a little blotter soaking up information and knowledge, and "feel" is an important adjunct to seeing.

   4. A child wandering through a department store with its mother is admonished over and over again not to touch things.

   5. Adults are exactly the same, in a measure, as you may ascertain when some new gadget or article is produced for inspection.

   6. What he means is that he wants to get it into his hands and feel it so as to become better acquainted.

   7. He doesn't mean "see," because he is already seeing it.

The sentence which violates paragraph unity is #_____.

The remaining six sentences should be in this order: #_____, #_____, #_____, #_____, #_____, #_____.

B. 1. My burning curiosity got the better of prudence and a certain reluctance to expose myself to physical pain.

   2. It seems that I had gone to an expert for tuition.

   3. I had been assigned to my first training-camp coverage, Dempsey's at Saratoga Springs, where he was preparing for his famous fight with Luis Firpo.

   4. I asked Dempsey to permit me to box a round with him.

   5. For days I watched him sag a spar boy with what seemed to be no more than a light cuff on the neck, or pat his face with what looked like no more than a caressing stroke of his arm, and the fellow would come all apart at the seams and collapse in a useless heap, grinning vacuously or twitching strangely.

   6. I had never boxed before, but I was in good physical shape, having just completed a four-year stretch as a galley slave in the Columbia eight-oared shell.

The sentence which violates paragraph unity is #_____.

The remaining five sentences should be in this order: #_____, #_____, #_____, #_____, #_____.

C. 1. It is all a man can do to get up after being stunned by a blow, much less fight back.

   2. From that afternoon on, also, dated my antipathy for the spectator at prizefights who yells: "Come on, you bum, get up and fight! Oh, you big quitter! Yah yellow, yah yellow!"

   3. And how a man is able to muster any further interest in a combat after being floored with a blow to the pit of the stomach will always remain to me a miracle of what the human animal is capable of under stress.

   4. I have never regretted these researches.

   5. Yellow, eh?

   6. But they do it.

The sentence which violates paragraph unity is #_____.

The remaining five sentences should be in this order: #_____, #_____, #_____, #_____, #_____.

NAME————————————————— DATE———————— READING RATE——————— W.P.M.

COMPREHENSION CHECK QUESTIONS

1. The mass media habit was specifically likened to (1) a tonic; (2) a security blanket; (3) a sleeping pill; (4) an addiction.   1. ————

2. The author refers to the portable (1) radio; (2) TV set; (3) record player; (4) cassette player.   2. ————

3. What program is mentioned by name? (1) I Love Lucy; (2) Sesame Street; (3) The F.B.I.; (4) Maude.   3. ————

4. As a sedative for children, the article mentions (1) warm milk; (2) paregoric; (3) poppy juice; (4) a pacifier.   4. ————

5. The author quotes from the writings of (1) Freud; (2) Bacon; (3) Thoreau; (4) McLuhan.   5. ————

Receptive Comprehension ————

6. This is mainly about (1) suggestions for measuring happiness; (2) the effects of the mass media; (3) evaluating life quality; (4) the difference between present and past cultures.   6. ————

7. The author's attitude toward the mass media is best described by what word? (1) critical; (2) objective; (3) hopeful; (4) uncertain.   7. ————

8. In his discussion of values, what seemed to be rated as most important? (1) our privacy; (2) our experience; (3) our security; (4) our intelligence.   8. ————

9. The purpose of discussing soap operas and comic strips was to show (1) how strongly they appeal; (2) how they confuse actuality with fiction; (3) how they give people an escape from reality; (4) how they interfere with the experiencing of life.   9. ————

10. Violence and delinquency were blamed primarily on (1) human nature; (2) television and comic books; (3) peer influence; (4) lack of parental guidance.   10. ————

(10 off for each mistake)   *Reflective Comprehension* ————

TOTAL READING COMPREHENSION SCORE ————

VOCABULARY CHECK QUESTIONS

		without context I	*with context* II
1. *diffuse*	(1) satisfied; (2) concentrated; (3) infrequent; (4) shy; (5) widespread.	1. ————	————
2. *cliché*	(1) sudden noise; (2) hiss; (3) order; (4) common expression; (5) argument.	2. ————	————
3. *motility*	(1) intention; (2) liveliness; (3) saying; (4) terrain; (5) group.	3. ————	————
4. *disparate*	(1) unlike; (2) important; (3) healthy; (4) vanishing; (5) prompt.	4. ————	————
5. *ineluctable*	(1) irregular; (2) attractive; (3) tasty; (4) inevitable; (5) chosen.	5. ————	————

(10 off for each mistake)   *Word Comprehension* without *contextual help* (I) ————

Word Comprehension with *contextual help* (II) ————

TOTAL WORD COMPREHENSION SCORE ————

EXERCISES

Noting transitional and connective devices: The efficient reader is alert to any words or phrases that let him follow with increased ease the path set by the writer. When a skilled reader reads, "To go back now to our general maxims. . . ," he knows he should look on the preceding development as somewhat of a digression from the main outline and the following paragraph as a return to another main division. Other words suggest cause, result, comparison, repetition, and the like, used in developing the subject. Enhance your alertness by classifying the following words and phrases taken from this selection, using the following divisions:

1. Addition	3. Repetition	6. Emphasis
2. Example	4. Comparison	7. Cause-effect
	5. Contrast	

(*Example:* "furthermore" would be classed as #1 — Addition)

a. "We have already stressed. . ." _____

b. "Further. . ." _____

c. "Even the most profound. . ." _____

d. "is thus weakened. . ." _____

e. "Sometimes it is argued. . ." _____

f. "For instance. . ." _____

g. "It seems more likely. . ." _____

h. "After all. . ." _____

i. "It is not so much an escape but. . ." _____

j. "Besides. . ." _____

k. "But mass media. . ." _____

Answers: a, 3; b, 1; c, 6; d, 7; e, 4 or 5; f, 2; g, 6; h, 6; i, 5; j, 1; k, 5.

Using the short survey: There are several different ways to survey just as there are different ways to read. One survey type is based on the likelihood that topic sentences usually come first. The short survey is based on the idea that the first paragraph and last paragraph are most revealing about what goes in between. The first paragraph normally points ahead so that the reader is aware of what is coming. The last paragraph either summarizes what has been said, points up its significance, or extends the coverage somewhat. Those points of major importance in between are often highlighted by headings in italics or heavier type.

With these things in mind, note the essential steps in making a short survey to get maximum information in minimum time.

1. Read the title, getting yourself properly oriented to its implications.
2. Read the first paragraph in entirety and not just the first sentence.
3. Read any headings or italicized portions.
4. Read the last paragraph in its entirety.

See what kind of overview you get by using this type of survey on Selection 17, as well as on other selections.

NAME_____ DATE_____ READING RATE_____ W.P.M.

COMPREHENSION CHECK QUESTIONS

1. Specific mention was made of (1) Tom Sawyer; (2) Oliver Twist; (3) Candide; (4) Moby Dick.   1. _____

2. You were cautioned against (1) reading too fast; (2) re-reading; (3) reading in bed; (4) looking up strange words.   2. _____

3. The author tried reading (1) Virgil's *Aeneid*; (2) Aristotle's *Poetics*; (3) Plato's *Republic*; (4) Goethe's *Faust*.   3. _____

4. Shakespeare got plots from reading (1) Sophocles' *Antigone*; (2) Herodotus' *History*; (3) Euripides' *Medea*; (4) Plutarch's *Lives*.   4. _____

5. The classics are called (1) the mirror of the soul; (2) the key to wisdom; (3) the diary of man; (4) the door to life.   5. _____

Receptive Comprehension _____

6. This article is mainly about (1) how to choose classics; (2) how to read classics; (3) the value of reading classics; (4) reading classics in big bites.   6. _____

7. He develops his points largely by (1) quoting authorities; (2) personal experience; (3) repetition; (4) making comparisons.   7. _____

8. The primary purpose is to get the reader to (1) act; (2) feel; (3) understand; (4) believe.   8. _____

9. Allen's feelings about classics are best described as (1) serious; (2) pleased; (3) reverent; (4) enthusiastic.   9. _____

10. You would infer that in school classics should be (1) taught differently; (2) introduced later; (3) avoided; (4) tied in with movies.   10. _____

(10 off for each mistake)   *Reflective Comprehension* _____

TOTAL READING COMPREHENSION SCORE _____

VOCABULARY CHECK QUESTIONS

		without context I	with context II
1. *exhilarating*	(1) changing; (2) hoping; (3) revealing; (4) exhausting; (5) stimulating.	1. _____	_____
2. *scurry*	(1) take; (2) cut; (3) scamper; (4) cover; (5) scatter.	2. _____	_____
3. *surmises*	(1) hints; (2) surges; (3) guesses; (4) excesses; (5) surprises.	3. _____	_____
4. *compiled*	(1) collected; (2) compared; (3) made; (4) filled; (5) paid.	4. _____	_____
5. *stigma*	(1) odor; (2) brand; (3) drop; (4) stake; (5) base.	5. _____	_____

(10 off for each mistake)   *Word Comprehension* without *contextual help* (I) _____

Word Comprehension with *contextual help* (II) _____

TOTAL READING COMPREHENSION SCORE _____

EXERCISES

Exploring factors affecting comprehension: After reading the preceding short selection, "Treat Causes, Not Symptoms," look at yourself more closely. Try to determine your major problems, then move toward solving them. Standardized test scores are particularly helpful if they are available. But this text is laid out to provide fairly complete evidence for helping you diagnose and assess most problems.

Under each of the following headings, record any concrete evidence available. Then, on the basis of your evaluation, look at the suggestions for dealing with the problem.

Vocabulary. Is this a major problem? To see, get some of the evidence down, as follows:

A. Enter the number you did correctly on the 20-item vocabulary test, p. 312. _____
   Enter the salary expectation figure from p. 316. _____
B. When you have completed any ten of the five-item Vocabulary Check Questions (a total of fifty items), enter the number you did correctly out of the fifty. _____
C. Turn to p. 151 and cover the column of words to the right of the column heading PREFIX. Try to supply the common meaning for each of the twenty prefixes listed. Check your answers by uncovering the column. Enter the number you did correctly out of the twenty. _____
D. Take your comprehension scores on the first ten selections read, average them, and enter the *average* score here. An average below 70 percent suggests vocabulary deficiency. _____

Now, looking over the evidence you have accumulated for rating your vocabulary, check one of the following three choices: No problem _____ Minor problem _____ Major problem _____.

Now what can you do to improve? Here are some suggestions. Check each when you have completed it.

1. Read the short selection "Context — Key to Meaning," p. 240, noting and applying relevant portions.
2. Read with particular emphasis the ten selections in Section VI on vocabulary for pertinent suggestions.
3. Complete the five-item Vocabulary Check Questions for each selection. Discover all unknown words and work them into your active vocabulary. Build added skill with context by using the first column (*without context*), then scanning the article to see how each word is used in context, putting a second set of answers in the column headed *with context*.
4. Read the article "A Master-Word Approach to Vocabulary," p. 150, and follow all suggestions given.
5. Do the vocabulary improvement exercises, pages 312 through 330.
6. For additional help, order the pocket-size vocabulary building game from Telstar, 366 North Prior Avenue, St. Paul, Minn. 55104. It provides a visualizing aid to unlock the meanings of over 30,000 common English words.

Interest. Is this a major problem? Again, check by getting some of the evidence down.

A. Look at the personal interest rating scale mentioned on p. 363. Use this scale with the first twenty selections you read, then average your ratings. If your average is above 2, interest should be no problem. If it is below 3, it looks like a major problem.
B. Check the relationship between your interest rating and comprehension. Does interest seem to make a consistent difference? Data from some 200 students using selections from an earlier edition of *Efficient Reading* should permit you to make meaningful comparisons. Notice that as articles are more difficult, interest tends to drop. If the drop is more pronounced with you, build stronger interests.

READING EASE GROUPING	AVERAGE INTEREST RATING	YOUR INTEREST RATING (AVERAGE)
Easy	2.109	_____
Fairly Easy	2.299	_____
Standard	2.346	_____
Fairly Difficult	2.359	_____
Difficult	2.381	_____
Very Difficult	2.454	_____

Looking back over this evidence, how would you rate interest? No problem _____ Minor problem _____ Major problem _____.

Now what can you do to improve interest level? Here are some specific suggestions. Check each when completed.

1. Read "The Importance of Being Interested" (Sel. 6) p. 14. _____
2. Apply the suggestions in the selections on pages 242 and 244. _____
3. Keep rating each selection read for interest, averaging each set of ten to see if there is improvement. _____

Difficulty. Is this a major problem? Look at the evidence.

A. Using the Flesch Reading Ease Score on page 362, figure your average comprehension for the first twenty selections read.
B. Compare your average with those from some 200 students who used an earlier edition of *Efficient Reading*.

READING EASE GROUPING	AVERAGE COMPREHENSION	YOUR AVERAGE COMPREHENSION
Fairly Easy	68.5	_____
Standard	67.5	_____
Fairly Difficult	65.2	_____
Difficult	67.4	_____

The relationship between ease and comprehension is not perfectly consistent, suggesting that other factors may be more important than difficulty. If, however, for you the relationship is consistent and the differences in comprehension are more pronounced, you know difficulty is a problem. Rate yourself as before: No problem _____ Minor problem _____ Major problem _____.

Now what can you do to deal with difficult material effectively?

Read selection 25, p. 59, and "Organization — Your Reading Satellite," p. 254.

Explorations of *rate*, as suggested on page 226, of *background*, of *concentration*, and *mechanical difficulties* — such as vocalizing, regressing, and perceiving — lend themselves to similar analysis.

NAME————————————————— DATE————————— READING RATE—————————— W.P.M.

COMPREHENSION CHECK QUESTIONS

1. Under a bluff reef there is a (1) tree branch; (2) submerged log; (3) wreck; (4) sand-bar.   1. ————

2. Mr. Higgins left Mark Twain but was hiding (1) below; (2) in the engine room; (3) behind a chimney; (4) behind a door.   2. ————

3. In the emergency, Twain (1) bumped against the shore; (2) yelled for Mr. Bixby; (3) rang the bell; (4) left the wheel.   3. ————

4. A reference was made to (1) Victoria Falls; (2) the Missouri River; (3) the Grand Canyon; (4) Niagara.   4. ————

5. The navigation of the Mississippi was for how many miles? (1) eight hundred; (2) eleven hundred; (3) twelve hundred; (4) fourteen hundred.   5. ————

Receptive Comprehension ————

6. This is chiefly about (1) learning to pilot a boat; (2) problems of understanding the river; (3) training a pilot; (4) the changing nature of the river.   6. ————

7. This would be classified primarily as (1) description; (2) narration; (3) exposition; (4) persuasion.   7. ————

8. To describe Mr. Bixby, which word seems best? (1) competent; (2) impatient; (3) easy-going; (4) excitable.   8. ————

9. To pilot a boat well, what seems to be most important? (1) intelligence; (2) calm nerves; (3) constant attention; (4) careful observation.   9. ————

10. What dictionary definition seems closest to the meaning of *read* as used in this selection? (1) interpret; (2) utter; (3) foretell; (4) acquire information.   10. ————

(10 off for each mistake)   *Reflective Comprehension* ————

TOTAL READING COMPREHENSION SCORE ————

VOCABULARY CHECK QUESTIONS

		without context I	*with context* II
1. *vaingloriously*	(1) helplessly; (2) bravely; (3) boastfully; (4) sadly; (5) openly.	1. ————	————
2. *prodigiously*	(1) generously; (2) smartly; (3) profanely; (4) marvelously; (5) properly.	2. ————	————
3. *imminent*	(1) famous; (2) impending; (3) imperishable; (4) steadfast; (5) manageable.	3. ————	————
4. *blandly*	(1) blankly; (2) tranquilly; (3) blamelessly; (4) loudly; (5) brightly.	4. ————	————
5. *void*	(1) vicious; (2) lacking; (3) complete; (4) victorious; (5) varied.	5. ————	————

(10 off for each mistake)   *Word Comprehension* without *contextual help* (I) ————

Word Comprehension with *contextual help* (II) ————

TOTAL WORD COMPREHENSION SCORE ————

EXERCISES

Exploring your rate-comprehension relationship: One of your first and most important moves in improving your reading is to explore the relationship between reading rate and comprehension. Such an exploration will let you know how important a factor rate is and, by implication, how important such matters as vocabulary, concentration, interest, and background are.

Beginning at about 100 words per minute, read ten selections of comparable difficulty (see Index According to Order of Difficulty, p. 362). Try to read each one about 60 wpm faster than you read the previous one. Then check your comprehension on each selection, plotting your results on the graph below. Keep increasing rate until comprehension drops to the 40 percent level or below, even if you have to call your activity skimming instead of reading. The resulting graph will provide evidence for a more intelligent approach to your reading improvement efforts. Specifically, it should answer the following three questions:

(1) Is it true that the slower you read, the better you comprehend?
(2) What is your present optimum speed for comprehension?
(3) What is your present best practice speed?

Generally speaking, the faster you read, within limits, the better you comprehend. Is this so with you? If it is, what are the limits? For most students, optimum comprehension comes at speeds somewhat above their slowest rates. A rapid drop-off as rate is increased indicates that rate is indeed of primary importance as a factor. A gradual drop-off or rather lengthy plateau area suggests that other factors are probably more important.

Further analysis of your graph record will suggest what those factors may be. For example, if comprehension never rises above a 60 or 70 percent level, despite wide variations in rate, you have reason to consider vocabulary as a possible limiting factor. If you do not drop below the 40 percent level, you have reason to conclude that you have an excellent general background and are able to pick up additional information even at extremely high rates. If your record is quite erratic, this suggests that differences in difficulty, background, or interest are more important than differences in rate, and should be explored further.

When you have completed your exploration, you should have definite answers to all three questions.

(1) Was your best comprehension score achieved at your slowest rate?
(2) At what specific rate or rates did you get your best comprehension, whether 70, 80, 90, or 100 percent?
(3) Finally, what is your present best practice speed? Your answer to this question depends on your answer to the preceding one. Your best present practice speed must be faster than the speed at which you now get best comprehension. After all, you don't want to waste precious time practicing what you already do well. No — you want to develop the skill to get that same comprehension but at speeds from 300 to 600 wpm faster than present speeds. To do that with maximum effectiveness, use the procedure described in "Swing Three Bats" (p. 236).

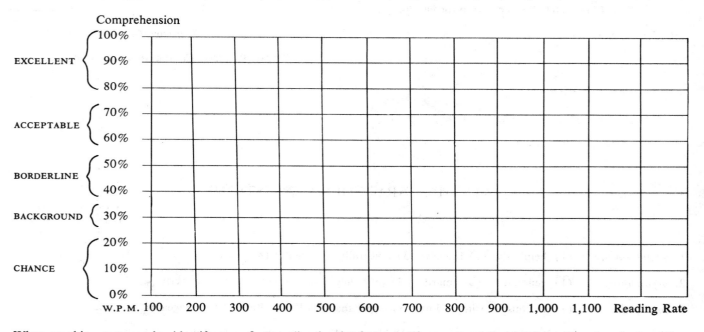

When graphing your results, identify your first reading by the figure *1*. Then connect the dot for each subsequent reading with the preceding one by a line, to indicate the order in which it was read. Results for a group of 100 students, following these directions with ten readings, show the following average changes: 197, 293, 359, 305, 306, 350, 411, 406, 432 and 467 wpm. Can you achieve a better than average range? Try a slower beginning rate as well as a faster final rate than indicated in the averages given above.

NAME————————————————————— DATE—————— READING RATE——————— W.P.M.

COMPREHENSION CHECK QUESTIONS

1. The patient referred specifically to (1) the parables; (2) Revelations; (3) the Gospels; (4) the Golden Rule.

   1. ————

2. The psychiatrist mentions (1) Carl Gustav Jung; (2) Freud; (3) Adler; (4) William James.

   2. ————

3. One of the fears we're born with was said to be fear of (1) furry objects; (2) loud noise; (3) falling; (4) large black objects.

   3. ————

4. Mention was made of the wife of (1) an enlisted man; (2) a pilot; (3) a gunner; (4) a reserve officer.

   4. ————

5. The psychiatrist refers to (1) Samson; (2) Jonah; (3) Job; (4) Luke.

   5. ————

Receptive Comprehension ————

6. The central idea is to read the Bible (1) for moral guidance; (2) to love your neighbor; (3) for helpful psychiatric insights; (4) to eliminate worry.

   6. ————

7. You would infer from the opening question "Do you — a psychiatrist — read the Bible?" that the patient was primarily expressing (1) curiosity; (2) pleasure; (3) approval; (4) surprise.

   7. ————

8. With regard to the Bible, greatest emphasis is put on (1) how to study it; (2) who should study it; (3) what verses to study; (4) when to study it.

   8. ————

9. The author would probably agree most fully that people need (1) security; (2) truth; (3) love; (4) joy.

   9. ————

10. Apparently, the author feels that the matter of most concern should be (1) love and hate; (2) conscious and subconscious; (3) guilt and innocence; (4) good and evil.

    10. ————

(10 off for each mistake)   *Reflective Comprehension* ————

TOTAL READING COMPREHENSION SCORE ————

VOCABULARY CHECK QUESTIONS

		without context I	*with context* II
1. *acute*	(1) severe; (2) clever; (3) active; (4) slow; (5) weighty.	1. ————	————
2. *insomnia*	(1) sleeplessness; (2) tiredness; (3) insight; (4) failure; (5) alertness.	2. ————	————
3. *futile*	(1) comic; (2) angry; (3) hostile; (4) useless; (5) stealthy.	3. ————	————
4. *camouflage*	(1) change; (2) disguise; (3) cover; (4) scared; (5) explode.	4. ————	————
5. *elemental*	(1) charitable; (2) lofty; (3) serious; (4) qualified; (5) fundamental.	5. ————	————

(10 off for each mistake)   *Word Comprehension* without *contextual help* (I) ————

Word Comprehension with *contextual help*   (II) ————

TOTAL WORD COMPREHENSION SCORE ————

EXERCISES

Developing specialized reading skills: Scanning: To function effectively, a mechanic needs many different tools. After all, he doesn't use a file to loosen a bolt or a wrench to tighten a screw. Similarly, to read and study effectively you need many different techniques, not just one.

Scanning is the technique to use when you want to find one small bit of information within a relatively large body of printed material. It fits the proverbial needle-in-the-haystack situation. It can and should be the fastest of the specialized reading speeds. The survey provides a quick, high-level view, skimming provides a lower-level view to bring more details into sight, and scanning zooms you in for a close, sharp view of only one detail.

With practice, you should scan accurately at from 10,000 to 15,000 wpm. Students in the Efficient Reading classes at the University of Minnesota scan initially, on the average, at about 1,500 wpm. After practice the class average moves up to about 15,000 wpm.

This text is laid out to help you make enviable progress toward that top-level performance. Your first move is to check both the speed and accuracy with which you now can scan. Use the following table to get your approximate rate. You can use it as it is with articles of approximately 2,000 words in length, such as Selections 37, 42, and 82. Then, dividing the figure in the time column by 2, you can also use it with selections of approximately 1,000 words in length, such as Selections 26, 28, and 79.

Scanning Time Wpm Rate	Scanning Time Wpm Rate
10 sec. — 12,000 wpm	60 sec. — 2,000 wpm
15 sec. — 8,000 wpm	80 sec. — 1,500 wpm
20 sec. — 6,000 wpm	90 sec. — 1,333 wpm
30 sec. — 4,000 wpm	100 sec. — 1,200 wpm
40 sec. — 3,000 wpm	120 sec. — 1,000 wpm
50 sec. — 2,400 wpm	140 sec. — 855 wpm

Sample scanning problem based on Selection 15, "In Other Words": Keeping an accurate count of your scanning time, scan this entire selection, "In Other Words," as rapidly as you can to find the answer to this question: How many times was the proper name *Pfungst* mentioned in the article? Determine your present scanning rate and accuracy.

A few weeks later, after additional practice, recheck your performance to see how much improvement you have made. For this recheck use the same selection, but try to answer this question: How many times does the abbreviation *IQ* appear? Again determine your rate and accuracy.

Scanning makes an ideal review technique in preparation for mid-terms or finals. It lets you check important details in the material to be covered. Perhaps even more important is the contribution that scanning makes to your development of vocabulary and comprehension. Here are suggestions for those uses.

Scan-checking to improve vocabulary: The five-item vocabulary tests for each selection are designed to help you make better use of context in arriving at word meanings. Getting word meaning from context is a rather specialized skill of the utmost importance. Use scanning to develop that skill. Take each five-item vocabulary test, putting your answers in the first column, headed *without context*. Then scan the selection rapidly, underlining each of the five words when you find them. Examine the context for clues to word meaning, changing any answers by entering revised answers in the second column, headed *with context*. If you make effective use of context, the answers in that second column should be perfect. If vocabulary is not a major problem, scan for only one word in each five-item test — the most difficult or strangest of the five. This will help you to become a more rapid and accurate scanner as well as to improve word mastery.

Scan-checking to improve receptive or reflective comprehension: If a certain type of math problem tends to give you difficulty, you need to work through some of that type very carefully, rethinking the problem until it is clear. This rethinking is equally useful in improving comprehension.

Here's how it works. Read a selection and finish the test as usual. Before checking the answers with the key in the back, select one or two questions — ones you feel least sure about — reread each and then scan through the selection as rapidly as possible until you find the exact place where the question is answered. In short, you check the accuracy, not by consulting the key but by returning to the article itself.

When you are dealing with one of the reflective-type questions, scanning is not quite so simple. With them you will seldom be able to find any one statement that answers the question. Here you need to scan for all bits of relevant evidence. Then by weighing one bit with another you can finally arrive at a tenable conclusion as to the best answer.

Such rethinking of difficult questions should eliminate or lessen present difficulties in handling similar questions, thus improving comprehension. For example, you may notice that the term *exposition* poses difficulties that will be cleared up as you notice the problem and check meaning.

Here are some sample general statements for use with any and all of the selections.

(1) Take any comprehension check question, reread it, then scan rapidly to find the exact spot where the question is answered.

(2) Take the most difficult reflective-type question. Reread it, then scan the entire selection for all relevant information. Weigh the evidence for and against each of the four choices before deciding which is best. You may want to imagine that you are in a debate, forced to prove to an unwilling believer that your answer is indeed the best.

NAME―――――――――――――――――――――― DATE――――――――― READING RATE――――――― W.P.M.

COMPREHENSION CHECK QUESTIONS

1. The author specifically speaks of feeding the mind (1) candy bars; (2) bonbons; (3) chocolate pudding; (4) sugar-plums.   1. ―――――

2. The article mentions eating at one sitting two or three (1) loaves of bread; (2) heads of lettuce; (3) cauliflowers; (4) beefsteaks.   2. ―――――

3. Specific reference is made to what kind of mind? (1) lean; (2) elegant; (3) fat; (4) mechanical.   3. ―――――

4. In the selection, mention was made of (1) Emerson's *Essays;* (2) Shakespeare's *King Lear;* (3) Gray's *Elegy;* (4) Pope's *Dunciad.*   4. ―――――

5. A specific rule was given for determining whether someone was (1) wise or foolish; (2) young or old; (3) educated or uneducated; (4) rich or poor.   5. ―――――

Receptive Comprehension ―――――

6. This is mainly about (1) reading a properly balanced fare; (2) selecting a varied reading fare; (3) thinking over what you have read; (4) spacing reading activities properly.   6. ―――――

7. The opening paragraphs were primarily to make us think about (1) the care lavished on our bodies; (2) the care we give to our mind; (3) how forgetful we are; (4) how important both body and mind are.   7. ―――――

8. The illustration of the thirsty haymaker was intended to remind us of the importance of (1) sufficient reading; (2) a wide variety of reading; (3) not reading too many kinds at once; (4) not reading too many of one kind of book.   8. ―――――

9. In essence, by "ticketing," the author means (1) buying; (2) using; (3) reading extensively; (4) labeling. 9. ―――――

10. His example of a "mental bun" suggested a way to test a person's (1) depth of reading interests; (2) mental health; (3) ability to concentrate; (4) taste for culture.   10. ―――――

(10 off for each mistake)   *Reflective Comprehension* ―――――

TOTAL READING COMPREHENSION SCORE ―――――

VOCABULARY CHECK QUESTIONS

		without context I	*with context* II
1. *ensue*	(1) enter; (2) take action; (3) follow; (4) charge; (5) report.	1. ―――	―――
2. *propensity*	(1) property; (2) fault; (3) statement; (4) inclination; (5) reason.	2. ―――	―――
3. *mastication*	(1) slicing; (2) chewing; (3) overcoming; (4) swallowing; (5) ruling.	3. ―――	―――
4. *impetus*	(1) search; (2) solution; (3) force; (4) method; (5) move.	4. ―――	―――
5. *ascertain*	(1) lead; (2) help out; (3) assert; (4) find out; (5) keep on.	5. ―――	―――

(10 off for each mistake)   *Word Comprehension* without *contextual help* (I) ―――――

Word Comprehension with *contextual help* (II) ―――――

TOTAL WORD COMPREHENSION SCORE ―――――

EXERCISES

Perceptual development: College and adult readers without special training habitually perceive words one at a time. Obviously one way to improve reading rate is to train yourself to take in two or more words at a quick look.

By using a 3 × 5 card and a daily paper, you can develop added perceptual span and accuracy. Just cover a headline in a column of print with the 3 × 5 card. Then jerk the card rapidly down and back to expose for a few seconds the first line of the headline. Repeat if necessary to get the complete line. Do the same thing with the next line and so on through the first paragraph of the news story.

For additional perceptual training, practice on the three-division and two-division lines below. Use the 3 × 5 card to cover the print, leaving only the black dot visible. Jerk the card quickly down and back to expose the phrase below for a few seconds. Try to read the entire phrase at one quick look. Ordinarily practice of this kind is provided by a tachistoscope. The procedure just described, however, is a close approximation and should show comparable results.

Three-Division

●
Carl Sandburg
            ●
        has often said
                    ●
                that every student
        ●
should learn how
            ●
        to read a newspaper
                    ●
                The other day
●
I heard a
        ●
    noted publisher declare
                ●
            that many college graduates
    ●
lack that ability.

Two-Division

●
First, the newspaper should
                            ●
                        and does help us
        ●
carry out our daily
                            ●
                        business. It puts the buyer
            ●
and seller of
                        ●
                    groceries, appliances, automobiles
        ●
in touch with
                            ●
                        each other, to
    ●
the mutual advantage
                        ●
                    of both.

Leaning on key details to formulate main ideas: Daily newspapers provide ideal exercise material for developing added skill in getting main ideas. Just cover the headline for any story, read the story — at least the first paragraph — , then write a headline that captures the essence in just four to six words. As an aid, think in terms of six key questions: Who? What? Why? When? Where? and How? Once you have answered those questions about the news story, ask yourself one more question. Of those six, which one or two seems most important? In this way you can decide which main idea or ideas deserve to dominate the headline.

Try this with the following brief paragraph of a news story:

> Farmers in central Minnesota reported serious crop
> damage yesterday as a result of an early morning
> frost combined with an unseasonably cold weekend.

Answer the six questions by looking back at that paragraph; then star the two you consider most important.

Who? _____   When? _____
What? _____   Where? _____
When? _____   How? _____

Finally, which of the following do you think actually appeared as headline for that story?

(1) CENTRAL MINNESOTA FARMERS
    SUFFER FROM BAD FROST

(3) SERIOUS CROP DAMAGE
    FOLLOWS EARLY FROST

(2) CROP DAMAGE CAUSED
    BY EARLY FROST

(4) FROST CAUSES CROP
    DAMAGE FOR FARMERS

(Headline #3 was actually used.)

NAME———— DATE———— READING RATE———— W.P.M.

COMPREHENSION CHECK QUESTIONS

1. The author discusses (1) reasons for reading; (2) lists of books to read; (3) the best time for reading; (4) ways to talk about reading.　1. ————

2. You're advised to buy (1) new books; (2) old books; (3) a wide variety of books; (4) best-sellers.　2. ————

3. Specific reference is made to (1) Ernest Hemingway; (2) Plato; (3) Thoreau; (4) Mark Twain.　3. ————

4. You're directed to (1) read in bed; (2) read with pencil in hand; (3) read book reviews; (4) read in a comfortable chair.　4. ————

5. The article has a quotation from (1) Shakespeare; (2) the Bible; (3) Francis Bacon; (4) Alexander Pope.　5. ————

Receptive Comprehension ————

6. This article is chiefly about (1) the value of reading; (2) tips on choosing books; (3) building a home library; (4) all of the preceding.　6. ————

7. The analogy to someone out walking was to suggest (1) the limits of fatigue; (2) the need for variety; (3) exercising your mind; (4) having a destination in mind.　7. ————

8. Apparently the chief reason to read classics lies in their (1) interest; (2) worth; (3) availability; (4) practicality.　8. ————

9. This article would best be classified as a (1) critique; (2) essay; (3) story; (4) summary.　9. ————

10. Coverage is best described as (1) one-sided; (2) comprehensive; (3) technical; (4) general.　10. ————

(10 off for each mistake)　　*Reflective Comprehension* ————

TOTAL READING COMPREHENSION SCORE ————

VOCABULARY CHECK QUESTIONS

		without context I	*with context* II
1. *demeaning*	(1) asking; (2) leaving; (3) lowering; (4) showing; (5) intending.	————	————
2. *ephemeral*	(1) effective; (2) short-lived; (3) feminine; (4) secure; (5) growing.	————	————
3. *peruse*	(1) open; (2) prevail; (3) turn; (4) read; (5) utilize.	————	————
4. *disport*	(1) display; (2) quarrel; (3) amuse; (4) split; (5) enter.	————	————
5. *decor*	(1) style of decoration; (2) distance; (3) etiquette; (4) mode of speech; (5) say emphatically.	————	————

(10 off for each mistake)

Word Comprehension without *contextual help* (I) ————

Word Comprehension with *contextual help* (II) ————

TOTAL WORD COMPREHENSION SCORE ————

WORD GROUPING EXERCISES

Can you read this?

THESE LINES ARE JUST AN EYE-CATCHING WAY
CHANGING THAT REALIZE TO YOU HELPING OF
YOUR PERCEPTUAL HABITS MAY SEEM DIFFICULT,
SOON VERY WILL INSIGHT AND PRACTICE BUT
BRING MASTERY OF THE CHANGES. READ THESE
WAY NEW THE IN — NOW AGAIN ONCE LINES FEW
SEE HOW QUICKLY YOU LEARN TO CHANGE?

Practice moving your eye down the middle of the column as you read.

Prove for yourself
why reading by phrases
aids comprehension
and is better than
word-for-word reading.
Notice what happens
when you read
one
word
at
a
time
or take time to
divide a word
into
syl-
-la-
-bles
as you read.

"Some books
are to be tasted,
others to be swallowed,
and some few
to be chewed
and digested;
that is, some books
are to be read
only in parts,
others to be read
but not curiously,
and some few
to be read wholly
and with diligence
and attention . . .
Reading maketh a full man,
conference a ready man,
and writing
an exact man." Bacon

Now try reading some square span.

Your eyes don't see	in narrow horizontal lines	but see an area	on all sides of the place	where they are focused.	Andrews, a student editor	at Southern Methodist University,	devised Square Span,
a way of modifying	the printed page	to fit man's natural	eye habits much better	than the ordinary arrangement	of printed words.	Tests show that	a majority of readers
could read it	with greater speed than	they could read	conventional printed matter.	At least it offers	an exercise in the grouping	of words that should	serve to discourage word-for-word tendencies.
Try a few more lines	just for additional	practice in grouping words	and in developing a rhythmic	eye movement across the page.	Adapting your reading speed	to the material	is the main thing
in reading.	It is as foolish	to speed through a	poem by Keats as it is	to slow to a snail's pace	in reading material obviously designed	to be read in a hurry.	
Experimental flashes with the tachistoscope	reveal that it is possible	to see five or six words	strung out in this manner	when flashed on a screen			
at 1/100 of a second.	Are you developing	suitable word-grouping habits?					

NAME_____ DATE_____ READING RATE_____W.P.M.

COMPREHENSION CHECK QUESTIONS

1. Emerson says that the theory of books is (1) dangerous; (2) ever-changing; (3) noble; (4) misunderstood.   1. _____

2. He specifically mentions (1) Cicero; (2) Milton; (3) Socrates; (4) Rousseau.   2. _____

3. The right use of a book is to (1) educate; (2) guide; (3) inform; (4) inspire.   3. _____

4. He calls genius the enemy of (1) thought; (2) change; (3) knowledge; (4) genius.   4. _____

5. One of the proverbs quoted is (1) Indian; (2) Arabian; (3) Greek; (4) Chinese.   5. _____

Receptive Comprehension _____

6. Emerson's chief concern is to tell us (1) how books are often abused; (2) how books have been overrated; (3) how closely books are related to the times; (4) how to deal with books properly.   6. _____

7. In the discussion of books, the allusion to a vacuum was to emphasize (1) the need for pure thought; (2) how life becomes truth; (3) the impossibility of excluding the perishable; (4) the effort demanded by reading.   7. _____

8. You would assume that readers should start with (1) their own principles; (2) accepted dogmas; (3) well-defined purposes; (4) authoritative guidance.   8. _____

9. Emerson sees change as (1) continuous; (2) difficult; (3) undesirable; (4) typical.   9. _____

10. The fig tree proverb was a reminder (1) to open your mind to books; (2) to read God directly; (3) to note similarities; (4) to set proper goals.   10. _____

(10 off for each mistake)   *Reflective Comprehension* _____

TOTAL READING COMPREHENSION SCORE _____

VOCABULARY CHECK QUESTIONS

		without context I	*with context* II
1. *transmuting* (1) delivering; (2) passing away; (3) changing; (4) quieting; (5) solidifying.	1.	_____	_____
2. *noxious* (1) advantageous; (2) new; (3) harmful; (4) adjoining; (5) old.	2.	_____	_____
3. *disparaged* (1) praised; (2) disappeared; (3) sent; (4) belittled; (5) disputed.	3.	_____	_____
4. *emendators* (1) healers; (2) beginners; (3) users; (4) improvers, (5) teachers.	4.	_____	_____
5. *efflux* (1) trial; (2) emanation; (3) exertion; (4) weakness; (5) likeness.	5.	_____	_____

(10 off for each mistake)   *Word Comprehension* without *contextual help* (I) _____

Word Comprehension with *contextual help* (II) _____

TOTAL WORD COMPREHENSION SCORE _____

EXERCISES

The Goal? Adaptability

What's a good car? One that's speedy? Easy to handle? Well designed? What about low initial cost, economy of operation, roominess, low maintenance, or riding ease? Perhaps you'll agree that no *one* factor provides a completely satisfying answer.

What's a good reader? Here, too, no one factor is enough. Speed isn't everything; neither is comprehension. More important than either one is the *ability to adapt* — to adapt rate to purpose and to a wide variety of reading materials. Adaptability, then, is the true mark of a good reader.

How do you measure adaptability? How better than by actually putting yourself into different reading situations to see how well you adapt? For example, using three articles of comparable difficulty, check your performance when reading normally, thoroughly, and rapidly.

To discover your normal leisure reading habits, read an article neither faster nor slower than you ordinarily do when you have some leisure and want to settle down comfortably with a magazine. Don't try to comprehend more or less than usual in that situation. When you have finished and taken the test, determine your reading rate and comprehension. Next, see how well you adapt yourself to the problem of getting meaning. In reading the next article, your purpose is to get as much comprehension as possible in a single reading. Keep track of reading time, but remember that it's comprehension you're after. With the last article, your purpose is to cover ground rapidly. Read it at your top rate. Although speed is your primary concern, check comprehension to see what price you ordinarily pay for haste.

These three sets of rate and comprehension scores provide a useful composite index of adaptability, a three-dimension picture of yourself as a reader. Careful analysis of these scores should reveal information of importance in directing future practice efforts and achieving maximum results. As Kettering once said: "A problem well-stated is a problem half-solved." In reading, that might well be paraphrased: "A problem *well-identified* is a problem half-solved."

For example, what about the range of reading rates at your command? Subtract your slowest rate from your top rate for that figure. Is it 200 wpm or more? If so, you're among the top 20 percent of adults *before* training in reading. If that figure is 50 wpm or less, you'll want to overcome your tendencies toward one-speed reading.

When reading at top speed, a rate under 300 wpm probably means vocalizing and regressing.

Did you get comprehension when that was your purpose? And did you get details as well as main ideas and inferences? Was comprehension consistently good or did it vary considerably? Consistently good comprehension without considerable range in rate may indicate an unwillingness to recognize the importance of both depth and breadth as you read, an overlooking of Bacon's dictum: "Some books are to be tasted, others to be swallowed, and some few to be chewed and digested."

Such an analysis touches significant facets of this thing called *adaptability*, so important in defining a good reader.

(500 words)

From James I. Brown, *Guide to Effective Reading*, D. C. Heath and Co., 1966.

COMPREHENSION CHECK QUESTIONS

1. The good reader is likened to a good (1) car; (2) motor; (3) driver; (4) model. 1. _____

2. You were told to use articles of comparable (1) column width; (2) difficulty; (3) length; (4) subject matter. 2. _____

3. Mention was made of (1) Byron; (2) Ford; (3) Lamb; (4) Kettering. 3. _____

4. Reference was made to (1) stuttering; (2) word-for-word reading; (3) the tachistoscope; (4) one-speed reading. 4. _____

5. A speed range of 200 wpm or more was said to put you among the top (1) 60 percent; (2) 40 percent; (3) 20 percent; (4) 5 percent. 5. _____

6. The primary purpose of this selection is to (1) define what is meant by a good reader; (2) define adaptability; (3) explain how to measure adaptability; (4) explain how to identify vocalizing difficulties. 6. _____

7. The emphasis in this selection is on (1) wisdom is power; (2) knowing thyself; (3) reading maketh a full man; (4) the reading man is the thinking man. 7. _____

8. The threefold check is intended to (1) eliminate reading difficulties; (2) identify reading difficulties; (3) test reading improvement; (4) determine reading potential. 8. _____

9. A vocabulary deficiency would be suggested by (1) consistently low comprehension; (2) consistently slow rate; (3) a drop in comprehension as rate is increased; (4) an increase in comprehension as rate is decreased. 9. _____

10. Difficulty with concentration would be suggested if (1) rapid reading brought better comprehension; (2) rapid reading did not affect comprehension; (3) normal rate brought better comprehension; (4) comprehension remained fairly constant. 10. _____

SCORE _____

Answers: 1, 1; 2, 2; 3, 4; 4, 4; 5, 3; 6, 1; 7, 2; 8, 2; 9, 1; 10, 1.

NAME————————————————————— DATE—————————— READING RATE——————————— W.P.M.

COMPREHENSION CHECK QUESTIONS

1. With reading, people tend to mutter something about (1) comprehension; (2) learning; (3) translating; (4) meaning.

   1. ———

2. The earliest readers were (1) scribes; (2) priests; (3) teachers; (4) wise men.

   2. ———

3. Specific mention was made of (1) Adam; (2) Eve; (3) Goliath; (4) Cain.

   3. ———

4. There was specific mention of the (1) Industrial Revolution; (2) Age of Reason; (3) American Revolution; (4) Civil War.

   4. ———

5. What was *not* mentioned as happening in the last half-century? (1) daily newspapers flourished; (2) books flooded the country; (3) magazines feeding a variety of interests appeared; (4) public and private libraries appeared.

   5. ———

Receptive Comprehension ———

6. This article is mainly to (1) discuss forces affecting reading; (2) recount the history of reading; (3) show how technology changed reading; (4) show how religion influenced reading.

   6. ———

7. The style is best described as (1) restrained; (2) stimulating; (3) objective; (4) semi-formal.

   7. ———

8. The ending quotation from Dr. La Brant emphasized that reading is most affected by (1) religion; (2) current developments; (3) discoveries in educational psychology; (4) the media.

   8. ———

9. The chief purpose is to (1) inform; (2) persuade; (3) entertain; (4) moralize.

   9. ———

10. The author implied that religion, in early days, (1) aroused interest in reading; (2) provided purpose for reading; (3) did not affect reading; (4) dominated reading.

    10. ———

(10 off for each mistake)   *Reflective Comprehension* ———

TOTAL READING COMPREHENSION SCORE ———

VOCABULARY CHECK QUESTIONS

			without context I	with context II
1. *portents*	(1) holes; (2) bags; (3) collections; (4) warnings; (5) parts.	1.	———	———
2. *aura*	(1) drill; (2) quality; (3) discipline; (4) tip; (5) flower.	2.	———	———
3. *secular*	(1) seasonal; (2) round; (3) worldly; (4) secret; (5) secure.	3.	———	———
4. *utilitarian*	(1) hard; (2) strong; (3) orderly; (4) useful; (5) useless.	4.	———	———
5. *agrarian*	(1) aged; (2) revolutionary; (3) smoothed; (4) cultivated; (5) landed.	5.	———	———

(10 off for each mistake)

Word Comprehension without *contextual help* (I) ———

Word Comprehension with *contextual help* (II) ———

TOTAL WORD COMPREHENSION SCORE ———

EXERCISES
SWING THREE BATS

Suppose you are a 200-word-a-minute reader. Realizing the distinct advantage of increased reading efficiency, you immediately set to work. Your goal? Double your present rate with the same or better comprehension.

Now, how do you go about reaching that goal? Well, how do you learn to play golf — or the piano? For one thing, by practicing. Paderewski once said: "I practice faithfully every day. If I miss one day, I notice it. If I miss two days, the critics notice it. And if I miss three, my audience notices it."

But that is hardly specific enough to be helpful. Take Henry Smith, freshman. Henry was one of those 200-word-a-minute readers, struggling to keep up in an assignment-filled world. His English teacher, sensing his problem, encouraged him to work on improving his reading. After three weeks of determined "practice," Henry reported disconsolately back to his teacher — *no real progress.*

Records of his practice session showed that only once — his second session — had he tried reading faster than 300 words a minute. But comprehension fell to a low of 30 percent, so for the remaining sessions he dropped back to his usual rate. To be sure, as he continued to practice, his comprehension rose from an initial 80 to 90 percent. But Henry's real need was for improvement in rate, and three weeks of fairly conscientious practice had not brought results.

But what had he been practicing? Suppose a hunt-and-peck typist wanted to improve her typing efficiency. Would she expect to master the touch system by practicing hunt-and-peck methods? And Henry — could he expect to master rapid reading by practicing slow reading?

Again, how to develop reading efficiency? What is best — a gradual increase in rate of about twenty-five words a minute every week or an immediate jump to double your present rate?

At first thought, a gradual increase might seem best. Yet that approach tends to reinforce old habits more than establish new ones. It may never provide the momentum needed for overcoming the inertia of long-established habits. Furthermore, since nothing succeeds like success, this method may result in loss of interest and discouragement. Jumping immediately to double your present rate has the advantage of a clean break with old habits. But failure to adjust immediately to this difficult new level often means frustration and discouragement.

There is still a third possibility, one which student records suggest is best. It is a zigzag pattern, embodying a rather sharp break from old habits with moves that reduce the accompanying frustration. Watch a batter swing three bats, throw two down, then step up and knock a homer. That one bat feels much lighter and easier to handle after swinging three. Try the same psychology in reading. Jump from your customary 200-word-a-minute rate to 300 words a minute before dropping back to 250. If 250 is your top speed, it will always seem uncomfortably fast. If 300 is top speed, 250 will soon seem much slower and easier reading.

Swing three bats!

From James I. Brown, *Guide to Effective Reading,* D. C. Heath and Co., 1966.

(500 words)

COMPREHENSION CHECK QUESTIONS

1. Critics noticed a difference when Paderewski missed practicing for (1) one day; (2) two days; (3) three days; (4) four days.   1. _____

2. Henry was encouraged to work on reading by (1) an English teacher; (2) a psychology teacher; (3) a counselor; (4) a high-school teacher.   2. _____

3. Henry's initial comprehension was (1) 80 percent; (2) 60 percent; (3) 40 percent; (4) not specifically mentioned.   3. _____

4. Jumping immediately to double one's present rate was said to have the advantage of (1) eliminating needless frustration; (2) giving one a feeling of immediate success; (3) making a clean break with old habits; (4) heightening interest.   4. _____

5. Before reporting back Henry practiced (1) two weeks; (2) three weeks; (3) four weeks; (4) five weeks.   5. _____

6. The chief purpose of this selection is to (1) suggest how improvement may best be made; (2) establish the importance of practice; (3) discuss the reasons for failure and discouragement; (4) stress the importance of rate.   6. _____

7. The Paderewski story was used to (1) stress the importance of swinging three bats; (2) emphasize the importance of practice; (3) explain Henry's failure; (4) stress the importance of daily effort.   7. _____

8. The analogy to the hunt-and-peck typist was intended to suggest (1) that Henry had been practicing the wrong things; (2) that Henry had not been working long enough to see results; (3) that reading is like typing; (4) that mechanical aids are particularly helpful.

9. You would infer from this selection that reading efficiency depends largely upon (1) a series of intensive practice sessions; (2) strong motivation and interest; (3) intelligence; (4) a specified practice procedure.   9. _____

10. As used in this selection, swing three bats means (1) work energetically; (2) coordinate your efforts; (3) look on practice as a game; (4) work beyond the desired level.   10. _____

SCORE _____

Answers: 1, 2; 2, 1; 3, 1; 4, 3; 5, 2; 6, 1; 7, 4; 8, 1; 9, 4; 10, 4.

NAME————————————————————— DATE———————— READING RATE———————— W.P.M.

COMPREHENSION CHECK QUESTIONS

1. It was said that (1) there is a single proven study method; (2) what works well with some students doesn't for others; (3) you need a different method for every subject matter area; (4) a how-to-study book is indispensable.   1. ————

2. If you get behind, you are advised to (1) get notes covering the missed material from another student; (2) skip to the material currently being covered; (3) skim over missed material; (4) catch up.   2. ————

3. At your first reading you are told to (1) underline main points; (2) circle unknown words; (3) make marginal notes; (4) use color-coded checks.   3. ————

4. When beginning a test, (1) outline each question before writing; (2) start right in on question 1; (3) start on the most difficult question; (4) read it through completely first.

5. How many rules are discussed at some length? (1) one; (2) two; (3) three; (4) four.   5. ————

Receptive Comprehension ————

6. The main idea is to (1) keep you from falling behind; (2) get you to mark your books; (3) help you do better on tests; (4) help you do better in school.   6. ————

7. Strongest emphasis is placed on (1) where to study; (2) proper management of study; (3) needed study aids and supplies; (4) the best time to study.   7. ————

8. The chief purpose of this selection was apparently to (1) guide; (2) clarify; (3) persuade; (4) evaluate. 8. ————

9. You would infer from this selection that the writers (1) were too unrealistic; (2) knew students well; (3) were too idealistic; (4) did not understand student problems.   9. ————

10. The tone of the selection is best described as (1) formal; (2) humorous; (3) straightforward; (4) imaginative.   10. ————

(10 off for each mistake)   *Reflective Comprehension* ————

TOTAL READING COMPREHENSION SCORE ————

VOCABULARY CHECK QUESTIONS

		without context I	*with context* II
1. *virtuous*	(1) brave; (2) truthful; (3) youthful; (4) righteous; (5) extraordinary.	1. ————	————
2. *incentive*	(1) encouragement; (2) reluctance; (3) distraction; (4) fine; (5) happening.	2. ————	————
3. *bout*	(1) bottle; (2) spell; (3) raft; (4) marker; (5) strike.	3. ————	————
4. *caricatures*	(1) pen drawings; (2) critical statements; (3) models; (4) falsified images; (5) ludicrous likenesses.	4. ————	————
5. *pseudo-students*	(1) sham students; (2) star students; (3) former students; (4) self-made students; (5) grad students.	5. ————	————

(10 off for each mistake)   *Word Comprehension* without *contextual help* (I) ————

Word Comprehension with *contextual help*   (II) ————

TOTAL WORD COMPREHENSION SCORE ————

EXERCISES

TREAT CAUSES, NOT SYMPTOMS

When you step into a doctor's office with a splitting headache, you expect more than an aspirin. That headache is usually a symptom of something that needs attention — something that is causing discomfort. A doctor, if he is to be genuinely helpful, must treat causes, not symptoms.

It helps to look at reading from this same vantage point. Suppose a student comprehends poorly and goes to a clinician for help. It will take more than the admonition, "Try to comprehend better" to bring results.

Poor comprehension is really a symptom — a symptom of what? That's the question which must be answered. Unfortunately the answer is likely to be complex, not simple. Many causes, not one, have to be examined.

For example, if a student reads that "Elizabeth is taciturn," he may not comprehend the statement because of a vocabulary deficiency. That's one important cause to check.

Sometimes a student may read a whole page or chapter and get very little. Why? Frankly because he was bored — had no real interest in it. Lack of interest, then, is another cause of poor comprehension.

Difficulty is still another factor accounting for low comprehension. The Flesch Reading Ease Score provides one method of determining difficulty, rating reading matter on a scale from 0 to 100 or from very easy to very difficult. Both word length and sentence length are used to determine difficulty.

A well-trained mechanic can often just listen to motor sounds and diagnose engine difficulties. He has had sufficient background and experience to do what one lacking that background would find impossible. In reading, also, low comprehension may be caused by inadequate background in a subject matter area.

And of course your reading rate affects comprehension. Reading either too rapidly or too slowly may affect comprehension adversely. For most students there is usually a "just-right" speed which provides maximum comprehension.

Lack of concentration is still another reason for low comprehension. Some readers have never developed proper techniques for dealing successfully with distractions, have never disciplined themselves to give concentrated attention to anything for any length of time. In this day of commercials, station breaks, and coffee breaks, we may be losing the ability to concentrate for extended periods of time.

This does not exhaust the list of causes, although those certainly deserve major attention. Other factors need to be kept in mind — temperature, noise, and movement, for example. Then there are the mechanics of reading — fixation patterns, regression patterns, vocalizings, word-for-word habits.

What does this add up to? Look closely and carefully at each of these possible causes. Try to decide which factor or combination of factors probably explains your low comprehension. Fortunately, without exception, you can do something about each of them. So set up a program for dealing with the causes underlying your symptoms. Then and only then can you begin to see good results.

(500 words)

From James I. Brown, *Guide to Effective Reading*, D. C. Heath and Co., 1966.

COMPREHENSION CHECK QUESTIONS

1. The article specifically mentions (1) a dentist; (2) a doctor; (3) an intern; (4) a receptionist.   1. _____

2. Poor comprehension is spoken of as (1) a symptom; (2) a disease; (3) a cause; (4) an accident.   2. _____

3. The Reading Ease Score mentioned was developed by (1) Flesch; (2) Fischer; (3) Flexner; (4) Garrison.   3. _____

4. The article mentions (1) a well-trained mechanic; (2) an experienced teacher; (3) a pilot; (4) a troubleshooter.   4. _____

5. The article mentions (1) wage hikes; (2) coffee breaks; (3) bonus gifts; (4) hypos.   5. _____

6. The central idea is to get you to (1) discover symptoms; (2) deal with causes; (3) improve comprehension; (4) check vocabulary deficiency.   6. _____

7. The allusion to station breaks was primarily to suggest (1) the importance of variety; (2) their effect on habits of concentration; (3) their encouragement of vocalization; (4) the importance of visual aids.   7. _____

8. A student who comprehends poorly (1) is reading too rapidly; (2) is not really interested; (3) is not concentrating; (4) may be doing none of these things.   8. _____

9. If your reading speed is not increasing, you should apparently try to (1) find out how to increase it; (2) try a new method; (3) discover why not; (4) work harder.   9. _____

10. Apparently, the most helpful move to insure progress is (1) careful self-analysis; (2) extensive practice; (3) a higher goal; (4) more work on vocabulary.   10. _____

SCORE _____

Answers: 1, 2; 2, 1; 3, 1; 4, 1; 5, 2; 6, 2; 7, 2; 8, 4; 9, 3; 10, 1.

NAME_____ DATE_____ READING RATE_____ W.P.M.

COMPREHENSION CHECK QUESTIONS

1. The reader was said to be about the size of a (1) magazine; (2) spiral-bound notebook; (3) ream of typing paper; (4) city telephone directory.   1. _____

2. The reader's weight was given in (1) ounces; (2) grams; (3) pounds; (4) kilograms.   2. _____

3. To get a book, you use (1) an electronic code; (2) a simple voice command; (3) an electronic title-finder; (4) an alphanumeric keyboard.   3. _____

4. The central storage area for this world library was located where? (1) Mt. McKinley; (2) Australian desert; (3) Brussels; (4) Egypt.   4. _____

5. The microprinted cards on which all documents are stored can take about how many book pages per single card? (1) 300; (2) 600; (3) 900; (4) not specified.   5. _____

Receptive Comprehension _____

6. This selection mainly (1) explains why the reader was developed; (2) describes its appearance; (3) points up its value; (4) explains its workings.   6. _____

7. The chief purpose is apparently to (1) entertain; (2) clarify; (3) stimulate; (4) evaluate. 7. _____

8. Points are developed largely through use of (1) definitions; (2) analogies; (3) personal examples; (4) specific details.   8. _____

9. The best word for describing the organization of this part of the story is (1) special; (2) analytical; (3) logical; (4) chronological.   9. _____

10. Apparently the most important thing about the reader is its (1) lightness; (2) efficiency; (3) mental stimulus; (4) ease of operation.   10. _____

(10 off for each mistake)   *Reflective Comprehension* _____

TOTAL READING COMPREHENSION SCORE _____

VOCABULARY CHECK QUESTIONS

		without context I	with context II
1. *eerie*	(1) high-pitched; (2) restrained; (3) loud; (4) soothing; (5) unsettling.	1. _____	_____
2. *surfeit*	(1) sufficient; (2) scarcity; (3) application; (4) excess; (5) factory.	2. _____	_____
3. *orgiastic*	(1) musical; (2) eccentric; (3) producing unrestrained activity; (4) calm; (5) noisy.	3. _____	_____
4. *provocation*	(1) training; (2) stimulation; (3) lying; (4) working; (5) opening.	4. _____	_____
5. *robots*	(1) controls; (2) thieves; (3) towers; (4) automatons; (5) keys.	5. _____	_____

(10 off for each mistake)

Word Comprehension without *contextual help* (I) _____

Word Comprehension with *contextual help* (II) _____

TOTAL WORD COMPREHENSION SCORE _____

EXERCISES

CONTEXT — KEY TO MEANING

When you come to an unknown word in your reading, what should you do? Eighty-four percent of the students in one college class answered — "look it up in the dictionary."

Take a closer look at that answer. Suppose you see the word *extenuate*. You consult the dictionary and find what? Not *the* meaning of *extenuate* but *four* meanings! Furthermore, the dictionary can never tell you exactly which meaning is intended.

Or take the common word *fast*. What does it mean? You answer — "quickly or rapidly," and you're quite right. But you're equally right if you say "firmly fastened." As a matter of fact, the one word *fast* is really not one word but twenty-one, all rolled into one. It has twelve meanings as an adjective, five as an adverb, two as a verb, and two as a noun. And that's talking in terms of the relatively small collegiate-size dictionary.

So — what does *fast* mean? You have to say *it all depends* — depends on the context, on the way the author used the word. To be sure, a dictionary should list all the different meanings. Even when a word is used in a new sense, that new meaning should eventually get into the dictionary, if it is used enough to become established. But unless the word has only one definition, we must always rely on context, not the dictionary, for its exact meaning. When you remember that the 500 most commonly used words have a total of 14,070 separate meanings, an aver-age of 28 per word — you can see why context must come first.

Furthermore, individuals vary widely in their ability to use contextual clues to arrive at accurate word meanings. In one class, for example, students took a difficult vocabulary test — first without any context to help, then a second time with sentence contexts for each word. Two students made identical scores of 30 the first time through. On the second time through one moved up to 40 but the other jumped up to 90. He had developed uncanny skill in getting word meanings through context. Obviously, that is a skill which deserves top priority. Research by Holmes accents its importance. He discovered that *vocabulary in context* contributed more to reading power than any other first-order factor isolated — 37 percent.

One sure way of developing that skill is to keep away from your dictionary until you have inferred a meaning from context alone. Then, and only then, should you turn to the dictionary for confirmation. If you go to the dictionary first you, by that move, discourage the development of the very skills and insights you need. Furthermore you'll find your interest is whetted by putting context first. You become more eager and alert to check your inference.

So — from now on — when you spot a strange word, look first at the context, formulate a tentative definition, *then* check it with the dictionary. You'll remember those new words much longer with that treatment. You'll also insure better comprehension.

From James I. Brown, *Guide to Effective Reading,* D. C. Heath and Co., 1966.

(500 words)

COMPREHENSION CHECK QUESTIONS

1. Specific mention is made of (1) a high school class; (2) a college class; (3) a TV class; (4) an English class. 1. ⎯⎯⎯⎯

2. *Fast* has how many different meanings? (1) 5; (2) 12; (3) 16; (4) 21. 2. ⎯⎯⎯⎯

3. The author specifically mentions (1) a collegiate-sized dictionary; (2) the *Oxford Dictionary;* (3) the Webster's dictionary; (4) a dictionary of slang. 3. ⎯⎯⎯⎯

4. In the use of contextual clues, individuals were said to (1) be about the same; (2) vary widely; (3) vary with I.Q.; (4) improve with age. 4. ⎯⎯⎯⎯

5. When first meeting a strange word, you are told to (1) look it up; (2) note any familiar prefix or root; (3) infer its meaning from context; (4) skip it and come back to study it later. 5. ⎯⎯⎯⎯

6. This is chiefly about (1) the relationship between context and meaning; (2) multiple word meanings; (3) kinds of context; (4) developing skill with context. 6. ⎯⎯⎯⎯

7. Primary emphasis is on (1) when context should be used; (2) how context should be used; (3) why context deserves priority; (4) what context includes. 7. ⎯⎯⎯⎯

8. The discussion of *extenuate* and *fast* illustrated (1) two different points; (2) somewhat the same point; (3) different kinds of dictionary entries; (4) how dictionaries differ. 8. ⎯⎯⎯⎯

9. You would infer from this that going to the dictionary first is most like (1) diving into deep water; (2) beginning a race; (3) using a crutch; (4) climbing a mountain. 9. ⎯⎯⎯⎯

10. You were most strongly cautioned against (1) consulting the dictionary first; (2) guessing at word meanings; (3) neglecting common words; (4) relying solely on context. 10. ⎯⎯⎯⎯

SCORE ⎯⎯⎯⎯

Answers: 1, 2; 2, 4; 3, 1; 4, 2; 5, 3; 6, 1; 7, 3; 8, 2; 9, 3; 10, 1.

240

NAME_____ DATE_____ READING RATE_____W.P.M.

COMPREHENSION CHECK QUESTIONS

1. One writer suggested we read Gibbon's *Decline and Fall* (1) in a day; (2) over a cup of instant coffee; (3) during breakfast; (4) at ten thousand words a minute.   1. _____

2. The average adult was said to read at about (1) 125 wpm; (2) 200 wpm; (3) 250 wpm; (4) 300 wpm.   2. _____

3. The author calls slow readers (1) good readers; (2) studious readers; (3) sloppy readers; (4) childish readers.   3. _____

4. The author refers specifically to (1) Voltaire; (2) Shakespeare; (3) Shelley; (4) Keats.   4. _____

5. To read the *Decline and Fall* at an average rate was said to take (1) 98 hours; (2) 83 hours; (3) 71 hours; (4) 64 hours.   5. _____

Receptive Comprehension _____

6. With respect to how fast to read, this discussion is mainly (1) a comparison of extreme views; (2) an evaluation of the advantages; (3) a realistic look at the whole question; (4) a defense of the middle ground or average position.   6. _____

7. The author's chief concern is with (1) speed; (2) over-all reading ability; (3) comprehension; (4) flexibility.   7. _____

8. The author is best described as (1) an extremist; (2) a theorist; (3) a pragmatist; (4) a conservative.   8. _____

9. The author most strongly favors (1) fast reading; (2) average reading speeds; (3) reading at speeds the material deserves; (4) using a variety of reading techniques.   9. _____

10. The writer believes that good reading is (1) natural; (2) God-given; (3) the result of learning; (4) a matter of intellect.   10. _____

(10 off for each mistake)   *Reflective Comprehension* _____

TOTAL READING COMPREHENSION SCORE _____

VOCABULARY CHECK QUESTIONS

			without context I	*with context* II
1. *blasphemy*	(1) seriousness; (2) loudness; (3) irreverence; (4) aimlessness; (5) rejection.	1.	_____	_____
2. *blitheness*	(1) nonsense; (2) sadness; (3) openness; (4) cheerfulness; (5) quietness.	2.	_____	_____
3. *reputable*	(1) restrained; (2) haphazard; (3) limited; (4) unpublished; (5) respectable.	3.	_____	_____
4. *ethereal*	(1) airy; (2) perfumed; (3) childlike; (4) proper; (5) continual.	4.	_____	_____
5. *mundane*	(1) moderate; (2) monetary; (3) generous; (4) heavenly; (5) practical.	5.	_____	_____

(10 off for each mistake)   *Word Comprehension* without *contextual help* (I) _____

Word Comprehension with *contextual help* (II) _____

TOTAL WORD COMPREHENSION SCORE _____

EXERCISES

CAPITALIZE ON INTEREST

What is interest? Witty defines it as a "disposition or tendency which impels an individual to seek out certain goals . . . ." Another authority calls it "a learned motive which drives an individual to act . . . ."

Impels, drives—those are the key words. Wrapped up in them you will discover the vital nature of interest. The best car ever made needs gasoline before it takes you anywhere. In the same way, the best mind needs a strong interest before it leads to outstanding achievement. Interest led Napoleon to become a military leader of world renown. Interest led Charles Darwin to discover the *Origin of Species.* Interest led Glenn Cunningham to overcome a major physical handicap and become a record-breaking mile runner. Just as gunpowder speeds a bullet toward its mark, so interest can speed you toward whatever goal you have in mind.

Take your reading. A comprehensive survey by Shaw of over 400 colleges and universities disclosed that an estimated 64 to 95 per cent of all college freshmen are handicapped by reading deficiencies. This suggests that no matter how well you read, you still probably read more slowly and ineffectively than you should—probably just because you are not interested enough in reading. You prefer TV, hunting, dancing or any of the other countless ways of spending time.

If this is so, what can you do about it? Specifically, how can you heighten your reading pleasure?

First, notice that people tend to like best those things which they do fairly well. If you are the worst bridge player ever, you will hardly look forward with interest to an evening of bridge—an evening of showing off your ineptitude.

That is equally true with reading—the better you read, the more you enjoy it. If you read slowly and painfully, you miss much of the fun. Your first step, then, is to develop added facility as a reader. This, in turn, means reading more than usual. It is almost that simple—to read better, you must read more.

At this point you may say, "But I don't want to read, let alone read more." Obviously, this is the time to make interest your ally—your driving force. What are your present strongest interests? Build on them for maximum help.

For example, if hunting is at the top of your list, start reading full-length books on that subject. Try *Hunter* or *Between the Elephant's Eyes.* You will be pleasantly surprised at how that interest in hunting will lead you through enough books to make you a more interested reader in general. Then gradually expand your interest in hunting to include such books as Maxwell's *Ring of Bright Water,* which stars two lively otters.

Each book read makes you a more proficient reader, makes the next one that much easier to read, and adds measurably to your general interest in reading.

So start now. Read a book every two or three weeks—one of your own choice, growing naturally out of your own present interests.

From James I. Brown, *Guide to Effective Reading,* D. C. Heath and Co., 1966.

(500 words)

COMPREHENSION CHECK QUESTIONS

1. The article mentioned (1) Strang; (2) Leedy; (3) Clark; (4) Witty.   1. _____

2. Reference was made to (1) *Man and Superman;* (2) *Origin of Species;* (3) *Voyage of the Beagle;* (4) *Story of Mankind.*   2. _____

3. Mention is made of (1) polo; (2) bridge; (3) rummy; (4) poker.   3. _____

4. You are told to build on your (1) favorite sport; (2) strongest interest; (3) educational background; (4) best subject matter area.   4. _____

5. Reference was made to (1) an arrow; (2) a dart; (3) an atomic bomb; (4) a bullet.   5. _____

6. This is mainly to (1) define interest; (2) discuss the importance of interest; (3) reveal a helpful connection between interest and reading; (4) urge the reading of more books.   6. _____

7. The author would apparently favor (1) more textbook reading; (2) having students select their own reading; (3) having the teacher assign an interesting novel; (4) providing a book list to choose from.   7. _____

8. You would infer that the most important aspect of interest is its (1) power; (2) variability; (3) universality; (4) individuality.   8. _____

9. The article implies that reading ability comes largely through (1) selected reading; (2) magazine reading; (3) careful reading; (4) varied reading.   9. _____

10. The article suggests that college courses in Efficient Reading should be for (1) poor readers; (2) average readers; (3) most students; (4) above-average students.   10. _____

SCORE _____

Answers: 1, 4; 2, 2; 3, 2; 4, 2; 5, 4; 6, 3; 7, 2; 8, 1; 9, 1; 10, 3.

NAME_____ DATE_____ READING RATE_____W.P.M.

COMPREHENSION CHECK QUESTIONS

1. The improvement of reading should serve (1) one function; (2) two functions; (3) three functions; (4) four functions.   1. _____

2. There is a quotation from (1) Darwin; (2) Milton; (3) Carlyle; (4) Shakespeare.   2. _____

3. In reading 100 words, college students regress an average of (1) 5 times; (2) 10 times; (3) 15 times; (4) 20 times.   3. _____

4. College students were said to be (1) omnivorous readers; (2) educated readers; (3) word-by-word readers; (4) fast readers.   4. _____

5. What one word was said to sum up our age best? (1) speed; (2) change; (3) nuclear; (4) frustrating.   5. _____

Receptive Comprehension _____

6. The chief focus of the article is on (1) habits that slow down reading; (2) making more reading time; (3) faster-than-comfortable reading; (4) methods for improving reading skill.   6. _____

7. The eye movement data was discussed primarily to show (1) how poorly college students read; (2) how time consuming regressions are; (3) what differences exist between ninth graders and college students; (4) how little one's habits change.   7. _____

8. The author implies that what contributes most toward managing higher reading speeds is (1) theory; (2) direction; (3) background; (4) experience.   8. _____

9. You would infer that present conditions demand (1) less reading; (2) a different kind of reading; (3) more careful reading; (4) more reading.   9. _____

10. In discussing the three reading brakes the author focuses largely on (1) defining the concepts; (2) noting cause-effect relationships; (3) underlining individual differences; (4) suggesting techniques for their elimination.   10. _____

(10 off for each mistake)   *Reflective Comprehension* _____

TOTAL READING COMPREHENSION SCORE _____

VOCABULARY CHECK QUESTIONS

		without context I	with context II
1. *integral*	(1) indispensable; (2) numerical; (3) extreme; (4) combined; (5) additional.	1. _____	_____
2. *plays havoc*	(1) fights; (2) aids; (3) ruins; (4) shelters; (5) acquires.	2. _____	_____
3. *regress*	(1) look back; (2) read again; (3) resume; (4) progress; (5) fixate.	3. _____	_____
4. *persist*	(1) remain; (2) cease; (3) convince; (4) distort; (5) pursue.	4. _____	_____
5. *imperative*	(1) majestic; (2) obligatory; (3) impassive; (4) disrespectful; (5) changeable.	5. _____	_____

(10 off for each mistake)   *Word Comprehension* without *contextual help* (I) _____

Word Comprehension with *contextual help* (II) _____

TOTAL WORD COMPREHENSION SCORE _____

EXERCISES

BUILDING SPECIFIC INTERESTS

Frank complained that he could not remember chemical symbols or formulas. Still he could reel off detailed information about big-league baseball for hours. How come? The secret, of course, was his strong interest in baseball.

Obviously, if you can build a fairly strong interest in any subject matter field, your mastery of it is greatly facilitated. Churchill divided people into two categories — "those whose work is work and whose pleasure is pleasure, and secondly, those whose work and pleasure are one." Interest makes the difference. Why not take full advantage of this in dealing with difficult subjects?

Suppose, for example, that you are taking chemistry but find it dull and uninteresting. This probably means you will avoid studying it and will be likely to do poorly or fail — unless you can develop an interest.

Try these positive suggestions to stimulate added interest in any subject.

First, cultivate the acquaintance of genuinely interested students. After a chemistry lecture, listen for a student who is talking with some enthusiasm and interest about a point raised in class. Fall into step with him or her. Suggest a cup of coffee. You'll be pleasantly surprised how soon some of that enthusiasm will rub off on you. Take the student who drew a bird-watcher for a roommate. At first he smiled to hear all the talk about birds. Two months later, however, he had bought binoculars and bird books and was himself going on early morning trips to identify birds. Fortunately, interest is contagious.

Second, read popular books on the subject. A man with no interest in art read Stone's book, *Lust for Life,* a biography of Vincent van Gogh. When he finished he amazed his wife by suggesting a visit to an art museum. Stefansson, the arctic explorer, traced his life-long interest in exploring to the reading of one book. Henri Fabre, famous French entymologist, is another whose life was changed by a book. Take the book *Crucibles: The Story of Chemistry,* by Jaffe. Read about the chemist Lavoisier, who lost his head on the guillotine. "It took but a moment to cut off that head, although a hundred years perhaps will be required to produce another like it." So said a contemporary. Such personal glimpses should take you back to your textbook with new zest and interest.

Third, spend extra time on dull, difficult subjects. The more you know about something, the more interested you become. If you know nothing about football you're not likely to be as interested as one who has watched many games and knows both players and rules.

Fourth, watch for educational TV shows or movies in the area of your low interest. The movie "Tom Jones" has stimulated many to read the book. In the same way, a movie about Pasteur can stimulate added interest in chemistry.

Now, get busy! Develop interest in specific subjects. More than anything else, this can change your outlook, can turn study from work to pleasure, can turn a potential *D* into a *B.*

From James I. Brown, *Guide to Effective Reading,* D. C. Heath and Co., 1966.

(500 words)

COMPREHENSION CHECK QUESTIONS

1. Frank was said to be interested in (1) baseball; (2) tennis; (3) football; (4) the Olympics.   1. _____

2. Which of the following was quoted? (1) Kennedy; (2) Stevenson; (3) Churchill; (4) Roosevelt.   2. _____

3. Reference was made to (1) a physicist; (2) a biologist; (3) an entymologist; (4) a sculptor.   3. _____

4. You were told to (1) listen to hi-fi; (2) collect stamps; (3) travel; (4) watch TV.   4. _____

5. How many specific suggestions were given? (1) none; (2) two; (3) three; (4) four.   5. _____

6. This dealt chiefly with (1) why interest should be cultivated; (2) how to develop interests; (3) the why and how of developing interests; (4) what specific interest should be developed.   6. _____

7. The quotation about "work and pleasure" was intended to point up (1) individual differences; (2) how interesting work really is; (3) the importance of interest; (4) how work stimulates interest.   7. _____

8. To develop interest in nuclear physics, which of the following books would be most helpful? (1) *College Physics;* (2) *Nuclear Physics;* (3) *The Atomic Structure of the Universe;* (4) *Our Friend the Atom.*   8. _____

9. Other things being equal, you would assume from this that the best grades are made by students who (1) are most interested; (2) study hardest; (3) are most intelligent; (4) have developed the most effective study habits.   9. _____

10. You would expect the writer to favor (1) a special hour for review; (2) two hours of preparation for every class hour; (3) provision for more leisure time; (4) less preparation time for interesting subjects.   10. _____

SCORE _____

Answers: 1, 1; 2, 3; 3, 3; 4, 4; 5, 4; 6, 3; 7, 3; 8, 4; 9, 1; 10, 4.

NAME_____ DATE_____ READING RATE_____W.P.M.

COMPREHENSION CHECK QUESTIONS

1. These super-speeds were said to put you where the (1) action is; (2) essence is; (3) substance is; (4) detail is.   1. _____

2. In the time normally taken to read one article in the usual fashion, you should be able to survey (1) 3 to 5, (2) 6 to 10; (3) 15 to 18; (4) 20 to 30.   2. _____

3. The bulk of our reading was spoken of as (1) expository; (2) persuasive; (3) descriptive; (4) narrative.   3. _____

4. For one example, specific mention was made of the word, (1) *rubles;* (2) *afghan;* (3) *steppes;* (4) *communes.*   4. _____

5. One intensive training session on scanning was said to get a class up to an average scanning speed of about (1) 4,000 wpm; (2) 9,000 wpm; (3) 14,000 wpm; (4) 22,000 wpm.   5. _____

Receptive Comprehension _____

6. This article mainly concerns (1) speed reading; (2) overviewing techniques; (3) special reading techniques; (4) the type of item to skip.   6. _____

7. By inference, the word *reading* is best defined as understanding (1) the details; (2) the main ideas; (3) the meaning from print; (4) every word.   7. _____

8. You would infer that these approaches should (1) be modified to suit the material being read; (2) be followed exactly; (3) all be used together; (4) be substituted for regular reading activities.   8. _____

9. The teeter-totter analogy was intended primarily to suggest (1) the need to balance slow and fast reading; (2) a way to counteract slow reading; (3) a way to improve comprehension; (4) the need to balance attention to details and main ideas.   9. _____

10. The visual example (TIE) was used to indicate the importance of (1) background; (2) experience; (3) perspective; (4) mind set.   10. _____

(10 off for each mistake)   *Reflective Comprehension* _____

TOTAL WORD COMPREHENSION SCORE _____

VOCABULARY CHECK QUESTIONS

		without context I	with context II
1. *paradox*	(1) self-sufficiency; (2) self-contradiction; (3) inactivity; (4) possessiveness; (5) a model.	1. _____	_____
2. *foreshadowing*	(1) darkening; (2) presaging; (3) hindering; (4) preferring; (5) following.	2. _____	_____
3. *expository*	(1) analytical; (2) poetic; (3) theoretical; (4) substantial; (5) explanatory.	3. _____	_____
4. *reiterates*	(1) repeats; (2) rejects; (3) compensates; (4) describes; (5) states.	4. _____	_____
5. *fulcrum*	(1) weight; (2) plank; (3) supply; (4) support; (5) movement.	5. _____	_____

(10 off for each mistake)   *Word Comprehension* without *contextual help* (I) _____

Word Comprehension with *contextual help* (II) _____

TOTAL WORD COMPREHENSION SCORE _____

EXERCISES

A good hunter doesn't rush into the woods, shooting aimlessly and muttering, "Maybe I'll hit something!" No — if he's hunting pheasants, that purpose dominates all his preparations, determining where, when, how and with what he hunts.

So it is with reading. If purpose is not crystal clear, the results will suffer. One freshman asked another, "What's the assignment about?" "About forty pages," was the reply. Hardly reflects a well-defined purpose, does it?

One way of looking at purpose is to think of reasons for reading. You might put reading for information first, with reading for understanding a close second — a move into depth. Your purpose? To go beyond facts into relationships that give them meaning, just as Sherlock Holmes noted clues, then built case-solving hypotheses. For a third purpose, there is entertainment, and for a fourth, stimulation. Just as a catalyst sparks a chemical reaction, so wide reading sparks new ideas. And, finally, you may read for inspiration. For generations, the Bible has inspired both nations and individuals.

But you must move from the general to the specific, to capitalize fully on purpose. For a specific purpose, turn to Lambuth's *Golden Book on Writing*: "Good writing may be acquired only by wide and intelligent reading. And in no other way whatsoever." Reading to become a better writer, to pass a psych quiz, to learn more about the stars or about yourself are all more specific purposes. Now you can see why it is said — "Tell me what you read and I'll tell you what you are."

Still another way of looking at purpose is in terms of the SPD Formula. In a sense, purpose in reading can only be determined after knowing something about the material to be read. The *S* stands for *Surveying* the material, the *P* for *Prereading* it — reading the first paragraph, topic sentences of following paragraphs, and final paragraph. This brings us to *D* — *Decide*. Only after the first two steps can you with intelligence decide to do one of four things — skip, skim, read, or study the material. This deserves thoughtful consideration.

What are the major advantages of accenting purpose? Well, it aids concentration, for one thing. Obviously, if you know the target, you can hit it more easily. Secondly, it aids memory. For example, experimental evidence shows that raising questions before reading — a way of sharpening purpose — improves both immediate and delayed recall, more so than reading plus re-reading.

Finally, Darwin's *Journal* adds eloquent testimony. After losing his taste for poetry and music, he wrote, pathetically — "If I had to live my life again, I would have made a rule to read some poetry and listen to some music at least once every week; for perhaps that part of my brain now atrophied would thus have been kept alive through use. The loss of those tastes is a loss of happiness . . . ."

To be sure, no one can live his life again. We can all, however, profit from the experience of others. As readers, we can always remember this: *Keep purpose uppermost.*

From James I. Brown, *Guide to Effective Reading*, D. C. Heath and Co., 1966.

(500 words)

COMPREHENSION CHECK QUESTIONS

1. Specific reference is made to hunting (1) ducks; (2) pheasants; (3) deer; (4) bears.   1. _____

2. How many specific reasons for reading were mentioned (1) none; (2) two; (3) three; (4) five.   2. _____

3. It was said that good writing may be acquired only by (1) practice; (2) special instruction; (3) reading; (4) heredity.   3. _____

4. Mention was made of (1) taking true-false tests; (2) raising questions before reading; (3) stating purpose in writing; (4) looking for a statement of purpose.   4. _____

5. A passage is quoted from the writing of (1) Malthus; (2) Darwin; (3) Solomon; (4) Emerson.   5. _____

6. The main idea is to get you to (1) look for a purpose; (2) emphasize purpose in reading; (3) apply the SPD Formula; (4) plan your life around purpose.   6. _____

7. The about-forty-pages anecdote points up primarily the (1) way to establish purpose; (2) way most students think; (3) need for a teacher-set purpose; (4) need for a purpose.   7. _____

8. You would assume from this article that Sherlock Holmes is famous largely because of (1) his nose for information; (2) his ability to go behind the facts; (3) the way he has inspired present-day detectives; (4) his influence on current mysteries.   8. _____

9. The reasons for reading were discussed in (1) the order of diminishing importance; (2) the order of frequency of appearance; (3) a general to specific order; (4) a specific to general order.   9. _____

10. The SPD Formula is based primarily on the assumption that to pass judgment on something demands (1) a well-developed critical faculty; (2) some knowledge of it; (3) good intelligence; (4) a strong degree of interest.   10. _____

Answers: 1, 2; 2, 4; 3, 1; 4, 2; 5, 2; 6, 2; 7, 4; 8, 2; 9, 3; 10, 2.

NAME—————————————————— DATE—————— READING RATE—————— W.P.M.

COMPREHENSION CHECK QUESTIONS

1. The author mentions (1) Bennett; (2) Maugham; (3) Stevenson; (4) Hardy.   1. ———

2. In reading, we're specifically told to (1) play a waiting game; (2) change character; (3) shift gears; (4) dream dreams.   2. ———

3. How many conditions for adult reading are discussed? (1) one; (2) two; (3) three; (4) four.   3. ———

4. Marya is a character in (1) *War and Peace*; (2) *Dover Beach*; (3) *Anna Karenina*; (4) *Fathers and Sons*.   4. ———

5. The author refers to (1) *Gone with the Wind*; (2) *Old McDonald's Farm*; (3) *Robinson Crusoe*; (4) *Growth of the Soil*.   5. ———

Receptive Comprehension ———

6. This article is mainly about (1) why we read; (2) conditions for adult reading; (3) recognizing the author's existence; (4) why we read and what is involved.   6. ———

7. The conditions for adult reading are arranged in order (1) from least to most important; (2) from the simple to the complex; (3) from the ordinary to the unusual; (4) from early to late in development.   7. ———

8. You might call this style (1) factual; (2) lively; (3) poetic; (4) impersonal.   8. ———

9. Least attention is given to (1) mastering basic reading skills; (2) the work of reading; (3) developing awareness of author; (4) living through reading.   9. ———

10. Uppermost in the author's mind is the fact that reading is extremely (1) difficult; (2) satisfying; (3) complicated; (4) practical.   10. ———

(10 off for each mistake)   *Reflective Comprehension* ———

TOTAL READING COMPREHENSION SCORE ———

VOCABULARY CHECK QUESTIONS

		without context I	*with context* II
1. *equanimity*	(1) fate; (2) equality; (3) calmness; (4) justice; (5) vagueness.	1. ———	———
2. *corollary*	(1) crown; (2) what follows; (3) petal; (4) heart attack; (5) wreath.	2. ———	———
3. *fraught*	(1) heavy; (2) free; (3) fresh; (4) filled; (5) friendly.	3. ———	———
4. *blasé*	(1) tired; (2) fat; (3) bored; (4) cheerful; (5) blasted.	4. ———	———
5. *amalgamates*	(1) improves; (2) molds; (3) melts; (4) joins; (5) establishes.	5. ———	———

(10 off for each mistake)   *Word Comprehension* without *contextual help* (I) ———

Word Comprehension with *contextual help* (II) ———

TOTAL WORD COMPREHENSION SCORE ———

Probing Paragraph Patterns

And so, to summarize, be sure to remember those three structurally oriented kinds of paragraphs just discussed.

Did that opening sentence confuse you? If it did, you will realize how important it is to be able to fit a paragraph into a proper framework of reference. Obviously, you — the reader — must be sensitive to the various kinds. An introductory paragraph, for example, should not be read in the same way as a transitional or concluding paragraph — the three kinds that provide key information about structure and emphasis.

The introductory paragraph normally has two functions — to arouse interest and suggest direction and content. It is as if the writer were to shine a flashlight in your face to attract attention — then turn the beam down the path to give you a quick glimpse of what is to be explored. As a reader, you must take full advantage of any and all directional cues so as to move without hesitation in the direction indicated by the writer.

And watch for transitional paragraphs. If read properly, they let you follow the writer with sure steps as he makes an abrupt change in his train of thought.

Finally, when you arrive at a concluding paragraph, slow down and take note. You may find a summary which brings together the very essence of what was said. Or, if the selection is short, you may have the main idea reiterated or put into a broader setting.

But this classification is incomplete. We need still another grouping to cover all varieties.

By far the greater number of paragraphs come under what might be called the expository type, particularly in textbook reading. They are the paragraphs which explain and develop ideas. Some such paragraphs contain one or more examples for clarification of a point. Some contain a mass of relevant details. Some may be built around a comparison or contrast. Black looks blacker when placed beside white. We see it better because of that juxtaposition. Analogy — a special kind of comparison — is another pattern to be noted. Life is like a river — with a beginning, a course, and an ending. Repetition or restatement is still another variety.

Each of these subvarieties can be dealt with more effectively if the reader has developed a sharpened awareness of them all. Often reading only a word or so will let him fit the paragraph into a frame of reference that lets him read it with much greater ease and understanding.

Finally, in addition to expository paragraphs, there are narrative, descriptive, and persuasive types. Narrative paragraphs usually give us action and people. Descriptive paragraphs give us a sensory view of life — let us feel, hear, see, smell, or taste it. And persuasive paragraphs are designed to get us to do something or believe something, thus going a step beyond plain explanation.

This quick look at two different categories of paragraph classification should help you read them with added effectiveness. The more familiar you are with common paragraph building block patterns, the better you can deal with them.

From James I. Brown, *Guide to Effective Reading,* D. C. Heath and Co., 1966.

(500 words)

COMPREHENSION CHECK QUESTIONS

1. The first classification mentioned covered what were called (1) narrative paragraphs; (2) transitional paragraphs; (3) complex paragraphs; (4) structured paragraphs. 1. _____

2. Specific mention was made of (1) a candle; (2) a flashlight; (3) an X ray; (4) a spotlight. 2. _____

3. When you read a concluding paragraph you are told to (1) slow down; (2) underline portions; (3) make notes; (4) guess what is coming. 3. _____

4. There is specific reference to (1) writing book reports; (2) reading *War and Peace*; (3) reading novels; (4) textbook reading. 4. _____

5. Narrative paragraphs were said to be characterized by (1) vivid details; (2) action; (3) sensory impressions; (4) a definite setting. 5. _____

6. In purpose, this is mainly to help you (1) read paragraphs more effectively; (2) become a better reader; (3) classify paragraphs more accurately; (4) recognize the importance of expository paragraphs. 6. _____

7. You would infer that the opening one-sentence paragraph was intended primarily (1) to introduce the subject; (2) to indicate content; (3) to confuse; (4) to awaken interest. 7. _____

8. You would infer that transitional paragraphs are most analogous to which highway sign? (1) Slow; (2) Curve; (3) Hill; (4) Cross Road. 8. _____

9. Most emphasis was placed on what kind of paragraph? (1) introductory; (2) expository; (3) narrative; (4) factual. 9. _____

10. Which of the following types of paragraphs is most likely to contain the word *because*? (1) persuasive; (2) expository; (3) concluding; (4) transitional. 10. _____

Answers: 1, 2; 2, 2; 3, 1; 4, 4; 5, 2; 6, 1; 7, 4; 8, 2; 9, 2; 10, 1.

NAME_____ DATE_____ READING RATE_____W.P.M.

1. The author once lived on a ranch in (1) Wyoming; (2) Texas; (3) Colorado; (4) Oklahoma.   1. _____

2. In college the author took (1) a Survey of English literature; (2) Psychology; (3) Beginning French; (4) Shakespeare.   2. _____

3. Her sorority sisters consider her (1) a bookworm; (2) an illiterate; (3) a wallflower; (4) a social butterfly.   3. _____

4. Mention is made of (1) Poe; (2) Mark Twain; (3) O. Henry; (4) Longfellow.   4. _____

5. In later life when she tries Dickens she (1) is disappointed; (2) is fascinated; (3) is mildly interested; (4) is unable to finish even one volume.   5. _____

Receptive Comprehension _____

6. The main idea of this selection is that (1) the classics should be read sooner; (2) an education actually interferes with reading pleasure; (3) even a bad education has advantages; (4) literature should be required in college.   6. _____

7. The author uses the word *illiteracy* to mean (1) inability to read; (2) inability to write; (3) lack of literary education; (4) an ignorant mistake in writing or speaking.   7. _____

8. This selection suggests that a major pleasure is that of (1) discovery; (2) conformity; (3) emotional involvement; (4) youthfulness.   8. _____

9. This selection divides itself most naturally into (1) A. Introduction, B. Body, C. Conclusion; (2) A. Early Life, B. Later Life; (3) A. The Cause, B. The Effect and Its Advantages; (4) A. Generalization, B. Specific Illustrations.   9. _____

10. You would infer from this selection that to get the utmost enjoyment from reading you should (1) start through a list of the world's classics; (2) take a literature course; (3) take an efficient reading course; (4) explore books for yourself.   10. _____

(10 off for each mistake)   *Reflective Comprehension* _____

TOTAL READING COMPREHENSION SCORE _____

VOCABULARY CHECK QUESTIONS

		without context I	*with context* II
1. *decorous*	(1) proper; (2) expensive; (3) elaborate; (4) old; (5) tidy.	1. _____	_____
2. *commiserate*	(1) begin; (2) injure; (3) detract; (4) sympathize; (5) force.	2. _____	_____
3. *savor*	(1) help; (2) interview; (3) restrain; (4) enjoy; (5) budget.	3. _____	_____
4. *beguiling*	(1) entertaining; (2) starting; (3) cheating; (4) begging; (5) studying.	4. _____	_____
5. *surfeit*	(1) excess; (2) entertainment; (3) modicum; (4) view; (5) touch.	5. _____	_____

(10 off for each mistake)   *Word Comprehension* without *contextual help* (I) _____

Word Comprehension with *contextual help* (II) _____

TOTAL WORD COMPREHENSION SCORE _____

EXERCISES

A New Look at an Old Method

Step into almost any efficient reading class. What do you find? What is perhaps the oldest, most widely used, yet newest approach in evidence? The answer? *Pacing!*

Most visual aids now in use, for example, are essentially pacing devices. Take the various sets of films for improving reading. They are but ways of getting you through print at projected speeds. Or take the various mechanical accelerators, using a shade, wire, bar, or band of light. Again, they are but machines to pace you through print. As you can see, almost every teacher of reading probably relies on some kind of pacing — films, accelerators, or stop watch.

The newest modification of this old approach comes in a highly commercialized course costing $495. Pacing is the heart of the course. The innovation is transforming the student's ubiquitous hand into a pacer and eliminating the need for machines or films.

Now why is pacing so common? Well, it works. I will never forget one student in my adult Efficient Reading class. At our first session when checking normal reading rate by having the class read a short selection, this young man plodded along at 80 wpm. The class waited patiently for him to finish, their average rate being 254, and the range, except for him, between 201 and 362 wpm.

After class I suggested he cancel the course. He looked at me in desperation. "I need this more than anyone," he said. I agreed but added that it was hardly fair to the others to have to wait for him. He begged to stay, saying, "You

won't have to wait. Pay no attention to me. I'll just get what I can." Well, I finally consented.

After seven weeks I noted an amazing change. The class had progressed nicely from 253 to 481 wpm, but he had shot from 80 to 460 wpm. I stopped him after class to ask what he was doing. He had wired his electric clock to the radio so that every time the sweep second hand passed twelve, the radio came on briefly. This let him know a minute had passed.

Fifteen minutes every night, *without fail,* he would read the *Reader's Digest* — approximately 500 words per page. At first he tried to read one column a minute. After a few weeks when he could manage that, he tried a whole page. This daily pacing had brought spectacular results. As he said, "You can't learn to read fast by practicing at slow rates."

Some students use a tape recorder to give themselves pacing signals. Others use book markers and oven timers to get themselves through a set number of pages. Still others enlist the help of a roommate, friend, or spouse.

So — ensure outstanding results from your own efforts through pacing. It can shut out distractions, heighten concentration, and provide invaluable experience at speeds faster than your usual. At first comprehension may suffer somewhat, but gradually, through practice, you will find yourself developing confidence and skill. Eventually your gains will become consolidated.

From James I. Brown, *Guide to Effective Reading*, D. C. Heath and Co., 1966.

(500 words)

COMPREHENSION CHECK QUESTIONS

1. The article mentions (1) overhead projectors; (2) accelerators; (3) eye-movement cameras; (4) graphs.   1. ———

2. One reading course costs (1) $195; (2) $295; (3) $395; (4) $495.   2. ———

3. The slow reader was asked to (1) cancel the course; (2) take another course; (3) take the course later; (4) get extra tutoring.   3. ———

4. Every night he paced himself for (1) 10 minutes; (2) 15 minutes; (3) 20 minutes; (4) 30 minutes.   4. ———

5. Pacing was said to (1) improve comprehension; (2) stimulate interest; (3) build background; (4) heighten concentration.   5. ———

6. The main idea is (1) to explain pacing; (2) to discuss various kinds of pacing; (3) to encourage the use of pacing; (4) to show how widely pacing is used.   6. ———

7. You would infer from this that films for speeding reading (1) are useless; (2) are only partially helpful; (3) need to be re-designed; (4) are quite helpful.   7. ———

8. What is apparently the chief reason for advocating the use of pacing? (1) its widespread use; (2) its use of interesting visual devices; (3) its effectiveness; (4) its novelty.   8. ———

9. The story of the slow reader was primarily intended to illustrate (1) the serious problems some students have; (2) the kind of results to expect; (3) a way to make a pacer; (4) the need for daily use.   9. ———

10. The major advantage of the hand as a pacer is apparently (1) its great flexibility; (2) its ever-present availability; (3) its elimination of costly machines; (4) its outstanding effectiveness.   10. ———

Answers: 1, 2; 2, 4; 3, 1; 4, 2; 5, 4; 6, 3; 7, 4; 8, 3; 9, 2; 10, 2.

NAME_____ DATE_____ READING RATE_____W.P.M.

COMPREHENSION CHECK QUESTIONS

1. Most students encountered were said to exhibit (1) simple reading disability; (2) emotional response to reading; (3) complex difficulties; (4) somewhat below average development.   1. _____

2. Ms. H. was said to spend what per cent of her working time on reading tasks? (1) one-tenth; (2) one-third; (3) one-half; (4) three-quarters.   2. _____

3. The increases described in the case of Ms. H. would save her (1) one day per week; (2) one week per month; (3) one day per month; (4) one hour per day.   3. _____

4. Benefits that Ms. H. was said to realize were stated in terms of (1) time saved; (2) time and money saved; (3) time, money, and personal development; (4) none of the above.   4. _____

5. In setting up a course of training the article recommends (1) a specific source of information; (2) a specific commercial agency; (3) a duplication of the Minnesota course; (4) professional assistance.   5. _____

Receptive Comprehension _____

6. The ultimate purpose of this article is (1) to publicize the Minnesota Efficient Reading Course; (2) to reveal the personal benefits possible through improved reading efficiency; (3) to prove that reading can be a "time stretcher"; (4) to encourage the installation of reading training programs by pointing out their value.   6. _____

7. This article is directed to the (1) professional individual; (2) teacher; (3) student; (4) executive.   7. _____

8. The author considers reading as (1) a skill generally mastered in the 4th grade; (2) a process that is refined only by education; (3) a simple skill; (4) a developmental process.   8. _____

9. Emphasized *least* in the training described was (1) guided practice; (2) visual training; (3) motivation; (4) psychology of reading.   9. _____

10. From this article you would infer that courses in efficient reading are at the present time (1) not readily available; (2) few, but increasing in number; (3) widespread and becoming more so; (4) limited to university campuses.   10. _____

(10 off for each mistake)   *Reflective Comprehension* _____

TOTAL READING COMPREHENSION SCORE _____

VOCABULARY CHECK QUESTIONS

		without context I	with context II
1. *tycoon*	(1) tropical storm; (2) animal; (3) machine; (4) magnate; (5) factory.	1. _____	_____
2. *esoteric*	(1) secret; (2) useful; (3) speedy; (4) legal; (5) complicated.	2. _____	_____
3. *optimum*	(1) visible; (2) hopeful; (3) opposite; (4) best; (5) rich.	3. _____	_____
4. *hypothetical*	(1) critical; (2) supposed; (3) sick; (4) actual; (5) hysterical.	4. _____	_____
5. *opportune*	(1) assumed; (2) fitting; (3) depressing; (4) approaching; (5) belated.	5. _____	_____

(10 off for each mistake)   *Word Comprehension* without *contextual help* (I) _____

Word Comprehension with *contextual help* (II) _____

TOTAL WORD COMPREHENSION SCORE _____

EXERCISES

Use the SSQ Formula

Before a new pitcher heads for the mound, he takes time to warm up. Before you begin reading, you too should do some warming up — some preparing.

When you sit down to study, those first few minutes are not too productive. Interest and concentration cannot be switched on and off, as a light switch. Unrelated thoughts have to be pushed out gradually, as you begin a new activity. Can you shorten this warm-up process? Yes — by the following formula.

Survey: This first step gives you the best possible overview in the shortest possible time. To survey an article or chapter, read the title, the first paragraph, all headings, italicized words, and the last paragraph. You should then have the bare essentials.

To illustrate, note the underlined parts here. They are what you would read in your survey. If you can read the entire 500-word selection in two minutes, it will take only twelve seconds to survey it. Or take a longer chapter from an anthropology text. Surveying the 7,650-word chapter means reading only 350 words — over twenty-one times faster than normal reading. This diving in headfirst — this sudden immersion — forces almost immediate concentration.

Skim: Skimming builds up an even stronger foundation. For this, read the title and first paragraph, as in the survey. Then read the first sentence and key words in all the following paragraphs, plus any headings, heavy-type or italicized words. When you reach the last paragraph, read it completely. As you see, this means rereading all parts covered in the survey, but taking an important next step. This selective reading of from 20 to 40 percent of the material, takes only about a fifth to a third your usual reading time. Note the parts in heavier type on this page. It marks what you would cover in skimming. Instead of two minutes, it should take only fifty-two seconds.

Question: Generally, a faster-than-comfortable reading speed means better-than-usual concentration. One student, however, slipped into an unfortunate habit, while trying to develop added concentration. He tried so hard to finish a certain number of pages in a limited time that he was not actually reading — just going through the motions. To break himself of this habit, he used this third step — raising questions.

More than anything else, a question is likely to drive unwanted thoughts out of mind. This tends to shorten the needed warming-up period. Raise questions both after surveying and after skimming the material. For example, take the reader who reads the title and consciously asks — "What does SSQ stand for?" He will obviously read with much more purpose than one who has not evidenced such curiosity. Naturally, when you survey and skim, much is missed. In a sense, however, this tends to encourage more questions than in normal reading, making this dynamic third step an almost automatic consequence of the first two.

So — use these prereading steps. Survey the material. Skim it rapidly. Then raise questions — ideal preparation for the reading to follow.

From James I. Brown, *Guide to Effective Reading*, D. C. Heath and Co., 1966.

(500 words)

COMPREHENSION CHECK QUESTIONS

1. The article mentions (1) a catcher; (2) a curve ball; (3) a fly; (4) a pitcher.
1. _____

2. The first few minutes of study were said to be (1) crucial; (2) important; (3) unimportant; (4) unproductive.
2. _____

3. Surveying this article was said to take (1) six seconds; (2) twelve seconds; (3) twenty seconds; (4) thirty-six seconds.
3. _____

4. Skimming is spoken of as (1) speed reading; (2) a useful substitute for reading; (3) useful only with textbook material; (4) selective reading.
4. _____

5. One student was said to (1) read too fast; (2) concentrate poorly; (3) go through the motions of reading; (4) spend too much time in skimming.
5. _____

6. This selection focuses mainly on (1) explaining the formula; (2) describing its origin; (3) encouraging its use; (4) pointing up its advantages.
6. _____

7. Major attention is placed on (1) the actual reading; (2) the selection of appropriate approaches; (3) the proper sequence of steps; (4) preparation for reading.
7. _____

8. The mention of the troubled student was to point up primarily the (1) need for a warm-up period; (2) danger in too much reading speed; (3) importance of concentration; (4) usefulness of questions.
8. _____

9. In the allusion, "diving in headfirst," the water is analogous to (1) meaning; (2) print; (3) the act of reading; (4) preparation for reading.
9. _____

10. You would infer that the reference to SSQ in the title was primarily to (1) aid memory; (2) summarize; (3) arouse interest; (4) save space.
10. _____

Score _____

Answers: 1, 4; 2, 4; 3, 2; 4, 4; 5, 3; 6, 3; 7, 4; 8, 4; 9, 2; 10, 3.

252

NAME_____ DATE_____ READING RATE_____ W.P.M.

COMPREHENSION CHECK QUESTIONS

1. In the past, the formula for success was (1) useful contacts; (2) intelligence; (3) good background; (4) hard work.   1. _____

2. The average high school graduate should know how many words from the short vocabulary quiz provided? (1) eight; (2) five; (3) two; (4) none.   2. _____

3. On the vocabulary test, the most recent high school graduates (1) showed a wide range of ability; (2) scored about average; (3) scored higher than the others; (4) had the lowest scores of all.   3. _____

4. The author speaks of teaching (1) political science; (2) freshman English; (3) literature; (4) economics.   4. _____

5. How much time each day should be spent in reading? At least (1) four hours; (2) two hours; (3) one hour; (4) forty-five minutes.   5. _____

Receptive Comprehension _____

6. The value of reading receiving most attention in this selection is the (1) practical; (2) recreational; (3) cultural; (4) intellectual.   6. _____

7. Vocabulary is stressed largely because words are (1) basic to all communication; (2) tools of thought; (3) useful socially; (4) helpful in getting good grades.   7. _____

8. The first consideration in encouraging one to read more is to provide (1) suitable instruction; (2) interesting reading; (3) additional incentives; (4) more "good" books.   8. _____

9. The survey of reading habits was mentioned largely to illustrate (1) the good taste of some students; (2) how reading interests change; (3) the value of pocket books; (4) the reason for decline in reading.   9. _____

10. To get children to read, parents should rely mostly on (1) direct advice; (2) example; (3) magazines; (4) book lists.   10. _____

(10 off for each mistake)   *Reflective Comprehension* _____

TOTAL READING COMPREHENSION SCORE _____

VOCABULARY CHECK QUESTIONS

		without context I	with context II
1. *extolled*	(1) extracted; (2) praised; (3) spoke out; (4) rang; (5) released.	1. _____	_____
2. *laggards*	(1) slow; (2) lazy; (3) stupid; (4) disabled; (5) tired persons.	2. _____	_____
3. *verbal*	(1) spoken; (2) written; (3) factual; (4) related to words; (5) active.	3. _____	_____
4. *correlation*	(1) correspondence; (2) confirmation; (3) correction; (4) figure; (5) average.	4. _____	_____
5. *induce*	(1) order; (2) refer; (3) try; (4) persuade; (5) lessen.	5. _____	_____

(10 off for each mistake)

Word Comprehension without *contextual help* (I) _____

Word Comprehension with *contextual help* (II) _____

TOTAL WORD COMPREHENSION SCORE _____

EXERCISES

NAPL. What does that mean? You don't know? No wonder — those letters need to be organized before they make PLAN. Now you see the important role of organization.

Organizing and reading must go hand-in-hand, if reading is to be truly effective. It helps to remember that reading is the reverse of writing; the writer sends, the reader receives. Fortunately, most writers try to organize their remarks carefully enough to insure clear, accurate communication. The reader, by trying to discover the writer's plan, gets as close as possible to his original meaning. Comprehension is thereby increased.

How is organization revealed? As a reader, you should become more sensitive to three kinds of special devices — typographical, rhetorical, and verbal. To make certain parts stand out, a writer may resort to CAPITAL LETTERS, **boldface type,** or *italics.* Or he may turn to such rhetorical devices as repetition, parallelism, or balance. Repeating a key word or phrase helps the reader fit what is said into a more orderly pattern. When Lincoln spoke of government "of the people, by the people, and for the people," he used parallelism to accent the three-fold pattern he wanted to emphasize. And Patrick Henry's "give me liberty or give me death," used balance to heighten the two-fold nature of that choice. Finally, verbal devices help the reader mark transitions, note methods of development, and discover outline form. The word *another,* for example, suggests a transition. *Consequently* suggests a development based on cause-and-effect relationships. And such words as *first* or *finally*

From James I. Brown, *Guide to Effective Reading,* D. C. Heath and Co., 1966.

are most useful indicators of outline form. All these devices, like road signs, help the reader keep on the track.

The other way is through noting paragraph structure. Major thought units are marked off by paragraphs. Each paragraph has a topic sentence, expressed or implied, plus supporting details. In outlining any article, rely heavily on paragraphing to make the plan clear.

What does organization contribute? When you have developed real skill in noting organization, the benefits fall into two categories — a sharpened awareness of certain key factors as well as improved ability in two areas.

A sharpened awareness of the thesis or main idea is one important benefit. Getting the main idea of this 500-word selection, for example, is greatly simplified by reducing the 500 words to a manageable skeleton — or outline. Organization also brings added awareness of the interrelationships between parts. Subordinate parts are seen as exactly that, their relationship to major divisions being more obvious.

Finally, organization improves both understanding and remembering. Knowledge and understanding are, in a sense, different. It is possible to know the facts but not understand what they mean. Organization helps here. And it contributes added retention. It is much easier to remember details if you have an outline as a frame of reference. It is easier, for example, to remember CAPITALS, **boldface type,** and *italics,* when they are grouped under the heading *Typographical devices.*

So, make organization a concomitant to reading. It can turn NEMAGIN into MEANING, the obscure into the obvious.

(500 words)

COMPREHENSION CHECK QUESTIONS

1. You were told to keep organizing and reading (1) as separate activities; (2) as consecutive steps; (3) hand-in-hand; (4) apart.   1. _____

2. Reading is spoken of as (1) the reverse of writing; (2) the spark for comprehension; (3) easier than writing; (4) the road to outlining.   2. _____

3. Reference was made to (1) Franklin; (2) Washington; (3) Monroe; (4) Lincoln.   3. _____

4. The special devices discussed were likened to (1) keys; (2) road signs; (3) timetables; (4) road maps.   4. _____

5. Parallelism is classed as a (1) typographical device; (2) verbal device; (3) rhetorical device; (4) paragraph device.   5. _____

6. This is mainly about (1) how organization is revealed; (2) what organization contributes to reading; (3) outlining techniques; (4) the role of organization in reading.   6. _____

7. The opening reference to NAPL (PLAN) was intended to show (1) how to organize; (2) the simplicity of good organization; (3) the importance of organization; (4) how slight changes make big differences.   7. _____

8. Two of the main divisions are marked off by (1) boldface type; (2) headings; (3) italics; (4) capital letters.   8. _____

9. The phrase, "make organization a concomitant to reading," apparently means to make it (1) a supplement; (2) an aid; (3) an end; (4) an accompaniment.   9. _____

10. Most attention is given to (1) how to organize; (2) what purpose it has; (3) when to organize; (4) what organization is.   10. _____

SCORE _____

Answers: 1, 3; 2, 1; 3, 4; 4, 2; 5, 3; 6, 4; 7, 3; 8, 3; 9, 4; 10, 2.

NAME_____ DATE_____ READING RATE_____W.P.M.

COMPREHENSION CHECK QUESTIONS

1. Mr. Z's office is (1) not specifically located; (2) in the basement; (3) on the ground floor; (4) on the third floor. 1. _____

2. Mr. Z. says he knows more about English usage than 90 per cent of the (1) college teachers; (2) linguists; (3) high school teachers; (4) professional writers. 2. _____

3. Mr. Z. mentions directions for a (1) coffee can; (2) butter carton; (3) cocoa can; (4) tea-bag label. 3. _____

4. Mr. Z's final copy is put on (1) blue paper; (2) yellow paper; (3) green paper; (4) bond paper. 4. _____

5. According to Mr. Z., the secret of writing directions is (1) selecting the exact words to fit the idea; (2) putting yourself in the reader's place; (3) creative imagination; (4) keeping your eye on the ball. 5. _____

Receptive Comprehension _____

6. The main idea of this selection is to (1) reveal Mr. Z's work habits; (2) emphasize the skill needed in writing directions; (3) show the importance of verbs in writing directions; (4) stress the importance of adjectives in directions. 6. _____

7. You would infer that the writer (1) accidentally noticed Z's office and stopped; (2) came purposely to see Mr. Z.; (3) had heard of Mr. Z. before; (4) stopped in at Mr. Z's request. 7. _____

8. You would infer that the best writing for directions is (1) simple and direct; (2) a matter of inspiration; (3) vivid and picture-making; (4) literary. 8. _____

9. You would infer that the conventions of punctuation are (1) actually unnecessary; (2) quite helpful; (3) not established firmly enough to merit study; (4) are less important than the purposes to be served. 9. _____

10. When Mr. Z. reads the copy which he has to revise, he apparently is reading primarily for (1) detail; (2) central idea; (3) understanding; (4) information. 10. _____

(10 off for each mistake)   *Reflective Comprehension* _____

TOTAL READING COMPREHENSION SCORE _____

VOCABULARY CHECK QUESTIONS

		without context I	with context II
1. *ventured*	(1) sold; (2) eyed; (3) wrote; (4) risked; (5) delayed.	1. _____	_____
2. *fluted*	(1) grooved; (2) perforated; (3) inserted; (4) excited; (5) flourished.	2. _____	_____
3. *affronted*	(1) affected; (2) added; (3) frightened; (4) aided; (5) offended.	3. _____	_____
4. *inconsistent*	(1) incongruous; (2) irregular; (3) unpleasant; (4) unintentional; (5) conservative.	4. _____	_____
5. *subtle*	(1) commonplace; (2) elusive; (3) nasty; (4) humorous; (5) friendly.	5. _____	_____

(10 off for each mistake)

Word Comprehension without *contextual help* (I) _____

Word Comprehension with *contextual help* (II) _____

TOTAL WORD COMPREHENSION SCORE _____

EXERCISES

1. *Capitals, italics, and quotation marks:* To check your handling of such marks, use the following passage. Encircle every letter that should be capitalized, underline every word that should be italicized, and insert quotation marks where they are needed.

When you have finished, turn back to the selection proper and compare your version with the original. Consult your handbook to resolve any differences between the two versions. In preparing a bibliography and making footnotes, you will want to know when to italicize and when to use quotation marks. The sooner you straighten out such matters, the more professional your reports will appear.

he stood up and unhooked it from the wall. blue paper, use it for all final o.k.'d directions, so as not to make a mistake and let one of the earlier versions—call them scratches—get out when there's a better one been done, he held the frame out to us. this one, i'll admit, is pretty good.

I like this one, he said, 'cause no adjectives and no plug. first line there got the concentration of a line from milton's samson, my favorite poem.

we noticed the adjective white before appearance, but knew now that it wasn't an adjective to mr. z. and, for that matter, to us any more. why so little punctuation? we asked. one period at the end and then only two hyphens in the first line.

2. *Active vs. passive verbs:* As Mr. Z. says, "Use active verbs whenever possible." In the following sentences change the underlined verbs from passive to active voice, making whatever other changes are necessary to complete the sentences. What is the difference in effect? Which one is least offensive in the examples below?

A. As the elevator on the third floor of the Business Associates Building at 1115–20 Horace Street was reached, the scratched black letters on the frosted glass were seen: Edward Zybowski—Best Directions Writer in the World.

_____

_____

B. The elevator was permitted to go down without us.

_____

C. As this was said, the rod was lifted that held the paper against the typewriter roller and the words were squinted at.

_____

_____

D. Not using adjectives was spoken of by you.

_____

3. *Directions:* Write some directions for a simple process such as tying a knot or necktie. Ask someone who does not know how to perform the process to attempt it with the help of your directions.

NAME———————————————————— DATE—————— READING RATE—————— W.P.M.

COMPREHENSION CHECK QUESTIONS

1. A well-written letter was said to have how many points of focus? (1) one; (2) two; (3) three; (4) four.   1. ————

2. Specific reference was made to (1) Samuel Johnson; (2) Shelley; (3) Wellington; (4) Walt Whitman.   2. ————

3. A prime minister was said to have addressed his queen as if she were (1) a commoner; (2) an equal; (3) an institution; (4) a public meeting.   3. ————

4. Mention is made of (1) the Lord's Prayer; (2) the Declaration of Independence; (3) the Gettysburg Address; (4) the Presidential Oath of Office.   4. ————

5. Procrustes was spoken of as a (1) prophet; (2) bandit; (3) merchant; (4) beggar.   5. ————

Receptive Comprehension ————

6. This selection is primarily to (1) explain how business and personal letters differ; (2) suggest how to write better letters; (3) discuss reasons for writing effective letters; (4) show the importance of word choice in letters.   6. ————

7. The introductory comment about labor-saving devices was to suggest that (1) they take time away from letter-writing; (2) they provide more time for letter-writing; (3) they should help us streamline letter-writing efforts; (4) they illustrate the rapidity of change.   7. ————

8. The reference to *incomprehensibility* was to suggest the (1) need for short words; (2) usefulness of long words; (3) way words are built; (4) need for the right word.   8. ————

9. The illustration of Procrustes was intended primarily to make what point? (1) be brief; (2) be exact; (3) don't be too exact; (4) don't be too brief.   9. ————

10. Apparently the chief concern in writing a business letter is to be (1) brief; (2) clear; (3) tactful; (4) interesting.   10. ————

(10 off for each mistake)   *Reflective Comprehension* ————

TOTAL READING COMPREHENSION SCORE ————

VOCABULARY CHECK QUESTIONS

		without context I	with context II
1. *uncouth*	(1) unhappy; (2) unsocial; (3) disobedient; (4) uncultured; (5) normal.	1. ————	————
2. *lucid*	(1) readily understood; (2) badly tangled; (3) fortunate; (4) glittering; (5) luxurious.	2. ————	————
3. *stodgy*	(1) impassive; (2) full; (3) alert; (4) sharply outlined; (5) dull.	3. ————	————
4. *audacious*	(1) daring; (2) quiet; (3) memorable; (4) hopeful; (5) customary.	4. ————	————
5. *opaque*	(1) clear; (2) obscure; (3) reflective; (4) opposite; (5) peaceful.	5. ————	————

(10 off for each mistake)   *Word Comprehension* without *contextual help* (I) ————

Word Comprehension with *contextual help* (II) ————

TOTAL WORD COMPREHENSION SCORE ————

EXERCISES

BE A PERFECT SPELLER IN 30 MINUTES
Norman Lewis

Can you become a perfect speller? Yes — if you are willing to memorize a few intriguing rules and give your memory a stimulating jolt. I have demonstrated again and again in my adult classes at the City College of New York that anyone who possesses normal intelligence and has had an average education should have no trouble in becoming a perfect speller in 30 minutes or even less!

What makes the task so easy and rapid?

1. Investigations have proved that 95 percent of our spelling mistakes occur in just 100 words. Not only do we all seem to misspell the same words, but we usually misspell them in just about the same way.
2. Correct spelling depends entirely on memory, and the most effective way I know of to train your memory is by means of association — or by *mnemonics* (pronounced *nemonics*).

If you are a poor speller, the chances are that you've developed a complex because you misspell some or all of the 100 words with which this article deals. When you have mastered this list by means of association and memory, 95 percent of your spelling difficulties will vanish.

So let's start with the 25 troublesome words listed below. In addition to the correct spelling of each of the words, you will find the simple mnemonic that will enable you to fix that correct spelling indelibly in your memory.

All right
   Two words, no matter what it means. Keep in mind that it's the opposite of all wrong.
Repetition
   The first four letters are the same as those in repeat.
Irritable, Inimitable
   Think of allied forms, irritate and imitate.
Recommend
   Commend, which is easy to spell, plus the prefix *re-*.
Ridiculous
   Think of the allied form, ridicule, which is usually spelled correctly, thus avoiding rediculous.
Despair
   Again think of another form — desperate — and so avoid dispair.
Stationery
   The word that means paper; notice the *er* in paper.
Stationary
   This means standing, so notice the *a* in stand.
Superintendent
   The superintendent in an apartment house collects the rent — thus you avoid superintendant.
Coolly
   You can spell cool — simply add the adverbial ending *-ly*.

Separate, Comparative
   Look for a rat in both words.
Supersede
   The only word in the language ending in *-sede*.
Succeed
Proceed
Exceed
   The only three words in the language ending in *-ceed*. In the order given here the initial letters form the first 3 letters in spell.
Cede, Recede,
Precede, etc.
   All other words with a final syllable sounding similar end in *cede*.
Procedure
   One of the double e's in proceed moves to the end in procedure.
Absence
   Think of the allied form absent, and you will not be tempted to misspell it abscence.
Conscience
   Science, plus the prefix *con-*.
Anoint
   Think of an ointment, hence no double n.
Ecstasy
   To *sy* (sigh) with ecstasy.
Analyze, Paralyze
   The only two non-technical words in the language ending in *-yze*.

Whether or not you have faith in your ability as a speller you will need only 30 seconds to overcome your difficulties with each of the 25 words in the list, or 12½ minutes all told. And as you probably misspell only some of the words, not the entire 25, you should be able to eliminate your errors in even less time. Just try spending 30 seconds, now, on each of the words you're doubtful about — then put your new-found learning to the test by filling in the missing letters in the same list of words which follows. To your delight, you'll find that it's not at all difficult to make a perfect score. Try it and see for yourself.

A—RIGHT	SUPER—
REP—TITION	SUC—
IRRIT—BLE	PROC—
INIMIT—BLE	EXC—
RE—O—MEND	PREC—
R—DICULOUS	PROC—DURE
D—SPAIR	AB—ENCE
STATION—RY (paper)	CON—NCE
STATION—RY (standing)	A—OINT
SUPERINTEND—NT	ECSTA—Y
COO—Y	ANAL—E
SEP—RATE	PARAL—E
COMPAR—TIVE	

(*continued on page 260*)

NAME————————————————— DATE————— READING RATE————— W.P.M.

COMPREHENSION CHECK QUESTIONS

1. The teacher's name was (1) Stamm; (2) Steele; (3) Stone; (4) Smith.   1. ———

2. Mention is made of reading a poem by (1) Keats; (2) Shelley; (3) Burns; (4) Byron. 2. ———

3. The teacher stirred their imagination by asking them how they would like to live in (1) England during the reign of Elizabeth; (2) Italy during the Renaissance; (3) Greece at the height of its glory; (4) France at the time of the French Revolution. 3. ———

4. For the good-bye party the boys prepared a (1) eulogy; (2) gift; (3) parody; (4) play. 4. ———

5. The class met in Room (1) 308; (2) 318; (3) 288; (4) 280. 5. ———

Receptive Comprehension ———

6. The purpose of this article is to (1) tell about an unusual character; (2) describe how he taught English; (3) suggest the importance of wide reading; (4) help us feel an appreciation for this character. 6. ———

7. The teacher's comment on the phrase "tender age" was (1) one of approval; (2) not given; (3) one suggesting lazy writing; (4) one suggesting a specific revision. 7. ———

8. His attempts to get them to see if they could improve on a poem were intended to lead to (1) a better understanding of the poem; (2) a better appreciation of literature; (3) an improvement in writing and speaking; (4) improvement of discussion techniques. 8. ———

9. His most important piece of advice was to (1) study; (2) work; (3) browse; (4) read. 9. ———

10. The article implies that we should read things of (1) personal interest; (2) recognized merit; (3) current interest; (4) literary worth. 10. ———

(10 off for each mistake)   *Reflective Comprehension* ———

TOTAL READING COMPREHENSION SCORE ———

VOCABULARY CHECK QUESTIONS

		without context I	*with context* II
1. *condescension*	(1) condemnation; (2) grief; (3) control; (4) insulation; (5) air of superiority.	1. ———	———
2. *melee*	(1) combining; (2) confused mass; (3) melting; (4) maturing; (5) orderly plan.	2. ———	———
3. *abhorred*	(1) clung to; (2) hated; (3) wandered; (4) gave up; (5) assumed.	3. ———	———
4. *bestow*	(1) give; (2) assign; (3) beset; (4) beg; (5) elevate.	4. ———	———
5. *concocted*	(1) finished; (2) exploded; (3) devised; (4) seasoned; (5) drank.	5. ———	———

(10 off for each mistake) *Word Comprehension* without *contextual help* (I) ———

Word Comprehension with *contextual help* (II) ———

TOTAL WORD COMPREHENSION SCORE ———

EXERCISES

Mere repetitious drill, however, will not teach you to spell correctly. If you drive a car or sew or do any familiar manual work, you know how your hands carry on automatically while your mind is far away. So if you hope to learn how to spell by filling pages with a word, about all you'll get for your trouble will be writer's cramp.

The only way to learn to spell the words that now plague you is to devise a mnemonic for each one.

If you are never sure whether it's *indispensible* or *indispensable*, you can spell it a thousand or a million times — and the next time you have occasion to write it you'll still wonder whether to end with *ible* or *able*. But if you say to yourself just once that *able* men are generally indispens*able*, you've conquered another spelling demon.

In the test below are another 25 words from the list of 100, each presented in both the correct form and in the popular misspelling. Go through the list quickly, checking what you consider the proper choices. In this way you will discover which of the 25 would stump you in a spelling test. Then devise a personal mnemonic for each word you failed to get right, writing your result in the margin of the page.

Don't be alarmed if some of your mnemonics turn out to be silly — the sillier they are, the easier to recall them in an emergency. One of my pupils, who could never remember how many *l*'s to put into tranquillity (or is it *tranquility?*), came up with this: "In the old days life was more tranquil, and people wrote with *quills* instead of fountain pens. Hence — *tranquillity!*" That is the preferred form, though either is correct.

Another pupil, a girl, who always chewed her nails over *irresistible* before deciding whether to end it with *ible* or *able*, suddenly realized that a certain brand of lipstick was called "*Irresistible*," the point being that the only vowel in *lipstick* is *i* — hence, *ible!* Silly, mnemonics, aren't they? But they work. Now tackle the test and see how clever — or silly — you can be.

Do These Words Stump You?

Listed below are the correct and incorrect spellings of 25 words commonly misspelled. Check a or b, whichever you think is correct. Then look at the answers to see how well you did.

1. (a) supprise,
   (b) surprise
2. (a) inoculate,
   (b) innoculate
3. (a) definitely,
   (b) definately
4. (a) priviledge,
   (b) privilege
5. (a) incidently,
   (b) incidentally
6. (a) predictible,
   (b) predictable
7. (a) embarassment,
   (b) embarrassment
8. (a) descriminate,
   (b) discriminate
9. (a) description,
   (b) discription
10. (a) pronounciation,
    (b) pronunciation
11. (a) occurence,
    (b) occurrence
12. (a) developement,
    (b) development
13. (a) arguement,
    (b) argument
14. (a) assistant,
    (b) asisstant
15. (a) grammer,
    (b) grammar
16. (a) parallel,
    (b) paralell
17. (a) drunkeness,
    (b) drunkenness
18. (a) suddeness,
    (b) suddenness
19. (a) dissipate,
    (b) disippate
20. (a) weird,
    (b) wierd
21. (a) baloon,
    (b) balloon
22. (a) noticeable,
    (b) noticable
23. (a) truely,
    (b) truly
24. (a) vicious,
    (b) viscious
25. (a) insistent,
    (b) insistant

By now you're well on the way to developing a definite superiority complex about your spelling. Remember: you want to spell correctly so that in correspondence you will not give your reader the impression your education has been sadly neglected. The conquest of the 100 words most commonly misspelled is not guaranteed to make you top man in a spelling bee, but it's certain to improve your writing and do a lot to bolster your ego.

So far you have worked with 50 of the 100 spelling demons. The remainder of the list appears below. Test yourself, and discover which words are your Waterloo. Study each one you miss, observe how it's put together, then devise whatever association pattern will fix the correct form in your mind.

Once you've mastered this list, you are a good speller. And — if you've truly applied yourself — your goal has been achieved in 30 minutes or less!

How Good Are You Now?

Here are fifty words which also frequently stump the expert speller. See how quickly you can master them by finding a simple association for each.

misspelling	vacillate	possesses
conscious	oscillate	professor
indispensable	forty	category
disappear	dilettante	rhythmical
disappoint	changeable	vacuum
corroborate	accessible	benefited
sacrilegious	accommodate	committee
persistent	license	grievous
exhilaration	panicky	judgment
newsstand	seize	plebeian
desirable	leisure	tariff
irresistible	receive	sheriff
tranquillity	achieve	connoisseur
dilemma	holiday	necessary
perseverance	existence	sergeant
until	pursue	irrelevant
tyrannize	pastime	

Answers: 1, b; 2, a; 3, a; 4, b; 5, b; 6, b; 7, b; 8, b; 9, a; 10, b; 11, b; 12, b; 13, b; 14, a; 15, b; 16, a; 17, b; 18, b; 19, a; 20, a; 21, b; 22, a; 23, b; 24, a; 25, a.

260

NAME————————————————————————— DATE——————————— READING RATE——————————— W.P.M.

COMPREHENSION CHECK QUESTIONS

1. The author talks about a (1) one-mile run; (2) two-mile run; (3) three-mile run; (4) four-mile run.   1. ————

2. Mention is made of the (1) Boston Marathon; (2) Clam Beach Run; (3) New York Marathon; (4) Olympic Marathon.   2. ————

3. The writer specifically mentions typing (1) "Chapter One"; (2) "The End"; (3) "Synopsis"; (4) "Story Outline."   3. ————

4. The writer's movie screen is located (1) on her desk; (2) inside her forehead; (3) on the ceiling; (4) on the back of her hand.   4. ————

5. Where was the woman in the imagined story? (1) on a raft; (2) on a sandy beach; (3) in a gorge; (4) at the edge of a cliff.   5. ————

Receptive Comprehension ————

6. The purpose of this article is to (1) tell you to start with "the"; (2) explain how to use your movie screen; (3) suggest how to begin writing; (4) show similarities between writing and running.   6. ————

7. Apparently the author is primarily a writer of (1) novels; (2) short stories; (3) magazine articles; (4) newspaper features.   7. ————

8. What was the point of the example of her friend with a contract for a juvenile mystery? The difficulty (1) of outlining; (2) of visualizing; (3) of starting; (4) of getting an acceptance.   8. ————

9. The reference to being surprised at meeting someone you'd heard of was to (1) suggest where to start a story; (2) point up the need to observe; (3) show how ideas grow; (4) prove the existence of a movie screen.   9. ————

10. Chief emphasis is on the (1) what; (2) when; (3) how; (4) why.   10. ————

(10 off for each mistake)

Reflective Comprehension ————

TOTAL READING COMPREHENSION SCORE ————

VOCABULARY CHECK QUESTIONS

		without context I	with context II
1. *sedentary*	(1) local; (2) segmented; (3) hard; (4) isolated; (5) sitting.	1. ————	————
2. *massive*	(1) bulky; (2) towering; (3) compacted; (4) dull; (5) metallic.	2. ————	————
3. *harrowingly*	(1) sharply; (2) distressingly; (3) rather; (4) smoothly; (5) aimlessly.	3. ————	————
4. *excruciatingly*	(1) often; (2) excitingly; (3) excessively; (4) hardly; (5) extremely.	4. ————	————
5. *albeit*	(1) despite; (2) beforehand; (3) in place of; (4) because; (5) although.	5. ————	————

(10 off for each mistake)

Word Comprehension without *contextual help* (I) ————

Word Comprehension with *contextual help* (II) ————

TOTAL WORD COMPREHENSION SCORE ————

EXERCISES

Finding words for what you observe: Observing may be thought of as a third channel of learning, one closely related to the signs and symbols present in our environment. We learn by reading, listening, and looking. If we sharpen our powers of observation and develop the vocabulary to express with sureness what we have observed, we are that much the better equipped to write and speak with effectiveness as well as to read and listen appreciatively.

1. The first suggestion is to *be specific*. Which of the following two sentences is more interesting to you?

> "We know of people being on a structure and observing the presence of vehicles that go over the structure for a space of time."
> "We hear of inquirers standing on London Bridge and counting the number of motor-buses, foot-passengers, lorries, and white horses that pass over the bridge in an hour."

Do you agree that the more specific account is better? If so, use the sharp, clear details, not the blurred generalization. Perhaps you are not interested in dating a "good-looking girl" but if you are told she is an ash blonde, has deep blue eyes, long curly eyelashes, and full, cherry-red lips, you may well change your mind. *Be specific.*

Think of all the synonyms you can, then select the one which makes the sharpest picture. Instead of having someone "move" down the street, think of synonyms of *move*—travel, disappear, walk, stride, trudge, etc. Then select the word which creates a picture.

2. The second suggestion is to record all the specific details possible in any simple scene. Aim at getting down 100 *specific sensory impressions*. The following headings will keep you from overlooking anything:*

SIGHT: *Form or Outline (as towering smokestacks)*:

_____   _____   _____
_____   _____   _____
_____   _____   _____

Motion or Position (as flitting sparrows):

_____   _____   _____
_____   _____   _____
_____   _____   _____

Shade or Color (as glowing red sky):

_____   _____   _____
_____   _____   _____
_____   _____   _____

SOUND (*as screech of car brakes*):

_____   _____   _____
_____   _____   _____
_____   _____   _____

SMELL (as of *hot rubber*):

_____   _____   _____
_____   _____   _____
_____   _____   _____

TOUCH (as of *cooling breeze*):

_____   _____   _____
_____   _____   _____
_____   _____   _____

TASTE (none noted):

_____   _____   _____
_____   _____   _____
_____   _____   _____

3. The last suggestion is to select those details from the large listing which create the dominant impression of the scene on the observer and weave them together into a coherent paragraph which will make the desired impression on the reader.

* This is the form suggested by F. S. Appel in his book, *Write What You Mean.*

NAME——————————————————— DATE—————— READING RATE—————— W.P.M.

COMPREHENSION CHECK QUESTIONS

1. You're told to do what about NCD? (1) use it; (2) avoid it; (3) begin with it; (4) conclude with it.   1. ————

2. You're told to (1) make an outline; (2) read extensively; (3) develop good interviewing techniques; (4) type even your first rough draft.   2. ————

3. There is specific mention of (1) Pascal; (2) Pope; (3) Shakespeare; (4) Virgil.   3. ————

4. The article refers to (1) an Audi; (2) a Cadillac; (3) a Rolls Royce; (4) a Mercedes.   4. ————

5. Specific reference is made to (1) *The Writer's Handbook*; (2) *The Elements of Style*; (3) *On Writing Well*; (4) *Better English*.   5. ————

Receptive Comprehension ————

6. This is primarily to (1) inspire; (2) persuade; (3) explain; (4) describe.   6. ————

7. The analogy to a baseball pitcher warming up was to get writers to (1) open with warm-up material; (2) throw away warm-up material; (3) reduce warm-up time; (4) enliven warm-up material.   7. ————

8. Introductions should be (1) interest-rousing; (2) avoided; (3) suspense-building; (4) humorous.   8. ————

9. Of the following phrasings, which would the author prefer? (1) Be brief; (2) It pays to be brief; (3) Conciseness is preferred; (4) You should never use unnecessary words.   9. ————

10. Most emphasis is placed on (1) getting to the point; (2) organizing well; (3) practice; (4) keeping moving.   10. ————

(10 off for each mistake)   *Reflective Comprehension* ————

TOTAL READING COMPREHENSION SCORE ————

VOCABULARY CHECK QUESTIONS

		without context I	*with context* II
1. *digress*	(1) ramble; (2) summarize; (3) decide; (4) scatter; (5) emphasize.	1. ————	————
2. *exposition*	(1) exposure; (2) exponent; (3) position; (4) description; (5) explanation.	2. ————	————
3. *configuration*	(1) list; (2) number; (3) limit; (4) form; (5) decision.	3. ————	————
4. *succinct*	(1) solid; (2) tight; (3) long; (4) aimless; (5) brief.	4. ————	————
5. *implicit*	(1) rash; (2) favorable; (3) defective; (4) suggested; (5) inserted.	5. ————	————

(10 off for each mistake)   *Word Comprehension* without *contextual help* (I) ————

Word Comprehension with *contextual help* (II) ————

TOTAL WORD COMPREHENSION SCORE ————

EXERCISES

Outlining your thoughts: One of the ten tips in this article reads, "Get your story in order." Of course that probably means making an outline. To prepare yourself for that task, turn to the short selection titled, "Organization — Your Reading Satellite," on page 254. Read it carefully, underlining all words and phrases that suggest the specific plan used. Then reconstruct in the blank outline form below what you think is the outline the writer used for that selection. Work carefully, for you want to learn as much as possible about outline form and procedure. Look back as often as you wish to the selection. When you have finished, compare your outline with the exact outline used by the writer of that selection. The original outline is on page 270.

OUTLINE FOR "ORGANIZATION — YOUR READING SATELLITE"

I. _____

II. _____

III. _____

    A. _____

        1. _____

            a. _____

            b. _____

            c. _____

        2. _____

            a. _____

            b. _____

            c. _____

        3. _____

            a. _____

            b. _____

            c. _____

    B. _____

        1. _____

        2. _____

IV. _____

    A. _____

        1. _____

        2. _____

    B. _____

        1. _____

        2. _____

V. _____

NAME_____ DATE_____ READING RATE_____W.P.M.

COMPREHENSION CHECK QUESTIONS

1. Of what the public reads and hears, what per cent is woefully repetitious? (1) ninety; (2) eighty; (3) seventy; (4) sixty.   1. _____

2. Who coined the man-bites-dog phrase? (1) Bogart; (2) Swift; (3) Wilde; (4) Butler.   2. _____

3. Proverbs and clichés were said to be (1) synonymous; (2) different; (3) have the same origin; (4) have the same appeal.   3. _____

4. What place was wonderful to visit but not to live in? (1) Athens; (2) Rome; (3) London; (4) Paris.   4. _____

5. Which one of the following individuals was *not* specifically mentioned? (1) Clifton Fadiman; (2) Edward VIII; (3) Samuel Butler; (4) John Milton.   5. _____

Receptive Comprehension _____

6. This article is mainly (1) a discussion of kinds of clichés; (2) a caution against using clichés; (3) a warning against insincerity; (4) a brief history of clichés.   6. _____

7. The title implies that clichés are (1) sometimes all right; (2) quick to become established; (3) a mess; (4) all of a kind.   7. _____

8. Clichés are useful to politicians primarily because (1)) they permit them to avoid meaning; (2) they identify one who can get down to brass tacks; (3) they put an audience to sleep; (4) they are so acceptable.   8. _____

9. The example, "None but the brave desert the fair," was to show (1) how familiarity adds interest; (2) how vividly clichés can communicate; (3) how clichés can become witticisms; (4) how to eliminate the commonplace.   9. _____

10. You would infer that a cliché is a cliché primarily because (1) it has been repeated so often; (2) it is so well established; (3) it is a certain age; (4) it lacks meaning.   10. _____

(10 off for each mistake)   *Reflective Comprehension* _____

TOTAL READING COMPREHENSION SCORE _____

VOCABULARY CHECK QUESTIONS

		without context I	*with context* II
1. *sententious*	(1) involved; (2) lengthy; (3) emotional; (4) thoughtful; (5) terse.	1. _____	_____
2. *jaded*	(1) polished; (2) colored; (3) dulled; (4) filled; (5) earnest.	2. _____	_____
3. *triteness*	(1) commonness; (2) pettiness; (3) trust; (4) vividness; (5) suspicion.	3. _____	_____
4. *felicitous*	(1) hearty; (2) well-chosen; (3) ordinary; (4) well-filled; (5) villainous.	4. _____	_____
5. *trope*	(1) turn of phrase; (2) triviality; (3) award; (4) measuring device; (5) lozenge.	5. _____	_____

(10 off for each mistake)

Word Comprehension without *contextual help* (I) _____

Word Comprehension with *contextual help* (II) _____

TOTAL WORD COMPREHENSION SCORE _____

EXERCISES

Spelling: Are common spelling errors putting you at a continual disadvantage? The following words taken from an exhaustive study by Pollock ("Spelling Report," *College English,* November, 1954) should provide an excellent check of your spelling ability. With the help of 599 college teachers of English in fifty-two colleges and universities, 31,375 misspellings were tabulated. The following words and word groups are those misspelled 100 or more times.

Get someone to dictate the following words and sentences to you as you try your hand at spelling these troublemakers. If you miss ten or more, you have reason to turn to the spelling section of your handbook or to the Pollock study for additional help. If you miss twenty or more, you will probably want the more detailed guidance of a book on improving your spelling.

receive	believe	referring
receiving	belief	
		success
exist	occasion	succeed
existence		succession
existent	lose	
	losing	privilege
occur		
occurred	write	environment
occurring	writing	
occurrence	writer	perform
		performance
definite	description	
definitely	describe	similar
definition		
define	benefit	professor
	benefited	profession
separate	beneficial	
separation		necessary
	precede	unnecessary

Those *two* were *too* tired *to* go along *too.*
They're getting *their* books to put *there.*
It's wagging *its* tail.
The problem of staff *personnel* is a very *personal* problem.
Then I walked farther *than* he did.
The school *principal* gave the *principal* speech on the subject, *Principles* of Education.
My *choice* is to *choose* the same thing that I *chose* before.

Improving your spelling: Make your own personal list of spelling troublemakers. Start with the words from the Pollock listing but keep adding to it as your papers are marked and as you continue to deal with new words. Review the list periodically.

Words I Misspell

_____ _____ _____ _____
_____ _____ _____ _____
_____ _____ _____ _____
_____ _____ _____ _____
_____ _____ _____ _____
_____ _____ _____ _____
_____ _____ _____ _____
_____ _____ _____ _____
_____ _____ _____ _____
_____ _____ _____ _____

NAME———————————————————— DATE———————— READING RATE———————— W.P.M.

COMPREHENSION CHECK QUESTIONS

1. The purpose of a résumé was said to be to get you (1) properly organized; (2) ready to compete effectively; (3) a job; (4) job interviews.   1. ————

2. You're told to (1) be a bit vague about what job you want; (2) summarize your job-related abilities; (3) use a specific job title; (4) stress willingness to learn.   2. ————

3. Be sure to (1) say references will be provided upon request; (2) list at least five references; (3) make no mention of references; (4) list both character and work references.   3. ————

4. Your work experience is spoken of as what part of your résumé? (1) core; (2) climax; (3) central part; (4) heart.   4. ————

5. One employment manager says he rejects what percentage of the résumés purely because of appearance? (1) 10%; (2) 15%; (3) 20%; (4) 25%.   5. ————

Receptive Comprehension ————

6. This article is mainly about what aspect of a résumé? (1) how you should write it; (2) what help you can get from books and professional writers; (3) why you should prepare it; (4) what you should do with it when it's completed.   6. ————

7. Most emphasis should be on (1) neatness; (2) your education; (3) what you've done; (4) your attitude.   7. ————

8. The points are developed primarily by (1) citing authorities; (2) repetition; (3) use of analogies; (4) use of details.   8. ————

9. You would infer that the résumé format (1) varies widely; (2) is firmly fixed; (3) still leaves room for originality; (4) is dictated by job requirements.   9. ————

10. You would call this style (1) involved; (2) dramatic; (3) informal; (4) lively.   10. ————

(10 off for each mistake)   *Reflective Comprehension* ————

TOTAL READING COMPREHENSION SCORE ————

VOCABULARY CHECK QUESTIONS

		without context I	*with context* II
1. *innovations*	(1) starts; (2) remarks; (3) notions; (4) novelties; (5) rules.	1. ————	————
2. *format*	(1) custom; (2) strength; (3) makeup; (4) formula; (5) content.	2. ————	————
3. *affiliations*	(1) profiles; (2) problems; (3) feelings; (4) connections; (5) orders.	3. ————	————
4. *curtailed*	(1) lengthened; (2) raised; (3) rounded; (4) cleaned; (5) shortened.	4. ————	————
5. *stilted*	(1) original; (2) stiffly formal; (3) stuffed; (4) highly dramatic; (5) suppressed.	5. ————	————

(10 off for each mistake)

Word Comprehension without *contextual help* (I) ————

Word Comprehension with *contextual help* (II) ————

TOTAL WORD COMPREHENSION SCORE ————

EXERCISES

1. *Translating from I-centered to you-centered English:* For both résumés and letters of application you need a strong you-centered approach. Look at the following actual letter of application received by Miller Cafeteria — one of the worst in their files. You can perhaps learn more from examining it critically than from examining one of the better examples.

Read it over. Then circle all the first person pronouns. Next, try to rewrite the letter so as to establish a strong you-centered point of view. That means eliminating as many of the first person references as possible or at least balancing any remaining *I*'s with *you*'s. Notice what a difference this makes.

Miller Cafeteria
Minneapolis, Minnesota

Dear Sir:

I am asking for a job that would give me experience in my field of Institutional Management. I could get the best experience possible in your cafeteria, due to its size and excellent management. Are there any vacancies for me at this time?

A position where I could start at the bottom and work up would be the most satisfactory to me. I would like all the opportunities available. My health is excellent, and I am single; therefore I could devote much of my time to the work given me.

May I come to your office next Tuesday morning at nine o'clock for an interview? If I have no reply, I shall come to your office at that time. Thanking you in advance, I am

Yours very truly,

_____

_____

_____

_____

_____

_____

_____

_____

_____

_____

_____

_____

_____

_____

_____

2. *Translating from technical to conversational English:* As is said in discussing résumés, "Use correct, straightforward English — active verbs, short and simple words." Practice the use of such language by translating difficult material into standard English. Psychologists emphasize that rephrasing the words of a textbook or lecture into your own nontechnical language is an excellent way to aid learning. Try it as part of your regular study routine.

In the space below, enter a difficult yet fairly short passage from one of your textbooks. Then, immediately after, translate the passage into simple English:

Text version:

Your version:

NAME_____ DATE_____ READING RATE_____ W.P.M.

COMPREHENSION CHECK QUESTIONS

1. Which book did Franklin have? (1) *Robinson Crusoe;* (2) *Gulliver's Travels;* (3) *Pilgrim's Progress;* (4) *Swiss Family Robinson.*   1. _____

2. His father's library contained mostly (1) religious books; (2) literary works; (3) novels; (4) practical volumes.   2. _____

3. Who was said to have discouraged Franklin from his verse-making? (1) his brother; (2) his friend; (3) his readers; (4) his father.   3. _____

4. Franklin attempted to imitate the prose found in (1) Plutarch's *Lives;* (2) Defoe's *Essays;* (3) Stevenson's *Essays;* (4) the *Spectator.*   4. _____

5. In comparing his version with the original, Franklin said he discovered (1) punctuation difficulties; (2) a vocabulary deficiency; (3) spelling problems; (4) sentence problems.   5. _____

Receptive Comprehension _____

6. This selection is chiefly to (1) explain his love of books; (2) tell why he decided to write prose, not poetry; (3) explain why he wanted to learn to write; (4) tell about the procedure he adapted to improve his writing.   6. _____

7. You would conclude that the chief reason for Franklin's turning away from writing poetry was (1) its difficulty; (2) its poor reception; (3) its poor financial return; (4) its lack of prestige.   7. _____

8. As a self-critic, Franklin was apparently (1) fairly accurate; (2) overly critical; (3) fairly generous; (4) quite unrealistic.   8. _____

9. The part about John Collins, another bookish boy, was mainly to indicate (1) how Franklin got interested in writing; (2) why one should avoid argumentation; (3) the value of arguing; (4) the influence of reading certain books.   9. _____

10. The primary purpose of the article was to (1) teach; (2) describe; (3) moralize; (4) evaluate.   10. _____

(10 off for each mistake)   *Reflective Comprehension* _____

TOTAL READING COMPREHENSION SCORE _____

VOCABULARY CHECK QUESTIONS

		without context I	*with context* II
1. *ingenious*	(1) naive; (2) frank; (3) mechanical; (4) trusting; (5) clever.	1. _____	
2. *confuting*	(1) predicting; (2) storing; (3) denying; (4) joining; (5) confounding.	2. _____	_____
3. *disputatious*	(1) argumentative; (2) displeasing; (3) productive; (4) stingy; (4) concerned.	3. _____	_____
4. *enmities*	(1) preliminaries; (2) foes; (3) laxatives; (4) antagonisms; (5) encouragements.	4. _____	_____
5. *amended*	(1) complained; (2) changed; (3) corrected; (4) added; (5) suggested.	5. _____	_____

(10 off for each mistake)   *Word Comprehension* without *contextual help* (I) _____

Word Comprehension with *contextual help*   (II) _____

TOTAL WORD COMPREHENSION SCORE _____

EXERCISES

1. Select from the following subjects five on which you have a strong opinion. Then write a sentence about each in which you express that opinion, either positively or negatively. (EXAMPLE: All people who use hard drugs should be imprisoned for a minimum of five years.)

   A. Drugs
   B. Welfare programs
   C. Pornography
   D. Mercy killing
   E. Sex education in the public schools
   F. Smoking
   G. Violence on television
   H. Freeways
   I. Abortion
   J. Homosexuality

   Now write a paragraph on each of the five subjects you chose in which you defend the *opposite* opinion from the one expressed in your sentence. Try to clear your mind of all prejudices and to present the case as convincingly and as objectively as you can.

2. Consider the effectiveness of the prose in the following brief passage from Frederick Jackson Turner's *The Frontier in American History*:

   > American democracy was born of no theorist's dream. It was not carried in the *Susan Constant* to Virginia, nor in the *Mayflower* to Plymouth. It came stark and strong and full of life out of the American forest, and it gained new strength each time it touched a new frontier.

   Now jot down in as few words as possible the basic idea in each sentence. (EXAMPLE: Democracy not of theoretical origin.) Put your notes aside for a few days. When you return to them, try writing the passage in complete sentences without looking at the original. Compare your version to Turner's. In what ways is your version weaker than, or superior to, his?

   Do the same thing with any other piece of writing you admire.

AUTHOR'S ORIGINAL OUTLINE FOR
"ORGANIZATION — YOUR READING SATELLITE"

I. The role of organization
II. Reading is the reverse of writing
III. How is organization revealed?
   A. Through special devices
      1. Typographical devices
         a. Capitals
         b. Bold-face type
         c. Italics
      2. Rhetorical devices
         a. Repetition
         b. Parallelism
         c. Balance
      3. Verbal devices
         a. To mark transitions
         b. To mark methods of development
         c. To mark outline form
   B. Through paragraph structure
      1. Topic sentences
      2. Supporting details
IV. What does organization contribute?
   A. Sharpened awareness
      1. Of main idea or thesis
      2. Of interrelationships
   B. Improved ability
      1. To understand
      2. To remember
V. Summary of purpose or role of organization

(Compare with your own version on page 264.)

NAME———————————————— DATE——————— READING RATE————— W.P.M.

COMPREHENSION CHECK QUESTIONS

1. Specific mention is made of (1) James Michener; (2) Kurt Vonnegut; (3) Saul Bellow; (4) William Styron.   1. ———

2. *The Complete Plain Words* was written by (1) Robert Louis Stevenson; (2) Sir Ernest Gowers; (3) Samuel Johnson; (4) Thomas Hardy.   2. ———

3. The word "involve" is called what kind of word? (1) careful; (2) superfluous; (3) thought; (4) multipurpose.   3. ———

4. What leader was said to have the common touch with language? (1) John Kennedy; (2) Winston Churchill; (3) Franklin D. Roosevelt; (4) Charles de Gaulle.   4. ———

5. Fowler set how many criteria for good writing? (1) five; (2) four; (3) three; (4) two.   5. ———

Receptive Comprehension ———

6. This article is mainly about how to (1) write what you mean; (2) write literature; (3) improve your writing style; (4) find the right words and use them well.   6. ———

7. Most emphasis is placed on (1) personal writing; (2) literary writing; (3) letter writing; (4) business writing.   7. ———

8. The advice given most emphasis is (1) be brief; (2) be specific; (3) be thoughtful; (4) be simple.   8. ———

9. The first section focuses chiefly on what aspect of writing? (1) the need; (2) the purpose; (3) the problems; (4) the solutions.   9. ———

10. You would infer that the best way to improve your writing would be to (1) study Fowler; (2) work at it; (3) think about it; (4) increase your vocabulary.   10. ———

(*10 off for each mistake*)   *Reflective Comprehension* ———

TOTAL READING COMPREHENSION SCORE ———

VOCABULARY CHECK QUESTIONS

		without context I	*with context* II
1. *reclusive*	(1) resting; (2) tired; (3) solitary; (4) agreeable; (5) recollecting.	1. ———	———
2. *havoc*	(1) destruction; (2) health; (3) war; (4) haste; (5) help.	2. ———	———
3. *nebulous*	(1) dark; (2) white; (3) large; (4) vague; (5) narrow.	3. ———	———
4. *lucid*	(1) lucky; (2) talkative; (3) profitable; (4) pertinent; (5) clear.	4. ———	———
5. *emulate*	(1) feel; (2) get rid of; (3) cover; (4) imitate; (5) conclude.	5. ———	———

(*10 off for each mistake*)   *Word Comprehension* without *contextual help* (I) ———

Word Comprehension with *contextual help* (II) ———

TOTAL WORD COMPREHENSION SCORE ———

EXERCISES

Sentence variety: The following sentences all follow a deadly, unvaried subject-verb pattern. By rearranging the various words in each sentence and making a few slight changes in wording, revise the following passage to get desirable variety of sentence pattern and form. Compare with the original when you finish.

Most educated people are, from time to time, called upon to act as writers. They might not think of themselves as such. They dash off a personal note. They dictate a memo. They are writers. They are practicing a difficult and demanding craft. They are facing its inborn challenge: to find the right words and put them in the right order. The thoughts they represent can then be understood.

Connecting ideas: No writer wants his reader to slip out of his article between sentences or paragraphs. Sentences must be closely connected so that the reader will pass easily from one to the next without losing continuity.

The skillful writer or speaker will see to it that at least one word in each sentence connects back to the preceding sentence or points ahead to the next one. Four common categories of words are used for this purpose:

1. Words and phrases such as *and, in contrast, but,* and *however,* which help the reader follow the thought easily.
2. Pronouns that refer back to a word in the preceding sentence.
3. Repetition of words or ideas.
4. Parallel structure — to connect sentences and ideas.

In the following paragraph, circle all words and phrases that serve a connective function. Classify each according to the four categories indicated above:

Paragraph	*Classification*
In the working world, bad writing is not only bad manners, it is bad business. The victim of an incomprehensible letter will at best be annoyed and at worst decide that people who can't say what they mean aren't worth doing business with. Write a sloppy letter, and it might rebound on you when the recipient calls for clarification. Where one carefully worded letter would have sufficed, you might have to write two or more.	

NAME——————————————————— DATE——————— READING RATE———— W.P.M.

COMPREHENSION CHECK QUESTIONS

1. The author attended what college? (1) Vassar; (2) Tarkio College; (3) Pomona College; (4) Park College.   1. ————

2. George is a (1) biologist; (2) chemist; (3) psychologist; (4) geneticist.   2. ————

3. One of George's illustrations was about (1) an angel food cake; (2) a magnet; (3) baking bread; (4) hybrid seed corn.   3. ————

4. Who was said to share the platform with George on occasion? (1) his wife; (2) their Siamese cats; (3) their dachshund; (4) his publisher.   4. ————

5. In writing the book, the author got some material from the (1) *World Encyclopedia;* (2) *Encyclopedia Britannica;* (3) *Syntopticon;* (4) *The Intelligent Man's Guide to Science.*   5. ————

Receptive Comprehension ————

6. This article was written essentially to (1) point up the need for popularizing science; (2) provide help in selecting an appropriate vocabulary; (3) describe the couple's stylistic differences; (4) suggest basic principles of effective writing.   6. ————

7. George's wife was most interested in making their book (1) popular; (2) accurate; (3) readable; (4) original.   7. ————

8. The reference to her advertising experience was intended primarily to explain (1) her background; (2) her interest in science; (3) her marriage; (4) her interest in practical matters.   8. ————

9. In this collaboration, apparently (1) each had an equal voice; (2) George supplied all content, his wife the form; (3) both content and form were matters of joint concern; (4) George probably had the final say about both content and form.   9. ————

10. You would infer that the finished book would have (1) rather long paragraphs; (2) no jokes; (3) a topic sentence to start each paragraph; (4) fairly short paragraphs.   10. ————

(10 off for each mistake)   *Reflective Comprehension* ————

TOTAL READING COMPREHENSION SCORE ————

VOCABULARY CHECK QUESTIONS

		without *context* I	*with* *context* II
1. *desiccated*	(1) dried out; (2) worn; (3) reckless; (4) removed; (5) torn up.	1. ————	————
2. *credo*	(1) small opening; (2) necktie; (3) depression; (4) statement of belief; (5) plume.	2. ————	————
3. *mutation*	(1) cut off; (2) pirate; (3) dumbness; (4) change; (5) principle.	3. ————	————
4. *opted*	(1) decided; (2) opened; (3) optical check; (4) lined up; (5) acted.	4. ————	————
5. *lucid*	(1) clear; (2) beautiful; (3) layoff; (4) level; (5) observant.	5. ————	————

(10 off for each mistake)   *Word Comprehension* without *contextual help* (I) ————

Word Comprehension with *contextual help* (II) ————

TOTAL WORD COMPREHENSION SCORE ————

EXERCISES

Managing degrees of informality: One important difference between formal and informal writing is the personal element. Term papers and reports are generally written in an impersonal style without any personal pronouns. Popular articles, on the other hand, are done in a personal style, since reader interest is an important consideration. For example, in formal writing, "experiments are performed," "the mixture is weighed," and "students are directed." In informal writing, "He performed the experiment," "I weighed the mixture," and "She directed the students."

A student should develop skill in expressing himself either formally or informally, using an impersonal or personal style when the situation demands. Translate the following passages into informal English by making them more personal. Use the first-person point of view. When you have finished each translation, check the original passage and compare the two versions.

Once upon a time a long time ago, satisfying the full science requirement at Pomona College was managed by taking a lecture course in chemistry. An A was received on the term paper, which had to do with the use of sulfur dioxide in preserving fruit. Thirty years later, the paper was rediscovered — in a beat-up carton that also contained a desiccated corsage — and it was given to my husband to read.

Scientific research, it was discovered, is a highly creative process. At its best, it proceeds via great leaps of imagination into the unknown; and the elegance and sophistication of the thinking behind such leaps was exciting. An attempt was made, therefore, to write excessively detailed accounts of research methods. For example, when the point about writing about discoveries that had been made possible by invention of the electron microscope was made, it was realized that to understand this instrument something should be known about the physical nature of light. Some independent research was undertaken on the subject. The result was three pages in which were summarized all of twentieth-century physics.

NAME_____ DATE_____ READING RATE_____ W.P.M.

COMPREHENSION CHECK QUESTIONS

1. Carnegie says that he learned his secret of easy public speaking (1) from a book; (2) in college; (3) in a public speaking course; (4) from experience.

   1. _____

2. Gay Kellogg was from (1) New Jersey; (2) New York; (3) New Concord; (4) New Haven.

   2. _____

3. The article contains (1) three rules; (2) five rules; (3) seven rules; (4) ten rules.

   3. _____

4. The late Ida Tarbell was spoken of as a distinguished (1) novelist; (2) biographer; (3) journalist; (4) lecturer.

   4. _____

5. The struggling young composer whom Gershwin met was working for (1) $35 a week; (2) $45 a week; (3) $55 a week; (4) $65 a week.

   5. _____

Receptive Comprehension _____

6. The purpose of this article is to (1) make us more effective speakers; (2) suggest how to organize and deliver an effective speech; (3) reveal the secret of effective public speaking; (4) explain where to find appropriate speech subjects.

   6. _____

7. The story about Ida Tarbell was used to illustrate the importance of (1) using illustrations; (2) rehearsing a speech; (3) knowing more about a subject than you need; (4) being yourself instead of imitating someone else.

   7. _____

8. The story about Gay Kellogg was used to illustrate the importance of (1) writing out the speech; (2) speaking from experience; (3) being yourself; (4) using illustrations.

   8. _____

9. The author implies that the difference between written and spoken English is (1) negligible; (2) important; (3) largely in subject matter; (4) largely in slanting for a specific audience.

   9. _____

10. The article suggests that if you are frightened when you make a speech (1) you are naturally shy; (2) you have not had enough speaking experience; (3) you have not prepared carefully enough; (4) you have not chosen a subject of real interest to yourself.

    10. _____

(10 off for each mistake)   *Reflective Comprehension* _____

TOTAL READING COMPREHENSION SCORE _____

VOCABULARY CHECK QUESTIONS

		without context I	*with context* II
1. *craved*	(1) wished; (2) unbalanced; (3) moved slowly; (4) desired intensely; (5) drugged.	1. _____	_____
2. *taut*	(1) tense; (2) ridiculed; (3) awkward; (4) very tall; (5) active.	2. _____	_____
3. *elicited*	(1) explained; (2) escaped; (3) eliminated; (4) hurried; (5) drew forth.	3. _____	_____
4. *irresistibly*	(1) regularly; (2) not compatible; (3) compellingly; (4) irrelevantly; (5) indecisively.	4. _____	_____
5. *sage*	(1) useful; (2) wise; (3) tangy; (4) bitter; (5) crafty.	5. _____	_____

(10 off for each mistake)   *Word Comprehension* without *contextual help* (I) _____

Word Comprehension with *contextual help* (II) _____

TOTAL WORD COMPREHENSION SCORE _____

EXERCISES

Remembering what you read: In this selection you are given seven rules to help in preparing a speech. What are they? How many can you remember without looking back at the selection? List all you can think of in the spaces below.

1.

2.

3.

4.

5.

6.

7.

Unless you are one in a million you did not list all seven with perfect accuracy. As a reader, what can you do to remember what you read more effectively? For one thing you can devise a learning or remembering aid.

For example, when daylight saving time starts in the spring, which way do you set your watch — ahead or back? Most people start a long process of reasoning that will eventually provide an answer. Others will use a mnemonic device or memory aid. Just think — *spring ahead, fall back* — and you will have little more trouble with remembering.

Can you name the five Great Lakes? If you have trouble thinking of them, try still another type of mnemonic device. Just think of the word *HOMES*. It will help you remember Huron, Ontario, Michigan, Erie, and Superior.

Take still another type of mnemonic device, one used often by doctors and medical students. How do they remember the twelve cranial nerves? They have a sentence that helps. The key is the first letter in each word. Here is the sentence: *On old Olympus' towering top, a fat-assed German viewed a hop.* How else does one remember *olfactory, optic, oculomotor, trochlear, trigeminal, abducens, facial, acoustic, glossopharyngeal, vagus, accessory, hypoglossal!*

Now, going back to the seven rules, try to work out some mnemonic device. Can you select a single letter to remind you of each — ones that would make one seven-letter word or two shorter words?

Write the word or words here and explain:

If that doesn't work out easily, try a seven-word sentence — each word to help you recall one of the seven points or rules. Write the sentence here:

Actually your efforts to manufacture a mnemonic device will do wonders in helping you remember, whether you come up with a device or not. Compare notes with other students to see what others devised.

Substituting narration for exposition: You may explain something by relying almost entirely on rather pure expository techniques, or you may lean very heavily on narration to make your explanation both interesting and clear.

Take some of the following topic ideas and explain them orally or in writing by using a narrative form:

A. Use illustrations to make your ideas interesting and clear.
B. Narration and exposition are different in several important respects.
C. Efficient reading is extremely important for the student (or businessman, or professional man).
D. Your voice is your fortune.
E. Background is important.

NAME——————————————————— DATE——————— READING RATE——————— W.P.M.

COMPREHENSION CHECK QUESTIONS

1. At first Twain used (1) 3 x 5 cards; (2) a full page of notes; (3) typed abbreviations; (4) calling-card-size notes.   1. ———

2. For a typical evening's lecture, Twain would memorize how many key sentence beginnings? (1) eleven; (2) eight; (3) five; (4) three.   2. ———

3. The article mentions (1) Reno; (2) Salt Lake; (3) Santa Fe; (4) Carson City.   3. ———

4. The nervous doctor lived in (1) Dubuque; (2) San Francisco (3) Des Moines; (4) Moline.   4. ———

5. You're told to include figures in the pictures (1) as captions; (2) coming out of people's mouths; (3) resting on a person's hand; (4) alongside the picture.   5. ———

Receptive Comprehension ———

6. This article is mainly about (1) making an outline; (2) identifying the central points; (3) speaking naturally; (4) keeping sequence in mind.   6. ———

7. It is primarily (1) narration; (2) exposition; (3) description; (4) persuasion.   7. ———

8. The organization is essentially (1) cause-effect; (2) problem-solution; (3) simple-to-complex; (4) by analysis.   8. ———

9. What is the tone of this essay? (1) enthusiastic; (2) realistic; (3) critical; (4) serious.   9. ———

10. The purpose of the opening bit about "strategy" is chiefly to (1) pose the problem; (2) provide humor; (3) introduce the subject; (4) arouse interest.   10. ———

(10 off for each mistake)   *Reflective Comprehension* ———

TOTAL READING COMPREHENSION SCORE ———

VOCABULARY CHECK QUESTIONS

		without context I	*with context* II
1. *dilemma*	(1) ruin; (2) limit; (3) decision; (4) predicament; (5) choice.	1. ———	———
2. *spontaneous*	(1) self-acting; (2) sponsored; (3) planned; (4) showy; (5) stimulating.	2. ———	———
3. *alleged*	(1) calmed; (2) walked; (3) supported; (4) declared; (5) reduced.	3. ———	———
4. *pathetic*	(1) pitiful; (2) paternal; (3) diseased; (4) sudden; (5) pastoral.	4. ———	———
5. *lurking*	(1) startling; (2) harmful; (3) lying in wait; (4) glaring sternly; (5) luring.	5. ———	———

(10 off for each mistake)   *Word Comprehension* without *contextual help* (I) ———

Word Comprehension with *contextual help*   (II) ———

TOTAL WORD COMPREHENSION SCORE ———

EXERCISES

1. *Substituting narration for persuasion or exposition:* Macaulay called narration "the mighty engine of argument." The next time you are to explain something or persuade someone of something, try using an anecdote or story to make your point.

   It is possible, for example, to explain that Coleridge was famous as a talker by mentioning that his London landlord offered him free quarters if he would stay on and talk, or by mentioning details of his success as a lecturer. The same point could also be made by a story. Coleridge once found Lamb hastening along a busy street and, drawing him into a doorway by a button, closed his eyes as was his habit, and started talking. Lamb, who was in a great hurry, cut off the button and left him. Hours later, so the story goes, Lamb found him in the same spot, holding the button and talking. True or not, the story serves well to remind us that Coleridge was a talker.

   Taking any of the following ideas (or others that may be suggested), make a point through use of a story you know or invent for the purpose:

Vocabulary brings success.	Your voice is your fortune.
Haste makes waste.	Knowledge is power.
Practice makes perfect.	Reading pays off.

2. *Preparing a story speech:* Using the suggestions in this selection as a basis of criticism, prepare a speech to fit the following situation. Find a story that would be appropriate whenever you happen to be called upon unexpectedly to "say a few words." Be prepared to tell it before the class at any time for their critical evaluation. Be sure to provide a transition from situation to story and another transition that will get you gracefully back into your seat. Here is a sample. Find or make up another to serve the same purpose.

   Friends, the last time anyone called upon me to make a speech, a man stopped afterward, gravely shook hands, then said, "Whoever told you you could speak?"

   I replied a bit sharply, "I'll have you know I've spent $8000 in speech lessons."
   He thought for a minute, then said, "I'd like you to meet my brother."
   "Why? Is he a speech teacher?"
   "No. He's a lawyer. He'll get your money back for you."
   I think you can see now why I make no more speeches.

   That gets you gracefully back to your seat, no matter what the situation — and makes you appear well in command of yourself. Now find another.

3. Go to the library to find a book of stories or anecdotes. List the titles of two such books below.

   1. _____

   2. _____

4. Review the book for the class, telling the funniest story you found. Notice how the stories are grouped and what aids are provided for finding an appropriate one for a given situation.

NAME_____ DATE_____ READING RATE_____W.P.M.

COMPREHENSION CHECK QUESTIONS

1. Laughton mentions reading Shakespeare's (1) *Merchant of Venice;* (2) *Comedy of Errors;* (3) *King Lear;* (4) *Twelfth Night.*   1. _____

2. He suggests (1) imitating different voices; (2) getting a group together to read plays; (3) reading *War and Peace;* (4) reading to children first.   2. _____

3. Laughton's list of favorites for reading aloud includes (1) Henry James; (2) Dickens; (3) Milton; (4) Hemingway.   3. _____

4. Laughton began reading to people (1) during the war; (2) when just a youngster; (3) while in college; (4) just before his first Hollywood movie.   4. _____

5. As a proper length for a reading period he suggests (1) 60 minutes; (2) 45 minutes; (3) 30 minutes; (4) 15 minutes.   5. _____

Receptive Comprehension _____

6. The principal purpose of this selection is to (1) suggest what we should read aloud; (2) tell us how to read aloud; (3) get us to read aloud; (4) suggest when we should read aloud.   6. _____

7. The opening anecdote about the college instructor and Shakespeare was used to show how reading aloud (1) requires careful editing; (2) brings enjoyment; (3) draws people closer together; (4) leads to rewarding talk.   7. _____

8. The writer places strongest emphasis on the need to (1) stick to it; (2) concentrate; (3) practice; (4) memorize short passages.   8. _____

9. Reference to the two young people reading *War and Peace* was used to illustrate (1) the need to discuss things read aloud; (2) the real way to enjoy reading aloud; (3) the importance of taking turns; (4) how reading aloud develops appreciation.   9. _____

10. You would infer that the writer would probably prefer (1) watching football; (2) seeing a movie; (3) listening to the radio; (4) playing games.   10. _____

(10 off for each mistake)   *Reflective Comprehension* _____

TOTAL READING COMPREHENSION SCORE _____

VOCABULARY CHECK QUESTIONS

		without context I	*with context* II
1. *confronted*	(1) denied; (2) judged; (3) appeared; (4) worked; (5) faced.	1. _____	_____
2. *solace*	(1) solitude; (2) solution; (3) encouragement; (4) sleep; (5) comfort.	2. _____	_____
3. *declaim*	(1) affirm; (2) detain; (3) resist; (4) claim after once repudiating the claim; (5) speak in rhetorical manner.	3. _____	_____
4. *savor*	(1) sorrow; (2) help; (3) appearance; (4) taste; (5) reason.	4. _____	_____
5. *elocution*	(1) omitting; (2) method of bringing about death; (3) art of oratorical speech; (4) lengthening; (5) art of effective instruction.	5. _____	_____

(10 off for each mistake)   *Word Comprehension* without *contextual help* (I) _____

Word Comprehension with *contextual help* (II) _____

TOTAL WORD COMPREHENSION SCORE _____

EXERCISES

1. Making subject and verb agree: Make necessary corrections in the following sentences to make subject and verb agree. Some sentences may be correct as they stand. Check any differences between your revision and the original with your handbook.

A. My first audiences was in Army hospitals.

_____

B. I am delighted to tell you that there is no hard and fast rules.

_____

C. Near the top of my own list of favorites is the Bible, Shakespeare, Charles Dickens, the Fables of Aesop, and the witty works of James Thurber.

_____

_____

D. Henry James and his rarefied vocabulary gets a wide berth from me.

_____

E. Mr. Dostoevski and I do poorly together, regardless of what his countless admirers says.

_____

_____

F. You know best how many evenings a week is free for reading.

_____

G. Old hands at this frequently find whole passages sticking in their memories.

_____

2. Bring to class a selection of particular interest to you for reading aloud.

3. Pocket book editions of plays are inexpensive enough to make them ideal for group reading. Together with other class members, prepare a portion of some play for reading to the class.

4. Checking mechanics: Make any necessary changes in the following passage—changes in punctuation, grammar, or spelling. Give yourself five points for each correction made.

But these is only my own preferances, the nice thing is, that you are bound by none of them.

If Milton defeats me. For you his words may turn handsprings. Time and again; when I have finished reading, to Groups in private homes; some one would fetch a book, and say. "do you know this?, and than read; far more beautifully than I could, a passage that has special meaning for him.

NAME——————————————— DATE——————— READING RATE——————— W.P.M.

COMPREHENSION CHECK QUESTIONS

1. There is specific mention of (1) trick questions; (2) crisis questions; (3) a red flag; (4) shoot-from-the-hip answers.   1. ————

2. The man applying for the comptroller job said his greatest weakness was (1) lack of strong interest; (2) dislike of computers; (3) hatred of detail; (4) lack of educational training.   2. ————

3. The author once recommended someone (1) confined to a wheelchair; (2) with a wooden leg; (3) with one arm; (4) who stuttered.   3. ————

4. The article discusses (1) pensions; (2) fringe benefits; (3) moving expenses; (4) health plans.   4. ————

5. One of the questions focused on (1) voice; (2) weight; (3) smoking; (4) age.   5. ————

Receptive Comprehension ————

6. The main focus is on (1) preparation; (2) company background; (3) personality; (4) relaxation.   6. ————

7. For this advice, the author relies chiefly on (1) his own personal experience; (2) business clients; (3) candidate feedback; (4) all the preceding about equally.   7. ————

8. The author's approach is best described as (1) positive; (2) objective; (3) casual; (4) vague.   8. ————

9. The coverage is (1) general; (2) abstract; (3) comprehensive; (4) limited.   9. ————

10. The primary intent is to (1) warn; (2) convince; (3) inform; (4) illustrate.   10. ————

(10 off for each mistake)   *Reflective Comprehension* ————

TOTAL READING COMPREHENSION SCORE ————

VOCABULARY CHECK QUESTIONS

		without context I	with context II
1. *empathy*	(1) superiority in rank; (2) lack; (3) force; (4) sharing of feelings; (5) gain.	1. ————	————
2. *candor*	(1) sweetness; (2) frankness; (3) thrift; (4) song; (5) container.	2. ————	————
3. *trepidation*	(1) tribute; (2) transom; (3) weakness; (4) concern; (5) fright.	3. ————	————
4. *dissertation*	(1) lengthy discourse; (2) distribution; (3) agreement; (4) change; (5) distraction.	4. ————	————
5. *pending*	(1) referring; (2) taking part in; (3) awaiting; (4) writing; (5) dividing into parts.	5. ————	————

(10 off for each mistake)   *Word Comprehension* without *contextual help* (I) ————

Word Comprehension with *contextual help*   (II) ————

TOTAL WORD COMPREHENSION SCORE ————

EXERCISES

Checking your voice: Make copies of the appropriate rating scale provided on this sheet. Have several persons who know you well rate you on all six points — points specifically mentioned in the article.

For Men

	Quite pronounced	More than average	Average	Less than average	Not noticeable
1. Mumbling	_____	_____	_____	_____	_____
2. Rasping	_____	_____	_____	_____	_____
3. Sullenness	_____	_____	_____	_____	_____
4. Tonal monotony	_____	_____	_____	_____	_____
5. Overloud	_____	_____	_____	_____	_____
6. Stilted accent	_____	_____	_____	_____	_____

For Women

	Quite pronounced	More than average	Average	Less than average	Not noticeable
1. Whining	_____	_____	_____	_____	_____
2. Shrillness	_____	_____	_____	_____	_____
3. Nasal tones	_____	_____	_____	_____	_____
4. Raucous and strident	_____	_____	_____	_____	_____
5. Baby talk	_____	_____	_____	_____	_____
6. Affected accents	_____	_____	_____	_____	_____

Self-analysis: Read aloud the first seven or eight paragraphs of this selection, using a cassette recorder to record your voice. Playing it back several times, make a personal evaluation of yourself. Ask others in your family to do the same, noting both good and bad characteristics. Then plan a program of improvement.

Surveying objectionable habits: You may wish to check further on those speech habits or defects that seem most objectionable. To do so, make an informal survey of students or faculty to see what they consider the six most objectionable speech characteristics. Is there agreement with the six specifically mentioned in the article?

NAME——————————————— DATE————— READING RATE————— W.P.M.

COMPREHENSION CHECK QUESTIONS

1. The preferred number for a discussion group as mentioned was (1) twenty-five; (2) twenty; (3) fifteen; (4) ten.

1. ———

2. Specific reference is made to (1) a timekeeper; (2) a Quaker influence; (3) the Supreme Court; (4) a devil's advocate.

2. ———

3. One role mentioned was that of a girl (1) getting home after a date; (2) asking for the family car; (3) interviewing for a job; (4) caught smoking in her room.

3. ———

4. Immediately after the role playing was said to come a (1) taped replay; (2) discussion; (3) replay with role changes; (4) written evaluation by participants.

4. ———

5. The advantages of role playing were said to be (1) one; (2) two; (3) many; (4) immeasurable.

5. ———

Receptive Comprehension ———

6. This article is mainly about how to (1) improve small group discussions and role playing; (2) solve delicate problems in human relations, (3) arrange new ground rules for small group discussions; (4) clarify purposes for discussions.

6. ———

7. What method of developing ideas does the author tend to use? (1) anecdotes; (2) exaggeration; (3) details; (4) statements of authorities.

7. ———

8. The purpose of this selection is primarily to (1) persuade; (2) describe; (3) evaluate; (4) explain.

8. ———

9. The chief purpose of the circular response pattern is to (1) create orderly discussion; (2) encourage the timid; (3) eliminate bad manners; (4) encourage more complete participation.

9. ———

10. In role playing, emphasis on make-believe is intended to get people to (1) sense problems; (2) be more relaxed; (3) feel the conflicts; (4) get rid of self-consciousness.

10. ———

(*10 off for each mistake*)

Reflective Comprehension ———

TOTAL READING COMPREHENSION SCORE ———

VOCABULARY CHECK QUESTIONS

		without context I	*with context* II
1. *pugilistic*	(1) snub-nosed; (2) talkative; (3) eloquent; (4) heavy-set; (5) belligerent.	1. ———	———
2. *lambaste*	(1) make fun of; (2) denounce; (3) cripple; (4) wail; (5) press together.	2. ———	———
3. *ire*	(1) irritation; (2) anger; (3) pain; (4) fault; (5) event.	3. ———	———
4. *consensus*	(1) general agreement; (2) action; (3) vote; (4) survey; (5) house-to-house canvass.	4. ———	———
5. *construed*	(1) sorted; (2) touched; (3) interpreted; (4) used up; (5) seized.	5. ———	———

(*10 off for each mistake*)

Word Comprehension without *contextual help* (I) ———

Word Comprehension with *contextual help* (II) ———

TOTAL WORD COMPREHENSION SCORE ———

EXERCISES

1. *Developing a rating scale for discussants:* Prepare a rating scale which includes five important characteristics of a good discussant. Compare individual lists in class, then make up a composite list after a careful discussion of the merits of the various suggestions. Use the final form in evaluating one or more discussions.

1. _____

2. _____

3. _____

4. _____

5. _____

2. *Analyzing radio or TV discussions:* Listen to a radio or TV round table or panel discussion involving two or more participants. Check the forward movement of the discussion and the frequency with which the participants follow the various suggestions made in this selection. Report a specific example from your listening which illustrates the application of one of those suggestions.

3. *Evaluating discussions in class:* Get a tape recording of a radio discussion and play it before the class. Follow with a critical evaluation of the discussion.

4. *Participating in classroom discussions:* Through discussion, decide on a current problem, local or national, which should lend itself well to discussion. Then, following the suggestions in Selection 48, see how effectively a discussion can be carried on. Some students can serve as critics and be asked to report at the conclusion of the discussion.

5. *Selecting discussion topics:* Prepare a list of six discussion topics which you feel would be particularly stimulating.

1. _____

2. _____

3. _____

4. _____

5. _____

6. _____

NAME_____ DATE_____ READING RATE_____W.P.M.

COMPREHENSION CHECK QUESTIONS

1. Miss Markham was said to be (1) a school principal; (2) a relative; (3) a counselor; (4) a school teacher.   1. _____

2. Cissa is the name of the author's (1) cat; (2) daughter; (3) neighbor; (4) friend.   2. _____

3. The author has a son named (1) Larry; (2) Russell; (3) John; (4) Lynn.   3. _____

4. Mention was made of (1) Moses; (2) Solomon; (3) Noah; (4) Cleopatra.   4. _____

5. One conversation reported had to do with (1) Hamlet; (2) Shylock; (3) Portia; (4) Ophelia. 5. _____

Receptive Comprehension _____

6. This is mainly about (1) listening; (2) being sincere; (3) keeping an open mind; (4) communication.   6. _____

7. The chief purpose of this article is to (1) entertain; (2) teach; (3) stimulate; (4) describe.   7. _____

8. The author makes most extensive use of (1) exposition; (2) narration; (3) persuasion; (4) description.   8. _____

9. The part of the article about Dr. Peale was intended to illustrate (1) the importance of valuing opinion; (2) the importance of registering no disapproval; (3) how to phrase questions; (4) how to combine telling and asking.   9. _____

10. *Most* importance is attached to (1) really caring; (2) keeping quiet; (3) asking leading questions; (4) asking questions.   10. _____

(10 off for each mistake)   *Reflective Comprehension* _____

TOTAL READING COMPREHENSION SCORE _____

VOCABULARY CHECK QUESTIONS

		without context I	*with context* II
1. *mull*	(1) cheat; (2) ponder; (3) pronounce; (4) read; (5) make.	1. _____	_____
2. *zany*	(1) wicked; (2) outlandish; (3) colorful; (4) windy; (5) cold.	2. _____	_____
3. *ineptness*	(1) awkwardness; (2) strangeness; (3) wildness; (4) vagueness; (5) willingness.	3. _____	_____
4. *incisive*	(1) questioning; (2) harsh; (3) rude; (4) dumb; (5) penetrating.	4. _____	_____
5. *provocative*	(1) chief; (2) brief; (3) stimulating; (4) proverbial; (5) near.	5. _____	_____

(10 off for each mistake)   *Word Comprehension* without *contextual help* (I) _____

Word Comprehension with *contextual help* (II) _____

TOTAL WORD COMPREHENSION SCORE _____

EXERCISES

Asking the right questions: Some questions seem to close more doors than they open, while others lead to a real dialogue. How good are you at the art of asking questions? Test yourself on this list of general questions by putting + beside the good ones, and — beside the poor ones.

1. What did you do today?   ———
2. Would you explain that to me?   ———
3. How was the party?   ———
4. How did you feel about that?   ———
5. Is something the matter?   ———
6. What would you have done?   ———
7. Do you love me?   ———
8. Why did you say that?   ———
9. Oh, really?   ———
10. For instance?   ———
11. Did you enjoy yourself?   ———
12. And then what happened?   ———
13. Is that so?   ———
14. What do you like best?   ———
15. Did you have a good day at the office? ———
16. Which book did you like best?   ———

(Answers at bottom of page.)

Noting conversation stimulators: Listen carefully to some conversations and jot down the specific questions that seemed to spark the most lively discussion. Try the same kind of analysis in a class or group discussion, trying to see what questions serve best as stimuli to talk. Remember some of the most interesting conversations you have ever had. What questions seemed to evoke an easy flow of communication?

Answers: the odd-numbered questions (1, 3, 5, etc.) are poor because they are conversation-stoppers usually answered by one or two words. The even-numbered questions are good ones because they call for thought-provoking answers that can send the conversational stone rolling downhill, initiating other topics for discussion.
If you put + by more than three odd-numbered questions, it may be time to revitalize your sense of curiosity.

NAME——————————————————— DATE——————— READING RATE——————— W.P.M.

COMPREHENSION CHECK QUESTIONS

1. The author specifically alludes to the conversation of (1) baseball enthusiasts; (2) artists; (3) families; (4) movie fans.   1. ————

2. The author lists (1) five rules; (2) eight rules; (3) ten rules; (4) twelve rules.   2. ————

3. The author belonged to (1) a conversation club; (2) a bridge club; (3) a dinner club; (4) an artist colony.   3. ————

4. Mention is made of (1) Eugene Field; (2) Ellis Parker Butler; (3) Edna St. Vincent Millay; (4) Alexander Pope.   4. ————

5. When the author read something aloud to get criticisms, he said he was helped most by (1) individual comments; (2) answers to specific questions; (3) watching their eyes or fingers; (4) noticing when they laughed.   5. ————

Receptive Comprehension ————

6. The purpose of this selection is to (1) help us become better conversationalists; (2) tell us what to avoid when we converse; (3) give us some necessary rules to guide our conversation; (4) suggest appropriate subjects for conversation.   6. ————

7. Apparently the secret of talking well is (1) reading widely; (2) thinking well; (3) listening intently; (4) talking distinctly.   7. ————

8. When a good conversationalist hears someone tell about running into another car, he will (1) narrate some similar story from his own experience; (2) ask about some of the details; (3) shift the conversation to less subjective matters; (4) make no comment until a more appropriate subject is introduced.   8. ————

9. The Japanese tea ceremony is used to illustrate the rule: (1) don't monopolize the conversation; (2) don't make dogmatic statements of opinion; (3) show an active interest in what is said; (4) avoid all purely subjective talk.   9. ————

10. The story about the guests who tried not to say anything destructive in tone for a day illustrated the need for (1) a Pollyanna attitude; (2) a limited amount of destructive talk; (3) eliminating unnecessary critical remarks; (4) looking on both the pleasant and unpleasant sides of life.   10. ————

(10 off for each mistake)   *Reflective Comprehension* ————

TOTAL READING COMPREHENSION SCORE ————

VOCABULARY CHECK QUESTIONS

		without context I	*with context* II
1. *dilate*	(1) hint; (2) expand; (3) refer; (4) close; (5) suffer.	1. ————	————
2. *interpolate*	(1) pronounce; (2) insert; (3) converse; (4) meet; (5) tempt.	2. ————	————
3. *desist*	(1) lose hope; (2) intend; (3) begin; (4) wish; (5) cease.	3. ————	————
4. *futile*	(1) useless; (2) old-time; (3) continuous; (4) easy; (5) easily fused.	4. ————	————
5. *self-effacement*	(1) pride; (2) confidence; (3) righteousness; (4) modesty; (5) egotism.	5. ————	————

(10 off for each mistake)   *Word Comprehension* without *contextual help* (I) ————

Word Comprehension with *contextual help* (II) ————

TOTAL WORD COMPREHENSION SCORE ————

EXERCISES

How to Pronounce a Word
Norman Lewis

No matter how carefully you try to conceal certain facts about yourself, your pronunciation gives you away. Only under the most unusual circumstances could an error cost you your job, your friends or your social standing, as some speech missionaries absurdly proclaim. But under ordinary circumstances an expert can draw from your pronunciation a number of interesting conclusions about your geographical background, your education, your cultural environment and your personality.

For instance, if you say something approaching *ahl* for all or *pak* for park, you are advertising that you grew up in or around Boston. If you call the city *Shi-kaw-go*, you are probably a native of the city, while if you say *Shi-kah-go*, you are more likely from the East.

Greezy for greasy may indicate that you have Southern or Western speech habits; a sharp *r* in *park* will similarly identify you with the Western part of the country, and the complete omission of the *r* in the same word will indicate your background as the Eastern seaboard. Explode your *t's* (*wett, hurtt*) or click your *ng's* (*singg ga songg, Longg gIsland*) and you almost reveal the street on which you live in the Bronx; or pronounce the three words *Mary, marry, merry,* and you name the section of the country in which you formed your linguistic habits — the West if you say these words almost identically, the East if the words are distinctly different in sound.

Your pronunciation of certain other words, for example *either, aunt, athletic, film, grimace, comparable* and *verbatim,* will reveal to the experienced ear more secrets than you may realize. By taking a few simple tests, we can arrive at a fairly accurate analysis of the impression your speech habits give to the world.

Do You Use Illiterate Forms?

Check in each case, in the test below, the form of the word which you habitually and naturally use. As this is not a test of knowledge but of speech patterns, you should be guided solely by what you believe you say, not by what you think is correct.

In the test, the first choice in each case is the illiterate form, the second choice the accepted or educated pronunciation. If you checked form (*b*) right down the line, or did not wander from this straight path more than a couple of times, you may feel assured your speech bears no stigma of illiteracy. If, however, you made several unfortunate choices, consider this a danger signal. As a further check on pronunciation habits, ask yourself whether you are guilty of saying *axed* for asked, *myoo-ni-SIP-'l* for municipal, *lyeberry* for library, *fasset* for faucet, *rassle* for wrestle, *drownd-ded* for drowned, or *lenth* and *strenth* for length and strength.

1. AVIATOR	(*a*) AVV-ee-ay-ter	(*b*) AY-vee-ay-ter
2. BRONCHIAL	(*a*) BRON-ikle	(*b*) BRON-kee-al
3. RADIATOR	(*a*) RADD-ee-ay-ter	(*b*) RAY-dee-ay-ter
4. VANILLA	(*a*) vi-NELL-a	(*b*) va-NILL-a
5. MODERN	(*a*) MOD-ren or MAR-den	(*b*) MOD-urn
6. FEBRUARY	(*a*) FEB-yoo-ar-y	(*b*) FEB-roo-ar-y
7. MISCHIEVOUS	(*a*) mis-CHEE-vee-us	(*b*) MISS-chi-vus
8. ATTACKED	(*a*) at-TACK-ted	(*b*) at-TACKT
9. ATHLETIC	(*a*) ath-a-LET-ic	(*b*) ath-LET-ic
10. ELM, FILM	(*a*) ellum, fillum	(*b*) elm, film
11. GENUINE	(*a*) JEN-yoo-wyne	(*b*) JEN-yoo-in
12. ZOOLOGY	(*a*) zoo-OL-o-gy	(*b*) zoe-OL-o-gy
13. COMPARABLE	(*a*) com-PAR-able	(*b*) COM-par-able
14. BOUQUET	(*a*) boe-KAY	(*b*) boo-KAY
15. HUMAN	(*a*) YOO-man	(*b*) HYOO-man
16. ROBUST	(*a*) ROE-bust	(*b*) ro-BUST
17. GARAGE	(*a*) ga-RAHDJ	(*b*) ga-RAHZH
18. CLANDESTINE	(*a*) CLAN-de-styne	(*b*) clan-DESS-tin
19. PREFERABLE	(*a*) pre-FER-able	(*b*) PREF-er-able
20. PLEBEIAN	(*a*) PLEE-bee-an	(*b*) ple-BEE-an

Reprinted with the permission of the author from *Coronet*, November 1946.

(*continued on page 290*)

NAME——————————————————— DATE——————— READING RATE——————— W.P.M.

COMPREHENSION CHECK QUESTIONS

1. The article mentions (1) Persian; (2) Asian; (3) Phrygian; (4) Greek.   1. ————

2. With 1,000 nouns and 1,000 verbs, the number of possible sentences would be (1) one million; (2) two million; (3) three million; (4) an unspecified number.   2. ————

3. The cartoon mentioned shows a child in what kind of shop? (1) magic; (2) toy; (3) candy; (4) book.   3. ————

4. Reference is made to: (1) Job; (2) Socrates; (3) Demosthenes; (4) David of the Psalms.   4. ————

5. Chomsky's theories are (1) universally accepted; (2) not accepted by all linguists; (3) still in the formative stage; (4) now outdated.   5. ————

Receptive Comprehension ————

6. This article is mainly about (1) personal language development; (2) Noam Chomsky; (3) creativity in language usage; (4) man talking.   6. ————

7. You would infer from the story of the Egyptian pharoah that he believed language (1) depends on race; (2) depends on nationality; (3) depends on inborn capacity; (4) depends on the surrounding language community.   7. ————

8. "Plato walks with the Macedonian swineherd" means (1) some have a special language gift, some haven't; (2) linguistic creativity is everyone's birthright; (3) education makes a difference; (4) Plato and the swineherd have a common language.   8. ————

9. You would infer from what you've read that the question you are now reading has probably (1) been asked before; (2) never been asked before; (3) been asked many times; (4) appeared elsewhere in this very book.   9. ————

10. This article was written primarily to (1) persuade; (2) entertain; (3) inform; (4) stimulate.   10. ————

(10 off for each mistake)   *Reflective Comprehension* ————

TOTAL READING COMPREHENSION SCORE ————

VOCABULARY CHECK QUESTIONS

		without context I	*with context* II
1. *primordial*	(1) principal; (2) most common; (3) earliest; (4) ordinary; (5) regular.	1. ————	————
2. *apocryphal*	(1) informal; (2) apologetic; (3) formal; (4) paralytic; (5) fictitious.	2. ————	————
3. *exploiting*	(1) exploring; (2) objecting; (3) making clear; (4) saying; (5) using productively.	3. ————	————
4. *arduous*	(1) devoted; (2) durable; (3) strenuous; (4) argumentative; (5) proud.	4. ————	————
5. *innate*	(1) acquired; (2) intense; (3) inborn; (4) inseparable; (5) uninteresting.	5. ————	————

(10 off for each mistake)   *Word Comprehension* without *contextual help* (I) ————

Word Comprehension with *contextual help* (II) ————

TOTAL WORD COMPREHENSION SCORE ————

EXERCISES

Do You Avoid Affected Speech?

Check, as before, the forms you habitually use in the test below.

1. Again	(*a*) a-GAYNE	(*b*) a-GEN
2. Either	(*a*) EYE-ther	(*b*) EE-ther
3. Vase	(*a*) vahz	(*b*) vayze or vayse
4. Tomato	(*a*) to-MAH-to	(*b*) to-MAY-to
5. Chauffeur	(*a*) SHO-fer	(*b*) sho-FURR
6. Aunt	(*a*) ahnt	(*b*) ant
7. Secretary	(*a*) SEC-re-tree	(*b*) SEC-re-terry
8. Rather	(*a*) rah-ther	(*b*) ra-ther (rhyme with *gather*)
9. Program	(*a*) pro-grum	(*b*) pro-gramm
10. Ask	(*a*) ahsk	(*b*) ask

Except for certain sections of New England and parts of the South, the second alternative offered in the above test is in every case the popular, current and standard form. Therefore, the greater the number of *b* pronunciations you checked, the more natural and unaffected will listeners consider your speech.

If you generally mix in social, business or geographical groups in which *ahnt, tomahto* and *eyether* are accepted pronunciations, you are relatively safe in using some or all of the *a* forms in the test. Nevertheless, you should bear in mind that these are not the pronunciations common to the majority of Americans and that you may occasionally run the risk of being thought "snooty" or supercilious by your more earthy listeners.

The third and last analysis, which appears below, is just for fun, and will serve to prove that we cannot become too fussy about "correct" pronunciation. These are "catch" words; that is, you are expected to get most of them

wrong. They are, with one exception, bookish words rarely used in everyday speech — thus there is no reason why you should be familiar with the dictionary pronunciations.

Most people taking this test will make seven or more errors. If you get more than three right, you may credit yourself with unusual language gifts. If you manage to come anywhere near a perfect score, you are absolutely phenomenal. To see how well you did, check with the inverted answers below the test itself.

In your own pronunciation, you are following the wisest course if you avoid uneducated forms and silly affectations. As an aid to improving pronunciation, you can consult the dictionary, study the simple rules of speech, observe and adopt the good pronunciation habits used by literate people.

The time you spend in improving your pronunciation will pay generous dividends. Actions, we are often told, speak louder than words. But the world bases its first impression of you on what you say — and *how* you say it.

1. Finis (the end) (*a*) FIN-iss, (*b*) fee-NEE, (*c*) FYE-niss

2. Eighth (the number) (*a*) ayt-th, (*b*) ayth

3. Secretive (concealing) (*a*) SEEK-re-tive, (*b*) se-KREE-tive

4. Cerebrum (portion of the brain) (*a*) SER-e-brum, (*b*) se-REE-brum

5. Dour (stern, forbidding) (*a*) rhyme with *poor*, (*b*) rhyme with *sour*

6. Congeries (a heap) (*a*) CON-je-reez, (*b*) con-JEER-ee-eez

7. Ignominy (disgrace) (*a*) IG-no-mi-ny, (*b*) ig-NOM-i-ny

8. Gramercy! (a Shakespearian exclamation) (*a*) GRAM-er-see, (*b*) gra-MUR-see

9. Vagary (whim) (*a*) VAG-a-ree, (*b*) VAY-ga-ree, (*c*) va-GARE-ee

10. Quay (a wharf) (*a*) kway, (*b*) kay, (*c*) key

Answers: 1, a; 2, a; 3, a; 4, a; 5, a; 6, b; 7, a; 8, b; 9, b; 10, c.

Remember — pronunciations change — dictionaries vary!

NAME_____ DATE_____ READING RATE_____ W.P.M.

COMPREHENSION CHECK QUESTIONS

1. The title of Conwell's lecture was (1) *America's Penniless Millionaire;* (2) *Acres of Diamonds;* (3) *The Story of Ali Hafed;* (4) *Opportunity Knocks But Once.*   1. _____

2. Conwell lived his early life (1) on a farm; (2) in a city; (3) in a small town; (4) in New Haven.   2. _____

3. In the Civil War Conwell was (1) an orderly; (2) a lieutenant; (3) a captain; (4) a major.   3. _____

4. Conwell was directly instrumental in the building of (1) a new church; (2) two new churches; (3) three new churches; (4) four new churches.   4. _____

5. Conwell delivered his famous lecture about (1) 1,000 times; (2) 2,000 times; (3) 4,000 times; (4) 6,000 times.   5. _____

Receptive Comprehension _____

6. The purpose of this article is to (1) explain the importance of cultivating your own back yard; (2) tell us about a famous speech; (3) tell us about Conwell; (4) suggest the importance of reading.   6. _____

7. The story of John Ring is used to demonstrate Conwell's ability to (1) command; (2) lay hold of symbols and fit them into his life; (3) keep an extravagant vow; (4) understand human nature and motives.   7. _____

8. Conwell apparently considered the most important communication skill to be (1) writing; (2) speaking; (3) listening; (4) reading.   8. _____

9. Conwell would probably agree that a man's success depends primarily on (1) the contacts he makes; (2) his environment; (3) being at the right place at the right time; (4) making the most of his opportunities.   9. _____

10. You would infer that the most effective exposition is (1) narrative; (2) descriptive; (3) humorous; (4) witty.   10. _____

(10 off for each mistake)   *Reflective Comprehension* _____

TOTAL READING COMPREHENSION SCORE _____

VOCABULARY CHECK QUESTIONS

		without context I	*with context* II
1. *diversity*	(1) category; (2) deity; (3) pleasure; (4) variety; (5) popularity.	1. _____	_____
2. *guises*	(1) plants; (2) guides; (3) secrets; (4) aspects; (5) creeds.	2. _____	_____
3. *intuitive*	(1) inborn; (2) intrusive; (3) useless; (4) fickle; (5) unwilling.	3. _____	_____
4. *tenaciously*	(1) temptingly; (2) temporarily; (3) moderately; (4) persistently; (5) quietly.	4. _____	_____
5. *stipulated*	(1) dotted; (2) paid; (3) drew; (4) estimated; (5) specified.	5. _____	_____

(10 off for each mistake)

Word Comprehension without *contextual help* (I) _____

Word Comprehension with *contextual help* (II) _____

TOTAL WORD COMPREHENSION SCORE _____

EXERCISES

1. Noting subtle degrees of emphasis: Many different shades of emphasis are reflected in the way that ideas are coordinated or subordinated in a sentence. An idea may be given added importance by being put into an independent clause, where it can stand alone as a complete statement or sentence. It can be given slightly less importance by putting it into a dependent clause, which cannot stand alone. If it deserves even less emphasis, the verb can be removed and the idea expressed in phrase form, either prepositional or verbal. Finally, if the idea deserves minimal emphasis, it can sometimes be boiled down to a single word.

Take this sentence: *A man was digging a ditch, and he had a big nose.* This contains two independent clauses connected with an *and.* In essence this suggests that the writer considered the two ideas of exact equal importance, putting them both into independent clauses. If the action is to get slightly more emphasis, the second clause could be made a dependent clause as follows: *The man who had a big nose was digging a ditch.*

For even less emphasis, see how the sentence reads when the dependent clause is made a phrase. *The man having a big nose was digging a ditch.* Finally, it is possible to move from a phrase to a single word, the sentence now reading: *The big-nosed man was digging a ditch.* In this rather subtle way a writer may communicate degrees of emphasis on ideas he is expressing — emphasis that you, the reader, should be aware of.

To develop that awareness more fully, try expressing shades of emphasis in the following sentence, using the patterns suggested in the model.

Conway's speech was fascinating, and *it could have made him a millionaire.*

Put the idea expressed in the first independent clause into a dependent clause.

_____

Now subordinate it further, making it a phrase of some kind.

_____

As a last move, boil the idea in the first clause into a single word.

_____

2. Getting proper emphasis through subordination: Revise the following sentences as directed, noting how proper subordination improves each one. When you have finished, check back to the original.

A. Subordinate by changing the italicized portion from an independent clause to a dependent clause, making any other changes necessary:

EXAMPLE: *He was making tens of thousands,* and he would rarely have more than a hundred ready dollars of his own. Though he was making tens of thousands, he would. . . .
(The dependent clause emphasizes the causal relationship present.)

A. 1. There is an event of his military service, and *it demonstrates his facility for laying hold of symbols.* . . .

2. *The Civil War broke,* and it was as if he had anticipated the opportunity to become "the recruiting orator of the Berkshires."

B. Subordinate by changing the italicized portion from an independent clause to a verbal phrase, making any other changes necessary:
1. He chips a corner, *and he finds an eye of blue-white fire* looking at him. . . .

2. It stands, very possibly, in our own boots, *and it wears our own socks.*

C. Subordinate by changing the italicized portion from a clause to a phrase of some kind, making any other changes necessary:
1. *It was the appointed day,* and he borrowed tools and came out.

2. *Eighteen months passed,* and he had been ordained their minister. . . .

NAME_____ DATE_____ READING RATE_____W.P.M.

COMPREHENSION CHECK QUESTIONS

1. Some of the experiments were conducted at (1) Yale; (2) Cornell; (3) Chicago; (4) Harvard.

    1. _____

2. One of the experimental speakers was (1) a salesman; (2) an accountant; (3) a taxi driver; (4) a musician.

    2. _____

3. Guessing age was done accurately (1) when speakers were over 40; (2) when speakers were under 40; (3) over the entire age range; (4) only by totally blind listeners.

    3. _____

4. As compared with radio, putting speakers behind a curtain (1) made no difference in accuracy; (2) actually resulted in a loss of accuracy; (3) added about 7 per cent more accuracy; (4) added about 14 per cent more accuracy.

    4. _____

5. Monotone is closely related to (1) maladjustment; (2) age; (3) physical health; (4) body build.

    5. _____

Receptive Comprehension _____

6. The purpose of this selection is (1) to suggest how best to train your voice (2) to show how accurately age can be judged from voice; (3) to indicate what your voice reveals about you; (4) to indicate how closely all experimental findings in this area agree.

    6. _____

7. The selection was organized primarily around (1) the various experimental studies; (2) the various characteristics studied; (3) a chronological sequence; (4) an evidence-to-conclusion basis.

    7. _____

8. Evidence was cited to show that (1) personality improvement led to voice improvement; (2) voice improvement led to personality improvement; (3) personality change did not affect voice; (4) voice change did not affect personality.

    8. _____

9. In this selection the points are developed chiefly through use of (1) anecdotes; (2) detail; (3) analogies; (4) repetition.

    9. _____

10. This article is aimed primarily at (1) psychologists; (2) college students; (3) adults; (4) women.

    10. _____

(10 off for each mistake)   *Reflective Comprehension* _____

TOTAL READING COMPREHENSION SCORE _____

VOCABULARY CHECK QUESTIONS

		without context I	*with context* II
1. *incredibly*	(1) helpfully; (2) unbelievably; (3) lastingly; (4) moderately; (5) slowly.	1. _____	_____
2. *invariably*	(1) inconstantly; (2) always; (3) invincibly; (4) usually; (5) softly.	2. _____	_____
3. *acute*	(1) keen; (2) attractive; (3) ugly; (4) real; (5) free.	3. _____	_____
4. *corroborated*	(1) consumed; (2) folded; (3) debased; (4) abated; (5) confirmed.	4. _____	_____
5. *nuances*	(1) new developments; (2) standards; (3) delicate variations; (4) annoyances; (5) loud voices.	5. _____	_____

(10 off for each mistake)   *Word Comprehension* without *contextual help* (I) _____

Word Comprehension with *contextual help* (II) _____

TOTAL WORD COMPREHENSION SCORE _____

EXERCISES

1. Getting variety by using both loose and periodic sentences: A periodic sentence is one in which the meaning is not completed until the end or nearly the end. A loose sentence is one which continues after a complete statement is made. Loose sentences are more conversational, periodic sentences more formal.

Change the following sentences from loose to periodic or from periodic to loose, noticing the difference in effect. Compare your version with the original, noting any differences.

Here, for example, is the opening sentence of Sigmund Spaeth's "Stabilizing the Language through Popular Songs":

(Periodic) "If you want to write a really popular song, one that will fall naturally from the lips of millions, be sure that somewhere in your chorus you assault the English language in no uncertain terms."

(Loose) Be sure you assault the English language in no uncertain terms somewhere in your chorus, if you want to write a really popular song, one that will fall naturally from the lips of millions.

A. (Loose) The estimates tended to be less accurate, however, in judging the ages of the persons who were over 45.

(Periodic) _____

_____

B. (Periodic) Voices having been broadcast over a public address system, the body build of the speakers was to be identified by the students.

(Loose) _____

_____

C. (Loose) His other senses seem to become more sensitive and acute, including hearing, when a person loses his sight, because he places greater reliance upon them.

(Periodic) _____

_____

D. (Loose) Harvard University scientists conducted a similar test in the United States, impressed by the findings of the Vienna study.

(Periodic) _____

_____

2. Getting variety by interrupting the normal sentence pattern of subject-verb-object: Revise the following sentences by placing part of the sentence so as to interrupt the normal pattern. Compare your versions with the original sentences in Selection 53.

A. The Psychological Institute of the University of Vienna conducted a fascinating experiment to test these findings.

_____

_____

B. The investigators believe this finding indicates that a slight degree of distortion was produced when the voices were transmitted over the radio.

_____

_____

C. Take the person who speaks in a dull monotone, for example.

_____

_____

NAME_____ DATE_____ READING RATE_____ W.P.M.

COMPREHENSION CHECK QUESTIONS

1. To cut down on talking, the husband suggested (1) chewing gum vigorously and constantly; (2) taping their lips; (3) using a word-rationing system; (4) taking turns talking with visitors.   1. _____

2. Specific mention was made of their (1) color TV; (2) open fire; (3) sunny patio; (4) stereo.   2. _____

3. Dan Blake told a long story about the (1) deer he shot; (2) accident he had; (3) train trip he took; (4) big bass he caught.   3. _____

4. The agreed signal to stop talking was to (1) touch the lips; (2) pull an ear; (3) touch the forehead; (4) clear the throat.   4. _____

5. The doctor diagnosed the husband as having (1) eye trouble; (2) sinus trouble; (3) hearing problems; (4) allergy problems.   5. _____

Receptive Comprehension _____

6. The chief purpose of this selection is to (1) entertain; (2) instruct; (3) explain; (4) stimulate.   6. _____

7. Which of the following statements is closest to the idea developed in this selection? (1) good listening makes good friends; (2) listen well to learn well; (3) good listening pays; (4) he who listens well, eats well.   7. _____

8. Which of the two seemed to take the leadership in their decision? (1) the husband, primarily; (2) both equally; (3) the wife, primarily; (4) first one, then the other.   8. _____

9. This selection would be most accurately classified as (1) exposition; (2) persuasion; (3) narration; (4) description.   9. _____

10. In style, you would call this selection (1) informal; (2) verbose; (3) humorous; (4) intimate.   10. _____

(10 off for each mistake)   *Reflective Comprehension* _____

TOTAL READING COMPREHENSION SCORE _____

VOCABULARY CHECK QUESTIONS

		without context I	*with context* II
1. *phlegmatic*	(1) small; (2) unemotional; (3) lively; (4) flattering; (5) show.	1. _____	_____
2. *chagrined*	(1) amused; (2) transformed; (3) pleased; (4) thanked; (5) humiliated.	2. _____	_____
3. *repercussion*	(1) blow; (2) sound; (3) repair; (4) rebounding; (5) censure.	3. _____	_____
4. *fiasco*	(1) authorization; (2) betrothed person; (3) complete failure; (4) conclusion; (5) award.	4. _____	_____
5. *moratorium*	(1) deferment; (2) burial; (3) bad situation; (4) payment; (5) inclination.	5. _____	_____

(10 off for each mistake)   Word Comprehension without *contextual help* (I) _____

Word Comprehension with *contextual help* (II) _____

TOTAL WORD COMPREHENSION SCORE _____

EXERCISES

Checking up on yourself as a listener: Suppose you try an experiment to see how you rate as a listener. Begin by taking the following twelve-item spelling quiz to see how many of the words you know how to spell accurately. To each of the following twelve words, you are to add an *-ing,* spelling the resulting combination on the line following the word, in the column headed *Initial Spelling.*

Spelling Quiz

Words	*Initial Spelling* (before listening)	*Final Spelling* (after listening)
1. din + ing		
2. shine + ing		
3. begin + ing		
4. quiz + ing		
5. unfurl + ing		
6. occur + ing		
7. label + ing		
8. man + ing		
9. droop + ing		
10. equip + ing		
11. profit + ing		
12. defer + ing		

When you have finished, do not check your answers. At this time you are to hand this text to someone else, asking him to read the rule that follows, while you listen carefully. Ask him to read it slowly twice, to make sure you understand the rule. After listening, spell the same twelve words, using the column headed *Final Spelling* and trying to apply the rule perfectly. If you understood and applied the rule, you should have a perfect score in the last column. This becomes, in a sense, a measure of your listening ability.

Here is the rule that is to be read aloud to you twice as you listen:

FINAL CONSONANT RULE: Words ending in a single final consonant, preceded by a single vowel, double the final consonant when a suffix beginning with a vowel is added and when the last syllable is accented. (Repeat the rule.)

Respell the words, using the column headed Final Spelling, applying the rule as accurately as possible. Now check both columns to see how many you got right.

What do your findings mean? Your scores for the two trials will put you into one of three categories. When ninety-two university students followed the same procedure, twenty-three were either slightly confused after listening to the rule or thoroughly confused, scoring from one to six points *lower* after listening to the rule. One student, for example, who scored 11 right the first time, spelled only 5 right in the second column.

Then nineteen of the ninety-two did not change at all after hearing the rule. One student scored 7 right the first time and 7 right after listening to the rule. This suggests a strong mind set that interfered with learning through listening.

Finally, the remaining fifty improved from one to five points after listening to the rule. One student improved from 7 to 12, a perfect score after listening to the rule.

Coming back to your own results, if you improved by one point, you have a somewhat better listening ability than found in the ninety-two students tested. If you improved to a perfect 12 in the second column, even if you moved up only from 11 to 12, you improved as much as possible.

If you scored any less than 12 right in the last column, ask yourself why. One student, in answering that question, wrote that he "didn't know what a consonant was." Word meaning was apparently part of his problem. Do you have a clear, accurate concept of what a syllable is, or a suffix, a vowel, or an accent? Any one of those may be a potential stumbling block.

Answers: 1, dinning; 2, shining; 3, beginning; 4, quizzing; 5, unfurling; 6, occurring; 7, labeling; 8, manning; 9, drooping; 10, equipping; 11, profiting; 12, deferring.

NAME————————————————— DATE————————— READING RATE——————————— W.P.M.

COMPREHENSION CHECK QUESTIONS

1. Rudolf lived in (1) Denmark; (2) Sweden; (3) Iceland; (4) Czechoslovakia.   1. ————

2. Mention was made of (1) Brahms; (2) Liszt; (3) Bach; (4) Chopin.   2. ————

3. Rudolf moored his boat (1) to an iron ring on a cliff; (2) to the steps; (3) to a jetty; (4) on a small rocky beach.   3. ————

4. The lighthouse keeper was expressly described as (1) muscular; (2) tall; (3) huge; (4) heavy-set.   4. ————

5. One thing they had for supper was (1) salmon; (2) coffee; (3) soup; (4) cheese.   5. ————

Receptive Comprehension ————

6. The chief purpose of this selection is to (1) get us to feel; (2) explain; (3) help us understand; (4) moralize.   6. ————

7. The fact that the lighthouse keeper used few words was made to seem (1) strange; (2) appropriate; (3) inappropriate; (4) ordinary.   7. ————

8. We would class this article as essentially (1) narration; (2) description; (3) exposition; (4) persuasion.   8. ————

9. The author characterized the lighthouse keeper (1) realistically; (2) cleverly; (3) critically; (4) movingly.   9. ————

10. The lighthouse keeper treated Rudolf (1) with courtesy; (2) as important; (3) with eager hospitality; (4) as strange.   10. ————

(10 off for each mistake)   *Reflective Comprehension* ————

TOTAL READING COMPREHENSION SCORE ————

VOCABULARY CHECK QUESTIONS

		without context I	*with context* II
1. *puny*	(1) young; (2) slight; (3) aged; (4) prompt; (5) harsh.	1. ————	————
2. *stolidly*	(1) impassively; (2) strongly; (3) strangely; (4) stoutly; (5) hopefully.	2. ————	————
3. *equable*	(1) erect; (2) misleading; (3) wandering; (4) serene; (5) fixed.	3. ————	————
4. *sparse*	(1) spasmodic; (2) petty; (3) meager; (4) spoken; (5) special.	4. ————	————
5. *poignant*	(1) pointed; (2) poised; (3) slow-moving; (4) prudent; (5) emotionally touching.	5. ————	————

(10 off for each mistake)   *Word Comprehension* without *contextual help* (I) ————

Word Comprehension with *contextual help* (II) ————

TOTAL WORD COMPREHENSION SCORE ————

EXERCISES

Listening and grades: What is the most important thing that education can do for you? This was one of the questions raised in a recent nationwide survey of the goals of education, as reported in the magazine *Phi Delta Kappan.* Results showed that the very first goal in order of importance, as indicated by those surveyed, was to "develop skills in reading, writing, speaking, and listening." The goal second in importance was to "develop pride in work and a feeling of self-worth."

Obviously reaching the second goal depends in large part on how well the first goal is achieved. The better you read, write, speak, and listen, the stronger your feelings of positive self-worth, security, and self-assurance. It is with these goals in mind that all the exercises in this text are designed expressly: to hasten your achievement in these areas of primary importance.

Actually the two assimilative skills of reading and listening can and should work most closely together, attention to one providing significant insights of importance to the other. Your academic success is dependent in large part on how skilled you are in assimilating by eye and ear.

The Commission on the English Curriculum points to the fact that "pupils from pre-school through college learn more frequently by listening than by any other means." Three separate studies made at Stephens College indicate that listening is more important than reading for success in 38 to 42 percent of the college courses taken by freshmen.

Additional evidence of the significance of listening comes from research based on the first standardized test of listening ability, the *Brown-Carlsen Listening Comprehension Test.* Research findings based on that test indicate that for a group of university sophomores grade point averages are related somewhat more closely to listening ability than to reading ability.

Evidence such as this suggests how important it is to know both what kind of reader and what kind of listener you are as you face problems of effective assimilation of information at the college and adult levels. Use this text for that purpose, in case you do not have standardized test scores providing specific percentile figures.

Use six selections — three that you read, three that are read aloud to you. For each, take the comprehension test and begin to note any differences between the reading and listening channels. A total of the three scores in each area, while not so reliable as standardized test scores, will still provide relevant evidence.

Listening Comprehension Scores	**Reading Comprehension Scores**
Selection #_____	Selection #_____
Selection #_____	Selection #_____
Selection #_____	Selection #_____
Total: _____	Total: _____

Are you about equally good as reader and listener? Are you a better listener than reader or a better reader than listener? The sooner you begin to find out, the sooner you can make desired adjustments. As a further aid, look more closely at the figures. Are the differences in performances caused by differences in difficulty, length, or interest?

For example, when forty-four students were given two short selections, one to be read silently, the other to be listened to, the average comprehension was slightly better in the reading situation. The average was 66 percent in reading, 58 percent in listening. Yet among the forty-four tested, one scored 80 percent in reading and only 20 percent in listening. On the same two selections, another student scored 50 percent in reading and 100 percent in listening.

NAME————————————————————— DATE——————————— READING RATE——————— W.P.M.

COMPREHENSION CHECK QUESTIONS

1. One conversation mentioned is overheard in the airport at (1) San Francisco; (2) Seattle; (3) Chicago; (4) Phoenix.   1. ————

2. What catastrophe was *not* mentioned? (1) Pearl Harbor; (2) sinking of the Titanic; (3) MGM Grand fire; (4) Johnstown flood.   2. ————

3. The divorce figure for each year is said to be (1) 250,000; (2) 500,000; (3) one million; (4) two million.   3. ————

4. What percent of our waking time is spent in communicating? (1) 55%; (2) 60%; (3) 70%; (4) 80%.   4. ————

5. Of the twenty most critical managerial competencies, listening actively ranks (1) at the very top; (2) next to the top; (3) third; (4) fourth.   5. ————

Receptive Comprehension ————

6. This selection is mainly about (1) the importance of listening; (2) the teaching of listening; (3) the effects of bad listening; (4) the need for listening in management.   6. ————

7. The opening three incidents are primarily to (1) arouse interest; (2) show that men are the poorest listeners; (3) suggest the prevalence of bad listening habits; (4) reveal the costly effects of poor listening.   7. ————

8. You would infer that the intended reading audience is (1) teachers; (2) the general public; (3) business personnel; (4) training directors.   8. ————

9. Points are developed largely by (1) description; (2) details; (3) comparison; (4) research findings.   9. ————

10. The style is essentially (1) lively; (2) inspirational; (3) conversational; (4) factual.   10. ————

(10 off for each mistake)   *Reflective Comprehension* ————

TOTAL READING COMPREHENSION SCORE ————

VOCABULARY CHECK QUESTIONS

		without context I	*with context* II
1. *quantitative*	(1) factual; (2) quarrelsome; (3) capable of measurement; (4) bulky; (5) explicit.	1. ————	————
2. *audits*	(1) sums; (2) drills; (3) examinations; (4) arrangements; (5) sounds.	2. ————	————
3. *reciprocate*	(1) receive; (2) summarize; (3) correct; (4) interchange; (5) prove.	3. ————	————
4. *misconstrue*	(1) build poorly; (2) suspect; (3) lie; (4) misunderstand; (5) miscalculate.	4. ————	————
5. *tortuous*	(1) winding; (2) painful; (3) slow; (4) hot; (5) arid.	5. ————	————

(10 off for each mistake)   *Word Comprehension* without *contextual help* (I) ————

Word Comprehension with *contextual help*   (II) ————

TOTAL WORD COMPREHENSION SCORE ————

EXERCISES

Checking your listening habits: Dr. Ralph G. Nichols, pioneer in the field of listening, has devised a special Listening Index for use in analyzing your bad listening habits. Check up on yourself — but be honest!

HOW WELL DO YOU LISTEN?

How often do you indulge in ten almost universal bad listening habits? Check yourself carefully on each one, tallying your score as follows:

For every "Almost always" checked, give yourself a score of   2
For every "Usually" checked, give yourself a score of   4
For every "Sometimes" checked, give yourself a score of   6
For every "Seldom" checked, give yourself a score of   8
For every "Almost never" checked, give yourself a score of   10

Habit	Almost Always	Usually	Some-times	Seldom	Almost Never	Score
1. Calling the subject uninteresting	_____	_____	_____	_____	_____	_____
2. Criticizing the speaker's delivery	_____	_____	_____	_____	_____	_____
3. Getting *over*stimulated by some point within the speech	_____	_____	_____	_____	_____	_____
4. Listening only for facts	_____	_____	_____	_____	_____	_____
5. Trying to outline everything	_____	_____	_____	_____	_____	_____
6. Faking attention to the speaker	_____	_____	_____	_____	_____	_____
7. Tolerating or creating distractions	_____	_____	_____	_____	_____	_____
8. Avoiding difficult expository material	_____	_____	_____	_____	_____	_____
9. Letting emotion-laden words arouse personal antagonism	_____	_____	_____	_____	_____	_____
10. Wasting the advantage of thought speed	_____	_____	_____	_____	_____	_____

TOTAL _____

TOTAL SCORE INTERPRETATION: Below 70 — You need training. From 70 to 90 — You listen well. Above 90 — You are extraordinarily good.

NAME——————————————————— DATE——————— READING RATE——————— W.P.M.

COMPREHENSION CHECK QUESTIONS

1. It was said that through efficient listening, American business could be (1) doubled; (2) tripled; (3) vastly improved; (4) none of the preceding.   1. ———

2. How many different kinds of questions were discussed? (1) only one; (2) two; (3) three; (4) four.   2. ———

3. How much did Herman sell the ashtray for? (1) $6; (2) $8; (3) $15; (4) $18.   3. ———

4. A specific reference was made to (1) Huck Finn; (2) Mark Twain; (3) Tom Sawyer; (4) Mickey Mouse.   4. ———

5. What was one of the topics specifically said to trigger emotion? (1) taxes; (2) politics; (3) nuclear power; (4) gun control.   5. ———

Receptive Comprehension ———

6. This selection is mainly about how to (1) ask the right questions; (2) control the emotions that interfere with listening; (3) improve your listening; (4) develop listening responsiveness.   6. ———

7. The six basic guidelines are arranged (1) in order of increasing importance; (2) in order of lessening importance; (3) in cause to effect order; (4) in no obvious order.   7. ———

8. The author's attitude is best described as (1) positive; (2) objective; (3) casual; (4) cautious.   8. ———

9. All six guidelines can best be summarized with the words (1) concentrate; (2) try harder; (3) be interested; (4) be unemotional.   9. ———

10. Points are developed largely through (1) pertinent details; (2) case history episodes; (3) contrast and comparison; (4) citing authorities.   10. ———

(10 off for each mistake)   *Reflective Comprehension* ———

TOTAL READING COMPREHENSION SCORE ———

VOCABULARY CHECK QUESTIONS

		without context I	*with context* II
1. *dynamic*	(1) static; (2) ruling; (3) creative; (4) original; (5) forceful.	1. ———	———
2. *rapport*	(1) motion; (2) portion; (3) harmony; (4) quickness; (5) gesture.	2. ———	———
3. *alienate*	(1) align; (2) travel; (3) alternate; (4) estrange; (5) treat.	3. ———	———
4. *prone*	(1) disposed to; (2) happy; (3) prepared; (4) afraid; (5) faint.	4. ———	———
5. *demeanor*	(1) record; (2) behavior; (3) experience; (4) attitude; (5) aptitude.	5. ———	———

(10 off for each mistake)   *Word Comprehension* without *contextual help* (I) ———

Word Comprehension with *contextual help*   (II) ———

TOTAL WORD COMPREHENSION SCORE ———

EXERCISES

1. *Listening vs. reading:* In the spaces below list the important advantages and disadvantages of learning through listening and learning through reading.

   A. Advantages:

   Of listening

   1.
   2.
   3.
   4.
   5.
   6.

   Of reading

   1.
   2.
   3.
   4.
   5.
   6.

   B. Disadvantages:

   Of listening

   1.
   2.
   3.
   4.
   5.
   6.

   Of reading

   1.
   2.
   3.
   4.
   5.
   6.

2. *Noting obstacle-words:* While serving with Air University, Norman Stageberg prepared an article, "Obstacle-Words in Group Discussion," for the *Journal of Communication*. This article discussed seven kinds of words which tend to cause delay and confusion in speaking-listening situations.

   Here is one of the important kinds which he discusses.

   Relative words. Relative words are words whose meanings are vague and fluctuating, and depend on what the word is related to or compared with. Take, for example, the adjectives *tall* and *short*. Is a six-story building tall or short? If it is located in a town of 4,000 and related to the one- and two-story buildings of the community, it will probably be called tall. If, however, the same building is located in a metropolis of 5,000,000 and is related to the surrounding skyscrapers, it will be considered short. Likewise, all opposite relative adjectives, e.g., *fast* and *slow, heavy* and *light, hot* and *cold,* can be used to describe exactly the same thing. Our indispensable *good* is a relative adjective. When it is stamped in purple on beef in "U.S. grade good," it means the second best of four grades. But in some mail-order catalogues, when applied to articles for sale, it means the lowest of three grades, the others being *better* and *best*. Here, then, *good* means poorest.

   List four relative words found in Selection 57. Does the author attempt to add other information or detail which makes them less relative?

Relative words	Other details to clarify?
1. _____	_____
2. _____	_____
3. _____	_____
4. _____	_____

NAME_____ DATE_____ READING RATE_____ W.P.M.

COMPREHENSION CHECK QUESTIONS

1. White collar workers are said to devote what percent of their working time to listening? (1) no figure given; (2) 40; (3) 25; (4) 12.   1. _____

2. One company mentioned as providing training in listening is (1) IBM; (2) Ford Motor Co.; (3) Remington-Rand; (4) Monsanto Chemical.   2. _____

3. The worst listeners thought that note-taking was synonymous with (1) summarizing; (2) noting main ideas; (3) noting facts; (4) outlining.   3. _____

4. One of the ten suggestions was to (1) get the facts; (2) sit toward the front; (3) exercise your mind; (4) involve your emotions.   4. _____

5. We are told that we live in a (1) "mechanized age"; (2) "noisy age"; (3) "jet age"; (4) "wordy age."   5. _____

Receptive Comprehension _____

6. This focuses mainly on (1) how to listen better; (2) reasons for poor listening; (3) the importance of listening; (4) the value of listening training.   6. _____

7. This is addressed primarily to (1) business people; (2) students; (3) women; (4) adults in general. 7. _____

8. By inference, an interesting speech should particularly stress the (1) novel; (2) unique; (3) useful; (4) colorful.   8. _____

9. The most important suggestion is apparently to (1) keep your mind open; (2) be flexible; (3) capitalize on thought speed; (4) hold your fire.   9. _____

10. The list of "red-flag" words was to develop the point that you should (1) resist distractions; (2) judge content, not delivery; (3) keep your mind open; (4) find areas of interest.   10. _____

(10 off for each mistake)   *Reflective Comprehension* _____

TOTAL READING COMPREHENSION SCORE _____

VOCABULARY CHECK QUESTIONS

		without context I	with context II
1. *component*	(1) constant; (2) comrade; (3) complex; (4) partial; (5) constituent.	1. _____	_____
2. *tactics*	(1) silences; (2) ideas; (3) taboos; (4) methods; (5) battles.	2. _____	_____
3. *inept*	(1) awkward; (2) crude; (3) erratic; (4) motionless; (5) infallible.	3. _____	_____
4. *recapitulation*	(1) summary; (2) statement; (3) analogy; (4) energy; (5) inflection.	4. _____	_____
5. *transpires*	(1) raises; (2) happens; (3) sees through; (4) changes; (5) snares.	5. _____	_____

(10 off for each mistake)

Word Comprehension without *contextual help* (I) _____

Word Comprehension with *contextual help* (II) _____

TOTAL WORD COMPREHENSION SCORE _____

EXERCISES

Rating yourself as a listener: Here are ten questions based on Dr. Nichols's research in the area of listening — questions that will serve nicely as an informal rating device. Check up on yourself. Answer each question with a *yes* or *no*.

1. Science says you think four times faster than a person usually talks to you. Do you use this excess time to turn your thoughts elsewhere while you are keeping general track of a conversation?   1. _____

2. Do you listen primarily for facts, rather than ideas, when someone is speaking?   2. _____

3. Do certain words, phrases, or ideas so prejudice you against the speaker that you cannot listen objectively to what is being said?   3. _____

4. When you are puzzled or annoyed by what someone says, do you try to get the question straightened out immediately — either in your own mind or by interrupting the speaker?   4. _____

5. If you feel that it would take too much time and effort to understand something, do you go out of your way to avoid hearing about it?   5. _____

6. Do you deliberately turn your thoughts to other subjects when you believe a speaker will have nothing particularly interesting to say?   6. _____

7. Can you tell by a person's appearance and delivery that he won't have anything worthwhile to say?   7. _____

8. When somebody is talking to you, do you try to make him think you're paying attention when you're not?   8. _____

9. When you're listening to someone, are you easily distracted by outside sights and sounds?   9. _____

10. If you want to remember what someone is saying, do you think it a good idea to write it down as he goes along?   10. _____

If you answer "NO" to all these questions, then you are that rare individual — the perfect listener. Every "YES" answer means that you are guilty of a specific bad listening habit.

Now you should know what habits, if any, need changing to make yourself a better listener, a move that will mean improved understanding, closer friendships, and increased general efficiency.

Comparing listening and reading time: Some years ago Paul T. Rankin made a survey of the time spent in communicating. Selecting sixty-eight adults, he asked them to keep a careful record, every fifteen minutes, of the amount of time spent in talking, reading, writing, and listening. Data collected over a two-month period led to the discovery that 70 percent of his subjects' waking day was spent in verbal communication. Of that communication time, listening made up 45 percent, reading 16 percent. But that was back in 1929.

What is true today with you? Make a survey of the time you spend in listening and reading during an average day. Compare your findings with those reported by Dr. Rankin.

NAME_____ DATE_____ READING RATE_____W.P.M.

COMPREHENSION CHECK QUESTIONS

1. The author says that most of us do not (1) hear as we should; (2) listen; (3) listen to friends; (4) listen to strangers.   1. _____

2. He quotes (1) Coleridge; (2) Shelley; (3) Keats; (4) Wordsworth.   2. _____

3. Listening is spoken of as (1) a very active business; (2) an automatic reaction; (3) varying with age; (4) varying with sex.   3. _____

4. The author specifically speaks of listening with our (1) imagination; (2) insights; (3) experience; (4) heart.   4. _____

5. He mentions opening a book and listening to (1) Socrates; (2) Aristotle; (3) Plato; (4) Hippocrates.   5. _____

Receptive Comprehension _____

6. This discussion is focused mainly on (1) how one should listen; (2) how similar listening and reading are; (3) how to become an active listener; (4) how listening enriches human experience.   6. _____

7. The two-line bit of poetry was used to remind us that (1) we can't help listening; (2) listening is mental and emotional; (3) listening is a physical thing; (4) listening is a matter of choice.   7. _____

8. You would assume you know a person is listening (1) from his silence; (2) from his vocal response; (3) from his internal changes; (4) from his muscular responses.   8. _____

9. The word "listen," as used in this selection; means essentially (1) reading as well as listening; (2) listening only; (3) hearing; (4) experience.   9. _____

10. Most emphasis is placed on the idea that individuals (1) do not listen; (2) simulate attention too often; (3) have major difficulties in listening; (4) are prisoners of their own experience.   10. _____

(10 off for each mistake)   *Reflective Comprehension* _____

TOTAL READING COMPREHENSION SCORE _____

VOCABULARY CHECK QUESTIONS

		without context I	with context II
1. *comatose*	(1) unconscious; (2) punctuated; (3) slow; (4) free-flowing; (5) hostile.	1. _____	_____
2. *biased*	(1) based; (2) stitched; (3) individualized; (4) prejudiced; (5) injured.	2. _____	_____
3. *inevitably*	(1) usually; (2) finally; (3) certainly; (4) completely; (5) elusively.	3. _____	_____
4. *code*	(1) creed; (2) supplement; (3) ending; (4) judgment; (5) system.	4. _____	_____
5. *inhibition*	(1) not hospitable; (2) commencement; (3) combination; (4) insert; (5) restriction.	5. _____	_____

(10 off for each mistake)

Word Comprehension without *contextual help* (I) _____

Word Comprehension with *contextual help* (II) _____

TOTAL WORD COMPREHENSION SCORE _____

EXERCISES

Effective listening depends in part on attitude, in part on actions. Here is another special Listening Index devised by Dr. Nichols to help you evaluate your listening habits and develop improved insights. For this one, think in terms of the more common face-to-face situations for listening.

ARE YOU A GOOD LISTENER?

	Almost Always	Usually	Occasionally	Seldom	Almost Never
Attitudes					
1. Do you like to listen to other people talk?	5	4	3	2	1
2. Do you encourage other people to talk?	5	4	3	2	1
3. Do you listen even if you do not like the person who is talking?	5	4	3	2	1
4. Do you listen equally well whether the person talking is man or woman, young or old?	5	4	3	2	1
5. Do you listen equally well to friend, acquaintance, stranger?	5	4	3	2	1
Actions					
6. Do you put what you have been doing out of sight and out of mind?	5	4	3	2	1
7. Do you look at him?	5	4	3	2	1
8. Do you ignore the distractions about you?	5	4	3	2	1
9. Do you smile, nod your head, and otherwise encourage him to talk?	5	4	3	2	1
10. Do you think about what he is saying?	5	4	3	2	1
11. Do you try to figure out what he means?	5	4	3	2	1
12. Do you try to figure out why he is saying it?	5	4	3	2	1
13. Do you let him finish what he is trying to say?	5	4	3	2	1
14. If he hesitates, do you encourage him to go on?	5	4	3	2	1
15. Do you restate what he has said and ask him if you got it right?	5	4	3	2	1
16. Do you withhold judgment about his idea until he has finished?	5	4	3	2	1
17. Do you listen regardless of his manner of speaking and choice of words?	5	4	3	2	1
18. Do you listen even though you anticipate what he is going to say?	5	4	3	2	1
19. Do you question him in order to get him to explain his idea more fully?	5	4	3	2	1
20. Do you ask him what the words mean as he uses them?	5	4	3	2	1

TOTAL SCORE ——————————

If your score is 75 or better, you are a *Good Listener.*
If your score is 50–75, you are an *Average Listener.*
If your score is below 50, you are a *Poor Listener.*

NAME_____ DATE_____ READING RATE_____ W.P.M.

COMPREHENSION CHECK QUESTIONS

1. The author likens the building up of small annoyances to the (1) straw that broke the camel's back; (2) drops that make a flood; (3) particles that dug the Grand Canyon; (4) particles that build up great deltas.　　　　　　　　　　　　　　　　　　　　　　1. _____

2. The wife reads him a bit about a New Jersey (1) dentist; (2) lawyer; (3) teacher; (4) policeman.　　2. _____

3. To patch up the quarrel the husband buys (1) a dozen roses; (2) a box of candy; (3) some jewelry; (4) her a dinner out.　　　　　　　　　　　　　　　　　　　　　　　3. _____

4. A comparison is made to (1) basketball; (2) baseball; (3) football; (4) volleyball.　　4. _____

5. One suggestion made is to (1) give up reading; (2) read in the office; (3) read in the bath; (4) turn up the hi-fi to drown out interference.　　　　　　　　　　　　　　　　　　5. _____

Receptive Comprehension _____

6. This is mainly to (1) explain the reason for this behavior; (2) help the husband deal with the problem; (3) warn couples to act wisely; (4) suggest the need for deception at times.　　6. _____

7. You would infer that females would be next most disturbed to see their males (1) playing bridge; (2) looking at TV; (3) fishing; (4) eating.　　　　　　　　　　　　　　　7. _____

8. Women interrupt largely as a matter of (1) habit; (2) thoughtlessness; (3) interest; (4) instinct.　　8. _____

9. This is addressed largely to (1) wives; (2) adults in general; (3) husbands; (4) marriage counselors.　9. _____

10. The suggestions are designed mainly to keep (1) both wife and husband happy; (2) the wife happy; (3) the husband happy; (4) the wife fooled.　　　　　　　　　　　　　　10. _____

(10 off for each mistake)　　　　　　　　　　　　　　　　*Reflective Comprehension* _____

TOTAL READING COMPREHENSION SCORE _____

VOCABULARY CHECK QUESTIONS

		without context I	*with context* II
1. *rampant*	(1) embankment; (2) slope; (3) breathless; (4) violent; (5) frightened.	1. _____	_____
2. *imprecations*	(1) impressions; (2) waves; (3) hints; (4) barriers; (5) curses.	2. _____	_____
3. *inertia*	(1) awkwardness; (2) inactivity; (3) inequality; (4) weight; (5) tension.	3. _____	_____
4. *manifested*	(1) manufactured; (2) kept; (3) revealed; (4) ordered; (5) filled out.	4. _____	_____
5. *bifurcation*	(1) twofold division; (2) every two years; (3) strain; (4) display; (5) secret.	5. _____	_____

(10 off for each mistake)　　　　　*Word Comprehension* without *contextual help* (I) _____

Word Comprehension with *contextual help* (II) _____

TOTAL WORD COMPREHENSION SCORE _____

EXERCISES

Using the radio to improve your listening: To develop improved concentration, accuracy, and skill in listening, put your radio to work. In the morning listen carefully to a fifteen-minute newscast, noting each story with a one- to five-word identifying phrase. When the broadcast is over, count the number of stories covered, turn your notes over, and see how many you can remember. Put a check after each story remembered. Record your results below.

Newscast	*Stories remembered*	*Details remembered*
1.		
2.		
3.		
4.		
5.		
6.		
7.		
8.		
9.		
10.		
11.		
12.		
13.		
14.		
15.		

With practice you should develop the ability to listen with enough skill to remember each story covered. The next step is to fill in the third column, headed *Details remembered*. See how many specific facts you can add for each story. When this is done for two or three weeks, improvement will be seen both in the second and third columns.

This practice lends itself well to class or group activity and works even better if the newscast is recorded and can be played back on a tape recorder or cassette. The entire group can listen, not even keeping a tally. After the newscast, the leader or teacher can give them the total number of stories covered, asking them to list the stories and to add as much factual information as possible.

The group can compare notes, try to resolve any differences in factual statement or opinion, and then listen again to the newscast. Such an exercise should also develop added awareness of details met in reading.

NAME_____ DATE_____ READING RATE_____W.P.M.

COMPREHENSION CHECK QUESTIONS

1. The author specifically mentions (1) a Mid-West drawl; (2) a Western twang; (3) an Eastern accent; (4) a Southern accent.   1. _____

2. The author's 89-year-old cousin is actually (1) delicate as a bluebell; (2) fragile as a sturdy oak; (3) deaf as a stone; (4) already vacant-eyed.   2. _____

3. One voice described is used in (1) discussing close neighbors; (2) addressing pets; (3) talking with teachers; (4) addressing auto mechanics.   3. _____

4. The author met Penny Pen (1) on a plane; (2) at a party; (3) on a train; (4) at a theatre.   4. _____

5. When talking with a doctor the author talks (1) with particular dignity; (2) in hushed tones; (3) in nervous monosyllables; (4) with animation.   5. _____

Receptive Comprehension _____

6. The purpose of this selection is to tell us about (1) regional accents; (2) personal experiences; (3) different types of people; (4) varying kinds of delivery.   6. _____

7. The humor of this selection lies largely in (1) situation; (2) surprise; (3) exaggeration; (4) puns. 7. _____

8. The material is organized largely (1) in order of climax; (2) in order of occurrence; (3) according to types; (4) according to frequency.   8. _____

9. The writer is primarily interested in getting us to (1) enjoy something; (2) do something; (3) believe something; (4) understand something.   9. _____

10. The writer develops points largely through (1) exposition; (2) comparisons; (3) literary allusions; (4) anecdotes.   10. _____

(10 off for each mistake)   *Reflective Comprehension* _____

TOTAL READING COMPREHENSION SCORE _____

VOCABULARY CHECK QUESTIONS

		without context I	*with context* II
1. *deferential*	(1) incomplete; (2) loud; (3) respectful; (4) eventful; (5) different.	1. _____	_____
2. *turbulent*	(1) foreign; (2) rigid; (3) violent; (4) new; (5) watery.	2. _____	_____
3. *hiatus*	(1) peak; (2) period; (3) gap; (4) road; (5) stream.	3. _____	_____
4. *dulcet*	(1) uninteresting; (2) peculiar; (3) moist; (4) sweet; (5) old.	4. _____	_____
5. *banalities*	(1) proverbs; (2) remarks; (3) greetings; (4) commonplaces; (5) lectures.	5. _____	_____

(10 off for each mistake)   *Word Comprehension* without *contextual help* (I) _____

Word Comprehension with *contextual help* (II) _____

TOTAL WORD COMPREHENSION SCORE _____

EXERCISES

Improving listening skill: One way of testing any idea is by trying it. Charles E. Irvin mentions some activities which have proved successful in the well-developed listening training program at Michigan State College. Try them yourself and decide which are most effective for you.

A. To make yourself "listening conscious" construct a *Code of Listening Manners.*

"Do's and Don'ts" of Acceptable Listening Deportment

1.   6.

2.   7.

3.   8.

4.   9.

5.   10.

B. Prepare a "listening inventory" of your strengths and weaknesses in the listening activity.

My Listening Inventory

Strengths   Weaknesses

1.   1.

2.   2.

3.   3.

4.   4.

5.   5.

6.   6.

C. List factors of distraction present in the classroom—anything which tends to take your mind off the subject. Discussion of such distractions often leads to the elimination of some and adjustment to others.

List of Distractions

1.

2.

3.

4.

5.

6.

D. Ask several people to write down the central idea in a talk. Compare and discuss any differences that arise.

E. Ask a speaker to prepare a short talk in which he uses at least three main points, each of which is supported by a different kind of evidence. Ask the listeners to draw a line down the center of their note sheet. As they listen they are to write down the main points on one side of the line, the development details on the other. Compare notes with the speaker afterward to see if there is agreement.

NAME_____ DATE_____ READING RATE_____W.P.M.

COMPREHENSION CHECK QUESTIONS

1. The first contestant didn't know the meaning of (1) decade; (2) century; (3) cupidity; (4) tragedy.   1. _____

2. Every time a contestant missed, the kitty was increased (1) an unspecified amount; (2) by $100; (3) by $1,000; (4) by double.   2. _____

3. The Quiz Master called one contestant (1) an imbecile; (2) an illiterate; (3) a pedant; (4) a charlatan.   3. _____

4. One contestant was a (1) private secretary; (2) stenographer; (3) clerk; (4) receptionist.   4. _____

5. One contestant was from (1) McClure; (2) England; (3) McClusky; (4) Ireland.   5. _____

Receptive Comprehension _____

6. The chief purpose of this selection is (1) to satirize; (2) to inform; (3) to describe; (4) to convince.   6. _____

7. The writer pokes fun chiefly at (1) stupidity; (2) radio; (3) sponsors; (4) announcers.   7. _____

8. You would infer that the studio audience is (1) not characterized sufficiently to permit generalizations; (2) not as smart as the contestants; (3) smarter than the contestants; (4) about equally as ignorant as the contestants.   8. _____

9. When the Quiz Master says, "and scores—hundreds—of other words as well," he apparently uses the word *hundreds* (1) for emphasis; (2) to talk down to the contestant; (3) to correct his first idea; (4) to confuse the contestant.   9. _____

10. The listener who tunes in on the show is best described as (1) sympathetic toward the Quiz Master; (2) sympathetic toward the contestants; (3) an objective listener; (4) an apathetic listener.   10. _____

(10 off for each mistake)   *Reflective Comprehension* _____

TOTAL READING COMPREHENSION SCORE _____

VOCABULARY CHECK QUESTIONS

		without context I	with context II
1. *contrive*	(1) forgive; (2) oppose; (3) assist; (4) manage; (5) continue.	1. _____	_____
2. *cupidity*	(1) love; (2) work; (3) hope; (4) greed; (5) fault.	2. _____	_____
3. *confreres*	(1) limits; (2) meetings; (3) secrets; (4) conflagrations; (5) associates.	3. _____	_____
4. *capacious*	(1) powerful; (2) playful; (3) hungry; (4) large; (5) complete.	4. _____	_____
5. *pandemonium*	(1) rain; (2) money; (3) tumult; (4) revenge; (5) assistance.	5. _____	_____

(10 off for each mistake)   *Word Comprehension* without *contextual help* (I) _____

Word Comprehension with *contextual help* (II) _____

TOTAL WORD COMPREHENSION SCORE _____

EXERCISES

Figuring your salary potential: To earn more money, learn more words. That pretty well sums up the point of Morton Winthrop's article, "Do You Know How Words Can Make You Rich?" His article contains the following twenty-item test. Take it, score it, and use those scores to predict your top income. Just circle the choice that comes closest to the meaning of the first italicized word to the left. Guess if you're not sure.

1. Did you see the *clergy?* / funeral / dolphin / churchmen / monastery / bell tower

2. Fine *louvers.* / doors / radiators / slatted vents / mouldings / bay windows

3. Like an *ellipse.* / sunspot / oval / satellite / triangle / volume

4. Dire *thoughts.* / angry / dreadful / blissful / ugly / unclean

5. It was the *affluence.* / flow rate / pull / wealth / flood / bankruptcy

6. Discussing the *acme.* / intersection / question / birth mark / perfection / low point

7. How *odious* / burdensome / lazy / hateful / attractive / fragrant

8. This is *finite* / limited / tiny / precise / endless / difficult

9. Watch for the *inflection.* / accent / mirror image / swelling / pendulum swing / violation

10. The *connubial state.* / marriage / tribal / festive / spinsterly / primitive

11. See the *nuance.* / contrast / upstart / renewal / delinquent / shading

12. Where is the *dryad?* / water sprite / fern / dish towel / chord / wood nymph

13. Will you *garner* it? / dispose of / store / polish / thresh / trim

14. A sort of *anchorite.* / religious service / hermit / marine deposit / mineral / promoter

15. *Knurled* edges. / twisted / weather beaten / flattened / ridged / knitted

16. It is *bifurcated?* / forked / hairy / two wheeled / mildewed / joined

17. Examining the *phthisis* / cell division / medicine / misstatement / dissertation / tuberculosis

18. *Preponderance* of the group. / absurdity / heaviness / small number / foresight / majority

19. Ready to *expound.* / pop / confuse / interpret / dig up / imprison

20. Staring at the *relict.* / trustee / antique table / corpse / widow / excavation

See page 316 for answers and predicted top income.

From *This Week* Magazine, Oct. 30, 1960.

NAME_____ DATE_____ READING RATE_____ W.P.M.

COMPREHENSION CHECK QUESTIONS

1. Words are specifically likened to (1) families; (2) trees; (3) personalities; (4) seeds.   1. _____

2. *Calculate* comes from a Latin word meaning (1) "cover"; (2) "hodometer"; (3) "vehicle"; (4) "pebble."   2. _____

3. From the Latin verb *spectare* have come English words to the number of about (1) 60; (2) 180; (3) 240; (4) 310.   3. _____

4. The word *companion* means literally one who (1) eats bread with you; (2) farms with you; (3) drinks with you; (4) walks with you.   4. _____

5. Specific mention is made of the Greek word appearing in English as (1) *ology;* (2) *graph;* (3) *philos;* (4) *phobia.*   5. _____

Receptive Comprehension _____

6. The purpose of this selection is to demonstrate the (1) importance of dictionary study; (2) fascination of words; (3) interesting role of Latin and Greek in our language; (4) close relationship between vocabulary and success.   6. _____

7. The one word that perhaps best illustrates the amazing vitality of language is the word (1) supercilious; (2) inspect; (3) inspire; (4) run.   7. _____

8. The authors emphasize (1) using the dictionary daily; (2) looking at words analytically; (3) falling in love with words; (4) studying classical elements.   8. _____

9. The discussion of the Latin verbs *spectare* and *spirare* is intended to suggest the importance of (1) roots; (2) definitions; (3) literal meanings; (4) Latin.   9. _____

10. You would conclude from this selection that vocabulary study time should be spent with (1) unknown words; (2) known words; (3) modern words; (4) all kinds of words.   10. _____

(10 off for each mistake)   *Reflective Comprehension* _____

TOTAL READING COMPREHENSION SCORE _____

VOCABULARY CHECK QUESTIONS

		without context I	*with context* II
1. *inordinately*	(1) recently; (2) excessively; (3) openly; (4) impatiently; (5) evenly.	1. _____	_____
2. *fastidious*	(1) fascinating; (2) fashionable; (3) dressy; (4) popular; (5) critical.	2. _____	_____
3. *static*	(1) motionless; (2) dynamic; (3) sharp; (4) bright; (5) dull.	3. _____	_____
4. *contrived*	(1) crushed; (2) restrained; (3) devised; (4) denied; (5) compared.	4. _____	_____
5. *prolific*	(1) powerful; (2) fruitful; (3) helpful; (4) favorable; (5) meager.	5. _____	_____

(10 off for each mistake)   *Word Comprehension* without *contextual help* (I) _____

Word Comprehension with *contextual help* (II) _____

TOTAL WORD COMPREHENSION SCORE _____

EXERCISES

1. Thought-structuring for mastery of new prefix, root, and suffix elements: Use this technique to determine the meanings of word elements without going to the dictionary. Suppose, for example, that you do not know the meaning of the prefix *pre-*. You can, of course, consult the dictionary, but it is far better to establish a way of thinking to achieve the same results. Here is the pattern to establish. Start thinking of some common words containing that prefix, define each, then see what meaning is common to all. For example, you might think of *preview, prepare,* and *precede,* meaning "to view before," "to make ready before," and "to go before." Obviously the meaning common to all probably belongs to the prefix common to all.

To develop added skill with this approach, do the following exercises with prefix, root, and suffix elements.

1. If *commingle* means to mingle _____

   and *compress* means to press or squeeze _____,

   the prefix *com-* probably means _____.

2. If *descend* means to come _____

   and *depress* means to press _____,

   the prefix *de-* probably means _____.

3. If *depart* means to go _____

   and *deprive* means to take _____,

   the prefix *de-* probably also means _____.

4. If *obstruct* means to work _____ something

   and *object* means to protest _____ something,

   the prefix *ob-* probably means _____.

5. If *hyperactive* means _____-active

   and *hypercritical* means _____ly critical,

   the prefix *hyper-* probably means _____.

6. If *portable* means able to be carried

   and *transport* to carry across,

   the root *portare* probably means _____.

7. If *attract* means to draw to

   and *extract* to draw out,

   the root *trahere* probably means _____.

8. If *tangible* means something that can be touched

   and *tangent* means touching,

   the root *tangere* probably means _____.

9. If *statuesque* means like a statue

   and *picturesque* means like a picture,

   the suffix *-esque* probably means _____.

10. If a *kitchenette* is a little kitchen

    and a *statuette* a little statue,

    the suffix *-ette* probably means _____.

2. Discovering variant forms: Some prefixes have several variant forms. If you are to put your prefix knowledge to full use, you must know all these forms well. That means, for example, recognizing *com-* in *collaborate* as well as in *compare.* Using your dictionary, find as many variant forms as possible for each of the following prefixes, the most changeable to be found.

Prefixes	Variant Forms
1. *ab-*	_____
2. *ad-*	_____
3. *in-*	_____
4. *com-*	_____
5. *sub-*	_____
6. *ob-*	_____
7. *syn-*	_____
8. *trans-*	_____
9. *ex-*	_____
10. *dis-*	_____

NAME_____ DATE_____ READING RATE_____W.P.M.

COMPREHENSION CHECK QUESTIONS

1. Vocabulary books are said (1) to sell well; (2) to sell poorly; (3) to be easy reading; (4) to be difficult reading.

            1. _____

2. The test accompanying this article was devised by (1) William Morris; (2) John Strachey; (3) Norman Lewis; (4) Wilfred Funk.

            2. _____

3. A widely accepted figure for the number of words in the English language is (1) 1,250,000; (2) 1,000,-000; (3) 750,000; (4) 500,000.

            3. _____

4. In building a vocabulary, crossword puzzles are said to be (1) extremely helpful; (2) moderately helpful; (3) useless; (4) of uncertain value.

            4. _____

5. The writer specifically mentions (1) Mark Twain; (2) Washington Irving; (3) Emerson; (4) Galsworthy.

            5. _____

Receptive Comprehension _____

6. The purpose of this selection is to help the reader (1) understand the power of words; (2) measure and increase his vocabulary; (3) enjoy reading the classics; (4) understand how many words he should know.

            6. _____

7. Word-building books are criticized for (1) their difficulty; (2) their artificiality; (3) their organization; (4) their length.

            7. _____

8. Crossword puzzles are criticized for (1) their repetition of certain words; (2) their over-simplification of definitions; (3) their concern with freak words; (4) no specified reason.

            8. _____

9. You would infer from this selection that the important thing to do is to read (1) certain books; (2) any books; (3) technical books; (4) the dictionary.

            9. _____

10. The chief reason for interest in words is (1) increased salary; (2) admiration for the fluent speaker; (3) the urge for self-improvement; (4) not discussed.

            10. _____

(10 off for each mistake)   *Reflective Comprehension* _____

TOTAL READING COMPREHENSION SCORE _____

VOCABULARY CHECK QUESTIONS

		without context I	*with context* II
1. *prowess*	(1) favor; (2) priority; (3) difficulty; (4) skill; (5) slowness.	1. _____	_____
2. *prestige*	(1) wealth; (2) privacy; (3) closeness; (4) education; (5) distinction.	2. _____	_____
3. *correlation*	(1) conflict; (2) likeness; (3) newness; (4) training; (5) argument.	3. _____	_____
4. *absorption*	(1) payment; (2) assimilation; (3) picture; (4) abuse; (5) relaxation.	4. _____	_____
5. *formidable*	(1) difficult; (2) shapely; (3) angry; (4) calm; (5) sincere.	5. _____	_____

(10 off for each mistake)   *Word Comprehension* without *contextual help* (I) _____

Word Comprehension with *contextual help* (II) _____

TOTAL WORD COMPREHENSION SCORE _____

EXERCISES

How to score yourself

Check your answers for the vocabulary test on pp. 141 and 142 against the key below.

	SECTION I					SECTION II			
1. u	6. k	11. e	16. o	21. y	1. b	6. r	11. g	16. u	21. c
2. d	7. p	12. j	17. r	22. b	2. m	7. n	12. d	17. x	22. v
3. c	8. g	13. s	18. a	23. i	3. p	8. f	13. a	18. q	23. w
4. m	9. x	14. l	19. n	24. t	4. l	9. o	14. s	19. j	24. h
5. q	10. w	15. f	20. v	25. h	5. y	10. i	15. t	20. k	25. e

SECTION III

1. d	6. b	11. c	16. a	21. b	26. a	31. b	36. d	41. b	46. c
2. c	7. b	12. d	17. c	22. b	27. b	32. a	37. b	42. a	47. a
3. b	8. c	13. d	18. b	23. a	28. d	33. d	38. a	43. c	48. b
4. d	9. d	14. d	19. d	24. b	29. a	34. c	39. d	44. a	49. d
5. a	10. a.	15. d	20. c	25. b	30. d	35. c	40. b	45. d	50. a

To score Sections I and II: Find the number of *correct* answers and multiply by 800. Thus if you had 30 *correct* answers, your score would be 24,000 for Sections I and II.

To score Section III: Count the number of *mistakes* you made and multiply this figure by 533. Deduct the total from 20,000. This is your score for Section III. Thus if you had 20 *mistakes,* you should deduct 10,660 from 20,000, which would give you a score of 9,340 for Section III.

Then add the scores for all three sections to find the *approximate* number of words in your recognition vocabulary. This number, under the example given, would be 24,000 plus 9,340, or 33,340 words—an excellent score for most people, as you will see below.

This test takes no account of the number of proper names and place names that may be included in your vocabulary. This part of one's vocabulary varies so greatly from person to person that no attempt to evaluate it is practicable.

Furthermore, most of us use, in addition to our general vocabulary, a jargon of our trade or profession, which may run from as few as fifty words to as many as a thousand or more in the case of law or medicine. It is safe to say, therefore, that a professional man's vocabulary will be substantially larger than this test may indicate.

On this test a rating of 15,000 words or better is excellent for a high school student. An adult high school graduate should score above 25,000 to rate "excellent." A college graduate should score well above 30,000, and a person who uses words regularly in his work—an author, newspaperman or clergyman, for example—should rate above 40,000.

1. *Paging Mrs. Malaprop:* In the following sentences there are some vocabulary slips. Cross out the inappropriate word and substitute the intended one.

   A. During the battle the soldier was wounded in a venerable spot. _____

   B. Because of their part in the escapade, they were dispelled from school. _____

   C. The deviation of a word is given in an unabridged dictionary. _____

   D. The entire crew of the ill-fated ship was taken into custardy. _____

   E. They tried in vain to distinguish the raging conflagration. _____

2. *Using the right word:* In the following sentences, select the word that should be used. Answers are below.
   A. This medicine should have a good (1. affect, 2. effect).
   B. The writer did not mean to (1. imply, 2. infer) that.
   C. With complete satisfaction, the worker (1. lay, 2. laid) down the hammer.
   D. The student (1. deprecated, 2. depreciated) their efforts.
   E. The press and radio seem (1. complementary, 2. complimentary) rather than competitive.

Answers to 1: A. vulnerable, B. expelled, C. derivation, D. custody, E. extinguish.
Answers to 2: A, 2; B, 1; C, 2; D, 1; E, 1. Check your dictionary if you missed any.

NAME————————————————————— DATE————————— READING RATE——————— W.P.M.

COMPREHENSION CHECK QUESTIONS

1. The author prefers to think in terms of what dictionary? (1) *Funk and Wagnalls;* (2) *Webster's New International;* (3) Thorndike-Barnhart; (4) *Webster's New World.*   1. ————

2. The article lists some words brought into our vocabulary by (1) playing the piano; (2) star gazing; (3) gardening; (4) sailing.   2. ————

3. Specific mention is made of the root (1) *auto;* (2) *nym;* (3) *lex;* (4) *floris.*   3. ————

4. The devil in "between the devil and the deep blue sea" is (1) a reference to a myth; (2) Satan; (3) a cliff overhanging the water; (4) a part of a boat.   4. ————

5. One of the rare words mentioned is (1) *alb;* (2) *podagra;* (3) *manubrium;* (4) *volute.*   5. ————

Receptive Comprehension ————

6. The main idea is to (1) help you improve your vocabulary; (2) stimulate interest in vocabulary development; (3) show how vocabulary grows; (4) describe four stages of vocabulary development.   6. ————

7. Most emphasis is on (1) firsthand experience; (2) daily effort; (3) frequent use; (4) attention to key roots and prefixes.   7. ————

8. Particular stress is on (1) reading aloud; (2) getting fun out of words; (3) correct pronunciation; (4) reading more.   8. ————

9. Mention of *nasturtium* and *nightmare* is to get us to (1) be more precise in definition; (2) develop interest in word origins; (3) pronounce words carefully; (4) notice spelling difficulties.   9. ————

10. Most of the main points are developed by (1) analogies; (2) stories; (3) specific details; (4) generalities. 10. ————

(10 off for each mistake)   *Reflective Comprehension* ————

TOTAL READING COMPREHENSION SCORE ————

VOCABULARY CHECK QUESTIONS

			without context I	*with context* II
1. *obsolete*	(1) colloquial; (2) stubborn; (3) worn out; (4) evident; (5) out of date.	1.	————	————
2. *recalcitrant*	(1) unruly; (2) hard; (3) reciprocal; (4) reassuring; (5) calculation.	2.	————	————
3. *lethargic*	(1) healthy; (2) lively; (3) dull; (4) deadly; (5) elevated.	3.	————	————
4. *lissome*	(1) lazy; (2) lisping; (3) irregular; (4) nimble; (5) messy.	4.	————	————
5. *alb*	(1) bird; (2) robe; (3) excuse; (4) holder; (5) powder.	5.	————	————

(10 off for each mistake)   *Word Comprehension* without *contextual help* (I) ————

Word Comprehension with *contextual help* (II) ————

TOTAL WORD COMPREHENSION SCORE ————

E e

⅃⅂	⅃	⅀	Ⅎ	Ⅎ	E	E	Ⅎ	E	E	Є	e	E	ℰ	e	ℓ
1	2	3	4	5	6	7	8	9		10	11	12	13	14	15

Phoenician   Greek   Roman   Medieval   Modern

Around 1000 B.C. *the Phoenicians and other Semites of Syria and Palestine began to use a graphic sign in the forms (1,2). They gave it the name* hē *and used it for the consonant* h. *After 900* B.C. *the Greeks borrowed the sign from the Phoenicians, gradually simplifying it and reversing its orientation (3,4,5,6). They also changed its name to* ē *and used it for the vowel* e. *Later they renamed the sign* epsilon, *"the short* e," *to differentiate it from* ēta, *which was reserved for the long* ē. *The Greek forms passed unchanged via Etruscan to the Roman alphabet (7,8). The Roman Monumental Capital (9) is the prototype of our modern capital, printed (12) and written (13). The written Roman form (8) developed into the late Roman and medieval Uncial (10) and Cursive (11), replacing linear with rounded shapes. These are the bases of our modern small letter, printed (14) and written (15).*

e, E (ē) *n., pl.* **e's** or *rare* **es, E's** or **Es. 1.** The fifth letter of the modern English alphabet. See **alphabet. 2.** Any of the speech sounds represented by this letter.

e, E, e., E. *Note:* As an abbreviation or symbol, *e* may be a small or a capital letter, with or without a period. Established forms or those generally preferred precede the definition. When no form is given, all four forms are in general use in that sense. **1.** E. earl. **2.** E Earth. **3.** east; eastern. **4.** e electron. **5.** e., E. engineer; engineering. **6.** E, E. English. **7.** e, e. Baseball. error. **8.** E excellent. **9.** e *Mathematics.* The base of the natural system of logarithms, having a numerical value of approximately 2.718... . **10.** The fifth in a series. **11.** E *Music.* **a.** The third tone in the scale of C major, or the fifth tone in the relative minor scale. **b.** The key or a scale in which E is the tonic. **c.** A written or printed note representing this tone. **d.** A string, key, or pipe tuned to the pitch of this tone.

each (ēch) *adj. Abbr.* **ea.** One of two or more persons, objects, or things considered individually or one by one; every: *Each man cast a vote.* —*pron.* Every one of a group of objects, persons, or things considered individually; each one. Usually regarded as singular: *Each presented his gift.* —*adv.* For or to each one; apiece: *ten cents each.* [Middle English *ech, ælc,* Old English *ælc, ǽghwile.* See **lik-** in Appendix.*]

Usage: *Each* (pronoun), employed as subject, takes a singular verb and related pronouns or pronominal adjectives in formal usage: *Each has his own job to perform.* This is true also when *each* is followed by *of* and a plural noun or pronoun: *Each of the boys has his own job.* Informally, especially in speech, such sentences sometimes take the form *Each . . . have their own job.* The plural construction is especially common when *each* refers to members of a group of men and women or boys and girls, and *their* is consequently felt to be more appropriate than *his.* On a formal level, however, a singular verb is required: *Each of them has a large following.* The alternative, *Each have large followings,* is termed unacceptable by 95 per cent of the Usage Panel. When *each* occurs after a plural subject with which it is in apposition, the verb is usually plural: *We each require much attention.* *O'Brien and Loeb each have large followings.* In examples involving compound subjects, such as the second, however, a singular verb sometimes occurs. Thus, the alternative construction, *O'Brien and Loeb each has a large following,* is acceptable to 69 per cent of the Panel, though most grammarians prescribe a plural verb. The phrase *each and every* is redundant and preferably replaced by either *each* or *every,* used singly. When it is used, however, *each and every* governs a singular verb and related words: *Each and every girl has an obligation to do her share.* See Usage note at **between.**

each other. 1. Each the other. Used as a compound reciprocal

pronoun: *They met each other* (each met the other). **2.** One another. See Usage note.

Usage: *Each other* occurs most often when the reference is to only two persons or things. Some grammarians recommend its restriction to such examples and prescribe *one another* in examples where more than two are involved. The distinction is not observed rigidly, however. Thus, the following is acceptable to 55 per cent of the Usage Panel: *The four partners regarded each other with suspicion.* Similarly, the construction *husband and wife should confide in one another* is acceptable to 54 per cent. The possessive forms are invariably written *each other's* (not *others'*) and *one another's.*

Eads (ēdz), **James Buchanan.** 1820–1887. American civil engineer and inventor.

ea·ger¹ (ē'gər) *adj.* **-gerer, -gerest. 1.** Intensely desirous of something; impatiently expectant: *an eager search for a familiar face in the crowd.* **2.** *Obsolete.* Tart; sharp; cutting. —See Usage note at **anxious.** [Middle English *egre,* sharp, keen, eager, from Old French *aigre,* from Latin *ācer.* See **ak-** in Appendix.*] —**ea'ger·ly** *adv.* —**ea'ger·ness** *n.*

Synonyms: *eager, avid, keen, anxious, earnest, fervid, zealous.* These adjectives describe a condition of mind marked by great interest, desire, or concern, or a manifestation of such a condition. *Eager* primarily suggests strong interest or desire. *Avid,* an intensification of *eager,* implies enthusiasm and unbounded craving. *Keen* suggests acuteness or intensity of interest or emotional drive. *Anxious* applies to interest or desire tinged by concern or fear. *Earnest* stresses seriousness of purpose and sincerity of motivation. *Fervid* emphasizes intensity of interest or desire, expressed in behavior that may be compulsive or overwrought. *Zealous* makes an even stronger implication of unbridled enthusiasm or concern, sometimes verging on fanaticism and unrestrained behavior.

ea·ger². Variant of **eagre.**

eager beaver. *Informal.* An industrious, overzealous person.

ea·gle (ē'gəl) *n.* **1.** Any of various large birds of prey of the family Accipitridae, including members of the genera *Aquila, Haliaeetus,* and other genera, characterized by a powerful hooked bill, long broad wings, and strong, soaring flight. **2.** A representation of an eagle used as an emblem, insignia, seal, or the like. **3.** A former gold coin of the United States having a face value of ten dollars. **4.** *Golf.* A score of two below par on any hole. [Middle English *egle,* from Old French *egle, aigle,* from Latin *aquila†.*]

eagle
Haliaeetus leucocephalus
Bald eagle

ea·gle-eyed (ē'gəl-īd') *adj.* Having keen eyesight.

eagle owl. A large Eurasian owl, *Bubo bubo,* having brownish plumage and prominent ear tufts.

Eagle Scout. The highest rank in the Boy Scouts.

ea·glet (ē'glĭt) *n.* A young eagle.

ea·gre (ē'gər, ā'-) *n.* Also **eag·er.** A tidal flood, a **bore** *(see).* [Perhaps ultimately from Old English *ēagor,* flood tide. See **akwā-** in Appendix.*]

Ea·kins (ā'kĭnz), **Thomas.** 1844–1916. American painter.

eal·dor·man (ôl'dər-mən) *n., pl.* **-men** (-mĭn). The chief magistrate of a shire in Anglo-Saxon England. [Old English *ealdormann,* prince. See **alderman.**]

Ea·ling (ē'lĭng). A borough of London, England, comprising the former administrative divisions of Acton, Ealing, and Southall. Population, 300,000.

-ean. Indicates of or pertaining to or derived from. Used chiefly with proper names; for example, **Caesarean, Tyrolean.** [Variant of **-IAN.**]

ear¹ (îr) *n.* **1.** *Anatomy.* **a.** The vertebrate organ of hearing,

ă pat/ā pay/âr care/ä father/b bib/ch church/d deed/ĕ pet/ē be/f fife/g gag/h hat/hw which/ĭ pit/ī pie/îr pier/j judge/k kick/l lid, needle/m mum/n no, sudden/ng thing/ŏ pot/ō toe/ô paw, for/oi noise/ou out/ŏŏ took/ōō boot/p pop/r roar/s sauce/sh ship, dish/

NAME————————————————— DATE——————— READING RATE ——————— W.P.M.

COMPREHENSION CHECK QUESTIONS

1. The writer's first job was as (1) refuse-collection person; (2) copy boy; (3) receptionist; (4) paper delivery person.

1. ————

2. Mention is made of a restaurant located in (1) San Francisco; (2) Los Angeles; (3) Berkeley; (4) Long Beach.

2. ————

3. The writer mentions (1) Jack the Ripper; (2) the Boston Strangler; (3) the Manson killings; (4) Bluebeard.

3. ————

4. In reference to a male person, specific mention was made of (1) smelly sweat socks; (2) a dingy sweat shirt; (3) grimy shirt collars; (4) baggy sweat pants.

4. ————

5. This writer is presently writing a book about (1) cattlemen; (2) southwest history; (3) Arizona; (4) rodeo.

5. ————

Receptive Comprehension ————

6. This selection is mainly focused on doing what about the desexing problem? (1) pointing up its presence; (2) suggesting a solution; (3) suggesting its insolubility; (4) pointing up its ridiculous effects.

6. ————

7. Points are developed largely through use of (1) contrast and comparison; (2) specific examples; (3) description; (4) analogies.

7. ————

8. The tone of this article is best described as (1) matter-of-fact; (2) dramatic; (3) humorous; (4) cynical.

8. ————

9. The primary purpose is to (1) make clear; (2) warn; (3) amuse; (4) explain.

9. ————

10. Transpersons were mentioned apparently (1) as further complications; (2) as supporters of the new trend; (3) as supporters of a return to gender; (4) as genderless persons.

10. ————

(10 off for each mistake)   *Reflective Comprehension* ————

TOTAL READING COMPREHENSION SCORE ————

VOCABULARY CHECK QUESTIONS

		without context I	*with context* II
1. *pervasive*	(1) contrary; (2) stubborn; (3) spreading; (4) persuasive; (5) personable.	1. ————	————
2. *generic*	(1) vague; (2) popular; (3) generous; (4) courteous; (5) universal.	2. ————	————
3. *replete*	(1) renewed; (2) well-filled; (3) replicate; (4) plain; (5) pleasing.	3. ————	————
4. *suffuses*	(1) satisfies; (2) suffers; (3) chokes; (4) overspreads; (5) substitutes.	4. ————	————
5. *lethargic*	(1) lethal; (2) light; (3) steady; (4) sluggish; (5) growing.	5. ————	————

(10 off for each mistake)   *Word Comprehension* without *contextual help* (I) ————

Word Comprehension with *contextual help*   (II) ————

TOTAL WORD COMPREHENSION SCORE ————

EXERCISES

Reading the dictionary: Dictionaries pack a tremendous amount of information into very compact form. For that reason they have to be read in a special way. To understand the problem and to move toward improving your mastery of the dictionary, check each of the following statements with the sample dictionary page on page 318 of this text. If the statement is in accord with the preferred usage sanctioned by the dictionary, mark it with a +. If it is *not* in accord, mark it with a −.

You consult the dictionary for information about plurals, spelling, hyphenation, word division, capitals, pronunciation, usage, derivation, synonyms, grammar, and abbreviations. See how effectively you read the dictionary with statements involving each of these headings.

Plurals

    1. Two eaglet were in the nest.   1. _____

Spelling

    2. How many e's are in *feed?*   2. _____

Capitals

    3. I know that he's an eagle scout.   3. _____

Hyphenation

    4. See that eagle-stone?   4. _____

Word Division

    5. The word *eaglet* should be divided after the *g.*   5. _____

Pronunciation

    6. The first syllable in *ealdorman* should be pronounced to rhyme with *eel.*   6. _____

Usage

    7. They hurt one another's feelings.   7. _____

    8. Each of the candidates has a large following.   8. _____

Derivation

    9. The word *eagle* is derived originally from the Old French.   9. _____

    10. The word *each* comes directly from Middle English.   10. _____

Synonym

    11. *Anxious* is the appropriate synonym of *eager* for the sentence: He is quite anxious to please his demanding and difficult constituency.   11. _____

Grammar

    12. Each and every book should be read completely.   12. _____

Abbreviations

    13. In baseball the abbreviation for *error* is *er.*   13. _____

Check your answers below. If you miss any items, you know that you have things to learn about reading the dictionary with accuracy.

The dictionary also serves as a miniature encyclopedia, as the following questions suggest. Answer them from the dictionary page.

    14. Where is Ealing?   14. _____

    15. What is the population of Ealing?   15. _____

    16. Who was Eakins?   16. _____

    17. What did Eads do?   17. _____

    18. What suffix is listed?   18. _____

    19. What is the technical name for an eagle owl?   19. _____

    20. Who reversed the orientation of E?   20. _____

Answers: 1, −; 2, +; 3, −; 4, −; 5, −; 6, −; 7, +; 8, +; 9, −; 10, +; 11, +; 12, −; 13, −; 14, London; 15, 300,000; 16, painter; 17, civil engineering; 18, -ean; 19, *Bubo bubo;* 20, the Greeks.

NAME_____ DATE_____ READING RATE_____W.P.M.

COMPREHENSION CHECK QUESTIONS

1. This account took place in (1) London; (2) Manhattan; (3) Chicago; (4) Los Angeles.
   1. _____

2. In the restaurant, the Old Man drank (1) beer; (2) whiskey; (3) tea; (4) ale.
   2. _____

3. In his office the Old Man had a photograph of (1) Jung; (2) Adler; (3) Coue; (4) Freud.
   3. _____

4. The journal the Old Man pulled out toward the end was written by (1) Jonathan; (2) Jonathan's wife; (3) Jonathan's sister; (4) Jonathan's fiancée.
   4. _____

5. Shortly after this conversation the Old Man (1) retired; (2) died; (3) moved; (4) became an invalid.
   5. _____

Receptive Comprehension _____

6. This article primarily shows (1) the importance of vocabulary; (2) how words can affect life; (3) how psychiatrists think and work; (4) how life affects choice of words.
   6. _____

7. This is primarily (1) persuasion; (2) exposition; (3) narration; (4) description.
   7. _____

8. You would assume that the young man probably (1) had arranged the meeting to get help with his problem; (2) had wanted to hide his problems from the Old Man; (3) had talked about them largely at the Old Man's urging; (4) had often gotten into difficulties.
   8. _____

9. The most important difference between the two phrases is in (1) the timing of their application; (2) the attention given to the mistakes; (3) the direction they tend to point; (4) the center-of-stage position.
   9. _____

10. The story about Jonathan was used to remind us to (1) profit from mistakes; (2) weigh all factors before judging; (3) act before it is too late; (4) work hard at the business of living.
    10. _____

(10 off for each mistake)   *Reflective Comprehension* _____

TOTAL READING COMPREHENSION SCORE _____

VOCABULARY CHECK QUESTIONS

		without context I	*with context* II
1. *gnome*	(1) column; (2) puzzle; (3) antelope; (4) spur; (5) dwarf.	1. _____	_____
2. *berated*	(1) rebuked; (2) deprived; (3) left; (4) begged; (5) judged.	2. _____	_____
3. *perverse*	(1) abundant; (2) uncertain; (3) contrary; (4) lucid; (5) impudent.	3. _____	_____
4. *ruefully*	(1) pleasantly; (2) roughly; (3) unruly; (4) mournfully; (5) ruddy colored.	4. _____	_____
5. *retrieve*	(1) carry; (2) recover; (3) reduce; (4) retain; (5) retrace.	5. _____	_____

(10 off for each mistake)

Word Comprehension without *contextual help* (I) _____

Word Comprehension with *contextual help* (II) _____

TOTAL WORD COMPREHENSION SCORE _____

EXERCISES

1. Sensing the power of words: Some years ago the *New York Times* carried an editorial headed "Vocabulary and Marks," which began by asking if there was any magic formula for getting high marks in college. The president of Stevens Institute, was quoted as saying that those students who worked on vocabulary their freshman year "were thereby enabled to do relatively better work in all their sophomore courses than their fellow classmen did. Those who improved most in vocabulary averaged three or four places nearer the top of their class during their sophomore year than during their freshman year. Conversely, all the men that did not improve at all in vocabulary averaged 7.5 places nearer the bottom of their class during the sophomore year." Apparently a new word a day keeps the low grades away!

Those results suggested the need to check the relationship between frequency of dictionary use and success in a single class, such as in a University of Minnesota Efficient Reading class. Since all students in such classes take a standardized reading test at the beginning and end of the course, any differences could be noted exactly. On the last day of class students were asked how frequently they had used their dictionary during the quarter. Those who said they had used a dictionary once a week or less improved on the pre- and post-test standardized score 11 percent. By comparison, those who said they had used a dictionary once a day or more improved 26 percent or 136 percent more than those who used a dictionary less frequently. In a reading improvement course, a new word a day keeps the low grades away also. Academically speaking, a student's best friend looks like the dictionary. Keep it handy. Use it frequently. It will pay off well. Don't underestimate the power of words.

2. Using words that smile and snarl: Our words usually reflect our attitudes. If a boy meets a thin girl and is favorably impressed, he is likely to use the word *slender* to describe her. If he is not impressed, the word *skinny* may slip out. They both mean the same thing; yet one has a favorable, the other an unfavorable, connotation. Yes, he can say she's a vision, but not she's a sight.

Observations	Favorable	Unfavorable
EXAMPLE: She is *thin*.	slender	skinny
1. He is *fat*.		
2. He *asked for* a favor.		
3. He made a *long speech*.		
4. She *spends money carefully*.		
5. Her hat was *different*.		

3. Using words that walk and live: Some words in common use today are actually mythological characters still living on in our language. Use your dictionary to discover the character behind each of the following words and the characterizing detail that gives the word its meaning.

Words	Characters	Characterizing Details
EXAMPLE: *herculean*	Hercules	strength (to do the difficult)
1. *tantalize*		
2. *procrustean*		
3. *panic*		
4. *venereal*		
5. *odyssey*		

4. Using words that fit: Many words can be used as more than one part of speech. In the following exercise, compose sentences for each part of speech indicated by the label. You may want help from your dictionary for this, distinctions of this kind being quite important.

Words	Sentences
EXAMPLE: *like* (as adj.)	You must pay a like sum to the other party.
1. *round* (as adj.)	
2. *round* (as noun)	
3. *round* (as v.t.)	
4. *round* (as prep.)	

NAME————————————————— DATE——————— READING RATE——————— W.P.M.

COMPREHENSION CHECK QUESTIONS

1. Bimbi was spoken of as (1) a safe blower; (2) an old-time burglar; (3) a second-story man; (4) a dope pusher.   1. ————

2. The author said he didn't know a verb from a (1) noun; (2) book; (3) hole in the ground; (4) house.   2. ————

3. The author felt that he should try to improve his (1) speech; (2) arithmetic; (3) grammar; (4) penmanship.   3. ————

4. How many words did he think he wrote while in prison? (1) two million; (2) a million; (3) half a million; (4) amount not specified.   4. ————

5. Lights out came at what time? (1) nine P.M.; (2) ten P.M.; (3) eleven P.M.; (4) no exact time given.   5. ————

Receptive Comprehension ————

6. The main focus is on how (1) Bimbi inspired Malcolm X; (2) Malcolm X developed his reading abilities and interests; (3) he developed his vocabulary; (4) strongly he was motivated.   6. ————

7. Malcolm X apparently felt that Bimbi was respected, largely for what reason? (1) age; (2) experience; (3) words; (4) personality.   7. ————

8. What subject of discussion attracted Malcolm X most strongly to Bimbi? (1) the science of human behavior; (2) Thoreau; (3) religion; (4) historical events and figures.   8. ————

9. Copying the dictionary seemed to please Malcolm X primarily because he (1) could remember the words easily; (2) improved his handwriting greatly; (3) learned words he didn't know existed; (4) found he could use them frequently.   9. ————

10. Of the following words, which best characterizes Malcolm X? (1) tough; (2) clever; (3) persistent; (4) sociable.   10. ————

(10 off for each mistake)   *Reflective Comprehension* ————

TOTAL READING COMPREHENSION SCORE ————

VOCABULARY CHECK QUESTIONS

			without context I	*with context* II
1. *quota*	(1) query; (2) figure; (3) proportional share; (4) large quantity; (5) pursuit.	1.	————	————
2. *expounded*	(1) crushed; (2) explained; (3) investigated; (4) transported; (5) tried.	2.	————	————
3. *emulate*	(1) hire; (2) sooth; (3) antagonize; (4) hinder; (5) imitate.	3.	————	————
4. *riffling*	(1) occurring frequently; (2) shooting; (3) opening; (4) leafing rapidly; (5) guessing.	4.	————	————
5. *dormant*	(1) sleeping; (2) uniformed; (3) worn; (4) carefully planned; (5) sympathetic.	5.	————	————

(10 off for each mistake)   *Word Comprehension* without *contextual help* (I) ————

Word Comprehension with *contextual help* (II) ————

TOTAL WORD COMPREHENSION SCORE ————

EXERCISES

Learning and using suffixes: Do you use four or five words to express an idea when one would do it more effectively? If so, put suffixes to work. For example, "capable of being read" boils down neatly into the word *readable* when you utilize the right suffix. Using the twenty suffixes listed below, enter the appropriate one in the blank in the right-hand column.

Suffixes: *-able, -al, -ate, -dom, -er, -esque, -ess, -ful, -ile, -ish, -ive, -less, -ly, -ock, -ory, -ose, -tion, -trix, -ule, -ulent.*

Phrases

1. A small hill or mound is a   hill_____.

2. The state of being wise is called   wis_____.

3. Of or pertaining to an infant is   infant_____.

4. Full of or characterized by fraud is   fraud_____.

5. One who is young is   youth_____.

6. A woman aviator is an   avia_____.

7. Something capable of being retracted is   retract_____.

8. If someone works without tiring, he is   tire_____.

9. A situation that lends itself to remedy is   remedi_____.

10. One who helps is a   help_____.

11. Something in the manner or style of a picture is called   pictur_____.

12. To cause something to become antique is to   antiqu_____.

13. A female lion is a   lion_____.

14. Something pertaining to a book is   book_____.

15. A minute globe is a   glob_____.

16. Having the nature of a commendation means   commendat_____.

17. To act toward instigating something is to   instiga_____ it.

18. A scheme full of grandeur is   grandi_____.

19. Action tending toward a conclusion is   conclus_____.

20. An object moved in the direction of heaven moves in a   heaven_____ direction.

Answers: 1, hillock; 2, wisdom; 3, infantile; 4, fraudulent; 5, youthful; 6, aviatrix; 7, retractable; 8, tireless; 9, remedial; 10, helper; 11, picturesque; 12, antiquate; 13, lioness; 14, bookish; 15, globule; 16, commendatory; 17, instigate; 18, grandiose; 19, conclusive; 20, heavenly or heavenward.

NAME＿＿＿＿＿＿＿＿＿＿＿＿＿＿＿＿ DATE＿＿＿＿＿ READING RATE＿＿＿＿ W.P.M.

COMPREHENSION CHECK QUESTIONS

1. This selection lists (1) ten master words; (2) twelve master words; (3) fourteen master words; (4) sixteen master words.   1. ＿＿＿

2. The Latin verb *plicare* means to (1) play; (2) fold; (3) place; (4) tease.   2. ＿＿＿

3. In our language, words derived from the Latin and Greek make up approximately (1) 20 percent; (2) 40 percent; (3) 60 percent; (4) 80 percent.   3. ＿＿＿

4. The relationship between the derivation and common definitions of a word is (1) identical; (2) remote; (3) varied; (4) close.   4. ＿＿＿

5. One of the following words is *not* discussed: (1) predilection; (2) explication; (3) cooperation; (4) prevarication.   5. ＿＿＿

Receptive Comprehension ＿＿＿

6. The purpose of this selection is to (1) encourage vocabulary building; (2) suggest the importance of Latin and Greek elements in our language; (3) describe a technique for improving one's vocabulary; (4) suggest how knowledge of certain classical elements makes spelling easier.   6. ＿＿＿

7. You would infer that *prescience* means (1) modern; (2) foreknowledge; (3) quietness; (4) intelligence.   7. ＿＿＿

8. Our common word *affect* probably contains an assimilated form of the prefix (1) a-; (2) abs-; (3) ad-; (4) af-.   8. ＿＿＿

9. If you wished to build a vocabulary quickly, several words at a time, probably the most useful part of a dictionary entry would be the (1) definitions; (2) derivation; (3) synonyms; (4) examples of words in contexts.   9. ＿＿＿

10. The phrase "vocabulary is a concomitant to success" probably means that vocabulary (1) results from success; (2) leads to success; (3) is unrelated to success; (4) goes along with success.   10. ＿＿＿

(10 off for each mistake)   *Reflective Comprehension* ＿＿＿

TOTAL READING COMPREHENSION SCORE ＿＿＿

VOCABULARY CHECK QUESTIONS

			without context I	with context II
1. *invaluable*	(1) cheap; (2) ordinary; (3) fairly valuable; (4) very valuable; (5) useless.	1.	＿＿	＿＿
2. *converting*	(1) reflecting; (2) carrying; (3) conversing; (4) meeting; (5) transforming.	2.	＿＿	＿＿
3. *partiality*	(1) bias; (2) portion; (3) speck; (4) follower; (5) partner.	3.	＿＿	＿＿
4. *intricacies*	(1) plans; (2) origins; (3) complexities; (4) peculiarities; (5) pledges.	4.	＿＿	＿＿
5. *touchstone*	(1) criticism; (2) hope; (3) diet; (4) criterion; (5) failure.	5.	＿＿	＿＿

(10 off for each mistake)   *Word Comprehension* without *contextual help* (I) ＿＿＿

Word Comprehension with *contextual help* (II) ＿＿＿

TOTAL WORD COMPREHENSION SCORE ＿＿＿

Using the master-word approach. What does it mean to *know* the twenty prefixes and fourteen roots in the master-word approach? Actually it means mastery of four kinds or levels of knowing — (1) memorization; (2) identification; (3) application; and (4) generalization.

Memorization. The first step or level of knowing is relatively easy. It means learning the common meaning or meanings of each prefix root element listed in the table on page 151. Memorizing those meanings will not take long. Just cover the answers in the Common Meaning columns, check to see how many meanings you know, then memorize the others perfectly. To review, turn to the table, cover the meaning column in order to supply the meanings yourself, and uncover the answers for an immediate check.

Since things learned by rote tend to be easily forgotten, work out a mnemonic aid to link each element meaningfully with its common meaning. Take the prefix *epi-*. What does it mean, commonly? Help yourself remember its meaning by thinking of a familiar word containing that prefix — a word where the meaning "upon" is so obvious that you no longer have to memorize. The association remembers for you. For example, you know perfectly well what an *epi*taph is. It's the inscription carved "upon" a tombstone. Take another example. You know what your epidermis is. It's the outermost layer of your skin — the "upon" layer, so to speak. Such words serve as mnemonic aids to link the prefix *epi-* with the meaning "upon," thus helping you remember.

Now devise a mnemonic aid for each prefix and root element in the table to insure a mastery of the first step in knowing — knowledge of common meanings.

Identification. It is not enough, however, to know the prefix or root meaning. You must also be able to identify the presence of an element as it appears in a word — otherwise knowing its meaning is useless. Most of the time the elements are rather easily spotted, but sometimes there are real difficulties. To see the problem more clearly, try the following quiz, dealing with one of the most difficult prefixes of all to identify.

Look at the following words, checking only the ones which you can identify as containing the prefix *ad-*:

1. accuse	___	8. associate	___
2. afferent	___	9. attract	___
3. agglutinate	___	10. ascend	___
4. allude	___	11. aspire	___
5. annex	___	12. astringent	___
6. acquire	___	13. agnate	___
7. arrive	___	14. adynamia	___

How well did you identify the prefix in question 14 — the prefix *ad-*? You should have checked all but the last one. All but the last contain a form of the prefix *ad-*. To be sure, this is perhaps the most difficult of all prefixes to identify. It is a reminder of the importance of knowing at the second level and of using the dictionary as a help in mastering this second step.

Look at the following dictionary entry for the prefix *ad-*. It should prepare you for the variant forms in the quiz.

ad–. Indicates motion toward; for example, **adsorb.** [Latin, from *ad,* to, toward, at. See **ad-** in Appendix.* In borrowed Latin compounds *ad-* indicates: 1. Motion toward, as in **advent.** 2. Proximity, as in **adjacent.** 3. Addition, increase, as in **accrue.** 4. Relationship, dependence, as in **adjunct.** 5. Intensified action, as in **accelerate.** Before *c, f, g, l, n, q, r, s,* and *t, ad-* is assimilated to *ac-, af-, ag-, al-, an-, acq-, ar-, as-,* and *at-;* before *sc, sp, st,* and *gn,* it is reduced to *a-.*]

Roots also show wide variations in form. Since it is important to relate prefix and root closely to the words containing those elements, suppose for the next exercise that you start with the variant forms of a root and come up with certain words containing those forms. In the preceding exercise you started with words and were to note those containing the prefix.

Take the root *facere,* meaning "to make or do." English words derived from that source are likely to have one of the following five forms: *fac, fic, fea, fec,* and *fas.* In the following exercise, for each of the phrase definitions supply a single word containing one of the five forms and fitting the definition. For example, what would you call "a building where things are made"? You would call it a *factory.* The word, derived from *facere,* does contain one of the five forms, the form *fac.* And it does fit the definition. Go ahead with the exercise.

Definitions	Words
1. not easily done	_____
2. made by hand or machinery	_____
3. a notable act or deed	_____
4. to make it easy to do	_____
5. tender attachment	_____
6. evil doer	_____
7. blemish or fault	_____
8. something without flaw	_____
9. conquer or overcome	_____
10. accepted style of doing	_____

(*Exercise continued on page 328*)

Answers: 1, difficult; 2, manufacture or fashion; 3, feat; 4, facilitate; 5, affection; 6, malefactor; 7, imperfection or defect; 8, perfect; 9, defeat; 10, fashion or fashionable.

NAME _____ DATE_____ READING RATE_____ W.P.M.

COMPREHENSION CHECK QUESTIONS

1. The author likens words to (1) arrows; (2) money; (3) diamonds; (4) magnets.   1. _____

2. Successful people usually (1) have large vocabularies; (2) read widely and well; (3) have a large library; (4) speak fluently and well.   2. _____

3. The writer discusses (1) no specific type of vocabulary; (2) two types of vocabulary; (3) three types of vocabulary; (4) four types of vocabulary.   3. _____

4. The author suggests (1) vocabulary flash cards; (2) a specific vocabulary-building book; (3) a vocabulary notebook; (4) use of a tape recorder.   4. _____

5. When you come across a new word in your reading you are told to (1) put a check in the margin and read on; (2) stop and consult the dictionary; (3) analyze it into prefix, root, and suffix; (4) write it down immediately.   5. _____

Receptive Comprehension _____

6. This selection is concerned chiefly with (1) how to improve your vocabulary; (2) defining what is meant by vocabulary; (3) establishing importance of vocabulary; (4) suggesting when a vocabulary can best be developed.   6. _____

7. Vocabulary exercises like those in this book are closely related to the suggestion in this selection to (1) write a sentence using the word; (2) review the words studied; (3) pronounce the words accurately; (4) get meanings from context.   7. _____

8. You would infer that this selection is probably taken from a complete text on (1) reading; (2) vocabulary-building; (3) composition; (4) communication.   8. _____

9. This selection is chiefly (1) narration; (2) description; (3) persuasion; (4) exposition.   9. _____

10. The specific suggestions for improving vocabulary at the end are listed in order of (1) importance; (2) difficulty; (3) effectiveness; (4) time.   10. _____

(10 off for each mistake)   *Reflective Comprehension* _____

TOTAL READING COMPREHENSION SCORE _____

VOCABULARY CHECK QUESTIONS

		without context I	with context II
1. *consider*	(1) select; (2) judge; (3) decide; (4) provide; (5) ponder.	_____	_____
2. *medium*	(1) source; (2) means; (3) process; (4) act; (5) ritual.	_____	_____
3. *assume*	(1) believe; (2) agree; (3) suppose; (4) trust; (5) say.	_____	_____
4. *block*	(1) reduce; (2) obstruct; (3) delay; (4) force; (5) eliminate.	_____	_____
5. *maintain*	(1) balance; (2) postpone; (3) increase; (4) sustain; (5) rely.	_____	_____

(10 off for each mistake)

Word Comprehension without *contextual help* (I) _____

Word Comprehension with *contextual help* (II) _____

TOTAL WORD COMPREHENSION SCORE _____

EXERCISES

Application. To a mathematician such words as *abscissa, exponential,* and *asymptote* are common. To a botanist, *mitosis, meiosis,* and *stomata* are equally so. But to a student just beginning to study higher mathematics or botany, such technical words are probably meaningless. One student during his first week in college came across the words *ebracteate* and *exospore* in a botany text and *extravasate* in geology; he heard a medical doctor use the word *exostosis.* Then in his general reading he came across the others listed below. How many of them do you know? Try the following quiz to see. Enter the answers in the column headed I.

		I	II
1. *ebracteate*	(1) with bracts; (2) without bracts; (3) rounded bracts; (4) pointed bracts; (5) stiff bracts.	1. _____	_____
2. *exospore*	(1) core; (2) source; (3) middle layer; (4) outer spore layer; (5) stem.	2. _____	_____
3. *extravasate*	(1) melt; (2) shrink; (3) solidify; (4) crack; (5) erupt.	3. _____	_____
4. *exostosis*	(1) outgrowth; (2) leg bone; (3) paralysis; (4) joint; (5) scab.	4. _____	_____
5. *ebullition*	(1) bruise; (2) boiling out; (3) seeping in; (4) repair; (5) warmth.	5. _____	_____
6. *elicit*	(1) draw forth; (2) make illegal; (3) hide; (4) prove; (5) close.	6. _____	_____
7. *expunge*	(1) dive in; (2) soak; (3) erase; (4) swim; (5) save.	7. _____	_____
8. *effete*	(1) worn out; (2) strong; (3) difficult; (4) shut in; (5) wealthy.	8. _____	_____
9. *exhume*	(1) moisten; (2) work; (3) put in; (4) pay for; (5) dig out.	9. _____	_____
10. *evulsion*	(1) hatred; (2) rotation; (3) lotion; (4) extraction; (5) description.	10. _____	_____

TOTAL SCORES: _____ _____

Before checking your answers, think back to what you did. Did you notice, for example, that all ten words began with an *e* — five of them with an *ex-*? Do you know what the prefix *ex-* commonly means? In short, did you apply some knowledge of prefixes as you took the test? If you did, your score should reflect that fact.

Now retake the same test, using column II for your answers. Consciously apply one additional bit of information — that all ten words contain a prefix meaning "out." Lean heavily on that prefix meaning as you retake the test. Check both sets of answers with the key.

You can see more clearly how this approach works. Once you know what a prefix or root means and can identify it accurately in a word, you are ready for the pay-off step — application. A group of seventy-eight adults tried the test without being encouraged to lean on prefix meaning. They were then told, as you were, that each word contained a prefix meaning "out." That knowledge improved their average score 36 percent.

A perfect score in the second column means that you applied your knowledge well. With the adults, while improvement was general, some scored only 70 or 80 the second time through. Since even a desk-size dictionary contains over a thousand words with a prefix meaning "out," the dramatic usefulness of this shortcut seems apparent.

Generalization. Even when you develop enviable ability with the first three steps, be sure not to overlook the fourth and last step — generalization. For example, by studying only twenty prefixes you can still learn things about all the other prefixes — if you know how.

Take the prefix *ad-*. See what happens when it combines with *lude* to make *allude.* Can you now generalize about another prefix — the prefix *com-*? If *com-* were to be added to *lude,* would the resulting word be *comlude, colude,* or *collude*? How accurately can you generalize?

Take still another kind of generalization. In a sense, you know the meaning of most prefixes — but you don't know that you know. For example, you may say you don't know exactly what the prefix *re-* means. Try some generalizing with this pattern. If to *reread* is "to read again" and *reheat* is "to heat again," you have reason to conclude that a common meaning of *re-* is "again." Generalizing on the basis of that sample, you now have a formula for discovering the meaning of any prefix or root.

Take the prefix *omni-*. What does it mean? Think of some words with *omni-*, such as *omnipresent, omnipotent,* or *omnivorous.* Use the formula to generalize. If *omnipresent* means "present in all places" and *omnipotent* means "all-powerful," apparently one meaning of *omni-* is "all." Finding the meaning common to any given prefix is like finding a common denominator in a math problem. Some generalizations are, of course, more complex and difficult than others. But as you develop improved insights, you develop the skill to handle much more difficult problems, just as in mathematics.

Answers: 1, 2; 2, 4; 3, 5; 4, 1; 5, 2; 6, 1; 7, 3; 8, 1; 9, 5; 10, 4.

NAME——————————————————————— DATE——————— READING RATE——————— W.P.M.

COMPREHENSION CHECK QUESTIONS

1. Dictionaries are spoken of specifically as (1) aids; (2) tools; (3) helpers; (4) friends.   1. ————

2. Specific mention is made of the (1) *American Heritage Dictionary*; (2) *Random House Dictionary of the English Language*; (3) *Century Dictionary*; (4) *Webster's New World Dictionary*.   2. ————

3. The author quotes Professor (1) O'Connor; (2) Bergen Evans; (3) Partridge; (4) Pei.   3. ————

4. The origin of what word is discussed? (1) *whooping crane*; (2) *ostrich*; (3) *heron*; (4) *gyasticutus*.   4. ————

5. The word *hyla* is from what language? (1) Latin; (2) Greek; (3) Arabic; (4) German.   5. ————

                                                                        Receptive Comprehension ————

6. The main idea is that dictionaries (1) contain a wealth of information; (2) should be better used by students; (3) are difficult reading; (4) provide fascinating information.   6. ————

7. The opening paragraphs about the steel square are intended primarily to do what with respect to the dictionary? (1) arouse interest in it; (2) suggest its complexity; (3) show its usefulness; (4) encourage its use.   7. ————

8. The "poll tax" illustration was to show (1) the difficulty of finding needed information; (2) the ignorance of students; (3) the easy availability of needed information; (4) the lack of acquaintance with larger dictionaries.   8. ————

9. You would infer that this selection is primarily addressed to (1) teachers; (2) freshmen; (3) graduate students; (4) general readers.   9. ————

10. Most emphasis is placed on the dictionary as (1) a holder of interesting information; (2) a problem-solver; (3) an aid in understanding technical words; (4) an introduction to linguistics.   10. ————

(10 off for each mistake)   *Reflective Comprehension* ————

                                             TOTAL READING COMPREHENSION SCORE ————

VOCABULARY CHECK QUESTIONS

		without context I	*with context* II
1. *lexicographer*	(1) analyst; (2) student; (3) typist; (4) dictionary compiler; (5) scientific editor.	1. ————	————
2. *philology*	Study of (1) medicine; (2) physics; (3) philosophy; (4) foreign languages; (5) words.	2. ————	————
3. *progenitor*	(1) prophet; (2) child; (3) origin; (4) forefather; (5) species.	3. ————	————
4. *impelled*	(1) driven; (2) imparted; (3) hindered; (4) begged; (5) implied.	4. ————	————
5. *assiduously*	(1) sharply; (2) heartily; (3) diligently; (4) hopefully; (5) helpfully.	5. ————	————

(10 off for each mistake)   *Word Comprehension* without *contextual help* (I) ————

                                    Word Comprehension with *contextual help*   (II) ————

                                             TOTAL WORD COMPREHENSION SCORE ————

EXERCISES

Answers to the 20-Word Quiz on page 312. Check your answers, then find your age group in the columns below, and you'll learn your probable peak future income. Don't be discouraged if you didn't score well — read the article for tips on how you can improve your vocabulary and your income potential.

1. *churchmen*	6. *perfection*	11. *shading*	16. *forked*
2. *slatted vents*	7. *hateful*	12. *wood nymph*	17. *tuberculosis*
3. *oval*	8. *limited*	13. *store*	18. *majority*
4. *dreadful*	9. *accent*	14. *hermit*	19. *interpret*
5. *wealth*	10. *marriage*	15. *ridged*	20. *widow*

Figure your top income by looking up the number of correct words under your age heading. Then adjust for inflation by adding 30 percent to the figures given.

Age 30 and Up

Score	
20–19	$36,500 and up
18–17	$24,300–$36,500
16–15	$16,200–$24,300
14–13	$12,200–$16,200
12–11	$ 8,500–$12,200
10–7	$ 6,500–$ 8,500
Below 7	Under $6,500

Age 21–29

Score	
20–17	$36,500 and up
16–15	$24,300–$36,500
14–13	$16,200–$24,300
12–11	$12,200–$16,200
10–5	$ 6,500–$12,200
Below 5	Under $6,500

Age 17–20

Score	
20–15	$36,500 and up
14–13	$24,300–$36,500
12–11	$16,200–$24,300
10–9	$12,200–$16,200
8–7	$ 8,500–$12,200
6–3	$ 6,500–$ 8,500
Below 3	Under $6,500

Age 13–16

Score	
20–12	$36,500 and up
11–10	$24,300–$36,500
9–8	$16,200–$24,300
7–6	$12,200–$16,200
5–4	$ 8,500–$12,200
3–2	$ 6,500–$ 8,500
Below 2	Under $6,500

Age 9–12

Score	
20–10	$36,500 and up
9–8	$24,300–$36,500
7–6	$16,200–$24,300
5–4	$12,200–$16,200
3–2	$ 8.500–$12,200
1	$ 6,500–$ 8,500
0	Under $6,500

Improving vocabulary through contextual clues: Wide reading is an invaluable aid to vocabulary development. This is particularly true if you sharpen your awareness of contextual clues by noting the following three common situations, so helpful in dealing with new and strange words.

(1) Words used in pairs, either similar or opposite pairs.
(2) Words surrounded by illustrative details that suggest meaning.
(3) Words followed or preceded by "remote synonyms" that make meaning clear.

For example, suppose you don't know what the word *octogenarian* means. If you find it in the following context of opposite pairs, meaning will be clarified: "Man or woman, millionaire or pauper, octogenarian or infant — all are affected by this new regulation." Or if you don't know the meaning of *lexicographers,* the meaningful details in the following context should help: "Lexicographers worked through the file marked 'new words' in an attempt to determine which words to include in the new desk dictionary." Such details strongly suggest that lexicographers are dictionary makers. As a last example, lean on a remote synonym to get the meaning of *lave:* "You must lave the area four times daily. The only way you can hope to alleviate the pain is by such regular bathing with warm water."

In the textbooks that you are studying, find two clearly defined illustrations of each of these three situations. Enter them below.

(1) Illustrations of word pairs:

    (a) _____

    (b) _____

(2) Illustrations of meaningful details:

    (a) _____

    (b) _____

(3) Illustrations of "remote synonyms":

    (a) _____

    (b) _____

NAME_____ DATE_____ READING RATE_____ W.P.M.

COMPREHENSION CHECK QUESTIONS

1. One young woman was attending (1) Chicago Medical School; (2) Jefferson Medical College; (3) Harvard Medical School; (4) Hahneman Medical College.   1. _____

2. How many years has the woman's movement been going on? (1) five; (2) ten; (3) fifteen; (4) twenty-five.   2. _____

3. The president of Radcliffe spoke of the present situation as a "crisis of (1) credibility"; (2) creativity"; (3) conflict"; (4) confidence."   3. _____

4. What newspaper is quoted? (1) *Chicago Tribune*; (2) *New York Times*; (3) *Washington Post*; (4) *Christian Science Monitor*.   4. _____

5. Specific reference is made to (1) share-time; (2) modeling schools; (3) flextime; (4) executive training programs.   5. _____

Receptive Comprehension _____

6. This selection is mainly about how to escape (1) the feminine mystique; (2) the feminist mystique; (3) the supermom image; (4) the remaining inequality.   6. _____

7. The example of the lovely "executive assistant" was to point up (1) how successful some women have become; (2) the progress in equal opportunity; (3) motherhood needs; (4) a growing problem.   7. _____

8. Primary focus is on the (1) causes; (2) gains; (3) solution; (4) problem.   8. _____

9. The author's opinions seem formed largely through (1) factual studies; (2) cited authorities; (3) personal contacts; (4) personal work experience.   9. _____

10. Apparently major emphasis should now be placed on (1) domestic equality; (2) equal job opportunity; (3) equal education; (4) motherhood needs.   10. _____

(10 off for each mistake)   *Reflective Comprehension* _____

TOTAL READING COMPREHENSION SCORE _____

VOCABULARY CHECK QUESTIONS

		without context I	*with context* II
1. *urgency*	(1) hindrance; (2) urbanism; (3) suffering; (4) insistence; (5) protection.	1. _____	_____
2. *queasiness*	(1) shakiness; (2) strangeness; (3) quickness; (4) suspiciousness; (5) uneasiness.	2. _____	_____
3. *illusory*	(1) illustrious; (2) unreal; (3) illegal; (4) similar; (5) illogical.	3. _____	_____
4. *viable*	(1) varied; (2) experienced; (3) workable; (4) unusual; (5) vibrating.	4. _____	_____
5. *demarcation*	(1) boundary; (2) standard; (3) demonstration; (4) demand; (5) destruction.	5. _____	_____

(10 off for each mistake)   *Word Comprehension* without *contextual help* (I) _____

Word Comprehension with *contextual help* (II) _____

TOTAL WORD COMPREHENSION SCORE _____

EXERCISES

With such matters as style, usage, punctuation, diction, spelling, and sentence structure in mind, make the best possible choices in the groupings that follow, circling your preferences.

These past few | (a) years, | I have been nagged by an uneasy feeling of | (a) urgency. | Listening to my own daughter and
| | (b) years | | (b) urgancy. |

(a) sons   (a) there   (a) whom   (a) I have   (a) when   (a) at
and others of   generation   met   lecturing
(b) sons,   (b) their   (b) who   (b) I've   (b) while   (b) in

(a) Universities   (a) proffessional   (a) world; (a) something seems *off,*
and attending   conferences around the   out of
(b) universities   (b) professional   (b) world, (b) I sense something *off,*

(a) focus —   (a) sense in which   (a) young people   (a) equity
going wrong, in the   these   are trying to live the
(b) focus,   (b) terms by which   (b) youngsters   (b) equality

(a) us   (a) womens'   (a) wanted. . . .
in the   movement
(b) we   (b) women's   (b) fought for. . . .

I sense | (a) victories, | we thought were | (a) won (a) yeilding | illusory | (a) gains; | I see new | (a) dimensions | to
| | (b) victories | | (b) won, (b) yielding | | (b) gains, | | (b) demensions |

(a) problems (a) which we   (a) were
thought   solved.
(b) problems, (b) we   (b) to be

When you have finished, check your version with the original in Selection 72. Consult a dictionary or an English handbook such as *The Heath Handbook of Composition* to clear up any problems. See how close you can come to writing like a professional.

NAME———————————————————— DATE—————————— READING RATE——————————— W.P.M.

COMPREHENSION CHECK QUESTIONS

1. What were the men digging? (1) a well; (2) a foundation; (3) a trench; (4) a hole.

    1. ————

2. There is a reference to (1) Hercules; (2) Adam and Eve; (3) Robinson Crusoe; (4) *Swiss Family Robinson.*

    2. ————

3. The author says the arts of the hand (1) are built on leisure; (2) are having a rebirth; (3) have disappeared; (4) are noticeably affected by economic conditions.

    3. ————

4. The citizens of Utopia worked in what kind of canning factory? (1) asparagus; (2) tomato; (3) bean; (4) pea.

    4. ————

5. Which of the following modes of travel was *not* mentioned? (1) dog-cart; (2) train; (3) mule; (4) car.

    5. ————

Receptive Comprehension ————

6. This selection is mainly to suggest (1) how machines save work; (2) the problem posed by machines; (3) (3) how machines provide leisure; (4) the proper use of machines.

    6. ————

7. The author believes that work is (1) worthwhile; (2) to be avoided at all costs; (3) unnecessary; (4) the author's attitude is unclear.

    7. ————

8. You would infer that as a hobby the author would consider carpentering (1) impractical; (2) satisfying; (3) work; (4) creative.

    8. ————

9. The purpose of this article is primarily to (1) predict; (2) inform; (3) convince; (4) entertain.

    9. ————

10. The style is best described as (1) lively; (2) chatty; (3) elevated; (4) direct.

    10. ————

(10 off for each mistake)

Reflective Comprehension ————

TOTAL READING COMPREHENSION SCORE ————

VOCABULARY CHECK QUESTIONS

		without context I	*with context* II
1. *drudgery*	(1) slowness; (2) force; (3) tiresome work; (4) idleness; (5) quaint humor.	1. ————	————
2. *antithesis*	(1) opposite; (2) aged; (3) hatred; (4) antiquity; (5) chant.	2. ————	————
3. *hedonists*	(1) rulers; (2) drug addicts; (3) unbelievers; (4) health-seekers; (5) pleasure-seekers.	3. ————	————
4. *interregnum*	(1) question; (2) power; (3) interference; (4) pause; (5) glory.	4. ————	————
5. *cumbrous*	(1) comfortable; (2) cumulative; (3) careful; (4) primitive; (5) unwieldy.	5. ————	————

(10 off for each mistake)

Word Comprehension without *contextual help* (I) ————

Word Comprehension with *contextual help* (II) ————

TOTAL WORD COMPREHENSION SCORE ————

EXERCISES

With such matters as style, usage, punctuation, diction, spelling, and sentence structure in mind, make the best possible choices in the groupings that follow, circling your preference.

(a) But   (a) said   (a) and   (a) "creative work?"

it may be   why not retain the machine   retain   Why not cultivate

(b) But,   (b) said,   (b) *and*   (b) "creative work"?

(a) sparetime   (a) Many people   (a) idea,   (a) solve,

anachronisms as a   hobby?   have played with this   it seems to   with such

(b) spare-time   (b) Many   (b) idea;   (b) solve

(a) ease,   (a) set by   (a) citizen   (a) we're

beautiful   the problems   the machine. The   of Utopia,

(b) ease   (b) given us by   (b) resident   (b) we are

(a) his   (a) two   (a) tomato-canning (a) factory,

told, coming home from   daily   hours of turning a handle in the

(b) their (b) 2   (b) tomato canning (b) factory;

(a) will deliberately revert   (a) primitive   (a) life   (a) their   (a) with

to a more   way of   and solace   creative instincts

(b) will revert deliberately   (b) primative   (b) living   (b) his   (b) using

(a) pottery glazing (a) handloom-   (a) And —   (a) absurdity —

a bit of fretwork,   or   weaving.   why is this picture an

(b) pottery-glazing (b) handloom   (b) And   (b) absurdity,

as it is, of course?

When you have finished, check your version with the original in Selection 73. See how close you are to writing like a professional.

NAME_____ DATE_____ READING RATE_____ W.P.M.

COMPREHENSION CHECK QUESTIONS

1. The unenviable Mrs. Jones was (1) in her mid-30's; (2) in her mid-40's; (3) in her late 20's; (4) of unmentioned age.   1. _____

2. Herb Smith was a (1) psychiatrist; (2) minister; (3) social worker; (4) medical doctor.   2. _____

3. One specific bit of advice was to pay more attention to (1) people; (2) books; (3) appearance; (4) political and social issues.   3. _____

4. Mention was made of a (1) large ant; (2) butterfly; (3) robin; (4) furry caterpillar.   4. _____

5. Norman Vincent Peale spoke of his own advice as (1) pious; (2) innovative; (3) practical; (4) religious. 5. _____

Receptive Comprehension _____

6. This selection is mainly about how to (1) avoid monotony; (2) live fully; (3) find love; (4) discover goodness.   6. _____

7. The phrase "horizontal living" apparently means (1) routine living; (2) intense living; (3) sustained and satisfying living; (4) intellectual living.   7. _____

8. The point of the story about Martha was to suggest the need to (1) give emotions full rein; (2) take our mind off ourselves; (3) develop a problem-solving attitude; (4) look at life more realistically.   8. _____

9. Writing a letter without an *I, me,* or *my,* was intended primarily to help (1) fight self-centeredness; (2) fight deadening routine; (3) set and meet challenges; (4) develop a different writing style.   9. _____

10. The magnifying glass episode was intended to show the need to (1) generate interest in living; (2) find beauty; (3) escape monotony; (4) get close to nature.   10. _____

(10 off for each mistake)   *Reflective Comprehension* _____

TOTAL READING COMPREHENSION SCORE _____

VOCABULARY CHECK QUESTIONS

		without context I	*with context* II
1. *futility*	(1) stuffiness; (2) success; (3) prospect; (4) enthusiasm; (5) uselessness.	1. _____	_____
2. *valid*	(1) venturesome; (2) accurate; (3) sound; (4) relaxing; (5) varied.	2. _____	_____
3. *mutely*	(1) silently; (2) markedly; (3) uniformly; (4) strongly; (5) stealthily.	3. _____	_____
4. *imperative*	(1) improper; (2) urgent; (3) hopeless; (4) unnecessary; (5) constructive.	4. _____	_____
5. *uncomprehensible*	(1) obscure; (2) without feeling; (3) compressed; (4) extended; (5) feeble.	5. _____	_____

(10 off for each mistake)   *Word Comprehension* without *contextual help* (I) _____

Word Comprehension with *contextual help*   (II) _____

TOTAL WORD COMPREHENSION SCORE _____

EXERCISES

With such matters as style, usage, punctuation, diction, spelling, and sentence structure in mind, make the best possible choices in the groupings that follow, circling your preference.

(a) "It's   (a) wide-spread   (a) said, "this nagging   (a) uneasyness,
         a very   thing," Dr. Herbert D. Smith
(b) "Its   (b) widespread   (b) said. "This nagging   (b) uneasiness,

                 (a) Life   (a) you, that   (a) we've   (a) capability to   (a) enjoy,
this feeling that   is hiding from   lost the
                 (b) life   (b) you; that   (b) you've   (b) capacity to   (b) enjoy

                             (a) existence. I   (a) think,   (a) susceptable
or appreciate the ordinary pleasures of   women are more
                             (b) existance. I   (b) think   (b) susceptible

           (a) men;   (a) men tend to be   (a) their work,   (a) partly because,
to it than   partly because   absorbed in
           (b) men —   (b) men, tend to be   (b) one's work,   (b) since,

                   (a) could   (a) hungry   (a) easier.
being more emotional, women   become emotionally
                   (b) can   (b) starved   (b) more easily.

           (a) say,   (a) Jones?   (a) commence   (a) a little,
"Now, what would I   to Mrs.   I think I'd   by trying to reassure her
           (b) say   (b) Jones.   (b) start   (b) a little.

       (a) tell   (a) understandible. . . ."
I'd   her that her feelings are
       (b) inform   (b) understandable. . . ."

When you have finished, check your version with the original in Selection 74. Consult your dictionary or an English handbook to clear up any problems.

NAME_____ DATE_____ READING RATE_____ W.P.M.

COMPREHENSION CHECK QUESTIONS

1. The two American matrons were looking for (1) Westminster Abbey; (2) the Tower; (3) St. Paul's Cathedral; (4) the Houses of Parliament. 1. _____

2. Nitrogen was said to make up about what percent of the air we breathe? (1) 40; (2) 60; (3) 80; (4) amount not given. 2. _____

3. The terrible smog that hit London came in (1) October; (2) November; (3) December; (4) January. 3. _____

4. Specific mention was made of (1) *Punch;* (2) the *Manchester Guardian;* (3) the *Times;* (4) the *London Daily News.* 4. _____

5. What were said to be coming upstream in the Thames once again? (1) salmon; (2) elvers; (3) cod; (4) mackerel. 5. _____

Receptive Comprehension _____

6. Chief emphasis is on the (1) economic costs of pollution; (2) causes and control of pollution; (3) changed appearance of London; (4) special English regard for animals and the location of the Houses of Parliament. 6. _____

7. The opening episode about the American matrons was intended primarily to (1) arouse interest; (2) show the fresh beauty of London; (3) indicate the amount of pollution in London; (4) show typical tourist reactions. 7. _____

8. The discussion of the chemistry involved in organic waste in the Thames was to show how (1) long it takes to pollute a river; (2) complex the problem is; (3) difficult it is to stop; (4) the smell came about. 8. _____

9. The author is apparently (1) an American; (2) a Canadian; (3) an Australian; (4) an Englishman. 9. _____

10. The primary purpose is apparently to (1) convince; (2) arouse to action; (3) entertain; (4) evaluate. 10. _____

(10 off for each mistake) *Reflective Comprehension* _____

TOTAL READING COMPREHENSION SCORE _____

VOCABULARY CHECK QUESTIONS

		without context I	*with context* II
1. *malignant*	(1) overly large; (2) magnificent; (3) harmful; (4) soothing; (5) sore.	1. _____	_____
2. *harass*	(1) harmonize; (2) protect; (3) hasten; (4) torment; (5) attempt.	2. _____	_____
3. *miasmas*	(1) floods; (2) storms; (3) antidotes; (4) headaches; (5) vapors.	3. _____	_____
4. *impinge*	(1) touch on; (2) improve; (3) regulate; (4) insult; (5) leave out.	4. _____	_____
5. *wreak*	(1) crash; (2) search; (3) wrinkle; (4) estimate; (5) inflict.	5. _____	_____

(10 off for each mistake) *Word Comprehension* without *contextual help* (I) _____

Word Comprehension with *contextual help* (II) _____

TOTAL WORD COMPREHENSION SCORE _____

337

EXERCISES

With such matters as style, usage, punctuation, diction, spelling, and sentence structure in mind, make the best possible choices in the groupings that follow, circling your preference.

(a) Now, that   (a) done,   (a) Londoners   (a) beauty,

much of the cleaning has been   delight in new

(b) Now that   (b) done   (b) Londoner's   (b) beauty

(a) beginning   (a) there   (a) had

but   with   was some uneasiness. We   become so accustomed to

(b) to begin   (b) their   (b) have

         (a) buildings, that   (a) people, felt   (a) their   (a) State.

the blackness of our great   many   that this was   proper

         (b) buildings that   (b) people felt   (b) its   (b) state.

       (a) Dean and Chapter   (a) St. Pauls'   (a) decided that   (a) london

When the   of   the new purity of the   air

       (b) dean and chapter   (b) St. Paul's   (b) decided, that   (b) London

       (a) huge   (a) Cathedral   (a) they   (a) prescribe

justified the   expense of cleaning the   stone,   asked the public to

       (b) corpulent   (b) cathedral   (b) it   (b) subscribe

       (a) money, for   (a) epistles   (a) Times

the necessary   many weeks afterwards   appeared in the   protesting the

       (b) money. For   (b) letters   (b) *Times*

(a) sacrifice.   (a) wreak   (a) familiar

How dare anyone   such a change on the dear   blackness of St. Paul's!

(b) sacrilege.   (b) wreck   (b) familar

When you have finished, check your version with the original in Selection 75. Consult your dictionary or an English handbook to clear up any problems.

NAME_____ DATE_____ READING RATE_____ W.P.M.

COMPREHENSION CHECK QUESTIONS

1. In the last ten years the total annual number of divorces was said to have (1) leveled off; (2) dropped slightly; (3) risen steeply; (4) doubled.

   1. _____

2. Second marriages tend to have (1) a longer life span that the first; (2) the same life span; (3) an unpredictable life span; (4) a shorter life span.

   2. _____

3. Today what percent of the low-birth-weight babies are born to mothers in their teens? (1) 25; (2) 20; (3) 15; (4) not given.

   3. _____

4. It is said that divorce hangs over a young wife (1) when she first becomes pregnant; (2) as soon as she's married; (3) even before the ceremony; (4) the minute she stops working.

   4. _____

5. It is said that a good marriage takes (1) money; (2) similar backgrounds; (3) hard work; (4) parental help.

   5. _____

Receptive Comprehension _____

6. The main idea is to (1) indicate the problem; (2) suggest ways of dealing with the problem; (3) encourage more parental guidance; (4) persuade people to postpone getting married.

   6. _____

7. What best describes the attitude taken here toward new-style alternates to marriage? (1) noncritical; (2) critical; (3) evasive; (4) encouraging.

   7. _____

8. What factor appears most likely to lead to divorce? (1) lack of education; (2) early marriage; (3) health; (4) children.

   8. _____

9. In tone this selection is (1) sarcastic; (2) straightforward; (3) somewhat flowery; (4) colloquial.

   9. _____

10. By implication, it would seem most important for young couples to (1) read for new insights and ideas; (2) spend more time apart; (3) watch TV together more; (4) plan things to do with each other.

    10. _____

(10 off for each mistake)   *Reflective Comprehension* _____

TOTAL READING COMPREHENSION SCORE _____

VOCABULARY CHECK QUESTIONS

		without context I	*with context* II
1. *peers*	(1) superiors; (2) inferiors; (3) parents; (4) equals; (5) strangers.	1. _____	_____
2. *fending*	(1) using; (2) complaining; (3) concluding; (4) destroying; (5) managing.	2. _____	_____
3. *interloper*	(1) runner; (2) eloquent plea; (3) foreigner; (4) intruder; (5) foreman.	3. _____	_____
4. *ambivalence*	(1) conflicting feeling; (2) dexterity; (3) pleasantness; (4) slow gait; (5) slumber.	4. _____	_____
5. *limbo*	(1) leg; (2) indeterminate state; (3) distress signal; (4) dialect; (5) distaste.	5. _____	_____

(10 off for each mistake)

Word Comprehension without *contextual help* (I) _____

Word Comprehension with *contextual help* (II) _____

TOTAL WORD COMPREHENSION SCORE _____

EXERCISES

With such matters as style, usage, punctuation, diction, spelling, and sentence structure in mind, make the best possible choices in the groupings that follow, circling your preference.

Marriage and early pregnancy   (a) are   the main   (a) reason   today why girls drop out of   (a) school.
                                       (b) is   (b) reasons   (b) school,

Perhaps   (a) returning.   (a) communities there   (a) no place   (a) high school
         never   In most   is   in the
perhaps   (b) to return.   (b) communities, there   (b) noplace   (b) high-school

              (a) young, married   (a) woman; let   (a) Often, too,
system for a   alone for a young mother.
              (b) young married   (b) woman, let   (b) Often too

                          (a) there   (a) schooling.   (a) gained,   by leaving
young husbands fail to go on with   The freedom
                          (b) their   (b) education.   (b) gained

                    (a) becomes   (a) work —   (a) self-supporting
home and school   the obligation to   to be   and,
                    (b) becoming   (b) work;   (b) self supporting

                 (a) father,   (a) means,   (a) very
for a young   to support a family. Lack of education in turn   that a   large
                (b) Father,   (b) means   (b) very,

(a) porportion   (a) married, live   (a) level
                       of the very young   at the poverty   without any
(b) proportion   (b) married live   (b) level;

                (a) on   (a) nor   (a) poverty and debt.
reserves to fall back   any hope of getting out of
                (b) to   (b) or   (b) poverty, and debt.

When you have finished, check your version with the original in Selection 76. Consult your dictionary or an English handbook to clear up any problems.

NAME_____ DATE_____ READING RATE_____W.P.M.

COMPREHENSION CHECK QUESTIONS

1. This essay starts with a reference to (1) Portsmouth; (2) the Bill of Rights; (3) the Code Napoleon; (4) Plymouth.   1. _____

2. The Arab child was spoken of as a lost (1) Mozart; (2) Chopin; (3) Beethoven; (4) Caruso.   2. _____

3. How many misunderstandings are discussed? (1) one; (2) two; (3) three; (4) four.   3. _____

4. In place of the hickory stick, we were said to have (1) the psychiatrist; (2) the counselor; (3) personality tests; (4) nothing.   4. _____

5. Toynbee said that all progress comes from (1) insight; (2) discipline; (3) challenge; (4) values.   5. _____

Receptive Comprehension _____

6. The main focus of the article is on the freedom to (1) determine our own goals; (2) think as we please; (3) realize our full potential; (4) set our own values.   6. _____

7. This discussion is organized primarily on a (1) problem-solution pattern; (2) cause-effect pattern; (3) question-answer pattern; (4) time-sequence pattern.   7. _____

8. The purpose of this article is to get us to (1) understand; (2) act; (3) believe; (4) evaluate.   8. _____

9. Judging from this article, any work on efficient reading should above all (1) be practical; (2) have set standards of achievement; (3) cover the widest possible number of techniques; (4) be demanding.   9. _____

10. The ending is best described as (1) a challenge; (2) a prediction; (3) a supplication; (4) a summary.   10. _____

(10 off for each mistake)   *Reflective Comprehension* _____

TOTAL READING COMPREHENSION SCORE _____

VOCABULARY CHECK QUESTIONS

		without context I	*with context* II
1. *nought*	(1) now; (2) newness; (3) nothing; (4) originality; (5) circular.	1. ____	____
2. *unprecedented*	(1) unsurpassed; (2) uncertain; (3) inexact; (4) customary; (5) pressured.	2. ____	____
3. *tenets*	(1) doctrines; (2) renters; (3) occupants; (4) lawyers; (5) structures.	3. ____	____
4. *ultimates*	(1) origins; (2) claims; (3) actions; (4) choices; (5) fundamentals.	4. ____	____
5. *discerned*	(1) disappeared; (2) perceived; (3) scowled; (4) heard; (5) soothed.	5. ____	____

(10 off for each mistake)   Word Comprehension without *contextual help* (I) _____

Word Comprehension with *contextual help* (II) _____

TOTAL WORD COMPREHENSION SCORE _____

EXERCISES

Review: With such matters as style, usage, punctuation (pn), diction, spelling, and sentence structure in mind, make the best possible choices in the groupings that follow. When you finish, check back to the article to note any differences. Consult your handbook or dictionary to clear up any problems that arise.

	(a) there	(a) 5th	(a) Freedom	(a) no pn
And yet		is a		
	(b) their	(b) fifth	(b) freedom	(b) -

	(a) no pn	(a) which
basic to those four		
	(b) -	(b) that

(a) we are in danger of losing (a) :

                            the freedom to be

(b) is in danger of being lost (b) ;

(a) *one's*   (a) St.   (a) discribes
(b) *your best.*   Exupéry
(c) *our*   (b) St   (b) describes

	(a) no pn	(a) sensitive-faced	(a) kid,
a ragged			Arab
	(b) ,	(b) sensitive faced	(b) child,

	(a) North African	
haunting the streets of a		town, as a lost
	(b) north African	

	(a) :	(a) he would never be	
Mozart			trained or developed.
	(b) ;	(b) never being	

(a) Was he free?   (a) "Nobody (a) grasped

                                            you by the

(b) Did he have freedom? (b) "No one (b) grabbed

	(a) still was	(a) ;
shoulder while there		time (b) : and
	(b) was still	(c) ,

(a) nought   (a) awake
             will   in you the sleeping poet or
(b) nothing   (b) awaken

	(a) which		(a) one
musician or astronomer		possibly inhabited	
	(b) that		(b) you

from the beginning."

NAME_____ DATE_____ READING RATE_____ W.P.M.

COMPREHENSION CHECK QUESTIONS

1. For what percent was time and energy expenditure said to be out of step with life goals? (1) 45; (2) 60; (3) 75; (4) 90.

    1. _____

2. One of the seven questions was specifically on (1) production of income; (2) environmental needs and life style; (3) sense of responsibility; (4) physical fitness as related to mental fitness.

    2. _____

3. Who was quoted? (1) Kennedy; (2) Pogo; (3) Peanuts; (4) Hitler.

    3. _____

4. At what age was parallel play said to be typical? (1) age 1; (2) age 2; (3) age 2 or 3; (4) age 3 or 4.

    4. _____

5. Reference was made to (1) Hollywood; (2) Utopia; (3) Great Britain; (4) San Francisco.

    5. _____

Receptive Comprehension _____

6. This selection is chiefly about how to (1) discover our problems; (2) solve our problems; (3) check up on our mental health; (4) strengthen our relationships with others.

    6. _____

7. The aphorism "physician, heal thyself" was used to develop the idea that self-examination (1) is difficult; (2) is common; (3) should be done by physicians; (4) is actually impossible to do.

    7. _____

8. The seven areas are ordered essentially on what basis? (1) from the global to the individual; (2) according to a developing time sequence; (3) from the particular to the general; (4) from most to least importance.

    8. _____

9. By implication, an avocation is considered primarily as a way of (1) avoiding problems; (2) gaining emotional fulfillment; (3) finding needed relaxation; (4) developing stronger self-reliance.

    9. _____

10. In style you would call this article (1) conversational; (2) lively; (3) dignified; (4) dreary.

    10. _____

(10 off for each mistake)

Reflective Comprehension _____

TOTAL READING COMPREHENSION SCORE _____

VOCABULARY CHECK QUESTIONS

		without context I	*with context* II
1. *autonomy*	(1) technical perfection; (2) independence; (3) motor-driven; (4) composite; (5) welfare state.	1. _____	_____
2. *castigate*	(1) punish; (2) discard; (3) evolve; (4) tear down; (5) smooth over.	2. _____	_____
3. *pre-empt*	(1) suggest; (2) spare; (3) turn over; (4) get beforehand; (5) force into submission.	3. _____	_____
4. *germane*	(1) relevant; (2) cultivated; (3) original; (4) infected; (5) weakened.	4. _____	_____
5. *hallmark*	(1) shipping label; (2) entryway; (3) engraving tool; (4) symbol of excellence; (5) gift.	5. _____	_____

(10 off for each mistake)

Word Comprehension without *contextual help* (I) _____

Word Comprehension with *contextual help* (II) _____

TOTAL WORD COMPREHENSION SCORE _____

EXERCISES

With such matters as style, usage, punctuation, diction, spelling, and sentence structure in mind, make the best possible choices in the groupings that follow, circling your preference.

         (a) clear that   (a) capacaty   (a) bring into existence   (a) significant emotional
It is   the   to   close,
         (b) clear, that   (b) capacity   (b) establish   (b) significant, emotional

                (a) are   (a) is   (a) clear (a) moreover
ties with others   characteristic of emotional maturity. It
                (b) is   (b) being (b) clear, (b) moreover,

             (a) effort, and   (a) pain of   (a) so
that the work, the   sometimes the   doing   is quite enough to discourage
          (b) effort and   (b) pain, of   (b) so,

(a) many. Especially (a) when
                              the trends in our society   (a) is   moving in the same direction. And
(b) many, especially (b) being that   (b) are

(a) yet, we   (a) disdainful   (a) superficiality   (a) "cocktail" (a) party, even
           are still   of the empty   of the
(b) yet we   (b) disdainfull   (b) superficially   (b) cocktail   (b) party. Even

                (a) illusion   (a) intimacy, which   (a) can
when lessened by the   of   alcohol   provide. . . .
              (b) allusion   (b) intimacy which   (b) could

               (a) others,   (a) image (a) your
Your relationships to   do indeed   relationship to yourself.
             (b) others   (b) mirror (b) you're

When you have finished, check your version with the original in Selection 78. Consult your dictionary on an English hand-book to clear up any problems.

NAME————————————————— DATE——————————— READING RATE——————— W.P.M.

COMPREHENSION CHECK QUESTIONS

1. What Shakespearean character was mentioned? (1) Caesar; (2) Antony; (3) Macbeth; (4) King Richard.   1. ————

2. In Canada, traffic accidents take the lives of how many people annually? (1) 4,000; (2) 6,000; (3) 8,000; (4) 10,000.   2. ————

3. In the U.S., what proportion of the drivers surveyed rated themselves as "above average"? (1) nine-tenths; (2) eight-tenths; (3) seven-tenths; (4) six-tenths.   3. ————

4. What driver is specifically mentioned? (1) a teenager with a girlfriend; (2) a grade-school teacher; (3) a respectable working man; (4) a department store clerk.   4. ————

5. Police talk about what syndrome? (1) the regular-fellow; (2) the not-my-fault; (3) the good-driver; (4) the other-guy.   5. ————

Receptive Comprehension ————

6. This selection is mainly to point up what about traffic accidents? (1) their seriousness; (2) their avoidability; (3) their frequency; (4) their widespread nature.   6. ————

7. It is organized roughly on what pattern? (1) cause-effect; (2) chronological; (3) problem-solution; (4) least to most important.   7. ————

8. The introductory paragraphs are intended to (1) establish the magnitude of traffic accident tolls; (2) show the international scope of the problem; (3) indicate the effect of alcohol; (4) show how laws are disregarded.   8. ————

9. Most emphasis is placed on (1) mechanical defects; (2) the complexity of driving skills; (3) lack of concentration; (4) undue haste.   9. ————

10. Primary concern seems placed on getting us to (1) understand; (2) act; (3) feel; (4) believe.   10. ————

(10 off for each mistake)   *Reflective Comprehension* ————

TOTAL READING COMPREHENSION SCORE ————

VOCABULARY CHECK QUESTIONS

		without context I	with context II
1. *peers*	(1) inferiors; (2) British nobility; (3) superiors; (4) youth; (5) executives.	1. ————	————
2. *carnage*	(1) massacre; (2) carnival; (3) fault; (4) accident; (5) paving.	2. ————	————
3. *juggernaut*	(1) judgment; (2) car; (3) junction; (4) irresistible force; (5) accident.	3. ————	————
4. *reprehensible*	(1) sad; (2) faulty; (3) deserving blame; (4) comprehensive; (5) representative.	4. ————	————
5. *syndrome*	Set of (1) records; (2) programs; (3) sins; (4) helps; (5) characteristics.	5. ————	————

(10 off for each mistake)   *Word Comprehension* without *contextual help* (I) ————

Word Comprehension with *contextual help* (II) ————

TOTAL WORD COMPREHENSION SCORE ————

EXERCISES

With such matters as style, usage, punctuation, diction, spelling, and sentence structure in mind, make the best possible choices in the groupings that follow, circling your preference.

       (a) plain   (a) might (a) say. But   (a) principal
Just   people acting carelessly, you   it is a   both of law and common
       (b) ordinary   (b) may (b) say, but   (b) principle

(a) mortality   (a) one's   (a) liable   (a) or
         that carelessness is no excuse when   actions are   to bring death   damage to
(b) morality   (b) ones'   (b) likely   (b) and

(a) another.   (a) ommission   (a) reprehensible equally   (a) human grief is caused.
         Sins of   and commission are   if
(b) others.   (b) omission   (b) equally reprehensible   (b) they cause human grief.

       (a) real and lasting   (a) say the experts,   (a) these things   (a) peoples'
The only   solution,   is to get   into
       (b) real, lasting   (b) so say the experts,   (b) it   (b) people's

(a) heads,   (a) skillful (a) task,   (a) continual   (a) todays
       that driving is a   requiring   care and concentration. A driver in
(b) heads   (b) skilled (b) task   (b) constant   (b) today's

      (a) called   (a) preform   (a) range (a) functions (a) at the same time . . . .
traffic is   to   a complex   of
      (b) called upon   (b) perform   (b) list   (b) jobs   (b) simultaneously . . . .

When you have finished, check your version with the original in Selection 79. Consult your dictionary or an English handbook to clear up any problems. See how close you are to writing like a professional.

NAME————————————————————— DATE——————————— READING RATE——————————— W.P.M.

COMPREHENSION CHECK QUESTIONS

1. How many collegiate dictionaries are most commonly recommended? (1) five; (2) four; (3) three; (4) two.

    1. ————

2. How many criteria are given for evaluating dictionaries? (1) five; (2) four; (3) three; (4) two.

    2. ————

3. The newest is the (1) *Webster's New World*; (2) *Webster's New Collegiate*; (3) *Funk & Wagnalls*; (4) *American Heritage*.

    3. ————

4. *Webster's New Collegiate* is called (1) prescriptive; (2) descriptive; (3) permissive; (4) balanced.

    4. ————

5. The best definitions are said to be found in (1) *Webster's New Collegiate*; (2) *Random House*; (3) *Webster's New World*; (4) *American Heritage*.

    5. ————

    Receptive Comprehension ————

6. This selection is mainly about what aspect of dictionaries? (1) comparing them; (2) how to choose one; (3) their use; (4) which size to choose.

    6. ————

7. It is addressed primarily to (1) teachers; (2) high school students; (3) college students; (4) the general public.

    7. ————

8. The criteria are arranged in what order? (1) order of appearance in the dictionary; (2) from least to most important; (3) from most to least important; (4) in no obvious order.

    8. ————

9. The article is best described as (1) subjective; (2) objective; (3) personal; (4) critical.

    9. ————

10. You would assume your choice should be based primarily on (1) comparing the dictionaries; (2) assessing your own needs; (3) matching personal needs with dictionaries; (4) personal inspection.

    10. ————

(10 off for each mistake)

Reflective Comprehension ————

TOTAL READING COMPREHENSION SCORE ————

VOCABULARY CHECK QUESTIONS

		without context I	*with context* II
1. *antonyms*	(1) new words; (2) archaic words; (3) opposites; (4) sound-alikes; (5) words often confused.	1. ————	————
2. *etymologies*	(1) studies; (2) origins; (3) dictionary entries; (4) parts of speech; (5) pronunciations.	2. ————	————
3. *criteria*	(1) credits; (2) aids; (3) skills; (4) criticisms; (5) standards.	3. ————	————
4. *format*	(1) general arrangement; (2) seriousness; (3) style; (4) illustrative material; (5) printing.	4. ————	————
5. *prefatory*	(1) preferential; (2) well-known; (3) premeditated; (4) predicted; (5) introductory.	5. ————	————

(10 off for each mistake)

Word Comprehension without *contextual help* (I) ————

Word Comprehension with *contextual help* (II) ————

TOTAL WORD COMPREHENSION SCORE ————

EXERCISES

With such matters as style, usage, punctuation, diction, spelling, grammar, and sentence structure in mind, make the best possible choices in the groupings that follow, circling your preference.

(a) First: (a) dictionary (a) will   (a) you   (a) than   (a) paperback.
    a hardcover   serve   much better   a
(b) First,   (b) Dictionary (b) should   (b) people   (b) then   (b) paper-back.

(a) Even though   (a) is more expensive,   (a) also more durable,
    it   it is   more convenient and more readable. Think of it
(b) Although   (b) costs more,   (b) more durable also,

(a) like a   (a) does
    businessman   the cost of equipment.
(b) as a   (b) thinks of

(a) In spite   (a) among   (a) is
    these similarities, some comparisons   the five   instructive. Below are five
(b) Despite   (b) between   (b) are

(a) criteria   (a) collegiate
    for evaluating a   dictionary.
(b) criterion   (b) college

(a) Beside   (a) identical   (a) words, and
    having about the   number of   costing, weighing and measuring about
(b) Besides   (b) same   (b) words and

(a) the same,   (a) is   (a) , all   (a) currently   (a) is possible.
    these dictionaries   all authoritative   stay as   as
(b) equally,   (b) are   (b) . All   (b) current   (b) possible.

When you have finished, check your version with the original in Selection 80. Consult your dictionary or an English handbook to clear up any problems. How close did you come to professional writing?

NAME——————————————————————— DATE——————————— READING RATE——————————— W.P.M.

COMPREHENSION CHECK QUESTIONS

1. The volumes sent to Macaulay were on the history of (1) Washington; (2) New England; (3) New York; (4) the United States.   1. ————

2. Macaulay specifically mentions (1) the House of Lords; (2) Royalists; (3) Tories; (4) Parliament.   2. ————

3. In England the supreme power was said to be in the hands of (1) the King; (2) an educated class; (3) the socially elite; (4) the wealthy class.   3. ————

4. Macaulay has seen England pass through critical hard times (1) five or six times; (2) three or four times; (3) one or two times; (4) only once.   4. ————

5. In referring to Jefferson he mentions (1) stories about his private life; (2) his Monticello expenditures; (3) his architectural passions; (4) his wife's indiscretions.   5. ————

Receptive Comprehension ————

6. This selection is focused mainly on what aspect of American democracy? (1) when it will fail; (2) why it will fail; (3) how it will fail; (4) who will be responsible for its failure.   6. ————

7. When Macaulay speaks of our Constitution as "all sail and no anchor," he apparently means it lacks (1) direction; (2) weight; (3) a guiding force; (4) stability.   7. ————

8. What chief condition was mentioned as distinguishing America from other Old World countries? (1) boundless fertile land; (2) sparse population; (3) a pioneering spirit; (4) widely diverse climates. 8. ————

9. In developing his points, Macaulay makes most use of (1) historical references; (2) personal opinions; (3) comparisons with England; (4) other authorities.   9. ————

10. Apparently the chief underlying reason for America's downfall will be (1) urbanization; (2) increased disparity between rich and poor; (3) economic situation; (4) rise of a demagogue.   10. ————

(10 off for each mistake)   *Reflective Comprehension* ————

TOTAL READING COMPREHENSION SCORE ————

VOCABULARY CHECK QUESTIONS

		without context I	*with context* II
1. *hustings*	(1) bustlings; (2) platform; (3) humps; (4) seats; (5) playing field.	1. ————	————
2. *spoliation*	(1) upheaval; (2) plundering; (3) helplessness; (4) change; (5) reconstruction.	2. ————	————
3. *indigent*	(1) scornful; (2) unwise; (3) disinterested; (4) needy; (5) indicated.	3. ————	————
4. *foreboding*	(1) prohibiting; (2) searching; (3) repelling; (4) preferring; (5) foretelling.	4. ————	————
5. *demagogue*	One who (1) prepares; (2) entertains; (3) mistrusts; (4) stirs up; (5) makes demands.	5. ————	————

(10 off for each mistake)   *Word Comprehension* without *contextual help* (I) ————

Word Comprehension with *contextual help* (II) ————

TOTAL WORD COMPREHENSION SCORE ————

EXERCISES

With such matters as style, usage, punctuation, diction, spelling, and sentence structure in mind, make the best possible choices in the groupings that follow, circling your preference.

      (a) Europe,   (a) dense,   (a) affect   (a) institutions
In   where the population is   the   of such   would be almost
      (b) Europe   (b) dense   (b) effect   (b) an institution

(a) instantaneous, what   (a) in France lately   (a) an   (a) 1848
               happened   is   example. In   a pure democracy
(b) instantaneous. What   (b) lately in France   (b) a   (b) 1848,

(a) established itself.   (a) there was reason   (a) spoliation:
           During a short time   to expect a general
(b) was established there.   (b) there existed reason   (b) spoliation,

(a) a national bankruptcy,   (a) soil,   (a) rising prices,
              a new partition of the   a
(b) a bankruptcy of the nation,   (b) ground, (b) a maximum of prices,

(a) ruinous load of taxation   (a) for the purpose of supporting
           laid on the rich   the poor in idleness. Such a system
(b) load of ruinous taxation   (b) in order to support

(a) in twenty years, would   (a) poverty-stricken   (a) the France
           have made France as   and barbarous as   of the
(b) would, in twenty years,   (b) poor   (b) was the France

(a) Carlovingian's.   (a) averted;   (a) there is a despotism,   (a) tribute,
        Happily the danger was   and now   a silent   an
(b) Carlovingians.   (b) averted,   (b) you'll find a despotism,   (b) tribune,

           (a) gone;
enslaved press. Liberty is   but civilization has been saved.
           (b) gone,

When you have finished, check your version with the original in Selection 81. How close did you come to professional writing?

NAME_____ DATE_____ READING RATE_____ W.P.M.

COMPREHENSION CHECK QUESTIONS

1. National security is spoken of as what specific kind of problem? (1) military; (2) conceptual; (3) logistical; (4) human relations.   1. _____

2. Which was *not* included under the heading of *critical services?* (1) communication; (2) transportation; (3) commerce; (4) politics.   2. _____

3. Specific reference was made to (1) the South Pole; (2) Antarctica; (3) Alaska; (4) Greenland.   3. _____

4. Specific mention was made of (1) Iraq; (2) Israel; (3) Egypt; (4) Ireland.   4. _____

5. The weapon mentioned in connection with Iran was (1) hostages; (2) a holy leader; (3) a revolution; (4) a general strike.   5. _____

Receptive Comprehension _____

6. The main focus is on (1) world natural biosphere; (2) military preparedness; (3) national security; (4) (4) Soviet-American confrontation.   6. _____

7. What seems the most telling argument for cessation of the arms race? (1) man-made environmental changes are approaching danger level; (2) new problems are indifferent to military force; (3) strictly military concept threatens world security; (4) polarization is bringing increased violence.   7. _____

8. Mention of the Soviet-Afghanistan conflict was to show (1) transportation and supply difficulties; (2) the degradation of farm lands; (3) the need for local support; (4) the failure of military options.   8. _____

9. Judging from this article, the author's response to a proposal to increase our defense budget would be to (1) strongly favor it; (2) tolerate it; (3) discourage it; (4) strongly discourage it.   9. _____

10. The author's chief purpose is to (1) convince us; (2) advise us; (3) frighten us; (4) inform us.   10. _____

(10 off for each mistake)   *Reflective Comprehension* _____

TOTAL READING COMPREHENSION SCORE _____

VOCABULARY CHECK QUESTIONS

		without context I	*with context* II
1. *millennia*	(1) 1,000 years; (2) million; (3) military; (4) concern; (5) millinery.	1. _____	_____
2. *viability*	(1) effect; (2) transportation; (3) truth; (4) ability; (5) practicality.	2. _____	_____
3. *multifarious*	(1) criminal; (2) complex; (3) many-sided; (4) faithful; (5) crowded.	3. _____	_____
4. *agenda*	(1) roll call; (2) agent; (3) list; (4) motion; (5) committee.	4. _____	_____
5. *vis-a-vis*	(1) visible; (2) in relation to; (3) vacant; (4) in addition to; (5) learned.	5. _____	_____

(10 off for each mistake)

Word Comprehension without *contextual help* (I) _____

Word Comprehension with *contextual help* (II) _____

TOTAL WORD COMPREHENSION SCORE _____

EXERCISES

With such matters as style, usage, punctuation, diction, spelling, and sentence structure in mind, make the best possible choices in the groupings that follow, circling your preference.

The problem of national (a) security, today, is (a) fundamentaly (a) conceptual in nature.
(b) security today (b) fundamentally (b) a conceptual problem. The question is

(a) if we can (a) expand our concept of the (a) national interest to include the integrity of the global systems
(b) whether (b) stretch our idea (b) interest of the nation

(a) which (a) sustain human society and life (a) too. Can we not (a) percieve that there (a) can't be any security for
(b) that (b) sustains (b) itself. (b) perceive (b) can be no

any (a) nation, if the planet itself (a) isn't safe? And that (a) world security has become the precondition
(b) nation (b) is at risk? (b) the security of the world

(a) upon which national defense rests? (a) Sure the point of departure for (a) an up-to-date defense policy is an
(b) for national defense? (b) Surely (b) a modern

understanding that national security (a) is (a) conceivable in these (a) last years of the (a) 20th century
(b) becomes (b) concievable (b) latter (b) twentieth

only (a) within the framework of (a) the larger scope of world security.
(b) inside (b) a wider world security.

When you have finished, check your version with the original in Selection 83.

NAME————————————————— DATE—————————— READING RATE——————————— W.P.M.

COMPREHENSION CHECK QUESTIONS

1. The sixfold job classification came from a professor from (1) Harvard; (2) Yale; (3) Columbia; (4) Johns Hopkins.　　　　　　　　　　　　1. ————

2. People attracted to realistic jobs are described as usually (1) talkative; (2) practical; (3) ambitious; (4) sociable.　　　　　　　　　　　　2. ————

3. The job of bookkeeper is classed as (1) a social job; (2) a realistic job; (3) a conventional job; (4) an investigative job.　　　　　　　　3. ————

4. Those attracted to artistic jobs are described as (1) dependable; (2) assertive; (3) social; (4) emotional.　　4. ————

5. Sales jobs come under the heading of (1) artistic jobs; (2) conventional jobs; (3) jobs of leadership; (4) social jobs.　　　　　　　　　5. ————

Receptive Comprehension ————

6. This selection is written chiefly to help readers (1) know the satisfactions of certain types of jobs; (2) know the key characteristics of success; (3) choose a career; (4) know what interest patterns to note.　　6. ————

7. The primary purpose is to (1) persuade; (2) teach; (3) clarify; (4) entertain.　　　　　　　7. ————

8. The style is best described as (1) colloquial; (2) straightforward; (3) dramatic; (4) inspirational.　　8. ————

9. Points are developed largely by (1) details from personal research findings; (2) the author's firsthand experience; (3) logical reasoning; (4) case histories.　　9. ————

10. Chief emphasis is on describing (1) job satisfactions; (2) educational backgrounds; (3) job characteristics; (4) personal attributes.　　10. ————

(10 off for each mistake)　　　　　　　　　　*Reflective Comprehension* ————

TOTAL READING COMPREHENSION SCORE ————

VOCABULARY CHECK QUESTIONS

		without context I	*with context* II
1. *robust*	(1) even-tempered; (2) tall; (3) full-bosomed; (4) vigorous; (5) ungainly.	1. ————	————
2. *tangible*	(1) actual; (2) twofold; (3) jumbled; (4) worn; (5) finished.	2. ————	————
3. *ambiguity*	(1) distinctiveness; (2) aimlessness; (3) inexactness; (4) helplessness; (5) continuity.	3. ————	————
4. *analytical*	(1) preparatory; (2) rearranged; (3) planned; (4) anatomical; (5) separating into parts.	4. ————	————
5. *introspective*	(1) reckless; (2) looking within; (3) thoughtful; (4) not essential; (5) active.	5. ————	————

(10 off for each mistake)　　　　*Word Comprehension* without *contextual help* (I) ————

Word Comprehension with *contextual help* (II) ————

TOTAL WORD COMPREHENSION SCORE ————

EXERCISES

SELF-SCORING CAREER COMPATIBILITY TEST

Your personality — the characteristics that define you as an individual — provide a clue to the type of career for which you are best suited.

How would you describe yourself? This little quiz is designed to let you become your own career counselor and see yourself as you really are.

To take this test, write 2 in the blank beside the word below that could usually be considered descriptive of you; 1 if sometimes applicable (or you are not sure). Leave blanks beside the words that definitely *do not apply* to you.

1. Adventuresome	F	26. Energetic	F	52. Popular	E
2. Ambitious	F	27. Enjoys puzzles	C	53. Practical	A
3. Analytical	C	28. Enthusiastic	F	54. Prefer a subordinate	
4. Argumentative	F	29. Flirtatious	F	role	B
5. Athletic	A	30. Frank	A	55. Prefer working with	
6. Attention-seeking	E	31. Friendly	E	people rather than	
7. Calm	B	32. Function best when activities are planned	B	machines	E
8. Challenged by ambiguous situations	C	33. Helpful	E	56. Problem- or task-oriented	C
9. Cheerful	E	34. Idealistic	D	57. Reserved	C
10. Competitive	F	35. Impractical	D	58. Risk-taking	D
11. Complicated	D	36. Impulsive	D	59. Rugged, strong	A
12. Confident of your own intellectual abilities	C	37. Independent	C	60. Scientifically inclined	C
		38. Inhibited	B	61. Self-confident	F
13. Conforming	A	39. Introspective	D	62. Sensitive to surroundings	D
14. Conscientious	B	40. Intuitive	D	63. Shy	A
15. Cooperative	E	41. Lacking in persuasive skills	C	64. Socially oriented	E
16. Creative-minded	C	42. Materialistic	A	65. Sports-minded	A
17. Curious	C	43. Mechanically adept	A	66. Stable in outlook and performance	A
18. Dependable	B	44. Non-conforming	D	67. Tactful	E
19. Disciplined	B	45. Obedient	B	68. Teaching-oriented	E
20. Discussion-oriented	E	46. Optimistic	F	69. Thrifty	A
21. Disinterested in physical activity	B	47. Orderly	B	70. Understanding with people	E
		48. Oriented toward the arts	D		
22. Disorderly (not "organized")	D	49. Original in thinking	C	71. Verbally skilled	F
23. Domineering	F	50. Persistent	A	72. Work well without public recognition	B
24. Efficient	B	51. Persuasive	F		
25. Emotional	D				

Scoring: Each item has a letter key (after the scoring space) which will be used to calculate your scores. Go back through the quiz and tally your score for each letter. For example, if you entered 2 for numbers 5, 13, 30, 42, 43, 50, 53, 59, 63, 65, 66, 69, you would write the figure 24 for your A total below. Then follow the same procedure for B, C, D, E and F.

A   B   C   D   E   F
Total ——— Total ——— Total ——— Total ——— Total ——— Total ———

Analyses: Each letter indicates a job category as follows:

A = Realistic Jobs   D = Artistic Jobs
B = Conventional Jobs   E = Social Jobs
C = Investigative Jobs   F = Jobs of Leadership

The analyses in Selection 83 will tell you more about each category.

You will probably find one category in which your score is considerably higher than the rest. This is the field in which you are likely to find the most satisfaction and success.

However, there may be more than one category in which you have a relatively high score. Some jobs fall directly into one category — "auto mechanic," for example, falls directly into the Realistic category (A), and "secretary" falls directly into the Conventional category (B). Other jobs fall in between — "art teacher," for example, falls about halfway between Artistic and Social, and "sales manager" falls about halfway between Jobs of Leadership (F) and Conventional Jobs (B).

Careful reading of the category in which you score highest will help you learn more about yourself.

From *If You Don't Know Where You Are Going You'll Probably End Up Somewhere Else* by David P. Campbell, Ph.D. © 1964 Argus Communications, a Division of DLM, Inc., Allen, TX 75002.

Appendix

ANSWERS

SELECTIONS BY NUMBER (1–42)

COMPREHENSION CHECK QUESTIONS

Q	1	2	3	4	5	6	7	8	9	10	11	12	13	14	15	16	17	18	19	20	21	22	23	24	25	26	27	28	29	30	31	32	33	34	35	36	37	38	39	40	41	42
1.	4	4	1	2	3	2	2	3	3	1	2	1	2	2	4	4	4	4	4	4	4	3	3	2	1	2	2	3	2	2	3	1	3	4	3	3	4	2	4	4	3	2
2.	3	1	2	4	4	1	4	4	1	4	4	2	1	4	3	3	3	3	3	2	3	1	1	4	2	3	2	3	4	3	4	2	3	4	1	2	1	1	2	2	1	4
3.	4	3	3	4	1	1	4	4	4	2	2	3	1	4	3	3	1	3	3	4	4	4	3	1	4	3	3	3	4	1	4	4	4	4	4	1	2	1	1	1	4	4
4.	4	3	4	4	1	4	4	4	2	2	3	1	3	4	4	4	3	4	4	3	2	3	2	1	2	3	2	2	1	2	1	1	2	2	1	4	2	2	4	4	4	2
5.	1	3	2	3	4	2	4	1	3	1	1	1	2	3	3	3	3	2	3	3	4	2	1	4	3	3	2	2	4	4	4	3	4	3	2	3	1	3	2	4	4	1
6.	2	3	1	3	2	3	2	3	4	4	2	4	4	2	2	2	2	2	4	4	3	3	3	2	4	2	3	2	3	2	3	2	1	2	3	3	4	2	3	2	3	4
7.	3	2	1	3	3	4	3	2	4	3	3	2	1	1	1	1	2	1	2	1	2	2	2	2	2	3	2	4	3	3	3	4	2	2	3	1	2	3	4	3	4	1
8.	1	2	1	2	2	2	4	1	2	2	2	1	4	3	3	4	4	2	1	3	4	1	1	2	4	2	3	3	1	1	2	1	2	1	1	2	3	2	3	3	2	3
9.	4	4	3	3	3	2	3	3	1	1	3	1	4	2	3	1	1	4	4	3	2	3	3	2	2	2	3	4	3	3	3	4	2	4	4	3	1	1	3	3	3	3
10.	1	1	2	1	1	4	3	3	2	4	3	4	1	1	1	1	1	2	1	4	2	2	2	3	3	3	3	2	4	2	3	3	2	2	2	1	3	3	3	2	2	2

VOCABULARY CHECK QUESTIONS

Q	1	2	3	4	5	6	7	8	9	10	11	12	13	14	15	16	17	18	19	20	21	22	23	24	25	26	27	28	29	30	31	32	33	34	35	36	37	38	39	40	41	42
1.	3	5	1	3	3	1	5	3	2	5	3	3	3	5	4	4	5	5	5	4	3	4	3	3	5	3	4	3	2	3	1	4	2	4	4	5	1	5	5	5	4	3
2.	2	3	2	5	4	2	4	4	3	5	2	5	2	4	3	1	5	5	3	3	2	3	1	2	4	4	4	1	3	2	4	1	1	1	1	2	5	3	3	3	4	1
3.	5	1	4	1	5	5	5	2	5	1	4	1	4	3	1	5	4	2	4	5	4	4	2	4	3	5	5	3	5	4	4	4	4	5	5	2	4	4	1	4	1	4
4.	4	2	2	3	3	1	2	4	4	4	2	4	3	3	2	2	1	4	2	2	3	2	3	5	2	2	1	1	1	3	1	2	1	1	1	1	5	5	2	4	5	5
5.	1	4	3	1	2	2	3	3	5	3	5	1	4	5	1	4	2	2	2	5	3	5	4	1	4	5	5	2	4	4	1	4	4	2	3	3	4	1	3	3	3	4

SELECTIONS BY NUMBER (43–83)

COMPREHENSION CHECK QUESTIONS

Q	43	44	45	46	47	48	49	50	51	52	53	54	55	56	57	58	59	60	61	62	63	64	65	66	67	68	69	70	71	72	73	74	75	76	77	78	79	80	81	82	83
1.	3	4	2	4	3	3	1	1	3	2	4	2	2	3	2	5	2	4	4	1	4	2	1	3	2	3	2	2	3	3	3	3	3	3	3	3	3	3	3	2	4
2.	4	1	2	2	3	2	1	1	1	3	3	2	3	3	4	5	4	4	3	3	4	3	3	2	4	2	1	3	3	3	3	4	1	4	2	1	4	4	4	1	2
3.	1	3	4	2	1	1	3	1	1	2	4	1	3	3	1	4	1	2	3	4	3	4	4	4	3	4	4	4	4	4	3	1	3	1	4	2	2	2	2	3	3
4.	2	2	1	1	2	3	2	3	4	3	3	4	4	4	3	3	3	3	3	3	2	3	2	3	3	3	3	2	3	2	1	1	1	1	3	4	4	2	4	4	4
5.	2	1	1	1	3	1	3	3	2	1	4	1	1	1	4	1	4	4	4	2	1	2	4	2	4	4	4	3	3	1	4	4	3	3	1	3	1	3	1	3	3
6.	4	2	4	3	4	3	4	2	3	3	3	2	2	3	2	2	2	2	2	2	2	2	2	4	2	3	1	1	4	4	2	2	2	2	3	4	1	2	1	3	3
7.	3	3	3	2	1	4	2	2	2	3	2	3	2	4	4	3	3	3	3	4	3	4	3	3	3	3	2	4	4	3	4	4	1	2	1	1	3	3	3	4	3
8.	1	2	2	3	1	2	2	2	2	1	1	1	1	1	1	4	1	4	4	3	2	2	3	3	3	2	3	3	1	4	4	2	2	4	4	1	4	4	4	4	1
9.	3	2	1	2	4	4	1	2	2	1	2	3	3	4	3	3	3	3	3	1	1	3	3	4	2	3	1	4	3	3	4	4	1	2	2	2	2	2	1	1	4
10.	4	4	4	1	1	3	1	3	3	3	3	2	3	1	3	3	3	1	4	4	3	1	3	1	4	4	4	1	1	4	1	1	2	1	1	3	3	3	3	3	4

VOCABULARY CHECK QUESTIONS

Q	43	44	45	46	47	48	49	50	51	52	53	54	55	56	57	58	59	60	61	62	63	64	65	66	67	68	69	70	71	72	73	74	75	76	77	78	79	80	81	82	83
1.	1	4	5	5	5	2	2	2	3	4	2	2	2	3	5	5	1	4	4	4	4	1	4	5	4	5	5	4	4	3	5	4	3	2	2	3	2	3	2	2	1
2.	4	1	5	5	2	2	2	5	5	2	1	5	1	3	2	2	3	5	3	4	2	3	5	1	5	5	5	5	5	1	3	5	4	1	1	2	3	2	4	4	4
3.	5	5	4	4	2	5	5	1	1	5	4	4	4	4	4	1	5	2	5	5	5	1	1	2	1	3	3	3	4	5	4	4	5	4	4	5	5	4	4	3	3
4.	4	3	1	5	1	1	1	1	4	5	3	3	3	4	1	2	3	4	4	4	3	2	3	3	3	4	3	4	4	1	2	4	1	2	2	1	1	1	5	5	5
5.	1	2	3	3	3	4	3	3	3	3	5	5	5	1	2	2	4	3	2	2	2	4	2	4	4	4	4	4	2	5	5	2	5	5	4	2	4	5	4	2	2

357

CONVERSION TABLE: Seconds to Words per Minute

The general procedure for getting word-per-minute rate is to divide the number of words by the reading time in seconds and then multiply that quotient by sixty. The conversion table provides, however, a convenient shortcut to that procedure for most reading times.

To use the table, find the figure in the left-hand column that is closest to your reading time. Then look along that line to the column headed by the number of the selection read to get your word-per-minute rate.

For reading times between one and two minutes (60 to 120 seconds), double your reading time before looking in the table. Then double the number in the table to get your rate.

For reading times over 420 seconds, divide your reading time by half before looking in the table. Then divide the number in the table by half to get your rate.

TIME IN SECONDS (AND MINUTES)	1	2	3	4	5	6	7	8	9	10	11	12	13	14	15	16	17	18	19
60(1)	1680	1620	1100	1210	3850	2250	2380	3000	1660	1320	1320	2400	2245	2108	1930	4470	1124	1290	1734
120(2)	840	810	550	605	1925	1125	1190	1500	830	660	660	1200	1123	1054	965	2235	562	645	867
130	775	746	508	558	1777	1038	1098	1384	766	609	609	1108	1036	973	891	2063	519	595	800
140	720	694	472	518	1650	963	1020	1284	711	566	566	1029	962	903	827	1916	482	553	743
150	672	648	440	484	1540	900	952	1200	664	528	528	960	898	840	772	1788	450	516	694
160	630	606	413	454	1444	843	893	1125	623	495	495	900	842	790	724	1676	422	484	650
170	593	572	388	427	1359	794	840	1059	586	466	466	847	792	744	681	1578	397	455	612
180(3)	560	540	367	403	1283	750	793	1000	553	440	440	800	748	703	643	1490	375	430	578
190	531	511	348	382	1216	710	752	947	524	417	417	758	709	665	609	1412	355	407	548
200	504	485	330	363	1155	675	714	900	498	396	396	720	674	632	579	1341	337	387	520
210	480	463	314	345	1099	642	680	856	474	377	377	686	641	602	551	1277	321	369	495
220	458	441	300	330	1050	612	644	818	453	360	360	655	612	575	526	1219	307	351	472
230	438	422	287	316	1004	587	621	782	433	344	344	626	586	550	503	1166	293	326	452
240(4)	420	405	275	303	963	563	595	750	415	330	330	600	562	527	483	1118	281	323	434
250	403	388	264	290	924	540	571	720	398	317	317	576	539	506	463	1073	270	309	416
260	388	373	254	279	888	519	549	692	383	305	305	554	518	486	445	1032	259	298	400
270	373	360	244	268	856	500	529	667	369	294	294	533	499	468	429	993	250	287	385
280	360	347	238	259	825	482	510	642	356	283	283	514	481	451	414	958	241	277	371
290	348	335	228	250	797	465	492	620	343	273	273	497	464	436	399	925	233	266	359
300(5)	336	324	220	242	770	450	476	600	332	264	264	480	449	422	386	894	225	258	347
310	325	313	213	234	745	435	461	580	322	256	256	465	435	408	374	865	218	249	336
320	315	303	207	227	722	422	446	563	312	248	248	450	421	395	362	838	211	242	325
330	305	294	199	220	699	409	433	545	302	240	240	436	408	383	351	813	204	234	315
340	296	286	194	213	679	397	420	530	293	233	233	424	396	372	341	789	198	228	306
350	288	278	189	207	660	386	408	514	284	226	226	411	385	361	331	766	193	221	297
360(6)	280	270	184	202	642	375	397	500	277	220	220	400	374	351	322	745	187	215	289
370	272	262	178	196	624	365	386	486	269	214	214	389	364	341	313	725	182	209	281
380	265	255	174	191	608	355	376	474	262	208	208	379	354	332	305	706	177	204	273
390	258	249	169	186	592	346	366	462	255	203	203	369	345	324	297	688	173	198	266
400	252	243	165	181	578	338	357	450	249	198	198	360	337	316	290	671	169	193	260
410	246	237	161	177	563	329	348	439	243	193	193	351	329	308	282	654	164	189	253
420(7)	240	231	157	173	550	321	340	429	237	186	186	343	321	301	276	639	161	184	248

SELECTIONS BY NUMBER

TIME IN SECONDS (AND MINUTES)	20	21	22	23	24	25	26	27	28	29	30	31	32	33	34	35	36	37	38	39	40	41
60(1)	1490	1866	2230	1454	1560	2090	1040	1734	1056	1180	1270	2280	1930	2110	2100	1390	1300	1950	1610	1375	1780	920
120(2)	745	933	1115	727	780	1045	520	867	528	590	635	1140	965	1055	1050	695	650	975	805	688	890	460
130	687	861	1029	671	720	964	480	800	487	545	588	1052	891	973	968	642	600	900	743	635	822	425
140	639	799	956	623	668	896	446	743	453	506	546	978	827	903	900	596	557	836	690	589	763	394
150	596	746	892	582	624	836	416	694	422	472	510	912	772	840	840	556	520	780	644	550	712	370
160	559	699	836	545	585	783	390	650	396	443	478	856	724	790	788	521	488	731	604	516	668	345
170	526	659	787	513	551	737	367	612	373	417	450	804	681	744	742	491	459	688	568	485	628	325
180(3)	497	622	743	485	520	697	347	578	352	393	425	760	643	703	700	463	433	650	537	458	593	307
190	471	589	704	459	492	660	328	548	333	373	403	720	609	665	664	439	410	616	508	434	562	291
200	447	560	669	436	468	627	312	520	317	354	383	684	579	632	630	417	389	585	483	412	534	276
210	426	533	637	415	444	597	297	495	302	338	364	652	551	602	600	397	369	557	460	393	509	263
220	406	509	608	396	425	570	283	472	288	322	347	622	526	575	570	379	353	532	439	375	485	251
230	389	485	582	379	408	545	270	452	275	308	332	594	503	550	548	363	337	509	420	359	464	240
240(4)	373	467	558	364	390	523	260	434	264	295	319	570	483	527	525	348	325	488	403	344	445	230
250	358	448	535	349	374	492	249	416	253	283	306	548	463	505	504	334	312	468	386	330	427	221
260	344	432	515	336	360	482	240	400	244	273	294	526	445	486	484	321	300	450	372	317	411	212
270	331	415	496	323	347	464	231	385	235	262	283	506	429	468	466	309	288	433	358	306	396	204
280	319	400	478	312	338	448	222	371	226	253	273	488	414	451	450	298	279	418	345	295	381	197
290	308	386	461	301	323	439	214	359	218	244	263	472	399	436	434	288	269	403	333	284	368	190
300(5)	298	373	446	291	312	418	208	347	211	236	255	456	386	422	420	278	260	390	322	275	356	184
310	288	359	432	282	302	404	201	336	204	228	247	442	374	408	406	269	251	377	311	266	345	178
320	279	350	418	273	293	392	195	325	198	221	239	428	363	395	394	261	243	366	302	258	334	173
330	271	339	405	265	284	380	190	315	192	215	232	414	351	383	382	253	238	355	293	250	324	167
340	263	329	392	257	275	369	183	306	186	209	225	402	341	372	372	245	229	344	284	243	314	162
350	255	319	382	250	267	358	178	297	181	202	219	390	331	361	360	238	222	334	276	236	305	158
360(6)	248	311	372	242	260	348	173	289	176	196	212	380	322	351	350	232	217	325	269	229	297	153
370	242	302	362	236	253	339	168	281	171	191	207	370	313	341	341	225	212	316	261	223	289	149
380	235	294	352	230	246	330	164	273	167	187	202	360	305	332	332	219	206	308	254	217	281	145
390	229	287	343	224	240	321	159	266	162	182	196	350	297	324	323	214	199	300	247	212	274	142
400	224	280	335	218	234	313	155	260	158	177	192	342	290	316	315	209	195	293	242	206	267	138
410	218	273	326	213	228	306	152	253	155	172	187	334	282	308	307	203	191	285	235	201	260	135
420(7)	213	267	319	208	222	299	149	248	151	168	182	326	276	301	300	199	186	279	230	196	254	131

TIME IN SECONDS (AND MINUTES)	42	43	44	45	46	47	48	49	50	51	52	53	54	55	56	57	58	59	60	61	62
60(1)	2015	1662	2320	1050	1430	1670	1704	2394	1930	1420	2530	1660	950	1320	1290	2210	2490	1434	1400	1380	1540
120(2)	1008	831	1160	525	715	835	852	1197	965	710	1265	830	475	660	645	1105	1245	717	700	690	770
130	925	767	1070	484	660	770	786	1105	890	655	1168	766	438	609	595	1020	1150	662	646	636	711
140	862	712	994	450	618	716	730	1026	828	609	1084	711	407	566	553	947	1071	615	600	592	660
150	805	665	928	420	572	669	682	958	772	568	1012	664	380	528	516	884	996	574	560	552	616
160	754	623	870	394	537	627	639	898	724	533	948	623	356	495	484	829	934	538	525	518	578
170	710	587	818	371	504	589	601	845	681	501	893	586	335	466	455	780	879	506	494	486	544
180(3)	672	554	773	350	477	556	568	798	643	473	843	553	317	440	430	734	830	478	467	460	513
190	635	525	733	332	451	527	538	756	609	448	798	524	300	417	407	698	786	453	442	436	486
200	604	499	696	315	429	501	511	718	579	426	759	498	285	396	387	663	747	430	420	414	462
210	575	475	660	300	408	477	487	684	552	406	722	474	271	377	369	631	711	410	400	396	440
220	549	453	633	285	390	456	465	653	526	387	690	453	259	360	351	602	680	391	382	376	420
230	525	434	605	274	373	436	445	625	503	370	660	433	248	344	326	577	650	374	366	360	402
240(4)	503	416	580	263	358	417	426	599	483	355	633	415	238	330	323	553	623	359	350	346	385
250	482	399	557	252	343	400	409	575	463	341	607	398	228	317	309	531	598	344	335	332	369
260	462	384	535	242	330	385	393	552	445	328	584	383	219	305	298	510	575	331	323	318	355
270	447	369	516	233	318	371	379	532	429	315	562	369	211	294	287	491	553	319	311	306	342
280	432	356	497	225	307	359	365	513	414	304	542	356	204	283	277	474	536	307	300	296	330
290	416	344	480	217	296	346	353	495	399	294	523	343	197	273	266	457	515	297	289	286	319
300(5)	403	332	464	210	286	332	341	479	386	284	506	332	190	264	258	442	498	287	280	276	308
310	389	322	449	203	276	322	330	463	374	275	490	322	184	256	249	428	480	278	271	266	298
320	377	312	435	197	268	312	320	449	362	267	474	312	178	248	242	414	467	269	263	258	289
330	365	302	422	191	260	302	310	435	351	258	460	302	173	240	234	402	453	261	254	250	280
340	355	293	409	186	252	293	301	422	341	251	447	293	168	233	228	390	440	253	247	244	272
350	345	285	397	180	245	284	292	410	331	244	434	284	163	226	221	379	427	246	240	236	264
360(6)	335	277	387	175	238	278	284	399	322	236	422	277	158	220	215	368	415	239	233	230	257
370	327	270	377	170	231	269	276	388	314	230	410	269	154	214	209	358	404	233	227	224	250
380	317	262	367	166	225	262	269	378	305	224	399	262	150	208	204	348	393	226	221	218	243
390	310	256	357	161	220	255	262	368	297	218	389	255	146	203	198	340	383	221	215	212	237
400	302	249	348	158	215	249	256	359	289	213	379	249	143	198	193	332	374	215	210	207	231
410	295	243	340	154	209	243	249	350	282	207	370	243	139	193	189	323	364	210	205	202	226
420(7)	287	237	331	150	204	238	243	342	276	203	361	237	136	186	184	316	356	205	200	197	220

TIME IN SECONDS (AND MINUTES)	63	64	65	66	67	68	69	70	71	72	73	74	75	76	77	78	79	80	81	82	83
60(1)	1380	890	1600	1125	1596	1720	1090	1380	2340	2210	1380	2654	1898	2225	934	3010	970	905	1140	2050	1750
120(2)	690	445	800	563	798	860	545	690	1170	1105	690	1327	949	1113	467	1505	485	453	570	1025	875
130	636	410	738	519	737	794	503	636	1080	1020	637	1225	876	1026	431	1389	448	418	526	946	808
140	592	380	686	482	684	737	467	592	1002	947	591	1137	813	953	400	1290	416	388	489	879	751
150	552	356	640	450	638	688	436	552	936	884	552	1062	759	890	374	1204	384	362	456	820	701
160	518	331	600	422	599	645	409	518	877	829	518	995	712	834	350	1129	364	339	428	769	658
170	486	311	566	397	563	607	385	486	825	780	487	937	670	785	330	1062	342	319	402	724	619
180(3)	460	297	533	375	532	573	363	460	780	737	460	885	633	742	311	1003	323	302	380	683	583
190	436	281	506	355	504	543	344	436	739	698	436	838	599	703	295	951	306	286	360	647	552
200	414	267	480	337	479	516	327	414	703	663	414	796	569	668	280	903	291	272	342	615	525
210	396	253	456	321	456	491	312	396	670	631	395	758	542	636	267	860	277	259	326	586	501
220	376	242	436	307	435	469	297	376	639	603	377	724	518	607	255	821	265	247	311	559	478
230	360	230	418	293	416	449	284	360	611	577	361	692	495	580	244	785	253	236	297	535	457
240(4)	346	222	400	281	399	430	273	346	595	553	345	664	475	556	234	753	243	226	285	513	438
250	332	214	384	270	383	413	262	332	561	530	331	637	455	534	224	722	233	217	274	492	421
260	318	206	369	259	368	397	252	318	540	510	318	612	438	513	216	695	224	209	263	473	405
270	306	198	356	250	355	382	242	306	520	491	307	590	422	495	208	669	216	201	253	456	390
280	296	191	343	241	342	368	234	296	501	474	296	569	407	477	200	645	208	194	244	439	376
290	286	184	331	233	330	356	226	286	484	457	285	549	393	460	193	623	200	187	236	424	363
300(5)	276	178	320	225	319	344	218	276	468	442	276	531	380	445	187	602	194	181	228	410	350
310	266	174	310	218	309	333	211	266	453	428	267	514	367	431	181	583	188	175	221	397	339
320	258	166	300	211	299	323	205	258	439	414	259	498	356	417	175	564	182	169	214	385	329
330	250	162	291	204	290	313	198	250	425	402	251	483	345	405	170	547	176	164	207	373	318
340	244	156	283	198	282	303	193	244	413	390	244	468	335	393	165	531	171	159	201	363	309
350	236	152	274	193	274	295	187	236	401	378	237	455	325	381	160	516	166	155	195	353	300
360(6)	230	148	267	187	266	287	182	230	390	368	230	442	316	371	156	502	162	151	190	342	292
370	224	144	260	182	259	279	177	224	380	358	224	430	308	361	151	488	157	147	185	333	289
380	218	140	253	177	252	272	172	218	370	349	218	419	300	351	147	475	153	143	180	324	276
390	212	136	246	173	246	264	168	212	360	340	213	408	291	342	144	463	149	139	175	316	270
400	207	133	240	169	239	258	164	207	351	332	207	398	285	334	140	452	146	136	171	308	263
410	202	130	234	164	234	252	160	202	343	323	202	388	278	326	137	440	143	133	167	300	256
420(7)	197	127	229	161	228	246	156	197	334	316	197	379	271	318	133	430	139	129	163	293	250

INDEX

According to Order of Difficulty

* Note to Instructors: nineteen selections contain item-analyzed tests with an average validity of .47 and a range from .21 to .78, approximating the acceptability of a standardized test.

PROGRESS RECORD

Students and teachers alike will find a Progress Record invaluable. Such a record helps spot specific reading strengths and weaknesses, points up growth and improvement, and heightens the personal satisfaction found in achievement.

Some students may wish to use only the columns for word-per-minute rate and Total Comprehension. Others may wish to keep a much more complete record. Space is provided for the following kinds of information:

1. DATE

2. SELECTION NUMBER

3. DIFFICULTY. As a measure of difficulty, enter the *Reading Ease Score* and *Classification* from the Index on page 362.

4. INTEREST RATING. Enter your personal Interest Rating for the selection. Enter a *1* if you think it is "very interesting," a *2* if "somewhat interesting," a *3* if "of average interest," a *4* if "somewhat uninteresting," and a *5* if "very uninteresting." The effect of interest on rate and comprehension is often a necessary aid to interpreting and understanding results.

5. RATE W.P.M. Enter your word-per-minute reading rate for the selection.

6. TOTAL COMP. Enter the Total Comprehension Score here — ten off for each of the questions missed.

7. R. E. INDEX. It is often desirable to have a single figure to indicate Reading Efficiency, an index that reflects both rate and comprehension factors. A Reading Efficiency Index may be obtained by multiplying word-per-minute rate by comprehension and dividing by one hundred. For example, if you read a selection at 320 words a minute with 60 percent comprehension, your Reading Efficiency Index would be 192. $\left(\dfrac{320 \times 60}{100} = 192 \right)$

8. PERCENT OF IMPROVEMENT. Improvement is sometimes best understood in terms of percentage gain. To determine the percent of improvement, subtract your initial Reading Efficiency Index from the last Reading Efficiency Index. The difference will be the number of points gained. Add two zeros to the number of points gained and divide that amount by the initial Reading Efficiency Index. The result will be your percent of improvement.

9. VOCABULARY. If you do the vocabulary check questions, both without and with the help of context, score them by taking ten off for each of the ten missed. If you just check vocabulary without context, take twenty off for each one missed and enter your scores.

The grouping of ten entry lines for ten selections is done to facilitate the averaging of any of the scores.

PROGRESS RECORD

	Date	Selection Number	Diffi-culty	Interest Rating	Rate W.P.M.	Total Comp.	R.E. Index	Percent of Improvement	Vocab-ulary
1.									
2.									
3.									
4.									
5.									
6.									
7.									
8.									
9.									
10.									

Average

1.									
2.									
3.									
4.									
5.									
6.									
7.									
8.									
9.									
10.									

Average

1.									
2.									
3.									
4.									
5.									
6.									
7.									
8.									
9.									
10.									

Average

PROGRESS RECORD

	Date	Selection Number	Diffi-culty	Interest Rating	Rate w.p.m.	Total Comp.	R.E. Index	Percent of Improvement	Vocab-ulary
1.									
2.									
3.									
4.									
5.									
6.									
7.									
8.									
9.									
10.									

Average

1.									
2.									
3.									
4.									
5.									
6.									
7.									
8.									
9.									
10.									

Average

1.									
2.									
3.									
4.									
5.									
6.									
7.									
8.									
9.									
10.									

Average

PROGRESS RECORD

	Date	Selection Number	Diffi- culty	Interest Rating	Rate W.P.M.	Total Comp.	R.E. Index	Percent of Improvement	Vocab- ulary
1.									
2.									
3.									
4.									
5.									
6.									
7.									
8.									
9.									
10.									
Average									

1.									
2.									
3.									
4.									
5.									
6.									
7.									
8.									
9.									
10.									
Average									

1.									
2.									
3.									
Average									

PACING AID SHEETS

(For pacing at 500, 750, 1,000, 1,500, or 2,000 W.P.M.)

The figures below will serve as a substitute for individual reading accelerator machines. Through use of the figures an individual or entire class can be paced through any selection in this text at speeds of 500, 750, 1,000, 1,500, or 2,000 words a minute, thus expediting the development of superior reading, scanning, and skimming skills.

At the signal "Begin," the individuals or class are to begin reading at what they feel is the indicated rate. When they should be finishing the first column, reading at that rate, say, "Next." If they have not quite finished, they are to skip the remaining portion of the column and start reading the next column somewhat faster. In that way as they are paced through a selection, they are able to adjust their rate as closely as possible to the paced rate.

Following the selection numbers and pages in the left-hand column, you will notice two sets of figures, one for each column of print for the selection. They indicate the time in minutes and seconds for reading the column at the speed given in the heading (e.g., @ 500, @ 750, etc.). For Selection #1, for example, the figures 0/43 and, for the second column, 1/29, mean that the first column should be finished in exactly zero minutes and 43 seconds and the second column in one minute and 29 seconds, or 46 seconds of additional time, since the time figures are cumulative. These figures would apply for pacing at 500 wpm. For pacing at 750 wpm, the signal "Next" would come after 29 seconds and, for the next column, after 1 minute.

For pacing at 2,000 wpm, divide each reading-time figure in the column headed @ 1,000 by two. (Similarly, for 3,000 wpm, divide the figure in the column headed @ 1,500 by two.)

SELECTION AND PAGE	1ST COLUMN @ 500	@ 750	@ 1000	@ 1500	2ND COLUMN @ 500	@ 750	@ 1000	@ 1500
#1	0/43	0/29	0/22	0/14	1/29	1/00	0/45	0/30
p. 4	2/24	1/36	1/12	0/48	3/21	2/14	1/41	1/7
#2	0/49	0/33	0/25	0/16	1/38	1/5	0/49	0/33
p. 6	2/25	1/36	1/12	0/48	3/14	2/10	1/37	1/5
#3	0/39	0/26	0/20	0/13	1/25	0/57	0/43	0/28
p. 8	1/50	1/13	0/55	0/37	2/12	1/28	1/6	0/44
#4	0/14	0/9	0/7	0/5	0/30	0/20	0/15	0/10
p. 9	1/30	1/0	0/45	0/30	2/25	1/37	1/13	0/48
#5	0/40	0/27	0/20	0/13	1/28	0/58	0/44	0/29
p. 11	2/23	1/35	1/12	0/48	3/23	2/15	1/41	1/8
p. 12	4/17	2/51	2/8	1/26	5/15	3/30	2/38	1/45
p. 13	6/13	4/9	3/7	2/4	7/8	4/45	3/34	2/23
p. 14	7/25	4/56	3/42	2/28	7/42	5/8	3/51	2/34
#6	0/22	0/15	0/11	0/7	0/46	0/31	0/23	0/15
p. 15	1/46	1/10	0/53	0/35	2/46	1/50	1/23	0/55
p. 16	3/38	2/26	1/49	1/13	4/30	3/0	2/15	1/30
#7	0/44	0/29	0/22	0/15	1/33	1/2	0/47	0/31
p. 18	2/29	1/40	1/15	0/50	3/24	2/16	1/42	1/8
p. 19	4/9	2/46	2/5	1/23	4/46	3/10	2/23	1/35
#8	0/39	0/26	0/19	0/13	1/24	0/57	0/43	0/28
p. 21	2/20	1/38	1/13	0/49	3/29	2/19	1/44	1/10
p. 22	4/23	2/55	2/12	1/28	5/24	3/36	2/42	1/48
p. 23	5/42	3/48	2/51	1/54	6/0	4/0	3/0	2/0
#9	0/20	0/13	0/10	0/7	0/46	0/31	0/23	0/15
p. 24	1/48	1/12	0/54	0/36	2/51	1/54	1/26	0/57
p. 25	3/5	2/4	1/33	1/2	3/39	2/13	1/40	1/6
#10	0/23	0/16	0/12	0/8	0/50	0/33	0/25	0/17
p. 26	1/46	1/10	0/53	0/35	2/38	1/46	1/19	0/53
#11	0/42	0/28	0/21	0/14	1/33	1/2	0/47	0/31
p. 28	2/7	1/25	1/4	0/42	2/38	1/46	1/19	0/53
#12	0/3	0/2	0/1	0/1	0/9	0/6	0/5	0/3
p. 29	1/7	0/44	0/33	0/22	1/59	1/18	0/58	0/39
p. 30	2/45	1/50	1/23	0/55	3/38	2/25	1/49	1/13
p. 31	4/14	2/49	2/7	1/25	4/48	3/12	2/24	1/36
#13	0/6	0/4	0/3	0/2	0/14	0/10	0/7	0/5
p. 32	1/19	0/54	0/39	0/27	2/24	1/36	1/12	0/48
p. 33	3/25	2/17	1/43	1/8	4/30	3/0	2/15	1/30
#14	0/38	0/25	0/19	0/13	1/25	0/57	0/43	0/28
p. 35	2/23	1/35	1/11	0/48	3/21	2/14	1/40	1/7
p. 36	3/47	2/31	1/53	1/15	4/13	2/49	2/7	1/24
#15	0/9	0/6	0/4	0/3	0/21	0/14	0/11	0/7
p. 37	1/19	0/53	0/40	0/26	2/16	1/30	1/8	0/45
p. 38	3/4	2/3	1/32	1/1	3/52	2/34	1/56	1/17

SELECTION AND PAGE	1ST COLUMN				2ND COLUMN			
	@ 500	@ 750	@ 1000	@ 1500	@ 500	@ 750	@ 1000	@ 1500
#16	0/47	0/32	0/24	0/16	1/42	1/8	0/51	0/34
p. 40	2/52	1/55	1/26	0/57	3/58	2/38	1/59	1/19
p. 41	5/4	3/23	2/32	1/41	6/14	4/9	3/7	2/5
p. 42	7/22	4/54	3/41	2/27	8/27	5/38	4/13	2/49
p. 43	8/46	5/48	4/23	2/54	8/57	5/58	4/28	2/59
#17	0/24	0/16	0/12	0/8	0/52	0/34	0/26	0/17
p. 44	1/32	1/2	0/47	0/31	2/15	1/30	1/7	0/45
#18	0/39	0/26	0/20	0/13	1/23	0/55	0/42	0/28
p. 46	2/3	1/22	1/1	0/41	2/35	1/43	1/17	0/52
#19	0/48	0/32	0/24	0/16	1/37	1/4	0/48	0/32
p. 48	2/31	1/41	1/16	0/50	3/28	2/18	1/44	1/9
#20	0/45	0/30	0/22	0/15	1/33	1/2	0/46	0/31
p. 50	2/16	1/30	1/8	0/45	2/59	1/59	1/39	1/0
#21	0/48	0/32	0/24	0/16	1/39	1/6	0/50	0/33
p. 52	2/43	1/48	1/21	0/54	3/43	2/29	1/52	1/14
#22	0/45	0/30	0/22	0/15	1/32	1/1	0/46	0/31
p. 54	2/28	1/28	1/14	0/49	3/24	2/16	1/42	1/8
p. 55	3/58	2/38	1/59	1/19	4/28	2/58	2/14	1/29
#23	0/7	0/5	0/4	0/2	0/18	0/12	0/9	0/6
p. 56	1/26	0/57	0/43	0/29	2/30	1/40	1/15	0/50
p. 57	2/44	1/49	1/22	0/54	2/55	1/56	1/27	0/58
#24	0/27	0/18	0/13	0/9	0/58	0/39	0/29	0/19
p. 58	1/59	1/20	1/0	0/40	2/59	1/59	1/29	1/0
p. 59	3/3	2/2	1/32	1/1	3/7	2/5	1/34	1/2
#25	0/35	0/23	0/17	0/12	1/16	0/50	0/38	0/25
p. 60	2/19	1/33	1/10	0/46	3/21	2/14	1/41	1/7
p. 61	3/47	2/32	1/54	1/16	4/11	2/47	2/5	1/24
#26	0/19	0/13	0/9	0/6	0/41	0/28	0/21	0/14
p. 62	1/23	0/55	0/42	0/28	2/7	1/24	1/3	0/42
#27	0/45	0/30	0/22	0/15	1/33	1/2	0/47	0/31
p. 64	2/32	1/41	1/16	0/50	3/28	2/19	1/44	1/9
#28	0/43	0/29	0/22	0/14	1/26	0/57	0/43	0/29
p. 66	1/46	1/10	0/53	0/35	2/7	1/24	1/3	0/42
#29	0/12	0/8	0/6	0/4	0/28	0/19	0/14	0/9
p. 67	1/6	0/44	0/33	0/22	1/46	1/11	0/53	0/35
p. 68	2/7	1/25	1/3	0/42	2/22	1/34	1/11	0/47
#30	0/21	0/14	0/10	0/7	0/44	0/29	0/22	0/15
p. 69	1/40	1/6	0/50	0/33	2/32	1/42	1/16	0/51
#31	0/48	0/32	0/24	0/16	1/38	1/6	0/49	0/33
p. 71	2/42	1/48	1/21	0/54	3/49	2/33	1/55	1/16
p. 72	4/12	2/48	2/6	1/24	4/34	3/2	2/17	1/31
#32	0/15	0/10	0/7	0/5	0/38	0/25	0/19	0/13
p. 73	1/34	1/3	0/47	0/31	2/34	1/42	1/17	0/51
p. 74	3/14	2/9	1/37	1/5	3/52	2/34	1/56	1/17
#33	0/41	0/27	0/20	0/14	1/19	0/53	0/40	0/26
p. 76	2/22	1/34	1/11	0/47	3/22	2/15	1/41	1/7
p. 77	3/49	2/33	1/55	1/16	4/13	2/49	2/7	1/24
#34	0/38	0/26	0/19	0/13	1/22	0/55	0/41	0/27
p. 79	2/22	1/35	1/11	0/47	3/18	2/12	1/39	1/6
p. 80	3/46	2/30	1/53	1/15	4/12	2/48	2/6	1/24
#35	0/11	0/8	0/6	0/4	0/28	0/18	0/14	0/9
p. 81	1/28	0/59	0/44	0/29	2/24	1/36	1/12	0/48
p. 82	2/34	1/43	1/17	0/51	2/47	1/52	1/23	0/56
#36	0/26	0/17	0/13	0/9	0/56	0/38	0/28	0/19
p. 83	1/46	1/11	0/53	0/35	2/36	1/44	1/18	0/52
#37	0/48	0/32	0/24	0/16	1/40	1/6	0/50	0/33
p. 85	2/39	1/46	1/19	0/53	3/37	2/24	1/48	1/12
p. 86	3/47	2/31	1/53	1/16	3/54	2/36	1/57	1/18
#38	0/29	0/20	0/15	0/10	1/2	0/41	0/31	0/21
p. 87	1/55	1/17	0/58	0/38	2/51	1/54	1/25	0/57
p. 88	3/2	2/2	1/31	1/1	3/13	2/9	1/37	1/4
#39	0/25	0/16	0/13	0/8	0/54	0/36	0/27	0/18
p. 89	1/50	1/13	0/55	0/37	2/45	1/50	1/23	0/55

SELECTION AND PAGE	1ST COLUMN				2ND COLUMN			
	@ 500	@ 750	@ 1000	@ 1500	@ 500	@ 750	@ 1000	@ 1500
#40	0/44	0/29	0/22	0/15	1/28	0/58	0/44	0/29
p. 91	2/24	1/36	1/12	0/48	3/22	2/15	1/41	1/7
p. 92	3/28	2/19	1/44	1/9	3/34	2/22	1/47	1/11
#41	0/32	0/21	0/16	0/11	1/8	0/45	0/34	0/23
p. 93	1/30	1/0	0/45	0/30	1/50	1/14	0/55	0/37
#42	0/21	0/14	0/10	0/7	0/43	0/29	0/22	0/14
p. 94	1/40	1/6	0/50	0/33	2/35	1/43	1/18	0/52
p. 95	3/18	2/12	1/39	1/6	4/2	2/41	2/1	1/21
#43	0/44	0/29	0/22	0/15	1/32	1/1	0/46	0/31
p. 97	2/28	1/39	1/14	0/49	3/20	2/13	1/40	1/6
#44	0/45	0/30	0/23	0/15	1/34	1/3	0/47	0/31
p. 99	2/35	1/43	1/17	0/51	3/35	2/23	1/48	1/12
p. 100	4/7	2/45	2/4	1/22	4/38	3/5	2/19	1/33
#45	0/5	0/3	0/3	0/2	0/15	0/10	0/7	0/5
p. 101	1/8	0/45	0/34	0/23	2/6	1/24	1/3	0/42
#46	0/43	0/29	0/22	0/14	1/29	0/59	0/45	0/30
p. 103	2/13	1/28	1/6	0/44	2/52	1/54	1/26	0/57
#47	0/42	0/28	0/21	0/14	1/29	1/0	0/45	0/30
p. 105	2/25	1/37	1/13	0/48	3/20	2/14	1/40	1/7
#48	0/44	0/30	0/22	0/15	1/35	1/3	0/48	0/32
p. 107	2/32	1/41	1/16	0/51	3/25	2/16	1/42	1/8
#49	0/42	0/28	0/21	0/14	1/40	1/0	0/45	0/30
p. 109	2/23	1/35	1/11	0/48	3/24	2/16	1/42	1/8
p. 110	4/6	2/42	2/3	1/21	4/47	3/12	2/24	1/36
#50	0/39	0/26	0/20	0/13	1/27	0/58	0/44	0/29
p. 112	2/33	1/42	1/16	0/51	3/29	2/19	1/44	1/10
p. 113	3/42	2/28	1/51	1/14	3/52	2/34	1/56	1/17
#51	0/20	0/14	0/10	0/7	0/45	0/30	0/23	0/15
p. 114	1/42	1/8	0/51	0/34	2/40	1/47	1/20	0/53
p. 115	2/46	1/51	1/23	0/55	2/50	1/54	1/25	0/57
#52	0/28	0/19	0/14	0/9	1/1	0/41	0/31	0/20
p. 116	2/7	1/25	1/4	0/42	3/7	2/4	1/33	1/2
p. 117	4/6	2/44	2/3	1/22	5/4	3/22	2/32	1/41
#53	0/45	0/30	0/22	0/15	1/31	1/0	0/45	0/30
p. 119	2/27	1/38	1/13	0/49	3/19	2/13	1/40	1/6
#54	0/38	0/25	0/19	0/13	1/26	0/57	0/43	0/29
p. 121	1/42	1/8	0/51	0/34	1/54	1/16	0/57	0/38
#55	0/25	0/17	0/12	0/8	0/53	0/35	0/27	0/18
p. 122	1/50	1/13	0/55	0/37	2/38	1/46	1/19	0/53
#56	0/44	0/29	0/22	0/15	1/31	1/1	0/46	0/30
p. 124	2/4	1/23	1/2	0/41	2/35	1/43	1/17	0/52
#57	0/4	0/3	0/2	0/1	0/13	0/9	0/6	0/4
p. 125	1/10	0/47	0/35	0/23	2/9	1/26	1/5	0/43
p. 126	3/9	2/6	1/35	1/3	4/2	2/41	1/1	1/21
p. 127	4/15	2/50	2/7	1/25	4/25	2/57	2/13	1/24
#58	0/20	0/13	0/10	0/7	0/44	0/29	0/22	0/15
p. 128	1/37	1/4	0/48	0/32	2/30	1/40	1/15	0/50
p. 129	3/26	2/17	1/43	1/4	4/14	2/50	2/7	1/25
p. 130	4/39	3/6	2/20	1/33	4/59	3/19	2/29	1/40
#59	0/16	0/10	0/8	0/5	0/33	0/22	0/17	0/11
p. 131	1/34	1/3	0/47	0/32	2/42	1/48	1/21	0/54
p. 132	2/47	1/52	1/24	0/56	2/52	1/55	1/26	0/58
#60	0/30	0/20	0/15	0/10	1/9	0/46	0/34	0/23
p. 133	1/59	1/20	1/0	0/40	2/48	1/52	1/24	0/56
#61	0/46	0/31	0/23	0/15	1/35	1/4	0/48	0/32
p. 135	2/10	1/27	1/5	0/43	2/46	1/50	1/23	0/55
#62	0/38	0/25	0/19	0/13	1/15	0/50	0/38	0/25
p. 137	2/2	1/21	1/1	0/41	2/55	1/56	1/27	0/58
p. 138	3/0	2/0	1/30	1/0	3/5	2/3	1/32	1/2
#63	0/31	0/21	0/16	0/10	1/11	0/47	0/35	0/24
p. 139	1/59	1/19	0/59	0/40	2/46	1/50	1/23	0/55
#64	0/39	0/26	0/20	0/13	1/24	0/56	0/42	0/28
p. 141	1/36	1/4	0/48	0/32	1/47	1/4	0/53	0/36

SELECTION AND PAGE	1ST COLUMN				2ND COLUMN			
	@500	@750	@1000	@1500	@500	@750	@1000	@1500
#65	0/37	0/25	0/19	0/12	1/22	0/55	0/41	0/27
p. 144	2/16	1/31	1/8	0/45	3/12	2/8	1/36	1/4
#66	0/43	0/29	0/22	0/14	1/30	1/0	0/45	0/30
p. 146	1/54	1/16	0/57	0/38	2/15	1/30	1/18	0/45
#67	0/10	0/7	0/5	0/3	0/27	0/18	0/14	0/9
p. 147	1/29	1/0	0/45	0/30	2/28	1/38	1/14	0/49
p. 148	2/50	1/53	1/25	0/57	3/12	2/8	1/36	1/4
#68	0/10	0/7	0/5	0/3	0/24	0/16	0/12	0/8
p. 149	1/26	0/57	0/43	0/29	2/28	1/38	1/14	0/49
p. 150	2/57	1/58	1/29	0/59	3/27	2/18	1/43	1/9
#69	0/12	0/8	0/6	0/4	0/27	0/18	0/14	0/9
p. 151	0/58	0/38	0/29	0/10	1/27	0/58	0/44	0/29
p. 152	1/48	1/12	0/54	0/36	2/11	1/28	1/6	0/44
#70	0/15	0/10	0/7	0/5	0/35	0/23	0/17	0/12
p. 153	1/28	0/59	0/44	0/29	2/19	1/33	1/9	0/46
p. 154	2/34	1/42	0/17	0/51	2/46	1/50	1/23	0/55
#71	0/24	0/16	0/12	0/8	0/51	0/34	0/25	0/17
p. 155	1/52	1/15	0/56	0/37	2/50	1/53	1/25	0/57
p. 156	3/43	2/29	1/52	1/14	4/41	3/7	2/20	1/34
#72	0/42	0/28	0/21	0/14	1/31	1/1	0/46	0/30
p. 158	2/26	1/38	1/13	0/49	3/26	2/18	1/43	1/9
p. 159	3/56	2/38	1/58	1/19	4/25	2/57	2/13	1/28
#73	0/6	0/4	0/3	0/2	0/20	0/13	0/10	0/7
p. 160	1/29	0/59	0/44	0/30	2/38	1/45	1/19	0/52
p. 161	2/42	1/48	1/21	0/54	2/46	1/50	1/23	0/55
#74	0/38	0/25	0/19	0/13	1/17	0/52	0/39	0/26
p. 162	2/21	1/34	1/11	0/47	3/21	2/14	1/41	1/7
p. 163	4/24	2/56	2/12	1/28	5/19	3/32	2/39	1/46
#75	0/44	0/29	0/22	0/15	1/30	1/10	0/45	0/35
p. 165	2/16	1/31	1/8	0/45	3/14	2/10	1/37	1/5
p. 166	3/20	2/17	1/43	1/7	3/48	2/12	1/54	1/16
#76	0/26	0/17	0/13	0/9	0/56	0/37	0/28	0/19
p. 167	1/55	1/17	0/58	0/38	2/52	1/59	1/26	1/0
p. 168	3/42	2/28	1/51	1/14	4/27	2/58	2/13	1/29
#77	0/47	0/31	0/23	0/16	1/36	1/4	0/48	0/32
p. 170	1/45	1/10	0/52	0/35	1/52	1/15	0/56	0/37
#78	0/31	0/21	0/16	0/10	1/2	0/41	0/31	0/21
p. 171	2/2	1/21	1/1	0/41	2/57	1/58	1/29	0/59
p. 172	3/53	2/35	1/56	1/18	4/51	3/14	2/26	1/37
p. 173	5/24	3/36	2/42	1/48	6/1	4/1	3/0	2/0
#79	0/5	0/3	0/3	0/2	0/12	0/8	0/6	0/4
p. 174	1/6	0/44	0/33	0/22	1/56	1/18	0/58	0/39
#80	0/33	0/22	0/17	0/11	1/18	0/52	0/39	0/26
p. 176	1/34	1/2	0/47	0/31	1/49	1/12	0/54	0/36
#81	0/22	0/15	0/11	0/7	0/43	0/29	0/22	0/14
p. 177	1/33	1/2	0/46	0/31	2/17	1/31	1/8	0/46
#82	0/47	0/31	0/23	0/16	1/31	1/1	0/46	0/30
p. 179	2/27	1/38	1/13	0/49	3/19	2/13	1/40	1/6
p. 180	3/43	2/29	1/52	1/14	4/6	2/44	2/3	1/22
#83	0/7	0/4	0/3	0/2	0/16	0/11	0/8	0/5
p. 181	1/2	0/42	0/31	0/21	1/50	1/13	0/55	0/37
p. 182	2/36	1/44	1/18	0/52	3/20	2/14	1/40	1/7
p. 183	3/25	2/17	1/43	1/8	3/30	2/20	1/45	1/10

1 2 3 4 5 6 7 8 9 0